THE
LEGAL
AND
REGULATORY
ENVIRONMENT
OF
BUSINESS

GEORGE D. CAMERON III
THE UNIVERSITY OF MICHIGAN

COLLEGE DIVISION South-Western Publishing Co.
Cincinnati Ohio

Sponsoring Editor: Jeanne R. Busemeyer
Developmental Editor: Carol A. Cromer
Production Editor: Rebecca Roby
Production House: Preface, Inc.
Cover and Interior Design: Craig LaGesse Ramsdell
Marketing Manager: Scott D. Person

LE61AA
Copyright © 1994
by SOUTH-WESTERN PUBLISHING CO.
Cincinnati, Ohio

ISBN: 0-538-81947-2
1 2 3 4 5 6 7 8 9 0 KI 2 1 0 9 8 7 6 5 4 3
Printed in the United States of America

Library of Congress Cataloging-in-Publication Data

Cameron, George Dana,
        The legal and regulatory environment of business/George D. Cameron III.
        p.   cm.
        Includes index.
        ISBN 0-538-81947-2
        1. Commercial law—United States. 2. Trade regulation—United States.
        3. Industrial law and legislation—United States.
    I. Title.
    KF889.C36   1994
    346.73'07—dc20
    [347.3067]   93-10864
                                                      CIP

 This book is printed on acid-free paper that meets Environmental Protection Agency
standards for recycled paper.

ITP South-Western is a subsidiary of ITP (International Thomson Publishing). The
trademark ITP is used under license.

ABOUT THE AUTHOR

George D. Cameron III is currently Professor of Business Law at The University of Michigan. He has also had international teaching experience through being a visiting professor at Beijing University of Political Science and Law. Professor Cameron taught U.S. and U.K. Contract Law and Corporation Law to Chinese lawyers and legal workers in Beijing, P.R.C. During three recent summers he also co-taught a law course for master's degree students from Erasmus University, Rotterdam, the Netherlands, who were studying in Ann Arbor.

Professor Cameron earned his B.A. and M.A. degrees from Kent State University. He received a Ph.D. in political science from The University of Michigan and a J.D. from The University of Michigan Law School.

Professor Cameron has won many scholarly honors and teaching awards, including the State of Michigan Undergraduate Teaching Award, the Tri-State Business Law Association's Best Paper Award, and two annual student awards for teaching excellence at the University of Michigan Business School.

PREFACE

T O THE INSTRUCTOR: LAW IN THE BUSINESS CURRICULUM—MOVING INTO THE 21ST CENTURY

Certain themes have been recurrent over the last few decades in business law education. One constant theme has been our need to establish, and reestablish, the relevance of our courses to the business curriculum. A second major recurring theme has been the dynamic tension between "Business Law" and "Legal Environment." The legal environment approach can be traced back to the AACSB standards, and perhaps to the critical reports on business education of the early 1960s. The AACSB was never specific about what it wanted, which has led to many differing interpretations of the meaning of "legal environment." For some, it has meant emphasis on the structure and procedure of legal institutions. For others, it has meant a focus on the regulatory public law areas rather than on the traditional private law areas such as contracts, commercial paper, and agency.

It does seem clear that there has been a long-term movement toward more "environmental" coverage in our courses. This is, of course, in tune with business reality, since government regulation is again on the increase. Our students must be prepared to deal with this higher level of governmental involvement in the workplace. These real-world changes may be part of the motivation behind the AACSB's use of "regulation," rather than "law," in the committee's draft of the new accreditation standards. In any event, we can no longer be satisfied with "business as usual" in our field.

On one dimension of our courses, we have been remarkably consistent. All texts present "the Law" as a series of legal topics. We may not agree on which legal topics ought to be taught, or in what sequence, but we all do seem to agree that we teach traditional legal topics. Even the legal environment texts teach the legal topics of public law and regulation; for example, antitrust law, unfair competition law, and securities law. In other words, we continue to teach the law as a set of the legal topics that we learned in law school. Because of this, many of our business school colleagues have difficulty relating to us and to our courses. A new approach seems to be indicated.

This text proposes a new paradigm—an organization of our legal materials to parallel the major functional areas of business. The Sherman Act, for example, says what it says. There is no way we can change that. But might it not make more sense to relate antitrust law to the marketing and organization functions of business than to teach "antitrust law," in splendid isolation, to business students? This text proposes to make those relationships.

To satisfy the need for coverage of legal institutions and legal process, the first six chapters deal with those topics. The text begins with chapters on the ethical, political, and constitutional framework within which our legal and business systems operate. It then covers the court system and civil procedure in much the same way as most texts. A full chapter on administrative agencies and administrative procedure follows. The introductory section concludes with a chapter combining tort law and criminal law.

It is difficult to imagine a more fundamental legal topic than contracts. Making contracts is the purpose of business. First, contracts are necessary to assemble the means of production, and then contracts are necessary to produce and distribute the business's product or service. This text's new approach does include two chapters on contract law. The first covers the making of contracts—agreement, consideration, and writing requirements. The coverage is not exhaustive, but it is reasonably complete. The second contracts chapter summarizes the major limitations on the enforcement of contracts—factors such as lack of capacity, lack of real consent due to fraud of force, and illegality. International comparisons are drawn where appropriate.

The final section of the book creates the new paradigm. Each of six major business functions is addressed—organization, finance, employment, production, marketing, and international operations. For each, there is a chapter on "the Law," as it relates to that topic, followed by a chapter on "regulation," as it impacts on that topic. The major focus of each law chapter is on the rules of the game—what are the legalities involved in organizing a business, for example. Each regulation chapter then covers the main limitations, restrictions, and governmental requirements imposed on that business function.

Anyone who has been teaching in a business school for very long is aware that there is some overlap among the major business disciplines, just as there is between law and regulation, and between contracts and sales. Human activities generally confound our attempts to place them in nice, neat categories. The six business functions chosen are generally recognized and used by our colleagues. The sequence in the text begins with the first steps—organizing the business, financing it, and hiring its personnel. The text then covers the production and distribution functions. Finally, international business operations are also subjected to the same dual coverage—international law, and the regulation of international trade.

To make this new approach as "user-friendly" as possible, many classic case illustrations have been retained. Due to the increased emphasis on regulation, many of the cases are from the U.S. Supreme Court, since it speaks the last word on the meaning of national statutes and administrative rules. Some cases from the 1990s are included to provide coverage of current developments. An effort has been made to edit the cases carefully, with the facts summarized, and with the Issue, Decision, and Rule clearly identified. Each case contains a brief excerpt from the opinion of the court to communicate the reality and the "flavor" of the case. Each case concludes with an ethical question about the conduct involved and/or the result.

In sum, the raw materials used for this new text are not different: constitutions, statutes, cases, regulations. The organization of those materials is very different, especially in the second and third parts of the text. The relationship of the materials to the functional areas of business is shown clearly and explicitly. The increased significance of the regulatory process to business operations is emphasized throughout the text. The importance of the ethical and political environments within which business operates is given increased coverage in the introductory section. International comparisons are made where appropriate.

As we prepare to move into the twenty-first century, it is clear that the successful business will spend much more time and effort managing its relationships with its external environment. Recognizing this new reality, the AACSB is demanding that academics devote more attention to those topics—ethics, regulation, and international concerns. This text provides the approach and the coverage to meet our new challenges.

■ LEARNING AIDS

Each chapter begins with Learning Objectives to help focus the student's attention on the important points which will be made in the chapter. The Preview of each chapter reinforces this focus on essentials and also provides an overview of the major legal problems to be discussed.

Important terms are bold-faced when introduced in the text. Significant points and definitions are further highlighted by margin notes. Cases provide real-life illustrations of the legal issues. Cases are edited for ease of use and clarity, and each includes a quoted excerpt from the actual opinion of the court. Studying law without reading some of the actual language of court opinions is analogous to studying Shakespeare without ever reading one of his plays or poems. The quoted excerpts give the reader the feel and flavor of the law. Selected charts and diagrams are also included as illustrations and explanations.

Each chapter is summarized in a Review section. End-of-chapter review questions on important points in the chapter are provided to reinforce learning. To enhance the ability of the student to apply the material to new situations, four case problems are also provided for each chapter. Additional readings are suggested for further study of the chapter topics.

A glossary of terms is included so a forgotten definition can be quickly recaptured. The index gives easy access to locations in the text where a particular legal problem or concept was discussed. The U.S. Constitution and excerpts from selected statues are also included as appendices for reference purposes.

■ STUDENT SUPPLEMENTS

A student workbook/study guide is available. It first restates the learning objectives for each chapter as a reinforcement of the chapter's goals. It then outlines the materials in the chapter. It contains a vocabulary review for each chapter to reinforce learning of the legal terminology. Review of text principles is provided in two different formats—true/false questions and multiple-choice questions. By using these reviews, the student verifies and reinforces knowledge of the legal materials in each chapter.

The instructor will also have available additional readings which can be provided to the student, either as assigned or as optional readings.

■ INSTRUCTOR SUPPLEMENTS

The instructor's manual includes an overview of each chapter to explain its objectives and its relationship to other parts of the text. Each chapter's Learning Objectives are explained, and a detailed outline of the chapter is given. Teaching Hints are provided as suggestions of how the chapter materials might be presented. Case diagrams are provided for each illustrative case. Answers are included for the review questions and problems at the end of the chapter. Supplementary diagrams and charts are provided in the form of transparency masters. For those instructors wishing to do a bit more with contract law, there are over forty overhead masters relating to contracts.

The test bank includes matching questions on terms and definitions. Questions on chapter materials appear in both true/false and multiple-choice formats. For those instructors wishing to test students' ability to analyze a new fact situation and to apply the legal rules to it, case questions are provided.

■ACKNOWLEDGMENTS

Thank you to the following faculty who reviewed manuscript for this text and provided helpful comments:

Dean Alexander
Miami-Dade Community College

Robert B. Bennett, Jr.
Butler University

Stanley R. Berkowitz
Northeastern University

H. Glenn Boggs
Florida State University

John W. Collis
St. Ambrose University

Michael Harford
Morehead University

Nancy Hauserman
University of Iowa

Eddie Kaminsky
University of Central Florida

J. Scott Kirkwood
Wingate College

Nancy R. Mansfield
Georgia State University

Donald O. Mayer
Oakland University

Debra Moon
DeKalb College

Ross D. Petty
Babson College

Steven Sher
Drexel University

Scott Sibary
California State University-Chico

Albert D. Spalding, Jr
Wayne State University

Roger D. Staton
Miami University

David L. Steele
University of Wisconsin-Eau Claire

Clyde D. Stoltenberg
University of Kansas

Charles R. B. Stowe
Sam Houston State University

Ronald L. Taylor
Metropolitan State College of Denver

Daphyne Saunders Thomas
James Madison University

Gary L. Tidwell
College of Charleston

Jules Scott Walker
Indiana Wesleyan University

Mary-Kathryn Zachary
West Georgia College

As you and your students use this text, your comments and suggestions would be welcome.

M ESSAGE TO THE STUDENT

This text represents the culmination of my thirty-two years of teaching. I have taught in all kinds of college and university settings—a small private business school, a large regional state university, and an internationally acclaimed research university. I have taught first-year students, sophomores, juniors, and seniors; graduate students; part-time evening students; and visiting foreign students. The highlight of my teaching experience, and my biggest challenge, was teaching U.S. and British Contract law and Corporation Law to a group of Chinese lawyers in Beijing.

All these experiences have their places in this textbook. Students at all levels want a text that is clearly written and interesting. Both students and instructors want a text that is accurate and reasonably complete. Of necessity, since this is an introductory text, not all details could be covered. But a wide range of legal topics is introduced, in reasonable detail, and with a high degree of accuracy. The international issues and the ethical focus should make the book both readable and relevant.

As you read the text, I urge you to keep looking for the big picture. How do the specific case examples relate to the main principles covered in the chapter? How do the chapters relate to each other? How do the legal problems being discussed relate to business operations? The objective, after all, is to provide you with an appreciation of how law and regulation impact on the operation of business institutions. No text can possibly give you all the answers you will need to navigate all the legal shoals you will encounter during your career. This text, and both you and I, will have succeeded if you are alerted to the major sorts of problems you will confront and are able to ask some of the right questions.

Happy reading.

George D. Cameron III

HOW TO ANALYZE A CASE

CITATION OF THE CASE

The citation for a case includes the names of the parties, the location of the court's opinion in a set of case reports, the court or state that decided the case, and the year of decision. For example, the citation for one case in this book is *Cucchi v. Rollins Protective Services*, 574 A.2d 565 (Pa. 1990). Anthony Cucchi and Grace Cucchi sued Rollins Protective Services. In the trial court, the plaintiff's name is always listed first, since that is the structure of the case at that stage. The plaintiff (Cucchi) is suing the defendant (Rollins Protective Services). Where there are multiple parties on either side of the case, the usual practice is to list only the first party in the citation for the case. In most states, the parties continue to be listed in that sequence through all appeals, regardless of which party brings the appeal. In some states, and in the federal courts, the party who brings the appeal is listed first in the citation of the appellate court's opinion. If Jones sues Smith in U.S. District Court, and Smith appeals the judgment to a U.S. Court of Appeals, the appellate case opinion is reported as *Smith v. Jones*. If

Jones then asks for review by the U.S. Supreme Court, the Supreme Court opinion is reported as *Jones v. Smith*.

The court's opinion in the *Cucchi* case is printed in Volume 574 of the *Atlantic Reporter*, second series, at page 565. The states are grouped regionally by the West Publishing Company into Atlantic, Northeastern, Northwestern, Pacific, Southeastern, Southwestern, and Southern. Opinions from all the appellate and supreme courts in each region are then printed in that regional reporter. For some states, the West regional reporter is also the state's official reporter system. Other states have an official state court reporter printed in addition to the West reporter. Cases decided by the Michigan Supreme Court, for instance, are found in the official state reporter (Mich.), as well as in West's regional *Northwest Reporter* (N.W.). Cases decided by the Michigan Court of Appeals are found in the official state reporter (Mich.App.), and in the *Northwest Reporter*. The *Cucchi* case is in the *Atlantic Reporter* because it was decided by the Pennsylvania Supreme Court. The *Cucchi* case was decided in 1990.

If a citation includes U.S. or S. Ct., such as 397 U.S. 294 or 110 S. Ct. 3117, the case was decided by the U.S. Supreme Court. Decisions by the U.S. Courts of Appeals are reported in the *Federal Reporter*, designated in citations as F. or F.2d.

F ACTS

The court's opinion will nearly always include a statement of the facts, that is, a summary of what happened. Who said what, who did what, who wrote what, and to whom, when, why? Who brought the lawsuit? What happened in the lower court or courts that have already considered the case? Which party is bringing the appeal? (Nearly all the case opinions in this text are from appellate courts.) Depending on the complexity of the case, the court's statement of the facts may take several pages. The fact statements in the cases in this book have been edited; they are not direct quotes of the court's statement s of what happened.

I SSUE(S)

The issue in the case is the legal question (or questions) presented to the appellate court for decision. It's a statement of the legal problem involved in the case. The court will have to answer this legal question in order to decide the case. In one of our first contract cases, *Lefkowitz v. Great Minneapolis Surplus Store*, the issue was whether two newspaper ads were offers to make contracts. Lefkowitz claimed that they were offers, and that he had accepted them, making two contracts with the store. He said that the store had then refused to sell him the merchandise and that he had been damaged as a result. If the ads were not offers, Lefkowitz loses the case. If they were offers, he wins—if he was an intended offeree (which is the second issue in the case). If Lefkowitz was a person for whom the offer was intended, and he did what the offer specified in order to accept, he wins. If the offer was not intended for him, he can't accept it, so he loses.

DECISION

The court's decision will resolve the issue and indicate who wins the case. An appellate court will indicate whether the lower court decided the case correctly, in which case its judgment will be affirmed. If the appellate court determines that the lower court decided the case incorrectly, the lower court's judgment will be reserved. Where there is a reversal, the appellate court may enter judgment for the other side, or it may decide that further proceedings are necessary in the lower court. Where further proceedings below are needed, the case is remanded to the lower court for further hearings, orders, or other proceedings.

RULE

The rule of law for each case in this text is stated separately. Courts do not usually state the legal rule they are using quite so clearly and separately. The court's opinion will contain the legal rule that is being used to decide the case, but the rule will be incorporated in a general discussion of why the case should be decided the way the court is deciding it. If the rule is from prior case law, the court will cite the case or cases where the rule originated. In this textbook, nearly all such citations to case precedents have been edited out of the court opinions. If the rule is derived from a statute, the court will cite the statute. Again, nearly all such citations have been eliminated from the sections of opinions quoted in this book.

DISCUSSION

This part of each example case in this textbook is quoted from the court's opinion. The court is telling you in its own words which facts it thought were important, what the rule is, why and how it applies, and who wins the case. In other words, the court is explaining and justifying its result.

C ONCURRING AND DISSENTING OPINIONS

Judges frequently disagree with each other. A judge may write a concurring opinion when he or she agrees with the majority's result but for a different reason. The concurring judge may also want to point out some other parts of the case which need added emphasis. A judge will write a dissenting opinion when disagreeing with the majority's result, as well as its reasoning. Only a few cases in this text include concurring or dissenting opinions.

E THICAL DIMENSION

As part of the text's emphasis on ethical awareness, an ethics question is included after each case. This question was not part of the court's opinion in the actual case. You are asked to consider the fairness of the legal rule or of the result it produced in the case. Sometimes you are asked your opinion on whether the conduct of one or both of the parties was ethical. Sometimes you're asked to think of a better policy or a more just result. There are no final "right" and "wrong" answers to such questions. Their purpose is to get you to consider the ethical dimensions of business decisions.

BRIEF CONTENTS

CONTENTS

■ 6 Public Wrongs and Private Wrongs   183

PART 2: CONTRACT LAW—FOUNDATION OF FREE ENTERPRISE   215

■ 14 Regulation of the Employment Relationship 413

■ 15 Law of Production 446

■ 18 Regulation of Marketing   540

■ 19 Law of International Business   569

THE ENVIRONMENT IN WHICH BUSINESS OPERATES

PART ONE

Part 1 provides an introduction to the legal system. Chapter 1 shows how society's standards for ethical and moral conduct came to be reflected in the common law system. Chapter 2 discusses the political system and the legislative process through which regulatory statutes are adopted. Chapter 3 examines the constitutional limits on the regulation and taxation of business. Chapter 4 is an overview of the legal system and the litigation process. Chapter 5 covers the development of administrative regulation and the requirements of administrative procedure. Chapter 6 summarizes the impact of tort law and criminal law on business operations.

Overall, the emphasis of Part 1 is on the origin of the laws and regulations which govern business and on the mechanisms by which those laws and regulations are enforced. Part 1 thus sets the stage for more specific discussions of how these laws and regulations relate to the major functional areas of business.

1

LAW
ETHICS
AND
SOCIETY

"A great society is a society in which [leaders] of business think greatly of their functions."
Alfred North Whitehead

LEARNING OBJECTIVES: After you have studied this chapter, you should be able to:

EXPLAIN the relationships between ethics, morals and laws.

DISCUSS several different ethical standards for human behavior.

UNDERSTAND how the common law developed in England and the United States.

DISCUSS several different legal theories used by U.S. scholars to define the role of judges.

EXPLAIN how ethical principles apply in the making of business decisions.

PREVIEW

Operating a business requires making decisions. Business decisions are made by human beings, sometimes individually, sometimes in a group. This chapter provides a framework for analyzing such decisions as a form of human conduct. Several of the ethical systems which have been developed over the centuries are presented in summarized form. These ethical tests can be used as a basis for judging whether a business decision was the "right" one to make.

This chapter also discusses the origin and development of the common law system in England and the United States. The system is based on customary practices, and it uses a jury of citizens to determine many questions where the "reasonableness" of someone's conduct is at issue. The system's supplementary rules of "equity," which govern special kinds of problems, are based on the principles of justice and fairness.

Finally, the chapter discusses the application of ethical standards to modern corporations, particularly those operating internationally.

SOCIETY'S RULES OF CONDUCT

Organized societies require rules of conduct for their members. Living and working together, we need to know what we can expect of each other. What rights do we have, and what duties do we owe? What behavior is required, what is expected, what is tolerated, what is prohibited?

Societies communicate these behavioral rules in various ways. Simpler rules may be communicated orally, from one generation to the next. Each new member of a society learns by observing the conduct of others, particularly the elder members. More complicated rules, such as those dealing with modern trade and industry, typically require written statements.

The form of government may affect the way in which behavioral rules are communicated. The government itself is usually a primary communicator of the rules. If the society is a monarchy, the king or queen simply announces the new or changed rule (perhaps with the advice and assistance of a trusted advisor or small group of advisors). In an oligarchy, the small group of persons in control of the government adopts the needed rules. In a democracy, the citizens vote to adopt the new rules or vote for representatives who will then adopt the new rules.

ETHICS, MORALS, LAWS

In modern society, we generally distinguish law from custom, although the two concepts do overlap to some extent. Our laws tell us what behavior is required and what behavior is prohibited and provide sanctions

Law requires or prohibits certain behavior.

for violation of these norms. Social customs tell us what behavior is expected, but the only penalty for violation is (perhaps) social disapproval. If someone says "Good morning," we expect a reply—out of courtesy and custom. A person who does not answer a cheerful greeting is not subject to any court penalty but may be described by others as a "grouch." In contrast, a person who makes a contract and then wrongfully fails to perform as promised is subject to legal sanctions by a court.

Ethics defines correct human behavior.

Ethics is the branch of philosophy which attempts to define standards for correct human behavior. Ethics, therefore, involves the development of a set of principles which can help us decide how to deal with each other. An unethical act is one which does not measure up to these expected standards. Generally, to be considered ethical in our culture, an action should promote such values as honesty, harmony, and fairness.

Morals are also principles of proper human behavior. In fact, for many purposes, ethics and morals are synonyms, since both are used to evaluate human actions against some standard. Ethics is generally used in connection with public, commercial relationships. We speak of "professional ethics," but not generally of "professional morals." The moral/immoral classification is often used in evaluating someone's private behavior, especially sexual behavior. We speak disapprovingly of someone as having "loose morals," not "loose ethics." An immoral person is usually thought to be guilty of more serious misbehavior than one who is unethical. The immoral person has usually committed a prohibited act. The unethical person has merely not done what is expected, that is, has not done what a "good" person would have done in the circumstances.

The murder of another human being is illegal, immoral (by most persons' standards), and unethical (although not usually so described). Telling a sick person that he "looks great" is not illegal, is probably not immoral, and would not generally be thought of as unethical. Driving on the wrong side of the road is illegal, but probably would not be defined as immoral or unethical by most people (at least if no one is being endangered). This last analysis could also be applied to a failure to stop for a stop sign, when there are no other vehicles or pedestrians near the intersection. The law describes violations of these "convenience" regulations as *malum prohibitum*, that is, they are bad simply because they are prohibited by law. Acts such as murder, in contrast, are *malum in se*. They are bad in themselves, inherently wrong.

Figures 1–1, 1–2, and 1–3 summarize these relationships in three different ways. People who hold the view shown in Figure 1–1, would say that all illegal actions are, by definition, also immoral, but that not all immoral actions are illegal. Those who hold this viewpoint consider all immoral actions to be unethical, but not all unethical actions to be immoral. Those who hold view 1 also consider all illegal actions unethical, but not all unethical actions illegal.

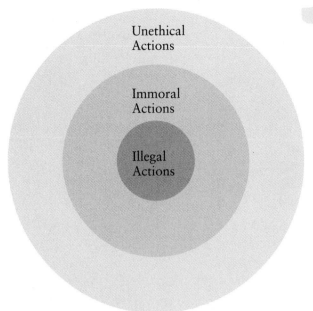

FIGURE 1–1
Some people view all illegal actions as immoral and all immoral acts as unethical.

People holding the view shown in Figure 1–2, think illegal, immoral, and unethical acts are basically separate, independent concepts. However, these people see overlap in certain situations.

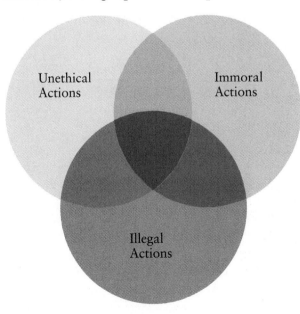

FIGURE 1–2
Some people view the concepts of illegal, immoral, and unethical acts as being independent, but having some overlap.

Other people have the view, illustrated by Figure 1–3, that some, but not all, illegal actions are also immoral. View 3 sees some, but not all, immoral actions as being illegal. Those who hold this viewpoint also see all illegal and immoral actions as being unethical. They do not, however, think all unethical actions are necessarily illegal or immoral.

FIGURE 1–3

Some people view all illegal or immoral actions as being unethical, but not every unethical act as being immoral or illegal.

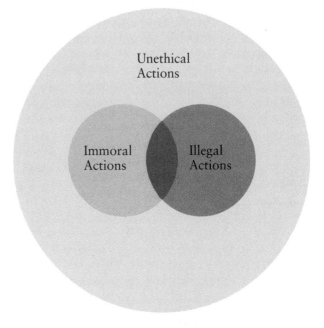

The following case further illustrates the relationships between and among these three concepts. It is an attempt to reconcile what is possible through modern medical science, with what is legal, moral and ethical.

WHITEHEAD-GOULD V. STERN

542 A.2d 52 (N.J. 1988)

Facts: The Sterns wanted children, but Mrs. Stern felt her health might be harmed if she became pregnant. Using a Michigan lawyer well-known for making such arrangements, the Sterns entered into a "surrogate parenting" contract with Mary Beth Whitehead. A doctor impregnated Mary Beth with Mr. Stern's sperm. The contract required Mary Beth to carry the baby to term and then to turn the baby over to the Sterns. In exchange for giving up all rights as the baby's mother, Mary Beth would receive $10,000. When the baby girl ("Baby M") was born, Mary Beth decided she wanted to keep her, thereby breaching the terms of the surrogacy contract. The trial court awarded custody of Baby M to the Sterns and denied Mary Beth all parental rights.

Issue: Is the surrogate parenting contract enforceable in court?

Decision: No, it is not. Trial court's judgment is modified, to permit visitation rights by Mary Beth.

Rule: Contracts which violate basic public policy should not be enforced, even if they are not specifically illegal.

Discussion: *By Chief Justice* WILENTZ:

"We find no offense to our present laws where a woman voluntarily and without payment agrees to act as a 'surrogate' mother, provided that she is not subject to a binding agreement to surrender her child. Moreover, our holding today does not preclude the legislature from altering the current statutory scheme, within constitutional limits, so as to permit surrogacy contracts. Under current law, however, the surrogacy agreement before us is illegal and invalid....

"We do not underestimate the difficulties of legislating on this subject.... Legislative consideration of surrogacy may also provide the opportunity to begin to focus on the overall implications of the new reproductive biotechnology—in vitro fertilization, preservation of sperm and eggs, embryo implantation, and the like....The problem can be addressed only when society decides what its values and objectives are in this troubling, yet promising, area."

Ethical Dimension

Was anyone acting unethically or immorally in this case? The doctor, for performing the medical procedure? The lawyer, for making the financial arrangements? Mary Beth, for agreeing to participate and then not keeping her word? Mr. Stern, for participating? Mrs. Stern, for encouraging the conduct of the others?

E THICAL SYSTEMS AND STANDARDS

Various philosophical, religious, and practical standards have been used over the years to try to define acceptable conduct. Of course, we do not have space here to discuss each of them fully. What follows is a series of brief summaries of several approaches to the problem of defining ethical conduct.

■ Aristotle's System

The Greek philosophers were much concerned with discovering, through the use of reason, the eternal values. Aristotle (384 to 322

B.C.) wrote important texts on both politics and ethics. He attempted to define the characteristics of the good person ("the high-minded man").

Aristotle defined a good person as one who respected truth and observed moderation.

This person valued honor above all else—deserved honor. Persons born into wealth or power, or acquiring it by accident, were not necessarily worthy of honor. Only good persons were worthy of honor. Good persons cared more for the truth than for what others thought of them. Good persons only reluctantly asked others for favors, but were always ready to give them. Good persons lived their own lives, not the lives others wanted them to live. They were open in their likes and dislikes, but they did not gossip or bear grudges. They did not follow the crowd on each new activity, but rather tried to do a few great and important things well. Above all, for Aristotle, "moral virtue is moderation or observance of the mean."

■ Biblical Standards

The Judeo-Christian religious tradition also provides a widely-known set of rules for human behavior.

THE TEN COMMANDMENTS

Many religious systems attempt to define correct behavior.

The story in the Old Testament of the Bible tells of Moses receiving the Ten Commandments on two tablets of stone, directly from God. God had both positive and negative commands: (1) You will have no other gods before Me; (2) You must not worship carved images of things in Heaven or on earth; (3) You must not make wrongful use of the name of God; (4) You must keep the Sabbath Day holy; (5) You must honor your father and mother; (6) You must not commit murder; (7) You must not commit adultery; (8) You must not steal; (9) You must not give false evidence against your neighbor; (10) You must not covet your neighbor's household or possessions.

For hundreds of millions of persons around the world, these are authoritative statements of required (or at least hoped-for) human behavior. Even non-religious persons would probably agree that our world would be a better place if all of us stopped killing, stealing, and lying. There are, however, many doctrinal disagreements on how the Commandments should be applied to specific situations. Some people believe that the prohibition against killing extends to military service in time of war; others do not. The employee in the next case wants to extend the "Thou shalt not kill" rule one step further—to a prohibition against making war weapons that can be used to kill. This interpretation, he claims, justifies his refusal to do the assigned work, and entitles him to claim unemployment benefits despite his voluntary resignation.

THOMAS V. REVIEW BOARD OF
INDIANA EMPLOYMENT SECURITY DIVISION

101 S. Ct.1425 (1981)

Facts: Thomas terminated his employment in the Blaw-Knox Foundry and Machinery Company when he was transferred from the roll foundry to a department that produced turrets for military tanks. He claimed his religious beliefs prevented him from participating in the production of war materials, so he quit his job. He then applied for unemployment compensation benefits from the state fund, since he was "unemployed." The Review Board denied him compensation benefits, because he had quit his job voluntarily, for personal reasons. The Indiana Court of Appeals ordered payment of benefits, but the Indiana Supreme Court reversed. Thomas petitioned the U.S. Supreme Court for further review.

Issue: Does the State's denial of unemployment compensation benefits to Thomas, a Jehovah's Witness who terminated his job because his religious beliefs forbade participation in the production of armaments, constitute a violation of his First Amendment right to free exercise of religion?

Decision: Yes. Judgment of Indiana of Supreme Court reversed. (Thomas wins.)

Rule: A person may not be compelled to choose between the exercise of a First Amendment right and participation in an otherwise available public program.

Discussion: *By Chief Justice* BURGER:

"Where the state conditions receipt of an important benefit upon conduct proscribed by a religious faith, or where it denies such a benefit because of conduct mandated by religious belief, thereby putting substantial pressure on an adherent to modify his behavior and to violate his beliefs, a burden upon religion exists. While the compulsion may be indirect, the infringement upon free exercise is nonetheless substantial....

"The mere fact that the petitioner's religious practice is burdened by a governmental program does not mean that an exemption accommodating his practice must be granted. The state may justify an inroad on religious liberty by showing that it is the least restrictive means of achieving some compelling state interest. However, it is still true that '[t]he essence of all that has been said and written on the subject is that only those interests of the highest order can overbalance legitimate claims to the free exercise of religion.'...

"The purposes urged to sustain the disqualifying provision of the Indiana unemployment compensation scheme are two-fold: (1) to avoid the widespread unemployment and the consequent burden on the fund resulting if people were permitted to leave jobs for 'personal' reasons; and (2) to avoid detailed probing by employers into job applicants' religious beliefs. These are by no means unimportant considerations.... [H]owever, we must conclude that the interests advanced by the state do not justify the burden placed on free exercise of religion.

"There is no evidence in the record to indicate that the number of people who find themselves in the predicament of choosing between benefits and religious beliefs is large enough to create 'widespread unemployment,' or even to seriously affect unemployment—and no such claim was advanced by the Review Board. Similarly, although detailed inquiry by employers into applicants' religious beliefs is undesirable, there is no evidence in the record to indicate that such inquiries will occur in Indiana, or that they have occurred in any of the states that extend benefits to people in the petitioner's position. Nor is there any reason to believe that the number of people terminating employment for religious reasons will be so great as to motivate employers to make such inquiries.

"Neither of the interests advanced is sufficiently compelling to justify the burden upon Thomas' religious liberty. Accordingly, Thomas is entitled to receive benefits unless, as the state contends and the Indiana court held, such payment would violate the Establishment Clause.

"The [Review Board] contends that to compel benefit payments to Thomas involves the state in fostering a religious faith. There is, in a sense, a 'benefit' to Thomas deriving from his religious beliefs, but this manifests no more than the tension between the two Religious Clauses which the Court resolved in *Sherbert* [the prior case dealing with this issue]...

"Unless we are prepared to overrule *Sherbert*..., Thomas cannot be denied the benefits due him on the basis of the findings of the referee, the Review Board and the Indiana Court of Appeals that he terminated his employment because of his religious convictions."

Ethical Dimension

Is it "ethical" to force other persons (taxpayers and the employers of Indiana) to pay for your own ethical choice?

OTHER RELIGIOUS RULES

Two other rules of religious origin are widely accepted as providing proper standards of human behavior. The Golden Rule—"Do unto others as you would have them do unto you"—states one basis for our actions toward others. Most of us want to be treated fairly and respectfully, and so we are told to treat others that way. We hope they will respond in kind. A second widely-quoted (but not so widely followed) lesson is "Love your neighbor as you love yourself." This standard directs us to respect the personal worth and value of each person.

■ The Kantian Imperative

The great German philosopher, Immanuel Kant, had another way of stating the most basic rule for human behavior. He called it the universal imperative: "Act always in such a way that you could compel your behavior to be universalized." In other words, each of us should behave the way we would want the whole world to behave. If we lie, we're saying we want the whole world to lie, rather than to try to tell the truth. If we steal, we're saying that we want the whole world to be thieves. With those patterns of behavior, we could never believe anyone, and no one's property would be safe. Under Kant's guideline, before we do something, we should ask, "Would I want everyone to behave this way?" If the answer is no, then we shouldn't do it either.

Kant's standard for human behavior was "the universal imperative."

■ The Utilitarianist Formula

Jeremy Bentham and a group of philosophers called the Utilitarianists constructed a formula to guide public policy. Decisions should be made based on what would produce "the greatest good for the greatest number." While this formula focuses mainly on decision-making by governmental agencies, it might also be used for decisions by individuals. The formula is, however, difficult to apply in any context.

First, it is often difficult to determine how many people are, in fact, going to be affected by a given decision—either positively or negatively. Second, it is difficult to decide the extent to which people will be positively or negatively affected. Third, people's perception of how they are affected may differ from the perception of the "decider." It may be useful to think about public policy decisions using this formula, but it is obviously a very complex standard for personal decisions.

The Utilitarianist's formula for making public policy decisions asked what would produce the greatest good for the greatest number of people.

■ The Publicity Test

Confronted with a problem, and trying to make the right decision, one might ask, "Am I willing to have my decision widely known?" Would you be willing to have your decision publicized on the front page of the morning paper? If the answer is no, perhaps you should rethink the

The publicity test asks if a decision could be publicized with pride.

decision. If your decision could stand up to public examination, it is probably the right one.

Another version of this test is the Family Knowledge Question. Would you want the other members of your family (or your close friends) to know how you had decided? Again, if you can feel proud of your decision in the company of those you care about the most, you have probably made the right decision.

Perhaps the primary value of both versions is the process of thinking about our decisions in terms of how others would view them. By doing so, we are at least forced to remember that many of our day-to-day decisions do have important ethical dimensions.

D EVELOPMENT OF THE COMMON LAW

For more serious violations of the expected standards of conduct, societies impose legal sanctions. The government, acting on behalf of the people as a whole, may prosecute the wrongdoer under the criminal law. (A **crime** is a wrong against the whole society.) Where the wrongful conduct has resulted in an injury to a specific person, that injured party can bring a private legal action against the wrongdoer. (A **tort** is a wrong against an individual, for which the law provides a remedy—usually the payment of money.)

Crime = a wrong against society.

Tort = a wrong against an individual.

In most European nations, a comprehensive legal code was adopted at some point in time. The legal rules were organized, systematized, and written in terms of generally applicable legal principles. The role of the judges in these nations was primarily that of applying their codes' legal rules to the facts of the particular cases as they arose.

■ Custom and Common Law

The legal system which developed in England over several centuries was quite different from those found in most of western Europe. In England, the king's judges gradually assumed **jurisdiction** (judicial power) over more and more kinds of cases. At first, the judges simply tried to apply the customary rules that the society had developed. Gradually, case decisions came to be written down—at first as brief summaries and eventually as the full texts of the judges' opinions. As the system matured, these prior decisions came to be used as guidelines for solving future cases. If the case to be decided was essentially the same as several others which had been decided in prior years, the current case was usually decided the same way. This approach thus emphasized consistency and predictability in the application of the "common law of the land."

The English legal system is based on prior judicial decisions, or precedents.

A great body of legal theories, rules, and doctrine thus came to be stated in the reported cases. The "body of the Law" was in the cases. Rules for many new situations could be developed by the judges, reasoning by analogy from the prior cases. If a slightly different new problem seemed to demand a different result from those reached in the prior cases, the judges could distinguish the new problem on its facts and modify the existing rule. When major change was needed, a statute was passed to deal with the specific problem. The working assumption of this case law system was that the prior decision(s) should generally be followed. This rule is spoken of as the **doctrine of precedent**, and is also summarized in the Latin phrase *stare decisis*: "let the decision stand." This system was transplanted to the English colonies in America and is the basis for the modern United States legal system.

The following case shows the interrelationship of custom, case law, and statute. Mrs. Byrd claims that she was injured due to her husband's negligence in maintaining his boat. Negligence is a tort, for which the injured party would normally be able to recover damages. Virginia, where the Byrds live, does not permit one spouse to sue the other for such injuries. This rule is called the doctrine of **interspousal immunity**.

BYRD V. BYRD

657 F.2d 615 (U.S. 4th Cir. Court of Appeals, 1981).

JUSTICE·UNDE[

Facts: Mrs. Byrd sued her husband for injuries she sustained on her husband's boat. She was sitting on a deck chair when it fell from the flying bridge of the boat. She claimed her husband was negligent in failing to fasten the chair securely or in failing to provide guard railings around the bridge. She sued in U.S. District Court, since the boat was in waters where the law of the sea applied. (The U.S. District Courts have authority to hear cases where **admiralty law**—the law of the sea—is involved.) The District Court dismissed the claim on the basis of interspousal immunity, which was still the law in Virginia. Mrs. Byrd appeals.

Issue: Should the court establish a national rule for such lawsuits, or should it apply the rule of the state where the injury occurred?

Decision: The Appeals Court announced a new national rule for these admiralty cases. There is no interspousal immunity. The District Court decision is reversed, and the case is **remanded** (sent back) to the District Court for further proceedings (a trial).

Rule: State law cannot impair national admiralty law or defeat an otherwise valid maritime claim. The application of state law here would do both. There is no interspousal immunity in admiralty cases.

Discussion: *Judge* MURNAGHAN *first noted that there was no U.S. statute, and no prior court decision on this point of law:*

"Whereas at one time interspousal immunity in tort actions was, without significant exception, the law of all the states, presently, in whole or in part, thirty-two states have abrogated the doctrine. On the other hand, eighteen states and the District of Columbia seem still to apply it generally. Moreover, in those states where the doctrine has been abrogated, even greater disunity exists. Some states have abolished the doctrine entirely. Others have abolished it only in cases of intentional torts. Still others have abolished it only in cases arising out of automobile accidents, or only in cases of outrageous, intentional torts, or some other class of cases. Clearly, reference to state law in deciding maritime tort suits between a husband and wife will not lead to uniform decisions....

"Negligence in the operation of a boat creates a federal right of recovery in all who are injured by the negligence.... Therefore, application of a state's law on interspousal immunity, if that state does not permit suits between spouses arising out of negligent torts as appellee husband contends that the law of Virginia did not, would operate to defeat a substantial admiralty right of recovery.... It is clear, therefore, that fashioning an admiralty rule dealing with interspousal immunity will further the goal of a uniform admiralty law....

"[I]nterspousal immunity is a common law doctrine, initiated by courts.... Although there are statements in some cases that it should only be abolished by legislative action, where, as here, there has been no previous consideration of the question of whether the doctrine applies at all in admiralty, this Court is as competent as any other within its respective jurisdiction to determine whether the doctrine is a wise one for establishment in the jurisdiction. Moreover, any decision which we make will establish an easily ascertainable and applied rule; it will not have the effect of leaving a complex field virtually unregulated....

"When we turn to the question of what the uniform admiralty rule should be, the answer seems plain. Interspousal immunity is a doctrine whose day has come and gone. One ancient foundation of the rule—that husband and wife are one flesh and that a wife cannot so separate herself from her husband's bodily corporation as to be capable of maintaining an action against him—"'cannot be seriously defended today.'"... The other mainstay of the doctrine—that the prevention of suits between spouses encourages familial harmony—is, we surmise, inapplicable here. In suits involving the negligent operation of an automobile, the great probability of insurance and the consequent presence of an indemnitor to blunt and absorb the distress which a suit between spouses might otherwise be expected to generate, has been a primary justification for the abrogation of the doctrine of interspousal immunity in such cases.... For marine accidents involving pleasure boats, the insurance picture is likely to be similar. Virginia, where the parties are domiciled, does not have in force a compulsory insurance law for motor cars or for pleasure boats. Still, the economic factors motivating both vehicle and boat owners to take out casualty insurance are very strong.

"Finally, we note that the general trend among the states is toward the abolition of interspousal immunity.... It would be anomalous and within the foreseeable future, creative of less rather than more harmony between state and federal law, to establish the doctrine of interspousal immunity as a living organism of the admiralty law at a time when the trend in the states is towards its abolition."

Ethical Dimension

Should one spouse be permitted to sue the other to collect insurance money which will benefit both of them?

■ Trial by Jury

Just as judicial custom was used as a source of legal rules, social customs became part of the law through the use of the trial by jury. The origins of the jury are not completely clear. One version has the jury being used as "oath-helpers" for one of the parties. Twelve citizens would swear under oath that they would believe the plaintiff if the plaintiff made statements under oath. A person known in the community as a truthful person could thus be believed in court. Another version has the jurors being summoned from the community to provide evidence about the dispute itself, since they knew "who owned the brown spotted cow" or "where the Smith/Jones property line was."

Our modern jurors are not supposed to be character witnesses or eyewitnesses. Witnesses will testify during the trial, of course. But they should not be sitting in the jury box. The modern jury is supposed to decide the case based only on the evidence presented in court. The jury brings to the case "the conscience of the community" and its common sense. After hearing the evidence, the lawyers' arguments, and the judge's instructions, the jurors decide which party's version of the facts is more likely to be correct. They decide based on their experiences

The jury decides the facts of the case, based on the evidence, arguments, and instructions.

(and the evidence) what conduct is "reasonable" and how much the plaintiff's injuries are worth (if there is liability). While the jury is not used in many cases in England today, it is still a very important part of the United States legal system. (See figure 1–4.)

FIGURE 1-4
The jury is important to the fact-finding process of the U.S. legal system.

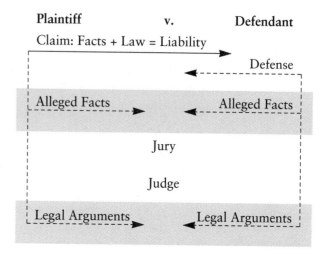

■ Ethics and Equity

A third distinguishing feature of the English legal system was its development of a supplementary set of courts called the **Equity**, or **Chancery**, Courts. Although the king's courts had assumed authority to hear a wide range of cases, they did not provide the kinds of relief or remedies to solve all types of problems. Their principal remedies were money damages and return of property wrongfully detained by another. These remedies solved most, but not all, problems. Persons who were being subjected to continued wrongdoing did not have an adequate remedy in a lawsuit for money damages. Persons who had contracted to buy unique items, where there was no second source available, did not have an adequate remedy in money damages. In these two cases, and in several others, the injured party's only recourse was to petition the king directly.

Equity developed as a supplement to the regular courts, to provide special remedies.

In very early times, the king may have heard such petitions himself. Quite often these petitions were directed to the crown's chief legal officer, the chancellor. The chancellor was empowered, in the king's name, to hear the dispute, to decide who was right, and to grant whatever relief was necessary to solve the problem. For the person threatened with a continuous wrong, the proper remedy was an **injunction**—a court order—in the king's name to stop. Then, if the wrongdoer disobeyed the court's order, fines and imprisonment for contempt of court could be used as further sanctions. Likewise, the person who had purchased a unique item wanted a court order **of specific performance** against the seller who was refusing to deliver. The court ordered the seller to perform the contract as agreed, by delivering the goods. If the seller then failed to do so, contempt of court sanctions could follow. Both of these remedies, as well as others developed by the equity courts, have major significance to modern business operations.

In most of our states today, there is no separate equity court. Delaware is an important exception. The Delaware Chancery Court is still organized as a separate court. It hears many important corporate disputes, since so many U.S. companies are incorporated in Delaware. In most states, the same judges hear both "law" and "equity" cases, using much the same procedure. On one point, however, there is still a difference—the right to a trial by jury. There is a constitutional right to have a civil case tried to a jury if the case is one "at common law." However, since there was no jury in the original equity courts, the constitutional guarantees for jury trial found in the national and state constitutions do not cover equity cases.

In deciding today whether a case will be heard by a jury, U.S. courts look to see what kind of relief the plaintiff is requesting. If it is money damages or return of property, the case is one "at common law," and each party has a constitutional right to have the case heard by a jury. If the plaintiff is asking for both money damages and an injunction, there will have to be a jury trial on the money damages aspects of the case if either party demands one. The judge will then decide any additional questions of fact raised by the injunction part of the case. If the plaintiff wants only an injunction (or specific performance), there is no constitutional right to a trial by jury at all. The trial judge would decide any disputed questions of fact in such a case. Similarly, if the plaintiff is seeking to enforce a new statutory right, unknown at common law, there is no constitutional right to a trial by jury. Workers' compensation cases, for instance, fall in this last category. Since the constitutional guarantee does not apply, the legislature is free to establish whatever method it wishes for handling disputes involving the new right. The legislature might decide to have these new cases tried to a jury, but it is not constitutionally required to provide a jury.

Most of our courts provide a right to trial by jury in civil cases only for those cases so triable when our Constitution was adopted.

⬛ UNITED STATES LEGAL THEORIES

Over the centuries, legal scholars in the U.S. and other western countries have developed several different theories to explain the nature of law and the law-making process. The relative strength of these theories has varied during our history, and expressions of each of them may be found in judicial opinions, legal texts, and law review articles. Fortunately for the law's predictability and stability, these theories are not totally opposed to each other, and they do contain many points of agreement.

■ Natural Law

Adherents of the natural law philosophy believe that there exists a body of "fundamental, unalterable, basic principles, uniformly applicable to all mankind, for the just governance of society." Murder is always wrong, whether it is committed by a jealous Cain against his brother Abel or by a crazed Hitler against a large portion of the Jewish population of Europe. Those who adhere to the natural law philosophy believe that these eternal standards of justice can be discovered by the use of one's reason. The standards can then be used as the benchmark by which current laws may be judged.

Natural law theory has been closely linked to the development of the U.S. legal system.

The natural law theory has been closely aligned with the development of the common law for many centuries. Thus, historically, it was the dominant school of legal thought in the United States. The task of the common law judge in developing a precedent was to discover and to apply these eternal principles to the case at hand. In addition, the American Revolution itself began with an appeal to these natural law principles. The Declaration of Independence states: "We hold these Truths to be self-evident, that all Men are created equal, that they are endowed by their Creator with certain unalienable Rights, that among these are Life, Liberty, and the Pursuit of Happiness...." Thus, the very ideals which are so basic to American democracy—freedom, equality, individualism—are closely tied to the concept of natural law.

Moreover, the Declaration goes on to recognize the natural law distinction between "just" laws and "unjust" laws as the basis for revolt against the British king. "That to secure these Rights, Governments are instituted among Men, deriving their just powers from the Consent of the Governed, that whenever any Form of Government becomes destructive of these Ends, it is the Right of the People to alter or to abolish it, and to institute new Government...." The ultimate sanction of the people against a government that is producing unjust laws is thus seen as the right to change and eliminate that government and to establish a new and just government. Natural law thus provides the standard against which the actions of existing governments can be judged.

■ Legal Realism

Legal realism is concerned with the actual results of court cases and how the judges decide them.

This theory is most succinctly expressed in Justice Holmes' famous quote: "The prophecies of what the courts will do in fact, and nothing more pretentious, are what I mean by the law." Holmes' theoretical perspective was from the point of view of the "bad man," who wished to know only what the courts would in fact do to him if he committed a certain act. The emphasis is on the law in action, its application, rather than the law as it is stated in statutes or cases. What the judge actually decides in the case at hand is the law, and not what legal scholars believe the rule to be. The law in action may or may not correspond to the law as stated in books.

Legal realism, then, is also an effort to predict the consequences of certain patterns of conduct, but the focus here is on the thought-processes of the judges who will decide actual cases rather than on abstract statements of legal principles. The training, experience, and mental set of the individual judge thus become more important parts of the prediction equation.

As the name implies, this group of theorists is more concerned with an accurate description of the "real" world of micro-law than with the ideal world of macro-law.

■ Legal Positivism

This legal theory is based on the writings of Mill, Bentham, and other political philosophers. Blackstone summarizes this view: all sovereign acts, and only sovereign acts, are the law. In a sense, this theory is also trying to describe legal reality; ideals of Right and Wrong, of the Just Society, are not really "the law." Only the rules for which governmental sanctions are provided are the law.

Legal positivism states that only the rules announced by governmental bodies are the law.

Moreover, adherents of this theory would argue, we cannot with certainty discover any eternal standards. Different persons' reasons will produce different sets of eternal truths, one person's no better than another's. However, society cannot function if each individual has the right and power to judge which rules will be obeyed and which will not. Freeway traffic could not move if each driver decided whether to drive on the right or the left side of the road or decided personally what was the appropriate speed limit.

This theory is correct in pointing out the fact that many of the "laws" enforced in modern society are only rules of convenience rather than applications of some eternal principle of justice. However, the danger inherent in this theory should also be apparent. If there are no eternal standards, and if anything passed by the sovereign power is the law and must therefore be obeyed, then there is no basis for condemning the actions of Nazi officials or Soviet keepers of the Gulag. Both governments enacted and enforced laws; millions of persons were imprisoned, starved, tortured, and killed in the name of enforcement of these laws. But since the sovereign power did these things, all were "legally" proper—if one follows positivism to its logical conclusion.

■ Sociological Theories

Another major group focuses on the law as an expression of the will of the people in a society. Although of more recent development, this theory is based in part on the studies of legal history done in the 1800s by Savigny and others. The emphasis here is on a judge's "creative choice" in shaping the law. The judge must look not only to precedent, in other words, but also to surrounding political, social, and economic factors, in deciding a case.

Sociological theories of the law focus on the social context within which legal rules are created.

Once again, the validity of this theory may depend on the emphasis one chooses. Surely a judge does need to be aware of the fact context within which a precedent was established and the fact context of the case at hand. Certainly in deciding whether to follow a precedent or to modify or reverse it, the judge needs to take into account the prevailing structure of society—how and when the precedent was decided. Presumably, common law judges have always done this, although there are instances where it seems that a precedent was being blindly followed rather than carefully examined.

At the other extreme, judicial "creativity" can be translated as judicial whim, arrogance, or caprice. Too much "creativity" and there is no legal system at all, only a hodgepodge of cases, each "creatively" decided.

■ Judicial Activism vs. Judicial Self-Restraint

A large part of the difference between and among the various theories centers on the role of the judge. One's adherence to one theory or the other may depend largely on how one views the judicial function. The more one trusts the judge, (presumably) the more power one would give the judge, and the more one would accept judicial decisions as a correct expression of the law.

Judges and lawyers disagree on the extent to which judges, rather than the legislature, should create new rules.

Supporters of an activist judiciary believe that there must be a governmental remedy for every (or nearly every) perceived social ill. They believe that the judges must take the lead if the legislative and executive branches refuse to act. The sociological and realist theories seem to provide the most support for this view. Persons wishing to restrain the judges to their more traditional role would argue that political solutions are the job of the political branches—the legislature and the executive. Supporters of judicial restraint believe that inaction by these political bodies means that the people do not desire changes. Further, the federal system implies that each state will have considerable freedom to experiment with particular social and economic arrangements. Logically, then, the judges should be very reluctant to substitute their ideas of public policy for those of the state legislatures.

Constitutional decision-making in the United States is further complicated by the conflict between conservative and liberal values. An activist conservative judge would be quite willing to strike down legislative limits on freedom of contract, such as required minimum wage laws. An activist liberal judge would quickly invalidate any limits on free speech. Judges following a philosophy of judicial self-restraint, whatever their political persuasion, would be more willing to balance off the restraint involved against the social objective to be served, and would be reluctant to second-guess a legislative judgment unless the restraint were a serious one.

As you read the case opinions in this book, you will see expressions of each of these philosophical viewpoints.

E THICS AND COMMERCIAL ACTIVITY

Of course, economic concerns are the primary driving force behind most business decisions. Will this course of action make our company more profitable? Which investment will produce greater income, both now and in the future? These are the kinds of questions which come immediately to mind when one thinks of "business decisions."

But business decisions often have effects on others—the company's workers, customers, suppliers, and the communities within which each of these groups lives and works. To what extent should such economic and non-economic concerns be factored into the business decision? It is at this point that ethical standards and business practice intersect.

Professional Codes of Ethics

Many professions, such as law and medicine, have their own codes of professional conduct. In some cases, compliance with these ethical standards is mandatory; in others, voluntary. A lawyer who violates the required standards of professional conduct may be barred from further practice or temporarily suspended. Official opinions as to the application of the standards to particular situations are published by many state bar associations as a guide to the lawyers practicing in that state.

Many professions have codes of ethical conduct for their members.

In contrast, the Preamble to the American Medical Association's "Principles of Medical Ethics" states: "[These principles] are not laws but standards by which a physician may determine the propriety of his conduct in his relationship with patients, with colleagues, with members of allied professions, and with the public." Noncompliance would not necessarily result in any sort of sanction against the offending doctor. Lawyers are probably in a unique position in most states in being subject to an actual loss of license to practice for violation of ethical norms.

Business Ethics

There are no similar, generally-applicable ethical standards for ordinary business operations. Of course, businesses are bound by the laws applicable to the various kinds of commercial transactions. And some companies do have their own codes of behavior for their own employees. But since there is no licensing/regulatory organization for businesses that is similar to the state bar associations for lawyers, there are no general ethical rules for ordinary businesses. The management of each business has to develop its own philosophy of how to treat its customers, suppliers, and employees.

Business ethics are difficult to define.

On many business questions, there are differences of opinion as to what constitutes ethical conduct. For example, is it ethical to advertise, on Saturday morning TV cartoon shows, products that appeal to young children? Most companies that sell such products do advertise that way, but is it proper to use powerful psychological tactics to influence unsophisticated young minds? Many people, both parents and non-parents, don't think so. To use another situation, is it ethical to manufacture and sell products that are legal, but are known to be harmful, such as cigarettes and alcoholic beverages? Some people would say no. Is it ethical to write commercials for such products, to convince people to buy and use the harmful products? Again, some people would say no, but billion-dollar industries are involved here.

For many such business decisions, what is legal and what many people would consider ethical do not necessarily correspond. Here is one more example, from contract law. There is usually no legal duty to make a full disclosure of all information to the other party to a contract. However, many people would probably say that it is unethical not to do so. Here again, each business and each person will have to construct an individual standard to follow.

■ Corporate Social Responsibility

There has been much talk in recent years of the "social responsibility" of corporations (and other business organizations). This phrase also means different things to different people.

Under a pure economic analysis, a corporation is nothing more than a legal device for conducting business (or other activities). It permits investors to pool their money for a joint activity without assuming personal liability for all the debts of the enterprise. It has no social purpose other than the successful operation of the enterprise—profit, in the case of the business corporation. The hope of profit was the reason for its formation and for the investments made by the individuals who bought its stock. It owes them, and society, nothing else.

There is disagreement over whether business corporations have a social role other than profit maximization.

Of course, in trying to gain profits, the business corporation must obey all the laws. But some commentators now believe that corporations owe society more than just obedience to the laws. In this view, corporations have a duty to use their tremendous economic power as a positive force for good. Under this "social welfare" model, corporate management should consider things other than simple profit maximization when making corporate decisions. It may make economic sense to close a particular plant, but what about the impact of that decision on the small town in which the plant is the main source of jobs? Shouldn't that social impact be factored into the equation somewhere? Those who believe in the "social welfare" model think that it should.

Even if there is no legal duty to the town and the workers, isn't there an ethical one? Compliance with the law is a minimum standard—the floor. Should it also be the ceiling? Shouldn't management do more than the required legal minimum? This is another area in which each company, and its managers, will have to make a personal decision.

One important point should be kept in mind in making these analyses of the corporation's social responsibility. Corporate managers are acting as trustees of someone else's (the stockholders') money. It is one thing to make a decision on non-economic grounds regarding the use of your own money. It is somewhat different to do so with the money others have turned over to you to manage to achieve economic results. Put in simplest terms, it's easy to be "charitable" with the money of others.

◼ International Corporate Conduct

The explosive growth of international trade has added a whole new dimension to the problem of defining ethical standards. U.S. managers are increasingly living and working abroad and negotiating and transacting business across national borders. Cultural differences produce different ethical standards, and linguistic differences make it difficult to resolve conflicting expectations.

U.S. supplier companies find that in some countries the managers of buyer companies expect large fees as part of the purchase transaction. In the buyer company's nation, such payments are customary, lawful, and expected. A supplier company which refuses to make such payments finds that its offer to do business is not even considered. What should the supplier do? Make the payment and compete for the business? Or forego the business (and the potential profit) because such payments are unethical by most western standards? This dilemma is partially resolved for managers of U.S. companies by the Foreign Corrupt Practices Act, which makes most such payments illegal. The U.S. company—and its managers—can be criminally prosecuted under U.S. law, even though the payment was lawful and customary in the country where made. This law has been widely criticized, both as an "imperialistic" attempt to impose U.S. standards on the rest of the world, and as an additional handicap for U.S. companies trying to compete abroad.

U.S. companies and their managers can be prosecuted here for bribes paid in other countries.

Another, much more difficult ethical judgment must be made in a very different international context. The U.S. has fairly strict health and safety regulations. Because of these regulations, many useful products cannot be sold here. Is it ethical to sell such products overseas, in countries without such regulations? The product is perfectly lawful where sold and is in demand. Customers want the product, and profits can be made. But a U.S. regulatory agency has banned the product's sale here. Those who make such export decisions should weigh the ethical dimension very carefully. Business managers will almost certainly have to make such decisions on a product-by-product basis.

Justice Doggett's separate opinion in the following case expresses many of these concerns. He agreed with the court's result, but he felt that some of these policy issues needed to be discussed.

DOW CHEMICAL CO. V. CASTRO ALFARO

786 S.W.2d 674 (Tex. 1990)

Facts: Domingo Castro Alfaro worked for Standard Fruit Company on its banana plantation in Costa Rica. He and 81 other employees claim they suffered personal injuries, including sterility, from being exposed to a pesticide which was manufactured by Dow and by Shell Oil and then sold by those companies to Standard Fruit. The 82 employees and their wives filed a lawsuit against Dow and Shell in Houston, Texas, in state court. Both defendants are incorporated in Delaware. However, Shell has its corporate world headquarters in Houston, and Dow operates the largest chemical plant in the United States in Freeport, Texas, about sixty miles from Houston.

Dow and Shell asked the Texas court to dismiss the case as being brought in an "inconvenient" location, since the injuries occurred in Costa Rica, to Costa Rica citizens. (The legal doctrine which permits courts to dismiss lawsuits on such grounds is called *forum non conveniens*.) A Texas statute says that personal injury actions "may be enforced" in Texas courts even though the injury occurred in another country. The pesticide at issue, dibromachloropropane (DBCP), was banned for use in the United States in 1977. Dow and Shell, both before and after the U.S. ban, shipped hundreds of thousands of gallons of DBCP to Standard Fruit in Costa Rica for use there. The estimated maximum recovery per worker for the injuries claimed here would be $1,080 in Costa Rica.

The Texas trial court did dismiss the case, on the basis of *forum non conveniens*. The Texas Court of Appeals reversed that decision, and sent the case back to the trial court for a trial on the merits of the plaintiffs' claims. Dow and Shell then filed a further appeal with the Texas Supreme Court.

Issue: Does the Texas statute in question abolish the doctrine of *forum non conveniens*?

Decision: Yes, it does. Judgment of the Court of Appeals is affirmed. (The case will be tried in Texas.)

Rule: There is an absolute statutory right to litigate such cases in Texas.

Dliscussion: *by Justice* RAY:

"The doctrine of *forum non conveniens* arose from [a similar rule] in Scottish cases.... The Scottish courts recognized that the [rule] applied when to hear the case was not expedient for the administration of justice.... By the end of the nineteenth century, English courts had 'accepted the doctrine.'...

"Texas courts applied the doctrine...in several cases prior to the enactment of article 4678 in 1913 [the section on which the current Texas statute was based]....

"Our interpretation of the [current statute] is controlled by... *Allen v. Bass*.... In *Allen* the court of civil appeals conferred an absolute right to maintain a properly brought suit in Texas courts....

"We conclude that the legislature has statutorily abolished the doctrine of *forum non conveniens* in suits brought under [this statute]."...

Mr. Justice DOGGETT, *concurring:*

"The [dissenting judges] are insistent that a jury of Texans be denied the opportunity to evaluate the conduct of a Texas corporation concerning decisions it made in Texas because the only ones allegedly hurt are foreigners. Fortunately, Texans are not so provincial and narrow-minded as these dissenters presume. Our citizenry recognizes that a wrong does not fade away because its immediate consequences are first felt far away rather than close to home. Never have we been required to forfeit our membership in the human race in order to maintain our proud heritage as citizens of Texas.

"The dissenters argue that it is inconvenient and unfair for farmworkers allegedly suffering permanent physical and mental injuries, including irreversible sterility, to seek redress by suing a multinational corporation in a court three blocks away from its world headquarters and another corporation, which operates in Texas this country's largest chemical plant.... [T]he 'doctrine' they advocate has nothing to do with fairness and convenience and everything to do with immunizing multinational corporations from accountability for their alleged torts causing injury abroad....

"The banana plantation workers allegedly injured by DBCP were employed by an American company on American-owned land and grew Dole bananas for export solely to American tables. The chemical allegedly rendering the workers sterile was researched, formulated, tested, manufactured, labeled and shipped by an American company in the United States to another American company. The decision to manufacture DBCP for distribution and use in the third world was made by these two American companies in their corporate offices in the United States. Yet now Shell and Dow argue that the one part of this equation that should not be American is the legal consequences of their actions....

"A *forum non conveniens* dismissal is often, in reality, a complete victory for the defendant.... 'In some instances ... invocation of the doctrine will send the case to a jurisdiction which has imposed such severe monetary limitations on recovery as to eliminate the likelihood that the case will be tried. When it is obvious that this will occur, discussion of the convenience of witnesses takes on a Kafkaesque quality—everyone knows that no witnesses ever will be called to testify.'... Empirical data available demonstrate that less than four percent of cases dismissed under the doctrine...ever reach trial in a foreign court....

"The abolition of *forum non conveniens* will further important public policy considerations by providing a check on the conduct of multinational corporations.... The misconduct of even a few multinational corporations can affect untold millions around the world. For example, after the United States imposed a domestic ban on the sale of cancer-producing...children's sleepwear, American companies exported approximately 2.4 million pieces to Africa, Asia and South America. A similar pattern occurred when a ban was proposed for baby pacifiers that had been linked to choking deaths in infants.... These examples of indifference by some corporations towards children abroad are not unusual.

"The allegations against Shell and Dow, if proven true, would not be unique, since production of many chemicals banned for domestic use has thereafter continued for foreign marketing."

Ethical Dimension

Is there any potential "unfairness" to defendants in such cases (permitting lawsuits here for injuries occurring in other countries)? Are there any possible adverse effects on the U.S. court system?

Closely related to this problem is the "unsavory customer" dilemma. Is it ethical to do business with a dictatorship? To sell it medical supplies, which will presumably benefit sick and injured people? To sell it telecommunications equipment, which will make it a more efficient police state? To sell it military weapons or nuclear technology, which might make it an international threat? To sell it computer technology, which might be used for either good purposes or evil ones? Over the years, several companies have earned large profits by dealing with the governments accused of various human rights violations. Is it ethical for us to support such companies with our investment dollars? To buy their products? To work for them? Again, each individual will have to make a personal decision on these points.

U.S. companies face ethical issues if they do business with dictatorial goverments.

REVIEW

All societies develop rules for the conduct of their members, indicating what conduct is required, expected, tolerated, and prohibited. Various moral and ethical systems have been developed over the centuries, many of them having a common core content. Even among persons claiming to follow a certain system, individual interpretations of the rules will vary.

The common law system has been closely linked with popular beliefs and customs for many centuries. Early court decisions were based on popular custom. The operating rule of the system is to follow established judicial custom, or precedents. The system continues to rely on the jury as a source of popular wisdom and common sense.

The common law system also developed the court of equity as a court of conscience, to remedy wrongs even though there was no previously established legal remedy. For many centuries, the common law was closely tied to the natural law doctrine, which tried to advance human justice towards an ideal justice. Other legal theories—realism, positivism, legal sociology—have more recently emphasized other factors in the judicial process. The conflict between judicial activism and judicial restraint remains an ongoing debate.

Professional and business decisions present many ethical dilemmas in today's internationally interdependent world. Science and technology permit us to do some things that perhaps ought not to be done, as in our tampering with human genetics. Complex ethical issues, for which there are no easy answers, confront today's business manager. Sensitivity to these ethical issues, and care and effort in dealing with them, have become important ingredients in long-term business success.

REVIEW QUESTIONS AND PROBLEMS

1. Should business decisions be based only on economic factors, or should other values be considered as well?

2. Pamela works for a government agency which regulates banks. She has been dating a secretary, Bert, who works for a regulated bank. Bert's bank, as a present for Secretaries' Week, gives him two tickets to a play. He asks Pamela to go with him. Would it be unethical for her to use one of these tickets?

3. A small freighter sinks during a hurricane, somewhere in the middle of the Atlantic Ocean. One lifeboat, designed to carry 12 people, is loaded with 15 people inside it, and with 8 more hanging onto its sides, but in the water. High winds and rough seas threaten to sink the boat if all 23 people continue to use it. If the lifeboat sinks, all 23 will probably drown. The officer in charge of the boat orders the 8 weakest persons pushed away from the boat, while the others row away. Those 8 drown; the 15 left in the boat survive. Did the officer make an ethical decision? Would your answer change if you knew that a rescue ship had arrived on the scene the very next morning?

4. Is it ethical for a medical doctor to perform any procedure which medical technology makes possible? What happens to frozen human embryos, which can be used to produce human beings, when the "parents" divorce or separate?

5. An inspector from the Department of Housing is checking a house to decide whether his agency should insure a mortgage on the house. The owner offers him a bottle of wine from the built-in wine cellar in the basement of the house. Should the inspector accept the wine? Suppose the offer was just a glass of wine while the inspection was in progress or while the inspector was sitting down writing up the report? Would your answer be different if the offer was for a cup of coffee, rather than a glass of wine?

6. Heidi was hired as a mail delivery person by the U.S. Post Office. She was a temporary employee for the summer before she started college in September. As the regular mail carriers took their vacations, she delivered the mail on their routes. Each morning, she was given a load of mail to deliver during that eight-hour day.

Heidi has found that she can deliver all the assigned mail in about five hours rather than the eight she is "supposed" to take. What should she do— go back to the office and ask for more mail to deliver, slow down so that it takes her eight hours, or just go home whenever she finishes each day? She realizes that since she is young and in good health, she may walk faster than some of the regular carriers she is replacing. She also realizes that she is only working in the job temporarily.

7. Over time, Eskimo society developed the practice of abandoning old people who could no longer contribute to the family group. These old ones were simply left to freeze to death. Is such a practice moral and ethical?

8. U.S. society currently spends millions, even billions, to prolong the lives of persons who are in comas or who are suffering horrible pain. Huge medical bills are incurred by families, or are imposed on the society as a whole, as a result of the desire to prolong life whenever possible. Is this practice ethical and moral? Is it ethical and moral to deprive a person of all possible means of sustaining life just because of financial costs?

9. About once a month, Rowena brings her supervisor home-made baked goods, such as rolls, cakes, bread or cookies. Should the supervisor continue to accept these small gifts?

2
THE
POLITICAL
SYSTEM

"Sell not virtue to purchase wealth, nor liberty to purchase power."
Benjamin Franklin

LEARNING OBJECTIVES: After you have studied this chapter, you should be able to:

IDENTIFY the major interest groups involved in the U.S. political process.

EXPLAIN how individuals and groups can influence the political process.

DISCUSS the role of political parties in the electoral process.

DESCRIBE the mechanics of elections in the United States.

EXPLAIN how the legislative process works.

P REVIEW

Large-scale involvement of government in economic affairs is a fact of life in modern America, and indeed, in nearly any other country one could name. In most areas of business, therefore, profitability depends in large measure on an ability to peacefully and creatively coexist with the government. This chapter discusses the American political process and the methods by which business can and does try to influence that process to produce favorable outcomes.

P ARTICIPATORY DEMOCRACY

The U.S. political system is based on consent of the governed.

The cornerstone of our governmental system is the "consent of the governed." This fundamental principle was stated in the Declaration of Independence. It is repeated in the Preamble to the U.S. Constitution: "We, the People of the United States...do ordain and establish this Constitution for the United States of America." Just so there could be no question, the rights involved in public participation in policy-making were reaffirmed in the First Amendment. The First Amendment provides that Congress shall make no law which restricts freedom of speech, or of the press, or of assembly, or of petition. All citizens were thus encouraged to participate—to speak out on public issues, to assemble to discuss them, to express their views to their representatives in government. A free press was felt to be absolutely essential to the democratic process—both as a forum for the expression of various points of view and as a watchdog on government officials.

The Declaration and the Constitution are magnificent statements of the great, enduring principles of democratic government. But two points are worth noting. First, there are limits even to the basic freedoms stated in the First Amendment. For example, freedom of speech does not give you the right to shout "Fire!" in a crowded theater. Freedom of the press is not a license for libel and slander of other persons. Freedom of assembly can be subject to reasonable time and place limits.

Second, full citizen participation is a goal, not necessarily a reality at a given point in time. When the Constitution was adopted in 1789, women did not have the right to vote. Neither did slaves or Native Americans. Even today, many people who are eligible to vote do not do so. Most of us never contact our representatives to express our views, or write a letter to our local newspaper. We complain a lot to each other, but most of us are not very active politically. Our system was designed to be effective when we participate.

INTEREST GROUPS

Political scientists identify coalitions of persons with similar interests or objectives as **interest groups** or **pressure groups**. Such groups may be organized for a variety of purposes. The groups or factions most frequently have an economic orientation, as noted by the authors of the *Federalist*: "(T)he most common and durable source of faction has been the various and unequal distribution of property." "Business" is only one of many such groups.

Business

American business constitutes the largest and most powerful, and yet at the same time most diverse, of these interest groups. Nearly all self-employed persons, including professionals such as doctors and lawyers, consider themselves to be "in business." Most managers, particularly those at the higher corporate levels, identify with the interests of the firm by which they are employed. (However, many white-collar employees have joined the ranks of organized labor in recent years.) Bankers, financiers, and brokers of both securities and real estate are also part of the business group. All these persons, together with their family members, plus corporate stockholders and their families, constitute a potentially gigantic pool of money, votes, and political workers.

Business is a very large, but diverse, interest group.

Of course, not all these people agree on all specific issues. No one agency or organization speaks for "business" as a whole. The National Association of Manufacturers does generally represent the views of most large manufacturing enterprises. Even within such a small subgroup, however, there may be differences on such issues as tariff policy and tax incentives between the auto and steel industries on the one hand and the aerospace and information industries on the other. Even within the same industry, not all firms agree on what governmental policy should be, any more than do all the citizens of a small town. Such differences of opinion are the very essence of politics.

Owners and managers of small businesses also have a set of priorities which may diverge considerably from those of the corporate giants. Small business wants free and equal access to the marketplace, including a fair share of government contracts. Small business wants the government to prevent monopolization by one or a few large firms. Small business may not favor the same sort of tax system as the large corporations.

Retailers in many industries are organized into their own trade associations—druggists, grocers, auto dealers, and others. Professionals such as doctors, dentists, lawyers, accountants, and realtors also have their own professional associations.

The Chamber of Commerce of the United States comes closest to being the voice of business as a whole. This group is a federation of several thousand other groups: state and local Chambers, industry groups, and trade associations. It attempts to formulate and to promote the business position on matters of nationwide scope, such as trade policy, tax laws, and labor and other regulation. An international Chamber of Commerce has also been organized. It provides a forum for businesses from many nations to exchange views and to work for common goals.

■ Farmers

In a sense, farmers are also part of "business," in that they are self-employed in an enterprise organized to make a profit. The nature and scope of the farming enterprise, however, make them a distinct interest group, even though they may agree with the business position on some issues. As producers of raw materials for the food-processing and textile industries, farmers want governmental policies which will help them get high prices for their crops. For years, the national government has subsidized some parts of agriculture, either by buying crops at a set minimum price or by paying farmers not to produce. As consumers of credit, fertilizers, and fuels, farmers want assured supplies of these items at stable, fair prices. The very high interest rates of recent years have contributed substantially to the decline in the number of small, family-owned farms.

NATIONAL FARM ORGANIZATIONS

Several different groups represent the interests of farmers.

There are several national farm organizations. The oldest and perhaps the largest is the National Grange, which still retains some aspects of a fraternal organization as well as functioning as an economic interest group. The Granger movement in the upper Midwest states in the 1870s and 1880s was primarily responsible for the laws regulating such businesses as grain elevators and railroads. It is probably strongest today in the Northeast and the Northwest, and in Ohio and Pennsylvania. A second national farm organization is the American Farm Bureau Federation. Its main constituencies are the corn and cotton farmers of the Midwest and the South, together with the land grant colleges and their agricultural services. The most radical of the three major farm groups is the National Farmer's Union (NFU). Its membership centers in the plains and mountain states and the upper Midwest. The members are generally younger and more heavily in debt. The NFU is more concerned with farming as a life-style and less concerned with farming as a business. The NFU also takes a more positive view of unions, with whom most of its members feel a certain degree of friendship. All three organizations are geared toward the individual farmer, whether old or new, wealthy or poor.

AGRIBUSINESS

None of the three national farm organizations just discussed really represents the newest phenomenon in American agriculture—the agribusiness. Increasingly, as more and more thousands of individual farmers leave farming, the dominant force in many sectors is the corporate farm. Economies of scale are such that only very large farming operations can make a profit from the land. Whether organized as subsidiaries of conglomerates or as independent corporations, such "farmers" are more closely allied with general business interests.

■ Labor

The obvious fellowship of all those who work with their hands and brains for wages paid by another provides a good deal of homogeneity to labor as an interest group. Even here, however, there are differences—between organized and unorganized, between blue-collar and white-collar, between public and private, between geographical regions, and between industries. Proposals for governmental action to prevent plant relocation sponsored by a northern union, might not be favored by unorganized workers in the Sun Belt states, where such plants are likely to relocate. Strikes by public school teachers for higher wages might not be received sympathetically by other workers (even unionized ones), who are also taxpayers and parents. (Such strikes are illegal in some states, but may occur anyway.)

The clearest voice of American labor is that of the American Federation of Labor-Congress of Industrial Organizations (AFL-CIO). Simply because it is organized, this merged federation has the most political clout—the most money to spend, the most votes, the most volunteer campaign workers. It should be noted, however, that less than twenty percent of all employees are members of unions. It is also worth noting that the AFL-CIO has had increasing difficulty in winning bargaining rights. In recent years it has won half or less of NLRB-sponsored elections. In the long run, a continued loss of economic power will mean a corresponding loss of political power.

The AFL-CIO is the largest labor organization.

With the return of the United Auto Workers to the AFL-CIO, the major "independent" union is the Teamsters. The Teamsters Union has been aggressively organizing employees in areas other than trucking and is the country's largest single union. While it may agree with the AFL-CIO on most labor issues, it showed political independence in 1972 by endorsing Richard Nixon for president, rather than the Democratic candidate endorsed by the AFL-CIO. For a variety of reasons, other state and local unions may also refuse to follow the AFL-CIO endorsements.

■ Veterans

About one out of every seven Americans over the age of sixteen is a veteran of military service. Veterans are typically cataloged as a separate interest group, but it is more difficult to identify issues which are specific to them. They are typically concerned about laws which grant veterans preference in applying for government jobs and which preserve veterans' civilian job seniority while on active duty. They want the government to continue programs for education, retraining, and rehabilitation, and insurance and medical benefits. Many, but by no means all veterans, favor a strong national defense. On most other issues, a veteran's position is likely to be determined by membership in other groups.

Veterans are represented by several organizations.

Most veterans' organizations are as much social clubs as pressure groups. The veterans' group with the most political clout historically was the Grand Army of the Republic, composed of Union veterans of the Civil War. Its role has been taken over to some extent by the American Legion, which does exercise considerable political power within the narrow range of issues on which it specializes. The Veterans of Foreign Wars limits its membership to those who have had overseas service, but its stance on most issues does not differ markedly from that of the Legion. The Disabled American Veterans is a still smaller group, composed of those with service-related disabilities. It is particularly concerned with medical, rehabilitation, and re-employment programs. The two smaller groups organized after World War II are the American Veterans (Amvets) and the American Veterans' Committee (AVC). Organizational positions taken by Amvets have not differed substantially from those of the older groups, but the AVC adopted a more radical stance on several issues. Most recently, the Vietnam Veterans of America (VVA) has been formed as a separate group. The unpopularity of the Vietnam War created special problems for many returning veterans. The VVA has attempted to address these concerns, by advocating increased counseling and rehabilitation programs.

■ Senior Citizens

Senior citizens form a large bloc of voters.

As more and more persons are living for a considerable time after retirement, the political power of older citizens has increased dramatically. More than 30 million persons are over 65, and a high percentage of them do vote. "Senior citizens" have a number of issues of prime concern. They are, of course, vitally interested in the continued solvency of the Social Security system. Any politician who advocates tampering with the system had better have a strong and convincing statement to justify proposed changes. The elderly are particularly susceptible to crimes of both force and fraud, so they are interested in programs for safe streets and public areas and for consumer protection against fraud. They are also concerned about public services such as transportation, parks, and recreation facilities. Senior citizens support government efforts to prevent age discrimination in employment and generally are not in favor of mandatory retirement at some specified age. By and large, these concerns are expressed in the voting booth. Senior citizens are still not a cohesive group, although an organization called the Gray Panthers has made some progress. Most recently, the American Association of Retired Persons (AARP) has emerged. AARP has several million members, for whom it provides a number of products and services. It has also become a powerful lobby group with a large Washington office.

◼ Ethnic Groups

The issue of most concern to members of ethnic groups is discrimination—in employment, in education, in access to services, and in all other areas. The "melting pot" is an idea whose time has come and gone. (See Figure 2–1.) Many ethnics no longer wish to be assimilated into the majority culture. Ethnics are generally proud of their differences. They may very well wish to strengthen, rather than diminish, their separate cultural identity. What is objectionable is not necessarily a recognition that differences exist, but rather the use of such differences as a basis for negative discriminatory treatment by employers

FIGURE 2–1

U.S. population–selected ancestry groups (1990 census)

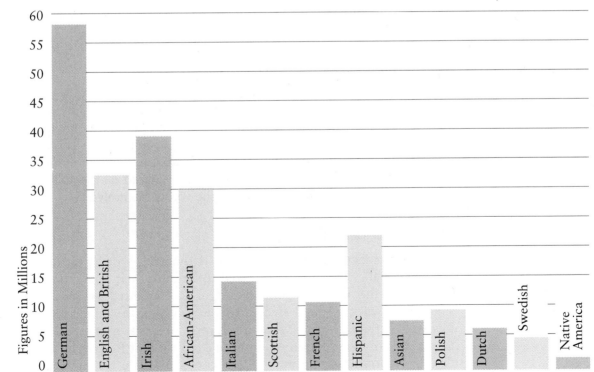

and other private and public agencies. A large share of the credit for the civil rights revolution of the last thirty years—both awareness of the problem and legislative and judicial solutions—must go to such organizations as the National Association for the Advancement of Colored People and the B'nai B'rith Anti-Defamation League.

Of course, each group has its own list of priorities based on the specific problems faced by its members. Culturally-biased employment and educational tests are examples. In the case of such groups as the Latinos, the bias is language-based. The most unique situation is that of the Native Americans, or American Indians. Although they are U.S. citizens and have the right to vote, they also retain a special status from the historical period when the tribes were dealt with by the U.S. government as sovereign nations. One of the primary concerns of many Indian tribes is the legal recognition of their treaty rights against the national and state governments.

■ Single Issue Groups

Rather than being organized on the basis of socio-economic status or ethnic background, many groups form to promote a single issue or group of issues. For instance, many separate groups were organized, both for and against, in the unsuccessful campaign for the adoption of the Equal Rights Amendment, which would have prohibited any gender-based discrimination by a state agency. There are similar opposing groups battling over the abortion issue. Such groups have organized to influence public decisions on such matters as school prayer, nuclear power, and national defense policy. The list is endless.

P UBLIC OPINION AND THE MEDIA

One of the primary objectives of most interest groups, indeed the very reason many of them come into being, is to influence public policy. The group may attempt to do so directly, by contacting legislators and administrators, or indirectly, by creating public opinion favorable to their cause. In those cases where the issue is placed on the ballot for direct vote, the appeal will be made to the voters themselves.

■ Letter Writing and Petitions

Voters may try to influence political leaders by contacting them directly.

One popular tactic of pressure groups is the letter-writing campaign. Members and sympathizers are asked to write to their public officials and request the desired action. Or people may be asked to sign a petition which will then be presented by the group to the public officials involved. Perhaps the most famous example of this sort of tactic is the Committee of One Million Against the Admission of Red China to the United Nations. Getting one million voters to agree on any specific issue is not an easy task, quite apart from the logistics involved. However, a communication from such a large number of voters is persuasive to a public official, especially if he or she was undecided on the issue.

Polls

Many large organizations are now involved in sampling the public's reaction to policy issues, either before or after decisions are made. The Gallup poll, the Harris poll, and polls by national news media are all published regularly. Polls are taken before elections to try to predict the winners. Polls are taken to gauge the public's approval of the incumbent president. Polls are taken of consumer confidence. In each case, the poll-taker, by using a statistical sample, is trying to discover how the public at large is reacting to a particular issue of public importance.

Polls show what the voters are thinking.

POLLS BY INTEREST GROUPS

In some instances, an interest group may conduct its own poll. One such poll which has gained considerable importance is the poll conducted on national security issues by the National Security Council (NSC). Even though it is a poll of NSC members, the numbers involved are significant, and the results are widely reported in newspapers and communicated to individual members of Congress. The NSC also uses the poll results as a basis for comparison of voter sentiment with the voting records of particular members of Congress. Several other organizations compile voting indexes for Congress, but they do not have similar poll data on voter sentiment. For those polls the only basis for comparison is whether one Congress-member is more or less liberal or conservative than another.

POLLS BY BUSINESS

Business, of course, also uses polling techniques in conducting marketing research. And in the broadest sense, the marketplace is itself a kind of "poll" of consumers' reactions to goods and services which are offered for sale. Consumers are making the ultimate "vote" by spending their hard-earned money for particular products or services. Just as the final test of a politician is the election result, the final test of a product is its acceptance in the marketplace. More recently, business has begun to make increased use of more sophisticated polling techniques to test employee attitudes, public perceptions of the company, and reaction to significant decisions such as plant location.

Advertising, Sponsorships, and Speech-Making

Business spends considerable sums of money to promote its products and services, both by advertising and by sponsoring events and perfor-

Advertising can be used to sell political ideas.

mances. These same tools can also be used to influence decisions on public policy, either directly or indirectly. An appeal can be made directly to the voters to support a particular ballot proposal or a particular candidate. Or "public issue" advertising can be used to try to create a climate of opinion favorable to a particular activity, such as the construction of nuclear power plants. Much good will toward business and (perhaps) a sympathetic ear for its views on public issues can be generated by business sponsorship of charitable and other community events, such as telethons and sporting events. All these devices can be used to try to overcome any automatic negativity attached to a proposal sponsored by business.

In addition to contributing their time, talents, and money, business people can have a substantial impact on public policy decisions by effectively communicating the business view of the issue. Many public policy decisions have business and economic implications—tax policy, labor policy, trade policy, environmental policy, and others. Both the voters and the governmental officials involved need (and usually want) information on these business and economic consequences. Business spokespersons who are articulate and available for meetings, TV appearances, and the like can have a very positive impact on the ultimate decision. Precisely because such business messages can be very effective, Massachusetts passed the statute at issue in the following case.

FIRST NATIONAL BANK OF BOSTON V. BELLOTTI

435 U.S. 765 (1978)

Facts: A Massachusetts statute prohibited corporations from making political contributions or expenditures except on ballot issues which materially affect their business. The statute further said that no ballot issue relating to taxation can materially affect corporate business. Violations of the statute could result in fines up to $50,000 for a corporation; up to $10,000 and/or a year in jail for executives.

First National Bank of Boston, another bank, and three business corporations challenged the constitutionality of this statute. They wanted to spend money to oppose a proposed amendment to the state constitution which would authorize a graduated income tax. Plaintiffs brought an action against the state attorney general, Bellotti, to have the statute declared unconstitutional. The state courts held for Bellotti. Plaintiffs asked the U.S. Supreme Court for further review.

Issue: May a state prohibit business corporations from spending money to publicize their views on political issues?

Decision: No. State court judgment for Bellotti is reversed.

Rule: The First Amendment protects the rights of listeners to hear, as well as speakers to discuss, various points of view on political issues.

Discussion: *By Justice POWELL:*

"The Constitution often protects interests broader than those of the party seeking their vindication. The First Amendment, in particular, serves significant societal interests. The proper question therefore is not whether corporations 'have' First Amendment rights and, if so, whether they are coextensive with those of natural persons. Instead, the question must be whether [the statute under consideration] abridges expression that the First Amendment was meant to protect. We hold that it does.

"The speech proposed by appellants is at the heart of the First Amendment's protection.

"The freedom of speech and of the press guaranteed by the Constitution embraces at the least the liberty to discuss publicly and truthfully all matters of public concern without previous restraint or fear of subsequent punishment.... In appellants' view, the enactment of a graduated personal income tax, as proposed to be authorized by constitutional amendment, would have a seriously adverse effect on the economy of the state. The importance of the referendum issue to the people and government of Massachusetts is not disputed. Its merits, however, are the subject of sharp disagreement.

"...'[T]here is practically universal agreement that a major purpose of [the First] Amendment was to protect the free discussion of governmental affairs.' If the speakers here were not corporations, no one would suggest that the state could silence their proposed speech. It is the type of speech indispensable to decision making in a democracy, and this is no less true because the speech comes from a corporation rather than an individual. The inherent worth of the speech in terms of its capacity for informing the public does not depend upon the identity of its source, whether corporation, association, union, or individual."

Ethical Dimension

How can a corporation—a "person" only for legal purposes—have a view on political issues? Exactly whose point of view is a corporation expressing? How is the "corporation's" position on a political issue determined?

P OLITICAL PARTIES

Political parties, at least the two major ones in the United States, are coalitions of interest groups and ordinary voters which have come together to try to win public office for their candidates. Political parties also provide organization for Congress and the state legislatures, making committee assignments and scheduling agenda items.

■ Major Parties

The Democrats and the Republicans have been our two major political parties since the Civil War.

Since the Civil War, politics in the United States has been dominated by the Republican and the Democratic parties. Because of the residue of bad feeling from the Civil War, the South had been a Democratic stronghold until quite recently. Even today, the Republican party in the South is not a viable challenger in many local elections, but change is still occurring. The Republicans have historically been strongest in the Midwest and the West.

NEW DEAL COALITION

A New Deal coalition assembled by Franklin D. Roosevelt consisted of labor, small farmers, and most of the minority ethnic groups, coupled with the solid South. This Democratic coalition held together with only minor defections until 1968, when many labor voters and some ethnics changed to the Republican party. High taxes, inflation, and crime were worrisome issues to these voters, and the Democratic national convention seemed to ignore its traditional leaders and supporters. Much of the South voted for Governor George Wallace of Alabama as an independent candidate for president in 1968. Without the choice of Wallace for president in 1972, many of his 1968 supporters voted for Richard Nixon. The nomination of a southerner, Jimmy Carter, as the Democratic candidate for president in 1976, at least brought the South back into the fold. The 1976 election is difficult to categorize, however, due to the impact of the Watergate scandal. (Both President Nixon and Vice-President Agnew had resigned. Gerald Ford, a longtime member of Congress who had been appointed Vice-President when Agnew resigned, became president when Nixon resigned. Thus the "incumbent" president in 1976 had not been elected to the job, or even to the vice-presidency.) The landslide victory of Republican Ronald Reagan in 1980 indicated that there are at least a large number of voters who are willing to switch their party support under certain conditions.

GEOGRAPHIC STRENGTH

Historically, since most of the "safe" Republican congressional seats were in the relatively conservative areas of the Midwest and West, and most of the "safe" Democratic seats were in the conservative South, the congressional leadership of each party tended to be more conservative than its presidential candidates. Until the election of 1964, the Republicans felt compelled to nominate presidential candidates who were "middle-of-the-road" enough to appeal to voters in the large states. Having conceded the South to the Democrats, and therefore having given them about half of the electoral votes needed to elect a president, the Republicans could not also concede the big-city states and still have a realistic chance of winning the presidency.

Historically, the Democrats have been strong in the South, the Republicans in the Midwest.

The nomination of Barry Goldwater in 1964 marked a turning point in Republican politics. Despite the aftermath of John F. Kennedy's assassination in 1963, which made many voters reluctant to vote for another change so soon, and despite some of the most viciously effective campaign ads ever, which portrayed Senator Goldwater as a mad nuclear terrorist, his "southern strategy" proved to be essentially correct. He did carry most of the states of the once-solid South and paved the way for a rebirth of the Republican party in those states. Few states can really be considered "solid" for either party now, at least in presidential elections.

LIBERAL AND CONSERVATIVE WINGS

There are still liberal and conservative wings in each party, although most liberals support the Democrats and most conservatives (at least outside the South) support the Republicans. There may also be other sorts of internal splits in each party. Most recently, members of Congress from both parties representing the older industrial states of the Northeast and Midwest have joined forces on matters of economic concern to their constituents. Some conservative Democrats, especially from the South, were vocal supporters of President Reagan's changes in tax and fiscal policy. One such Democrat, Congressman Phil Gramm of Texas, was stripped of his seniority by the Democratic leadership in the House. He resigned his seat, and was later elected as a Republican senator from Texas.

■ Minor Parties

For both the U.S. Senate and the U.S. House of Representatives, the candidate with the most votes is elected. The "single member district" thus makes it difficult for a narrowly-based party to gain representation in the Congress. New York, for example, has had a Liberal Party for many years, but the Liberals usually endorse the Democratic candidates for national office. In the 1970s a Conservative Party appeared as an additional ballot choice in New York and actually elected its candidate for U.S. Senator, James Buckley, with the help of Democrats and independents.

In the election of 1912, the "Bull Moose" wing of the Republican Party got more electoral votes for its presidential candidate, Theodore

Roosevelt, than the regular Republican candidate, William H. Taft. However, Woodrow Wilson received more than either of them and was elected. Strom Thurmond received the electoral votes of some southern states as the "Dixiecrat" candidate in 1948 (he was later elected Republican Senator from South Carolina). George Wallace received comparable popular vote totals in these southern states in 1968 and also ran strongly in several northern states. In the 1992 election, independent candidate Ross Perot received about 20 percent of the popular vote and actually outpolled the incumbent president, George Bush, in a few states.

Minor parties have often provided the momentum for reform.

Even though they do not win national office, minor party candidates can be effective voices for reform. If particular proposals seem to be generating substantial popular support, they will probably be adopted by one or both major parties sooner or later. Neither major party can hope for electoral success if it continuously refuses to recognize the problems perceived by significant voting blocs. Norman Thomas, who ran several times for president as the Socialist candidate, claimed that FDR's New Deal took over most of the ideas which the Socialists had been advocating for years.

■ Party Reforms and Party Discipline

One of the Washington slogans which one hears frequently is "Those who go along, get along." The implication is clear: a member of Congress who wishes to be an effective representative must cooperate with the party's leadership. If one does not "vote right" most of the time, particularly on issues important to the party leaders, one does not get the best committee assignments or a place on the agenda for one's pet bill. How tightly the system works in any single session of Congress, of course, depends on the leaders' personalities and on external and institutional factors.

Today, senators and representatives feel freer to vote independently.

During most of the 1950s, for example, two Texas Democrats, Lyndon Johnson in the Senate and Sam Rayburn in the House, exercised very effective party control as majority leaders. They turned out the votes when they had to do so. If they wanted something done, it nearly always did get done. Others might have disagreed with their agenda, but there was no question as to who was in charge. In the 1960s, leadership passed to two far less dominant personalities— Senator Mike Mansfield and Speaker of the House John McCormack. Organizational changes meant that committee chairs had less power. The campaign spending reforms of the 1970s provided candidates with sources of substantial campaign funds, free of party strings. These changes meant that members were likely to be more independent and that the congressional leadership could not always deliver a majority vote on legislation.

SUPREME COURT DECISIONS ON APPORTIONMENT

The greatest reform came as the result of U.S. Supreme Court decisions
on legislative apportionment. Traditionally, the line-drawing for districts within a state for the state's own legislature and for the U.S.
House of Representatives had been left to each state's political bodies—its own legislature and its governor. As a result of various compromises with the existing power blocs, district lines were drawn to over-
represent rural areas, somewhat under-represent cities, and grossly
under-represent the newer suburban areas. The persons who did the re-
districting after each U.S. census were the same people who benefitted
by the unfair apportionment, so changes occurred very slowly. Figure
2–2 shows how our population has shifted from rural areas to the suburbs and central cities.

Then, in 1962, the U.S. Supreme Court revolutionized this whole
process by stating that the U.S. Constitution required legislative districts to be approximately the same size in population. Even if a state
had two houses in its legislature, the districts for each had to be of approximately the same size population. This series of court decisions
thus resulted in a massive shift of political power from the rural areas

FIGURE 2–2
*U.S. population shifts
political power to the
suburbs = need for reap-
portionment.*

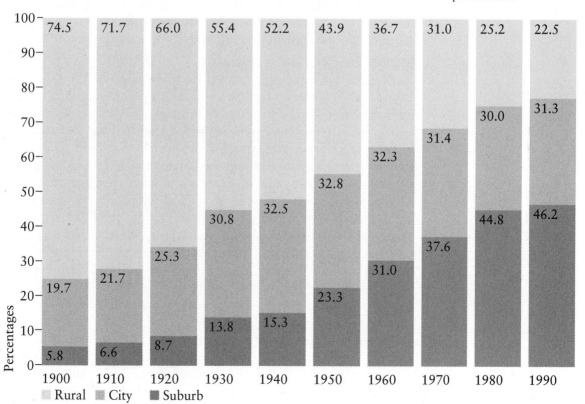

Source: U.S. Bureau of the Census

to the suburbs and cities. One of the leading cases in this series is *Reynolds v. Sims*.

JUSTICE·UNDEF

REYNOLDS V. SIMS

377 U.S. 533 (1964)

Facts: Plaintiffs are voters from Jefferson County, Alabama; defendants are various state and political party officials charged with administering elections. In 1961, plaintiffs filed a lawsuit in U.S. District Court, alleging that the Alabama legislature was apportioned in a constitutionally unfair manner. Only 25.1 percent of the population lived in counties which could elect a majority of the Senate; only 25.7 percent in counties which could elect a majority of the House of Representatives. Population-variance ratios of up to 40-to-1 existed for the Senate; up to 16-to-1, for the House. The District Court ruled for plaintiffs.

Issue: Do these differences in legislative apportionment violate the Equal Protection Clause of the Fourteenth Amendment?

Decision: Yes. Judgment for plaintiffs affirmed.

Rule: The Equal Protection Clause requires that both houses of a state legislature must be apportioned on a population basis, in districts of approximately equal size.

Discussion: *By Chief Justice* WARREN:

"Legislators represent people, not trees or acres. Legislators are elected by voters, not farms or cities or economic interests. As long as ours is a representative form of government, and our legislatures are those instruments of government elected directly by and directly representative of the people, the right to elect legislators in a free and unimpaired fashion is a bedrock of our political system. It would appear extraordinary to suggest that a State could be constitutionally permitted to enact a law providing that certain of the State's voters could vote two, five, or ten times for their legislative representatives, while voters living elsewhere could vote only once. And it is inconceivable that a state law to the effect that, in counting votes for legislators, votes of citizens in one part of the State would be multiplied by two, five, or ten, while the votes of persons in another area would be counted only at face value, could be constitutionally sustainable. Of course, the effect of state legislative districting schemes which give the same number of representatives to unequal numbers of constituents is identical. Overweighting and overvaluation of the votes of those living here has the certain effect of dilution and undervaluation of the voters living there. The resulting discrimination against those individual voters living in disfavored areas is easily demonstrable mathematically. Their right to vote is simply not the same right to vote as that of those living in a favored part of the State. Two, five, or ten of them must vote before the effect of their voting is equivalent to that of their favored neighbor. Weighting the votes of citizens differently, by any method or means, merely because of where they happen to reside, hardly seems justifiable. One must be ever aware that the Constitution forbids 'sophisticated as well as simpleminded modes of discrimination'."

Justice HARLAN, dissenting:

"These decisions...have the effect of placing basic aspects of state political systems under the pervasive overlordship of the federal judiciary. Once again, I must register my protest....

"The Court's constitutional discussion...is remarkable...for its failure to address itself at all to the Fourteenth Amendment as a whole or to the legislative history of the Amendment pertinent to the matter at hand. Stripped of aphorisms, the Court's argument boils down to the assertion that appellees' right to vote has been invidiously 'debased' or 'diluted' by systems of apportionment which entitle them to vote for fewer legislators than other voters, an assertion which is tied to the Equal Protection Clause only by the constitutionally frail tautology that 'equal' means 'equal.'

"Had the Court paused to probe more deeply into the matter, it would have found that the Equal Protection Clause was never intended to inhibit the States in choosing any democratic method they pleased for the apportionment of their legislatures. This is shown by the language of the Fourteenth Amendment taken as a whole, by the understanding of those who proposed and ratified it, and by the political practices of the States at the time the Amendment was adopted. It is confirmed by numerous state and congressional actions since the adoption of the Fourteenth Amendment, and by the common understanding of the Amendment as evidenced by subsequent constitutional amendments and decisions of this Court before Baker v. Carr... made an abrupt break with the past in 1962."

Ethical Dimension

Why shouldn't the people in a state be able to apportion their state legislature the way they want to?

EFFECT OF REFORM

Supreme Court decisions on legislative apportionment have drastically changed the composition of the House of Representatives

The result of all these changes has been to produce a Congress which is substantially less controllable than before. In one sense, this is a very positive development. We want our representatives to vote independently, rather than to simply follow a party line. In another sense, however, it makes the job of governing much more difficult. If no one is really in charge, it is difficult to agree on a legislative agenda, let alone to develop and adopt proposals for dealing with the agenda.

E LECTIONS

The electoral process is at the heart of democratic theory. Popular rule requires popular approval of the leadership (at least on election day). Elected representatives are then expected to represent their constituents, both by following the policy preferences expressed by the voters, and by leading and educating the voters. The age-old dilemma of the elected official is whether to vote one's conscience—for what one believes is the correct policy choice—or to vote the way the constituents prefer. The representative should be expected to exercise his or her best judgment, particularly since the representative often has access to much more complete information than most voters. In practice, however, it is often very difficult to explain one's vote on such emotional issues as decreasing Social Security benefits or raising the retirement age.

■ Nomination of Candidates

Individual candidates may be self-selected, or may be asked to run for office by a party or an interest group. Quite typically, nominating petitions are required. The prospective candidate must file petitions containing the signatures of a certain number of registered voters from the district to be represented. For larger electoral units, the requirement is usually phrased in terms of a certain percentage of the votes cast in the last general election.

PRIMARY ELECTIONS AND PARTY CAUCUSES

Political party candidates are usually chosen by primary elections or caucuses.

If more than one candidate seeks the nomination of one party for the same office, the choice between them may be made either by holding a primary election or by a party caucus. The caucus is a closed party meeting, at which only party members, or delegates selected by party members, will vote to select the official party candidate. The primary election may be open to all registered voters, or closed, so that only registered or declared members of the party can vote. Only Republicans vote in the closed Republican primary to choose Republican candidates, and Democrats do the same in the closed

Democratic primary. The party organizations usually prefer to have closed primaries, since there is less chance of selecting a candidate who disagrees with the party's general philosophy on the issues. With an open primary, there is always the danger that members of the other party may cross over to vote for the person they perceive to be the weakest candidate to try to improve their own chances in the general election.

NATIONAL NOMINATING CONVENTIONS

For the presidential nomination, both major parties use the national nominating convention. Convention delegates are selected by state party organizations, either by primary or by caucus. Minor parties may also use nominating conventions for their presidential candidates. The delegates may be selected in the same way as those of the major parties or in some other way.

■ Election of Candidates

After all the TV ads, the posters, the speeches, the coffee hours, the hand-shaking, and the baby-kissing, the decision is finally made by the voters, one at a time, in the privacy of the voting booth. Each vote is a combination of likes and dislikes, pros and cons, and perceptions of the issues, the candidates, and the parties, as seen by the individual voter. In recent years, "exit polling" has been developed by the news media and other organizations, to try to discover which issues in particular motivated the voters. Such surveys can provide useful information to the parties and the candidates about how they are perceived by the voters (or at least how the voters said they perceived them). It is undoubtedly true that a popular candidate for president (or for governor) at the top of the ticket will mean additional votes for legislative and other candidates of that party. But it is also true that many voters are quite willing to split their votes between the parties, even office by office. The days when party bosses could deliver large batches of votes for the entire ticket are probably gone forever. Increasingly, election is a matter of having the right candidate make an effective presentation of the right issues—at the right time.

States generally decide who can vote in political elections.

In general, the states set the rules for participation in elections. Even as to members of the U.S. House of Representatives and Senate, the Constitution gives the states the power to specify the "times, places and manner of holding elections." However, as is true with all state actions, the states' election rules must comply with due process and equal protection standards. In addition, the 26th Amendment provides for a uniform voting age of eighteen for national elections. To ensure that all citizens had the right to participate in electing public officials, Congress passed the Voting Rights Act in 1965.

The following case involves a challenge to Hawaii's prohibition against "write-in" voting (writing on the ballot the name of a person not listed as a candidate).

JUSTICE·UNDE[

BURDICK V. TAKUSHI

112 S. Ct. 2059 (1992)

Facts: Burdick is a registered voter in the city and county of Honolulu. In 1986, only one candidate filed nominating petitions to run for the Hawaii House of Representatives from Burdick's district. Burdick wrote to state officials and inquired about write-in voting. He received a copy of an opinion letter by the state attorney general, which said that Hawaii's election law did not permit write-in voting. He then filed a lawsuit in U.S. District Court, asking the court to order the state to permit write-in votes. The U.S. District Court issued the injunction, but the U.S. Court of Appeals reversed. Burdick then asked the U.S. Supreme Court for further review.

Issue: Does Hawaii's failure to provide write-in voting violate the constitutional rights of registered voters?

Decision: No, it does not. No injunction will be issued against the state.

Rule: A state may impose reasonable, nondiscriminatory regulations on the right to vote.

Discussion: *By Justice* WHITE*:*

"[Burdick] proceeds from the erroneous assumption that a law which imposes any burden upon the right to vote must be subject to strict scrutiny. Our cases do not so hold.

"It is beyond cavil that 'voting is of the most fundamental significance under our constitutional structure.'... It does not follow, however, that the right to vote in any manner and the right to associate for political purposes through the ballot are absolute.... The Constitution provides that the States may prescribe '[t]he Times, Places and Manner of holding Elections for Senators and Representatives.' ...and the Court therefore has recognized that States retain the power to regulate their own elections.... Common sense, as well as constitutional law, compels the conclusion that government must play an active role in structuring elections; 'as a practical matter, there must be a substantial regulation of elections if they are to be fair and honest and if some sort of order, rather than chaos, is to accompany the democratic processes.'..."

"Election laws will invariably impose some burden upon individual voters. Each provision of a code, 'whether it governs the registration and qualifications of voters, the selection and eligibility of candidates, or the voting process itself, inevitably affects—at least to some degree—the individual's right to vote and his right to associate with others for political ends.'... Consequently, to subject every voting regulation to strict scrutiny and to require that the registration be narrowly tailored to advance a compelling state interest, as [Burdick] suggests, would tie the hands of States seeking to assure that elections are operated equitably and efficiently....

"A court considering a challenge to a state election law must weigh 'the character and magnitude of the asserted injury to the rights protected by the First and Fourteenth Amendments that the plaintiff seeks to vindicate' against 'the precise interests put forward by the State as justifications for the burden imposed by its rule,' taking into consideration 'the extent to which those interests make it necessary to burden the plaintiff's rights.'...

"Although Hawaii makes no provision for write-in voting in its primary or general elections, [its] system...provides for easy access to the ballot until the cutoff date for the filing of nominating petitions, two months before the primary. Consequently, any burden on voters' freedom of choice and association is borne only by those who fail to identify their candidate of choice until days before the primary....

"[W]hen a State's ballot access laws pass constitutional muster as imposing only reasonable burdens on First and Fourteenth Amendment rights—as do Hawaii's election laws—a prohibition on write-in voting will be presumptively valid, since any burden on the right to vote for the candidate of one's choice will be light and normally will be counterbalanced by the very state interests supporting the ballot access scheme.

"In such situations, the objection to the specific ban on write-in voting amounts to nothing more than the insistence that the State record, count, and publish individual protests against the election system or the choices presented on the ballot through the efforts of those who actively participate in the system. There are other means available, however, to voice such generalized dissension from the electoral process: and we discern no adequate basis for our requiring the State to provide and to finance a place on the ballot for recording protests against its constitutionally valid election laws.

"'No right is more precious in a free country than that of

having a voice in the election of those who make the laws under which, as good citizens, we must live.'... But the right to vote is the right to participate in an electoral process that is necessarily structured to maintain the integrity of the democratic system.... We think that Hawaii's prohibition on write-in voting, considered as part of an electoral scheme that provides constitutionally sufficient ballot access, does not impose an unconstitutional burden upon the First and Fourteenth Amendment rights of the State's voters."

Ethical Dimension

Is it fair and "democratic" to offer voters only one choice in an election, as was happening in 30 to 40 percent of the state House districts in Hawaii?

◼ Ballot Proposals

Citizens may vote directly on legislation.

At least for state and local elections, ballot proposals of various sorts provide another important source of citizen input into the governing process. Many tax and revenue decisions may be made in local elections. Local ballots may also contain proposed ordinances on such topics as landlord-tenant relationships, pet control, drug restrictions, and environmental controls. Proposals to amend state constitutions are quite frequently submitted to the voters. These proposals may come from the state legislature (usually called a **referendum**) or from the voters themselves (through a process called the **initiative**).

In some cases, the state legislature may wish to avoid taking responsibility for deciding an emotional issue. The referendum is one way to try to defuse voter retribution against the legislators who voted the "wrong way" on the issue. Groups who feel that their views on tax and fiscal policy, or other issues, are not being represented can use the initiative to place the issue on the ballot. While the complicated wording of these ballot proposals and the claims and counter-claims of proponents and opponents may tend to confuse the issue, referenda and initiatives are useful safety valves in the political process.

◼ Money and PAC-Men

Modern electioneering is complex and costly. Only the wealthiest or the most solidly entrenched incumbent candidates may avoid soliciting the substantial sums of money needed to run an effective political campaign. Inflation has meant increased costs for such mundane political raw materials as postage stamps, telephones, and paper. For candidates for state-wide offices and those from big cities, television commercials are virtually required, and TV time is very expensive. Increasingly, sophisticated computer techniques are being used to identify likely supporters of particular issues and candidates and to prepare requests for contributions and support. These solicitations can also be very effective, but they too are expensive.

The reaction to the Watergate scandal accelerated the campaign reform movement which had begun in the late 1960s. Since a large part of the Watergate problem seemed to result from unrestricted campaign contributions, and the use of such funds to corrupt the political process, new restrictions were imposed. An attempt was made to restrict the influence of individual campaign contributions, and to provide for a more "democratic" method of financing political campaigns by using "political action committees" or PACs. PACs were created to allow many individuals to make small contributions to offset the influence of large corporate and individual donors.

Political action committees now play an important part in financing political campaigns.

As is often the case, reality has turned out to be something quite different from the vision of the reformers. The cry now is that the PACs themselves are the danger. Critics say that PACs "have covered politics with a money sludge that could sink the democratic process as it is generally understood"; that their "contributions, although legal, have become the equivalent of the millions of dollars in illegal campaign funds donated by Richard Nixon's rich friends in 1972." In the congressional election of 1982, for example, PACs reportedly contributed $80 million, most of it to incumbents, out of the $280 million spent by all House and Senate candidates. The need for such funds has continued to increase. Congressional candidates spent a total of $400 million in the 1990 election.

The potential for corruption of the political process by PAC-money can be seen in the following case-study. The Federal Trade Commission regulates advertising and other business practices to prevent fraud and deception. (FTC regulation will be discussed more fully in Chapter 18.) In 1982, Congress was considering a bill which would have exempted licensed professionals from the control of the FTC. Three professional organizations—the American Medical Association, the American Dental Association, and the American Optometric Association—contributed $4.9 million to congressional campaigns that year. Late in 1982, the House of Representatives voted 245 to 155 to approve the exemption bill. Nearly all of the 245 voting in favor had received some PAC-money from the three organizations. Of those who received $10,000 or more, 103 of 124 voted in favor and nine more did not vote. The bill ultimately failed in the Senate. The very high correlation between favorable votes on this bill and significant contributions from the PACs favoring it suggests that money still influences public policy decisions.

The congressional sponsors of the PAC approach to campaign financing apparently did not foresee the possibility of rapid multiplication of the number of funds, each of which, under the law, can give the maximum to any particular candidate. The number of PAC funds leaped from 600 in 1974 to 3,500 in 1982 to 6,800 in 1992. One congressman, Dan Rostenkowski of Illinois, received some $445,000 in the 1982 election. He happened to be chairman of the House Ways and Means Committee, which writes the tax laws. Senator Warren Rudman of New Hampshire, who led the 1982 fight against the FTC exemption bill in the Senate, retired in 1992 without having achieved further reform of the PACs. For those concerned about the integrity of the democratic process, the dominance of PAC-money is a continuing problem.

The next case illustrates the constitutional difficulties involved in limiting spending in political campaigns. Several important First Amendment principles are impacted by such legislation.

BUCKLEY V. VALEO

424 U.S. 1 (1976)

Facts: Concerned about the large amounts of money being spent in political campaigns, Congress passed the Federal Election Campaign Act in 1971. The Act limited the amount an individual or group could contribute to a candidate's campaign, the amount a candidate could spend personally, the amount an individual could spend to support a candidate, and the total amounts that could be spent in political campaigns. James Buckley, several other political candidates, and various parties and interest groups challenged the constitutionality of the Act. Francis Valeo was the Secretary of the Senate and a member of the Federal Elections Commission which was set up to administer and enforce the Act. Plaintiffs asked the U.S. District Court to enjoin enforcement of the Act. The District Court and the U.S. Court of Appeals upheld the Act.

Issue: Do the Act's restrictions violate the First Amendment?

Decision: The limitations on spending violate the First Amendment; the limits on contributions do not.

Rule: The First Amendment does not allow substantial and direct restrictions on the ability of candidates, citizens, and associations to engage in protected political expression.

Discussion: *By the Court:*

"The Act's contribution and expenditure limitations operate in an area of the most fundamental First Amendment activities.

Discussion of public issues and debate on the qualifications of candidates are integral to the operation of the system of government established by our Constitution. The First Amendment affords the broadest protection to such political expression in order 'to assure [the] unfettered interchange of ideas for the bringing about of political and social changes desired by the people.'... Although First Amendment protections are not confined to 'the exposition of ideas...there is practically universal agreement that a major purpose of that Amendment was to protect the free discussion of governmental affairs....of course includ[ing] discussions of candidates....' In a republic where the people are sovereign, the ability of the citizenry to make informed choices among candidates for office is essential, for the identities of those who are elected will inevitably shape the course that we follow as a nation. As the Court observed in *Monitor Patriot Co*....'it can hardly be doubted that the constitutional guarantee has its fullest and most urgent application precisely to the conduct of campaigns for political office.'

"The First Amendment protects political association as well as political expression. The constitutional right of association...stem[s] from the Court's recognition that '[e]ffective advocacy of both public and private points of view, particularly controversial ones, is undeniably enhanced by group association.' Subsequent decisions have made clear that the First and Fourteenth Amendments guarantee 'freedom to associate with others for the common advancement of political beliefs and ideas,' a freedom that encompasses '[t]he right to associate with the political party of one's choice'...

"A restriction on the amount of money a person or group can spend on political communication during a campaign necessarily reduces the quantity of expression by restricting the number of issues discussed, the depth of their exploration, and the size of the audience reached. This is because virtually every means of communicating ideas in today's mass society requires the expenditure of money...

"By contrast with a limitation upon expenditures for political expression, a limitation upon the amount that any one person or group many contribute to a candidate or political committee entails only a marginal restriction upon the contributor's ability to engage in free communication. A contribution serves as a general expression of support for the candidate and his views, but does not communicate the underlying basis for the support. The quantity of communication by the contributor does not increase perceptibly with the size of his contribution, since the expression rests solely on the undifferentiated, symbolic act of contributing....

"In sum, although the Act's contribution and expenditure limitations both implicate fundamental First Amendment interests, its expenditure ceilings impose significantly more severe restrictions on protected freedoms of political expression and association than do its limitations on financial contributions."

Ethical Dimension

Should candidates solicit campaign contributions from companies they might be regulating, if elected? Should they accept such contributions, if offered by the companies?

APPOINTMENT OF GOVERNMENT PERSONNEL

Most government employees are not elected, even in our democracy. They are appointed, either by the executive acting alone or with the approval of the Senate. Most of the two million-plus employees of the national government are hired in much the same way as employees of other large organizations.

Patronage

Another favorite Washington motto is "To the victor belong the spoils." The winning party, in other words, gets to distribute the governmental largesse—jobs, contracts, buildings, projects of various kinds. Historically, the distribution of this **patronage** (the jobs and projects) was a very important source of political power.

Here again, substantial changes, commencing even before the turn of the century, have drastically reduced the ability of the winning party to "reward its friends and punish its enemies." Only those persons who exercise major policy-making authority can be replaced at the will of the president. Members of the president's cabinet, for instance, can be removed by the president at any time. The vast majority of national, state, and local government employees are covered by civil service rules, union contracts, or both. These employees cannot automatically and arbitrarily be replaced after each electoral change. Further, the U.S. Supreme Court held in 1976 that there are limits to what may be required even of non-civil service personnel as a condition to continued employment.

What then remains of patronage? There are still virtually complete replacements in policy-making and advisory positions by each new administration. These positions include cabinet secretaries, ambassadors, agency heads, and the like. Judicial vacancies are particularly prized for key supporters who happen to be lawyers. Government contracts are generally subject to competitive bidding requirements, but there are many loopholes in the laws. Funding priorities remain a matter for legislative and executive discretion. So do many items of administrative action. Most government jobs may have been insulated from the spoils system, but there are still plenty to go around.

The winning political party my appoint persons to policy-making and advisory governmental jobs.

■ Office of Presidential Personnel

Writing in 1988, Bradley Patterson (who had himself served on the White House staffs of three presidents) estimated that the Office of Presidential Personnel was responsible for over 6,000 appointments. Some of these, of course, require Senate confirmation. Cabinet secretaries, under-secretaries, assistant secretaries, ambassadors, U.S. attorneys, and marshalls all need to be confirmed. So do U.S. judges and the members of certain boards and commissions. Patterson estimated that over 1,000 part-time members of boards and commissions did not need confirmation, however. Nor do the nearly 600 White House and executive branch staff appointed directly by the president. In addition, another 2,300 persons are appointed to non-career positions by the heads of cabinet departments and various agencies and, likewise, need no Senate confirmation.

The Office of Presidential Personnel works with the president to select candidates for government jobs.

It is the Office of Presidential Personnel (OPP) that manages this tremendous job on behalf of the president. It describes the positions to be filled and the skills and talents they require. It identifies and recruits candidates for these positions. It makes sure, after the inauguration of the new president, that these positions are indeed vacant and available for the new appointees. It manages the selection process (with input from senior White House staff and others), and puts the nominee through background checks by the FBI, the IRS, members of the president's party, Congress, and perhaps other persons. Once selected (and confirmed, if necessary), the new staff person is oriented to the position by the OPP. Finally, OPP is responsible for ongoing evaluation of staff performance. The sheer size of this recruitment and control job requires systematization and computerization.

▋EGISLATIVE PROCESS

In a common-law legal system, the legislature is the primary agent for changes in the law. It is true that a court is not prohibited from reversing one of its precedents, but that happens infrequently. Indeed, courts

Legislation is the primary change mechanism in a common-law legal system.

will sometimes express dissatisfaction with the precedent rule and specifically suggest that the matter be presented to the legislature for possible changes. In the fifty-odd years since the New Deal, Congress and the state legislatures have passed statutes which have resulted in massive structural changes in our economy and society. Those changes provide the basis for much of the rest of this book. This section considers the process by which a proposal becomes a law. Although some of the procedures vary, the process is quite similar at both the national and state levels. Figure 2–3 presents a flow chart of the major steps in the legislative process.

■ Origin of Bills

Most major bills, under current practice, are originated by the executive branch or one of the major independent agencies. Congress, of course, also investigates problems on its own initiative, and legislation may be introduced as the result of such investigations. In these cases, the staffs of the Senators and Representatives sponsoring the bill will take a primary role in drafting the bill and in preparing supporting materials. Some sources indicate that as many as 20,000 bills may be introduced in a single session of Congress. However, many of these are "private bills," designed to produce a particular result for a particular constituent. Some identical bills may be counted twice in the House,

FIGURE 2–3
How a bill becomes a law.

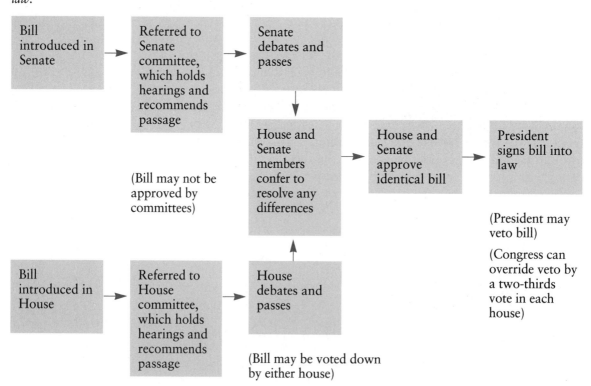

where several members may each introduce the same bill. By any standard, however, the number of bills is tremendous.

◼ Introduction of the Bill

Article I, section 7 of the Constitution specifies that all revenue bills shall be introduced first in the House. With that exception, a bill may be introduced in either the House or the Senate. Quite commonly, the bill is introduced in both houses simultaneously. Only members of Congress can introduce bills; and each bill must be introduced in each house. Each new bill is then referred to the appropriate committee for initial discussion, hearings, and investigation. The choice of the appropriate committee is usually quite clear. Occasionally, however, political factors may enter into the decision, and the bill's sponsors may try to get it referred to a committee which seems more favorably disposed towards the bill.

◼ Committee Action

Each house has a number of standing committees, which in turn each have a number of subcommittees. The committee's action generally determines the fate of a bill. The committee's failure to take action usually means that the bill is dead, although the members of that house have the power to order the bill out for debate, by passing a **discharge petition**. On the other hand, a committee's recommendation, after investigation, that a bill be passed, will also usually be followed by Congress. The committee members' recommendations are given deference because they are usually based on more intense study than has been given to the bill by the other members of Congress. Also, reciprocal trust and respect permit allocation of an otherwise overwhelming workload. Each house of Congress always has the power to reject the bill after floor debate, or the bill may be killed by a successful filibuster in the Senate. Knowing that the committee's endorsement usually means passage by that house, each side will try to present convincing testimony during the committee hearings on the bill, and will try to persuade committee members to vote their way on the bill. Lobbyists, agency representatives, and congressional staff will all be very active during this process. The votes that finally count, however, are the votes on the floor of each house.

Most work on a bill occurs in the committee to which it is referred.

◼ House of Representatives Action

A bill which is reported out of committee for action by the House of Representatives is placed on one of three schedules—the House calendar, for non-fiscal legislation; the Union calendar, for fiscal legislation; or the Private calendar, for private bills. Bills come up for debate and floor action in turn, but the order may be changed by two-thirds vote on certain days, by action of the House Rules Committee, or by unanimous consent at any time.

Debate in the House is limited, since a simple majority vote can close debate at any time. Speakers' schedules are usually agreed to by the floor leaders of each party. Historically, the House Rules Committee controlled floor action almost completely, since it set the terms of the debate and the choices of action in its "rule" which brought the bill up for debate and action. It might issue a rule which prohibited all amendments, for example. This historic power has been lessened to some extent by recent reforms.

■ Senate Action

The Senate is a much smaller group (100 members, as opposed to 435 representatives), and, as a result, it functions in a less formal manner than the House. Senate rules still permit unlimited debate, although a filibuster can now be stopped by a two-thirds vote of those present. After such a vote for "**cloture**" (closure) of debate, each Senator may speak for no more than one hour, and then a vote must be taken on the bill. As in the House, committee recommendations on legislation are usually followed, since the majority party controls a majority on each committee. If the parties are of approximately equal strength, however, five or six defecting Senators could change the result of the vote. Bills dealing with important regional concerns may produce votes along regional rather than party lines. Emotional issues such as school prayer and abortion regulation may find senators voting their conscience rather than their party's official position (if indeed the party takes a position on such issues). With only 100 senators, each one's vote is much more important than the vote of one of the 435 representatives.

■ Conference Committees

Conference committees resolve any differences between the two houses' versions of legislation.

Where the bills passed by the House and the Senate do not contain identical language, one house must accept the other's version, or a conference committee must be appointed to work out the differences. Usually, one house simply repasses the bill with the other's language; a conference committee is required in only one of ten cases.

Each house usually appoints five members when a conference committee is required. The conference committee engages in a give-and-take process to try to arrive at language which will be acceptable to a majority in each house. If the House passed the bill with a 100-vote majority, for example, the House conferees might be able to agree to language which would cost them 20 or 30 votes, in order to preserve a two-vote majority in the Senate. The conference report is taken back to each house, where it may only be voted up or down, but not amended. Either house may direct further negotiations by its conferees.

IMMIGRATION AND NATURALIZATION SERVICE V. CHADHA

103 S. Ct. 2764 (1983)

Facts: Jagdish Rai Chadha was an East Indian who was born in Kenya and held a British passport. He was lawfully admitted to the United States in 1966 on a nonimmigrant student visa. His visa expired on June 30, 1972. On October 11, 1973, the District Director of the Immigration and Naturalization Service ordered Chadha to show cause why he should not be deported for having remained in the United States for a longer time than permitted. Pursuant to § 242(b) of the Immigration and Nationality Act (Act), a deportation hearing was held on January 11, 1974. Chadha conceded that he was deportable for overstaying his visa, and the hearing was adjourned to enable him to file an application for suspension of deportation under § 244(a)(1) of the Act. Section 244(a)(1) provides that the attorney general may suspend a deportation in cases of extreme hardship, and the AG did so in this case. [The nature of Chadha's alleged "hardship" does not appear in the Supreme Court's opinion, although it is stated that he married a U.S. citizen in 1980, while his court appeal was pending.] Section 244(c)(2) says that either house of Congress can override the AG's decision by a resolution. The House of Representatives passed such a resolution. Chadha challenged the constitutionality of the "one-house" override provision.

Issue: Does action of one house of Congress under § 244(c)(2) violate the Constitution?

Decision: Yes, it does. (Chadha gets to stay in the United States.)

Rule: Explicit and unambiguous provisions of the Constitution prescribe and define the respective functions of the Congress and of the Executive in the legislative process.

Discussion: *By Chief Justice* BURGER:

"The Constitution sought to divide the delegated powers of the new federal government into three defined categories, legislative, executive and judicial, to assure, as nearly as possible, that each Branch of government would confine itself to its assigned responsibility. The hydraulic pressure inherent within each of the separate Branches to exceed the outer limits of its power, even to accomplish desirable objectives, must be resisted....

"Since it is clear that the action by the House under § 244(c)(2) was not within any of the express constitutional exceptions authorizing one House to act alone, and equally clear that it was an exercise of legislative power, that action was subject to the standards prescribed in Article I. The bicameral requirement, the Presentment Clauses, the President's veto were intended to erect enduring checks on each Branch and to protect the people from the improvident exercise of power by mandating certain prescribed steps. To preserve those checks, and maintain the separation of powers, the carefully defined limits on the power of each Branch must not be eroded. To accomplish what has been attempted by one House of Congress in this case requires action in conformity with the express procedures of the Constitution's prescription for legislative action: passage by a majority of both Houses and presentment to the President."

Ethical Dimension

Is it fair for the immigration authorities to treat some people (Chadha) differently than others?

◼ Presidential Action

If both houses have passed the bill in identical form, it is then sent to the president for signing. If the president signs the bill, it becomes part of the "law of the land." If the president vetoes the bill, it is returned to the house where it originated, with a statement of objections. Congress can override the president's veto by repassing the bill with a two-thirds majority in each house. Even where the bill was originally passed by a two-thirds margin, it may not receive that margin after a presidential veto. Members of the president's party will be reluctant to cast an opposing vote on an important issue, and even members of the other party may think twice before doing so.

If the president neither signs nor vetoes the bill within ten weekdays after receiving it, the bill becomes law without this signature. But if Congress adjourns during that ten-day period, the bill is dead. This presidential inaction at the end of a session is called a **pocket veto**.

The president must sign or veto a bill as a whole.

Perhaps the most significant aspect of this process is the tradition of denying the president an **item veto**. That is, the president must accept or reject the bill as a whole, not merely veto the objectionable parts, as many state governors can. As a result, Congress loads unrelated special "riders" onto necessary appropriations bills and other key legislation, calculating that the president will not veto them. As long as the riders are not too objectionable or too numerous, the president probably will not veto the bill. Many pieces of special legislation become law in this manner. For example, a certain "breeder" reactor was funded for years because a key senator demanded it as the price for his support of the appropriations bills, and the president lacked the power to strike out those funds from the bills. Likewise, U.S. tax bills quickly become a 'Christmas tree,' with presents and decorations for everyone, since the president lacks (at least by tradition) an item veto. A court test of this power might be desirable, since the Constitution is not totally clear on this point.

◼ Appropriations

If the new law is one which requires funding, as nearly all do, the enactment of the law does not end the legislative process. Another bill must be passed appropriating funds for the new program or agency. Low (or no) funding could cripple the new program. The opponents of a new program thus have two turns at bat—the original bill and its subsequent appropriation. Once again, passage of the original bill does not necessarily insure adequate funding. Legislators may wish to go on record as supporting a popular program by voting to pass the original bill. When it comes time to spend the money to fund the new program, however, some members may back away, not wishing to appear too liberal with the taxpayers' money. Annual appropriations mean an annual struggle for scarce funds.

◼ Review and Oversight

It is very difficult to terminate an agency or program once it is established. People come to rely on the presence of the agency or program, both for employment and for benefits; those constituencies become voices for its continuance. Votes, money, and influence are used to try to reward congressional friends and to punish congressional opponents.

Nevertheless, Congress can and does exercise some control over its programs and agencies. The appropriations process itself is one form of review. The Government Accounting Office also serves a watchdog function by making recommendations for improvements in policies and procedures. Most cases of blatant abuse will surface sooner or later in the press, if nowhere else; Congress may then be forced to respond to the pressure of public opinion. Finally, in the recent climate of deregulation, agencies and programs are being challenged to justify their existence and expenditures. There have been significant structural changes at the national level; others are pending. At the state level, many states are considering **sunset legislation**, under which a program or agency would terminate automatically after a certain number of years, unless reenacted by the legislature.

REVIEW

It is the political process which produces the laws which regulate business activity. By all indications, tomorrow's business managers will have to live with more government regulation rather than less. Business can, however, play a role in the development and implementation of regulations. By participating in the political process, business managers may be able to help produce regulations which are reasonable and workable.

Tomorrow's managers should therefore have an understanding of how the political process works. They need to know who the other major players are and the methods by which public opinion can be influenced. They should be aware of the important role played by political parties. They need to understand the electoral system, which chooses our political leaders. Finally, they need to appreciate the complex process by which a bill becomes a law. Armed with such information, managers are in a much better position to deal with the regulators in a constructive way.

REVIEW QUESTIONS AND PROBLEMS

1. What is the difference between an interest group and a political party? How do these two types of organizations relate to each other?

2. What are the arguments for and against limiting contributions to political campaigns?

3. Why is it important for everyone to have access to the nominating process for political candidates, as well as a vote in the final elections?

4. What is "patronage"? Why is it important to business?

5. Why is it so difficult to get legislation passed by Congress?

6. How do interest groups influence public policy?

7. As part of its job to reduce product-related injuries, the U.S. Consumer Product Safety Commission (CPSC) requires manufacturers to file reports of any known accidents involving their products. Sylvio, Inc., which makes electrical products, filed the required accident reports, but asked that they be kept confidential. Several months later, a consumer group, Users United, demanded that the CPSC disclose the contents of these reports (and others). Users United also wants the CPSC statistical analysis of accident frequency. Sylvio asked a U.S. District Court to issue an injunction prohibiting such disclosure. How should the court rule? Explain.

8. Northeast Power owns and operates an electric utility business. It uses oil, natural gas, and water power to generate the electricity it sells in several states. As a result of lobbying by Naturelovers, Inc., an environmental group, the state legislature of one of these states passed a statute which prohibited the sale of electricity generated through the use of the state's rivers to customers outside the state. Northeast Power sues in U.S. District Court to have the statute declared invalid. What result, and why?

9. Grace was the city attorney for a small town. When a new city council was elected, Grace was fired, because she belonged to the losing political party.

Grace thinks that her rights have been violated by this action, even though she was not covered under the state's civil service law. Does she have a basis for a lawsuit? Discuss.

10. Energy Systems was organized to construct a large pipeline which would carry crushed coal from coal mines in northern states to utility companies in southern states. Since the pipeline would require large amounts of water, various state agencies had to give their approval. An environmental impact statement was also required by national law. Rival Railroad saw the proposed pipeline as a threat to its very profitable business of transporting coal by rail. Rival therefore refused to grant Energy Systems the right to cross its tracks (there was no way around them). Rival also decided to appear before all public bodies which had to approve Energy Systems' plans, and to offer arguments as to why the pipeline should not be built. After several years and many millions of dollars, Energy Systems gave up its plans. One of the coal-producing states then filed an antitrust case against Rival. The state claimed that Rival was guilty of trying to monopolize the coal-carrying business. Rival says that it cannot be criminally prosecuted for simply presenting its views to public agencies. Who is right, and why?

SUGGESTIONS FOR FURTHER READING

Greenhouse, "Ex-Justice Thurgood Marshall Dies at 84," *New York Times* (January 25, 1993): A–1.

Parshall, "The Feuding Fathers," *U.S. News & World Report* (February 1, 1993): 53.

Richards, "In Search of a Consensus on the Future of Campaign Finance Laws: California Medical Association v. Federal Election Commission," *American Business Law Journal* 20 (Spring 1982): 243.

3
THE CONSTITUTIONAL SYSTEM

"A constitution states or ought to state not rules for the passing hour, but principles for an expanding future."

Benjamin Cardozo

LEARNING OBJECTIVES: After you have studied this chapter, you should be able to:

DEFINE the basic constitutional doctrines of Federalism and Separation of Powers.

EXPLAIN the constitutional limitations on national regulation of business.

DISCUSS the constitutional limitations on state regulation of business.

IDENTIFY the constitutional limitations on state taxation of business.

EXPLAIN how federalism limits state regulation of business.

P REVIEW

The fifty-five delegates to the Constitutional Convention who came together in Philadelphia in the summer of 1787 had differing views on many of the specific issues which they faced. However, most of them shared a common set of experiences and some common assumptions about the role of government. Almost exclusively, the delegates were drawn from the commercial and large agrarian interests along the Atlantic seaboard. They generally agreed that something needed to be done to remedy the perceived defects of the Articles of Confederation. These defects included lack of adequate funding for the national government, lack of national power to regulate interstate and foreign commerce, and lack of a national judiciary. At least initially, the delegates disagreed on what specific changes needed to be made in the governmental structure, but they nearly all operated on the basis of similar views of the nature of government.

As a result of their knowledge of English constitutional history and their own colonial experience, they generally distrusted concentrated governmental power. The delegates believed government should be limited; it should be representative; and it should be popular. Limited government meant that only certain tasks should be assigned to the public sector; all else should remain in the hands of private organizations and individuals. Representative government meant that there was no room for hereditary positions; elected assemblies should control most basic functions. Popular sovereignty meant that government ultimately derived its power from the people, whether or not all persons actually voted in elections. Government was legitimate only if it was based on the "consent of the governed." These common experiences and assumptions eventually led to the adoption of a system based on two constitutional principles—federalism and separation of powers. Figure 3–1 provides an overview of our constitutional structure.

F EDERALISM

Federalism prevents accumulation of power by dividing authority between a national government and local or regional governments. This division can be accomplished in several ways, but two patterns predominate in existing federal systems. In one, the national government receives only specific powers, with the residue reserved to the several regions. In the other, the regions are assigned specific tasks, with the residue of governmental power being given to the national government. The U.S. Constitution adopted the first pattern. As stated in the Tenth Amendment, all powers not assigned to the national government, nor prohibited to the states, are reserved to the states or to the people.

Federalism divides governmental powers between a central unit and regional governments.

FIGURE 3–1
Constitutional structure

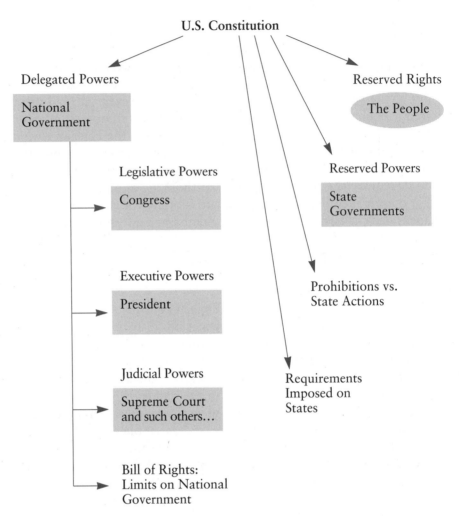

U.S. Constitution

Delegated Powers

National Government

Legislative Powers

Congress

Executive Powers

President

Judicial Powers

Supreme Court and such others...

Bill of Rights: Limits on National Government

Reserved Rights

The People

Reserved Powers

State Governments

Prohibitions vs. State Actions

Requirements Imposed on States

■ Relationship Between National Government and the States

National rules supersede state and local laws.

The most basic, and most significant, legal principle involved in the relationship between the national government and the states is expressed in the "supremacy clause" found in Article VI of the Constitution. The Constitution itself, all national laws "made in pursuance thereof," and all treaties made "under the authority of the United States" are the supreme law of the land. Judges in all states are bound to apply these supreme laws, regardless of any conflicting state law. Within its proper constitutional sphere, then, the legal acts of the national government supersede any conflicting state laws.

The problem in the following case is the definition of the "proper" sphere of the national government. Specifically, the question is whether the national government can do things to implement a treaty which it is not otherwise specifically authorized by the Constitution to do.

MISSOURI V. HOLLAND

252 U.S. 416 (1920)

JU STICE · UNDER

Facts: Congress passed a statute to regulate the hunting of migratory game birds. This act was held unconstitutional by two lower courts, since the Constitution had not given Congress regulatory power over this topic. The U.S. government then entered into a treaty with Great Britain (which then had power over Canada's foreign relations). The treaty obligated both parties to pass legislation regulating the hunting of migratory game birds. Congress enacted such legislation in 1918. Missouri sued U.S. game warden Ray Holland to prevent him from enforcing the 1918 statute. The U.S. District Court dismissed the case; Missouri appealed.

Issue: Does the 1918 statute exceed the power of Congress?

Decision: No. Judgment for Holland affirmed. (The statute is valid.)

Rule: The states have all powers not delegated to the national government, but the national government does have the power to make and implement treaties.

Discussion: *By Justice* HOLMES:

"It is said that a treaty cannot be valid if it infringes the Constitution, that there are limits, therefore, to the treaty-making power, and that one such limit is that what an act of Congress could not do unaided, in derogation of the powers reserved to the States, a treaty cannot do. An earlier act of Congress that attempted by itself and not in pursuance of a treaty to regulate the killing of migratory birds within the States had been held [unconstitutional] in the District Court....

"Acts of Congress are the supreme law of the land only when made in pursuance of the Constitution, while treaties are declared to be so when made under the authority of the United States.... We do not mean to imply that there are no qualifications to the treaty-making power; but they must be ascertained in a different way. It is obvious that there may be matters of the sharpest exigency for the national well-being that an act of Congress should not deal with, but that a treaty followed by such an act could, and it is not lightly to be assumed that, in matters requiring national action, 'a power which must belong to and somewhere reside in every civilized government' is not to be found.... [W]e may add that when we are dealing with words that are also a constituent act, like the Constitution of the United States, we must realize that they have called into life a being the development of which could not have been foreseen completely by the most gifted of its begetters.... The case before us must be considered in the light of our whole experience, and not merely in that of what was said a hundred years ago. The treaty in question does not contravene any prohibitory words to be found in the Constitution. The only question is whether it is forbidden by some invisible radiation from the general terms of the 10th Amendment." [The Court found that it wasn't.]

Ethical Dimension

Does this decision mean that the national government can do anything it wishes, simply by negotiating a treaty on that subject? Should it be able to do so?

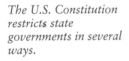

EXCLUSIVE FEDERAL FUNCTIONS

The U.S. Constitution restricts state governments in several ways.

The Constitution specifically prohibits the states from exercising some governmental functions—those which would clearly be an interference with the sovereignty of the national government. States may not issue money or regulate which forms of money are "legal tender" in payment of debts. States may not enter into treaties with foreign powers or maintain armies and navies (unless approved by Congress). States may not, without the consent of Congress, tax any exports or imports, except as absolutely necessary for their inspection systems. There are also other specific prohibitions.

POLITICAL PROCESSES OF THE STATES

There are several sections of the Constitution that impact on states' political processes. The Fifteenth Amendment precludes a state from limiting voting rights on the basis of race; the Nineteenth does the same for sex. The Twenty-fourth Amendment prevents the states from using a poll tax to prevent citizens from voting in primary or final elections for president, senator, or representative. The Twenty-sixth Amendment makes eighteen the national voting age.

NATIONAL JUDICIAL POWER

Another significant legal element was added by the Eleventh Amendment. Ratified in 1795, it stated that the national judicial power did not extend to lawsuits brought against a state by citizens of another state, or of a foreign country. The Supreme Court, after the adoption of the amendment, held that a lawsuit by a foreign government against a state was also barred from the federal courts.

◼ Relationships Between and Among States

Article IV of the Constitution contains two important legal rules concerning the duties which the states owe each other. One rule relates to the extradition of persons accused or convicted of crimes. Article IV requires that a criminal fugitive who is caught in another state "shall on demand of the executive authority of the state from which he fled, be delivered up, to be removed to the state having jurisdiction of the crime." While the use of the word *shall* indicates that this is a mandatory provision, the U.S. Supreme Court ruled in 1861 that this section only declared a "moral duty." There have been other instances of Governors' refusals to return accused defendants and convicted escapees, although usually the second state complies with the request. Similar arrangements between nations exist as the result of specific treaties, although not all crimes are extraditable under all treaties.

The U.S. Constitution requires the states to respect each others' laws and court decisions.

The second of these rules concerning duties states owe to each other is the key to our dual court system: "Full faith and credit shall be given in each state to the public acts, records, and judicial proceedings of every other State." In this instance, the courts do enforce the word *shall* as imposing a mandatory, legal duty on the courts of other states. Where enforcement action is requested in a second state on a court judgment from the first state, a court in the second state can ask only the basic question of whether the judgment was based on adequate jurisdiction in the court which issued it. If the issuing court in the first state had jurisdiction over the subject matter of the suit and over the parties, the court in the second state has no choice; it *must* enforce the first court's judgment, just as it would one of its own.

◼ SEPARATION OF POWERS

The concept of dividing governmental powers between executive, legislative, and judicial branches had been rather fully explained by the French political theorist, Montesquieu. His view that liberty could be assured only where the same person or body did not exercise all three groups of governmental functions was very appealing to the American leaders. The abuses of power by the English King and his royal governors, and to some extent even by Parliament, reinforced the view of Madison and others that the Constitution should include a series of "chains" to restrain arbitrary governmental actions.

Not only does the Constitution distribute powers among the three branches, but it also uses other structural devices to guard against one group's being able to take control of the entire structure in a moment of panic or emotion. Each branch is selected differently and is thus responsible to different constituencies. Members of the House of Representatives are elected from local districts. Senators were to be selected by the state legislatures. (The change made by the Seventeenth

The U.S. Constitution divides national governmental power among the executive, legislative, and judicial branches.

Amendment, which provides for direct election of the senators by the state's voters, also separates them from the locally-elected representatives.) The president is chosen by the Electoral College, made up of representatives selected by each state, in a total number equal to that state's congressional delegation. The federal judiciary is selected by the president and confirmed by the Senate. In addition to providing for these differing constituencies and methods of selection, the Constitution also provides for different terms of office: representatives, two years; senators, six years, with one-third elected each two years; the president, four years; the judges, "during good behavior." As a result of these structural arrangements, a coalition of interests would have to sustain its majority status over a period of time, and at several levels, in order to gain complete control of the governmental machinery.

Each of the three branches of government exercises some control over the other two.

Further, "separation of powers" did not mean that each branch was to operate in splendid isolation from the others. Rather, a kind of dynamic tension among the branches was desired, to try to make sure each stayed within its assigned sphere. The actual operation of the system is usually described by the phrase "checks and balances." Many actions require coordination between two branches. Each branch exercises some control of the other two. And all three are aware that they function within a total system. As stated most succinctly by Justice Brandeis in his dissent in *Myers v. United States*, 272 U.S. 52 (1926): "...(S)eparation of powers was adopted...not to promote efficiency but to preclude the exercise of arbitrary power. The purpose was not to avoid friction, but, by means of the inevitable friction incident to the distribution of the governmental powers among three departments, to save the people from autocracy."

■ Relationship Between Executive and Legislature

One way to summarize this relationship is with the phrase, "The president proposes, and Congress disposes." That is, of course, a greatly oversimplified summary of the actual legislative process. It is true, today, that many legislative proposals originate from one of the executive departments, or from one of the independent administrative agencies. Congress, however, also conducts hearings on topics of its own choice and initiates many legislative proposals. On the other hand, Congress does not finally "dispose" of legislative matters, since the president may still veto the bill, thus checking the will of Congress. The veto may, of course, be overridden by a two-thirds vote in each house of Congress.

Congress controls the president through its appropriation of funds.

Congress further checks the executive branch, since Congress holds the purse-strings. By appropriating less money for a particular activity, it may curtail executive and administrative action. Within these budgetary limits, however, the president (or the independent administrative agency) determines enforcement policy and decides, in large part, how the laws will be administered.

Further, the president is the national leader, visible and newsworthy. A president skilled in the use of the media is in a position to influence national opinion, and ultimately, the will of Congress. The president is also the national party leader, and is thus in a position of real political strength if that party has a majority in one or both houses of Congress. Even without such majority party control, the president still speaks for a broad national consensus, and the members of Congress know that. By virtue of the office, the president is in charge of the operation of the national government. Thus the president is in a position to dispense certain "benefits"—government appointments, government contracts, government construction. Members of Congress who vote against the president on key bills may not see their pet projects funded as quickly, or at all. Favors for their constituents may not be granted as readily, or at all. Congress is generally aware of which side its collective and individual bread is buttered on, and the president has most of the butter.

One other aspect of this relationship also deserves mention. Congress does have the ultimate control over the president—the power of impeachment. The House of Representatives indicts, and the Senate decides the case, with a vote of two-thirds of those present being required for removal. Until the Watergate scandal of the Nixon years, many people were inclined to write off the impeachment power as unrealistic and unworkable. The nearly successful impeachment of Andrew Johnson after the Civil War (he escaped by one vote) was dismissed as a phenomenon of those unique times. Watergate showed that impeachment is a real control, even though it may be contemplated only under extraordinary provocation. If the vast majority of the American people and their congressional representatives are convinced that their president has lost control and is running amok, they *do* have the power to indict, convict, and remove that chief executive.

■ Relationship Between Executive and Judiciary

On the surface, it would seem that the president exercises substantial control over the federal courts, since the president appoints the federal judges for what are, in effect, life terms (during "good behavior"). In practice, this control through appointment may or may not be effective. Only by very careful screening can a president determine the judicial candidate's philosophy. Even then, the judge may change views once appointed. The basically conservative President Eisenhower appointed two of the most liberal judges ever to sit on the Supreme Court—Chief Justice Earl Warren and Justice William Brennan. In addition to undergoing presidential screening, the candidate must be approved by the Senate. In practice, that has meant that the senior Senator of the president's political party has a veto over judicial

The President appoints federal judges, subject to confirmation by the Senate.

appointments from his or her state. Even at the Supreme Court level, the president does not have a free hand. As recently as 1987, President Reagan's nomination of Judge Robert Bork was defeated by a determined and vociferous political coalition.

Perhaps equally as significant as the appointment control is the prosecutorial control. The courts are, after all, passive agencies. They can do nothing on their own; they must be presented, by others, with a "case or controversy." If the executive branch chooses not to pursue a particular matter in court, the courts do not hear it, unless it involves an issue where a private party may be the plaintiff. Even where a private party may also mount a legal challenge, the case is presented to the courts in a far different posture than would be the case if the government itself were the complainant. In some measure, then, the executive branch determines what kind of cases the courts will hear and decide.

To the extent that the case may be brought to court, however, the courts have the ultimate control over the executive branch—the power to declare the president's actions unconstitutional. Actions by the president or a deputy, or by one of the independent administrative agencies, may generally be challenged by any affected parties as being unconstitutional, not in accordance with relevant legislation, or both. While the president and the executive branch have a good deal of discretion in enforcing the laws, there are some outer limits, and the courts have maintained these limits and will continue to do so as necessary.

The following case involves the president's powers as commander in chief of the armed forces.

JUSTICE·UNDEI

DELLUMS V. BUSH

752 F. SUPP. 1141 (U.S. DISTRICT Ct., D. C. 1990)

Facts: Iraq invaded Kuwait on August 2, 1990. On November 8, President Bush announced a substantial troop buildup in the Persian Gulf, to provide an "adequate offensive military option." Congress had not been asked for a declaration of war against Iraq. On November 19, Ron Dellums and other members of Congress filed this lawsuit, asking the court to enjoin President Bush from any offensive action against Iraq, unless and until Congress declared war on Iraq.

Issues: Is this a "political question," which a court lacks power to decide? Is there an existing dispute, which the court must resolve?

Decision: No. A court has the judicial power to determine the meaning of the U.S. Constitution, including the definition of "war."

No. Neither the president nor Congress has made a final decision yet, so it is not clear that there is any dispute at all. The request for an injunction is denied.

Rules: The courts have the power to determine the meaning of all parts of the Constitution, including the definition of "war." The courts will not try to anticipate disputes which do not yet exist.

Discussion: *By Judge* GREENE:

"Although...the Court rejects several of defendant's objections to the maintenance of this lawsuit, and concludes that, in principle, an injunction may issue at the request of Members of Congress to prevent the conduct of a war which is about to be carried on without congressional authorization, it does not follow that these plaintiffs are entitled to relief at this juncture. For the plaintiffs are met with a significant obstacle to such relief: the doctrine of ripeness....

"No one knows the position of the Legislative Branch on the issue of war or peace with Iraq; certainly no one, including this Court, is able to ascertain the congressional position on that issue on the basis of this lawsuit brought by fifty-three members of the House of Representatives and one member of the U.S. Senate. It would be both premature and presumptuous for the Court to render a decision on the issue of whether a declaration of war is required at this time or in the near future when the Congress itself has provided no indication whether it deems such a declaration either necessary, on the one hand, or imprudent, on the other....

"It would hardly do to have the Court, in effect, force a choice upon the Congress by a blunt injunctive decision, called for by only about ten percent of its membership, to the effect that, unless the rest of the Congress votes in favor of a declaration of war, the President, and the several hundred thousand troops he has dispatched to the Saudi Arabian desert, must be immobilized. Similarly, the President is entitled to be protected from an injunctive order respecting a declaration of war when there is no evidence that this is what the Legislative Branch as such—as distinguished from a fraction thereof—regards as a necessary prerequisite to military moves in the Arabian desert....

"Given the facts currently available to this Court, it would seem that as of now the Executive Branch has not shown a commitment to a definitive course of action sufficient to support ripeness. In any event, however, a final decision on that issue is not necessary at this time."

Ethical Dimension

Should there be any limits to the president's power to move U.S. military forces around, as commander-in-chief?

●

■ Relationship Between Legislature and Judiciary

The most controversial aspect of this relationship is surely the power of the courts to declare acts of Congress unconstitutional. The power of judicial review of legislation is often criticized as being "undemocratic" and a "usurpation" by the courts. In fact, it is neither. As argued by Alexander Hamilton in *Federalist* number 78, a written Constitution logically requires an interpreter, a body to referee disputes among the various branches of government, and the U.S. Supreme Court is clearly the logical agency for that role. Nothing was specifically stated in the Constitution granting that power, because it was assumed it was obvious. Further, the delegates to the Constitutional Convention certainly expressed again and again their fear of "mobocracy"—the rule of the mob, the danger that a "pure" democracy would degenerate into a populist dictatorship. Judicial review is thus implicit in the written Constitution, which sets limits on what the popularly elected representatives can do. In any event, for better or worse, judicial review is now an established part of our constitutional system. Legislative, as well as executive, acts may be struck down by the courts.

Congress controls the judiciary by defining the powers of the courts.

Congress exercises certain controls over the judiciary. In addition to the Senate's participation in the appointment process, as described previously, Congress also determines the jurisdiction of the various federal courts and their level of funding. Article III of the Constitution does provide that the judges' compensation "shall not be diminished during their continuance in office." However, it can be argued that a failure to receive a raise which corresponds to the rate of inflation is a "diminution" in a very real economic sense. This provision, of course, says nothing about the level of expenditures which Congress may authorize for clerks, secretaries, research assistants, supplies, office facilities, and all the other operating expenses of the courts. These expenses may be decreased without violating Article III. Lower appropriations to the executive enforcement agencies would also indirectly influence the work of the courts, since the enforcement officers would not be able to prosecute as many actions in their areas of responsibility. Lower funding for the Federal Trade Commission, for example, would almost certainly mean fewer FTC cases brought to the courts.

Congress' authority to control which cases can be heard by which courts is its ultimate control, although this authority has rarely been used specifically for "control" purposes. Congress may create such courts under the Supreme Court as it wishes and may give them whatever jurisdiction it wishes. Article III does specify the original jurisdiction of the Supreme Court: cases in which a state is a party, and cases affecting ambassadors, ministers, or consuls of other nations. This jurisdiction is no longer exclusive; concurrent jurisdiction is given to the District Courts, which nearly always hear such cases initially. All other jurisdiction of the Supreme Court is appellate, "both as to law and fact, with such exceptions, and under such regulations as the Congress shall make." While these provisions seem to give Congress a blank check to control an unpopular Supreme Court, it has been difficult in practice to convince a majority of Congress that such political maneuvering is in the national interest. Further, the president would have to sign such legislation, which he might not do if it appears to be an obvious political attack on the Court.

One other possible, but improbable, "control" on the Supreme Court is changing the number of justices. There is nothing sacrosanct about the number nine; Congress could provide for fewer or more justices (and has done so on occasion). Here again, however, such changes are likely to be quickly perceived as blatant political attempts to control the Court. Even Franklin Roosevelt, with his immense political power, was unable to push his Court-packing plan through Congress, despite large Democratic majorities in both houses. Even the members of Roosevelt's own party were reluctant to permit him to appoint enough justices to assure approval of the economic programs which Congress was enacting. The Supreme Court, in sum, is an institution with a strong political constituency of its own.

C ONSTITUTIONAL LIMITATIONS ON NATIONAL REGULATION

In our political system, the U.S. Constitution sets the outer limits for governmental regulation of business. Not all regulations approved by Congress and the president (or by a state's legislature and governor) are necessarily constitutional. The difficult and exasperating task of drawing the constitutional line in specific cases is assigned to the judiciary, and ultimately, to the U.S. Supreme Court.

Both federalism and separation of powers limit the activities of the national government.

The two fundamental principles of our constitutional scheme—federalism and separation of powers—provide some limitations on the national government's power to regulate the economy. Either or both principles may be used to invalidate specific acts of the legislative or executive branches.

Federalism as a Limitation

The national government is, as stated, a government of delegated powers, with all residual powers remaining in the several states, or with the people themselves. Any action by the national government must therefore be justified as falling under one of the Constitution's grants of power. The interpretation of the commerce clause over the years has been so broad that it is hard to imagine, as a practical matter, any activity that is still "purely local." At least in theory, however, it would still be possible for the Court to hold a particular regulation unconstitutional on this basis. A teenager operating a lawn-mowing service might be local enough to fall outside interstate commerce, but his mower almost certainly moved in interstate commerce. So did the gasoline to run it, if it's a power mower. When the Court decided in 1942 that a farmer who raised 239 bushels of wheat on 11.9 acres, solely for his own use, was sufficiently linked to interstate commerce to justify regulation, it didn't leave very many local activities outside national power. (The "farmer" case is *Wickard v. Filburn,* 317 U.S. 111.)

It's also possible, in a specific case, that a national regulation might be ruled unconstitutional because it infringes on the federalism principle itself, that is, that it unduly interferes with the operation of the state governments as independent, sovereign entities within their own sphere. Here again, the Court has generally taken a liberal view of national power, several times stating that the Tenth Amendment is but a "truism." It has, however, used the federalism principle to prevent national taxation of some state governmental activities. After initially ruling the other way, the Supreme Court also decided that federal courts could not develop their own rules of tort law and contract law. More recently, the Court prevented the national government from applying its wage and hour regulations to state government employees. Although this last decision was later reversed, national agencies have had to recognize that this Tenth Amendment "truism" may still have some residual constitutional force.

■ Separation of Powers as a Limitation

The dividing lines between the legislative, executive, and judicial branches are not clear. They were not meant to be. The object of the framers was not to produce the most efficient governmental mechanism, but rather one in which absolute power could not be acquired by any small group. Although the three branches are in theory co-equal, and although Thomas Jefferson and others have argued that each ought to be the judge of the constitutionality of its own actions, the U.S. Supreme Court has become the umpire of our system. It is the Court which decides whether the executive branch or Congress has overstepped its constitutional bounds.

On rare occasions, there is a direct boundary dispute between the Congress and the executive branch. There have been several recent situations in which Congress demanded disclosure of information by a member of the executive branch, while the president insisted that the information be kept confidential. Ultimately, the U.S. Supreme Court will have to decide whether the need for confidentiality in law administration outweighs the congressional need for disclosure to exercise its oversight function.

The Court even has to decide boundary disputes involving the judicial branch. One of the parties to a lawsuit, for instance, asks for the discovery of certain confidential government documents and claims that they are essential to the case. The government administrator claims that the documents are privileged and refuses to disclose them. The trial court hearing the case will make the initial decision on whether the documents must be disclosed, but ultimately the Supreme Court sets these boundary lines, too.

■ Limitations in the Bill of Rights as a Whole

The U.S. Supreme Court decided at an early date that the Bill of Rights applied as guarantees only against the national government, not against the states. Both the historical record and the language used are quite clear on this point. The fear of many citizens, expressed after the Constitutional Convention, was that the proposed national government would become too powerful, that we were simply replacing a foreign tyrant with a domestic one. A Bill of Rights was promised by the supporters of the proposed Constitution as a means of offsetting these arguments and gaining votes for ratification. The very first amendment begins: "Congress shall make no law...." It is thus easy to see why these prohibitions and guarantees could be drafted in such absolute terms. It simply was not the job of Congress, or other agencies of the national government, to regulate speech and the press; if there were to be any such regulations, they were to issue from the state and local governments. It is only much later, through an expansive reading of the due process clause of the Fourteenth Amendment, that most of the Bill of Rights guarantees and prohibitions came to be applied to the states. (See Figure 3–2 for a summary of the protections found in the Bill of Rights.)

The Bill of Rights limits the national government.

■ First Amendment Limitations

At least in the view of some justices, a strong presumption of invalidity attaches to any regulation which interferes in any substantial way with the freedoms guaranteed by the First Amendment: speech, press, religion, assembly, petition. Even though other justices do not use this absolutist approach and are somewhat more willing to recognize the need to regulate these freedoms under some circumstances, the Court has been vigilant in protecting First Amendment rights. If a serious challenge can be mounted under the First Amendment, a regulation stands a good chance of being ruled unconstitutional, even though most of the justices apply a "weighing" approach. The public interest in the regulation must be very strong to justify the infringement of First

The First Amendment contains several specific limitations on the national government.

FIGURE 3–2

The Bill of Rights provided guarantees essential to gaining ratification for the constitution.

THE BILL OF RIGHTS FIRST TEN AMENDMENTS TO THE CONSTITUTION	
First	Freedom of speech, press, assembly, religion No establishment of religion
Second	Right to keep and bear arms
Third	No soldiers in private homes
Fourth	No unreasonable searches and seizures No search warrants unless on probable cause
Fifth	Indictment for crime by Grand Jury required No double jeopardy No self-incrimination Due process of law required Just compensation required if private property taken
Sixth	Speedy and public criminal trial required Trial by jury for crimes Notice of charges required Right to confront and cross-examine witnesses Right to require witnesses to appear Right to counsel
Seventh	Right to trial by jury in civil cases at common law
Eighth	No excessive bail No excessive fines No cruel and unusual punishment
Ninth	Constitution's list of rights is not exclusive
Tenth	Powers not given to national government, nor prohibited to states, are reserved to states, or to the people

Amendment rights. Moreover, the regulation adopted must be no more burdensome than is necessary to accomplish the public purpose.

FREEDOM OF SPEECH AND OF THE PRESS

Publishing businesses have the double protection of both the speech and the press clauses, but even here some regulations have been sustained. These freedoms do not provide absolute immunity from liability for defamatory statements which are published. However, if the person defamed is a "public figure" (in the eyes of the Court), malice or at least gross negligence on the part of the publisher must be proved. There are some limits on the publication of obscenity, although the boundaries are hard to draw. As Justice Potter Stewart wrote in 1963: "I can't define obscenity, but I know it when I see it." The judicial interest in having access to all the facts in both criminal and civil cases has generally outweighed any claim of privilege for communications from "informants." There are other limits in other legal areas.

The Court has recently been involved in defining the rights of individuals and corporations to engage in "commercial speech," and of corporations to engage in the more traditional political debate. The *Bellotti* case in Chapter 2 raised these issues. With the adoption of reform legislation dealing with campaign financing, the Court has been confronted with a whole new range of First Amendment issues. Not only freedom of speech, but also freedom of petition and freedom of assembly/association may be involved in these cases. The *Buckley* case in Chapter 2 illustrates these problems. The many split decisions in these cases indicate that the boundary lines are still in a state of flux.

The next case involves an attempt by Congress to limit "editorializing" by publicly funded, "educational" broadcasting stations.

F.C.C. V. LEAGUE OF WOMEN VOTERS OF CALIFORNIA

104 S. Ct. 3106 (1984)

Facts: Congress set out in 1967 to support and promote the development of noncommercial, educational broadcasting stations. The Public Broadcasting Act of 1967 established the Corporation for Public Broadcasting (CPB), a nonprofit corporation authorized to disburse government funds to noncommercial television and radio stations in support of station operations and educational programming. Section 399 of that act forbids any "noncommercial educational broadcasting station which receives a grant from the Corporation" to "engage in editorializing."

Pacifica Foundation is a nonprofit corporation that owns and operates several noncommercial educational broadcasting stations in five major metropolitan areas. Its stations have received and are presently receiving grants from the CPB and are therefore prohibited from editorializing by the terms of § 399. In April 1979, Pacifica brought this suit in U.S. District Court challenging the constitutionality of § 399. The District Court ruled that § 399's ban on editorializing violated the First Amendment. The government appealed directly to the Supreme Court.

Issue: Does the prohibition against editorials violate the First Amendment?

Decision: Yes. Judgment for Pacifica is affirmed.

Rule: The freedom of speech and of the press guaranteed by the Constitution embraces at least the liberty to discuss publicly and truthfully all matters of public concern without previous restraint or fear of subsequent punishment.

Discussion: *By Justice* BRENNAN:

"The fundamental principles that guide our evaluation of broadcast regulation are by now well established.... [W]e have long recognized that Congress, acting pursuant to the Commerce Clause, has power to regulate the use of this scarce and valuable national resource. The distinctive feature of Congress' efforts in this area has been to ensure through the regulatory oversight of the FCC that only those who satisfy the 'public interest, convenience and necessity' are granted a license to use radio and television broadcast frequencies....

"[T]he restriction imposed by § 399 is specifically directed at a form of speech—namely, the expression of editorial opinion— that lies at the heart of First Amendment protection.... 'Freedom of discussion, if it would fulfill its historic function in this nation, must embrace all issues about which information is needed or appropriate to enable the members of society to cope with the exigencies of their period.'...

"The editorial has traditionally played precisely this role by informing and arousing the public, and by criticizing and cajoling those who hold government office in order to help launch new solutions to the problems of the time. Preserving the free expression of editorial opinion, therefore, is part and parcel of 'our profound national commitment...that debate on public issues should be uninhibited, robust, and wide-open.'...

"In sum § 399's broad ban on all editorializing by every station that receives CPB funds far exceeds what is necessary to protect against the risk of governmental interference or to prevent the public from assuming that editorials by public broadcasting stations represent the official view of government. The regulation impermissibly sweeps within its prohibition a wide range of speech by wholly private stations on topics that do not take a directly partisan stand or that have nothing whatever to do with federal, state or local government."

Ethical Dimension

Why isn't it permissible for the government to specify the terms under which it will grant money to a TV or radio station?

●

FREEDOM OF RELIGION

Freedom of religion has historically been of most interest to retail businesses which wish to operate seven days a week but are forbidden to do so by state or local laws. More recently, the Court has had to consider such labor law matters as whether an employee's refusal to work on Sunday justified discipline or discharge (it does, at least in some cases), and whether the National Labor Relations Act applies to professors in a private religious school (it does not, at least not usually). (These issues will be discussed in more detail in Chapter 14.)

Potentially, claims under the religion clause may crop up in a number of different contexts. Further definition by the Court may be needed on the scope of the religious fund-raising exemption under the national securities laws, for example. This right also intertwines with freedom of speech and of assembly when religious groups (or groups claiming to be such) seek to use public and private property for speeches, rallies, and other evangelistic activities. Claimed tax-exempt status may need close monitoring by the Court, as well. Is anyone who claims to be a minister a minister for tax purposes? Suppose the person has a "doctor of divinity" degree from a diploma mill—is the person then tax-exempt? Not all these situations have direct business significance, of course, but rules announced in one context have a strange way of appearing in new guises in other contexts.

■ Procedural Limitations

Particular regulations may also be challenged for violating the procedural guarantees stated in Amendments Four, Five, Six, and Seven. Courts have generally given a restrictive interpretation to the Seventh Amendment. The constitutional right to a trial by jury in *civil* cases applies only to those specific types of cases which were recognized at common law. As to any other, newly-created statutory rights, Congress (or the state legislature) is free to provide whatever method of trial it wishes, subject only to the basic requirement of due process.

The Bill of Rights specifies procedural requirements for civil and criminal cases.

Chapter 5 will discuss administrative due process in some detail. As noted there, statutory and administrative regulations which impose criminal or quasi-criminal penalties against specific defendants must include many of the same procedural guarantees as a regular criminal trial. Files and buildings may not be searched, and evidence seized, in violation of the Fourth Amendment's guarantee against unreasonable searches and seizures. Serious criminal charges must be brought by a grand jury, in accordance with the Fifth Amendment. Individuals may not be forced to be witnesses against themselves, directly, although they may be required to produce certain records, from which evidence can be derived. Both individuals and corporations are protected by the various provisions of the Sixth Amendment: speedy and public trial where the alleged offense was committed; knowledge of the nature of the accusation; confrontation with accusers; favorable witnesses subpoenaed; assistance of counsel. In general, procedural shortcuts are not permitted, although the Court may permit alternative procedures to be used if a strong public policy case is presented for them.

■ Due Process and Just Compensation Limitations

Some judges and commentators have tried to distinguish "mere" property rights from "human rights" such as freedom of speech and religion. Some Supreme Court Justices have, at various times, spoken of the First Amendment freedoms—as opposed to others listed in the Bill of Rights—as being "preferred." These justices are thus willing to strike down most restrictions on free speech, for example. At the same time, they permit Congress to limit other constitutional rights if a valid reason for doing so can be shown. It is a bit difficult to see how the First Amendment freedoms were intended to be "preferred," since the right to private property was mentioned twice, and protected in two different ways, in the Fifth Amendment. No person may be deprived of life, liberty, or property, without due process of law. And private property may not be taken for public use, without just compensation.

TAKINGS CLAUSE

Private property can be taken for public use only if just compensation is paid.

The "takings" clause has been greatly expanded by the Supreme Court, particularly by its decision in *Berman v. Parker*. Historically, "public use" was a clear enough concept—public parks, schools, streets, fire stations, and the like. To permit the implementation of urban renewal plans, however, a Supreme Court majority held in *Berman* that "public use" meant the same thing as "public purpose." There was a public purpose to be served in taking the private property of one owner and reselling it to another private owner for "renewal." If "use" and "purpose" mean the same thing, then the only limitation on the seizure of private property is the government's willingness to pay for it. Almost by definition, any takings program adopted by an appropriate governmental agency would involve a public purpose. However, there would not necessarily be a public use of the land so acquired. (For a more recent application of the takings clause, see the *Lucas* case in Chapter 16.)

SUBSTANTIVE DUE PROCESS

Beginning in the 1850s, state and national courts used the constitutional requirement of "due process" to strike down legislation. This line of decisions indicated that regulatory laws would be unconstitutional if the judges thought them "unreasonable." The substance of the law, as well as its procedural aspects, would be reviewed by the courts. In effect, the judges were substituting their views of public policy for those of Congress and the state legislatures. This approach was followed by the Supreme Court until the late 1930s.

Substantive due process, at least in the context of economic regulations, has been largely repudiated by the Supreme Court in subsequent decisions. Much of the force of the due process clause of the Fifth Amendment has also been removed by Supreme Court interpretations. The due process clause is no longer much of a barrier to the adoption of economic regulations. For some time now, a majority of the Court has apparently agreed to defer to the legislative will where regulation of "mere" property rights is involved. It is still theoretically possible to challenge national regulations on due process grounds, but the probability of success is not great, unless a First Amendment freedom is also at issue.

S UPREME COURT REVIEW OF STATE REGULATION

The same concerns and disagreements over constitutional interpretation which were discussed in the context of the Court's review of national economic regulations, also apply when the Court reviews state regulations. The same dichotomy has existed between the absolutists and the balancers. There is the same concern over deciding constitutional questions needlessly. On many occasions, the Court has used reasoning developed in one context to help decide cases arising in the other context.

There are, however, some differences between interpreting national power and interpreting state power. In the first place, the states hold the residue of governmental powers in our federal system. All powers not delegated to the national government are retained by the states or by the people. It is thus necessary in many cases to determine what has been delegated in order to determine what remains. Second, the Constitution contains some specific prohibitions against certain kinds of state action, prohibitions which do not apply to the national government. Third, even though the states retain all residual governmental powers, the states are parts of a larger whole. Individualized regulations which might be entirely proper for a separate sovereignty may not be feasible for the individual units in a federal system. Fourth, each of us is a citizen of the United States, as well as of our particular state. As such, the national government has a direct responsibility to each of us, and we have one to it. This concept of national citizenship also limits state action.

The states retain all governmental powers not delegated to the national government, nor prohibited to them by the U.S. Constitution.

C ONSTITUTIONAL PROHIBITIONS AGAINST STATE ACTION

As noted previously, the national Constitution contains several prohibitions against various types of state action. Any of these specific clauses, if applicable, can be used to challenge the legality of a particular state regulation of business activity.

■ Contracts Clause

States are prohibited by Article I, Section 10 from passing any law which impairs the obligation of contracts. This provision was added to

No state is permitted to pass any law which would impair the obligation of a contract.

prevent the states from passing retroactive laws which would change the rules of the game after persons had entered into legal relationships in good faith reliance on prior law. Just as a person cannot be criminally prosecuted for an act which was lawful when done, a state should not be able to invalidate contracts which were legal when made. It is unfair in either case to change the rules in the middle of the game.

Another clause of Article I, Section 10 prohibited the states from making anything but gold and silver coin legal tender in payment of debts. This clause meant that the states could not favor debtors by forcing creditors to accept paper money of questionable value. These provisions were inserted at the urging of Hamilton and others, who saw the need to put the finances of the new country on a sound basis.

What is surely the most famous case under the contracts clause is *Trustees of Dartmouth College v. Woodward*, 4 Wheaton 518 (1819). The college had been chartered in 1769 by King George III. When the state of New Hampshire attempted to impose new controls on the college, a lawsuit resulted. The Supreme Court held that corporate charters, issued by the government itself. were subject to the contracts clause. The Court also said that New Hampshire continued to be obligated on this contract as the successor to the English Crown. Chief Justice John Marshall, writing the Court's opinion, also provided us with what has become the classic definition of a corporation:

"A corporation is an artificial being, invisible, intangible, and existing only in contemplation of law. Being the mere creature of law, it possesses only those properties which the charter of its creation confers upon it, either expressly or as incidental to its very existence. These are such as are supposed best calculated to effect the object for which it was created. Among the most important are immortality, and, if the expression may be allowed, individuality; properties, by which a perpetual succession of many persons are considered as the same, and may act as a single individual. They enable a corporation to manage its own affairs, and to hold property without the perplexing intricacies, the hazardous and endless necessity, of perpetual conveyances for the purpose of transmitting it from hand to hand. It is chiefly for the purpose of clothing bodies of men in succession with these qualities and capacities that corporations were invented and are in use. By these means, a perpetual succession of individuals are capable of acting for the promotion of the particular object, like one immortal being."

Less than twenty years later, the Supreme Court substantially restricted the operation of the contracts clause. The Court held that a legislative grant or charter would not be implied to be exclusive, except where that result was clearly intended. In several cases, the Court has made clear that the state cannot "contract" so as to divest itself of the essential attributes of sovereignty, including the police power. If all "contracts" remain subject to the state's general police power, the contracts clause is no longer a substantial barrier to state regulation of business. In 1934, the Court even decided that a state legislature could pass the very sort of pro-debtor legislation which the clause was originally designed to prevent, provided the emergency were great enough. Many people saw that decision as the death-knell of the contracts clause. In the 1978 *Allied Structural Steel* case, however, the Court used the contracts clause to strike down another Minnesota statute, this one regulating company pension plans. This more recent case shows that the contracts clause is not dead; it was only dormant, waiting for the right case.

■ Compacts and Treaties

Section 10 of Article I also prohibits the states from entering into agreements with each other, or with foreign governments, without the consent of Congress. Multi-state agreements on such matters as pollution control are permissible, if Congress agrees. Similar, such agreements could be entered into with Canada or Mexico, for example, with congressional consent. Only the national government, however, may enter into a **treaty**. (As an agreement between countries, a treaty binds the entire nation and is part of the supreme law of the land.) States are likewise prohibited from coining money and issuing bills of credit.

■ State Taxes

A state may tax imports and exports only to the extent "absolutely necessary for executing its inspection laws," unless Congress consents to the imposition of a higher tax. To protect national commerce, there is also a similar restriction against state taxation of ships ("duty of tonnage").

The major battle-cry of the American Revolution was "No taxation without representation." In the last three decades, however, the states have moved aggressively to impose a variety of taxes on interstate businesses. These businesses are potentially the perfect taxpayers—they have clearly identifiable assets and income, but they do not have the vote. Of course, a tax which some businesses perceive as excessive might result in their withdrawal from a particular state. Likewise, the existence of a certain tax might lead a business to decide not to commence operations in the first place. As more and more states have imposed similar forms of taxes, however, a corporation no longer has the luxury of doing business only in tax-free areas. In hundreds of cases, especially since the turn of the century, corporate taxpayers have challenged the validity of particular state taxes. Despite these many precedents, this remains a fertile field for litigation. Since states have governmental powers only within their own territories, there are many complex constitutional questions as to what sorts of taxes they may impose on multi-state business operations.

■ Constitutional Requirements for State Taxes

State taxes on multistate transactions must be properly apportioned.

In order to pass constitutional muster, a state tax must comply with three requirements: (1) there must be a taxing "nexus" in the state, that is, the event or activity which is being taxed must have occurred within the state; (2) the tax may not discriminate against interstate commerce; and (3) where the tax is imposed on multi-state activities, an apportionment formula must be used which allocates to the taxing state only a fair share of the taxable subject-matter. The business against which the tax is assessed may thus challenge it on any or all of these grounds.

■ Discrimination/Burden

States taxes cannot discriminate against interstate commerce, nor unduly burden it.

The Court has not always used exactly the same formulation of this second test in deciding whether a state tax is valid. It is quite clear that a tax which discriminated against interstate commerce would be held unconstitutional, and that such discrimination could be found either in the actual language of the statute or in the administration of the statute. At some point, however, even a non-discriminatory tax may become an undue burden to an interstate business and thus be ruled invalid. Perhaps this is only another way of saying that the impact of the tax is discriminatory, even if the language of the act is not. If, for example, a city imposes a flat annual license fee on all sales representatives who solicit orders there, the tax has a very different impact on local and out-of-state firms. The local business would pay only one annual fee; one operating in many cities could be forced to pay many fees. If each city's fee is a flat rate, without reference to the amount of sales there, the burden on interstate commerce is obvious. The Court held such a fee unconstitutional in *Nippert v. Richmond*, 327 U.S. 416 (1946). Such decisions do not mean that a state can place no burdens on interstate commerce, since as Justice Frankfurter observed, both the tax itself and the costs of compliance impose real burdens on the taxpayer. *Any* tax is a burden. The Court won't permit "undue" burdens, which in effect encourages litigation on this point.

■ Apportionment

As noted above, apportionment is required in some tax situations. It would hardly be fair for each state in which an airline operated to be able to tax the entire value of its airplane fleet. Assuming that the airline is regularly operating in a state, however, that state should be able to impose its personal property tax, based on the privilege of using those planes within the state. Not all the planes are in the same state all year, and conceivably, some of the planes may not enter the taxing state at all during the year. How, then, to impose a fair tax burden?

The Court has upheld personal property taxes under such circumstances, if the state applies an equitable apportionment formula. The Court has not required such formulas to be uniform, although it has suggested in several opinions that it would give relief from multiple taxation where such could be proved to have occurred.

The potential for multiple taxation may be seen in the following hypothetical case: Southwind Airlines operates in six states and serves 96 cities. State Number One, a geographically large state, uses an apportionment formula based on route miles flown over the state. On that basis, State One taxes half the value of Southwind's airplane fleet. State Two, where half of Southwind's passenger boardings occur, uses boardings as the basis for apportionment and taxes half of the planes' value. State Three, where 16 of the cities served by Southwind are located, uses a formula based on number of stops within the state, and taxes one-sixth of the planes' value. State Four, a small state, simply divides by the number of states served by Southwind, and taxes one-sixth of the planes' value. State Five, an industrial state, uses a formula based on freight tonnage and taxes half of the planes' value. State Six uses a formula based on a combination of these factors, which permits it to tax one-third of the planes' value. Each of these is, presumably, a reasonable basis for allocation, if taken in isolation. In combination, however, Southwind is paying state personal property taxes on over two hundred percent of the value of its fleet. In other words, it's paying personal property taxes on twice as many planes as it actually owns!

State apportionment formulas need not be uniform.

The problems involved in working out a fair apportionment formula for taxation of movable personal property are difficult enough, but they pale into insignificance in comparison with those involved in taxation of income derived from multi-state operations. At least one can know how many planes are owned, and, within a reasonable degree of certainty, their value. With state taxation of interstate income, not only may there be wide variation in the apportionment formulas used, there may also be widely different definitions of exactly what is being taxed. Is it gross income, net income, gross sales, net sales, gross profit, net profit, or what? Even if two or more states used the same phrase, they might still define it quite differently. The myriad accounting problems involved in a determination of a business's revenues might be answered differently from state to state. Is a LIFO or a FIFO system to be used for inventories? Are reserves for depreciation, bad debts, and the like to be recognized? Are extraordinary gains and losses to be included? What about capital gains? What about dividend income from subsidiaries? From unaffiliated companies? Questions such as these need to be answered by each taxing authority. In general, the U.S. Supreme Court has taken a hands-off attitude to these problems and has permitted each state to work out its own system. Congress has been "studying" the problem of state taxation of interstate income for at least thirty years, but no set of national standards has been adopted.

The fears expressed by Justice Frankfurter have been realized. At some point, the present crazy-quilt of state tax laws does become a serious barrier to multi-state business operations. For the present, businesses need to weigh these factors carefully in making the decision to expand across state lines.

The following case is a recent example of this on-going problem.

JUSTICE · UNDER

ALLIED-SIGNAL, INC. V. DIRECTOR, DIVISION OF TAXATION

112 S. Ct. 2251 (1992)

Facts: Bendix was a Delaware corporation, with its corporate headquarters in Michigan. It did business in all 50 states and in 22 foreign countries. Its main business is the manufacture of aerospace and automotive parts. ASARCO is a New Jersey corporation with its corporate headquarters in New York. It is one of the world's largest producers of nonferrous metals.

Bendix bought 20.6 percent of the stock of ASARCO in the late 1970s. While Bendix owned the ASARCO stock, the companies were operated as completely separate businesses. When Bendix resold the stock in 1981, it made a profit of $211.5 million. The state of New Jersey, where Bendix does conduct some business, included this gain when the state calculated how much state tax Bendix owed in New Jersey. Bendix sued for a refund of this portion of the New Jersey income tax it had paid for 1981. The New Jersey courts held that the stock-sale profit was properly included as "income" for New Jersey state tax purposes. Bendix has since been sold to Allied-Signal, which is now claiming the refund.

Issue: Can a state include all the income of an out-of-state corporation when it applies the state's income tax apportionment formula?

Decision: No, it cannot do so. Allied-Signal gets the refund it requested.

Rule: A state cannot tax a non-domiciled corporation's income which is derived from business activity that is unrelated to its operations in the taxing state.

Discussion: *By Justice* KENNEDY:

"Among the limitations the Constitution sets on the power of a single State to tax the multi-state income of a nondomiciliary corporation are these: there must be 'a "minimal connection" between the interstate activities and the taxing state,'...and there must be a rational relation between the income attributed to the taxing State and the intrastate value of the corporate business. Under our precedents, a State need not attempt to isolate the intrastate income producing activities from the rest of the business; it may tax an apportioned sum if the corporation's multistate business is unitary.... A State may not tax a nondomiciliary corporation's income, however, if it is 'derive[d] from "unrelated business activity" which constitutes a "discrete business enterprise".'...

"The principle that a state may not tax value earned outside its borders rests on the fundamental requirement of both the Due Process and Commerce Clauses that there be 'some definite link, some minimum connection, between a state and the person, property or transaction it seeks to tax.'... The reason the Commerce Clause includes this limit is self-evident: in a Union of 50 States, to permit each State to tax activities outside its borders would have drastic consequences for the national economy, as businesses would be subject to severe multiple taxation. But the Due Process Clause also underlies our decisions in this area. Although our modern due process jurisprudence rejects a rigid, formalistic definition of minimum connection..., we have not abandoned the requirement that, in the case of a tax on an activity, there must be a connection to the activity itself, rather than a connection only to the actor the State seeks to tax.... The present inquiry focuses on the guidelines necessary to circumscribe the reach of the State's legitimate power to tax. We are guided by the basic principle that the State's power to tax an individual's or corporation's activities is justified by the 'protection, opportunities and benefits' the State confers on those activities....

"Because of the complications and uncertainties in allocating the income of multistate business to the several States, we permit States to tax a corporation on an apportionable share of the multistate business carried on in part in the taxing State. That is the unitary business principle. It is not a novel construct, but one which we approved rather a short time after the passage of the Fourteenth Amendment's Due Process Clause....

"[I]f anything would be unworkable in practice, it would be for us now to abandon our settled jurisprudence defining the limits of state power to tax under the unitary business principle. State legislatures have relied upon our precedents by enacting tax codes which allocate intangible nonbusiness income to the domiciliary State.... Were we to adopt New Jersey's theory, we would be required either to invalidate those statutes or authorize what would be certain double taxation. And, of course, we would defeat the reliance interest of those corporations which have structured their activities and paid their taxes based upon the well-established rules we here confirm. Difficult questions respecting the retroactive effect of our decision would also be presented.... New Jersey's proposal would disrupt settled expectations in an area of the law in which the demands of the national economy require stability....

"Application of the foregoing principles to the present case yields a clear result.... There is no serious contention that any of the three factors upon which we focused in [a prior case] were present. Functional integration and economies of scale could not exist because, as the parties have stipulated, 'Bendix and ASARCO were unrelated business enterprises each of whose activities had nothing to do with the other.'... Moreover, because Bendix owned only 20.6% of ASARCO's stock, it did not have the potential to operate ASARCO as an integrated division of a single unitary business, and of course, even potential control is not sufficient.... There was no centralization of management....

"Furthermore, contrary to the view expressed...by the New Jersey Supreme Court..., the mere fact that an intangible asset was acquired pursuant to a long-term corporate strategy of acquisitions and dispositions does not convert an otherwise passive investment into an integral operational one. Indeed, in [a prior case] we noted the important distinction between a capital investment which serves an investment function and one which serves an operational function.... If that distinction is to retain its vitality, then...the fact that a transaction was undertaken for a business purpose does not change its character.... [Other states have] argued that intangible income could be treated as earned in the course of a unitary business if the intangible property which produced the income is 'acquired, managed or disposed of for purposes relating on contributing to the taxpayer's business.'... In rejecting that argument we observed: 'This definition of unitary business would destroy the concept. The business of a corporation requires that it earn money to continue operations and to provide a return on its invested capital. Consequently all of its operations, including any investments made, in some sense can be said to be "for purposes relating to or contributing to the [corporation's] business." When pressed to its logical limit, this conception of the "unitary business" limitation becomes no limitation at all.'...

"Apart from semantics, we see no distinction between the 'purpose' test we [have already] rejected...and the 'ingrained acquisition-divestiture policy' approach adopted by the New Jersey Supreme Court.... The hallmarks of an acquisition which is part of the taxpayer's unitary business continue to be functional integration, centralization of management, and economies of scale.... [T]hese essentials could respectively be shown by transactions not undertaken at arm's length..., a management role by the parent which is grounded in its own operational expertise and operational strategy..., and the fact that the corporations are engaged in the same line of business.... It is undisputed that none of these circumstances existed here....

"In sum, the agreed-upon facts make clear that under our precedents New Jersey was not permitted to include the gain realized on the sale of Bendix's ASARCO stock in the former's apportionable tax base."

Ethical Dimension

Is it ethical for corporate managers to structure operations to minimize the corporation's liability for state income tax?

F EDERALISM AS A LIMITATION ON STATE REGULATION

The principle of federalism itself imposes some limits on the regulatory powers of the states. In those areas assigned by the Constitution to the national government, the national regulations must prevail over those of the states. Much litigation occurs over the setting of the boundaries on the states' powers which remain.

National Monopolies

Some areas require a uniform national rule almost by definition. Most of these are set out in the Constitution as being subject to exclusive national jurisdiction. The operation of the postal system, the armed forces, and the patent and copyright system are some of the government functions where uniformity is desirable. Even though not specifically set out in the Constitution, there may be other areas where a uniform rule is necessary. It would be extremely cumbersome, to say the least, if each state were free to decide for itself whether motor vehicles were to travel on the right-hand or the left-hand side of the highway.

Conversely, even though specifically set out in the Constitution, some national powers may still permit state action within a limited scope. For example, while Congress is given the power to establish uniform national rules on bankruptcy, it may defer to the states' laws for the definitions of exemptions (property which the debtor need not turn over to the bankruptcy proceeding).

◼ Commerce Clause versus State Police Power

States may regulate business activities to promote citizens' health, safety, and welfare.

Congress is given the power "To regulate Commerce with foreign Nations, and among the several States and with the Indian Tribes." The commerce clause has been, and continues to be, one of the major limitations on the states' power to regulate business. The demarcation line between legitimate exercises of a state's power to regulate for the promotion of its citizens' health, safety, morals, and welfare and unconstitutional burdens on the flow of interstate commerce is not an easy one to draw. The question has been litigated many, many times. Some general principles have been fairly well established. The application of these principles to specific fact combinations, however, provides a continuing source of disagreement among the justices.

The Court has generally recognized that the many and varied subjects of commerce fall into three categories, for regulatory purposes: those which may be regulated only by the national government, those which may be regulated only by the states, and those which are subject to regulation by both levels of government. Exclusive areas of national jurisdiction would include such matters as the establishment of our international trade policy, including tariffs and treaties; airplane navigation; and space satellite communications. As noted above, it is difficult to find commercial activities which do not somehow at least "impact" on interstate commerce under the Court's precedents. If babysitters and window-washers are subject to congressional power under the commerce clause, it's hard to imagine who would not be. If a farmer growing wheat for his own use can be regulated under the commerce clause, can our home vegetable gardens be far behind?

What is left for exclusive state regulation are the general rules of commercial law: torts, contracts, sales, commercial paper, business organizations, and the like. Even here, however, federal regulation is occurring. The traditional state rules for contract formation are now subject to several "consumer protection" regulations adopted by the Federal Trade Commission. Corporations may still be chartered by the states, but the issuance and transfer of their securities is subject to comprehensive national regulation as well. Even in the area of family law, clearly intended by the framers to be "reserved to the States respectively, or to the people," some national incursions have taken place. Even those areas of commercial and personal law, in other words, might be better described today as areas of dual jurisdiction, rather than "exclusively state."

◼ Dual Jurisdiction

Of the thousands of interpretations of the commerce clause by state supreme courts and the U.S. Supreme Court, most have involved business activities which were subject to regulation by both the national government and the states. In attempting to adjust the respective interests of the national and state governments, the Supreme Court has noted that three different situations may exist: (1) national regulation may preempt state regulation; (2) national regulation may exist, but not preempt state regulation; (3) there may be no national regulation at all as to a particular subject-matter. The states' power is somewhat different in each of these situations. Figure 3–3 summarizes the range of possible relationships between national and state regulation of interstate commerce.

In many areas, national and state governments both have regulatory powers.

REGULATION OF INTERSTATE COMMERCE	
CONGRESS	**STATES**
I. Expressly preempts	= States cannot regulate
II. Legislates (Comprehensive)	= States cannot regulate
III. Legislates (Non-comprehensive)	= States can regulate, but:
	A] Cannot conflict
	B] Cannot discriminate
	C] Cannot be undue burden
	D] Cannot be arbitrary
	E] Cannot violate due process
	F] Cannot violate equal protection
IV. No legislation	= (Same as III)
V. Expressly delegates	= (Same as III)

FIGURE 3–3
The relationship between national and state regulation depends on the nature of the legislation involved.

If Congress acts within its constitutional authority to regulate a subject of commerce, that statute becomes part of the "supreme law of the land." If Congress specifically declares that it intends to preempt the particular field of commerce, the states are then prohibited from interfering with the congressional regulatory scheme. These are relatively easy cases to decide, since the only issue is whether Congress had the authority to pass the statute. More difficult preemption issues are presented when there is no clear expression of congressional intent. The Court must then decide whether the statute (along with any implementing administrative regulations) presents such a comprehensive scheme that preemption must be presumed. How "comprehensive" the national regulation must be in order for the Court to imply an intent to preempt state laws is a question which must be answered on a case-by-case basis.

Even if there is no express or implied congressional intent to preempt state regulation, the state must act within certain limits. The state could not adopt a regulation which was inconsistent with the policy expressed in the national law. Nor could the state adopt a regulation

National regulation may preempt state power to regulate the same subject.

which placed an undue burden on the free flow of interstate commerce. Finally, the state may not impose a regulation which discriminates against interstate commerce in favor of local businesses. That, too, would restrict the free flow of commerce throughout the nation.

Even though Congress has not acted and the subject is a "local" one, a state could not unduly burden interstate commerce or discriminate against it. Congressional inaction would not validate burdensome or discriminatory state regulation. In such a case, there would just not be a national standard against which to judge the state's action for inconsistency.

In the *Morales* case, all eight justices who participated agreed that Congress did intend to expressly preempt state regulation. The five majority justices think Congress meant to preempt all state regulation "relating" to airline fares. The three dissenters think Congress meant to preempt only state regulation of the fares themselves.

MORALES V. TRANS WORLD AIRLINES, INC.

112 S. Ct. 2031 (1992)

Facts: Before 1978, the Civil Aeronautics Board (CAB) was empowered by the Federal Aviation Act of 1958 to regulate interstate air fares and to take action against deceptive trade practices. The 1958 Act contained a "savings clause" which let the states regulate intrastate fares and enforce their own laws against deceptive trade practices. The 1978 Airline Deregulation Act, however, included a provision which expressly prohibited the states from enforcing any law "relating to rates, routes, or services" of any air carrier.

In 1987 the National Association of Attorneys General (NAAG) adopted a set of detailed standards for airline advertising—the Air Travel Industry Enforcement Guidelines. The attorneys general of seven states, including Texas, then sent letters to several major airlines, including TWA, announcing that they intended to sue to enforce the states' "guidelines." (Dan Morales was the Texas Attorney General at the time the case was filed.) The airlines sued in U.S. District Court in Texas, asking the court for an injunction against enforcement of the guidelines. The court issued an injunction against Texas and thirty-three other states. The U.S. Court of Appeals affirmed. Morales asked the U.S. Supreme Court for further review.

Issue: Does the Airline Deregulation Act preempt state regulation of airline advertising of fares, as well as state regulation of the fares themselves?

Decision: Yes, it does. Judgment affirmed. (The injunction stands.)

Rule: State enforcement actions having a connection with or reference to airline "rates, routes, or services" are expressly preempted by the 1978 Act.

Discussion: *By Justice SCALIA:*

"As we have often observed, '[p]re-emption may be either express or implied, and is compelled whether Congress' command is explicitly stated in the statute's language or implicitly contained in its structure and purpose.' The question, at bottom, is one of statutory intent, and we accordingly 'begin with the language employed by Congress and the assumption that the ordinary meaning of that language accurately expresses the legislative purpose.'...

"Section 1305(a)(1) expressly preempts the States from 'enact[ing] or enforc[ing] any law, rule, regulation, standard, or other provision having the force and effect of law relating to rates, routes, or services of any air carrier.'... For purposes of the present case, the key phrase, obviously, is 'relating to.' The ordinary meaning of these words is a broad one—'to stand in some relation, to have bearing or concern, to pertain, refer, to bring into association with or connection with'...—and the words thus express a broad preemptive purpose.... State enforcement actions having a connection with or reference to airline 'rates, routes, or services' are preempted under...1305(a)(1).

"[Morales] raises a number of objections to this reading, none of which we think is well taken. First, he claims that we may not use our interpretations of identical language in ERISA [the Employment Retirement Income Security Act] as a guide, because the sweeping nature of ERISA pre-emption derives not from the 'relates to' language, but from 'the wide and inclusive sweep of the comprehensive ERISA scheme,' which he asserts the ADA does not have.... This argument is flatly contradicted by our ERISA cases, which clearly and unmistakably rely on express pre-emption principles and a construction of the phrase 'relates to.'...

"[Morales] contends that § 1305(a)(1) only pre-empts the States from actually prescribing rates, routes, or services. This simply reads the words 'relating to' out of the statute. Had the statute been designed to pre-empt state law in such a limited fashion, it would have forbidden the States to 'regulate rates, routes, and services.'...

"Next, [Morales] advances the notion that only State laws specifically addressed to the airline industry are pre-empted, whereas the ADA imposes no constraints on laws of general applicability. Besides creating an utterly irrational loophole (there is little reason why state impairment of the federal scheme should be deemed acceptable so long as it is effected by the particularized application of a general statute), this notion similarly ignores the sweep of the 'relating to' language.

"Last, the State suggests that the pre-emption is inappropriate when state and federal law are consistent. State and federal law are in fact inconsistent here—DOT [the U.S. Department of Transportation] opposes the obligations contained in the guidelines, and Texas law imposes greater liability—but that is beside the point. Nothing in the language of § 1305(a)(1) suggests that its 'relating to' pre-emption is limited to *inconsistent* state regulation....

"It is hardly surprising that [Morales] contests most of his case on such strained readings of § 1305(a)(1), rather than contesting whether NAAG guidelines really 'relat[e] to' fares. They quite obviously do.

"One cannot avoid the conclusion that...the guidelines 'relate to' airlines rates. In its terms, every one of the guidelines enumerated above bears a 'reference to' air fares.... And, collectively, the guidelines establish binding requirements as to how tickets may be marketed if they are to be sold at given prices....

"Although the State insists that it is not compelling or restricting advertising, but is instead merely preventing the market distortion caused by 'false' advertising, in fact the dynamics of the air transportation industry cause the guidelines to curtail the airlines' ability to communicate fares to their customers.... As the FTC [Federal Trade Commission] observed, '[r]equiring too much information in advertisements can have the paradoxical effect of stifling the information that customers receive.'... Further, [guideline] § 2.4, by allowing fares to be advertised only if sufficient seats are available to meet demand or if the extent of unavailability is disclosed, may make it impossible to use this marketing process at all. All in all, the obligations imposed by the guidelines would have a significant impact upon the airlines' ability to market their product, and hence a significant impact upon the fares they charge."

Ethical Dimension

Why should airline management object to complying with the states' guidelines for the fair advertising of the airlines' rates and services?

■ Fourteenth Amendment Limitations

State regulations may also be challenged under any of the three guarantees contained in the Fourteenth Amendment: "privileges and immunities," "equal protection," and "due process." If any of these three provisions is found to have been violated, the regulation in question is invalid. Figure 3–4 outlines these three requirements and the three different tests of "equal protection" used by the courts.

THE FOURTEENTH AMENDMENT

No State Shall:
- Make any law abridging the privileges and immunities of U.S. citizens.
- Deprive any person of life, liberty, or property without due process of law.
- Deny any person the equal protection of its laws.

14TH AMENDMENT EQUAL PROTECTION TESTS

Strict Scrutiny Test:
1. *Compelling* public interest
2. No alternative means
3. Necessary to achieve objective
4. No more intrusive than needed

Intermediate Test(s):
1. Important public interest
2. Substantially related

Rational Basis Test:
1. Valid public interest
2. Rationally related

FIGURE 3–4
The Fourteenth Amendment provides protection from state regulations.

PRIVILEGES AND IMMUNITIES

The privileges and immunities clause protects only citizens, not aliens and not corporations. Thus, a state law which prohibited land ownership by aliens would not be unconstitutional under this clause, although it might violate one or both of the other two. The number of activities which are privileges and immunities under this section, and which a state can thus restrict to citizens only, has been limited in recent years. A state may no longer prevent aliens from practicing law in the state, for example, if the alien meets all other qualifications. The Court has even prevented the states from denying certain public benefits to unlawful aliens. Alien children who are in the country unlawfully must, for example, be given access to the state's free public schools. The right to vote and to run for political office, and, perhaps, to serve on juries, may still be limited to citizens only. Most business operations transactions, however, almost certainly fall under one of the other two clauses.

EQUAL PROTECTION

The equal protection clause has never meant that a state must treat all persons exactly alike; different standards may be, and are, imposed. This clause does mean that any differences in treatment must be rational; there can be no arbitrary or invidious discrimination. The state, in other words, must be prepared to justify the differential.

States can treat persons differently only if there is a valid basis for the classification.

The Court has developed two standards by which a state's differential treatment may be judged: the "strict scrutiny" test and the "rational basis" test. The strict scrutiny test is applied where a state regulation impacts on "fundamental rights" or on a "suspect class." (Racial classifications by a state are "suspect" almost by definition.) **Strict scrutiny** means that the state will have to show a compelling reason for the regulation. The state will also have to convince the Court that there is no feasible alternative way to accomplish the purpose of the regulation, and that the regulation is as minimally burdensome as it can be. A regulation which interferes with the free exercise of religion, for example, could be justified only by the state's showing a "compelling public need" for the regulation.

Most economic regulations will probably be tested under the less rigorous "rational basis" test. Here, a state need only show that it had a rational basis for adopting the regulation and that the regulation does serve the state's objectives. Under this second test, a regulation may be valid even though it has an uneven impact on certain persons.

More recently, some courts have suggested an "intermediate scrutiny" test. The rationale for this "halfway house" is that there are circumstances under which such factors as age and sex may legitimately be considered by government regulations. As usually defined, this test requires only that the regulation be reasonably related to a proper government purpose. Establishing minimum and maximum ages for military service, for instance, might be perfectly legitimate. A minimum age requirement for jury service might also be proper.

Not all the justices have subscribed to this dual approach, nor have they applied the tests in exactly the same way from case to case. Moreover, there is a bitter and continuing controversy over whether an intent to discriminate must be shown in order to invalidate a state regulation. If a state acts in good faith, follows regular procedure, and has a legitimate objective to be served, is its regulation invalid simply because it produces a differential impact on a "suspect class"? The justices do not agree on this point.

DUE PROCESS OF LAW

States must provide all persons with due process of law.

The due process clause of the Fourteenth Amendment is the vehicle by which the Court has gradually made nearly all of the protections of the Bill of Rights applicable to the states. Some justices and constitutional scholars have argued that this clause automatically incorporates all of the exact provisions from the Bill of Rights, but that is not the approach that the Court has actually taken. The Court has declared that the clause has both a procedural and a substantive content. Procedurally, states must guarantee the basics of a fair trial, whether it be a civil case or a criminal case. The Court has not required, however, that each of the specific procedural provisions of the Bill of Rights must be followed by the states. For instance, the charges may be conveyed to a state criminal accused by means of a formal statement from a prosecutor (called an "**information**"), rather than by a grand jury indictment, as required by the Fifth Amendment. Also, the states are free to use their own tests for determining when a party in a civil case has the right to a trial by jury, rather than using the test derived from the Seventh Amendment. On the procedural side, therefore, the Court has taken a common-sense, pragmatic approach: Is the state's procedure basically fair, under the standards of a civilized society? If so, it should pass constitutional muster if challenged.

It is now well established that the due process clause also has a substantive content. Some state regulations are invalid simply because of the subject-matter which they purport to regulate, even though they were properly adopted and even though they provide fair procedures for making decisions. Again, the Court has spoken of "preferred freedoms" (those listed in the First Amendment) as being beyond the states' power to regulate, unless a strong justification is shown. On the other hand, where the regulation applies to mere property and contract rights, some justices (perhaps most of them) will defer to the legislative will, so long as the regulation has some rational purpose. Just as was true in interpreting the Bill of Rights, not all justices follow this "split-level" approach, or apply it the same way in all contexts if they do follow it.

The following case deals with "commercial speech." State regulation of this area continues to be a very troublesome topic.

POSADAS DE PUERTO RICO ASSOC. V. TOURISM CO.

478 U.S. 328 (1986).

Facts: The island of Puerto Rico has a unique legal status as a U.S. "commonwealth"—much more than a colony, but not quite a state. It has its own governor, legislature, and courts. A 1948 act makes casino gambling lawful on the island, but prohibits casino advertising which is directed to the local residents of the island. Local ads directed at tourists on the island are permitted, even if such ads might also be seen by residents. Other forms of legal gambling, such as horse racing and the state's own lottery, may advertise freely to both tourists and residents.

Posadas, a Texas partnership, is authorized to operate a casino in its Holiday Inn in Puerto Rico. It paid two fines for violating the advertising restrictions. It could have lost its license to operate if it had not paid. It then filed a lawsuit, asking the Puerto Rico court to declare the law unconstitutional. It claimed that the law violated its rights to free speech, due process, and equal protection. The Puerto Rico Superior Court upheld the law (as it interpreted the law more narrowly). The Puerto Rico Supreme Court refused an appeal, saying that no substantial constitutional question was raised. Posadas then sought further review by the U.S. Supreme Court.

Issue: Does the statute violate the First Amendment (as applied to the states, and to Puerto Rico, through the Fourteenth Amendment)?

Decision: No, it does not. Judgment of the Puerto Rico courts is affirmed.

Rule: Commercial speech may be regulated, to a limited extent, to achieve valid state (or "commonwealth") purposes.

Discussion: *By Justice REHNQUIST:*

"[C]ommercial speech receives a limited form of First Amendment protection so long as it concerns a lawful activity and is not misleading or fraudulent. Once it is determined that the First Amendment applies to the particular kind of commercial speech at issue, then the speech may be restricted only if the government's interest in doing so is substantial, the restrictions directly advance the government's asserted interest, and the restrictions are no more extensive than necessary to serve that interest....

"The first of these three steps involves an assessment of the strength of the government's interest in restricting the speech. The interest at stake in this case...is the reduction of demand for casino gambling by the residents of Puerto Rico.... The [Puerto Rico] Tourism Company's brief before this Court explains the legislature's belief that '[e]xcessive casino gambling among local residents...would produce serious harmful effects on the health, safety and welfare of the Puerto Rico citizens, such as the disruption of moral and cultural patterns, the increase of local crime, the fostering of prostitution, the development of corruption, and the infiltration of organized crime.'... These are some of the very same concerns, of course, that have motivated the vast majority of the 50 states to prohibit casino gambling. We have no difficulty in concluding that the Puerto Rico

Legislature's interest in the health, safety, and welfare of its citizens constitutes a 'substantial' governmental interest....

"[Posadas] argues, however, that the challenged advertising restrictions are underinclusive because other kinds of gambling...may be advertised to the residents of Puerto Rico. [This] argument is misplaced for two reasons. First, whether other kinds of gambling are advertised in Puerto Rico or not, the restrictions on advertising of casino gambling 'directly advance' the legislature's interest in reducing demand for games of chance.... Second, the legislature's interest...is not necessarily to reduce demand for all games of chance, but to reduce demand for casino gambling.... In other words, the legislature felt that for Puerto Ricans the risks associated with casino gambling were significantly greater than those associated with the more traditional kinds of gambling in Puerto Rico....

"We also think it clear...that the challenged statute and regulations satisfy the last step of the...analysis, namely, whether the restrictions on commercial speech are no more extensive than necessary to serve the government's interest. The narrowing constructions of the advertising restrictions announced by the Superior Court ensure that the restrictions will not affect advertising of casino gambling aimed at tourists, but will only apply to such advertising when aimed at the residents of Puerto Rico....

"[T]he Puerto Rico Legislature surely could have prohibited casino gambling by the residents of Puerto Rico altogether. In our view, the greater power to completely ban casino gambling necessarily includes the lesser power to ban advertising of casino gambling....

"It would surely by a Pyrrhic victory for casino owners such as [Posadas] to gain recognition of a First Amendment right to advertise their casinos in Puerto Rico, only to thereby force the legislature into banning casino gambling altogether. It would just as surely be a strange constitutional doctrine which would concede to the legislature the authority to totally ban a product or activity, but deny to the legislature the authority to forbid the stimulation of demand for the product or activity through advertising on behalf of those who would profit from such increased demand."

Ethical Dimension

Is it fair to single out one form of gambling and to apply advertising restrictions only to it?

REVIEW

Separation of powers and federalism are the twin foundations of the U.S. Constitution. The Constitution also contains several prohibitions against action by the states, or by any agency of government. It states a number of specific substantive and procedural rights which each person is entitled to receive. Ultimately, the scope and meaning of the various powers, prohibitions, rights, and limitations will be decided by the U.S. Supreme Court. The Court serves as the final umpire in deciding what the Constitution means, at least until it is amended by the special procedure provided in the Constitution itself.

Although for the last fifty years the Supreme Court has taken an expansive view of the national government's power to regulate business, the U.S. Constitution still provides a number of important limitations. Especially in those areas where business regulation impacts on First Amendment freedoms, there is a very real possibility that the regulation can be overturned through a court challenge to its constitutionality.

Similar limitations exist on state regulation. In addition, there may be state constitutional grounds to challenge the regulation. U.S. or state constitutional issues can be raised in court. Of course, the financial costs and the possible adverse publicity need to be weighed carefully before filing such a lawsuit. The legal bases for a challenge do exist, however, and some state (and national) regulations are invalidated by the courts.

REVIEW QUESTIONS AND PROBLEMS

1. What are the two tests for validity of regulations under the Equal Protection Clause? Why is this distinction important to business?

2. How is the right to own private property protected in the Constitution?

3. Why is the First Amendment important to business?

4. How does Federalism impact on business operations?

5. What are the constitutional limitations on state taxation of business?

6. It is sometimes said that the power of Congress over interstate commerce is absolute. What is meant by that statement?

7. Bakeslow Company sells stuffed turkeys in several states. The U.S. Department of Agriculture requires companies to put the net weight of the stuffed bird on the package. A state law requires that the product labels state both the net weight of the stuffed bird and the net weight of the unstuffed bird. Bakeslow asked the USDA for approval of a label which would satisfy the state requirements. The USDA refused. Rather than asking for an administrative review or a court review of the USDA decision, Bakeslow sued in the U.S. District Court to have the state law declared unconstitutional. How should the court rule, and why?

8. Mary and Larry Garza bought a home. The bank which was financing their purchase required a lawyer's opinion that they would receive a valid title to the real estate from the seller. Mary and Larry contacted several local lawyers. None would do the legal work for less than one percent of the sales price, which was the minimum fee "suggested" by the state lawyers' association. Mary and Larry filed an antitrust lawsuit against the state lawyers' association, claiming that it was fixing prices. The lawyers' association says that real estate purchases are purely local transactions, and thus not within the reach of Congress under the Commerce Clause. Therefore, the lawyers claim, the national antitrust acts are not applicable to them. Is this a valid argument? Explain.

9. Passive People United (PPU), an organization opposed to all use of force in international disputes, wanted to pass out leaflets stating these views. PPU asked the owner of a large shopping mall for permission to distribute their leaflets at the mall. She refused to grant permission. PPU wants to file a lawsuit to gain access to the mall. The U.S. Supreme Court has already ruled that property owners have the right to control access to their land. Is there any other basis for such a lawsuit? Discuss.

10. In an attempt to promote energy conservation, a state public service commission adopted a regulation which prohibited any advertising by an electric utility company which would advocate the increased use of electricity. Zappo Electric Company, which sells electric power, immediately filed a lawsuit which challenged this regulation on constitutional grounds. Do they have a case? Why or why not?

SUGGESTIONS FOR FURTHER READING

Boren, "Suits Against States in Federal Court: The Current Fourteenth Amendment Controversy," *American Business Law Journal* 25 (Winter 1988): 701.

Fox, "Due process and Student Academic Misconduct," *American Business Law Journal* 25(Winter 1988): 671.

4
THE
LEGAL
SYSTEM

"Laws are a dead letter without courts to...define their true meaning and operation."
Alexander Hamilton

LEARNING OBJECTIVES: After you have studied this chapter, you should be able to:

IDENTIFY the major courts in the federal court system, and their functions.

INDICATE the types of cases which are assigned to the federal courts and the state courts.

EXPLAIN the concept of court jurisdiction.

OUTLINE the main steps in the process of litigating a case.

DISCUSS the various forms of alternate dispute resolution.

DEFINE forum-selection and choice-of-law clauses.

P REVIEW

In no other nation do the courts play so great a social role as in the United States. A 1992 story in *The Economist* compared the number of lawyers per capita in various countries. (See Figure 4–1.) We have more than twice as many lawyers per capita as Great Britain, more than three times as many as Japan, and more than six times as many as France. Of the two million-plus lawyers in the world, nearly forty percent are in the United States. Our legal system absorbs a much greater share of our GNP than that of any of our major international trade competitors. The same *Economist* story indicates that the total costs for processing civil injury cases are six times greater in the United States than in Japan. The U.S. legal process is the subject of numerous TV shows, movies, and novels. Because of their power of judicial review, as discussed in the previous chapter, our courts are important shapers of national policy. In sum, courts in the United States play significant political, economic, and social roles.

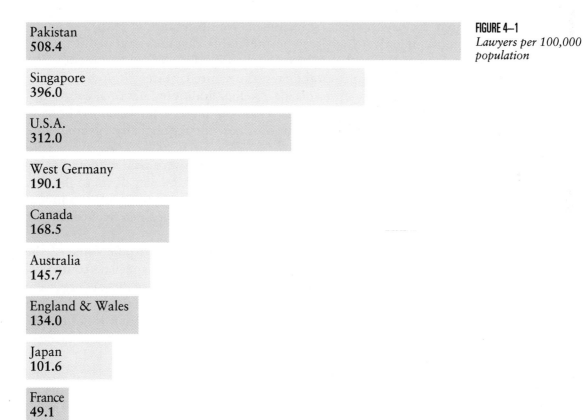

Pakistan
508.4

Singapore
396.0

U.S.A.
312.0

West Germany
190.1

Canada
168.5

Australia
145.7

England & Wales
134.0

Japan
101.6

France
49.1

India
34.4

FIGURE 4–1
Lawyers per 100,000 population

Derived from information reported in *The Economist*, July 18, 1992, p.4

This chapter discusses the structure of our courts and the process by which they hear and decide civil (as distinguished from criminal) cases. You will examine the organization of the federal courts and the state courts, the relationship between the two sets of courts, and the procedure which is used for the trial of civil cases. There are many specific differences from state to state, but this chapter will provide a general overview of court structure and civil procedure.

D UAL COURT SYSTEMS

One of the unique features of the U.S. governmental structure is the existence of a complete set of national courts, in addition to the court systems of the fifty states. As a result, the litigants in many cases may have a choice of using a national court or a state court.

■ Federalism for the Courts

It must have seemed fairly clear to the drafters of the Constitution that the new national government would require at least a supreme court, if only to referee the inevitable disputes that would occur between the various branches and levels of government. The Constitution thus establishes the United States Supreme Court. Congress is then left to decide whether additional national courts will be needed. (State courts were already in place, established by the state governments. The Constitution does not require any specific state court structure.)

It is possible to have a federal system of government without having a complete set of national courts reaching all the way down to the trial court level. Canada and Germany, for example, have only a national supreme court. All trials and intermediate appeals in such countries occur in provincial or *lander* (state) courts.

Congress first created a national trial court to take some of the workload off the Supreme Court. An intermediate appellate court level and several specialized courts were added later. Since these courts were established under the authority of the federal Constitution, they are generally referred to as the "federal" courts. (Although it is not technically precise, this usage is so widespread among courts and lawyers that this text will also use the term.)

The federal courts and the state courts exist in parallel systems.

In general, the federal (national) court system is separate and distinct from the state court systems. It is a parallel system, rather than a supervisory system. Figure 4–2 shows this parallelism, with the main federal courts on the left and the court system of a typical large state on the right. (Not all states have an intermediate court of appeals.) Each system hears the cases assigned to it. Many types of cases can be heard by either court system. The Constitution says that the following types of cases may be brought in the federal courts:

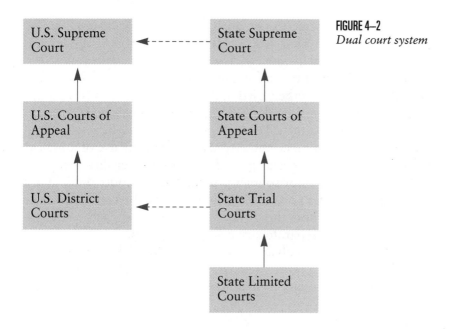

FIGURE 4–2
Dual court system

- cases arising under the Constitution, treaties, or national statutes;
- cases affecting ambassadors and other representatives of foreign governments;
- cases in which the United States is a party;
- cases between two or more states;
- cases between a state and citizens of another state;
- cases between citizens of different states;
- cases between citizens of the same state claiming land under conflicting land grants from different states;
- cases between a state or its citizens and a foreign government or its citizens.

The Eleventh Amendment states that the federal courts can not hear cases "commenced or prosecuted" against a state by citizens of another state or another country.

A plaintiff wishing to file a lawsuit in a U.S. District Court would thus have to show that the case fell into one of the listed categories. Congress has the power to further define these categories. Cases between citizens of different states (**diversity of citizenship** cases), for instance, must now involve $50,000 or more to be heard in a U.S. District Court. Congress may also specify that cases arising under a statute it passes may be brought only in the federal courts, either a U.S. District Court or a specialized court. If it does not do so, the U.S. Supreme Court held in 1990, such cases may also be filed in an appropriate state court.

The U.S. Supreme Court is the final authority on the meaning of the U.S. Constitution, so it can review state court rulings on constitutional points. A state court decision which violates the Constitution could be

The federal courts may hear ordinary contract and tort cases if the parties are from different states and at least $50,000 is involved.

The U.S. Supreme Court can review state court decisions which raise issues under the U.S. Constitution.

overturned by the Supreme Court. Also, at the trial court level, a case which could have been filed in a U.S. District Court but was instead begun by the plaintiff in a state court, can be removed to an appropriate U.S. District Court. If the defendant requests removal and this petition is granted, the case is then tried in the U.S. District Court. Any appeals would then be heard by the U.S. Court of Appeals and (perhaps) by the U.S. Supreme Court. The federal courts also have a limited power of review over state criminal trials, through the use of a **habeas corpus** proceeding. This special procedure tests the legality (constitutionality) of a person's imprisonment. If the federal court finds that a prisoner was not given a constitutionally fair trial, the court can order a release. Aside from these three control mechanisms, each court system should respect the separate authority of the other.

The following case involves a potential conflict between the state courts and the federal courts. Texaco, the party who lost in a state court, asked a federal court to invalidate the state's requirements for filing an appeal.

JUSTICE·UNDER

PENNZOIL CO. V. TEXACO, INC.

107 S. Ct. 1519 (1987)

Facts: In a Texas state court decision, Texaco lost the largest civil case in history (over $10 billion in damages). Texaco found that it would have to post an amount equal to the judgment in order to file an appeal. Ten billion dollars was more than the entire net worth of the company. (Many small nations don't have a GNP that large!) Texaco felt that this Texas procedural rule was denying it due process, so it filed its own lawsuit in U.S. District Court in New York, where it had its home office. Texaco asked the U.S. District Court in New York to enjoin Pennzoil from enforcing the Texas state court judgment in favor of Pennzoil. The U.S. District Court granted the injunction, and the U.S. Court of Appeals for the Second Circuit affirmed. Pennzoil then asked the U.S. Supreme Court to review the injunction case.

Issue: Should federal courts issue injunctions against state court proceedings where there has been no final state decision in the case?

Decision: No, they should not. The injunction decision is reversed, and the case is sent back to the U.S. District Court with instructions to dismiss Texaco's complaint.

Rule: Federal courts should defer to state court proceedings which are still in process.

Descussion: *By Justice POWELL:*

"Both the District Court and the Court of Appeals failed to recognize the significant interests harmed by their unprecedented intrusion into the Texas judicial system. Similarly, neither of those courts applied the appropriate standard in determining whether adequate relief was available in the Texas courts....

"Another important reason for abstention [noninterference] is to avoid unwarranted determination of federal constitutional questions.... This concern has special significance in this case. Because Texaco chose not to present to the Texas courts the constitutional claims asserted in this case, it is impossible to be certain that the governing Texas statutes and procedural rules actually raise these claims. Moreover, the Texas constitution contains an 'open courts' provision...that appears to address Texaco's claims more specifically than the due process clause of the Fourteenth Amendment. Thus, when this case was filed in Federal Court, it was entirely possible that the Texas courts would have resolved this case on state statutory or constitutional grounds, without reaching the federal constitutional questions Texaco raises in this case.... [A]bstention in situations like this 'offers the opportunity for narrowing constructions that might obviate the constitutional problem and intelligently mediate federal constitutional concerns and state interests.'...

"In sum, the lower courts should have deferred...to the pending state proceedings. They erred in accepting Texaco's assertions as to the inadequacies of Texas procedure to provide effective relief. It is true that this case presents an unusual fact situation, never before addressed by the Texas courts, and that Texaco urgently desired prompt relief. But we cannot say that those courts, when this suit was filed, would have been any less inclined than a federal court to address and decide the federal constitutional claims. Because Texaco apparently did not give the Texas courts an opportunity to adjudicate its constitutional claims, and because Texaco cannot demonstrate that...the Texas courts were not then open to adjudicate its claims, there is no basis for concluding that the Texas law and procedures were so deficient that...abstention is inappropriate. Accordingly, we conclude that the District Court should have abstained."

Ethical Dimension

Is it fair to force a company to defend itself in the other company's home state? Is it fair to force the losing party to post a large sum of money with the court in order to appeal the judgment?

As a result of this decision by the U.S. Supreme Court, Texaco decided to go into bankruptcy to protect its assets from seizure and sale by the state courts. A settlement was eventually worked out, by the terms of which Texaco paid cash and other assets to Pennzoil. The total value of the settlement was variously estimated at $1.5 to $3 billion. Texaco then emerged from bankruptcy and continued its normal business operations.

■ Choice of Law in Federal Courts

Substantive law declares rights and duties. It specifies what a person needs to do to organize a corporation, or what two parties must do to form a valid contract. **Procedural law** specifies the steps by which a lawsuit is heard. As a rule, a court hearing a case uses its own procedural law, but difficult questions can arise as to whose substantive law applies.

Federal courts use their own civil procedure rules. The Constitution, various national statutes, and the Federal Rules of Civil Procedure (FRCP) will determine the details for the trial of the civil case—whether a jury is available, how many jurors are used, how they are chosen, how many of them must agree on a verdict, what evidence is admissible, and so on. Similarly, the federal courts will use their own criminal procedure rules. Crimes against national law can be tried only in the federal courts, and state crimes can be tried only in the state courts. There are thus no "choices" about which procedural law to use or which substantive criminal law to use.

In diversity of citizenship cases, U.S. courts generally choose the same substantive legal rules as would a state court in that state.

Some civil cases, such as those involving diversity of citizenship, can be tried either in the federal courts or in the state courts. In such cases, a decision must be made as to which body of substantive civil law to apply. If one person claims to have been injured by the negligent conduct of another, and the case is brought in a federal court because the parties are from different states, whose law of negligence should apply? Should the trial court use the negligence law of the plaintiff's home state, that of the defendant's home state, or is there a national law of negligence which should be applied? The federal courts originally began to develop their own rules for contract, property, and tort (personal injury) cases. These earlier precedents were overruled in 1938 by the *Erie Railroad* case, in which the U.S. Supreme Court decided that there is no national law on these matters. The federal trial court hearing such a case should apply the same rules as would a state trial court in the state where the federal court is located. If a state court would use its own state's rules, so should a federal court. If a state court would use the law of another state, so should a federal court hearing one of these "diversity of citizenship" cases.

■ Choice of Law in State Courts

State courts generally have the power to hear civil cases based on national law, as well as those based on state law. If a national statute is involved in the case, the state court hearing it would use that statute, as interpreted by the federal courts. A final interpretation of such a statute by the U.S. Supreme Court would be binding on all state courts. In the same way, U.S. Supreme Court interpretations of the U.S. Constitution and of treaties would also be binding on state courts.

Multistate transactions can raise some very difficult choice-of-law questions. For example, suppose that Company A and Company Z enter into a contract. Company A is incorporated in Delaware, but has its home office in New York. Company Z is incorporated in Texas and also has its home office there. The contract is negotiated by representatives of the two companies in Chicago, Illinois. The contract requires Company A to deliver a shipment of goods to one of Company Z's plants in California. If a dispute which results in a lawsuit arises between them, which state's law should be used?

Over the years, courts have developed some general principles to solve these problems. Questions about the validity of a contract are usually decided according to the law of the place where the contract was made. Questions about whether a contract was properly performed are usually decided according to the law of the place of performance. Questions about whether proper corporate procedures were followed (and most other internal corporate matters) are usually decided according to the law of the state of incorporation. Historically, lawsuits for personal injury were governed by the law of the place where the alleged wrong occurred. While some states may still follow this rule, at least for some injury cases, many states now use a "grouping-of-contacts" approach for personal injury cases. Under this newer approach, a court will try to decide which state has the strongest interest in the outcome of the case, based on the residence of the parties, the location of the alleged wrong, and other factors. The law of that state will then be used to determine whether the defendant is liable for the alleged wrong.

International transactions can add a whole new level of complications. Many of the same general principles noted above are also used in international disputes. In addition, treaties have been negotiated between some nations on these issues. If there is a treaty in force between the governments of the parties to the dispute, the treaty rules would normally be used to decide which nation's law applied. The treaty might also provide for the application of some international rule, such as the U.N. Convention on Contracts for International Sale of Goods (CISG). Treaties may or may not permit the parties to a contract to select the body of law they wish to have applied to any disputes.

F EDERAL COURT SYSTEM

As now structured, the federal court system consists of the Supreme Court, the courts of appeal, the district courts, and several specialized courts.

■ U.S. District Courts

The district court is the trial court in the federal court system. Crimes against national law are tried here. Civil cases which involve claims under the U.S. Constitution or national statutes or regulations may be brought here. Civil cases where the parties are from different states can be tried here if at least $50,000 is at issue. (The required amount has been raised twice since the *Erie* case was decided.) Generally, any case falling in one of the constitutional categories listed earlier in this chapter can be tried in the district court.

The U.S. District Court is the main trial court in the federal system.

Each state has at least one U.S. district court located there. Large states have two or more; Texas and California have four each. (See Figure 4–3.) There may be more than one U.S. district court judge in a district. Districts with large populations, and therefore large case loads, may have eight or ten judges. Assigned to each U.S. district court is a U.S. attorney, to prosecute any criminal cases and to represent the national government in any other matters arising in the district. Each district also has a U.S. marshal to serve court papers and to carry out other court orders. Assistant attorneys, deputy marshals, and clerical staff are hired as needed.

U.S. MAGISTRATE

Attached to each district court is a U.S. Magistrate, functioning as a kind of subsidiary court. The magistrate can hold preliminary hearings on criminal charges, set the amount of bail for the accused, and handle other similar functions for the court.

U.S. BANKRUPTCY COURT

Article I of the Constitution gives Congress the power to establish uniform laws on bankruptcy. (The substantive law of bankruptcy will be covered in Chapter 12.) When Congress passed a new bankruptcy statute in 1978, it included a section which established bankruptcy courts. A bankruptcy court is attached to each district court, and is given authority to hear all bankruptcy cases arising within that district. The Supreme Court held in 1982 that certain parts of the 1978 statute were unconstitutional. The problem was that these new judges were given jurisdiction over some cases arising under Article III, but did not enjoy the constitutional protections of Article III judges. The bankruptcy judges had only fourteen-year terms of office, rather than appointment for life ("on good behavior"). This conflict was removed by the Federal Courts Improvement Act of 1984, so the bankruptcy courts are now functioning again. Appeals from a bankruptcy court's decision go first to its district court, and then to the court of appeals for that circuit. Ultimately, these decisions, too, are subject to review by the Supreme Court.

■ U.S. Courts of Appeals

The intermediate appellate courts in the federal system are the courts of appeals. The country is divided geographically into eleven "circuits" that each contain three or more states. (See Figure 4–3.) There is one court of appeals for each of these circuits. There is also a twelfth separate Court of Appeals for the District of Columbia, since it is the location of the main offices for most U.S. administrative agencies, such as the National Labor Relations Board and the Federal Communications Commission. In addition to these twelve circuit courts, a new Court of Appeals for the Federal Circuit was created in 1982 to hear appeals from the specialized federal courts and the Patent Office.

The U.S. Courts of Appeals hear appeals from the District Courts and from administrative agencies.

Appeals from the U.S. District Courts and administrative agencies are heard by panels of three judges. There may be a dozen or more appeals-court judges in a given circuit, depending on the number of appeals being filed there. The party losing on appeal to a three-judge panel can request a hearing before all the appeals judges in the circuit. Such a rehearing is called a **hearing *en banc***.

No trials are held in the Courts of Appeals, and no witnesses appear before them. The U.S. Courts of Appeals have no power to review state court decisions. Appeals are based on the record from the federal trial court or the administrative agency. Each party is permitted to file a brief—its written arguments for or against the trial court's decision. Usually, there is also an opportunity for a short oral argument before the three-judge panel.

■ U.S. Supreme Court

The Constitution does give the Supreme Court the power to act as trial court in cases in which a state is a party and in those involving foreign diplomatic personnel. The Supreme Court usually declines to act in these cases, however, since they can also be heard by a district court. Congress, by statute, specifies what kinds of cases can be reviewed by the Supreme Court.

For most cases, Supreme Court review is discretionary. The party asking for review files a **petition for certiorari** with the Court, setting forth its reasons for requesting review. If at least four of the nine justices think that the case is important enough, the petition is granted. Each party then files a brief and is usually given time for oral

The Supreme Court hears cases after granting a petition for certiorari.

FIGURE 4-3 *United States Courts of Appeal and United States District Courts*

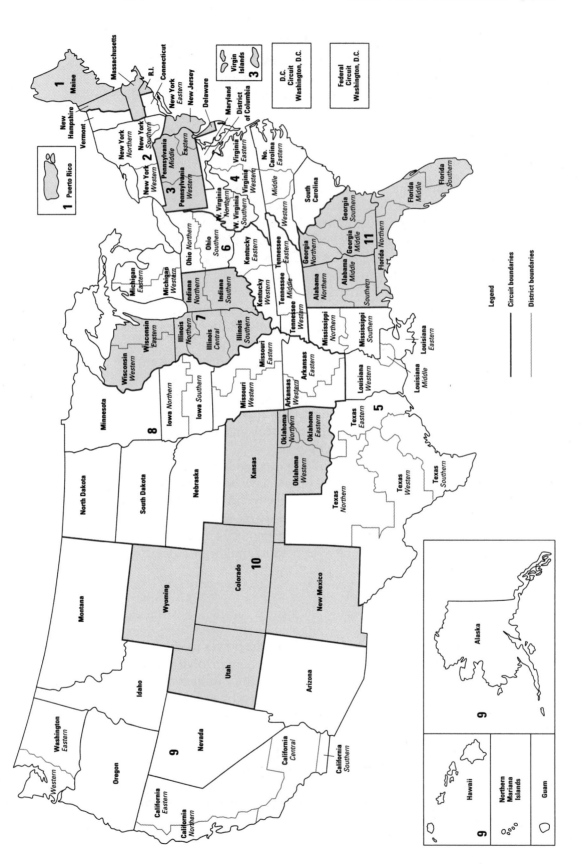

argument. Several thousand petitions are filed each year; the Court agrees to hear a few hundred cases.

The Supreme Court reviews decisions by Courts of Appeals and final decisions from the state courts which involve issues of national law. In a few exceptional cases, there may be a direct appeal from a U.S. District Court.

■ U.S. Specialty Courts

Congress has established a number of specialized courts to decide cases arising out of the various activities of the national government. The Court of Military Appeals reviews court-martial convictions of members of the armed services. The Tax Court handles tax disputes between the Internal Revenue Service and taxpayers. The Claims Court hears certain kinds of claims against the national government and its agents. The Court of International Trade adjudicates tariff and similar trade disputes. As noted above, the Court of Appeals for the Federal Circuit was set up to hear appeals from the Claims Court and the Court of International Trade, as well as patent and trademark cases. The basic justification for creating these specialized courts is to provide judges who have some expertise on these very technical topics. Figure 4–4 diagrams the overall federal court system.

Several federal specialty courts have been established to hear special categories of cases.

■ Selection of Federal Judges

As noted in Chapter 2, federal judges are appointed by the president, with the advice and consent of the Senate. In practice, the senior senator of the president's political party needs to approve any appointments of U.S. District judges from that senator's state. If there is no senator of the president's party in a particular state, the president has the greater discretion, but must still have the nominee approved by the entire Senate. For appointments to the U.S. Court of Appeals, the senators of the president's party from the states in the particular circuit will usually confer. It is customary for the appeals judges to represent all of the states in the circuit, but there may be more judges from a large state than from a small one. This practice of clearing judicial nominees with a state's senators is called **senatorial courtesy.**

Nominees for the U.S. Supreme Court are handled quite differently. There is no senatorial courtesy for these appointments. The Senate as a whole debates the nominee's qualifications. If the president's party has a majority in the Senate, the nominee will usually be confirmed. If not, there may be a bruising partisan battle, as happened recently when President Reagan nominated Circuit Judge Robert Bork for a vacancy on the Supreme Court. Bork's nomination was defeated.

Judges of the specialized federal courts are also nominated by the president and confirmed by the Senate. They do not have life terms, however, but rather are appointed for a number of years.

FIGURE 4–4
This diagram shows the overall structure of the federal court system, including specialty courts.

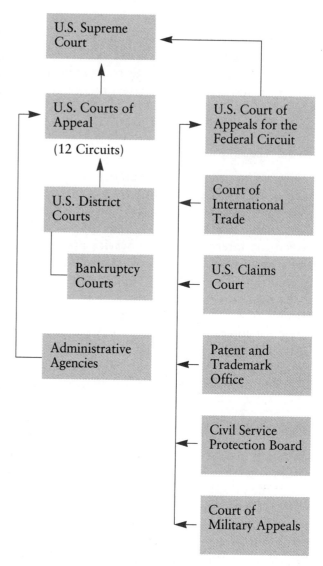

S TATE COURT SYSTEMS

States differ greatly in area, population, history, and customs. As a result, their court structures also vary considerably. So do their civil procedure rules. What follows is a general outline, rather than the structure of a particular state.

State Limited Trial Courts

Many states have special trial courts to hear minor disputes.

Most of the larger states and many smaller ones have special trial courts to hear minor cases. Parking violations, traffic offenses, and other minor criminal cases are heard in these courts. Defendants accused of major crimes may be brought before these judges for an initial hearing and the setting of bail, but serious criminal cases must be heard in the "regular" trial courts. For civil cases, there is usually a maximum dollar amount on the claims that can be heard—$10,000, for example. These courts usually cannot issue injunctions. Juries are usually used, but they may be only six-person, rather than twelve-person, juries.

Small claims divisions may be part of these limited trial courts, or they may be organized separately. If they are separate, the judge may or may not be a lawyer. Historically, minor traffic cases and small civil cases were heard by **justices of the peace**, who were usually not lawyers. Many states have now abolished the "J.P." courts and provided small claims courts staffed by legally trained judges.

Many states also have separate courts for cases involving wills and decedents' estates, divorces, and similar family and juvenile matters. A few states are now creating courts to handle only business cases.

■ State General Trial Courts

All states have a trial court with the general power to hear civil and criminal cases. If there is a separate limited trial court, the general trial court hears felony criminal cases and civil cases involving larger sums of money and requests for injunctive and other special relief. Juries are used here, at least for most cases. There will probably be twelve jurors, although some states may use smaller juries here, too. In some states, these general trial courts also hear appeals from some of the limited courts in their districts. Figure 4–5 shows the major categories of state civil cases filed in 1990.

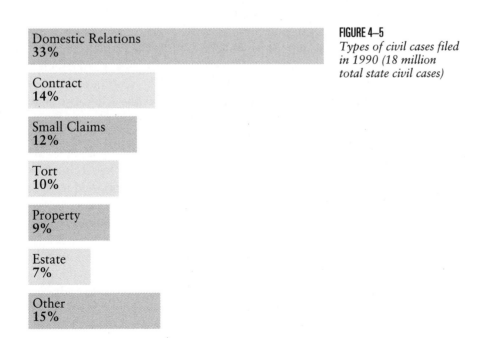

Domestic Relations
33%

Contract
14%

Small Claims
12%

Tort
10%

Property
9%

Estate
7%

Other
15%

FIGURE 4–5
Types of civil cases filed in 1990 (18 million total state civil cases)

State Intermediate Appellate Courts

In some of the smaller states, there may be no intermediate appellate court. Appeals go directly from the trial court to the state supreme court. Most of the larger states do have intermediate appellate courts. Their functions are similar to those of the U.S Courts of Appeals.

State Supreme Courts

Each state has a supreme court, although the title varies from state to state. Its rulings are the final word on points of state law, unless and until a new state statute is passed or the state constitution is amended. Where points of national law are involved, the decision of a state supreme court may be reviewed by the U.S. Supreme Court, as indicated earlier. Many state supreme courts exercise general supervision of the state's court system. Some also supervise the state bar association (the lawyers' organization).

State supreme courts usually hear appeals as one body, with all judges participating, rather than sitting in three-judge panels as the intermediate appellate courts do. Typically, there are seven or nine judges on a state supreme court, but the number may be higher or lower.

Selection of State Judges

Some states follow the pattern used for federal judges—appointment by the executive, followed by Senate confirmation. In most states, the governor can at least appoint when a vacancy occurs.

Most state judges are selected through some form of election.

Most states use some form of election, but there are wide variations. In some states, judicial candidates are identified by political party. In others, judges are nominated by the political parties, but appear on a separate "non-partisan" judicial ballot. The newest method, combining features of the appointive system and the non-partisan election, originated in Missouri and has been widely recommended by groups favoring reform of judicial selection. Under the **Missouri Plan,** the governor appoints each judge by selecting one name from a list of three presented by a non-partisan board of nomination. At the next election, the new judge's name is placed on the ballot, and the voters are simply asked to vote *Yes* or *No* on whether the judge will be retained for a full term. If the vote is *Yes*, the judge is elected for the specified term of office, usually six or eight years. If the vote is *No*, the process begins again. Under this system, judicial candidates do not run against each other, but are judged on their qualifications and their records.

Procedures for removal of incompetent judges also differ widely. Some states have provisions for holding recall elections, in which the voters make the decision. In some states, judges may be removed by the state legislature's passing a concurrent resolution. Such a resolution usually requires at least a two-thirds majority in each house. The third procedure for removal is impeachment, following the national model. The state House of Representatives votes to impeach Judge X, who would then be "tried" by the state Senate. At the national level, a two-thirds vote of the U.S. Senate is required to remove a judge or other official. This two-thirds requirement may or may not be used in the states. (At the national level, there have been only a dozen or so such removals of U.S. officials in our entire 200-year history.)

C IVIL PROCEDURE

Here again, there are many specific differences, both from state to state, and between the state courts and the federal courts. Since their adoption in 1938, however, the Federal Rules of Civil Procedure (FRCP) have had a strong influence on state civil procedure. Many states now follow the FRCP on most procedural points. The procedural differences which remain would be a major factor in a lawyer's decision to file suit in one court as opposed to another, where a choice was possible. Figure 4–6 presents a general outline of the major steps involved in a civil case.

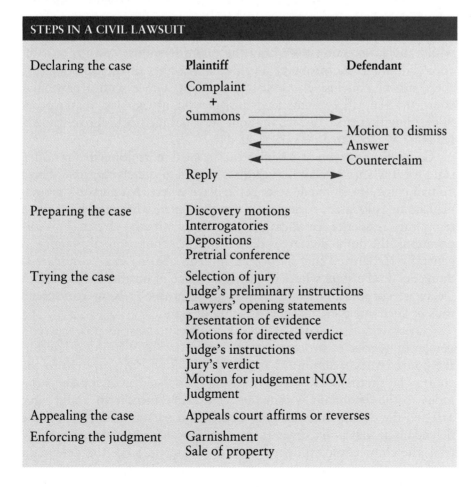

FIGURE 4–6
This table presents a general outline of the steps in a civil case.

STEPS IN A CIVIL LAWSUIT		
Declaring the case	**Plaintiff**	**Defendant**
	Complaint + Summons ⟶	
	⟵	Motion to dismiss
	⟵	Answer
	⟵	Counterclaim
	Reply ⟶	
Preparing the case	Discovery motions	
	Interrogatories	
	Depositions	
	Pretrial conference	
Trying the case	Selection of jury	
	Judge's preliminary instructions	
	Lawyers' opening statements	
	Presentation of evidence	
	Motions for directed verdict	
	Judge's instructions	
	Jury's verdict	
	Motion for judgement N.O.V.	
	Judgment	
Appealing the case	Appeals court affirms or reverses	
Enforcing the judgment	Garnishment	
	Sale of property	

■ Deciding Where to Sue

The plaintiff's lawyer's first job is to decide where to file the lawsuit. There may be alternatives. In a multi-state transaction, two or more states may be possible places for a trial. If the parties are from different states and at least $50,000 is at issue in the dispute, the U.S. District Courts can be used. Even within a single state, there may be several appropriate locations (**venues**) for a trial.

To secure a valid judgment, the plaintiff must select a court which has **jurisdiction** (power) to hear this kind of case and which has jurisdiction over the parties to the lawsuit. The first type of judicial power is called **subject-matter jurisdiction**; the second is called **personal jurisdiction**.

For state court systems, subject-matter jurisdiction is simple enough. The plaintiff's lawyer has to read the state constitution and statutes to find out which courts can hear which kinds of cases. In order to use the U.S. District Courts, the plaintiff must have a claim based on national law, or must show "diversity of citizenship"—parties from different states, and $50,000 at issue.

To render a valid judgment, a court must have jurisdiction over the litigants and over the subject matter of the case.

Personal jurisdiction is much more complicated. Usually, to render a binding judgment, a court must have jurisdiction over *both* parties, not just the plaintiff. (Divorce cases are a notable exception; a court with valid jurisdiction over only the plaintiff spouse can grant a divorce, although the property and parental rights of the other spouse could not be conclusively decided.) By filing a case with a particular court, the plaintiff consents to its jurisdiction, at least for the purposes of deciding that case. But what about personal jurisdiction over the defendant? Where can a person be sued?

Generally, a person or business can be sued in its **domicile**, or home, state for any sort of claim, regardless of where the claim arose. For a human being, the domicile state is the place where that person's permanent home is located. A person is not domiciled where there is only a temporary residence for vacation, school, or military service. For corporations, the domicile state is the state of incorporation, although it is generally recognized that a corporation can also have a "commercial domicile" in the state where its principal place of business is located. A Delaware corporation which had its home offices in New York could thus be sued in either state for any kind of claim.

Our system also recognizes that a court can assert its power over a person by **service of process** within that state. Plaintiff files a lawsuit; the court issues a **summons** to the defendant to appear before the court. The sheriff then "serves the court process" by giving the summons to the defendant within the state. Since the sheriff could have arrested the defendant, the court clearly had personal power over the defendant at that point. Even if the defendant left the state prior to the trial, the court could still enter a valid judgment, since the defendant had been subjected to its authority. This principle was reaffirmed by the U.S. Supreme Court in 1990, in *Burnham* v. *Superior Court* (495 U.S. 604).

Of course, a defendant can be sued anywhere that person consents to be sued. Such consent may be given expressly, as part of a contract. Out-of-state businesses are usually required to give such consent as part of registering to do local business in a state. Consent may also be implied from a person's conducting certain activities within a state, such as operating a motor vehicle.

What about the person who comes into a state, commits a wrong, and then flees the state before a summons can be served? To deal with the problems caused by these out-of-state, non-resident defendants, states have passed **"long-arm"** statutes. These statutes provide for a limited personal jurisdiction over persons who have had certain **minimum contacts** with persons or things within the state. Lawsuit jurisdiction is limited to claims which arise out of the relationship established within the state. A person who makes a contract in the state can be sued in the state for claims arising out of that contract. A person who commits a tort (civil injury) in the state can be sued in the state for that wrong. A person who owns real estate (or tangible personal property, in some states) can be sued for claims relating to the property. A person who insures a risk which was located in the state when the insurance policy became effective can be sued in the state for those insurance claims. A director or officer can be sued in the state of incorporation for claims relating to performance as director or officer. These statutes do not require the consent of the defendant or personal service of process on the defendant within the state. The defendant will be notified by registered mail if there is an address available; otherwise, notification may be by advertisement in a local paper. If a state court has such limited personal jurisdiction over nonresidents, so does a U.S. District Court in that state when it is hearing diversity of citizenship cases.

Long-arm statutes permit lawsuits against out-of-state, non-resident defendants who have established minimum contacts in the state hearing the case.

All state court processes must provide the "due process of law" required by the Fourteenth Amendment to the Constitution. The U.S. Supreme Court thus has the final word on what sort of activity within a state is a sufficient minimum contact to provide the basis for a lawsuit. As usually stated, the test is whether the state's procedure complies with "traditional notions of fair play and substantial justice." Based on what was done in the state where the lawsuit has been filed, could the out-of-state defendant reasonably have anticipated being haled into court there? In one very important decision in 1980, the Supreme Court said that the presence of a product in a state, in and of itself, was not a sufficient basis for suing the out-of-state seller there. (The product had been bought from a retail seller in another state and then taken into the "lawsuit" state by the buyer.) In a subsequent case, the Court split 4 to 4, with one justice not participating, on whether a manufacturer who puts products into the "stream of commerce," knowing that they will be widely distributed, can be sued in any location where the product causes injury. State courts also disagree on this "stream of commerce" theory, as seen in the *Wiles* case.

WILES V. MORITA IRON WORKS LTD.

530 N.E.2d 1382 (Ill. 1988)

Facts: Astro Packaging Co. bought four machines from Morita Iron Works, a Japanese manufacturer. The machines were delivered to Astro in Japan and became its property there. Two of the machines were then shipped to Astro's plant in New Jersey, and two were sent to Astro's Illinois plant, where Floyd Wiles worked. Floyd was injured while he was using one of the machines. Floyd sued Morita in Illinois, claiming that his injuries were caused by defects in the machine. Morita had no offices, facilities, or personnel in Illinois. There was no evidence that Morita knew that its machines would be sent to Illinois. The trial court dismissed the case for lack of jurisdiction, but the appeals court reversed, holding that there was jurisdiction over Morita.

Issue: Is the presence of defendant's product in the state a sufficient connection to provide the basis for a lawsuit there?

Decision: No, it is not a sufficient connection. Case dismissed.

Rule: The defendant must "purposefully avail itself" of the privilege of doing business in the state in order to be suable there.

Discussion: *By Justice* CLARK:

"[W]e believe that even under the broader version of the stream of commerce theory there were no minimum contacts between defendant Morita and the State of Illinois. Under the facts presented in the instant case, an exertion of personal jurisdiction over this defendant by the Illinois courts would...be inconsistent with due process. Under either interpretation of the stream of commerce theory, it is clear that purposeful availment of the forum's market requires, at a *minimum*, that the alien defendant is '*aware* that the final product is marketed in the forum State.' The record in this case is totally devoid of any evidence that the defendant was aware either during contract negotiations or at the time of delivery of the products to Astro in Japan that Astro intended to transport two of the air cell formers to Illinois, or that Astro even had a plant in Illinois. Without any evidence of such knowledge on the part of the defendant, on this basis alone we would have to conclude, under either theory that [Morita] made no effort, directly or indirectly, to serve the market for its product in Illinois and that the air cell formers were, therefore, brought into Illinois solely by the unilateral act of Astro. 'The unilateral activity of those who claim some relationship with a nonresident defendant cannot satisfy the requirement of contact with the forum State.' The fact that the defendant now knows the machines were sent to Illinois, as revealed in the defendant's affidavit, is of no consequence in the determination of whether this defendant has purposefully availed itself of the privilege of conducting activities within Illinois."

Ethical Dimension

Is it ethical for a business to structure its distribution system to avoid lawsuits in other countries?

Jurisdiction refers to the power of a court to decide the case. The term *venue* refers to the proper location within a state for the trial. Usually, the place where the wrong occurred, or where the defendant was located (if a resident of the state), would be the appropriate place for the trial. If a fair trial cannot be had there, venue can be changed to a different location within the state.

■ Declaring the Case

Once a decision has been made as to where to file the lawsuit, plaintiff's attorney prepares a **complaint** and files it with the court. The complaint states plaintiff's version of the facts (what allegedly happened) and the legal basis for recovery from the defendant (why the defendant is liable). The court then issues a summons, ordering the defendant to appear before the court if the defendant wishes to contest the charges. The summons and a copy of the complaint are given to the defendant, served either in person or by registered mail. There is a specified time period within which the defendant must respond to the charges.

Plaintiff begins the case by filing a complaint.

The defendant may respond in various ways. It may ask the court to dismiss the complaint—for lack of jurisdiction, or other reasons. For most claims, for example, there is a limited time period after the occurrence in which a lawsuit must be filed. If this **statute of limitations** period has elapsed, the defendant can generally have the lawsuit dismissed. The defendant may also try to show, by **affidavits** (sworn statements) and other documents (checks and receipts, for instance) that there is really no factual dispute at all. If that is the case and the

Defendant may respond to the complaint in various ways.

facts are clearly in the defendant's favor, the defendant is entitled to a **summary judgment** (judgment in the defendant's favor, without a trial). For example, if the defendant can prove to the court with a canceled check that the alleged debt has in fact been paid, there is no need for a trial, and the case should be decided in favor of the defendant automatically. If the defendant does not get a favorable ruling on these preliminary motions, it can file an **answer**, which denies the truth of some or all of the claims stated in the complaint. The defendant can also file a **counterclaim**, which is its own case seeking recovery from the plaintiff. (The defendant in effect says: "Not only do I not owe you; you owe me.") Counterclaims are quite common in contract cases and auto accident cases. Each party claims the other was the wrongdoer.

The plaintiff is then given a chance to file a **reply**, which responds to any new issues raised by the defendant in the answer or counterclaim. Modern civil procedure stops at this point, except for a limited time period within which the parties are permitted to amend the pleadings already filed. Some states permit additional pleadings. Usually, a party wishing a jury trial must request one in writing sometime during the pleading stage.

■ Preparing the Case

Both parties are given the chance to discover evidence prior to trial.

During the period between the filing of the pleadings and the trial of the case (which could be as long as several years), the trial court and the parties will be preparing the case for trial. **Depositions** (statements) will be taken from witnesses under oath. Each party can force the other to answer **interrogatories** (lists of specific questions). Each party can file discovery motions, asking the court to order the other party to produce documents, business records, physical evidence, or names. Under the FRCP, and in most states, the basic idea is that all relevant evidence should be made available to both sides prior to trial. That way, many cases may be settled, saving everyone's time and money. If the case does have to go to trial, there will be no unfair surprises by either side.

The FRCP and most state procedures also provide for a **pre-trial conference**. The trial judge meets with both parties and their lawyers and makes a last effort to settle the case. If no settlement can be agreed on, at least some of the facts may be agreed on by the parties, so some time can be saved. The judge will also try to make sure that all evidence has been made available, and that both parties are ready to go to trial.

■ Trying the Case

Jurors are selected to determine the facts of the case.

If the case does go to trial, the first job is selecting a jury if one has been requested. Depending on the state, jury lists may be prepared from voter registrations, motor vehicle driver licenses, and/or telephone listings. The court clerk then selects names at random, and the court notifies those persons that they must appear for jury duty. Names are then drawn from this group for each case. Prospective jurors may be asked to fill out a brief personal background statement. Using the personal statement and other information, the lawyers are usually permitted to ask the jurors questions about their qualifications. Depending on the state, the lawyers may ask the questions directly, or may be required to submit the questions to the trial judge. This process of questioning the prospective jurors is called **voir dire**. Either party may ask the court to remove any juror **for cause**—prior knowledge about the case, prior relationship with one of the parties or lawyers, and the like. Each party is also given a limited number of **peremptory challenges** (no specific reason for dismissing the juror has to be stated). A lawyer might not be able to show actual bias or prejudice in a prospective juror, but might still feel that the person would not view the client's case favorably. In that situation, the lawyer might use a peremptory challenge.

The lawyers are usually permitted to make brief opening statements to the jury as to the nature of the case and the evidence. The plaintiff's case is presented first—witnesses, documents, and physical evidence. There are detailed and complicated rules about what kinds of evidence can be admitted. If one party objects to the introduction of a piece of physical evidence, or to a question or witness, the trial judge will have to make a ruling on whether the particular evidence is admissible. The plaintiff's witnesses can be cross-examined by the defendant's attorney. The defendant then presents its case. The plaintiff's lawyer can cross-examine the defendant's witnesses. Each side is permitted to make closing arguments to the jury. The trial judge then instructs the jury as to what the law is and what their options are. In some states, the trial judge is also allowed to comment on the evidence presented.

Either party may move for a **directed verdict**. This motion asks the trial judge to instruct the jury to bring in a verdict for one side or the other, since there is really no dispute on the facts as presented. If the plaintiff has failed to present evidence to support the claims, the defendant should receive a directed verdict. Likewise, if the plaintiff has introduced evidence to support the claim, and the defendant has not contradicted any of it, the plaintiff should get a directed verdict.

If the trial judge does not grant either side's motion, the jury then goes to a private room to discuss the case and to make its decision, or **verdict**. On most points, the plaintiff bears the **burden of proof**, that is, it must convince the jury that its side of the case is at least slightly more persuasive than the defendant's version of what happened. This standard of proof is usually described as a "preponderance of the evidence." (In contrast, the standard of proof in a criminal case is "beyond a reasonable doubt.") If dollar damages are claimed, the jury will also determine the amount.

The trial judge has a limited power to overrule a jury verdict which is contrary to the evidence presented.

In most cases, the trial judge enters the court's **judgment** on the basis of the jury's verdict. If one of the lawyers feels that the jury has reached a result that is contrary to the evidence, a motion for judgment notwithstanding the verdict (**judgment N.O.V.**) can be filed with the trial judge. This motion asks the trial judge to enter a judgment for one side despite the jury's verdict for the other side. It should be granted only where there is no possible factual basis for the verdict. If the jury has come in with a clearly incorrect dollar amount, a motion for **additur** (more damages) or for **remittitur** (lower damages) can be filed with the court. The *Moran* case illustrates the judgment N.O.V., and its limitations.

JUSTICE·UNDE

MORAN V. FABERGÉ, INC.

332 A.2d 11 (Md. 1975)

Facts: Randy Williams, age fifteen, was staying with Mr. and Mrs. Grigsby. She invited Nancy Moran (age seventeen) and several other friends over to the house. The group at first gathered in the family room area of the basement, but then everyone left except Randy and Nancy. There was a Christmas-tree-shaped candle on the shelf behind the couch. After deciding that the candle was not scented, Randy said, "Well, let's make it scented." With that, she grabbed a drip bottle of Fabergé Tigress cologne which Mrs. Grigsby had put in the basement as an air freshener and began to pour the perfume onto the lighted candle. A burst of flame badly burned Nancy. She sued Fabergé, for failing to include a warning on the perfume label. The jury found for her, but the trial judge granted Fabergé's motion for a judgment N.O.V. Nancy Moran appealed from the trial judge's ruling.

Issue: Was the judgment N.O.V. proper in this case?

Decision: No, it was not. The jury verdict for Nancy will be reinstated.

Rule: A judgment N.O.V. is proper only if there is no evidence in the trial record to sustain the jury's verdict.

Discussion: *By Judge* DIGGES:

"It is our opinion then, that the totality of the evidence presented in this case, viewed most favorably toward [Nancy Moran], was legally sufficient to enable the jury to find that Fabergé's failure to place a warning on its Tigress cologne 'drip bottle' constituted actionable negligence. We say this because there was evidence presented at trial which, if accepted as true, tends to show that Fabergé's Tigress cologne possessed a latent danger of flammability; that Fabergé, through its officials, knew or should have known of this danger; that it is normal to find in the home environment both flame and cologne; that it was reasonably foreseeable to Fabergé that the flame and the cologne may well come in contact, one with the other, so as to cause an explosion which injures a person who happens to be standing nearby—Nancy; and that a reasonably prudent manufacturer, knowing of its product's characteristics and propensities, should have warned consumers of this latent flammability danger."

Ethical Dimension

Should a manufacturer be held liable for failing to warn users of obvious dangers? Should a manufacturer be held liable for failing to warn of possible dangers from unintended uses?

■ Appealing the Case

In general, appeals are based on alleged errors of law committed by the trial court judge. (The scope of review for an equity case may be somewhat broader, depending on the state.) The appeals court is not reviewing the jury's verdict on the evidence, but rather the various rulings made by the trial court judge during the course of the trial. Should a particular witness have been permitted to answer a certain question or to testify at all? Should a motion to dismiss the case have been granted? Should a jury have been used—or a particular juror seated on the panel? And so on.

Appeals courts generally only review the questions of law decided by the trial judge.

The appeals court generally has three options. It can affirm the trial court judgment, if it feels no material error has been shown. (A material error would be one that had, or might have had, a significant impact on the outcome of the case.) If it does find a material error, it can enter its own judgment for the other party. (Minor technical errors would normally not be a basis for reversal.) Or, as frequently happens, the appeals court does find a material error, but thinks that further proceedings are necessary at the trial level. In this last situation, the appeals court will remand (send back) the case to the trial court—with instructions to correct the error.

■ Enforcing the Judgment

Once there is a final judgment in the case, it must be enforced. If money is to be paid, wages and bank accounts can be **garnisheed**; that is, a third party who owes money to the judgment debtor can be ordered to pay it to the court to satisfy the unpaid judgment. The judgment debtor's property can be seized under court order and sold to pay the judgment. If the court has ordered someone to do something, there may not be compliance with the order. When that happens, contempt of court proceedings may be commenced. The party against whom the order is directed may be fined or jailed until there is compliance.

Valid judgments from one state must be enforced in all other states.

As noted in Chapter 3, court judgments are entitled to full faith and credit in all other states—if, and only if, they are based on valid jurisdiction. If there is no jurisdiction, other states are not constitutionally required to enforce the judgment. (Even though not required to do so, other states might recognize the first state's judgment anyway.) The *Keck* case illustrates this point, as well as the definition of *domicile* and the special jurisdictional rule for divorce cases. (To grant a valid divorce, the court only has to have valid jurisdiction over the plaintiff spouse. In contrast, in most cases, jurisdiction over both parties is required for a valid judgment.)

KECK V. KECK

309 N.E.2d 217 (Ill. 1974)

Facts: James Keck was married to Dolores Keck. They resided in Illinois. James decided he wanted a divorce, and filed a petition in Chicago. Dolores did not want a divorce—for religious reasons. She asked the court to order separate maintenance, so that James would be required to support her, even though they would be living apart. At that point, James went to Nevada, stayed there for six weeks, and got a Nevada divorce. He then came back to Chicago and asked that the Illinois courts recognize his Nevada decree of divorce. The trial court said the Nevada decree was invalid, but the appeals court said it must be given full faith and credit. Dolores appealed to the state supreme court.

Issue: Is the Nevada divorce decree entitled to full faith and credit?

Decision: No, it is not. Dolores is still married to James (in Illinois).

Rule: To be valid, a divorce decree must be based on domicile of the plaintiff spouse. Domicile is more than physical presence; it is a matter of intent.

Discussion: *By Justice DAVIS:*

"[T]he evidence presented...overcame the presumption of such domicile created by the introduction into evidence of the

Nevada divorce decree. It is well established that the question of domicile is largely one of intention and that to establish a new domicile a person must physically go to a new home and live there with the intention of making it his permanent home.... Here plaintiff lived in Nevada only two months, he returned immediately upon obtaining his decree, he retained his apartment in Chicago and returned there, he retained his job in Chicago and returned to it, he retained his Chicago bank accounts and his Illinois driver's license. Within one or two days after arriving in Nevada, he contacted a lawyer about getting a divorce. The evidence presented to the trial court clearly supports the conclusion that the plaintiff went to Nevada for the purpose of obtaining a divorce and with the intent of returning to Illinois. The plaintiff did not establish a *bona fide* domicile in Nevada, and the trial court was warranted in concluding that the Nevada decree was invalid and in denying it full faith and credit."

Ethical Dimension

Is it proper for a state court to grant a divorce if only one spouse requests it?

■ Enforcing International Judgments

For judgments from other nations, there is no "full faith and credit" requirement. International judgments are recognized on the basis of reciprocity: "You recognize mine and I'll recognize yours." While most foreign judgments are probably enforced on this basis, there could be sharp cultural differences from country to country which would prevent enforcement of specific types of judgments.

A LTERNATE DISPUTE RESOLUTION

Only those agencies vested with the power of government can force persons to participate in their decision-making processes. The "alternatives" discussed below are all voluntary; the parties must agree to participate. Some states now do require a pre-trial review of some types of cases—medical malpractice, for example—to deter frivolous cases. A plaintiff who files a lawsuit to harass the defendant (a competing business, for example) will probably not voluntarily agree to any form of alternate dispute resolution. For the harasser, the disadvantages listed below are the very things which make filing a lawsuit such an effective weapon.

■ Disadvantages to Litigation

The litigation process has several distinct disadvantages for business persons. First, a lawsuit will normally involve a delay of many months, perhaps even several years, before it is finally brought to trial and decided. Appeals can take additional years. Meanwhile, the relationship between the two parties to the dispute is that of adversaries. It is difficult, if not impossible, to have a continuing business relationship while fighting each other in court.

Second, a lawsuit is public. Records of transactions, names of suppliers and customers, business plans—everything—is now out in the open, fair game for the curious, the press, and the competition. Courts do have some discretion on closing files and court proceedings, but are usually reluctant to do so. The chances are that the trial will produce unwanted publicity, at least, and disclosure of key business secrets, at worst.

Third, with the use of a jury, there is an added element of uncertainty in the decision process, which is already uncertain enough. Probably, the jurors will not be familiar with the nature of the business transactions involved in the dispute. They may take a totally unexpected view of the evidence presented, despite the arguments of the lawyers and the instructions of the judge. This extra uncertainty makes it even more difficult to predict the outcome of the case.

Finally, there is the tremendous expense involved. Tens of thousands, hundreds of thousands, or even millions of dollars can be used in preparing and presenting a complex case. In addition to the actual costs of lawyers, witnesses, documents, and the like, management's time is being used to prepare the case, not to produce the business's normal line of goods and services. The litigation process is usually dysfunctional to ongoing business operations.

For all these reasons, business people have developed alternate methods of settling their disputes. Some have been in use for years; others are newer devices.

■ Mediation

One of the earliest non-court devices for dispute resolution is to employ a trusted third party to help the parties reach a settlement themselves. This third person is not actually given power to decide the dispute, but only to suggest possible compromises and alternatives. A mediator often helps the parties to get past personalities, and to focus on what is really at issue between them. In many cases, if the parties can be persuaded to look at their dispute rationally, they can arrive at a compromise solution. The use of some form of mediation is especially favored in other cultures, particularly Oriental ones.

■ Arbitration

Another traditional alternative to the lawsuit is arbitration, in which the parties do agree to let a third party decide their dispute. Many commercial contracts, especially in international trade, include a clause providing for arbitration of any disputes. The parties could also agree to arbitration after the dispute arises, if there is no such provision in their original contract. One person or a panel of three may serve as arbitrator. These persons are usually experienced and familiar with the type of dispute involved. Evidence is presented in private. Procedure is usually much less formal than would be used in court, and there is no jury. The arbitrator's decision is final unless fraud or a clear mistake of law is shown. If necessary, the winning party can go to court to get enforcement of the arbitrator's award.

Arbitration is increasingly being used as an alternate method of settling disputes.

Historically, English and American courts did not favor arbitration agreements. The courts were reluctant to see their own authority limited and jury trials waived. A court might thus refuse to enforce an arbitration agreement or might severely limit its application. Today, little of this judicial hostility remains. Part of the change in attitude has been prompted by statutes, at both the national and state levels. The Federal Arbitration Act, for example, provides that arbitration agreements "shall be valid, irrevocable, and enforceable, save upon such grounds as exist at law or in equity for the revocation of any contract." The following case interprets this act, in the context of a customer/stockbroker arbitration agreement.

SHEARSON/AMERICAN EXPRESS, INC. V. McMAHON

107 S. Ct. 2332 (1987)

Facts: From 1980 to 1982, Eugene and Julia McMahon were customers of Shearson, a brokerage firm registered with the Securities and Exchange Commission. Julia signed two arbitration agreements, which provided for arbitration of any controversy relating to the brokerage accounts which the McMahons had with Shearson. In 1984, the McMahons filed a lawsuit against Shearson and Mary Ann McNulty, their account representative at Shearson. They claimed that Mary Ann had made false statements to them, had not told them material facts, and had engaged in fraudulent trading on their accounts at Shearson. They alleged violations of Section 10(b) of the Securities Exchange Act, the SEC's Rule 10b-5, the Racketeer Influenced and Corrupt Organizations Act, and fraud and breach of fiduciary duty under state law.

Shearson asked the court to enforce the arbitration agreement. The U.S. District Court held that the RICO claim was not arbitrable but that all of the other claims were. The U.S. Court of Appeals said that the securities law claims were not subject to the arbitration agreement either. Shearson asked the U.S. Supreme Court for further review.

Issue: Does the arbitration agreement cover plaintiffs' claims under the national securities acts and under the RICO Act?

Decision: Yes, as to both. Judgment of the Court of Appeals is reversed, and the case is remanded for appropriate orders (to enforce the arbitration agreement).

Rule: Statutory rights, as well as common law rights, are governed by a valid arbitration agreement.

Discussion: *By Justice* O'CONNOR:

"The Arbitration Act...establishes a 'federal policy favoring arbitration,'...requiring that 'we rigorously enforce agreements to arbitrate.'... This duty to enforce arbitration agreements is not diminished when a party bound by an agreement raises a claim founded on statutory rights.... Absent a well-founded claim that an arbitration agreement resulted from the sort of fraud or excessive economic power that 'would provide grounds "for the revocation of any contract",'...the Arbitration Act 'provides no basis for disfavoring agreements to arbitrate statutory claims by skewing the otherwise hospitable inquiry into arbitrability.'...

"To defeat application of the Arbitration Act in this case, therefore, the McMahons must demonstrate that Congress intended to make an exception to the Arbitration Act for claims arising under RICO and the Exchange Act, an intention discernible from the text, history, or purposes of the statute....

"When Congress enacted the Exchange Act in 1934, it did not specifically address the question of the arbitrability of § 10(b) claims. The McMahons contend, however, that congressional intent to require a judicial forum for the resolution of § 10(b) claims can be deduced from § 29(a) of the Exchange Act, ...which declares void '[a]ny condition, stipulation, or provision binding any person to waive compliance with any provision of [the Act].'...

"[W]e reject the McMahons' argument that § 29(a) forbids waiver of § 27 of the Exchange Act.... Section 27 provides in relevant part: 'The district courts of the United States...shall have exclusive jurisdiction of violations of this title or the rules and regulations thereunder, and of all suits in equity and actions at law brought to enforce any liability or duty created by this title or the rules and regulations thereunder.'

"The McMahons contend that an agreement to waive this jurisdictional provision is unenforceable because § 29(a) voids the waiver of 'any provision' of the Exchange Act. The language of § 29(a), however, does not reach so far. What the antiwaiver provision of § 29(a) forbids is enforcement of agreements to waive 'compliance' with the provisions of the statute. But § 27 itself does not impose any duty with which persons trading in securities must 'comply.' By its terms, § 29(a) only prohibits waiver of the substantive obligations imposed by the Exchange Act. Because § 27 does not impose any statutory duties, its waiver does not constitute a waiver of 'compliance with any provision' of the Exchange Act under § 29(a)....

"In the exercise of its regulatory authority, the SEC has specifically approved the arbitration procedures of the New York Stock Exchange, the American Stock Exchange, and the NASD, the organizations mentioned in the arbitration agreement at issue in this case. We conclude that where, as in this case, the prescribed procedures are subject to the Commission's...authority, an arbitration agreement does not effect a waiver of the protections of the Act....

"Unlike the Exchange Act, there is nothing in the text of the RICO statute that even arguably evinces congressional intent to exclude civil RICO claims from the dictates of the Arbitration Act. This silence in the text is matched by silence in the statute's legislative history. The private treble-damages provision...was added to the House version of the bill after the bill had been passed by the Senate, and it received only abbreviated discussion in either House.... There is no hint in these legislative debates that Congress intended for RICO treble-damages claims to be excluded from the ambit of the Arbitration Act....

"In sum, we find no basis for concluding that Congress intended to prevent enforcement of agreements to arbitrate RICO claims. The McMahons may effectively vindicate their RICO claim in an arbitral forum, and therefore there is no inherent conflict between arbitration and the purposes underlying [RICO]. Moreover, nothing in RICO's text or legislative history otherwise demonstrates congressional intent to make an exception to the Arbitration Act for RICO claims. Accordingly, the McMahons, 'having made the bargain to arbitrate,' will be held to their bargain. Their RICO claim is arbitrable under the terms of the Arbitration Act."

Private Judge

The parties may agree to hire a private judge to hear their case.

Speed, secrecy, and expertise can also be achieved by hiring a judge to hear and decide the dispute outside the regular court system. Typically, these persons are retired judges. Again, they can be chosen for their knowledge of commercial law and their reputation for fairness. The normal rules of evidence usually do apply here, but the trial is private. The judge is paid by the parties, who agree to abide by the decision. If they do not, an enforcement order can be obtained from the regular courts, just as is true for an arbitration award.

Mini-Trial

The newest alternative is the mini-trial, which combines some features of mediation and some parts of arbitration. A neutral third party, expert in the field, is chosen by the parties to the dispute. Each side presents the essentials of its case. The presenter for each side has been given authority to settle the dispute after hearing the other side's arguments and evidence. If the parties do not settle at that point, the third party expert gives an opinion as to what the probable court result would be if the case were litigated. The parties may then negotiate further, but there is no guarantee of a decision. The hope is that the responsible manager on each side will be able to come to a settlement after looking at the other side of the case objectively.

Other Contractual Litigation Controls

The parties to a contract may provide that any dispute will be resolved according to the law of a particular state or country.

Rather than provide for some form of ADR, the parties may simply specify in their contract that disputes will be heard by the courts in a particular state or country. This sort of provision is called a **forum-selection clause.** They may also wish to designate the law of a particular state or country as being applicable to the contract. This would be a **choice-of-law clause.** Such provisions are especially useful in international agreements. In many international transactions, the laws of several nations might be involved, as the contract is being negotiated and performed across several national boundaries. Time-consuming and costly litigation could be required just to determine where a case could be brought and what law would apply. The parties can thus save themselves time and money, if a dispute does later arise, by including such "choice" provisions in their contract.

Recognizing these motivations, courts today are generally willing to enforce such contract clauses. The strongest case for validity is a situation where the parties specifically negotiated for the "choice" clause. Even without specific negotiations, however, a court may be willing to enforce a "choice" clause if it is convinced that the choice is fair and reasonable under the circumstances. The next case illustrates that point.

CARNIVAL CRUISE LINES, INC. V. SHUTE

111 S. Ct. 1522 (1991)

Facts: Eulala Shute and her husband bought tickets for a cruise on the Tropicale, a ship operated by Carnival. The Shutes lived in the State of Washington and bought the tickets through a travel agent located there. The travel agent sent their payment to Carnival, at its headquarters in Miami, Florida. Carnival prepared the tickets and sent them back to the Shutes. On the face of each ticket was a statement indicating that it was subject to the conditions on the back. Statements on the back of the ticket said that the customers accepted all printed terms by accepting the ticket and that any disputes "shall be litigated, if at all, in and before a Court located in the State of Florida, USA, to the exclusion of the Courts of any other state or country."

The Shutes boarded the ship in Los Angeles for the cruise to Puerto Vallarta, Mexico. While the ship was in international waters off the Mexican Coast, Eulala was injured when she slipped on a deck mat during a tour of the ship's galley. The Shutes filed a lawsuit in the U.S. District Court in the State of Washington. Carnival asked the court for summary judgment, on the basis of the forum-selection clause on the tickets. It also claimed that it was not subject to personal jurisdiction in the state. The District Court ruled in its favor on the jurisdiction argument. The U.S. Court of Appeals reversed, holding that there was jurisdiction and that the forum-selection clause was not enforceable because it was not freely bargained for. Carnival asked the U.S. Supreme Court for further review.

Issue: Is the forum-selection clause valid, even though it was not specifically negotiated by these parties?

Decision: Yes, it is. Judgment of the Court of Appeals is reversed.

Rule: A reasonable forum-selection clause may be enforced, even though it appears in a form contract.

Discussion: *By Justice BLACKMUN:*

"In this context, it would be entirely unreasonable for us to assume that [the Shutes]—or any other cruise passenger—would negotiate with [Carnival] the terms of a forum-selection clause in an ordinary commercial cruise ticket. Common sense dictates that a ticket of this kind will be a form contract the terms of which are not subject to negotiation, and that an individual purchasing the ticket will not have bargaining parity with the cruise line....

"Including a reasonable forum clause in a form contract of this kind may well be permissible for several reasons: First, a cruise line has a special interest in limiting the fora in which it potentially could be subject to suit. Because a cruise ship typically carries passengers from many locales, it is not unlikely that a mishap on a cruise could subject the cruise line to litigation in several different fora.... Additionally, a clause establishing ex ante the forum for dispute resolution has the salutary effect of dispelling any confusion about where suits arising from the contract must be brought and defended, sparing litigants the time and expense of pretrial motions to determine the correct forum, and conserving judicial resources that otherwise would be devoted to deciding these motions.... Finally, it stands to reason that passengers who purchase tickets containing a forum clause like that at issue in this case benefit in the form of reduced fares reflecting the savings that the cruise line enjoys by limiting the fora in which it may be sued....

"In the present case, Florida is not a 'remote alien forum,' nor—given the fact that Mrs. Shute's accident occurred off the coast of Mexico—is this dispute an essentially local one inherently more suited to resolution in the State of Washington than in Florida. In light of these [factors], and because [the Shutes] do not claim lack of notice of the forum clause, we conclude that they have not satisfied the 'heavy burden of proof'...required to set aside the clause on the grounds of inconvenience.

"It bears emphasis that forum-selection clauses contained in form passage contracts are subject to judicial scrutiny for fundamental fairness. In this case, there is no indication that [Carnival] set Florida as the forum in which disputes were to be resolved as a means of discouraging cruise passengers from pursuing legitimate claims. Any suggestion of such a bad-faith motive is belied by two facts: [Carnival] has its principal place of business in Florida, and many of its cruises depart from and return to Florida ports. Similarly, there is no evidence that [Carnival] obtained [the Shutes'] accession to the forum clause by fraud or overreaching. Finally, [the Shutes] have conceded that they were given notice of the forum provision and, therefore, presumably retained the option of rejecting the contract with impunity. In the case before us, therefore, we conclude that the Court of Appeals erred in refusing to enforce the forum-selection clause."

Ethical Dimension

Is it fair to force the Shutes to travel to Florida to litigate their claim? Would it be fair to require Carnival to defend suits wherever its passengers live?

REVIEW

The national government and each of the state governments maintain a complete set of courts. In many cases, there will be choices available because several trial locations are possible. The court actually hearing the case will use its own procedural rules. There are still some important differences in procedural rules for civil cases, both among the states and between the state courts and the federal courts. Court judgments from one state, if based on jurisdiction over the parties and the dispute, must be given full faith and credit in all other states. Litigation is costly, uncertain, inconvenient, public, and dysfunctional to normal business operations. These defects have led to the development of alternate dispute resolution methods—mediation, arbitration, private judges, and mini-trials. The parties may also wish to simplify the litigation process by specifying a forum and an applicable law in their original contract.

REVIEW QUESTIONS AND PROBLEMS

1. Explain the relationship between the federal courts and the state courts.

2. To what extent are decisions by the courts in one state enforceable in other states?

3. Under what circumstances can a company located in one state be sued in another state?

4. What difference does it make whether a case is heard in the federal courts or in the state courts?

5. Why are alternative methods of dispute resolution becoming more popular for settling business disputes?

6. What is diversity of citizenship jurisdiction? Why is it important to business firms?

7. Deutsche Motors Company (DMC) sells its cars in all states in the U.S. DMC is incorporated in Germany and makes its cars there, but delivers some of them to various wholesalers and retailers throughout the United States. It advertises heavily in all national media in the United States. It has sales representatives throughout the United States. Takisha bought a DMC car in Boston, Massachusetts. She drove her new car to Cleveland, Ohio, for a business meeting. She was involved in a serious accident there; she says she was injured because the car's air bag did not function properly. Takisha sues both DMC and the Boston car dealer in Ohio, claiming that her new car was defective. The Boston car dealer moves to dismiss the case against it, for lack of jurisdiction. How should the court rule, and why?

8. Flying Fleet, Inc. operates its airline business in several Midwestern states. It is incorporated in Delaware, but its corporate home office and the home airport for its planes is Detroit, Michigan. Herman, a Michigan resident, was injured when a Flying Fleet plane had a very rough landing in Omaha, Nebraska. Herman brings a lawsuit in U.S. District Court in Detroit. He alleges the airline's negligence caused the crash. Flying Fleet says the U.S. District Court in Detroit does not have jurisdiction. Who is right, and why?

9. Assuming that Herman finds the right court to hear his lawsuit, what law will be used to determine whether the airline was at fault? Explain.

10. Sokel Company was hired to do electrical work on a construction project by the general contractor, Seuss Corp. Their contract specified that any dispute arising between them would be submitted to arbitration. Seuss later claimed that the work was not being done properly and refused to let Sokel continue with the job. Sokel sued in court to collect what it claimed was due for work already performed. Seuss moved to dismiss the court case. How should the trial judge rule on this motion? Explain.

SUGGESTIONS FOR FURTHER READING

Cox & Tandford, "An Alternative Method of Capital Jury Selection," *Journal of Law & Human Behavior* (June 1989): 167.

Cutler, Penrod & Dexter, "The Eyewitness, the Expert Psychologist, and the Jury," *Journal of Law & Human Behavior* (September 1989): 311.

Goodwin & Rovelstad, "Rules of Evidence and the Marketing Expert: An Analysis of a Marketing Study Used in Court," *American Business Law Journal* 14 (Spring 1976): 25.

Henkel, "The Civil Jury—Modification or Abolition?," *American Business Law Journal* 14 (Spring 1976): 97.

"What's Happened to the Due Process Among the States?: Pretrial Publicity and Motions for Change of Venue in Criminal Proceedings," *American Journal of Criminal Law* (Winter 1990): 175.

5
THE REGULATORY SYSTEM

"What a charming life that was, that dear old life in the Navy when I kept grocery on a gunboat. I knew all the regulations and the rest of them didn't. I had all of my rights and most of theirs."

Thomas B. Reed
Speaker of the House, 1890-92, 1895-99

LEARNING OBJECTIVES: After you have studied this chapter, you should be able to:

OUTLINE the historical development of administrative agencies.

DISCUSS the advantages and disadvantages of agency policy-making.

IDENTIFY the different functions performed by agencies.

EXPLAIN the need for and the steps in a trial-type hearing by an agency.

DISCUSS the role of the courts in reviewing agency actions.

P REVIEW

The drafters of the Declaration of Independence, out of "a decent respect to the opinions of mankind," included in the document a list of their grievances against the English king. One of the charges was that "He has erected a multitude of new offices, and sent hither swarms of officers to harass our people and eat out their substance." One can only wonder at what the reaction of Jefferson and the other drafters would be if they returned today and saw what has developed under their replacement government. Our business and personal activities are regulated by government to a degree that would have been unimaginable in 1776. We are indeed subject to a "multitude of new offices," with "swarms of officers." Yet for all its significance, the relationship between business and politics was little studied until quite recently. Writing in 1959 Robert Dahl found that "only about a dozen articles" dealing with business had been published in the *American Political Science Review* in the preceding fifty years.

Agencies are created by the executive branch, Congress, and by the states to deal with problems which market mechanisms do not seem to be handling properly. Some agencies administer regulations in certain general areas, such as labor relations or securities issuance. Some are created to regulate specific industries, such as transportation and communication, to ensure safety and access. Many of them are free of direct control by the president. Since the administrative agency is one of the primary contact points between business and government, business practitioners need some awareness of how these agencies operate. This chapter focuses on the development of the independent federal regulatory agencies, their functions, their problems and their future. It will also review administrative agency procedure in adjudications, including the scope of court review of the agency's action.

T YPES OF FEDERAL REGULATORY AGENCIES

Regulatory bodies come in a variety of shapes and sizes and from a variety of sources. The following discussion outlines the major types of administrative agencies which regulate business operations.

■ Executive Departments

In the broadest sense, the departments of government represented in the president's Cabinet are administrative agencies. In popular speech, and indeed for many technical purposes, the terms *executive* and *administrator* are used interchangeably. Webster defines *administrator* as "a person who has executive work or ability" and *executive* as "a person, group of people, or branch of government empowered and required to administer the laws and affairs of a nation." The national executive power of the United States is vested in the president by Article II of the Constitution. The president is in turn free to assign responsibility for specific functions to the various Cabinet departments and other appointed officials.

Most of the bureaus and agencies which are directly subordinate to the president and the Cabinet departments have only limited rule-making and adjudicatory functions. Their primary job is administering the laws in their area of jurisdiction. Typically, these agencies investigate only to the extent necessary to ensure compliance with "their" laws. Although such agencies usually have not been given broad rule-making, or legislative, powers, their regulatory decisions do have significant business impacts. As one example, the wood products industry is heavily dependent on the timber management decisions of the U.S. Forest Service and the Bureau of Land Management.

Most executive departments have limited power to make adjudications.

■ Independent Commissions

Much of the growth in the regulation of American business occurred outside the regular executive departments, as Congress established independent regulatory commissions. From Congress's standpoint, the main advantage of the independent commission is that it does not increase the accumulation of power in the executive branch. In addition, because the independent commission is not subject to direct presidential control, it is better able to implement the policy which Congress expressed in the statute which created it. Commissioners who are experts in the complex technological fields being regulated can be appointed. It was felt that persons of the same caliber might not wish to serve in a Cabinet department, where they could be fired at the pleasure of the president. The high level of expertise and professionalism possessed by these independent commissioners would enable them to decide complex and technical questions with speed and flexibility. These experts would also be more able to make the detailed rules needed to regulate these technical areas. Moreover, Congress could not put every detail in the basic statutes. Agencies could fill in the details and take some of the decision workload off the courts. In addition, it would probably not be constitutional to delegate rule-making authority to the courts. Even if the delegation problem could have been solved, the courts would not have been particularly suited to the rule-making function. Finally, the independent commission, by combining legislative policy and administrative policy, would be able to coordinate the adoption and the enforcement of regulations.

Independent commissions were established to regulate complex technological fields.

Beyond all these claimed advantages, however, lies another reason for the growth of the independent regulatory commission. Many of the regulatory statutes were passed by Congresses dominated by liberal Democrats during periods when the courts were dominated by conservatives. There was a fear that leaving the application of regulations to the courts would not produce the same sort of results as would assigning these functions to an independent commission. The courts were not sympathetic to many of these new economic regulations and, until the late 1930s, struck them down with regularity whenever they had the opportunity. The courts, in sum, would not necessarily have provided the aggressive but flexible enforcement necessary to make the new regulations effective.

D EVELOPMENT OF REGULATORY AGENCIES

Our existing regulatory agencies were not all created at one time, according to some master plan. Agencies have been created under various administrations, and for various reasons.

■ First Wave

Early regulatory commissions included the ICC and the FDA.

The movement toward regulating by independent commission began slowly enough. After the creation in 1887 of the Interstate Commerce Commission (ICC) to deal with the tremendous problems generated by railroad expansion, more than twenty years passed before the device was used again. The Food and Drug Administration was created in 1907, but it was not really independent of the executive branch.

Woodrow Wilson's first administration saw the adoption of statutes setting up the Federal Reserve Board (FRB) in 1913 and the Federal Trade Commission (FTC) in 1914. While it is true that the FRB was not given complete control of banking and finance (the Department of the Treasury and the Comptroller of the Currency also have significant areas of control), it is independent of executive direction.

The FTC provides the clearest case of congressional preference for commission over court. For most of its history (until the 1970s), the FTC was content to proceed mainly on a case-by-case basis, with its staff of trial examiners hearing cases in which unfair trade practices were alleged. While the FTC Act did make unfair trade practices unlawful as a matter of national law, there was no particular reason for assigning such cases to an independent commission. There is nothing so inherently complex about such trials that the regular courts would be unsuited to hear them. What was clearly at work here was the congressional preference. The regular judges, trained in the common law, would not provide the same sort of vigorous enforcement as would a commission. As it turned out, the FTC was not all that vigorous either until its rejuvenation in the 1970s, when it began to exercise rule-making power more frequently.

■ New Deal Agencies

With an overwhelming mandate from the voters to do something about national economic conditions, Franklin D. Roosevelt's administration

created new agencies almost as fast as a computer programmed to produce permutations of the alphabet. Not all of these, of course, were
true independent commissions. Some were more tightly controlled by
the executive departments. Nor were all really regulatory in the normal
sense of the word. The Tennessee Valley Authority, for example, was
really a government-operated power company on a grand scale.

Among the more important agencies created during the 1930s are
the Federal Deposit Insurance Corporation (FDIC), the Federal
Communications Commission (FCC), the Securities and Exchange
Commission (SEC), the National Labor Relations Board (NLRB), the
Federal Power Commission (FPC), and the Civil Aeronautics Board
(CAB). The FDIC was important in restoring confidence in the national
banking system, but it is not the same kind of independent regulatory
commission as the other five. The other five, along with the ICC, made
up what were often referred to as the "Big Six" regulatory commissions. All of the six held hearings, adopted regulations, and adjudi-
cated disputes. In each instance, the members of the board or commission were independent of direct presidential control. Although the regulated industries—transportation, communication, power, securities—
were not nationalized, they were now subject to uniform national policies. As for the NLRB, it was responsible for a revolution in labor relations. The great successes enjoyed by the new industrial unions in the
1930s were due in large part to the NLRB and its Act. (One of the popular slogans was: "FDR wants *you* to join the Union!") The Big Six set
the tone of government relations with business until the 1960s.

*Many important
agencies date from the
New Deal period.*

■ New Activism

Anyone who lived through the 1960s and 1970s will remember the
Vietnam War as the social issue of that period. Vietnam dominated our
national consciousness, and our personal and institutional discourse,
as few events have. For the most part, however, business and government were partners, rather than adversaries, in the Vietnam affair.
Many businesses made large profits from the war, and some indicated
that they felt they had a duty to supply war materials even if it were
not profitable to do so. (Dow Chemical was finally pressured into
holding a stockholder referendum on its manufacture of napalm. See
*Medical Committee for Human Rights v. Securities and Exchange
Commission*, 432 F.2d 659.) Most of the anti-war sentiment directed
against participating businesses came not from government, but from
outside activists, who attempted to use stockholder meetings and public opinion to change corporate policies. The SEC was involved in these
exchanges only to ensure that proper proxy and voting procedures
were being followed. Otherwise, the government was not a party to
these debates on corporate morality. Perhaps the Vietnam War's greatest legacy, from a business standpoint, was a new recognition of the

importance of public and shareholder relations. Corporate managements can be changed, or be persuaded to change, by an aroused shareholder-public.

From the regulatory standpoint, the 1960s and 1970s were the years of the underdog—consumers and minorities, individual workers and citizens. The new issues of concern were discrimination and health and safety. At the same time our country was spending billions of dollars and thousands of lives in Vietnam, President Johnson pledged to create the Great Society here at home. What followed was a new wave of legislation, the like of which had not been seen since the New Deal. The election of Richard Nixon in 1968 did not appreciably slow this new legislative onslaught.

More recently created agencies include the EPA, OSHA, the CPSC, and the EEOC.

Many of the most controversial regulatory agencies date from this period—the Environmental Protection Agency (EPA), the Occupational Safety and Health Review Commission, the Consumer Product Safety Commission (CPSC), and even the Equal Employment Opportunity Commission (EEOC). The major focus of this group of agencies was on general problems rather than on the regulation of specific industries. Concern for the maintenance and improvement of our environment has fostered what some people see as an overzealousness at the EPA. Critics feel that the EPA's target is always the ideal—the maximum that is technologically achievable—whatever the cost. As a result, businesses (and entire communities) have been devastated. Similar concerns are voiced against OSHA. Critics charge that OHSA has not been in tune with the real world of work, that it has taken an absolutist and unrealistic view of its mission. While no one would argue against employees' having a reasonably safe place in which to work, absolute safety does not exist in this world. Some dangerous jobs do need to be performed. In its early years, OSHA also lost much credibility by expending considerable effort and money on ensuring compliance with such things as a required design for toilet seats and a specified height for mounting fire extinguishers. If government regulation is to be successful, it must be sensible and cost-effective.

The controversy surrounding the EEOC is of a different sort. While few would argue against the idea of equal treatment for all in the work force, there is sharp disagreement over the extent to which members of minority groups should be given employment preference now to make up for discrimination which occurred in the past. There is also continuing argument over what proofs should be required in a discrimination case. These problems are more fully discussed in Chapter 14.

■ Reform and Deregulation

Even before the election of Ronald Reagan in 1980, efforts were underway to reevaluate national regulatory policies. Faced with a severe economic recession, many businesses, individuals, and communities raised questions about the costs of environmental and safety regulations. International competitors have preempted many domestic and foreign markets and threaten to continue to do so. To what extent have our regulatory policies disadvantaged us as competitors in an international economy? In addition to these concerns, one does not have to be a corporate director to wonder about the Big Brother attitude exhibited by some agencies. When the EPA uses spy cameras mounted in airplanes and flies over businesses to try to detect violations, many people perceive a potential threat to civil liberties.

The new attack on regulation is proceeding on several fronts. There is an increase in court challenges to both the substance and the procedure of regulations. The drive for legislative reform is aimed at gaining a fairer, more objective administrative decision. One aspect of this drive is to stop the practice of paying "public interest" advocates' legal fees. While this practice generates much work (and money) for a certain class of lawyers, it may not be a positive contribution to enlightened agency decision-making. Shaping agencies' policies through lawsuits begun by small, vocal special interest groups may not produce results which are desired and needed by most of society.

Deregulation of several areas occurred in the late 1970s and the 1980s.

At least as important as ending the payment of plaintiffs' lawyers' fees is the passage of the Equal Access to Justice Act of 1980 (EAJA). For small business, the EAJA is the most significant regulatory reform ever enacted. Corporations with a net worth of $5 million or less and individuals with a net worth of $1 million or less, either of whom employ 500 or fewer people, may now be reimbursed by the agency for court costs and reasonable attorney fees involved in successfully defending themselves against civil actions by government agencies. Prior to this act, many small businesses could be bullied into accepting unfair agency decisions simply because of the costs involved in defending the action. Not all defenses are reimbursed. The agency can avoid reimbursing the costs if it can convince a trial court that its enforcement action was justified. What the EAJA does is to provide a warning to the enforcement agencies: Be prepared to prove that your action was brought in good faith and with a reasonable basis—or pay the defendant's costs.

In addition to appointing regulators who took a more conservative approach, the Reagan administration was committed to a reexamination of the whole process of agency regulation. Cost-benefit analyses were ordered for many regulations. Greater consultation with the businesses concerned, it was hoped, might produce more rational, and therefore more enforceable, regulations. Finally, further areas which might be ripe for de-regulation were examined. The role of free markets has been increased in several major industries already—airlines, oil and gas, broadcasting, railroads, and trucking. Whether the deregulation of industries such as trucking and airlines has produced net benefits to society is still being debated.

Many of these trends continued under the Bush administration, even though it also adopted many new regulations. A White House Council on Competitiveness, chaired by the vice-president, was established. The Council's job, in consultation with business leaders, was to make sure that regulations designed to protect workers and consumers did not prevent U.S. industry from competing in the global marketplace. One of President Clinton's first actions after he took office in 1993 was to abolish this Council.

On another front, the National Federation of Independent Business has sponsored legislation which would (1) require agencies to provide a written cost-benefit analysis of proposed regulations; (2) publish proposed regulations six months prior to their effective date; and, (3) provide for a congressional veto of such regulations by a joint resolution. It now seems only a question of time until this or similar legislation is enacted.

AGENCY FUNCTIONS

The unique feature of the independent administrative agencies, which have been called the "headless fourth branch of government," is that they combine all the functions of the other three branches. These agencies investigate to determine whether further regulations or enforcement actions are required; they legislate, by filling in the general provisions of their creating statutes with detailed regulations; they administer and enforce their creating statute and their own regulations; and they adjudicate disputed matters—deciding rates, licenses, and violations. This combined-functions approach has both advantages and disadvantages.

Agency Investigations

Many agencies have authority to conduct investigations.

Agencies are authorized to conduct investigations for a number of purposes. They need to investigate to discover violators in their area of enforcement. They need information in order to develop regulations, to set rates, and to grant licenses. In many cases, they are charged by Congress with the responsibility for gathering information and transmitting it periodically to Congress. In conducting its investigation, an agency may be able to subpoena witnesses and documents; to require the filing of reports; to inspect business premises, books, and records; and to make copies of business documents.

Courts have generally been reluctant to imply the existence of an agency's power to subpoena, so such power must normally be specifically stated in the agency's creating statute. Once so stated, however, most courts today would interpret the subpoena power quite broadly. Courts are generally willing to enforce an agency's subpoena if the data sought are relevant to any lawful agency purpose and will usually accept the agency's allegations at face value. In other words, the burden of proof is on the defendant to show that the requested information is irrelevant to any lawful agency purpose. The demand must be reasonably specific, as specific as possible under the circumstances, and must not be unduly burdensome to the defendant when weighed against the value of the information to the agency. The data cannot be subpoenaed if to do so would violate the defendant's trade secrets or if the information is otherwise privileged. The privilege against self-incrimination does not apply to corporations or labor unions, only to individuals, so corporate or union officers could be ordered to produce evidence which is incriminating to the organization. Corporate or union officers could likewise be required to produce corporate or union records which are incriminating as to themselves. They could claim a privilege only as to the production of their own private papers, not as to the organization's documents. Even as to privileged evidence, a grant of immunity from prosecution suspends the privilege, and the evidence must then be produced even if other adverse consequences, such as a non-criminal enforcement order from the agency, followed.

As was discussed in Chapter 3, where physical inspection of business premises is demanded, the protections of the Fourth Amendment do apply. Any search and seizure must be reasonable, as determined ultimately by the courts. As for the probable cause required for the issuance of a search warrant, the courts have generally been quite liberal.

In an investigatory proceeding (as opposed to an adversary one), a witness is not on trial, and therefore need not be given the right to counsel or the right to confront adverse witnesses and present defense witnesses. These limits on due process are discussed in the *Groban* case.

IN RE GROBAN

352 U.S. 330 (1957)

Facts: A fire occurred on the premises of a business owned and operated by Groban and his associates. The Ohio State Fire Marshal conducted an investigation into the causes of the fire and summoned Groban and the others as witnesses. They refused to testify without the presence of their lawyer. Acting under his statutory authority, the Fire Marshal had them jailed for refusal to testify. They petitioned the Ohio courts for a writ of habeas corpus (which challenges the legality of a person's detention). The Ohio courts refused to issue the writ, and Groban and his associates appealed to the U.S. Supreme Court.

Issue: Do witnesses in an administrative investigation have the right to counsel?

Decision: No, they do not. The Ohio courts' denial of their habeas corpus petition is affirmed by the U.S. Supreme Court.

Rule: The full requirements of due process for a court proceeding do not apply in administrative investigations.

Discussion: *By Justice* REED:

"It is clear that a defendant in a state criminal trial has an unqualified right, under the Due Process Clause, to be heard through his own counsel.... Prosecution of an individual differs widely from administrative investigation of incidents damaging to the economy or dangerous to the public. The proceeding before the Fire Marshal was not a criminal trial, nor was it an administrative proceeding that would in any way adjudicate appellants' responsibilities for the fire. It was a proceeding solely to elicit facts relating to the causes and circumstances of the fire. The Fire Marshal's duty was to 'determine whether the fire was the result of carelessness or design,' and to arrest any person against whom there was sufficient evidence on which to base a charge of arson. The fact that appellants were under a legal duty to speak and that their testimony might provide a basis for criminal charges against them does not mean that they had a constitutional right to the assistance of their counsel. Appellants here are witnesses from whom information was sought as to the cause of the fire. A witness before a grand jury cannot insist, as a matter of constitutional right, on being represented by his counsel, nor can a witness before other investigatory bodies. There is no more reason to allow the presence of counsel before a Fire Marshal trying in the public interest to determine the cause of a fire. Obviously in these situations evidence obtained may possibly lay a witness open to criminal charges. When such charges are made in a criminal proceeding, he may then demand the presence of his counsel for his defense. Until then his protection is the privilege against self-incrimination.... This is a privilege available in investigations as well as in prosecutions.... We have no doubt that the privilege is available in Ohio against prosecutions as well as convictions reasonably feared.... The mere fact that suspicion may be entertained of such a witness, as appellants believed existed here, though without allegation of facts to support such a belief, does not bar the taking of testimony in a private investigatory proceeding.

"It may be that the number of people present in a grand jury proceeding gives greater assurance that improper use will not be made of the witness' presence. We think, however, that the presumption of fair and orderly conduct by state officials without coercion or distortion exists until challenged by facts to the contrary. Possibility of improper exercise of opportunity to examine is not in our judgment a sound reason to set aside a State's procedure for fire prevention. As in similar situations, abuses may be corrected as they arise; for example, by excluding from subsequent prosecutions evidence improperly obtained....

"The sole assertion of a constitutional violation that appellants relied upon before the Ohio Supreme Court and the only one open on the record here—the authorization in §3737.13 [of the Ohio Revised Code] of the exclusion of counsel while a witness testifies—is not well founded. We hold that appellants had no constitutional right to be assisted by their counsel in giving testimony at the investigatory proceeding conducted by the Fire Marshal, and that §3737.13, insofar as it authorizes the exclusion of counsel while a witness testifies, is not repugnant to the Due Process Clause of the Fourteenth Amendment."

Ethical Dimension

Is it fair for a government agency to use its powers to investigate, and not provide the witnesses it summons with full due process protections?

Agency Legislation

A large part of the rationale for the existence of administrative agencies stems from their ability to use their expert knowledge to provide the detailed regulations needed in each area. Statutes creating the agencies express the congressional policy objectives in very broad terms and then delegate to the agencies the power and the duty to fill in the details. When its investigations uncover problems, the agency may respond by adopting a general rule to deal with the problem or by bringing an enforcement action against particular persons or businesses.

Many agencies have the power to adopt rules which have the force of law.

Agency rule-making differs from agency adjudication in several important aspects. Rules adopted will apply prospectively—to future conduct, as opposed to adjudication, which is based on past conduct. (This is one of the main advantages of an agency over a court: the agency, by adopting a rule, can prohibit conduct in advance; a court generally must wait for a wrong to occur and then try to provide a remedy if an injured party complains.) Rules will apply, generally, to a whole class of parties or cases, as opposed to an adjudication of the rights of the specific parties before the agency in a contested proceeding. Any sanctions for violation of rules adopted can be imposed only after a further, adversary hearing, as opposed to an adjudication, which is the adversary hearing. Finally, the agency is not bound by any record in adopting a rule. Rather, a rule is based on the agency's policy choice as well as on the record. In general, an agency rule can only be challenged on the basis that it is arbitrary, that it exceeds the agency's power, or that the agency failed to follow proper procedure in adopting it. By contrast, an agency's decision in an adjudication must be based on the record.

Agencies legislate three different types of rules: procedural rules, interpretive rules, and legislative rules. **Procedural rules** are adopted by the agency to govern its own internal operations. Once adopted, they must be followed by the agency until they are changed. A formal hearing is generally not required prior to the adoption, although an agency may provide an opportunity for the submission of written comments. The Administrative Procedure Act (APA) states that no notice and hearing are required for interpretive rules either, but the line between interpretive rules and **legislative** (substantive) **rules** is not always easy to draw. The idea behind **interpretive rules** is that the agency should be able to provide some official guidelines to its enforcement policy. In the case of the Internal Revenue Service, for example, a "revenue ruling" which outlines the IRS position on a particular question of tax law may be issued. Such interpretations do not necessarily have the force of law, at least not until sanctioned by a court, but they do indicate how the IRS views those issues. In contrast, a regulation adopted by the IRS after notice and hearing *is* part of the tax law—if constitutional and authorized.

Formal hearings are not always required prior to agency rule-making.

Even for legislative/substantive rules, a trial-type hearing is not always required, and the agency has broad discretion in establishing the format of any hearing. Advance notice of the proposed rule-making must be given in the *Federal Register*, which is the official legal news publication of the national government. In addition to notices of agency hearings, the proposed regulations themselves are published. At least some opportunity for written comments must usually be given. The rule as adopted must then be published in the *Federal Register* thirty days before its effective date. Such publication is constructive notice of the rule's existence to all those affected.

Agencies involved in rate-making activities are usually required to follow the procedures for legislative/substantive rules. The affected parties normally have to be given notice and an opportunity to participate in the rate-making process. Again, however, the agency would not necessarily be bound by the hearing record, since policy choices could also be involved in the setting of rates.

■ Agency Enforcement and Adjudication

Agencies, unlike courts, not only provide many of the substantive rules, but also prosecute violations of the rules. The agency itself also decides whether its rule has been violated. The agency is thus, in a very real sense, both prosecutor and judge—although different members of the agency's staff would be performing these two functions. The requirements of administrative due process in conducting a trial-type hearing are discussed in detail later in this chapter.

C ONTROLS ON AGENCIES

Since agencies exercise a multiplicity of functions, in violation of the traditional American doctrine of separation of powers, there has been much concern over establishing effective controls over agency action. The goal is to give the agency sufficient elbow room within which to exercise its discretion, while at the same time providing effective checks against any possible abuse of discretion. This balance is a difficult one to strike and may be set differently for different agencies, or for the same agency at different times. Figure 5–1 presents an overview of the controls on agencies.

■ Legislative Controls

Congress has the ultimate power to control any agency which it creates. An agency's creating statute may be amended to change its substantive or procedural rules, or to withdraw part of its jurisdiction. Strong lobbying efforts were made in 1982, for example, in support of a bill which would have exempted doctors, dentists, and optometrists from FTC jurisdiction. A change could also be made in the structure of the agency, for example, by appointing additional members after a

Agencies are subject to various congressional controls.

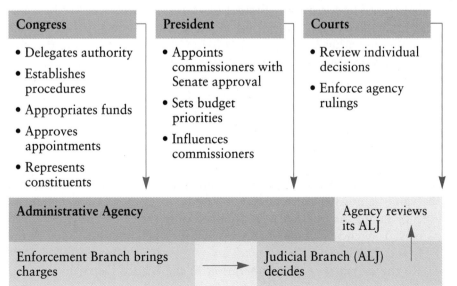

FIGURE 5–1
Controls on agencies

Congress	President	Courts
• Delegates authority	• Appoints commissioners with Senate approval	• Review individual decisions
• Establishes procedures	• Sets budget priorities	• Enforce agency rulings
• Appropriates funds	• Influences commissioners	
• Approves appointments		
• Represents constituents		

Administrative Agency   Agency reviews its ALJ

Enforcement Branch brings charges   →   Judicial Branch (ALJ) decides change in the statute. In the extreme case, the agency might be abolished altogether, as happened with the Civil Aeronautics Board.

Congress may also influence the agency's administration in those instances where appointments of agency personnel are subject to approval by the Senate. Another form of legislative control is control of the agency's budget. By raising or lowering appropriations, Congress can expand or contract the agency's operations.

Congress has also passed several statutes which control agencies' use of information in their possession. The Freedom of Information Act requires that most records of the national government be open to the public. (Many states have similar statutes.) There are limited exceptions for national security and law enforcement information, for business trade secrets, and for personal medical and financial records. Generally, however, agencies must disclose their data if requested to do so. Congress did adopt the Privacy Act to try to prevent the unauthorized disclosure of personal information, but widespread use of computers has largely frustrated the act's purpose. Congress tried again, by passing the Right to Financial Privacy Act, which requires individual permission or a court order before the national government may access personal information held by financial institutions. Even under this act, however, no permission or court order is required for Internal Revenue Service proceedings, grand jury investigations, civil litigation, or verification of information in connection with government loans or loan guarantees.

■ Executive Controls

The president, having the responsibility to appoint the top level administrators at most agencies, has a significant impact on enforcement policy. The president is usually limited by statute, however, as to the number of members of the same political party that can be appointed to the agency's governing board or commission. Moreover, the board members' terms of office are typically longer than the president's four year term, so there may be holdovers from a prior administration. (Some board members may not stay for their full terms, however.) Also, as with judges, there is no guarantee that an agency member, once appointed, will continue to agree with the president's policies.

The president has only a limited power to remove members of independent agencies.

As discussed in Chapter 2, the president has only a limited removal power for board members of the independent agencies. While Cabinet members can be removed at will, for any reason or for no reason at all, the same removal power does not extend to agency board members. Agency board members can be removed only for cause shown, at least as regards agencies which exercise quasi-judicial functions, such as the FTC and the SEC.

To the extent that the cooperation of the Justice Department is required in an enforcement proceeding, the president could affect agency policy by refusing such cooperation. Such an approach might involve significant political costs, however, and would probably only be used in an extreme case. To the extent that the president has influence in Congress, he might also indirectly affect the agency's budget and other activities.

■ Judicial Controls

The major justification for permitting the agencies to exercise multiple powers, including rule-making, is that the agencies' actions are subject to judicial review. It is true that nearly all agency actions are reviewable by the courts, but the courts are generally supposed to defer to the agency's expertise within its regulatory area. Such "deference" does have limits, as seen in several cases in this chapter. The effectiveness of judicial review of contested agency cases is discussed more fully later in this chapter, in connection with the trial-type hearing.

Courts generally defer to agencies' expertise in their area of authority.

The following case deals with judicial review of an agency's *failure* to act, and also discusses the issues of standing and ripeness.

HER MAJESTY THE QUEEN IN RIGHT OF ONTARIO V. U.S. ENVIRONMENTAL PROTECTION AGENCY

912 F.2d 1525 (D.C. Cir. Court of Appeals, 1990)

Facts: Section 115 of the U.S. Clean Air Act establishes a procedure to prevent U.S. air pollution from causing acid rain in Canada. When the EPA administrator has reason to believe such harm is occurring, the administrator is to give notification to the governor of the state from which the pollution is originating that the state's clean air program must be improved.

In January 1981, administrator Douglas Costle sent letters to Secretary of State Edmund Muskie and Senator George Mitchell. In each letter, Costle said that U.S. pollution was causing acid rain in Canada and that the EPA staff was investigating which states should receive the required notification. When the EPA did nothing further, several states and private parties filed a lawsuit in U.S. District Court for the District of Columbia. The plaintiffs claimed that the EPA had a duty to make findings and to issue the required notifications. The District Court ordered the EPA to do so within 180 days. On appeal, in 1985, the Court of Appeals reversed, stating that the Costle findings were "rules" under the Administrative Procedure Act. Since Costle had not held hearings as required by the APA, the "rules" were invalid.

On April 7, 1988, the Province of Ontario, several states, and various environmental groups filed rule-making petitions with the EPA, requesting that it take action on the acid rain problem. After several months, an EPA assistant administrator (Clay) wrote letters to the petitioners, indicating that he felt that the EPA did not have enough data to notify specific states that it was their pollution which was causing the acid rain in Ontario. Clay also said that the EPA would not hold a separate proceeding on whether Canada was "endangered," but would wait until it could identify the sources of the air pollution. Petitioners now ask the Court of Appeals to review the EPA's non-action.

Issue: Are the non-action letters a "final agency action" so that the case is "ripe for review"?

Decision: Yes, they are, as to the EPA's decision that it must identify specific states to be notified in order to initiate Section 115 proceedings. (But the EPA wins on the merits as to whether it should act at this time.}

Rule: Administrative inaction which has the same effect on the parties as a formal denial of relief is also "final agency action," and therefore it is also subject to judicial review.

Discussion: *By Judge* BUCKLEY:

"To determine finality, courts must decide 'whether the agency's position is definitive and whether it has a direct and immediate...effect on the day-to-day business of the parties challenging the action.'... The inquiry seeks to distinguish a tentative agency position from the situation where 'the agency views its deliberative process as sufficiently final to demand compliance with its announced position.'... When an agency position is merely tentative, judicial intervention may 'den[y] the agency an opportunity to correct its own mistakes and to apply its expertise' and 'leads to piecemeal review which at the least is inefficient and upon completion of the agency process might prove to have been unnecessary.'...

"Although the EPA emphasizes that it has taken no final action with respect to the petitions, 'agency inaction may represent effectively final agency action that the agency has not frankly acknowledged.'... When administrative inaction has the same impact on the rights of the parties as an express denial of relief, judicial review is not precluded.... Similarly, the absence of a formal statement of the agency's position, as here, is not dispositive. An agency may not, for example, avoid judicial review 'merely by choosing the form of a letter to express its definitive position on a general question of statutory interpretation.'...

"On applying the foregoing principles, we conclude that the Clay letters represent final agency action as to the EPA's interpretation of section 115. In other words, although...the EPA concededly made no final decision on petitioners' request that the section 115 remedial process be initiated, it clearly and unequivocally rejected, on the basis of its construction of section 115, petitioners' requests for a separate proceeding limited to the endangerment and reciprocity findings....

"The EPA also asserts that even if it is deemed to have taken final action, the petitions are not ripe for review.... Under the Supreme Court's [test], we consider 'both the fitness of the issues for judicial decision and the hardship to the parties of withholding court consideration.' The ripeness doctrine generally prevents courts from becoming 'entangled' in 'abstract disagreements over agency policy' and from improperly interfering in the administrative decision making process.... The EPA contends that neither part of the ripeness test is satisfied here.

"The first prong of the test, fitness for review, measures the interests of both court and agency in postponing review.... We consider such factors as whether the issue presented is purely legal, whether consideration of the issue would benefit from a more concrete setting, and whether the agency's action is sufficiently final....

"The issue presented is a purely legal question of statutory interpretation—that is, whether section 115 obliges the EPA to promulgate endangerment and reciprocity findings even when it is unable to follow through with notification to specific States. Petitioners do not challenge the technical and factual aspects of the EPA's acid rain research; they challenge only its failure to take action under section 115 on the endangerment and reciprocity issues. Our resolution of the question will not benefit from the development of further information; nor will it interfere prematurely with the EPA's own consideration of the issue, as the Clay letters represent a definitive statement of the agency's position....

"[The Acid Precipitation Act of 1980] initiated a ten-year program, commonly known as the National Acid Precipitation Assessment Program,...that is designed to identify the causes and sources of acid rain, to evaluate its environmental, social, and economic effects, and to assess potential methods of control.... We note that the final NAPAP report is due in December 1990. At oral argument the EPA pointed to this study as evidence of specific research being conducted that could enable the agency to take action under section 115; the EPA also asserted that the report should provide it with a sufficient basis to make a reasoned decision on the petitioners' rule making petitions.

"It is in part on the basis of this information that we conclude that the EPA's delay in acting on the petitions has been neither arbitrary, nor capricious, nor contrary to law."

Ethical Dimension

Was it ethical for our government to wait ten years before doing anything about acid rain?

REQUIREMENT OF A TRIAL-TYPE HEARING

One of the major issues in the operation of administrative agencies revolves around the need for a trial-type hearing. If such a hearing is required, agency action will be delayed. Agency personnel and other resources must be devoted to holding the hearing. Final agency action will be limited by the evidence introduced during the hearing. Clearly, agencies have much at stake in the decision on where this line should be drawn.

■ Constitutional Requirement

As previously indicated, not all administrative agency decisions will require a trial-type hearing. In general, the distinction is drawn between legislative facts and adjudicative facts. If the agency is acting in its legislative capacity, deciding questions of policy within its discretion, with its decision to be generally applicable, a trial-type hearing is not required. In other words, if it is rule-making rather than adjudicating, it need not hold a trial-type hearing. As a rule, the agency may make its general policy decisions on whatever basis it wishes, as long as it is acting within the scope of its enabling statute.

An agency is generally required to hold a trial-type hearing when it decides the rights of specific persons.

However, when the agency applies its own general rules or the provisions of its statute to a specific person or persons, a trial-type hearing is usually required. In these proceedings, the decision will have an individual impact, based on individual facts. Who did what, where, when, how, and with what motive or intent are the kinds of facts which would be determined by a jury in a court trial. A trial-type hearing is therefore required to determine such facts. Thus, an agency decision directed against an individual requires a trial-type hearing. The *Hannah* case is an illustration of this distinction.

HANNAH V. LARCHE

363 U.S. 420 (1960)

JUSTICE·UNDER

Facts: The U.S. Civil Rights Commission held a hearing in Shreveport, Louisiana, to investigate charges that African American citizens were being denied their voting rights. State voting registrars and private citizens were summoned for questioning at this hearing. The commission's procedural rules provided that the names of complainants did not have to be disclosed and that persons called to testify, including those against whom charges had been filed, did not have the right to confront and cross-examine other witnesses. Both the registrars and the private citizens who were summoned filed lawsuits in U.S. District Court in Louisiana, challenging the constitutionality of the commission's procedural rules. An injunction against the commission was granted in each case. The commission (John Hannah, chairman) asked for review by the U.S. Supreme Court.

Issue: Do the Civil Rights Commission's rules violate due process of law?

Decision: No, they do not. No court injunction should be issued to prevent the commission from holding its hearings.

Rule: Full due process protections do not have to be given in agency investigations.

Discussion: *By Chief Justice* WARREN:

"'Due process' is an elusive concept. Its exact boundaries are undefinable, and its content varies according to specific factual contexts. Thus, when governmental agencies adjudicate or make binding determinations which directly affect the legal rights of individuals, it is imperative that those agencies use the procedures which have traditionally been associated with the judicial process. On the other hand, when governmental action does not partake of an adjudication, as for example, when a general fact-finding investigation is being conducted, it is not necessary that the full panoply of judicial procedures be used. Therefore, as a generalization, it can be said that due process embodies the differing rules of fair play, which through the years, have become associated with differing types of proceedings. Whether the Constitution requires that a particular right obtain in a specific proceeding depends upon a complexity of factors. The nature of the alleged right involved, the nature of the proceeding, and the possible burden on that proceeding, are all considerations which must be taken into account. An analysis of these factors demonstrates why it is that the particular rights claimed by respondents need not be conferred upon those appearing before purely investigative agencies, of which the Commission on Civil Rights is one.

"It is probably sufficient merely to indicate that the rights claimed...are normally associated only with adjudicatory proceedings, and that since the Commission does not adjudicate, it need not be bound by adjudicatory procedures. Yet...the court below implied that such procedures are required since the Commission's proceedings might irreparably harm those being investigated by subjecting them to public opprobrium and scorn, the distinct likelihood of losing their jobs, and the possibility of criminal prosecutions. That any of these consequences will result is purely conjectural. There is nothing in the record to indicate that such will be the case or that past Commission proceedings have had any harmful effects upon witnesses.... However, even if such collateral consequences were to flow from the Commission's investigations, they would not be the result of any affirmative determinations made by the Commission, and they would not affect the legitimacy of the Commission's investigative function.

"On the other hand, the investigative process could be completely disrupted if investigative hearings were transformed into trial-like proceedings, and if persons who might be indirectly affected by an investigation were given an absolute right to cross-examine every witness called to testify. Fact-finding agencies without any power to adjudicate would be diverted from their legitimate duties and would be plagued by the injection of collateral issues that would make the investigation interminable. Even a person not called as a witness could demand the right to appear at the hearing, cross-examine any witness whose testimony or sworn affidavit allegedly defamed or incriminated him, and call an unlimited number of witnesses of his own selection. This type of proceedings would make a shambles of the investigation and stifle the agency in its gathering of facts.

"In addition to these persuasive considerations, we think it is highly significant that the Commission's procedures are not historically foreign to other forms of investigation under our system. Far from being unique, the Rules of Procedure adopted by the Commission are similar to those which...have traditionally governed the proceedings of the vast majority of governmental investigating agencies....

"From what we have said, it is obvious that the District Court erred in both cases in enjoining the Commission from holding its Shreveport hearing. The court's judgments are accordingly reversed, and the cases are remanded with direction to vacate the injunctions."

Ethical Dimension

What are the dangers of permitting government agencies to listen to "faceless accusers"?

■ Statutory Requirement

The agency's own statute, or the Administrative Procedure Act, may require a hearing before the agency takes certain action. An award or a revocation of a license, for example, may require a hearing under the applicable statute. Even here, however, many individual cases may be disposed of by the application of a general rule, without holding a formal hearing. Where the FCC had adopted a valid general rule which provided that no more than five broadcast outlets should be held by one person, for instance, it could summarily reject an application from a company which already controlled that many. Even where individual licenses have already been granted, the courts have held that general modifications can be made without the necessity of a trial-type hearing.

■ Procedural Shortcuts and Temporary Actions

In some situations, an agency may take provisional action immediately, subject to further proceedings. Administrative due process may be satisfied if there is an opportunity to challenge the summary decision later, in administrative or judicial review proceedings. At least for businesses, if not for individuals, the burden may be cast on the affected party to show the need for a formal hearing.

Summary proceedings are clearly justified where there is an immediate threat to public health and safety, as for example, with contaminated food. Banking and stock-trading activities may be suspended in advance of a formal hearing, where reasonable cause is shown. In all of these cases, the necessity for speedy action to protect the public welfare outweighs the general requirement for a hearing in advance of agency action. The validity of the agency's action can be reviewed later, but the threat to the public needs to be met immediately.

An agency can take immediate action to meet an emergency and then hold a hearing on the matter.

■ Right-Privilege Distinction

Older cases draw the distinction between an individual's rights, such as freedom of speech, and privileges, which are granted at the discretion of the government. Privileges are analogous to gifts, under this analysis. They are received under such terms and conditions as the donor (government) may decide, and the donor has the power to change the terms and conditions at any time—unilaterally. Rights, on the other hand, may not be withdrawn or infringed on by the government or its agencies without due process of law—which would usually mean a trial-type hearing.

Older cases held that agencies did not have to hold a hearing prior to revoking a privilege.

Since there is such a sharp difference in the legal results under this approach, categorization becomes very important. What is a "right," and what is a "privilege"? Government lawyers, defending unilateral agency actions, will of course argue that the dispute involves a privilege and that the agency's action without a hearing was therefore lawful. Most government benefit programs would probably be classified as privileges under this analysis. (After all the statements about our retirement "rights," it's interesting to read the government's arguments in Social Security cases. According to these arguments, there is no contractual right to Social Security.) The courts generally held that there was no right to government employment, either, so that government employees could be subjected to restrictions, such as the ban against political activity.

In more recent cases, the U.S. Supreme Court has indicated that it may be prepared to abandon the distinction between rights and duties altogether. If that occurs, at least minimal due process requirements will have to be met before any agency action is taken which adversely affects individuals. The *Goldberg* case discusses these points.

GOLDBERG V. KELLY

397 U.S. 294 (1969)

Facts: Kelly and other recipients of welfare benefits sued in U.S. District Court, alleging that New York permitted welfare officials to terminate these benefit payments, for various reasons, without a hearing. Goldberg is the New York City Commissioner of Social Services. After the lawsuits were filed, the city and state amended their procedures to require notice and a hearing. Plaintiffs also challenged the constitutional adequacy of the amended procedures. The District Court held that a pre-termination hearing was required and that it must comply with constitutional due process, which these procedures did not.

Issue: Is a constitutional due process hearing required before a government benefit can be terminated?

Decision: Yes. Judgment for plaintiffs affirmed.

Rule: Constitutional requirements apply to a decision to terminate welfare benefits. There is no distinction between a "right" and a "privilege" in this context.

Discussion: *By Justice* BRENNAN:

"For qualified recipients, welfare provides the means to obtain essential food, clothing, housing, and medical care.... Thus the crucial factor in this context—a factor not present in the case of the blacklisted government contractor, the discharged government employee, the taxpayer denied a tax exemption, or virtually anyone else whose governmental entitlements are ended—is that termination of aid pending resolution of a controversy over eligibility may deprive an *eligible* recipient of the very means by which to live while he waits. Since he lacks independent resources, his situation becomes immediately desperate. His need to concentrate upon finding the means for daily subsistence, in turn, adversely affects his ability to seek redress from the welfare bureaucracy.

"Moreover, important governmental interests are promoted by affording recipients a pre-termination evidentiary hearing. From its founding the Nation's basic commitment has been to foster the dignity and well-being of all persons within its borders. We have come to recognize that forces not within the control of the poor contribute to their poverty. This perception, against the background of our traditions, has significantly influenced the development of the contemporary public assistance system. Welfare, by meeting the basic demands of subsistence, can help bring within the reach of the poor the same opportunities that are available to others to participate meaningfully in the life of the community. At the same time, welfare guards against the societal malaise that may flow from a widespread sense of unjustified frustration and insecurity. Public assistance, then, is not merely charity, but a means to 'promote the Blessings of Liberty to ourselves and our Posterity.' The same governmental interests that counsel the provision of welfare, counsel as well its uninterrupted provision to those eligible to receive it; pre-termination evidentiary hearings are indispensable to that end....

"The requirement of a prior hearing doubtless involves some greater expense, and the benefits paid to ineligible recipients pending decision at the hearing probably cannot be recouped, since these recipients are likely to be judgment-proof. But the State is not without weapons to minimize these increased costs. Much of the drain on fiscal and administrative resources can be reduced by developing procedures for prompt pre-termination hearings and by skillful use of personnel and facilities. Indeed, the very provision for a post-termination evidentiary hearing in New York's Home Relief program is itself cogent evidence that the State recognizes the primacy of the public interest in correct eligibility determinations and therefore in the provision of procedural safeguards. Thus, the interest of the eligible recipient in uninterrupted receipt of public assistance, coupled with the State's interest that his payments not be erroneously terminated, clearly outweighs the State's competing concern to prevent any increase in its fiscal and administrative burdens. As the District Court correctly concluded, '[t]he stakes are simply too high for the welfare recipient, and the possibility of honest error too great, to allow termination of aid without giving the recipient a chance, if he so desires, to be fully informed of the case against him so that he may contest its basis and produce evidence in rebuttal.'...

"The city's procedures presently do not permit recipients to appear personally with or without counsel before the official who finally determines continued eligibility. Thus a recipient is not permitted to present evidence to that official orally, or to confront or cross-examine adverse witnesses. These omissions are fatal to the constitutional adequacy of the procedures."

Ethical Dimension

Should a hearing be required before *any* government decision is made? (The U.S. Supreme Court ruled in 1976 that a hearing was *not* required prior to the termination of Social Security disability benefits, where the termination was subject to later review, with retroactive payments made if the termination was incorrect. *Mathews* v. *Eldridge*, 424 U.S. 319.)

●

■ Preliminary Investigation and Administrative Discretion

For many agencies, a formal enforcement hearing occurs only after charges are filed by the agency's prosecuting arm. When a claim of an unfair labor practice is received at one of the field offices of the NLRB, for instance, the staff makes a preliminary investigation. If it decides that no violation has occurred, no charges are filed with the Board itself and no hearing occurs. The Office of the General Counsel of the NLRB has the final word on whether a complaint issues and a hearing is held. By statute, that decision is not reviewable, either by the Board itself or by the courts. The General Counsel might be persuaded to issue a complaint, but cannot be ordered to do so. Only if a complaint is issued will a hearing be held before one of the NLRB's administrative law judges. An agency, in other words, may be able to dismiss most cases by simply not filing a formal charge.

■ Settlement

As is true generally in both civil and criminal cases, a full hearing may not be necessary because the parties agree to a settlement of the agency proceeding. Many of the same factors are at work to encourage settlement of agency matters as exist in the courts: the difficulty of proof, the uncertainty of outcome, congestion and delay, and adverse publicity. For these and other reasons, the business or individual against whom the administrative charges have been brought may wish to settle. In general, settlements are encouraged here just as they are in the courts, and the prosecutorial staff of the agency has the same discretion in deciding to settle as would a prosecuting attorney in a criminal case.

Consent decrees are widely used by agencies as an enforcement tool. The defendant company does not actually admit to having engaged in any illegal conduct, but agrees not to do so in the future. The public is saved the expense of a formal hearing, but the improper conduct is stopped. For the company, it not only saves the expense and adverse publicity of a hearing; it also avoids any finding or admission of guilt. If individual civil cases are brought against the company later on in the courts, those plaintiffs must prove their entire case; the consent decree supplies no admission or evidence of guilt. For the rest of the industry, the agency has indicated that certain kinds of conduct will not be tolerated and that formal charges may be brought if such conduct is discovered. In this last sense, a consent decree can serve as a sort of preventive medicine for the whole industry. The FTC and the SEC, in particular, have made considerable use of consent decrees.

Many agencies use consent decrees as an enforcement tool.

E LEMENTS OF A TRIAL-TYPE HEARING

One of the claimed advantages for agency proceedings, as opposed to court trials, is that the agency can use a less formal hearing procedure. Since technical experts, rather than jurors, would be making the fact decisions, most of the technical rules of evidence would not be necessary. The experts would presumably be able to sort out which witnesses had first-hand knowledge and which were merely repeating what they had heard from others. While there is a certain informality to many agency hearings, minimal due process standards must still be followed to ensure a fair hearing.

Administrative due process includes many of the same elements as due process in criminal and civil court proceedings: adequate notice of the charges, the right to confront and cross-examine accusers, the right to counsel, the right to present evidence and arguments, and an impartial decision-maker who must decide the case on the basis of the evidence in the record. Because these elements may operate a bit differently in the administrative agency context, we now consider each in more detail. A final element of due process, the right to review of the initial decision, is considered in the next section. Figure 5–2 provides an outline of the steps in an agency's trial-type hearing.

■ Notice of Charges

Persons against whom agency action is to be taken must receive notice of the charges.

The defendant ("respondent') must be fully informed of the charges against it in time to prepare an answer to them. The courts have generally taken a liberal view of this requirement, however, and will hold that it has been satisfied if the respondent is made aware of the thrust of the agency's case at any time before it must submit its own proofs. The Administrative Procedure Act's rule that the respondent be given notice of "matters of fact and law asserted" by the agency has been

FIGURE 5–2
Procedure in an NLRB case

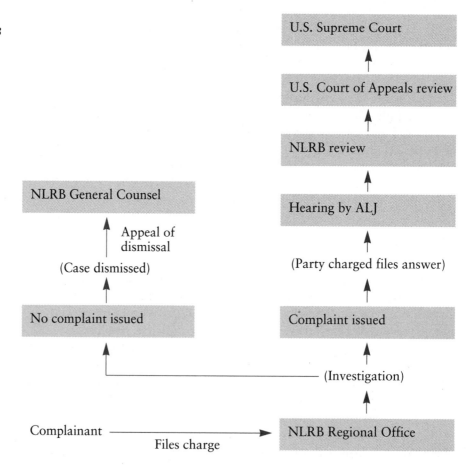

loosely interpreted. Generally, the agency's proofs may vary from the pleadings, and the pleadings can usually be amended to conform to the proofs. As a result, in many cases the actual nature of the charges is not known until the case is well under way.

Notice of an agency proceeding is usually sent by mail, unlike court process, where personal service is the preferred method. For parties whose interest in the proceeding is less direct, constructive notice in the *Federal Register* may be used. Where there is a statutory requirement to notify the public generally, TV ads and press releases are sufficient notice. Notice must be given to "indispensable parties," but that phrase is not always easy to define. Competitors may or may not be such. Where environmental and land use restrictions are at issue, it is difficult to draw geographical lines as to who is "indispensable." Courts generally have considerable discretion as to which "interested parties" will be allowed to participate in their proceedings.

■ Confrontation

Secret accusations are alien to our system of law. The accused is entitled to know who is making the charges, to hear the accuser testify, and to cross-examine the accuser and other adverse witnesses. The right of confrontation is one of our primary methods of getting at the truth. Justice Douglas outlined the dangers of secret accusations in *Peters* v. *Hobby*, 349 U.S. 331 (1955), a case in which Dr. Peters had been fired by the Public Health Service after questions had been raised as to his loyalty:

Dr. Peters was condemned by faceless informers, some of whom were not known even to the Board that condemned him. Some of these informers were not even under oath. None of them had to submit to cross-examination. None had to face Dr. Peters. So far as we or the Board know, they may be psychopaths or venal people...who revel in being informers. They may bear old grudges. Under cross-examination their stories might disappear like bubbles. Their whispered confidences might turn out to be yarns conceived by twisted minds or by people who, though sincere, have poor faculties of observation and memory.

For all these reasons, the concept of a fair hearing must include the right of confrontation and cross-examination. A related problem concerns the question of whether the hearing shall be public or private. The Sixth Amendment requires a speedy and public trial for criminal cases; is there a similar requirement for agency proceedings? In general, an agency is given considerable latitude in deciding on the format of its hearings, but there is generally a strong public policy argument in favor of open hearings. Secrecy in government provides the opportunity for abuse by government. In nearly all cases, the agencies have decided in favor of public hearings, even if some or all of the respondents want

An agency hearing must normally provide for the right to confront and to cross-examine witnesses.

closed hearings. Only where trade secrets or similar privileged evidence is involved would there be a good argument for closed hearings.

■ Counsel

Persons charged by an agency with a violation of the law must usually be given the right to counsel.

The right to representation by counsel is also deeply ingrained in our legal system. In criminal cases, not only does the defendant have the right to retain counsel of its own choosing, but free legal counsel must be provided if the defendant cannot afford to pay. Witnesses who are summoned to appear before grand juries, on the other hand, are not entitled to counsel, since they are not on trial. The grand jury is merely investigating to see whether a crime may have been committed and who may have committed it. Only when criminal charges are brought against a specific person or persons does the right to counsel arise. The problem in the agency setting is to determine when an agency is merely conducting a general investigation and when it is proceeding against a specific person. In light of the independent agencies' combination of functions, this is not always easy to do. If a formal complaint has been filed, the right to counsel should apply to the ensuing agency proceeding, whatever it is called. On the other hand, if the agency is simply engaged in gathering data about the regulated industry, those summoned to testify probably do not have to be given the right to counsel.

■ Defense Case

Inherent in the concept of a hearing is the presentation of both sides of the issues; indeed, that is the whole purpose of having a hearing. There is normally no dispute over the basic idea here, but disputes may arise over the extent to which the agency must assist the respondent in presenting its case.

In a sense, the agency's dilemma here is no different from that faced by a prosecutor in a criminal case. Is the primary function of that office merely prosecution, or is it making sure that justice is done? Is the officer primarily advocate or truth-seeker? In most specific terms, to what extent does the prosecutor have a duty to find, and produce, both sides of the case? This moral and legal dilemma is heightened for the multipurpose agency, which is functioning as both prosecutor and judge. The public interest would demand an obligation to find and produce all relevant information bearing on the proceeding. In practice, however, there is always the danger that the agency staff, in particular, may get swept up in prosecutorial zeal.

One specific area of concern relates to the agency's use of its subpoena power to compel testimony by witnesses requested by the respondent. The APA seems to sanction such subpoenas: "Agency subpoenas authorized by law shall be issued to any party upon request and, as may be required by rules of procedure, upon a statement or showing of general relevance and reasonable scope of the evidence sought." The APA generally tries to put the agency and the respondent on the same footing as to the ability to get data through subpoenas. Under the APA, all evidentiary requirements and privileges should apply equally to each side. While extensive delays through unending pre-hearing discovery need not be tolerated, the respondent would usually be able to force production of data shown to be relevant and reasonable in scope. Such data could include information in the agency's own files, too, unless it is classified or otherwise privileged.

■ Administrative Law Judge

The initial decision-maker for the agency, the trial examiner or hearing examiner, is now usually called an **administrative law judge** (ALJ). The title may be a bit more impressive, but the function is the same. This person makes the initial determination of what the facts are in the case, how the law applies to those facts, and what the disposition of the case will be.

Due process requires that the decider be unbiased and that the decision be based on evidence in the record. Of course, the ALJ should be disqualified where there is a demonstrated personal bias against a respondent, or a direct (or substantial indirect) financial interest in the outcome of the proceeding. Prior employment by the respondent would also normally result in disqualification. On the other hand, the fact that the ALJ has a particular philosophy about regulation would usually not be grounds for disqualification, any more than liberal or conservative judges are disqualified by their views. Some people continue to feel that the combination of functions within the agency inherently biases their proceedings, but this view has not prevailed in the courts. Unless there is evidence of improper consultations or influence in the particular case, the unification of functions within the agency as a whole will not be a sufficient basis for overturning the decision.

Due process means that the person deciding the case must be unbiased.

A more serious problem exists when the ALJ merely makes a recommended decision, which is then transmitted to the agency itself for final action. If the agency itself makes the decision based on a certified record, or if it hears only appeals from the ALJs' decisions, which are otherwise final, the responsibility for a decision *based on the record* is clear. But with the intermediate procedure, it is not clear that the person making the decision has indeed "mastered the record." With this procedure, the agency staff will usually prepare a memorandum which includes a summary of the record and proposed findings of fact, conclusions of law, and decision. The respondent may likewise submit recommendations, but there is a real danger that the agency may simply rely on its own staff memo in deciding the case. The staff memo is not made part of the record and it is not generally available to the respondent.

The danger under this intermediate procedure, in other words, is that the decision may be made without consideration of the whole record, on the basis of recommendations from only one side. As a solution to this problem, the Hoover Commission, which was established to study government operations, recommended that the ALJ's decisions be final. Appeals to the agency itself could occur on questions of law, matters of policy, or clearly erroneous findings of fact.

R EVIEW OF INITIAL DECISION

Part of due process is the opportunity for at least one level of review of the initial decision. In the administrative agency context, review may occur by the agency itself and/or by the courts.

Agency Review

The decision of an ALJ is generally reviewable by the agency.

Some of the problems involved in the division of authority between the ALJ and the agency itself have already been noted. There is no uniform rule on the exact division of functions between the two agency decision levels. What occurs is sometimes called a "split-level" trial decision, that is, both the ALJ and the agency really make fact decisions based on the record. Certainly in the majority of cases the agency would sustain the ALJ, but it could also reverse a dismissal of a complaint or a finding of a violation. Many agency statutes provide that the agency has the same decision power as if it had heard the case initially. Such language gives the ultimate responsibility for the *right* decision in the case, not just a review of whether the ALJ made a *possible* decision based on the record. The difference is vital to the scope of the review undertaken. The findings of the ALJ are entitled to special weight in evaluating the testimony of witnesses, since the ALJ saw and heard the witnesses. The agency may reverse its own ALJ, however, if the agency can explain why the original decision was wrong.

Judicial Review

Most agency decisions in contested cases can be reviewed by the courts.

Typically, agency decisions are reviewable by the courts. In some cases, the agency must ask for court enforcement of its orders; this provides a court review. Some agency statutes provide for court review of agency orders. Respondents may also seek court review by suing agency officials for damages, by asking for an injunction against agency action, or by seeking a declaratory judgment of the invalidity of the agency's statute or regulations. While matters requiring the exercise of administrative discretion may not be reviewable, there is a general presumption in favor of the reviewability of administrative actions. This presumption is even strong enough to overcome some statutory statements indicating agency actions are not reviewable. Some of the factors which a court may consider are the agency's need for discretion, the personal interests affected by the agency's action, the availability of other methods of preventing administrative abuse, and the relative expertise of the agency as opposed to the courts. Agencies have no special expertise in interpreting the law, for example, so such agency decisions are nearly always reviewable by a court.

STANDING, EXHAUSTION, AND RIPENESS

Agency actions may be challenged only by persons who have **standing** to do so. By the APA definition, this includes "any person suffering legal wrong because of any agency action, or adversely affected or aggrieved by such action within the meaning of the relevant statute." This requirement is intended to preclude actions by persons who wish to harass the agency, or who are merely curious, or who have no real stake in the outcome of the agency proceeding. The test for the court, then, is whether the person seeking review is "aggrieved in fact." Is the interest "arguably within the zone of interests protected or regulated by the statute or constitutional guarantee in question"? The court must find that the person seeking review has sustained an "injury in fact, economic or otherwise."

In general, a person affected by an agency proceeding is required to pursue all internal review procedures available within the agency before asking for court review. This requirement is called **exhaustion of administrative remedies.** This rule is usually also applied to challenges to the applicability of the agency's statute to the business in question or to the validity of the agency's complaint. Where the challenge is based on constitutional or jurisdictional grounds, however, there are many cases permitting review without exhaustion of administrative remedies. The courts thus retain considerable discretion in deciding whether or not to grant immediate review.

The **ripeness for review** requirement merely means that a genuine case or controversy has arisen, which demands court review. Historically, U.S. courts have refused to give advisory opinions on the interpretation of statutes in hypothetical situations which might arise. The courts have felt that they have enough real cases to decide; they don't need to concern themselves with hypotheticals. Also, the case or controversy requirement, like the standing requirement, ensures that the parties have a real stake in the outcome and are not simply wasting the court's time and everyone's money. Our courts do, however, issue **declaratory judgments,** which define the rights of the parties without ordering anyone to do anything. An insurance company might bring such an action to determine its liability under an existing policy, for instance. That would be a real case, and the parties would have something at stake. The *Lujan* case discusses several of the above points.

Persons wishing to have a court review an agency's decision must show that they are affected by it and that they have exhausted all review steps within the agency.

JUSTICE·UNDER

LUJAN V. NATIONAL WILDLIFE FEDERATION

110 S. Ct. 3177 (1990)

Facts: The national government owns about one-third of all the land in the United States. Various statutes have authorized private citizens to acquire ownership of, or rights in, these public lands. Congress has also authorized the president to "withdraw" public lands from these statutory programs and to "reserve" those lands for public use exclusively. To coordinate land-use policies, Congress in 1976 passed the Federal Land Policy and Management Act. The FLPMA established a general policy of multiple use of public lands. Pursuant to the FLPMA, the Secretary of the Interior (Lujan) and the Interior Department's Bureau of Land Management (BLM) conducted studies, classified public lands, and revoked some earlier presidential "withdrawals." More public lands were thus made available for multiple use.

National Wildlife Federation (NWF) filed this lawsuit in the U.S. District Court in the District of Columbia in 1985. NWF alleged that Lujan and his agency had violated the FLPMA, the National Environmental Policy Act, and the Administrative Procedure Act. NWF specifically objected to administrative actions that would have opened some lands to mining. The District Court granted a preliminary injunction against changing any classification in effect on January 4, 1981. The Court of Appeals affirmed. Hearing the case on the merits, the District Court granted Lujan's motion for summary judgment, since the NWF lacked standing to sue. The Court of Appeals reversed this decision. It felt that the affidavits of two NWF members, stating that they used land "in the vicinity" of the affected national lands, was enough to prevent a summary judgment. Lujan asked the Supreme Court for further review.

Issue: Does plaintiff (NWF) have standing to sue?

Decision: No, it does not. Judgment of the Court of Appeals is reversed.

Rule: A general statement that persons use land "in the vicinity of" the affected national lands is not sufficient to show that they were actually affected by decisions regarding the national lands.

Discussion: *By Justice* SCALIA:

"[NWF] does not contend that either the FLPMA or NEPA provides a private right of action for violations of its provisions. Rather [it] claims a right to judicial review under § 10(a) of the APA, which provides: 'A person suffering legal wrong because of agency action, or adversely affected or aggrieved by agency action within the meaning of a relevant statute, is entitled to judicial review thereof.'... This provision contains two separate requirements. First, the person claiming a right to sue must identify some 'agency action' that affects him in the specified fashion; it is judicial review 'thereof' to which he is entitled. The meaning of 'agency action'...is...'the whole or a part of an agency rule, order, license, sanction, relief, or the equivalent or denial thereof, or failure to act.'... When, as here, review is sought not pursuant to specific authorization in the substantive statute, but only under the general review provisions of the APA, the 'agency action' in question must be 'final agency action.'...

"Second, the party seeking review...must show that he has 'suffer[ed] legal wrong' because of the challenged agency action, or is 'adversely affected or aggrieved' by that action 'within the meaning of a relevant statute.' [NWF] does not assert that it has suffered 'legal wrong,' so we need only discuss the meaning of 'adversely affected or aggrieved...within the meaning of a relevant statute.'... [W]e have said that to be 'adversely affected or aggrieved...within the meaning' of a statute, the plaintiff must establish that the injury he complains of (*his* aggrievement, or the adverse effect *upon him*) falls within the 'zone of interests' sought to be protected by the statutory provision whose violation forms the legal basis for his complaint....

"Rule 56(e) [of the Federal Rules of Civil Procedure] provides: 'When a motion for summary judgment is made and supported as provided in this rule, an adverse party may not rest upon the mere allegations or denials on the adverse party's pleading, but the adverse party's response, by affidavits or as otherwise provided in this rule, must set forth specific facts showing that there is a genuine issue for trial. If the adverse party does not so respond, summary judgment, if appropriate, shall be entered against the adverse party....

"We assume, since it has been uncontested, that the allegedly affected interests set forth in the affidavits—'recreational use and aesthetic enjoyment'—are sufficiently related to the purposes of [NWF] that it meets the [standing] requirements...if any of its members do....

"We also think that whatever 'adverse effect' or 'aggrievement' is established by the affidavits was 'within the meaning of the relevant statute'.... The relevant statute, of course, is the statute whose violation is the [basis] of the complaint—both the

FLPMA and NEPA. We have no doubt that 'recreational use and aesthetic enjoyment' are among the *sorts* of interests those statutes were specifically designed to protect. The only issue, then, is whether the facts alleged in the affidavits showed that those interests of *Peterson and Erman* [the two individual NWF members] were actually affected.

"The Peterson affidavit averred; 'My recreational use and aesthetic enjoyment of federal lands, particularly those in the vicinity of South Pass—Green Mountain, Wyoming have been and continue to be adversely affected in fact by the unlawful actions of the Bureau and the Department.'... Erman's affidavit was substantially the same as Peterson's, with respect to all except the area involved; he claimed use of land 'in the vicinity of Grand Canyon National Par[k], the Arizona Strip (Kanab Plateau), and the Kaibab National Forest.'...

"At the margins there is some room for debate as to how 'specific' must be the 'specific facts' that Rule 56(e) requires in a particular case. But where the fact in question is the one put in issue...—whether one of [NWF's] members has been, or is threatened to be, 'adversely affected or aggrieved' by Government action—Rule 56(e) is assuredly not satisfied by averments which state only that one of [NWF's] members uses unspecified portions of an immense tract of territory, on some portions of which mining activity has occurred or probably will occur by virtue of the governmental action. It will not do to 'presume' the missing facts because without them the affidavits would not establish the injury that they generally allege....

"As we discussed earlier, the 'Land Withdrawal Review Program' is not an identifiable action or event. With regard to alleged deficiencies in providing information and permitting public participation, as with regard to the other illegalities alleged in the complaint, [NWF] cannot demand a general judicial review of the BLM's day-to-day operations."

Ethical Dimension

Is it fair for a governmental agency to take action without substantial input from interested citizens?

●

SCOPE OF JUDICIAL REVIEW

As administrative agencies have become more established and more professional, courts have become more reluctant to second-guess their decisions. Courts will still exercise their review power on questions of constitutional standards, statutory interpretation, and procedural fairness. Arbitrary, capricious, or excessive agency action will of course be overturned. Other than these obvious cases, courts may also reverse agency decisions in accordance with certain established rules for review.

In general, the agency's findings of fact must be sustained if they are supported by substantial evidence in the record, taken as a whole. An agency reviewing the decision of its own ALJ is generally free to second-guess the ALJ's interpretation of the facts and to make what it feels is the "right" decision. A court reviewing an agency's decision is not supposed to substitute its judgment of what is the right decision for that of the agency. The agency's decision should be sustained if it is a *possible* decision, based on the record taken as a whole. The decision can be reversed if the agency failed to exercise its expertise, if it made unwarranted assumptions, or if the decision is not based on substantial evidence. As the Supreme Court has defined substantial evidence, it "is more than a scintilla, and must do more than create a suspicion of the existence of the fact to be established. 'It means such relevant evidence as a reasonable mind might accept as adequate to support a conclusion,'...and it must be enough to justify, if the trial were to a jury, a refusal to direct a verdict when the conclusion sought to be drawn from it is one of fact for a jury."

Agency decisions are normally upheld if they are supported by substantial evidence in the record.

The method of court review, the reputation of the agency for fairness and expertise, the amount of discretion given to the agency, and the language of the statute itself may also impact on the scope of review exercised in particular cases. The *American Textile* case, which appears later in this chapter, discusses the "substantial evidence" test as the standard for judicial review of an agency decision.

■ Role of Company Counsel

Administrative agency procedure is both different from and similar to court procedure. It is complex enough that counsel should be involved from the beginning of any significant proceeding. Agencies are required to abide by certain minimum constitutional and statutory standards, and court review is generally available to cure agency excesses. Where a company's business is involved with an agency on a regular basis, counsel should review the company's policies and procedures periodically to try to discover possible short-cuts which might be developed for dealings with the agency. All management personnel should have some appreciation of the agency's procedures, so they know what costs and delays may be involved in dealing with the agency.

■ PROBLEMS AND CRITICISMS

Regulation of business through independent administrative agencies has produced strong criticism, both from within and from without the business community. Questions have been raised about the functioning of these agencies from their inception, and many problems continue today.

■ Delegation of Legislative Authority

Historically, the major constitutional question which had to be settled was whether legislative power, assigned by the Constitution to Congress, could be delegated to another body. The courts originally said that the power to make a law could not be delegated, only the power to provide administrative rules for its implementation. Courts today recognize, however, that legislative power does need to be delegated in some situations. The question remains: when, and on what terms?

Courts will now permit broad delegations of legislative authority, provided that the statute doing so includes adequate standards or guidelines for administrative action. A statute simply giving an agency legislative power, with no limits and with no statement of the policy objectives to be served, would most likely still be held unconstitutional by the courts. The courts have not formulated a hard and fast rule as to how precise the statutory guidelines have to be, but they have developed some of the factors that may be considered in testing the statute.

There are some limits on how much of its legislative authority Congress can delegate to any agency.

A court deciding such a case would certainly look at the industry or area being regulated—how much technical expertise is needed in this field? The more technical and less legal the case, the more discretion is likely to be permitted to the agency. Some areas, such as rate-setting in the power industry, have traditionally required and been given a wide range of discretion. New and complex technologies may also require considerable room for the agency's expertise. Where a statute uses language that has been previously interpreted by the courts, a similar delegation is likely to be upheld. If the agency is required by the statute to hold hearings at which opposing views can be presented, it is likely to be permitted more discretion than if it were making its decisions after internal discussion only. In general, the federal courts have been more liberal in permitting delegations than have state courts. A state court could still take a strict view of legislative delegations under the state's own constitution.

■ Democracy and Administrative Responsibility

There is an inherent conflict between democratic government and the existence of unelected, independent administrators. The debate over how best to control our administrative colossus, or whether it is in fact controllable at all, has been an ongoing one for at least fifty years. Carl J. Friedrich, a well-respected political scientist, thought that it was enough to have a dedicated and professional group of administrators who acted in accordance with their own set of standards. In contrast, Herman Finer, also an eminent political scientist, believed that we could not rely on such professionalism, but should provide institutional structures to ensure administrative responsibility and accountability. To quote Montesquieu, the French theorist who is generally given credit for originating the separation of powers concept: "Virtue itself hath need of limits." In a democracy, in other words, "good government is not an acceptable substitute for self government." We cannot simply rely on the good will and sound discretion of the administrative professionals. They work for us. We need mechanisms to tell them what we want them to do, and to hold them accountable if they fail to do it.

Exactly what form these accountability mechanisms might take is not clear. Many agencies already have an internal complaint procedure; some have a person or board patterned after the Swedish "ombudsman." The ombudsman generally has authority to receive and to mediate complaints against the agency. Perhaps the most widespread suggestion is to have a more activist oversight by the various congressional committees in charge of each regulatory area. Certainly, the Governmental Accounting Office has the capacity to produce studies of the effectiveness of the various agencies, which might then be used to influence public opinion and Congress. It may be that we are entering the twilight of the independent regulatory commission and that most commissions will be abolished, or at least placed under the control of the president, who is directly responsible to us every four years. One increasingly popular mechanism is the sunset law provision. Included in the statute which creates the agency, a sunset law provision forces the agency to justify its existence and its regulatory program to Congress periodically. If the agency cannot do so, and Congress fails to pass legislation re-authorizing the agency, it is automatically abolished.

Agencies need to be held accountable.

▇ Institutional Bias

A related problem concerns the combined structure of the independent agency: how can one expect a fair hearing from the same person that is bringing the enforcement proceeding to begin with? Originally, there was widespread belief that such a combination of duties violated one of the most basic elements of due process—an unbiased decision-maker. Gradually, as the agency form has become more familiar, much of this fear has dissipated. As the agencies' membership has changed, business has learned that its interests may be taken into account by more sympathetic administrators. Today, most observers probably do not see bias due to combined functions as the most serious problem existing in administrative agency regulation.

■ Administrative "Overfeasance"

Some administrators can be criticized for not doing their jobs (nonfeasance), or for doing them poorly (misfeasance). What seems to be an even greater problem, and even more significant than the "bias" just discussed, was described by Professor Finer as "overfeasance"—going beyond assigned duties. Persons in an institutional setting may be inclined to engage in empire-building. How much more likely is this process to occur in the agency setting, where the "experts" have been charged by Congress with the duty of "cleaning up" a marketplace mess? Both the academic literature and the popular press abound with examples of agency arrogance, insensitivity to real-world problems, total unconcern with the costs of compliance, and similar attitudinal deficiencies. Taxpayers' dollars are awarded by an agency for a study of the frisbee ($375,000), or for a cotton subsidy to the Queen of England ($68,000). Consumers must pay greatly increased prices for fresh tomatoes when an agency official decides that all tomatoes sold in the U. S. must be of minimum size, and thereby bars up to half of Mexico's tomato crop from sale here. Businesses (and all of us to whom the costs are passed along) are forced to pay billions of dollars simply to comply with the paperwork costs imposed by the regulators.

Cost-benefit analyses are used to evaluate some agency regulations.

Requiring agencies to do cost-benefit analyses would help solve some of these problems. However, there are inherent limitations in cost-benefit analyses, too. One obvious problem is establishing a price for a human life which is saved by a safety regulation—just how much is a person "worth" in dollars and cents? How about the "value" of a wetland, or a redwood forest which has been growing for hundreds of years? While it may be difficult to put a price tag on many intangible values, forcing a weighing of objectives and costs does at least make an agency aware of the possible adverse impact of its actions. The *American Textile* case discusses some of these cost-benefit issues.

JUSTICE · UNDE

AMERICAN TEXTILE MANUFACTURERS INSTITUTE, INC. V. DONOVAN

452 U.S. 490 (1981)

Facts: Passed in 1970, the Occupational Safety and Health Act is intended to "assure so far as possible every working man and woman in the Nation safe and healthful working conditions." The Occupational Safety and Health Administration (OSHA) is established under the Secretary of Labor (Donovan) to enforce the Act. OSHA is authorized to adopt standards for the use of hazardous materials in the workplace. In 1978, OSHA adopted a standard for exposure to cotton dust, which is generated by the manufacture of cotton products. When inhaled by the worker, cotton dust can cause a number of respiratory problems.

The American Textile Manufacturers Institute (ATMI) challenged the adoption of the standard, claiming that OSHA was required to prove a reasonable relationship between the costs and benefits of its standard. The Secretary of Labor claims that the act requires OSHA to adopt a standard which will eliminate any significant risk of substantial health impairment, and that a standard need only be economically and technically feasible. The Court of Appeals for the District of Columbia agreed with Donovan. ATMI asked for further review by the U.S. Supreme Court.

Issue: Does the Occupational Safety and Health Act require a reasonable relationship between the costs of a safety standard and its benefits? Was the agency's standard supported by substantial evidence in the record as a whole?

Decision: No, to the first question. Yes, to the second. Judgment for the Secretary of Labor is affirmed.

Rule: The act requires safety standards to provide the maximum protection which is feasible. A Court of Appeals ruling on the substantial evidence test should be reversed only where the Supreme Court thinks the test has been grossly misapplied.

Discussion: *By Justice BRENNAN:*

"The plain meaning of the word 'feasible' supports [Donovan's] interpretation of the statute. According to Webster's Third New International Dictionary of the English Language 831 (1976), 'feasible' means 'capable of being done, executed, or effected.'... Thus, § 6(b)(5) directs the Secretary to issue the standard that 'most adequately assures...that no employee will suffer material impairment of health,' limited only by the extent to which this is 'capable of being done.' In effect, then...Congress itself defined the basic relationship between costs and benefits, by placing the 'benefit' of worker health above all other considerations save those making attainment of this 'benefit' unachievable. Any standard based on a balancing of costs and benefits by the Secretary that strikes a different balance than that struck by Congress would be inconsistent with the command set forth in [the Act]. Thus, cost-benefit analysis by OSHA is not required by the statute because feasibility analysis is....

"Section 6(f) of the Act provides that '[t]he determinations of the Secretary shall be conclusive if supported by substantial evidence in the record considered as a whole.'... [ATMI] claim[s]

(1) that OSHA underestimated the financial costs necessary to meet the Standard's requirements; and (2) that OSHA incorrectly found that the Standard would not threaten the economic viability of the cotton industry....

"OSHA derived its cost estimate for industry compliance with the Cotton Dust Standard after reviewing two financial analyses.... The agency carefully explored the assumptions and methodologies underlying the conclusions of each of these studies. From this exercise the agency was able to build upon conclusions from each which it found reliable and explain its process for choosing its cost estimate....

"Therefore,...we cannot say that the Court of Appeals in this case 'misapprehended or grossly misapplied' the substantial evidence test when it found that 'OSHA reasonably evaluated the cost estimates before it, considered criticisms of each, and selected suitable estimates of compliance costs.'...

"The Court of Appeals found that the agency 'explained the economic impact it projected for the textile industry,' and that OSHA has 'substantial support in the record for its...findings of economic feasibility for the textile industry.' On the basis of the whole record, we cannot conclude that the Court of Appeals 'misapprehended or grossly misapplied' the substantial evidence test."

Ethical Dimension

Is it ethical for a firm to argue that it should not be required to give its workers the maximum feasible health protection?

■ Personnel Problems

Personnel problems exist in any enterprise. Indeed, one of the key ingredients in managerial success is the ability to select, train, and motivate employees. Two rather different personnel problems exist in the agencies, and to some extent, throughout government service.

Appropriate controls over agency personnel are necessary to ensure responsible behavior.

The civil service system was adopted to prevent the excesses of the spoils system—politically motivated hirings and firings. As the civil service system has developed, it has made promotion or discipline for any reason other than "time in grade" very difficult. The *Wall Street Journal* reported the case of a $25,000-a-year staff economist who was actually doing no work for his agency. When questioned by one of President's Carter's new appointees at the agency, the economist admitted that all he was doing was writing his own free-lance magazine articles. In response to the Carter appointee's statement that he would "spend whatever time it takes" to solve the problem, the economist said: "You'll see. I'll wait you out just like I did all the others." The *Journal* used this story to illustrate its conclusion that the national government has become "a bureaucracy nearly devoid of incentives and largely beyond anyone's control." The *Journal's* editors are not alone in feeling that there is too little positive incentive to do a good job and too little disincentive from doing a poor one. If the agencies are to receive the sort of professional staff work which is needed to perform their complex regulatory tasks, civil service rules must allow for appropriate personnel controls.

A totally different sort of problem exists with respect to the top level administrative personnel. Since these are appointive positions, there tends to be considerable turnover. While the president may not be able to remove all of these persons overnight, they need not be reappointed at the end of their terms, either. In many cases, these top managers take a considerable pay cut when they are recruited from industry. Since they usually view the government job as temporary, they do not want to sever all their industry ties—or poison the waters from which they may be drinking again in a few years. The result is a sort of symbiosis between the regulators and the regulated, a particularly likely occurrence where the agency regulates only one industry. The potential danger is that this friendliness may lead to a less vigorous enforcement of the agency's regulations. At the extreme, the agency may be "captured" by the industry it was set up to regulate, as top personnel shuffle back and forth.

Again, the stories are legion. A GAO report in 1974 prompted a congressional investigation in which nineteen Federal Power Commission officials were found to be in "technical" violation of conflict-of-interest rules. Others under investigation included seven administrative law judges, including the chief judge, who owned forty-five shares of "prohibited" stock in a railroad company. In 1976, what was described as a "mini-Watergate" occurred at the Federal Energy Administration, when the FEA and the natural gas industry withheld information from Congress, and the Deputy Administrator's testimony was described by one Congressman as "an arrogant pack of lies." Newton Minow, former FCC chairman, who described television as a "vast wasteland," went to work for a Chicago law firm which represented CBS, one of the main targets of his earlier criticism. Manuel Cohen, proponent of tough enforcement as chairman of the SEC, brought a number of SEC staff lawyers with him to a Washington law firm, where he negotiated a settlement with the SEC on behalf of Northrop, which was accused of making illegal overseas payments. Nicholas Katzenbach, former Attorney General, became general counsel for IBM and negotiated a favorable settlement of the antitrust charges filed against it. As the bloom wore off the government's efforts

The interchange of top personnel between a regulatory agency and the regulated industry may create the appearance of less vigorous law enforcement.

to regulate energy, there was an exodus from the Department of Energy to private industry. James Schlesinger, the former Secretary, became an energy consultant to Lehman Brothers. Another former energy "czar," Frank Zarb, became a partner in Lazard Freres and the cofounder of a new energy corporation. And so it goes. Not even President Reagan's ad hoc committee of top corporate executives, the Private Sector Survey on Cost Control, was immune from this phenomenon. Executives from Dow Chemical studied the EPA; insurance managers studied social security; defense contractors studied the military; agribusiness executives studied programs in the Agriculture Department. Such use of persons with direct conflicts of interest makes it difficult for the public to accept the validity of the commission's findings.

THE FUTURE OF AGENCY REGULATION

It has been suggested several times in this chapter that the high point of regulation by independent agencies has passed. Deregulation and sunset laws are now the hot topics of public debate. It seems quite unlikely, however, that we will ever return to the days of the Robber Barons and the "public-be-damned" attitude of the late 1800s and the early 1900s. Shareholders, employees, consumers, and the public as a whole are too sophisticated to allow repeal of all protective regulations. If an agency does not file complaints, competitors or other affected private persons may do so. Even if we agree with former President Reagan that we want the government "off our backs and out of our pockets," that does not mean we are willing to accept adulterated food, worthless drugs, dangerous and shoddy products, or poisoned air and water. Somewhere between these extremes there must be a viable compromise, a level of regulation which is technically feasible, economically sustainable, and politically acceptable. Finding that balance is one of the major challenges of both business and government as we proceed toward the twenty-first century.

REVIEW

Business activities in the United States are heavily regulated by a variety of administrative agencies. Independent boards and commissions such as the NLRB and the FCC, as well as various agencies under the cabinet departments are involved in the regulatory process.

Agencies investigate to discover problems and violations. Many of them have rule-making, or legislative authority. All of them try to enforce the laws. They are themselves subject to various financial, personnel, and political controls by the courts, the legislature, and the executive.

To try to ensure fairness in agency activities, due process requirements are imposed on agencies. Minimum constitutional standards must be met before agency action can be taken. In addition, many agency enforcement proceedings are subject to the requirements of the Administrative Procedure Act. Where a trial-type hearing is required, the person accused of a violation must be notified of the charges, given the right to confront the accuser and the right to present a defense case, with the assistance of legal counsel. The hearing officer or administrative law judge must be unbiased, and there must be an opportunity for court review of the decision.

Over the years, there has been much criticism of agency activities. Some of these charges may be valid; others may not. There seems little likelihood that all agency regulation will end. Business needs to work with government to ensure that needed regulations are fair and effective.

REVIEW QUESTIONS AND PROBLEMS

1. What is meant by the "substantial evidence" standard for judicial review of administrative action? Why is this rule important to business firms?

2. What is the difference between an agency's "procedural rules," "interpretive rules," and "legislative rules"?

3. Why is the Equal Access to Justice Act important to business?

4. What is the scope of an agency's subpoena power? Why is this issue significant to businesses?

5. What is involved in a "trial-type" agency hearing? When is the agency required to hold one?

6. Why is the right of confrontation of witnesses important in agency proceedings?

7. Seniors United is an organization which was formed to protect the rights of older citizens. The Medicaid program of the national government provides money to states that pay hospital and medical expenses for poor people, many of whom are elderly. Under this program, the amount of assistance given to a person depends on that person's own financial resources; the more personal wealth, the lower the Medicaid payments. Some states' regulations provide that the personal wealth of a claimant's spouse will also be counted as available to that claimant. Seniors United filed a lawsuit challenging these regulations, claiming that an individual hearing is required for each claimant. How should this lawsuit be decided?

8. A state established a Public Utilities Commission (PUC) to regulate all public utility companies operating in the state (electricity, natural gas, heating oil, telephones, and similar utilities). To protect the environment by discouraging excess use of fossil fuels, the PUC adopted a regulation which prohibited advertising by power companies. Burning Tree Power Company (an electric utility) filed a lawsuit claiming this regulation was invalid. Should this agency regulation be upheld? Explain.

9. To stimulate the national economy, Congress passed a statute creating the National Recovery Administration and authorizing it to adopt industry-wide regulations which would "remove obstructions to the free flow of commerce" and "promote cooperative action among trade groups in the various industries."

Once set up, the NRA did in fact adopt such regulations for several industries, including the poultry industry. Quick-Chick, Inc., a chicken processor, was prosecuted for violating several of these regulations. Quick-Chick claimed that the regulations were unconstitutional. What result, and why?

10. A state university (E.S.U.) is governed by a Board of Regents. The state has an Open Meetings Act which requires that most official meetings of governmental bodies must be open to the press and the public. As part of its search for a new university president, the E.S.U. Board of Regents held private meetings of small groups of the Board (never a majority of the seven members). Candidates for the job were interviewed at these meetings, and the candidates' qualifications were then discussed. All seven members of the Board then held a public meeting at which they announced they had selected Hermoine as the new university president. The local newspaper and several students filed a court action challenging the legality of the Board's action under the Open Meetings Act. What should happen in this case. and why?

SUGGESTIONS FOR FURTHER READING

Adler, Klitzman & Mann, "Shaping Up Federal Agencies: A Basic Training Program for Regulators," *Journal of Law & Politics* (Winter 1990): 343.

Bagby, "Administrative Investigations: Preserving a Reasonable Balance Between Agency Powers and Target Rights," *American Business Law Journal* 23 (Fall 1985): 319.

Singer, "Due Process and Student Suspension—Goss v. Lopez," *American Business Law Journal* 13 (Fall 1975): 266.

Spiller, "Politicians, Interest Groups, and Regulators: A Multiple-Principals Agency Theory of Regulation, or 'Let Them Be Bribed'," *Journal of Law & Economics* (April 1990): 65.

6
PUBLIC
WRONGS
AND
PRIVATE
WRONGS

"Due process of law does not have a fixed meaning.... Representing a profound attitude of fairness between man and man, and more particularly between the individual and government, 'due process' is composed of history, reason, the past course of decisions, and stout confidence in the strength of the democratic faith which we profess. Due process is not a mechanical instrument. It is not a yardstick. It is a delicate process of adjustment inescapably involving the exercise of judgment by those whom the Constitution entrusted with the unfolding of the process."

Justice Felix Frankfurter

LEARNING OBJECTIVES: After you have studied this chapter, you should be able to:

EXPLAIN the difference between a crime and a tort.

DISCUSS the major constitution limitations on criminal law and procedure.

IDENTIFY the major areas of potential tort liability for businesses.

DEFINE the major defenses against liability for negligent torts.

DISCUSS the potential tort liability of sellers of professional services.

183

P REVIEW: CRIMES, TORTS, AND PERSONS LIABLE

Like other members of our society, businesses and their employees might commit wrongful acts. Wrongs might be committed by a business organization against its employees and by employees against the business. Wrongs might also be committed against third parties during the course of business operations. Finally, wrongs such as fraudulent failure to pay taxes might be committed against society as a whole. This chapter covers both the nature of the acts which are defined as crimes and torts and the procedures for trying a person accused of committing a crime.

Crimes and Torts

Crime and tort overlap.

The legal areas of crime and tort overlap. Many **crimes** (wrongs against society as a whole) also involve a **tort** (a wrong against a specific victim). The wrongdoer can be prosecuted by the state government or the national government for the wrong against society. Our legal system keeps this case separate from the private lawsuit which can be brought by the victim for tort damages. An unjustified physical attack against another person, for example, is both a crime (assault and battery) and a tort (also called assault and battery). Counterfeiting money is a crime against national law, but no tort has been committed unless some of the counterfeit money is passed along to an unknowing victim in place of the real thing. Making false statements about someone's reputation or behavior is the tort of libel (if written) or the tort of slander (if oral), but there is usually no criminal offense involved. Thus, a wrongful act may be a crime against national law, a crime against state law, and a tort—or only one or two of these.

Vicarious Liability

As we will discuss in more detail in Chapter 9, persons who have agents or employees working for them may be held civilly liable for the wrongful acts of those representatives. If the wrongful act was done while the agent or employee was doing the assigned job, the person for whom the work was being done, as well as the agent or employee, is liable. This sort of liability, called **vicarious liability**, is imposed just because of the relationship between the two persons; it does not require proof that "the boss" actually did anything wrong. Vicarious liability is usually imposed for torts by agents and employees.

Vicarious liability is usually not imposed for crimes, only for torts.

As a rule, no one can be held criminally liable just because of the conduct of another person. Most crimes require proof of criminal intent. The person committing the criminal act has that intent, but usually intent cannot be transferred to another person. Of course, if one person ordered another to commit a crime, or counseled it, or helped plan it, both persons would be prosecuted. Some regulatory statutes impose criminal penalties (usually only fines) for violations, without the government's having to prove a specific intent to violate the statute. A store selling packages that did not state the correct weight of the contents is guilty of violating state law even if the weight shortage is simply a mistake. For this sort of regulatory violation, managers and other officers of the business may be held liable for personal fines, in addition to the fines against the business.

CRIMINAL LAW

As noted above, criminal acts may be committed during the course of business operations. Most of these are based on fraud and trickery rather than force and violence.

Felonies and Misdemeanors

Serious crimes (usually defined as those for which a prison term of one year or more, or the death penalty, may be imposed) are called **felonies**. Less serious crimes, for which punishment is usually a fine or short-term confinement in a local jail, are called **misdemeanors**. Both types can be found in national criminal law, as well as in criminal law of the states. In addition, the U.S. Constitution defines the crime of treason as waging war against the U.S., or giving its enemies aid and comfort.

Felonies typically include crimes which involve force and violence, thus creating the threat of serious physical injury to other persons. Murder, burglary, armed robbery, arson and the like would be defined as felonies in most states. Misdemeanors include such offenses as driving a motor vehicle too fast, or disturbing the peace by making excessive amounts of noise.

Businesses may be the victims in crimes such as robbery or burglary, but would normally not be committing crimes of this sort.

White Collar Crimes

The phrase **"white collar crime"** describes the kind of wrong based on fraud and cheating, rather than on force. Because these crimes typically occur in business/commercial situations, they are labelled "white collar." The bank robber who uses a gun and forces the bank tellers to hand over money is committing a crime of force. The bank employee who secretly steals a few "samples" is also committing a crime (the white-collar crime of embezzlement), even though no force is being used against another human being. Even the use for personal gain of secret information about one's company by trading in the company's stock, is a criminal offense (insider trading).

White collar crimes normally involve fraud rather than force.

Crimes involving computers have become an increasingly common problem for businesses. Since computers are so widely used to store information and to transfer data and money, there are many new opportunities for theft. Criminals trained in computer use may be able to steal or to destroy data by wrongfully accessing someone's files. Money may be illegally transferred out of someone's account. Wrongful access to the computer running a state lottery might enable the criminals to print out fake tickets containing the winning numbers. Computer crimes may be prosecuted under general criminal statutes prohibiting theft and embezzlement or under special statutes outlawing wrongful computer access and the like. Computer crime is difficult to detect and also difficult to prosecute.

White collar crime would also encompass violations of various regulatory statutes by businesses and their managers. Included here would be crimes under the environmental laws, the packaging and labelling laws, the computer-privacy laws, the business-registration laws, and similar statutes. In the following case, Acme Markets and its president (Park) were accused of violating the national Pure Food and Drug Act, which is one of the few criminal statutes that do not require specific criminal intent.

U.S. V. PARK

421 U.S. 658 (1975)

Facts: Park was president of Acme Markets, Inc., which owns and operates 12 food warehouses and 874 retail stores. Acme has 36,000 employees. The U.S. Food and Drug Administration sent Acme and Park a notice that two of its warehouses were unsanitary. Park told the warehouse managers to clean their buildings. Some cleaning was done, but there were still problems when the FDA inspector came back to check. Violations were then issued against both Acme and Park. Acme pleaded guilty. After trial, Park was found guilty as charged. He appealed.

Issue: Can a corporate CEO be held criminally liable for the company's regulatory violations?

Decision: Yes. Trial court conviction is affirmed.

Rule: Any corporate employee who has a responsible role in the regulatory violation can be held criminally liable.

Discussion: *By Chief Justice* BURGER:

"The rule [that corporate employees who have a responsible share in the furtherance of the transaction which the statute outlaws are subject to the criminal provision of the Act] was not formulated in a vacuum...[T]he principle had been recognized that a corporate agent, through whose act, default, or omission the corporation committed a crime, was himself guilty individually of that crime. The principle has been applied whether or not the crime required consciousness of wrongdoing, and it has been applied not only to those corporate agents who themselves committed the criminal act, but also to those who by virtue of their managerial positions or other similar relations to the act could be deemed responsible for its commission...."

[In this case, by his own admission, Mr. Park was responsible for "any result which occurs in our company," since he was the CEO.]

Ethical Dimension

Is it fair to hold a CEO criminally liable for anything that goes wrong within the corporation? Was Park meeting his moral responsibility by delegating the clean-up to the same managers who were responsible for the problem in the first place?

Courts (and most members of the public) generally feel that cheating someone out of some money, or violating a regulation, is a less serious matter than assaulting someone with a knife or a gun. Persons convicted of serious, violent crimes will frequently receive prison sentences. White collar criminals typically have to pay fines and to perform community service, but have usually not been sent to prison. There is some evidence that this approach is changing. Blatant violators of the antitrust laws or the environmental laws now stand a good chance of going to prison. Professionals who are required to be licensed, such as lawyers and doctors, may lose their right to practice their profession when convicted of a serious crime.

■ Constitutional Limits on Criminal Law

In addition to the procedural requirements discussed in the next section, the U.S Constitution also contains limits on what sort of conduct can be made criminal. Both the national government and the states are prohibited from infringing on First Amendment rights and similar personal freedoms. Criminal laws which do so can be challenged as unconstitutional by defendants accused of violating them.

To be constitutionally valid, a criminal law must also clearly state the conduct which is being prohibited. A reasonable person must be able to determine what kinds of acts are wrongful, so those actions can

Criminal statutes must be unambiguous so everyone can know what is prohibited.

be avoided. If the criminal statute is vague and ambiguous, it will usually be declared unconstitutional. In the following Supreme Court case, the criminal defendant [R.A.V.] raised both these issues against the St. Paul city ordinance under which he was being prosecuted.

R.A.V. V. CITY OF ST. PAUL, MINNESOTA

60 U.S.L.W. 4667 (1992)

Facts: The city of St. Paul adopted an ordinance which prohibited the display of any symbol which "arouses anger, alarm, or resentment in others on the basis of race, color, creed, religion or gender." The ordinance specifically prohibited Nazi swastikas and burning crosses.

In the "predawn hours" of June 21, 1990, R.A.V. and several other teenagers taped several broken chair legs together in the form of a cross. They then soaked the cross with a flammable liquid and set it on fire on the lawn of an African-American family, across the street from R.A.V.'s house. R.A.V. was charged with violation of "bias-crime" ordinance, as well as several other crimes. R.A.V. filed a motion with the trial court for dismissal of the charge under the ordinance. He claimed the ordinance was "overbroad," and that it regulated the "content" of "speech." The trial court granted his motion and dismissed that charge. The Minnesota Supreme Court reversed that decision. The state supreme court said that the ordinance only prohibited "fighting words," which the U.S. Supreme Court had previously said that a state or city could do. The state supreme court said that the content-regulation was valid here because the ordinance was narrowly drawn to meet a compelling state interest. R.A.V. asked the U.S. Supreme Court for further review.

Issue: Can the government prohibit some types of "offensive" speech, but not others?

Decision: No. Judgment of the Minnesota Supreme Court is reversed.

Rule: The government can not regulate speech on the basis of its content, prohibiting some types and permitting other types.

Discussion: *By Justice SCALIA:*

"The First Amendment generally prevents government from proscribing speech...or even expressive conduct...because of disapproval of the ideas expressed. Content-based regulations are presumptively invalid.... From 1791 to the present, however, our society, like other free but civilized societies, has permitted restrictions upon the content of speech in a few limited areas, which are 'of such slight social value as a step to truth that any benefit that may be derived from them is clearly outweighed by the social interest in order and morality.'... We have recognized that 'the freedom of speech' referred to by the First Amendment does not include a freedom to disregard these traditional limitations.... Our decisions since the 1960's have narrowed the scope of the traditional categorical exceptions for defamation...and for obscenity..., but a limited categorical approach has remained an important part of our First Amendment jurisprudence....

"[T]he exclusion of 'fighting words' from the scope of the First Amendment simply means that, for purposes of that Amendment, the unprotected features of the words are, despite their verbal character, essentially a 'nonspeech' element of communication. Fighting words are thus analogous to a sound truck: Each is...a 'mode of speech'...; both can be used to convey an idea; but neither has, in and of itself, a claim upon the First Amendment. As with the sound truck, however, so also with fighting words: The government may not regulate use based on hostility—or favoritism—towards the underlying message expressed....

"When the basis for the content discrimination consists entirely of the very reason the entire class of speech at issue is proscribable, no significant danger of idea or viewpoint discrimination exists. Such a reason, having been adjudged neutral enough to support exclusion of the entire class of speech from First Amendment protection, is also neutral enough to form the basis of distinction within the class. To illustrate: A state might choose to prohibit only that obscenity which is the most patently offensive in its prurience—i.e., that which involves the most lascivious displays of sexual activity. But it may not prohibit, for example, only that obscenity which includes offensive political messages....

"Applying these principles to the St. Paul ordinance, we conclude that, even as narrowly construed by the Minnesota Supreme Court, the ordinance is facially unconstitutional. Although the phrase in the ordinance, 'arouses anger, alarm or resentment in others,' has been limited by the Minnesota Supreme Court's construction to reach only those symbols or displays that amount to 'fighting words,' the remaining, unmodified terms make clear that the ordinance applies only to 'fighting words' that insult, or provoke violence, 'on the basis of race, color, creed, religion or gender.' Displays containing abusive invective, no matter how vicious or severe, are permissible unless they are addressed to one of the specified disfavored topics. Those who wish to use 'fighting words' in connection with other ideas—to express hostility, for example, on the basis of political affiliation, union membership, or homosexuality—are not covered. The First Amendment does not permit St. Paul to impose special prohibitions on those speakers who express views on disfavored subjects."

Ethical Dimension

Doesn't government have duty to protect its citizens against the sort of "hate speech" involved in this case? Is the Supreme Court saying that government cannot do so?

C RIMINAL PROCEDURE

Our system surrounds the accused with legal protections. Both the national and the state constitutions list many specific procedural steps which must be followed, as well as an overall requirement of due process.

■ Due Process of Law

Criminal cases must follow fair procedures.

The original and basic meaning of *due process of law* is "fair procedure." In the context of a criminal trial, that means the accused must be notified of the charges, must have the assistance of counsel, must be permitted to argue a defense case and to confront and cross-examine the accusers, must be judged impartially on the evidence presented, and must have an opportunity for appeal.

Perhaps stating this general requirement and implying these basic standards would have been enough. But our Founding Fathers had enough direct experience with arbitrary royal courts during the colonial period that they were taking no chances with the new national government they were creating. Criminal trials by the new national courts would also have to provide a number of specific procedural guarantees to the accused.

■ Specific Guarantees

The Fourth Amendment prohibits unreasonable searches of property and seizures of evidence. As now interpreted by the U.S. Supreme

Court, improperly seized evidence is inadmissible in a later criminal trial, although there are some exceptions to this rule. Warrants from a court for such searches are not to be issued except on probable cause (the belief that there is such criminal evidence), and the warrant must "particularly" describe the place to be searched and the persons or things to be seized.

Since the accused is presumed innocent until proven guilty during the trial, it is generally improper to keep the accused in jail until the trial. Most criminal defendants are given the opportunity to post **bail** (a sum of money left with the court to guarantee they will appear for trial) and then released. If they do not appear for trial, the money is forfeited to the public treasury. The Eighth Amendment prohibits a court from requiring "excessive" bail. In other words, the amount of money required must bear some relation to the seriousness of the crime and the probability that the defendant may flee the country to avoid punishment. Murder is generally not a bailable offense, and persons who are allegedly involved in high-level narcotics transactions may have to post very large amounts as bail. On the other hand, persons who have no prior criminal record and have substantial connection to the community may be released on their own pledge (recognizance) to return for trial.

The Bill of Rights contains several specific procedural requirements for criminal cases.

The Sixth Amendment guarantees the accused a speedy and public trial. The trial must be by jury, in the place where the alleged crime was committed. If the accused does not think there can be a fair trial in that location, a request can be filed with the court asking that the trial be moved to another location ("venue"). The Sixth Amendment also requires that the accused be informed of the charges, be given legal counsel, have the right to confront the accusers, and have the help of the court to force testimony by defense witnesses.

In addition to the basic due process requirement, the Fifth Amendment also requires the use of a grand jury for serious crimes ("capital or otherwise infamous" crimes). The prosecuting attorney must first convince a majority of twenty-three citizens that there is probable cause to believe that a crime has been committed and that the particular accused has committed it. The grand jury hears this preliminary evidence and votes a "true bill," or an **indictment** of the accused. When (and if) that happens, the defendant is then bound over for trial. At the arraignment hearing before a judge, the accused will be asked to plead to the charges—guilty, not guilty, or *nolo contendere*. The Latin phrase **nolo contendere** basically means "no contest"; the accused does not admit guilt, but agrees to punishment. The prosecution and the defense may agree to a guilty plea or a no contest plea on a lesser charge to avoid the expense and uncertainty of a trial.

If there is a trial, the defendant cannot be forced to testify against himself or herself. Corporations do not enjoy this particular protection, since a corporation cannot of itself do anything at all. Everything *it* does, it does through employees and agents. Those persons can be forced to testify against it—their corporation, but not to incriminate themselves personally.

Finally, the defendant cannot be tried twice for the same crime (double jeopardy). Once the defendant is found not guilty that's the end—at least for that alleged crime, and all "lesser included offenses." A person who is found not guilty of murder could not be re-tried for manslaughter, or for assault with a deadly weapon, based on the same occurrence. On the other hand, it is possible that the same act might be a crime under both state and national law, so that in reality two separate and distinct offenses were committed. In that case, there could be one criminal trial for each crime, national and state. There could also be a separate civil trial for damages by the victim who was harmed.

The Supreme Court's decision in Dr. Sheppard's case shows that, in addition to all the specific procedural guarantees, there is an underlying requirement. Due process of law requires that the trial as a whole must be basically fair.

JUSTICE · UNDER

SHEPPARD V. MAXWELL

384 U.S. 333 (1966)

Facts: Dr. Sam Sheppard was tried and convicted of the murder of his pregnant wife, Marilyn, after a "circus" trial in state court in Cleveland, Ohio. Headline stories in the newspapers had accused him of not cooperating with the investigation and said his family had thrown up a "protective ring" around him. One story said someone was "getting away with murder." The County Coroner was criticized for not holding an inquest into the wife's death. An inquest was held the next day—in a high school gymnasium. In front of the room was a long table occupied by reporters, TV and radio personnel, and broadcasting equipment. The inquest was broadcast live, with microphones at the witness chair and the coroner's chair. Sheppard was brought into the room and searched by police in front of several hundred spectators. His counsel were present during the three-day hearing, but were not permitted to participate. When his chief counsel tried to have some documents put in the record, he was forcibly ejected from the room by the coroner, who was then cheered, hugged, and kissed by ladies in the audience.

After the Ohio Supreme Court affirmed his conviction, Sheppard filed a habeas corpus petition with the U.S. District Court, challenging the legality of his stay in jail. The District Court held for him, but the U.S. Court of Appeals reversed.

Issue: Did Sheppard receive a fair trial (due process of law)?

Decision: No, He did not. The habeas corpus petition must be granted. (Sheppard was released from prison. The State of Ohio could try him again for the murder, since the first trial was nullified. He was acquitted when he was tried again.)

Rule: The jury must be given an opportunity to decide the case based on the evidence presented in court, without being unduly distracted or prejudiced by the news media.

Discussion: *By Justice* CLARK:

"With this background the case came up for trial two weeks before the November general election at which the...trial judge...was a candidate to succeed himself. Twenty-five days before the case was set, 75 [people] were called as prospective jurors. All three Cleveland newspapers published [their] names and addresses.... As a consequence, anonymous letters and telephone calls, as well as calls from friends, regarding the impending prosecution were received by all of the prospective jurors. The selection of the jury began on October 18, 1954.

"The courtroom in which the trial was held measured 26 by 48 feet. A long temporary table was set up inside the bar, in back of the single counsel table. It ran the width of the courtroom, parallel to the bar railing, with one end less than three feet from the jury box. Approximately 20 representatives of newspapers and wire services were assigned seats at this table by the court. Behind the bar railing there were four rows of benches. These seats were likewise assigned by the court for the entire trial. The first row was occupied by representatives of television and radio stations, and the second and third rows by reporters from out-of-town newspapers and magazines.... Representatives of the news media also used all the rooms on the courtroom floor, including the room where jurors were ordinarily called and assigned for trial. Private telephone lines and telegraph equipment were installed in these rooms so that reports from the trial could be speeded to the papers....

"There can be no question about the nature of the publicity which surrounded Sheppard's trial. We agree, as did the Court of Appeals, with the findings of Judge Bell's opinion for the Ohio Supreme Court:

Murder and mystery, society, sex, and suspense were combined in this case in such a manner as to intrigue and captivate the public fancy to a degree perhaps unparalleled in recent annals. Throughout the preindictment investigation, the subsequent legal skirmishes, and the nine-week trial, circulation-conscious editors catered to the insatiable interest of the American public in the bizarre.... In this "Roman Holiday" for the news media, Sam Sheppard stood trial for his life.

"Indeed, every court that has considered this case, save the court that tried it, has deplored the manner in which the news media inflamed and prejudiced the public.

"Since the state trial judge did not fulfill his duty to protect Sheppard from the inherently prejudicial publicity which saturated the community and to control disruptive influences in the courtroom, we must reverse the denial of the habeas petition. The case is remanded to the District Court with instructions to issue the writ and order that Sheppard be released from custody unless the State puts him to its charges again within a reasonable time."

Ethical Dimension

Is it proper for the news media to editorialize (or even report) on a criminal case before the jury has made its decision? Which is the higher priority, freedom of the press or the right to a fair trial?

T ORT LAW

Businesses and their agents and employees may also commit torts against other persons. Sometimes intentional wrongs are done to others. More frequently, the injured party's claim is based on **negligence**— the defendant's alleged failure to use reasonable care in performing activities. In some cases, such as the sale of defective products, the business can be held strictly liable. The usual court remedy for tort is money compensation to the injured party. Where an intentional wrong has been committed, punitive damages may be awarded, as a kind of punishment to the bad person, who meant to do injury. Where there is a threat of continuing wrongdoing, an injunction against that conduct can be issued by the court.

■ Intentional Torts

Intentional torts are those in which the wrong was done on purpose.

This category includes all those situations where one person does harm to another "on purpose." It also includes cases in which the defendant acted recklessly, in total disregard of the rights and safety of others, even though the defendant did not intend to cause harm to a specific person. Punitive damages can be awarded to victims of intentional torts, both to punish the defendants and to deter others from doing similar intentional wrongs.

Intentional torts can be committed against the physical person of another, against one's reputation, or against one's property. **Assault** occurs when one person's actions put another person in fear of bodily harm. **Battery** occurs when there is any unauthorized touching of another's body, either with the wrongdoer's body, or with a weapon or missile. **False imprisonment** is committed when one person illegally interferes with the freedom of movement of another. A business may be liable for assault and battery where an agent or employee becomes involved in a physical dispute with a customer during the course of business. A store which unreasonably detains a customer suspected of shoplifting might have to pay damages for false imprisonment. Other than these two situations, businesses will probably not be committing these intentional torts.

Businesses which are engaged in publishing information do need to know the law relating to libel and slander, however. **Libel** occurs when false information about someone is published in written form. If the false data is conveyed in oral form, the tort of **slander** has been committed. If the subject person is a "public figure," such as a politician, there is no tort liability unless the false information was published maliciously. *Malice* in this sense can be inferred where the falsity of the information was known prior to its publication or where it was published with "reckless disregard" for its truth or falsity. This special standard exists because comment on matters of public concern is encouraged and protected by the First Amendment. Public figures can't be thin-skinned. As former President Harry Truman once said, "If you can't stand the heat, get out of the kitchen!"

By definition, both libel and slander involve the publication of *false* information. Truth is, therefore, a complete defense in most states. *True* statements are not libelous or slanderous, although they may cause much embarrassment, or even wreck marriages or careers. (A few states do require, in addition, that the true statement be published with "good motives.") There is another tort that may be used against persons who snoop and spy, "dig up the dirt," and then publish it to humiliate and embarrass the subject. Even though what is published is true, it may be possible to collect damages from the snoop for **invasion of privacy**. Not everything that one does or says is necessarily the public's business. Even public figures have some right to privacy, as the following case shows. Similar issues are raised when a person's name or likeness is used for commercial purposes without permission. Cases involving employees' privacy are discussed in Chapter 13.

Publishing false information about a person constitutes libel or slander.

JUSTICE·UNDE

GALELLA V. ONASSIS

487 F.2d 986 (U.S. 2nd Cir. Court of Appeals, 1973)

Facts: Ron Galella takes "candid" photos of famous people. He aggressively pursued Jackie Kennedy Onassis, widow of President John Kennedy—and her two children. When he jumped out from behind some bushes to take a picture of young John, who was riding his bike, Galella was arrested by Secret Service officers who were protecting the little boy. Galella was not convicted, and he sued the officers for false arrest. He also sued Mrs. Onassis, claiming that they were acting under her orders. The lawsuit against the officers was dismissed, since they were performing their official duties. Mrs. Onassis counterclaimed for an injunction to prevent Galella from harassing her and the children. The trial court granted the injunction.

Issue: Has Galella exceeded his privilege of reporting the news?

Decision: Yes, he has. He should be enjoined from interfering in the lives of Mrs. Onassis and her children.

Rule: The First Amendment does not give anyone the right to commit crimes and torts.

Discussion: *By Judge* SMITH:

"Galella's action went far beyond the reasonable bounds of news gathering. When weighted against the de minimis public importance of the daily activities of the defendant, Galella's constant surveillance, his obtrusive and intruding presence, was unwarranted and unreasonable. If there were any doubt in our minds, Galella's inexcusable conduct toward defendant's minor children would resolve it.

"Galella does not seriously dispute the court's findings of tortious conduct. Rather, he sets up the First Amendment as a wall of immunity protecting newsmen from any liability for their conduct while gathering news. There is no such scope to the First Amendment right. Crimes and torts committed in news gathering are not protected....

"The injunction, however, is broader than is required to protect the defendant. Relief must be tailored to protect Mrs. Onassis from the 'paparazzo' attack which distinguishes Galella's behavior from that of other photographers; it should not unnecessarily infringe on reasonable efforts to 'cover' defendant. Therefore, we modify the court's order to prohibit only (1) any approach within twenty-five (25) feet of defendant or any touching of the person of the defendant Jacqueline Onassis; (2) any blocking of her movement in public places and thoroughfares;

(3) any act foreseeably or reasonably calculated to place the life and safety of defendant in jeopardy; and (4) any conduct which would reasonably be foreseen to harass, alarm, or frighten the defendant....

"Likewise, we affirm the grant of injunctive relief to the government, modified to prohibit any action interfering with Secret Service agents' protective duties. Galella thus may be enjoined from (a) entering the children's schools or play areas; (b) engaging in action calculated or reasonably foreseen to place the children's safety or well-being in jeopardy, or which would threaten or create physical injury; (c) taking any action which could reasonably be foreseen to harass, alarm, or frighten the children; and (d) from approaching within thirty (30) feet of the children....

"As modified, the relief granted fully allows Galella the opportunity to photograph and report on Mrs. Onassis' public activities. Any prior restraint on news gathering is miniscule and fully supported by the findings."

Ethical Dimension

Should there be any limits on gathering and publishing the news? Should "public figures" have any privacy rights, or are all their activities newsworthy?

One of the torts which Galella was accused of committing was **intentional infliction of emotional distress.** He had driven a speedboat dangerously close to Mrs. Onassis while she was swimming, and had harassed her and the children in various ways. Actions committed with the intent of disturbing another person's mental well-being can be sanctioned under this tort. In recent years, it has also been used by employees claiming emotional stress caused by an alleged wrongful discharge, or harassment on the job. Those types of cases are discussed in the chapters dealing with employment.

■ Torts Involving Property

Businesses may be victims or wrongdoers as to torts involving property. An agent or employee who took a short-cut across someone's land to save a few minutes in making a pizza delivery would commit the tort of **trespass.** An injunction could be issued to prevent such conduct from continuing, and damages could be collected, although the award would probably be quite small. Wrongful interference with an owner's right to personal property, such as a car or a promissory note, is called

Wrongful interference with a property owner's rights is a tort—either trespass or conversion.

conversion. A creditor business that wrongfully repossessed collateral could be sued for the tort of conversion, whether the wrongful repossession was done intentionally or by mistake. A repair shop which sold an item left only for repair could also be sued for conversion—again, whether or not the wrongful sale was intentional or mistaken. (In both of these last situations, if the wrongful action was intentional, punitive damages can be collected in addition the value of the item of property.) Conversion would also cover an employee's wrongful use of a firm's trade secrets, such as formulas or customer lists.

Most states now also recognize a tort called **intentional interference with economic relations.** Where a business induces a customer to breach an existing contract with one of the business's competitors, this tort has been committed. Competing for business is an inherent part of the free enterprise system, but there are limits to what can be done in the name of competition. As will be discussed in the chapters on distribution, various other "competitive" torts may also be committed by a business that is not aware of these legal limits.

Property owners may commit torts due to conditions on their property which injure others.

There are many cases in which businesses have been sued for the tort of **nuisance,** meaning that some part of the business operation is interfering with other property owners' rights to use and enjoy their real estate. A business which is polluting a stream with chemical run-off, for instance, could be enjoined from continuing to do so and could be required to pay damages to landowners downstream.

In addition to its potential liability to persons off the business premises, a business owes certain duties to persons who come onto the land. **Invitees** are persons who come onto the premises for the benefit of the landowner, at the landowner's "invitation." For person who are business invitees, such as customers and clients, the business must provide a reasonably safe store or office within which to do business. An injured invitee could collect damages if the business had not taken reasonable steps to inspect, clean, and maintain the premises, and if the injury occurred as a result of that failure. For **licensees**—persons who are on the premises with the owner's express or implied permission, but not for the owner's benefit—the landowner owes only a duty to warn of *known* hazards. A social guest who is injured in your home generally has no case for tort damages unless injured by a condition of which you were aware and of which you failed to warn your guest. ("Watch out for the second step, Roger; it's a little loose.") Today, some states do not distinguish between invitees and licensees, but require a landowner to exercise reasonable care towards all persons who are on the premises lawfully. As to **trespassers**—those who come on your land without any right at all—your only duty is not to cause them injury intentionally. Most states continue to maintain at least this distinction. The landowner's negative duty towards trespassers is at issue in the following case.

KATKO V. BRINEY

JUSTICE · UNDER

183 N.W.2d 657 (Iowa 1971)

Facts: Bertha Briney inherited her parents' home in 1957. She and her husband Edward tried to maintain the property, but no one lived there from 1957 to 1967. Over that period, there were several break-ins at the vacant house. The Brineys finally set up a "spring-gun" inside the house. When someone pulled the door open, a cord would pull the trigger on a shotgun aimed at the door. Katko and a friend had broken into the house and were searching for any valuable items that might be there. When Katko opened the bedroom door, the gun shot him in the leg. He sued in tort, and was awarded $20,000 actual and $10,000 punitive damages.

Issue: Have the Brineys committed a tort against Katko, a trespasser?

Decision: Yes, they have. Jury verdict for Katko is sustained.

Rule: Deadly force cannot be used merely to protect property. A property owner cannot intentionally injure trespassers.

Discussion: *By Chief Justice* MOORE:

"The main thrust of defendants' defense in the trial court and on this appeal is that 'the law permits use of a spring gun in a dwelling or warehouse for the purpose of preventing unlawful entry of a burglar or thief.'...

"In the statement of issues the trial court stated plaintiff and his companion committed a felony when they broke and entered defendants' house. In instruction 2 the court referred to the early case history of the use of spring guns and stated under the law their use was prohibited except to prevent the commission of felonies of violence and where human life is in danger. The instruction included a statement [that] breaking and entering is not a felony of violence....

"The overwhelming weight of authority, both textbook and case law, supports the trial court's statement of the applicable principles of law.

"Prosser on Torts, Third Edition, pages 116–118, states:

The law has always placed a higher value upon human safety than upon mere rights in property. It is the accepted rule that there is no privilege to use any force calculated to cause death or serious bodily injury to repel the threat to land or chattels, unless there is also such a threat to the defendant's personal safety as to justify self-defense.... Spring guns and other man-killing devices are not justifiable against a mere trespasser, or even a petty thief. They are privileged only against those upon whom the landowner, if he were present in person would be free to inflict injury of the same kind...."

Ethical Dimension

Should a person who is injured while commiting a crime be able to collect damages from the victim? Why should the law care so much about trespassers? Should the landowners here be able to use deadly force to protect their farm?

▆ Negligent Torts

Negligence occurs when one person's carelessness causes injury to another.

Each of us, whoever we are and whatever we are doing, owes the other members of society a general duty to use reasonable care to avoid injuring others. Whether driving a car, mowing a lawn, or using a charcoal grill to cook dinner, we are required to be reasonably careful. Another person who is injured because we fail to use reasonable care can sue us and collect damages. To win a lawsuit for negligence, the plaintiff must show (1) that the defendant owed a duty of care; (2) that the defendant breached that duty; (3) that the breach of duty was the proximate cause of the plaintiff's injury; and, (4) that the plaintiff sustained damages. If there is such a lawsuit, a jury (or a judge) will decide whether the injury occurred because of a failure to use reasonable care.

EXISTENCE OF DUTY AND BREACH OF DUTY

Whether a particular person owes a duty to do specific things is a question of law, to be decided by the trial judge. Is the plaintiff one of a class of persons who might be exposed to unreasonable risk of harm by the defendant's actions? If no duty exists, the trial judge should enter a judgment for the defendant without the necessity of a trial. If a duty is found to exist because of the relationship between the plaintiff and the defendant, then the trial judge must consider the standard of care. The standard of care is usually described as that of a reasonable person under the circumstances of the particular case.

The jury (if one is used) will then determine whether the defendant met the required standard of care. The jury will probably be instructed that the reasonable person is a hypothetical or fictional person who is supposed to represent the community's standard. Several of these points are at issue in the *Eimann* case.

EIMANN V. SOLDIER OF FORTUNE MAGAZINE, INC.

880 F.2d 830 (U.S. 5th Cir. Court of Appeals, 1989)

JUSTICE · UNDE[

Facts: John Wayne Hearn placed an ad in Soldier of Fortune Magazine (SOF), which focuses on military activities. The ad ran in the September, October, and November issues. It stated: "EX-MARINES—67–69 'Nam Vets, Ex-DI, weapons specialist-jungle warfare, pilot, M.E., high risk assignments, U.S. or overseas. (404) 991-2684." Hearn testified that he and another ex-Marine placed the ad to recruit Vietnam veterans for bodyguard and security work. About 90 percent of the callers who responded to the ad wanted to hire someone for criminal activities. An oil company which called did want ten bodyguards, and Hearn placed seven men with that company.

Robert Black had been trying to convince four of his friends or co-workers in Bryan, Texas, to kill his wife (Sandra), or help him kill her. When Black called Hearn, he initially asked about getting bodyguard work through Hearn. Later, he hinted about having Hearn kill his wife. Hearn eventually agreed to do so, and did, for $10,000. Hearn also killed Black's girlfriend's husband and her sister's ex-husband. Sandra's son Gary and Sandra's mother Marjorie Eimann sued SOF and its parent corporation, Omega Group, for wrongful death. The plaintiffs claimed that SOF had been negligent in publishing the ad. The jury awarded Eimann $1.9 million in compensatory damages and $7.5 million in punitive damages. SOF appeals.

Issue: Does a "military-oriented" magazine owe a duty to investigate the persons who place ads for personal services?

Decision: No. Judgment reversed. (SOF is not liable.)

Rule: Requiring a publication to investigate each ad submitted would impose an unreasonable burden on the freedoms of speech and the press.

Discussion: *By Judge DAVIS:*

"In essence, a duty represents a legally enforceable obligation to conform to a particular standard of conduct.... Whether the defendant in a negligence action owes a duty involves consideration of two related issues: (1) whether the defendant owes an obligation to this particular plaintiff to act as a reasonable person would in the circumstances; and (2) the standard of conduct required to satisfy that obligation...."

"Texas courts have applied risk-utility balancing tests in resolving both aspects of the duty question. Thus, in deciding whether an actor owes a duty of reasonable care to the public at large, the Supreme Court of Texas has weighed the risk, forseeability and likelihood of injury from certain conduct against the conduct's social utility and the burden of guarding against injury....

"Similarly, Texas courts have applied risk-utility analysis in determining the second duty issue—whether a defendant who owes an established duty of reasonable care to specified parties must take precautions against particular dangers.... Courts have described this aspect of duty as the defendant's obligation to protect those parties against unreasonable risks.... A risk becomes unreasonable when its magnitude outweighs the social utility of the act or omission that creates it....

"In assessing the threatened harm we note that 'nearly all human acts...carry some recognizable but remote possibility of harm to another.'... The SOF classified ads presented more than a remote risk. Of the 2,000 or so personal service classified ads that SOF printed between 1975 and 1984, Eimann's evidence established that as many as nine had served as links in criminal plots. Of these nine, the evidence revealed that SOF staffers had participated in at least two police investigations of crimes in which classified ads had played a role; other crimes tied to the ads received varying amounts of media coverage....

"The standard of conduct imposed by the district court against SOF is too high; it allows a jury to visit liability on a publisher for untoward consequences that flow from his decision to publish any suspicious, ambiguous ad that might cause serious harm. The burden on a publisher to avoid liability from suits of this type is too great: he must reject *all* such advertisements.

"The range of forseeable misuses of advertised products and services is as limitless as the forms and functions of the products themselves. Without a more specific indication of illegal intent than Hearn's ad or its context provided, we conclude that SOF did not violate the required standard of conduct by publishing an ad that later played a role in criminal activity."

Ethical Dimension

Is it ethical for a publisher to provide a forum through which persons may be hired for criminal activities?

BURDEN OF PROOF AND PRESUMPTIONS

The plaintiff has the burden of proof as to the defendant's negligence. Generally this means that the jury must be convinced that the preponderance of the evidence is on the plaintiff's side. In other words, the jury must be persuaded that the plaintiff's version of what happened is at least somewhat more likely than the defendant's version.

Plaintiff must prove that defendant's lack of care directly caused the injury.

The plaintiff may be aided by certain presumptions. In some situations, the law assumes that proof of one fact implies the existence of another fact, unless the opposing party can produce another explanation. Negligence may be proved by circumstantial evidence, usually described here by the Latin phrase *res ipsa loquitur* (the thing speaks for itself). The presumption of negligence arises where (1) the accident is of a kind which ordinarily does not happen without someone's negligence; (2) the defendant would be responsible for any negligence associated with the apparent cause of the accident; and, (3) the possibility of plaintiff's own conduct contributing to the occurrence is eliminated. The collapse of a building, without any external stress, would normally "speak for itself." On the other hand, someone's falling down the stairs would not necessarily presume any negligence on the part of the building's owner.

PROXIMATE CAUSE

The third element of the negligence case (after duty and breach) is described by the phrase **proximate cause**. In order to hold the defendant liable, it is necessary for the plaintiff to show that the defendant's conduct did in fact cause the plaintiff's injury. That proof is necessary, but not sufficient, to establish the defendant's liability. The law also requires proof that the defendant's conduct was the proximate cause of the plaintiff's injury. As a matter of policy, the courts have placed some outer limits on a person's liability for the end results of actions or omissions. Proximate cause implies a relationship close in time and space and also a direct cause-and-effect relationship.

Courts generally do not impose liability where the plaintiff's injury is the result of an abnormal intervening cause which could not have been foreseen. Courts also apply various rules to make sure that there is a reasonably close connection between the defendant's act and the plaintiff's injury. There is probably no single test which covers all possible cases.

DEFENSES TO NEGLIGENCE

If the injured plaintiff was also partly at fault, the law originally did not permit recovery, due to the theory of **contributory negligence**. If Sam and Joan were both driving carelessly, and both contributed to cause the car accident, neither could collect from the other. Some states still follow this rule. Most states, however, now use the doctrine of

Plaintiff's own negligence may prevent collection of some or all of the damages sustained.

comparative negligence, under which the party who was mostly at fault would have to pay at least part of the other party's damages. If Sam had been 90 percent at fault for the accident, and Joan only 10 percent, she would collect 90 percent of her damages (or perhaps only 80 percent, depending on how this rule is applied in the particular state).

Another frequently used defense is **assumption of risk**. If a person is aware of the risk of injury, but voluntarily goes ahead and participates in the risky activity, there may be no liability if injury does in fact occur. Adequate warnings of the risk involved may thus prevent liability if a person accepts the risk and is injured. For example, someone who developed a fear of heights while sky-diving probably has no claim for mental stress against the operator of the sky-diving service. On the other hand, what is "assumed" under this doctrine are the normal risks involved in the activity. A bungee-jumper whose safety cord snapped because of a defect would not have assumed the risk of that kind of occurrence.

■ Strict Liability in Tort

Strict liability is imposed on a person who exposes the public to unusual risks of harm.

Historically, **strict liability**, or liability without proof of negligence or fault, was imposed in only two situations: the keeping of dangerous wild animals and the performance of extra-hazardous activities. The common factor in these situations is that a person is exposing society to an unreasonable risk of harm and therefore ought to be held liable for any damages that are in fact sustained, even if there is no proof of negligence. Both of these cases involve unusual situations. A person who has a tiger in captivity, either as a special exhibit or as a mascot for a sports team, is imposing an extra risk of injury on society. No matter how or why the tiger gets loose, the owner is held accountable for any injury it causes. This rule may also be applied to impose liability on the owners of ferocious dogs, such as dobermans or pit bulls.

Similarly, if a business is doing blasting work with dynamite or is smashing down buildings with a large steel ball, society is being exposed to an unusual danger. The business that engages in these lawful, but very dangerous activities should have to pay for any damages caused. Since it is not necessary to prove negligence in these cases, the defendant's proof of reasonable care is not a defense.

A related doctrine, known as **attractive nuisance**, imposes liability on a landowner who permits conditions on the property that lure young children onto the property and cause their injury. Even though the young child is technically a trespasser, the landowner (or occupier) is liable for the injury which occurs. Examples of attractive nuisance would include old cars, refrigerators, or machinery, or (perhaps) bodies of water. To small children, these may look like interesting places to play, and the danger would not be apparent.

During the 1960s and 1970s, state courts extended strict liability to manufacturers and sellers of defective products. This form of strict liability will be discussed in Chapters 15, 16, and 17.

◼ No-Fault Auto Statutes

Many negligence cases arise out of auto accidents. As of 1991, thirteen states had no-fault statutes for motor vehicle accidents as a substitute for lawsuits trying to establish negligence. With millions of cars on our streets and highways, accidents occur frequently. Much court time is used in trying to determine which driver was "at fault," that is, which one's negligence caused the accident. If a trial is required, several years will probably elapse before there is a final decision. Since legal time is expensive—lawyers, judges, jurors, and administrators all have to be paid—processing costs take a large share of any damages award.

No-fault auto accident laws require each driver to bear any personal loss, regardless of which one caused the accident.

The basic idea of no-fault is that each driver (or his or her insurance company) should pay for any personal losses; neither can sue the other, since "fault" is not relevant. They were both involved; each pays for his or her own losses (or files an insurance claim). Some no-fault states do permit tort lawsuits where there is death or permanent bodily injury. Some also permit a tort lawsuit to collect the amount of the insurance deductible where there is property damage.

In the *Fisher* case, the tree owner apparently did not understand how no-fault worked.

JUSTICE·UNDE[R]

FISHER V. LOWE

333 N.W.2d 67 (Mich. 1983)

Facts: Karen Lowe lost control of the car she was driving and ran it into William Fisher's "beautiful oak tree." The car was owned by Larry Moffet and insured by State Farm. Despite the state's having a no-fault auto accident law, Fisher sued all three—Lowe, Moffet, and State Farm. The trial court granted summary judgment for Lowe and Moffet because of the no-fault law, and for State Farm because it had not been properly served with court process. Fisher appealed.

Issue: Can the owner of the tree sue the owner and driver of the car?

Decision: No, such lawsuits are not permitted under the no-fault system.

Rule: Negligence is not relevant in motor vehicle accident cases, under a no-fault system.

Discussion: *The court seemed to think this was a frivolous lawsuit, and so announced its decision in a poem by Judge* GILLIS:

"We thought that we would never see
A suit to compensate a tree.
A suit whose claim in tort is prest
Upon a mangled tree's behest;
A tree whose battered trunk was prest
Against a Chevy's crumpled crest;
A tree that faces each new day
With bark and limbs in disarray;
A tree that may forever bear
A lasting need for tender care.
Flora lovers though we three,
We must uphold the court's decree.
"Affirmed."

Ethical Dimension

What incentive is there for safe driving, if one is not held liable for the results of one's careless driving?

■ Immunities

Historically, for public policy reasons, some persons and institutions could not be sued for their torts. The three major groups which enjoyed such immunity were governmental units, charitable organizations, and families.

Governments generally cannot be sued for torts without their consent to be sued.

Under the early common law, governmental (or "sovereign") immunity was summed up in the phrase "the king can do no wrong." Since the king was "sovereign," that is, he possessed ultimate governmental power, he could not be sued in the courts he had created, at least not without his consent. Although Parliament ultimately became the supreme governing body in England, and although the U. S. Constitution makes the people the ultimate source of governmental power, this doctrine of sovereign immunity from lawsuits has continued to the present day.

In 1946, Congress passed the Federal Tort Claims Act, which does give us permission to collect from the national government in some cases—a claim for property damage caused by the driver of a post office vehicle, for example. Various statutes and regulations also provide mechanisms to settle contract claims against the national government. Agents of the government can be sued in certain instances. Whether state governments and their agents are suable depends on the law of each state. There is considerable variation on this point.

Charitable agencies also used to be immune from tort suits. Charities perform important social functions—caring for the poor and the sick, educating the young, teaching moral and ethical values. Their funds are limited, usually based on private contributions. It did not seem to make sense to subject such organizations to tort liability.

Today, in most states, charities can be sued for torts they commit. The modern view is that it is not fair to deny compensation to an injured person, simply because a charity committed the tort. The charity can use some of its funds to buy liability insurance, just as the rest of us do.

Traditionally, the courts also refused to recognize lawsuits by one family member against another. Judges generally felt that such problems should not be resolved in court, but within the family, perhaps with religious or other counseling help. There is also the danger that such lawsuits are really just attempts to get money from an insurance company that has issued a policy covering "homeowner's liability." On the other hand, a parent or spouse guilty of intentional physical abuse of a family member should not be immune from lawsuits just because of the relationship. And the same argument can be made if one family member negligently injures another: the wrongdoer should pay, and the victim should be compensated. Today, most states will permit such intra-family lawsuits, relying on the courts to sort out the fake claims from the real ones.

■ Tort Liability of Professionals

Persons engaged in professions such as law, medicine, and engineering are required to exercise reasonable care in doing their work. Failure to measure up to professional standards is usually described as **malpractice**. Malpractice is thus a case of professional negligence. The general rules discussed above for a negligence case also apply to professional malpractice. Originally, the standard of care was measured according to that of a reasonable practitioner in the locality where the particular defendant was practicing. Now, however, a national standard for the profession as a whole is used in most cases.

Professional malpractice is the negligent performance of professional services.

States disagree sharply over how far this duty of care extends, especially with respect to the duty of professional accountants. All states agree that a duty of care is owed to the client and to specifically contracted-for third parties (persons who were intended to receive and use the client's financial statements). Some states also extend the accountant's duty to third parties whose reliance on the financial statements was foreseen by the accountant. A third group of states goes even further, holding the accountant liable to any third party whose reliance on the financial statements should have been foreseen. Presumably, any person entering into any sort of commercial relationship with the accountant's client would fall into this last group. Figure 6–1 shows the relative scope of these three rules. The *Rosenblum* case illustrates the "reasonably forseeable" rule.

States disagree over how far a professional duty of care extends beyond the client.

FIGURE 6–1
How far does CPA's duty extend?

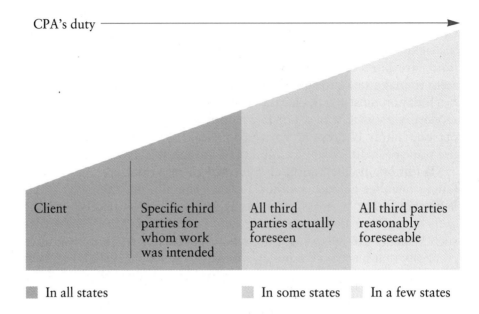

CPA's duty

| Client | Specific third parties for whom work was intended | All third parties actually foreseen | All third parties reasonably foreseeable |

■ In all states   ■ In some states   In a few states

JUSTICE·UNDE[R

ROSENBLUM V. ADLER

461 A.2d 138 (N.J. 1983)

Facts: Giant, Inc., operated retail stores and shops. Touche, Ross prepared its audited annual financial statements from 1969 through 1972. Touche also prepared the financial statements for Giant's stock offering in December, 1971. Rosenblum was negotiating a merger with Giant from November, 1971 until they reached an agreement on March 9, 1972. Giant had falsified many of its records, but Touche never discovered these frauds. When Giant went bankrupt, Rosenblum sued Touche (Adler and all of the other Touche partners in New Jersey) for fraud, negligence, and breach of warranty. The trial court denied Touche's motion to dismiss the negligence claim as to the 1972 financial statements. Touche appeals.

Issue: Does an accountant's duty of care extend to third parties whose use of the financial statements should have been foreseen?

Decision: Yes, it does. Judgment affirmed.

Rule: An accountant owes a duty of care to all third parties whose reliance on the financial statements should have been foreseen. (Note: This is a New Jersey court ruling: other states may follow different standards as discussed above.)

Discussion: *By Justice SCHREIBER:*

"The imposition of a duty to foreseeable users may cause

accounting firms to engage in more thorough reviews. This might entail setting up stricter standards and applying closer supervision, which should tend to reduce the number of instances in which liability would ensue. Much of the additional costs incurred either because of more thorough auditing review or increased insurance premiums would be borne by the business entity and its stockholders or its customers....

"When the defendants prepared the Giant audit, they knew or should have known that Giant would probably use the audited figures for many proper business purposes. They knew that it was to be incorporated in Giant's annual report, a report that would be transmitted to each Giant stockholder, and would be filed with the SEC in conjunction with Giant's proxy solicitation material for its annual stockholder meeting. The defendants also knew or should have known that the audited financial statements would be available and useful for other proper business purposes, such as public offerings of securities, credit, and corporate acquisitions. These were clearly foreseeable potential uses of the audited financials at the time of their preparation. Giant and the defendant auditors knew that these financial statements would be used at least until the next financial statements had been audited and released.

"Defendants became aware of plaintiffs' existence and their intended use of these statements before plaintiffs relied on the accuracy of these financials. The defendants knew that the merger agreement included a representation that the prospectus used for the public offering in December 1971 contained no untrue statement of a material fact and did not omit to state any material fact. The defendants knew that this prospectus included their opinion that the financials had been prepared in accordance with generally accepted accounting principles and fairly represented Giant's financial condition. The defendants' representations were of a continuing nature and their obligation was a continuing one....

"Irrespective of whether the defendants had actual knowledge of Giant's proposed use of the 1972 audit in connection with the merger, it was reasonably foreseeable that Giant would use the audited statement in connection with the merger and its consummation. This is particularly so since the defendants were familiar with the merger agreement and had been engaged by Giant to audit the books and records of the plaintiffs' enterprises for the purpose of the merger. The trial court properly denied defendants' motion."

As will be discussed more fully in Chapter 10, the national securities acts require that companies selling securities on the national exchanges or in interstate commerce must make certain disclosures. Among the documents which must be publicly filed are certified financial statements. CPAs who certify such financials can also be held liable under the securities acts if the statements contain material errors. The CPA firm can, however, avoid such liability if it proves that it exercised reasonable care in the preparation of the financial statements. Here, too, the test is based on a national standard.

■ Tort Reform Legislation

Faced with medical doctors who refuse to accept maternity patients, with drug companies who refuse to produce needed vaccines, and with manufacturers who stop making existing products and don't develop new ones, some state legislators have begun to wonder whether tort liability has been carried too far by the courts. If pregnant women and their babies can't get medical care because doctors are afraid of being sued, is society as a whole being well-served by the tort system? If no one is willing to assume the huge liability risk associated with football helmets, are we better off without any football games at all? How about vaccines against such diseases as polio, measles, mumps, and chicken pox? If there are no manufacturers of the vaccines, we go back to the days when thousands died of these diseases, and tens of thousands suffered. At the same time, persons whose carelessness has caused injury to others should be held accountable for their wrongful actions.

State legislatures have passed a variety of statutes limiting tort liability.

State legislatures have tried to deal with these difficult issues in various ways. Some have passed statutes limiting the amount of damages which can be collected for "pain and suffering." Some have shortened the time period within which a lawsuit must be filed (the **Statute of Limitations** period). Some have imposed higher standards of proof of negligence. No-fault systems have also been suggested for some areas of liability. The national government is also interested in tort reform, in part because the costs imposed by the tort system have a large impact on our ability to compete in the international marketplace. Thus far, efforts at reform have been hit-or-miss, at best. Even where reform statutes have been passed, some of them have been ruled unconstitutional by the courts. The organized bar, particularly plaintiffs' lawyers, continue to oppose nearly all efforts at tort reform.

■ Business Liability for Civil Penalties

Several important national statutes impost civil penalties for violations. The national antitrust laws, for example, provide for treble (triple) damages for violations. A person injured by illegal price-fixing or other antitrust violations can collect three times the actual damages proved. The purpose of statutes like these is two-fold: to discourage the wrongful conduct by providing an extra penalty and to encourage private parties to bring lawsuits by awarding them the extra damages. Various other national and state statutes may specify such penalties.

One of the most widely used penalties statutes is the Racketeer Influenced and Corrupt Organizations Act (RICO). RICO was originally passed by Congress to deal with organized crime's infiltration of legitimate businesses. It was worded so broadly, however, that it covers all sorts of business disputes. As a result, plaintiffs' lawyers have used it in a wide variety of cases. From the plaintiff's standpoint, RICO's attraction is the treble damages it provides for a violation. RICO may be invoked whenever there are multiple violations of the mail fraud, wire fraud, or other federal statutes.

Business may be liable for civil penalties under statutes such as RICO and the antitrust laws.

REVIEW

The law provides a mechanism for redressing wrongs. Wrongs against society as a whole are punished through the criminal law. Criminal penalties range from fines, to community service, to imprisonment, to—ultimately—death. Wrongs against specific individuals are remedied through the tort system. The tort system recognizes liability based on intentional conduct, on negligent conduct, and on strict liability. Remedies for tort include injunctive relief, actual damages, and punitive damages. Deterrence of wrongful conduct is an objective of both systems, although criminal law focuses on punishing the wrongdoer, while tort law focuses on compensating the injured party. Businesses may be wrongdoer or victim under either system. In both systems, the challenge is to strike the right balance between the claims of the victim, the rights of the accused defendant, and the needs of society as a whole.

REVIEW QUESTIONS AND PROBLEMS

1. What differences are there between a crime and a tort? What similarities?

2. What are the requirements of "due process of law" in a criminal case?

3. What liabilities does a business have to persons who come onto its premises?

4. What is the difference between "defamation" and "invasion of privacy"?

5. How is "comparative negligence" different from "contributory negligence"? Why is this difference important to business firms?

6. When are professionals performing services liable to their clients?

7. Marker Motors and its advertising agency, Pride Productions, offered $100,000 to Babs, the famous rock star, if she would sing in the new TV commercial being prepared to advertise Marker's cars. Babs refused. Marker and Pride then contacted one of Babs' back-up singers and asked her to imitate Babs' voice and to sing the TV commercial. When Babs heard the commercial on TV, she was furious, and sued Marker and Pride. The defendants claimed that Babs had no case, since they had not violated the U.S. copyright laws (nothing protected had been copied). What result, and why?

8. Great Oil Company was a smaller independent, engaged in refining and distributing petroleum products in most of the western states. Most of Great's stock was owned by Larry, who was interested in selling out and retiring. Larry was contacted by Herman, chairman of Pennsy Oil, about selling his Great stock to Pennsy Oil. The two men agreed "in principle" that the deal would be beneficial to both sides and tentatively set a price of $90 per share for all of Larry's stock in Great Oil. Portia, the CEO of Rex Oil, heard that Larry's Great Oil stock was for sale and that the deal with Pennsy Oil had not yet been finalized. She contacted Larry and offered him $110 per share, and so he sold his Great Oil stock to Rex Oil. Pennsy sues Rex Oil for intentional tort. What should happen in this case? Explain.

9. Hilda owns and operates an amusement park. There are various rides, games, and displays in the park. One ride, "Tugboat Annie," features a small tugboat on which the patrons ride from one small lake to another by means of a six-foot deep canal. This area is surrounded by a low fence, and signs are posted which warn patrons not to cross the fence or to wade or swim in the water. Four-year-old Rocky wandered away from his parents, and was later found in the canal—drowned. Rocky's parents sued the amusement park. Do they have a tort case? Discuss.

10. Winnie was employed by Money Morning, a financial paper, as a stock market analyst. Winnie's column of stock tips and news appeared in the paper on Tuesdays and Thursdays. Apparently, her advice was followed by a number of investors, because stocks usually went up or down in response to her advice to buy or sell. Winnie and her friend Cato devised a plan to make some extra money by anticipating these stock market price changes. Winnie would tell Cato in advance what recommendations she would be making, and Cato would buy or sell those stocks before the public read Winnie's column in the paper. When they were criminally prosecuted by the U.S. Government for mail and wire fraud, Winnie and Cato claimed that they had not stolen any "property" as required for conviction under these statutes. Has a crime been committed? Discuss.

SUGGESTIONS FOR FURTHER READING

Bucy, "Corporate Ethos: A Standard for Imposing Corporate Criminal Liability," *Minnesota Law Review* 75 (April 1991): 1095.

Cherry, "Negligence: An Expanding Cause of Action Against Builders for Used Home Defects," *American Business Law Journal* 26 (Spring 1988): 167.

Drechsel & Moon, "Corporate Libel Plaintiffs and the News Media: An Analysis of the Public-Private Figure Distinction After Gertz," *American Business Law Journal* 21 (Summer 1983): 127.

Jennings, Reckers & Kneer, "The Auditor's Dilemma: The Incongruous Judicial Notions of the Auditing Profession and Actual Auditor Practice," *American Business Law Journal* 29 (Spring 1991): 99.

CONTRACT LAW – FOUNDATION OF FREE ENTERPRISE

PART TWO

Part 2 summarizes contract law. Contracts are the mechanism through which business objectives are achieved. Coverage of contract law is therefore essential to an understanding of the legal environment of business. Without contracts there is no "business" in any meaningful sense of the term. Chapter 7 covers the essentials of making an enforceable contract – an agreement, an exchange of considerations, a signed writing. Chapter 8 then presents the major limitations on the enforcement of contracts – problems such as lack of contractual capacity, mistake, fraud, and illegality. Since nearly every business transaction in the functional areas in Part 3 is based on a contract, Part 2 is also a necessary preliminary to Part 3.

7

FORMATION AND ENFORCEABILITY OF CONTRACTS

"Words are more plastic than wax."
Socrates

LEARNING OBJECTIVES: After you have studied this chapter, you should be able to:

IDENTIFY the three essential elements of an enforceable contract.

OUTLINE the process involved in the formation of an agreement.

EXPLAIN the meaning and application of consideration in a contract.

DISCUSS the situations which require written evidence of a contract.

DEFINE the parol evidence rule.

P REVIEW: FREEDOM OF CONTRACT, FREE ENTERPRISE, AND DEMOCRACY

Freedom of contract is one of the key concepts in our free enterprise economic system. The ability to make our own economic decisions accounts for much of the freedom we enjoy in the United States. We choose where (and when) we work, and we are generally free to leave if we get a better offer from another employer. If we want to open our own business, we are generally free to do so, subject only to minimal legal requirements. As consumers, we decide what to buy, when, and where—from a vast array of competing choices. It is precisely because we are free to choose which contracts we will make that sellers of goods and services must satisfy our expectations. If we have choices, and one supplier is not doing the job, we will simply take our business somewhere else.

Freedom of contract is a key part of free enterprise.

T YPES OF CONTRACTS

A **contract** is an agreement between two (or more) parties which the law recognizes as imposing binding obligations on each. Contracts are categorized in various ways: As to the structure of the contract and the mutuality of obligation, contracts are classified as bilateral or unilateral. In a **bilateral contract**, each party makes a promise to the other. Both parties are bound to perform, or neither is. In a **unilateral contract**, one party makes a promise, offering some benefit if another party will perform some specified act. No one is bound to perform the act, but if someone does, the other party must deliver the promised benefit in exchange. An offer of a $50 reward for the return of a lost cat is the offer of a unilateral contract. No one promises to look for the cat, and no one is bound to do so. If someone does find and return the cat, the offeror is legally bound to pay the $50.

A bilateral contract is an exchange of promises

A **voidable contract** is one in which one of the parties has the option to disaffirm the bargain, to back and out and to require a redelivery of any benefits already exchanged. Minors who make contracts and persons who are defrauded have this option to disaffirm. **Void agreements** are those which are totally without legal effect, such as a contract involving the commission of a crime. **Unenforceable contracts** are those for which the law gives no court remedy. Examples of this third group would be oral contracts where a writing was required for enforcement or contracts which had become unenforceable because one of the parties had gone through bankruptcy or because the period of time within which to file a lawsuit for breach of the contract had elapsed. **Valid contracts** are those which are fully enforceable against both parties because all of the essential elements are present.

A voidable contract may be disaffirmed by one of the parties.

E LEMENTS OF COMMERCIAL CONTRACTS

Contracts require an agreement, consideration, and in some cases, a signed writing.

Each party must consent to the formation of a contract. There must, in other words, be an agreement between them.

Generally, the law only requires someone to perform a promise made when that person has received something in exchange for the promise. This second part of the contract formula is called consideration. As a rule, a promise of "something for nothing" is not enforceable as a contract.

For some special types of contracts, there is a third requirement—a signed writing. If a contract is one of these types, a court will generally refuse to enforce the contract if it is not in writing.

Each of these three legal requirements is examined below in greater detail.

Agreement

Many agreements are not contracts. Two persons may agree to have dinner together on Saturday, without intending their informal arrangement to be legally binding. Family members may agree among themselves as to who does which household chores. This sort of agreement is also not intended, nor reasonably understood, as a binding contract. Even in business, there may be such informal understandings and customs. An employer might give each employee a fruit basket on the employee's birthday without being bound to do so. In a business setting, however, there is a possibility that a court might interpret an informal arrangement as an implied contract or as an implied term of a later contract between the parties.

Not all agreements are contracts.

While not every agreement is a contract, the reverse is not true. In order for there to be a contract, there must be an agreement between two or more persons. The agreement, in turn, is composed of two parts—an offer and an acceptance. Someone must make an offer to do something—to enter into a contract. The person to whom the offer was made must agree to the proposal—must accept the offered terms.

When disputes arise over whether an agreement had been reached, one of three main questions is usually at issue. First, was an offer made? One party will argue that there is no contract because no offer was made to begin with. Second, was the offer still open for acceptance, or had it already ended? Again, one party will say that there is no contract because the offer (if there was one) had terminated. Third, was there an effective acceptance? One party will claim that a response did not really agree to the terms in the offer, and thus, there is no contract. The law provides some fairly detailed rules for each of these points.

CONTENTS OF OFFER

Obviously, there are many, many business and personal communications which are not offers of contracts. Even where the parties are, or may be, interested in a commercial relationship, they may exchange several preliminary communications before someone finally makes an offer. A company wishing to buy goods or services may ask several potential suppliers for price information. Neither the request for a price nor the price quote in response is considered an offer, in most cases. The buyer company simply wants information; the seller companies merely supply it. Neither the question nor the answers are offers of contracts.

Promise. To be an offer, the communication must contain a promise—a commitment to do business if the specified terms are met. Advertisements which merely quote prices on described merchandise would thus not be offers—legally—since there is no specific promise to sell. States' false advertising statutes do, however, provide criminal penalties if reasonable quantities of the advertised product are not in fact available for sale.

An offer must contain a promise.

Offeree and Terms. In addition to a promise to do business, an offer will usually identify the person(s) to whom it is directed—the offeree(s). If an offer is made publicly, and contains no limitation, it is assumed that any member of the public may accept it. The method of acceptance is frequently, but not always, specified in the offer. The duration of the offer (for how long is it open?) may or may not be included. Of course, the terms must be stated specifically enough that a court can determine what commitments have been made and can give a remedy if those commitments are not met.

The *Lefkowitz* case is a classic illustration of the definition of an offer. The Minnesota court finally decided that the general rule noted above (that ads and similar price quotations are not offers) did not apply because these particular ads did contain promises.

LEFKOWITZ V. GREAT MINNEAPOLIS SURPLUS STORE

86 N.W.2d 689 (Minn. 1957)

Facts: Great Minneapolis Surplus Store ran newspaper ads on two successive weeks. The first ad stated:

SATURDAY 9 a.m. SHARP
3 BRAND NEW
FUR COATS
Worth up to $100.00
First Come
First Served
$1
EACH

The second ad stated:

> SATURDAY 9 a.m.
> 2 BRAND NEW PASTEL
> MINK 3-SKIN SCARVES
> Selling for $89.50
> Out they go
> Saturday..Each . . .$1.00
> 1 BLACK LAPIN STOLE
> Beautiful,
> Worth $139.50 . . .$1.00
> FIRST COME
> FIRST SERVED

Lefkowitz was the first in line each Saturday when the store opened. He tried to buy a coat the first week and the black lapin stole the second week. The store refused to sell, claiming that the ads were not offers and that they were intended for women only. The trial court awarded Lefkowitz $138.50 in damages.

Issues: Were the ads offers? Was Lefkowitz an intended offeree?

Decision: Yes. Yes. Judgment affirmed.

Rule: An ad which contains a promise is an offer. When an offer is made publicly, all members of the public are intended offerees.

Discussion: *By Justice* MURPHY:

"The test of whether a binding obligation may originate in advertisements addressed to the general public is whether the facts show that some performance was promised in positive terms in return for something requested....

"[W]here the offer is clear, definite, and explicit, and leaves nothing open for negotiation, it constitutes an offer, acceptance of which will complete the contract. Whether in any individual instance a newspaper advertisement is an offer rather than an invitation to make an offer depends on the legal intention of the parties and the surrounding circumstances. We are of the view on the facts before us that the offer by the defendant of the sale of the Lapin fur was clear, definite, and explicit, and left nothing open for negotiation. The plaintiff having successfully managed to be the first one to appear at the seller's place of business to be served, as requested by the advertisement, and having offered the stated purchase price of the article, he was entitled to performance on the part of the defendant. We think the trial court was correct."

Ethical Dimension

Is it fair to advertise items and then not sell them as advertised?

DURATION OF OFFER

Offers do not last forever. Even if no termination date is specified, the offer will end when a reasonable time elapses. What is a reasonable time depends on the facts of the particular situation. In a dispute, one party will argue that there is no contract because a reasonable time had passed before the offeree tried to accept the offer. The other party will claim that the offer was still open.

Offers end after a reasonable time if no ending date is stated.

Where the offer did specify a termination date, another kind of problem may arise. If the offeror promised to keep the offer open until a certain date, can the offer be revoked prior to that date? Generally, it can be, as long as the revocation is communicated to the offeree before that party sends back an acceptance. Unless the offeror is paid something in exchange for promising to keep the offer open, there is no contract to do so. This sort of preliminary contract, in which value is given to the offeror in return for keeping the offer open, is called an **option**. Options are used in real estate transactions, and could be used for other contracts as well. For sales of **goods** (tangible, movable items), the Uniform Commercial Code (UCC) says that a merchant is bound to keep its offer open, if it said in a signed writing that it would do so. This is called a **firm offer**. Under the UCC, a **merchant** is a dealer in goods of the kind involved in the transaction, or someone who is held out as having special knowledge about them, or someone who is represented by an agent who is held out as having such special knowledge. The merchant is not, however, bound to keep any offer open for more than three months.

A merchant may be bound to keep an offer for goods open.

TERMINATION OF OFFER

A revocation does not take effect to end the offer until the communication is received by the offeree. However, an offer is impliedly terminated if the specific thing to which the offer relates is destroyed before the offer is accepted. For example, Smith offers to sell Jones a certain used car. While Jones is still considering the offer, but before she accepts it, the car is wrecked. Smith's offer is impliedly ended, since the car is no more. If Jones learned that Smith had sold the car to Green before Jones accepted, the offer to sell to Jones would also be impliedly revoked.

If Jones rejects the car offer, her rejection ends the offer when Smith receives the rejection. The same result occurs if Jones sends Smith a **counteroffer**, that is, a proposal of different terms. For instance, Jones says she will buy, but at a lower price. When Smith gets the

A counteroffer ends the original offer.

counteroffer, his original offer to sell is terminated. Smith could now make a contract by accepting the counteroffer, but Jones could not change her mind and accept Smith's original offer. Jones' counteroffer killed the original offer; the ball is now in Smith's court.

CONTENTS OF ACCEPTANCE

As a rule, an acceptance must agree to all the terms contained in the offer. Changing any of them, or deleting any of them, or adding other terms, means that the response is not really an acceptance at all, but only a counteroffer. Lawyers call this the **"mirror-image" rule**: to be an acceptance, the response must be a mirror-image of the offer. To accept, an offeree must agree to the whole deal as proposed. An offeree cannot pick the favorable terms, reject the rest, and still insist that there is contract.

As a rule, an acceptance must be a mirror image of the offer.

For all contracts except for the sale of goods, a non-mirror-image response is a counteroffer, which ends the original offer. For goods, the UCC says that a positive response which contains different or additional terms is still an acceptance, unless the response includes express counteroffer language. To be a counteroffer under the UCC, the response must not only state changes; it must specify that there is no contract unless the changes are agreed to by the original offeror. As a rule, if there is no specific condition in the acceptance document, the contract would be made on the terms of the original offer. The changes would merely be proposals for addition to the contract, to which the original offeror would not have to respond, and which would not become part of the contract unless the original offeror expressly agreed. If both parties in the goods contract are merchants, non-material additions would become part of their contract unless the original offeror-merchant objected to them. Even if both buyer and seller are merchants, material changes (such as warranty disclaimers or arbitration clauses) would not become part of their contract unless expressly agreed to by the offeree-merchant.

DORTON V. COLLINS & AIKMAN CORPORATION

453 F.2d 1161 (U.S. 6th Cir. Court of Appeals, 1972).

Facts: Frank Dorton and J.A. Castle were partners who operated a retail carpet store, "The Carpet Mart," in Kingsport, Tennessee. In a series of more than fifty-five transactions during 1968, 1969, and 1970, Carpet Mart bought carpets from Collins & Aikman, a carpet manufacturer. Collins & Aikman was incorporated in Delaware and owned a plant in Dalton, Georgia. All the carpets were supposed to be made of 100 percent Kodel polyester fiber. Carpet Mart says that, after a customer complained in 1970, it learned that some of the carpets had been made with a cheaper, inferior fiber. Carpet Mart sued in state court in Tennessee for actual and punitive damages of $450,000. Collins & Aikman first had the case removed to U.S. District Court on the basis of diversity of citizenship and then argued that the lawsuit could not proceed until arbitration had occurred.

Arbitration clauses appeared in small print on the reverse side of the acknowledgement forms sent by Collins & Aikman to Carpet Mart. Oral orders had been telephoned to the Georgia plant, either by one of the partners or by a Collins & Aikman salesman. Plant personnel verified the prices on the order and Carpet Mart's credit and then mailed back an acknowledgement form. The Acknowledgement form stated on the front: "The acceptance of your order is subject to all of the terms and conditions on the face and reverse side hereof, including arbitration, all of which are accepted by the buyer; it supersedes buyer's order form, if any." The form further provided that it became a contract when the buyer signed it, received the goods, or "otherwise assented to the terms and conditions hereof." Carpet Mart received these acknowledgements, received the various carpet shipments, and never objected to any of the terms in the acknowledgements. The U.S. District Court refused to order arbitration. Collins & Aikman appealed.

Issue: Had Carpet Mart "agreed" to the arbitration clauses?

Decision: No. Case remanded for further specific findings of fact.

Rule: Additional terms in an acceptance are proposals for addition to a contract for the sale of goods. They do not become part of the contract without the other party's express consent unless they are non-material and both parties are merchants.

Discussion: *By Judge* CELEBREZZE:

"In reviewing this determination by the District Court, we are aware of the problems which courts have had in interpreting Section 2–207. This section of the UCC has been described as a 'murky bit of prose,'…as 'not too happily drafted,'…and as 'one of the most important, subtle, and difficult in the entire Code, and well it may be said that the product as it finally reads is not altogether satisfactory.'… Despite the lack of clarity in its language, Section 2–207 manifests definite objectives which are significant in the present case.…

"[U]nder Subsection (1) [of 2–207] a contract is recognized notwithstanding the fact that an acceptance or confirmation contains terms additional to or different from those of the offer or prior agreement, provided that the offeree's intent to accept the offer is definitely expressed,...and provided that the offeree's acceptance is not expressly conditioned on the offeror's assent to the additional or different terms....

"Assuming, for purposes of analysis, that the arbitration provision was an addition to the terms of The Carpet Mart's oral offers, we must next determine whether or not Collins & Aikman's acceptances were 'expressly made conditional on assent to the additional...terms.' In order to fall within this proviso,...an acceptance must be *expressly* conditional on the offeror's *assent* to those terms.... [The proviso] was intended to apply only to an acceptance which clearly reveals that the offeree is unwilling to proceed with the transaction unless he is assured of the offeror's assent to the additional or different terms therein....

"Regardless of whether the District Court finds Collins & Aikman's acknowledgment forms to have been acceptances or confirmations, if the arbitration provision was additional to, and a material alteration of, the offers or prior oral agreements, The Carpet Mart will not be bound to that provision absent a finding that it expressly agreed to be bound thereby."

[The Court of Appeals said that the District Court needed to make specific findings on three points: were the arbitration clauses agreed to as part of the oral orders, or were they "additional" terms; were they "material" changes, if they were additional; were they expressly agreed to by Carpet Mart, if they were additional and material. It seems fairly clear that Carpet Mart will win this case.]

Ethical Dimension

Is it fair for a buyer to accept delivery of the goods without agreeing to the seller's additional terms?

●

TIMING OF ACCEPTANCE

An acceptance is usually effective when mailed.

Unlike offers and rejections and revocations of offers, which are effective only when and if received, an acceptance is presumed to take legal effect when the communication is properly sent. Lawyers call this presumption the **"mail-box" rule.** A letter of acceptance forms the contract at the instant it is mailed. Both parties are bound at that point in time. Neither can change the contract, nor back out, without the consent of the other.

The mail-box rule assumes that the address on the letter is correct and that it contains sufficient postage. It also assumes that the offeror did not specify a different rule for acceptances. Since the offeror controls the terms of the offer, the offeror can specify whatever rule it wishes for acceptances.

There is no mail-box presumption where the offeree first sends a letter of rejection or counteroffer. That first negative response does not end the offer until received by the offeror. The offeree who then wishes to accept must get an acceptance to the offeror before the rejection/counteroffer arrives. If the acceptance is received first, there is a contract; if not, the would-be acceptance is only another counteroffer. For example, Brown mails a rejection on May 3, which will arrive on May 8. The receipt of the rejection on May 8 will terminate the offer. If Brown wishes to change her mind and accept the offer, she must get her acceptance to the offeror before he receives the rejection on May 8. If her second communication is received after the first one, there is no contract. Brown has made a counteroffer, but it would have to be accepted by the offeror in order for there to be a contract.

Finally, the mail-box rule assumes that the offeree uses the same method of communication as the offeror, or at least a reasonable alternative method. If the offeree uses an unreasonable method of communicating the acceptance, there is no mail-box effect. The unreasonable response is effective only when and if received (and only if the offer is still open at that point). If the offeror requires a particular method of acceptance, only that method can be used. Any other type of response would be a counteroffer.

INTERNATIONAL RULES

Persons negotiating contracts across international boundaries need to be aware that other countries may not follow the same rules on these issues. Customs differ, and so do statutes in particular countries. Treaties, such as the Convention on Contracts for the International Sale of Goods (CISG), may govern commercial relationships between persons in nations which have agreed to the treaty.

The CISG may apply to contracts for the international sale of goods.

The French offeror of a commercial contract, for example, is required to keep the offer open for some period of time—a rule similar to the UCC. England, however, still follows the general common law rule, which allows an offeror to revoke the offer any time prior to an effective acceptance. Most nations require a mirror-image for an acceptance, but a specific country's law could be different. The mail-box rule for acceptances may or may not be applied in France, depending on the circumstances of the particular negotiations. Because of these and many other potential differences, persons engaged in such contract negotiations need to state their intentions very clearly. (There may also be differences from country to country as to whether the parties can overide the normally applicable contract rules by so specifying in their contract.)

Consideration

As noted earlier, our legal system generally does not enforce a promise unless something of value was given in return for it. Stated another way, a promise to make a gift is usually not enforceable as a contract. The law almost always requires that there be a bargain, an exchange of benefits (or burdens).

MEANING OF THE CONSIDERATION REQUIREMENT

Something of value must be given in exchange, in order for a promise to be binding as a contract.

The basic meaning of the legal term **consideration** is value—the thing of value that is given in exchange for a promise. In the most typical case, the promises which the parties exchange provide the consideration for each other. The buyer's promise to pay the money for the used car is consideration for the seller's promise to deliver the car, and vice versa. A promise to make a gift of the car would not be enforceable as a contract because the car owner would be receiving no consideration in return. In general, the parties are free to make any sort of bargain they wish, and they can determine what they wish to be the basis of their exchange. The *Porporato* case illustrates these principles.

PORPORATO V. DEVINCENZI

261 Cal. App. 2d 670 (Cal. 1968)

Facts: Annie Marie Porporato was John Porporato's daughter-in-law. John let his son and Annie live in a new house John had built in San Francisco. John "idolized" his grandson and visited frequently. John's son was killed in military action in 1943. Annie was then visiting her family in Omaha, Nebraska, and decided to stay there and raise her son. John begged her to return to San Francisco so he could be near his grandson. John promised Annie he would leave her the house when he died, if she would return to San Francisco and raise her child there. She did so. When John died twenty years later, Annie discovered that John's will in fact in left the house to Anita DeVincenzi. Annie sued for specific performance of John's promise.

Issue: Did Annie Porporato provide consideration in exchange for her father-in-law's promise to leave her the house when he died?

Decision: Yes. Annie Porporato wins. She gets the house.

Rule: Doing an act at the promisor's request provides consideration for the promise made in return.

Discussion: *By Justice* CHRISTIAN:

"[T]he consideration she exchanged for the promise now sued upon was her agreement—in 1945—to do as the decedent asked. The proper time for testing the adequacy of consideration is as of the formation of the contract, and the court may consider 'such factors as the relationship of the parties, their friendship, love, affection, and regard for each other, and the object to be attained by the contract.' [Annie's] promise was exchanged for the decedent's: and in a…contract 'Mutual promises are concurrent considerations….' Her agreement to raise her son near the decedent was manifestly a 'benefit conferred, or agreed to be conferred, upon the promisor…to which the promisor [was] not lawfully entitled' and as such was a good consideration for the decedent's promise to her.…

"It is true that [Annie] did not uproot herself from elsewhere to keep her promise, but only remained in San Francisco, where she had already lived for several years. But the complaint also alleges that [she] was in Omaha when her husband was killed, and that she believed at the time that her interests and those of the child would be best served if she remained there with her own family and friends and obtained employment which was available to her there: nevertheless, she came back to San Francisco in reliance upon the decedent's promise.

"According to the allegations of the complaint, [Annie] returned to San Francisco as a new widow with an infant, entering a new and wholly different mode of life which cannot justly be characterized as merely 'remaining' in her former home, as contended by [DeVincenzi]. Her return to California was a significant change of position. That being so, she sufficiently pleads an estoppel [i.e., the defendant cannot insist that the promise is unenforceable because it is not in writing]; having alleged that she gave 20 years of her own life and the childhood years of her son in keeping her bargain, she will suffer 'unconscionable injury' if she is not permitted to enforce the contract."

Ethical Dimension

How ethical is it to make a promise of benefits, and then not deliver the benefits? Are there any circumstances under which the father-in-law would be justified in not leaving Annie the house?

COMPLIANCE ALTERNATIVES

There are several exceptional situations in which the courts will enforce a promise even though there is no bargain, or return value.

A person who has led another to rely on a promise may be bound to fulfill the promise.

Promissory Estoppel. Most courts would enforce a promise which led the other party to make a substantial change in legal position, in reasonable reliance on the promise. The promisor has not requested the performance as the price of the promise. The promise was made, and the promisee believed it and did something which would not otherwise have been done. In the *Porporato* case, by contrast, the move back to San Francisco was specifically requested by the father-in-law as the price for his leaving the house to Annie. There was clearly a bargain between Annie and her father-in-law. Even if there had been no bargain, it would not be fair to refuse to perform the promise after someone had relied on it and done something substantial that would not otherwise have been done. This change-of-position-in-reliance rule is usually referred to as **promissory estoppel**. The promisor is estopped, or prevented, from making the no consideration argument and avoiding liability on the promise, where the promise has been reasonably relied on by the promisee. Some courts use the phrase **detrimental reliance** to describe this rule. The case which the plaintiff-promisee must prove is essentially the same under either description.

Seals. Under the old common law rules in England, if a person signed and sealed a written document, it was conclusively presumed that value had been given for the promises made in the document. The person making promises in a signed and sealed writing could not raise the no-consideration argument in court when sued for nonperformance of the promise. Only a few of our states follow this rule today. In about half the states, the seal on a document (the word "seal," or the initials "L.S.") raises a rebuttable presumption that a promisor received value in exchange for the promises it contains. This means that the promisor has the burden of proving that there was in fact no value given in return for the promises. In the other half of the states, a sealed writing is treated the same as one without a seal; the promisee has the burden of showing what value was given for the promises made. This last rule is also used by the UCC for sales of goods contracts.

Both the UCC and other statutes have certain exceptions to the consideration requirement.

Statutory Exceptions. Some statutes (sections of the UCC, and other statutes) provide that certain promises are binding even though no consideration is given in return for them. As explained above, a goods merchant is bound to keep its offer to buy or sell goods open for the time period it states—up to three months—even though it receives nothing of value in return for that promise. The UCC also states that a claim for breach of contract can be settled by a simple written and signed statement which waives (gives up) the claim. Further, the UCC permits the parties to a goods contract to modify it any way they wish, later on, as long as they both agree to the modification. There does not have to be a new exchange of considerations; the modification can be totally one-sided, as long as both parties agree to it. These, and similar promises, are binding without any consideration simply because the statute says so.

LEGAL SUFFICIENCY OF CONSIDERATION

To make sure that there is a real bargain, and not just the promise of a gift dressed up in contract language, the courts have developed some fairly detailed rules. The basic test is that there must be a legally sufficient consideration—a thing or performance which the law recognizes as having enough value to support a return promise. This thing or performance need not have any recognized commercial value, so long as the court is convinced that it had real value to the parties. Annie Porporato's act of moving back to live in San Francisco is exactly the benefit that her father-in-law requested, even though the act does not have any specific market value.

Generally, the parties decide what things have value for their contract.

Pre-printed legal forms frequently contain a statement that "$1.00" has been given in exchange for certain promises. This is nearly always a sham, and is so treated by the courts. If all Porporato had was a promise by her father-in-law on such a form, she would not have received the house. Her father-in-law would just have made a gift promise, not a contract. The fake dollar figure is called **nominal consideration**; it is not legally sufficient, as the basis for a contract. On the other hand, if the parties have in fact set a real price for the promised performances, but simply wish to keep the dollar amount private, a statement that "$1.00 and other good and valuable consideration" has been given may not be a mere sham. As the next case shows, the courts are willing to examine the actual transaction to see whether it was a sham or was a genuine business transaction.

O'NEILL V. DELANEY

92 Ill. App. 3d 292 (Ill. 1980)

Facts: O'Neill claims that he bought a very valuable painting from his good friend James DeLaney, and that he now owns it free and clear of any claims by Jeannette DeLaney, James' wife. When questioned on the witness stand during the trial, O'Neill said that he paid ten dollars and "good and valuable" consideration. When asked what he meant by "good and valuable," he answered that he meant the "love and affection" which Mr. DeLaney felt towards him. The DeLaneys had no children, and O'Neill said that Mr. DeLaney considered him "like a son." Jeanette DeLaney claims the painting is still owned by her and James and is an asset whose value will have to be allocated as part of their divorce proceeding.

Issue: Is O'Neill a buyer of the painting or a donee (receiver of a gift)?

Decision: O'Neill loses; he was at best a donee. He does not own the painting.

Rule: To be a buyer of the painting, O'Neill would have to have given real value (legally sufficient consideration) for it.

Discussion: *By Justice LOREN:*

"An offer, an acceptance, and consideration are the basic elements of a contract. Consideration to support a contract is any act or promise which is of benefit to one party or disadvantage to the other. Whether there is consideration for a contract is a question of law for the court. Generally, courts will not inquire into the sufficiency of the consideration which supports a contract. However, where the amount of consideration is so grossly inadequate as to shock the conscience of the court, the contract will fail.... In such extreme cases,...'the stated consideration is a mere pretense' and no contract exists....

"Generally, a spouse has an absolute right to dispose of his or her property during marriage without the concurrence of the other spouse. Moreover, the spouse may do so even if the transfer is made for the express purpose of minimizing or defeating the marital interests of the surviving spouse. There is only one exception to this rule: when the transaction is merely 'colorable' or 'illusory' and is tantamount to fraud. This fraud, as explained by our supreme court, relates to the absence of a present intent to transfer title and ownership of the property, not the presence of an intent to defeat the marital interest or right of the other spouse.

"In the present case, the painting was purportedly sold to the plaintiff on August 18, 1970, for $10 and other good and valuable consideration. Plaintiff expressly testified that 'other good and valuable consideration' meant the love and affection plaintiff and James Paul DeLaney had for one another. In Illinois, love and affection does not constitute legal consideration. Thus, the only remaining valid consideration for the transaction was the tender of $10. As we noted above, the adequacy of the consideration must be determined as of the time of entering the contract. Plaintiff stated that at the time he purchased the painting, it was worth $100,000 if not authenticated and several hundred thousand dollars if authenticated as an original Rubens. James Paul DeLaney told him at the time of transfer that the painting was an original Rubens. A purchase price of $10 for such a valuable work of art is so grossly inadequate consideration as to shock the conscience of this court, as it did the trial court's. To find $10 valid consideration for this painting would be to reduce the requirement of consideration to a mere formality. This we will not do. By finding this to be inadequate consideration, we are not trying to protect one party against a bad deal entered into voluntarily, but rather are questioning the existence of the alleged contract.

"We hold that no valid sales contract existed between plaintiff and defendant James Paul DeLaney. Both the grossly inadequate consideration and the conduct of plaintiff and James Paul DeLaney demonstrate that this sales contract was colorable and a mere pretense. No present intent to transfer title to the painting existed here. Accordingly, the order of the circuit court is affirmed."

Ethical Dimension

Should one spouse be permitted to "sell" assets for nominal amounts without the consent of the other spouse?

●

Similar rules prevent enforcement of promises given in exchange for the performance of already-owed legal duties, or for things which have already been given in the past. **Past consideration** (things given or done previously) is not consideration for a promise made today. There is no bargain in this sort of situation. And promising to do something you already have to do anyway is not consideration for a return promise; this is the **pre-existing duty rule**. A promise of new or added benefits is not enforceable unless something new or additional is being received in exchange. For this reason, modifications of existing contracts must generally provide new benefits to each side, or the modification is not enforceable. The UCC rule for goods contracts discussed above is an exception to the general rule. Modifications of contracts for land, services, securities, or anything other than goods must have new consideration to each party.

Performances already done or already due do not provide exchanged value for a new promise.

Usually, the existence of a moral obligation underlying the promise is not a sufficient basis for enforcing the promise. **Moral consideration** is legally sufficient, however, in three situations. Most states do enforce promises made to charitable organizations, on the basis that there is a moral obligation to support such efforts. Second, most states will enforce a new promise made to pay an old debt which was discharged in bankruptcy, but never paid. (Where the debtor is a consumer, the bankruptcy court has to approve such reaffirmation of discharged debts.) There is still a moral obligation to pay one's debts. The same rationale is used to enforce a new promise to pay an old debt which has become unenforceable because the creditor waited too long to try to enforce it in court.

INTERNATIONAL RULES

Many other countries do not require an exchange of values to enforce a contract.

The consideration requirement is part of the Anglo-American common law system. It is not found in the Civil-Law systems of continental Europe, or in the legal systems in other parts of the world which are based on the Civil-Law system. Thus, in France or Germany, a promise could be contractually enforceable even without a bargained-for exchange of values. The promise of a gift could be enforceable if there were a legitimate reason (*causa*) for making the promise.

■ Writing Requirements

The third requirement for an enforceable contract applies to some, but not all, types of transactions. In 1677 the English Parliament passed a statute to prevent "frauds and perjuries." (**Perjury** is lying in court, while testifying under oath.) This "**Statute of Frauds,**" as it came to be known, was an attempt to prevent the enforcement of contracts which were never really made, but which were enforced because a jury believed perjured court testimony. Parliament's solution was to require a signed writing for certain types of contracts—real estate, promises to pay another person's debt, promises impossible to perform in less than one year, and sales of goods over a specified amount.

Some contracts are not enforceable without a signed writing.

These same categories have been carried over by most of our states. The UCC requires a writing for a sale of goods of $500 or more; for goods with a price of less than $500, an oral contract is fully enforceable. The UCC also requires any contract for investment securities (stocks and bonds) to be in writing, as well as sales of intangibles such as patents and copyrights if the price is $5,000 or more. The UCC further provides that a security interest against personal property as collateral must be in writing and signed by the debtor, unless the creditor (secured party) keeps possession of the collateral.

CONTENTS OF SIGNED WRITING

The traditional rule was (and is) that the writing must contain all the material terms of the contract and be signed by the party to be charged on the contract. In a real estate contract, for instance, the signed writing would have to include the parties, the property, the price and the payment terms—the four *P*'s.

The UCC does not require all terms be stated in the signed writing.

The UCC has greatly liberalized this old rule for sales of goods contracts. The writing must indicate that there is a sale of the goods, but only the quantity of goods being sold is required to be stated. All other terms—the price, the delivery date, warranties—are optional. (If the parties do not specify, the UCC will assume that a reasonable market price, a reasonable time for performance, and certain minimum quality warranties were intended.) For stocks and bonds, both the quantity and the price of the securities must be included. Of course, the UCC does require that the writing be signed by the party against whom enforcement of the contract is sought.

The following case involves the application of the statute of frauds to the transfer of a lease on a commercial building.

HYMAN FREIGHTWAYS V. CAROLINA FREIGHT CARRIERS CORP.

942 F.2d 500 (U.S. 8th Cir. Court of Appeals, 1991)

Facts: Hyman and Carolina both leased space at a trucking terminal in Hillside, Illinois, from Bellemeade Development Corporation. Hyman's lease would not end until October 31, 1989, but it wanted to move to another facility. Through a real estate agent, Phyllis Sutker, Hyman and Carolina corresponded about a possible assumption of Hyman's lease by Carolina. In a letter dated July 25, 1988, Sutker told Carolina that Hyman would be vacating the property by August 31, 1988. Hyman signed a lease on its new location on or about August 1. On August 5, Carolina sent Sutker a fax which stated in part: "Please use this letter to confirm our phone conversation earlier today, wherein we agreed to assume the Lease...between Hyman...and Bellemeade.... The effective date of the Lease Assignment will be approximately September 15, 1988, the actual date to be determined by mutual consent once Hyman has totally vacated the leased premises. The Lessor shall prepare an assignment document immediately for the approval and signatures of all parties, including Lessee, Lessor and Assignee."

An assignment of the lease was prepared, but the document was never signed. Hyman moved out over a three-day period, October 15–17, and gave its building keys to a Carolina employee at that time. On October 31, Carolina wrote to Hyman that it was withdrawing its offer to take over Hyman's lease. Hyman could not find anyone else to take over the lease and had to make the rest of the rental payments. Hyman sued Carolina in Minnesota state court. Carolina had the case removed to U.S. District Court, which then entered a summary judgment for Carolina. Hyman appeals.

Issue: Is the August 5 fax an adequate signed writing?

Decision: No, it is not. Judgment affirmed.

Rule: To enforce a contract for real estate, there must be a signed writing which contains all the material terms.

Discussion: *By Judge* GIBSON:

"An assignment of the Hyman space, being for a term longer than one year, would be an interest in land that would have to be evidenced by a writing to comply with the Illinois statute of frauds.... The only writing between the parties signed by the party to be charged (Carolina) is the August 5 fax, and thus that document controls this case; either it evidences a contract or it does not. We agree with the district court that it does not because, contrary to Illinois law, the date-of-assignment term was left open for future negotiation, which makes the purported agreement unenforceable.... 'When any essential term of an agreement is left to future negotiation, there is no binding contract.'...

"While Hyman urges that the term was identified as the date of Hyman's vacation of the premises—a date determinable by an event—we simply cannot avoid the language of the fax that the date was 'to be determined by mutual consent once Hyman has totally vacated the leased premises.'... That amounts to nothing more than an agreement to agree. Had the parties actually agreed to a lease assignment on the date of Hyman's vacation of the premises, they could be said to have so contracted. However, the only arguably sufficient writing (the August 5 fax) does not admit of such a simple solution.... This single correspondence in a series of negotiations is insufficient to evidence a contract for an interest in land.

"We do not doubt that the parties intended to reach an agreement on a lease assignment, and perhaps at one time they even believed they had reached one. Hyman suggests that we must give effect to this intent of the parties under Illinois case law. We disagree; Hyman's authorities are distinguishable because they proceed from the existence of a contract. In this case, Hyman's argument skips a necessary step; there must first be a contract evidencing the intent of the parties before a court can effectuate that intent. We cannot take the supposed intent of the parties to create the contract and independently supply that contract's terms. The law requires a writing evidencing a contract, not a writing evidencing intent to enter into a contract. The August 5 fax is evidence only of the latter; the former simply never came about."

Ethical Dimension

On the facts given, was it ethical for Carolina to change its mind and to refuse to go through with the assumption of the lease?

ENFORCEMENT ALTERNATIVES

Full performance may require performance of the other party's oral promise.

The original English statute of frauds, and the state statutes which copied it, did not provide any alternatives to the signed writing. Courts did, however, develop some limited exceptions to the writing requirement. In some states, an admission in court that the oral contract was made by the person being charged on the contract will permit enforcement. If a person has fully performed one side of an over-one-year contract, the other side's performance should be enforced. If there has been only partial performance, the fair value of that partial performance should be paid.

For real estate, if the buyer has been permitted to take possession and has made valuable, permanent improvements to the land, the oral contract is usually enforced. Some states permit enforcement of the oral real estate contract if the buyer has taken possession and has paid part of the contract price.

UCC STATUTORY ALTERNATIVES TO THE WRITING

If both parties to the goods contract are merchants, the UCC permits either to send the other a writing in confirmation of their prior oral contract. If the writing is sufficient to enforce the contract against the sender merchant, it also makes the contract enforceable against the receiver merchant, unless the receiver sends back written notice of objection to its contents within ten days after it is received. Similar confirmations can be used in securities transactions—by anyone (not just by merchants or brokers). The securities confirmation must contain the price as well as the quantity and be signed by the sender.

The UCC has several alternatives to the signed writing.

Admission in court is specifically listed in the UCC as an acceptable alternative to the signed writing for enforcement of goods or securities contracts. Where there has been partial delivery or partial payment, a reciprocal portion of the contract can be enforced on that basis. If the goods are not divisible (an item such as a car or airplane), a down payment accepted by the seller would make the entire contract enforceable, even without a signed writing.

Finally, sellers of custom-made goods are protected by a UCC section which permits them to enforce an oral contract if they have made a substantial start on making or acquiring the special goods before the buyer tries to repudiate the oral contract.

The following case discusses the UCC's "confirmation" alternative.

SIERENS V. CLAUSEN

328 N.E.2d 559 (Ill. 1975)

Facts: Edwin Clausen had been a farmer for thirty-four years. He was raising 150 acres of soybeans and 180 acres of corn. He had been selling his crops to grain elevators for the last five years. Kenneth Sierens and James Thompson claimed that Clausen had made two oral contracts with them to sell them a total of 3,500 bushels of his soybeans. They said that they had sent Clausen a written confirmation of these oral contracts. The trial court held

that the Statute of Frauds had not been satisfied because a farmer is not a merchant. The Court of Appeals affirmed.

Issue: Is a farmer who sells his own grain a merchant under the UCC?

Decision: Sierens wins on this point. Clausen is a merchant. (The case is sent back to the trial court to give Sierens a chance to prove that an oral contract was agreed to by Clausen.)

Rule: A merchant is defined as including a person who by his occupation holds himself out as having special knowledge about the goods involved in the transaction.

Discussion: *By Justice GOLDENHERSH:*

"The practice of grain and soybean growers in selling their products in the manner described in plaintiffs' amended complaint is well known and widely followed. We know of no reason why under the circumstances shown here the defendant, admittedly a farmer, cannot at the time of the sale be a 'merchant.' On this record we hold that he was a merchant and that Section 2–201 of the Uniform Commercial Code applied to those transactions.

"In his motion to strike the complaint defendant has attacked the sufficiency of the written confirmations of the agreements sent by plaintiffs. We have examined the documents and hold them to be sufficient under the provisions of Section 2–201 of the Uniform Commercial Code.

"Although for purposes of the motion all facts well pleaded are taken as true, defendant's letter 'repudiating' the agreements, which appears in the record as an exhibit attached to plaintiffs' amended complaint, purports to raise the question whether the parties entered into the oral contracts. Although we have determined as a matter of law defendant's status and the sufficiency of the confirmations, the remaining question is one for the trier of fact."

Ethical Dimension

Is it ethical to agree to something orally, and then use the Statute of Frauds as a defense because you never signed anything?

INTERNATIONAL RULES

Since much of our law on these points was copied from English law, there are still many similarities. Many other countries, including France, the (former) U.S.S.R., and the People's Republic of China, also recognize that some contracts need to be in written form to be enforceable, but their categories are not the same as ours.

Perhaps the most important international rule is found in the Convention on Contracts for the International Sale of Goods, which does not require a writing for goods transactions between citizens of nations which have signed the treaty. A goods contract between a U.S. firm and a French firm, for example, would not have to be in writing, regardless of the price of the goods. If such parties wanted to require written proof of their transaction, they would have to so specify during their negotiations with each other.

The CISG does not require a signed writing.

PAROL EVIDENCE RULE

There is one last point regarding writings that needs explanation. For any type of contract, if the parties have signed a writing which they intend to be the complete statement of the agreed terms, the courts generally do not permit either of them to add to or modify those terms. No **"parol"** (oral or written proofs "outside" the document) evidence will be heard to vary or contradict the terms contained in the final writing. This rule does not prevent the parties from modifying their deal later; it just prevents them from trying to prove that something "extra" was agreed to during the negotiations.

Prior "extra" promises can usually not be enforced where a writing states it is final.

A party can try to show that no contract should be enforced because of the existence of one of the defenses against liability discussed in the next chapter. "Outside" evidence can also be introduced to clear up an ambiguity in the written contract. One of the parties may also try to prove that there has been a mistake in writing up the terms expressly agreed to. What the parol evidence rule prohibits is evidence which adds on or changes terms in a complete, final written contract. Note the size of the attempted add-on in the *Shepherd Realty* case.

SHEPHERD REALTY CO. V. WINN-DIXIE MONTGOMERY, INC.

418 So. 2d 871 (Ala. 1982)

Facts: In 1971 Winn-Dixie entered into a twenty-year lease for a 30,000 square foot food supermarket in a shopping center. A "merchants association" for all the stores in the shopping center was organized in 1974. The association set monthly dues at twenty cents per square foot of floor space in the individual store. Winn-Dixie voluntarily paid these dues for five years, although there was no clause in its lease which specifically required it to do so. All other store leases did contain such a clause. When the dues were raised to twenty-eight cents per square foot in 1979, Winn-Dixie objected to paying the higher amount, and eventually, to paying any dues at all. Shepherd

Realty, the landlord, sued to declare the lease in default. Shepherd Realty claims payment of dues can be required under a "Rules and Regulations" paragraph (#42) in the lease.

Issue: Can Shepherd Realty try to prove that Winn-Dixie had agreed to join the merchants association, even though its lease contained no such provision?

Decision: Winn-Dixie wins. They do not have to pay dues to the association.

Rule: If the writing is intended as final, it cannot be contradicted by adding on terms.

Discussion: *By Justice* EMBRY:

"There was no error in the trial court's ruling that Winn-Dixie was not required to be a member of the Brookwood Village Merchants Association. There is no specific language in the lease requiring Winn-Dixie to join the merchants association. Furthermore, the record reflects that specific language requiring such membership was found in the leases of other tenants of Brookwood Village but not in the Winn-Dixie lease.

"Shepherd Realty vigorously argues that paragraph 42 of the lease should be construed as requiring Winn-Dixie to become and remain a member of the merchants association. Upon a careful reading of that paragraph, together with the other terms of the lease, we conclude that paragraph 42 cannot be construed as requiring Winn-Dixie's membership in the association. Rather, we conclude that this paragraph, on its face, only provides a means by which Shepherd Realty may compel Winn-Dixie to comply with rules affecting the normal operation of Brookwood Village Convenience Center of a nature regarding parking, maintenance, etc., insofar as its premises and appurtenant facilities are concerned. Once a contract between two parties is reduced to writing, absent mistake or fraud, the courts must construe the contract as written. 'Furthermore, in the absence of ambiguity, the court cannot interpret the contract but must take it as it is written.'...

"Paragraph 33 of the lease also militates against a liberal construction of paragraph 42. [It] provides: 'The written lease contains the complete agreement of the parties with reference to the leasing of the demised premises except plans and specifications for tenant's store and related improvements to be formally approved by the parties prior to the effective date of this lease.'

"We agree with Winn-Dixie that 'Paragraph 33 clearly indicates the lease constitutes the complete agreement between the parties.'

"The trial court was correct in refusing to admit parol evidence to show the 'true intent' of the parties. It is fundamental that the parol evidence rule prohibits the contradiction of a written agreement by evidence of a prior oral agreement. The rule provides, generally, that when the parties reduce a contract to writing, intended to be a complete contract regarding the subject covered by that contract, no extrinsic evidence of prior or contemporaneous agreements will be admissible to change, alter, or contradict such writing."

Ethical Dimension

Is it fair to hold parties to the terms in a writing they have both signed and agreed on as final?

REVIEW

Freedom of contract is one of the keystones of our modern economic system. Both companies and individuals make numerous contracts every day. A large supermarket or department store is probably making thousands of contracts every business day. Knowing the rules for entering into an enforceable contract is thus important for effective business operations.

Making a contract requires entering into an agreement and having an exchange of legal values as the result of that agreement. The formation of an agreement requires that one party make an offer to do business and that the other party accept that offer while it is still open and available for acceptance. For some important types of contracts, such as those for land or for goods with a price of $500 or more, a signed writing is generally required in order for the contract to be enforceable in court. The contract formula is thus: agreement + consideration + (sometimes) signed writing = enforceable contract.

REVIEW QUESTIONS AND PROBLEMS

1. Explain the "mirror-image" rule. Does it apply in all contracting situations?

2. Define the term "promissory estoppel." How is it applied to contracts?

3. Why is the parol evidence rule important to contracting parties?

4. Explain the difference between "pre-existing duty" and "past consideration."

5. What differences are there between the writing requirements imposed by the original Statute of Frauds and those found in the UCC?

6. What is the significance of the "mail-box rule"?

7. Louise was employed as a supervisor for Zarro Electric. Zarro had a contract to do the electrical work on a large construction project. Louise was assigned to supervise the job. She claims that Zarro's owner, Harvey, promised her that she would get a bonus of fifty percent of any cost savings Louise could generate in doing the work. (Whatever difference there was between the estimated cost for the job and the actual cost, half would be paid to Louise.) Louise's crew did exceed the production standards required by their union contract and saved Zarro $35,000. Harvey now says that Louise has provided no consideration for any "bonus," and refuses to pay anything extra to Louise. Can Louise sue and collect? Why or why not?

8. Gina taught mathematics at Normal College. She was originally appointed as a lecturer, but became an associate professor when she received her Ph.D. in 1989. Gina claims she was promised lifetime employment, beginning with a three-year contract. Normal has notified Gina that she will not be reappointed for the 1992–93 school year. Gina filed a lawsuit alleging breach of contract. Normal moves to dismiss the case, since Gina has nothing in writing except monthly statements which show her pay and deductions. How should the court rule? Explain.

9. Adam and Eve Edwards mailed a signed, written offer of purchase to Jerry and Terri Baker, who owned a piece of real estate which they had advertised as being for sale. Jerry and Terri signed the purchase offer form on the bottom, indicating that they accepted it, and mailed it back to Adam and Eve. The very next day (before Adam and Eve had received the returned form), Jerry and Terri got a much higher offer for the land from another buyer. Jerry called Eve on the telephone and told her that her offer was rejected. Two days after the telephone call, Adam and Eve did receive the purchase form that Jerry and Terri had signed. Adam and Eve sue to enforce the contract; Jerry and Terri claim there is no contract. Who is right, and why?

10. Henrietta wanted to go into business, as a franchisee of Red Robin Stores. Red Robin's representative told her that they would build a store for her in Mhilly, Minnesota, but that she would have to invest $100,000. To qualify as a franchisee, she would also have to have at least six months experience as a retail manager. Henrietta sold her home outside Minneapolis, moved to Mhilly, bought a small hardware store and operated it for nine months, then sold it and bought a building site for her Red Robin Store. When she called Red Robin and told them she had the money, the experience, and the building site, she was told that she would have to invest $200,000. Henrietta did not have the additional capital and sued for breach of the original agreement. Red Robin says that there never was a contract, because they never received anything from Henrietta. How should the court resolve this dispute? Discuss.

SUGGESTIONS FOR FURTHER READING

Highsmith and Havens, "Revocation of Acceptance and the Defective Automobile: The Uniform Commercial Code to the Rescue," *American Business Law Journal* 18 (Summer 1980): 303.

Metzger and Phillips, "Promissory Estoppel and the Evolution of Contract Law," *American Business Law Journal* 18 (Summer 1980): 139.

Nathan, "Grappling with the Pre-Existing Duty Rule: A Proposal for a Statutory Amendment," *American Business Law Journal* 23 (Winter 1986): 509.

8
LIMITATIONS ON FREEDOM OF CONTRACT

*"[F]oresight may be vain: The best-laid schemes o'
mice an' men gang aft agley [often go astray]."*
Robert Burns

LEARNING OBJECTIVES: After you have studied this chapter, you should be able to:

EXPLAIN the impact of lack of contractual capacity on a contract.

IDENTIFY the different types of mistakes and their impact on a contract.

EXPLAIN what is meant by impossibility, impracticability, and unconscionability.

DISCUSS the effect on a contract of a misrepresentation of fact by one party.

DEFINE duress and undue influence as they relate to contracts.

IDENTIFY various types of illegality as they impact on contracts.

P REVIEW

Some contracts are not enforced.

While our legal system gives us wide latitude in deciding what contracts we wish to make, there are some outer limits. Bargains which involve the commission of a crime or tort, or which are otherwise prohibited, are not enforced. The law also wants to make sure that both parties have fully and freely consented to the arrangement. Therefore the law does not enforce contracts based on force or fraud, or, sometimes, mistake. Increasingly, the courts are also unwilling to enforce grossly unfair contracts. In addition, there are rules to insure that both parties are capable of understanding the transaction to which they are agreeing; that is, that they have the "mental capacity" to make a contract.

L ACK OF CONTRACTUAL CAPACITY

Every person is presumed to have mental capacity. A person alleging a lack of such capacity has the burden of proving it. Where someone does enter into a contract while suffering from a mental disability, the contract is generally either void or voidable. Similar rules apply to persons who lack contractual capacity due to age or legal status.

Mental Disability, Intoxication, or Drug Influence

Contracts made by a person lacking mental capacity are voidable or void.

The most obvious case in which a person's contracts should not be binding occurs when one party lacks understanding because of mental disease or mental defect. If the person has been declared mentally incompetent by a court and has had a legal guardian appointed, the guardian is to make all contract and property decisions for the mentally ill person while the disability lasts. Attempts to contract by the mentally ill person are totally null and void. If money or other property is actually transferred, it should be returned. If no legal guardian has yet been appointed, such contracts are voidable by the mentally ill person after recovery, or by a guardian when one is appointed. Here again, if property has been transferred, it should be returned.

Where a guardian has been appointed, a court will have ruled on the person's lack of mental capacity. Otherwise, the general test is whether the person, at the time of contracting, was able to understand the nature and consequences of the transaction. This same basic test is used where it is alleged that someone was intoxicated or under the influence of drugs at the time of contracting. Whatever the specific reason for the lack of mental capacity, if the person did not understand what was going on, the resulting contract should not be enforceable by the other party.

■ Minority

The law gives the same kind of choice (to disaffirm the contract) to persons who lack full understanding because of age. Such persons are called **minors**, or "legal infants." The original common law rules drew the line at age twenty-one. In most states today, the age of contract majority is the same as the voting age—eighteen. There may, however, be different ages at which other legal acts, such as getting married, making a will, or purchasing alcoholic beverages, are permitted.

A person under eighteen who makes a contract is thus given the choice of disaffirming it while still a minor or for a reasonable time after reaching the age of majority. What is a reasonable time is a question of fact to be decided in each specific case. One case involving purchase of a car said that disaffirmance four months after majority was still within a reasonable time; a similar case said ten months was too long, particularly where the person had made ten monthly installment payments during that time. Most states have a different rule for real estate transactions: the minor must wait until the age of majority and then disaffirm within a reasonable time. If the minor does not disaffirm, the contract is **ratified** and the minor is bound to perform it.

Contracts by persons under age are usually voidable.

Where the minor (or former minor) does disaffirm within the proper time, the other party must return all things received from the minor. If the other party no longer has the actual item, its fair value must be paid to the minor. Conversely, most states do require the minor to return what was received, but only if the minor still has that same item at the time of disaffirmance. Some states do require the minor to pay for use value while the minor had the item or depreciation which has occurred, but most states do not.

■ Necessaries

A seller who has supplied the minor with such necessities as food, clothing, shelter, or medical care can collect the reasonable value of the item from the minor. Reasonable value cannot exceed the contract price; it might be substantially less, as determined by a jury. This alternative enforcement is available only to the extent that the item was actually used by the minor prior to disaffirmance of the contract. And it is available only if the seller can show that the item was actually a necessary to the particular minor in question. A minor who is **emancipated**, that is, free from parental control and support, will need to make contracts for the necessities of life. A minor who is still dependent upon parents or guardians will normally not need to do so. Whether an apartment was a necessary is at issue in the following case. As the Nebraska court notes, emancipation does not mean that the minor has full contractual capacity. It only means that the minor is free of parental control and support. An emancipated minor is still a minor, but will be liable for the reasonable value of any necessaries purchased.

A person who sells necessaries to a minor can collect reasonable market value.

WEBSTER STREET PARTNERSHIP V. SHERIDAN

368 N.W.2d 439 (Neb. 1982)

Facts: On September 18, 1982, Webster Street leased an apartment to two minors, Matthew Sheridan and Pat Wilwerding. The boys wanted to try living on their own for a while. They paid a $150 security deposit, $100 rent for the rest of September, and $250 for October. Sheridan became an adult on November 5. The boys moved back home on November 12. Webster Street sued for damages for breach of contact: $500 rent for November and December, $20 for utilities, $40 for garage rental, $46.79 for clean-up, $24.15 for advertising for a new tenant; $150 re-rental fee. Webster Street claimed $630.94, after it deducted the $150 security deposit. It won in the Municipal Court, but the District Court said Webster Street owed the boys $3.25. The boys then filed a further appeal with the state supreme court.

Issue: Was the apartment a necessary for Sheridan and Wilwerding?

Decision: No. Landlord collects nothing, and must refund all money paid.

Rule: It is not necessary for the minor to make a contract for items which are available from parents or guardians.

Discussion: *By Chief Justice* KRIVOSHA:

"As a general rule, an infant does not have the capacity to bind himself absolutely by contract.... The right of the infant to avoid his contract is one conferred by law for his protection against his own improvidence and the designs of others.... The policy of the law is to discourage adults from contracting with an infant; they cannot complain if, as a consequence of violating that rule, they are unable to enforce their contracts.... 'The result seems hardly just to the [adult], but persons dealing with infants do so at their peril. The law is plain as to their disability to contract, and safety lies in refusing to transact business with them.'

"However, the privilege of infancy will not enable an infant to escape liability in all cases and under all circumstances. For example, it is well established that an infant is liable for the value of necessaries furnished him.... An infant's liability for necessaries is based not upon his actual contract to pay for them but upon a contract implied by law, or, in other words, a quasi contract....

"The undisputed testimony in this case is that both were living away from home, apparently with the understanding that they could return home at any time.... It would therefore appear that in the present case neither Sheridan nor Wilwerding was in need of shelter but, rather, had chosen to voluntarily leave home, with the understanding that they could return whenever they desired. One may at first blush believe that such a rule is unfair. Yet, on further consideration the wisdom of the rule is apparent. If, indeed, landlords may not contract with minors, except at their peril, they may refuse to do so. In that event, minors who voluntarily leave home but who are free to return will be compelled to return to their parents' home—a result which is desirable. We therefore find that both the municipal court and the district court erred in finding that the apartment, under the facts in this case, was necessary.

"Having therefore concluded that the apartment was not a necessary, the question of whether Sheridan and Wilwerding were emancipated is of no significance. The effect of emancipation is only relevant with regard to necessaries. If the minors were not emancipated, then their parents would be liable for necessaries provided to the minors....

"If, on the other hand, it was determined that the minors were emancipated and the apartment was a necessary, then the minors would be liable. But where, as here, we determine that the apartment was not a necessary, then neither the parents nor the infants are liable and the question of emancipation is of no moment.

"Because the rental of the apartment was not a necessary, the minors had the right to avoid the contract, either during their minority or within a reasonable time after reaching their majority.... Disaffirmance by an infant completely puts an end to the contract's existence, both as to him and as to the adult with whom he contracted.... Because the parties then stand as if no contract had ever existed, the infant can recover payments made to the adult, and the adult is entitled to the return of whatever was received by the infant."

Ethical Dimension

Is it ethical for a minor to make a contract and then refuse to go through with it on the basis of minority? Does it make any difference whether the other party knew it was dealing with a minor?

●

■ Misrepresentation by Minor

Occasionally, minors lie about their age during contract negotiations. What effect do such misrepresentations have on their liability? States do not agree on what should happen in such cases.

*Minors who lie about
their ages when making
contracts are liable in
some states.*

Some states prevent the minor from disaffirming a contract if there has been misrepresentation of age. "Johnny said he was over eighteen, so we will hold him to the contract he made on that basis." Because sellers of cars and other goods might be tempted to use this argument in every minority case, at least one state holds a minor to the contract only if the misrepresentation of age is made in a separate signed writing. Most states will permit the minor to disaffirm the contract.

Another group of states permits the lying minor to disaffirm, but also permits the other party to sue for the tort of fraud. The minor has lied, and the other party is injured financially when the minor disaffirms. The states which do not let the other party sue in tort think that it is more important to protect the minor from unwise contracts than to protect sellers who deal with minors.

■ Other Special Capacity Rules

*Other persons may also
have a special legal
status.*

At common law, based on the legal fiction that the husband and wife were one person, the married woman lacked legal capacity to contract. The husband could be held liable for the fair value of necessaries his wife purchased for the family, but otherwise her contracts were totally void. Today, nearly all states give a married woman the same contractual powers as her husband.

Aliens lawfully in this country enjoy nearly all the same rights as citizens, except for voting and running for political office. If they qualify, they have the right to practice professions such as law and medicine. The national government has passed an act to prevent employers from hiring aliens who are not lawfully in this country or who do not have permission to work here.

Special rules may also exist for other groups. New York, for instance, had a statute which prohibited criminals from making a profit on their crimes by selling their story to the media. (The obvious constitutional problem with this statute was its violation of freedom of the press. It was ruled invalid on that basis by the U.S. Supreme Court.)

■M ISTAKE

All kinds of mistakes can occur during the process of negotiating, writing, and performing a contract. If one of the parties can prove that such a mistake did occur, the courts will generally try to work out a fair result in light of all the circumstances. In many cases, however, the courts do enforce the bargain as made. Some risk is inherent in the bargaining process, and both parties are presumed to know that when they enter into their contract.

■ Mutual Mistake in Basic Assumptions

In some situations, both parties are mistaken about some basic fact which was important to their contract. Something which they both assumed to be true turns out not to be so. If their whole deal hinged on the existence of this fact, the courts will usually say that there is no contract. In effect, they did not make the contract they both thought they had made: there is no contract at all. The *Beachcomber Coins* case illustrates this kind of mistake.

There is no contract if both parties are mistaken as to a material assumption.

BEACHCOMBER COINS, INC. V. BOSKETT

400 A.2d 78 (N. J. 1979)

Facts: Beachcomber is a retail coin dealer. It bought what was supposed to be a rare 1916 dime from Boskett. The *D* stamped on the coin meant that it had originated at the Denver, Colorado, branch of the U.S. mint. When Beachcomber later tried to resell the coin for $700, the customer determined that the *D* had been stamped on by someone other than the U.S. mint. The coin was a fake, although neither Boskett nor Beachcomber Coins had realized it at the time. Beachcomber sued Boskett to rescind their contract of sale. The trial judge held for Boskett, on the basis that Beachcomber had assumed the risk of non-genuineness.

Issue: Is there a contract if both parties were mistaken as to the identity of the thing being bought and sold?

Decision: No. Judgment reversed. The seller must refund the contract price and take back the fake coin.

Rule: If both parties are mistaken as to the identity of the subject-matter of the contract, there is no contract.

Discussion: *By Judge* CONFORD:

"[N]egligent failure of a party to know or to discover the facts as to which both parties are under a mistake does not preclude rescission or reformation on account thereof. It is undisputed that both parties believed that the coin was a genuine Denver-minted one. The mistake was mutual in that both parties were laboring under the same misapprehension as to this particular, essential fact. The price asked and paid was directly based on that assumption. That plaintiff may have been negligent in his inspection of the coin (a point not expressly found but implied by the trial judge) does not, as noted above, bar its claim for rescission.

"Defendant's contention that plaintiff assumed the risk that the coin might be of greater or lesser value than that paid is not supported by the evidence. It is well established that a party to a contract can assume the risk of being mistaken as to the value of the thing sold. The *Restatement* states the rule this way: 'Where the parties know that there is doubt in regard to a certain matter and contract on that assumption, the contract is not rendered voidable because one is disappointed in the hope that the facts accord with his wishes. The risk of the existence of the doubtful fact is then assumed as one of the elements of the bargain.'

"However, for the stated rule to apply, the parties must be conscious that the pertinent fact may not be true and make their agreement at the risk of that possibility. In this case both parties were certain that the coin was genuine. They so testified. Plaintiff's principal thought so after his inspection, and defendant would not have paid nearly $450 for it otherwise. A different case would be presented if the seller were uncertain either of the genuineness of the coin or of its value if genuine, and had accepted the expert buyer's judgment on these matters."

Ethical Dimension

Is it ethical for a seller to insist on enforcing a contract where the thing sold turns out not to be what the parties both thought it was?

Material Unilateral Mistake

In some cases, a party who submits an obviously mistaken offer can withdraw it.

In cases where there is a **unilateral mistake**—a mistake by only one of the parties—the contract is usually enforceable as negotiated. However, in at least one sort of contracting situation, the courts may also rule that one party's mistake will produce the no-contract result. Public works projects, such as road construction or bridge building, are typically awarded to the lowest of several bidders. What happens if the low bidder has made a mathematical error in adding up the figures in its bid? Is it bound to do the job for the mistaken low price or be liable for breach of contract? The answer is probably no, at least if the error is so big that the other party must have known that there had been a mistake. Several cases have given relief for this kind of error, even though it is all one party's fault.

Mistake in Integration

Mistakes can also occur in writing up the contract. Typographical errors do happen, even in lawyers' offices. As long as both parties agree that the writing is mistaken, there is no problem. Simply write up a new document.

What if one party insists that the writing is correct, and the other says it is wrong? There is a strong presumption that a written, signed document is correct. But if there is clear evidence that it does contain a mistake, a court has the power to correct the document and then to enforce the real terms of the contract.

■ Mistake in Performance

What happens when one party to a contract performs at the wrong time and place or for the wrong person? Difficult problems can occur, and the courts simply have to do the best job they can of working out a fair result.

Mistakes made in performing a contract may be difficult to correct.

Where money is paid to someone by mistake, the solution is obvious: the money must be returned. But suppose a crew from a paving company, sent to black-top a driveway at 210 South Seventh Street, does the job by mistake on my driveway at 210 North Seventh Street? If I'm at home and see them doing the job and don't tell them anything, I owe the fair market price of the job. But suppose I'm not at home— then what? Probably, I have received a free black-top job, since it was their mistake and I had no chance to tell them I didn't want it. Suppose instead that the crew had been sent by a wrecking company to tear down the house at 210 South Seventh, and they tear down mine—by mistake? This question is a little harder to answer, but I should at least receive the current fair value of my house. A court might force the company who made the mistake to pay the cost of rebuilding a similar house and might also hold it liable for tort damages. As far as possible, the innocent party should be put back in the situation which existed before the mistake was made.

■ IMPOSSIBILITY OR IMPRACTICABILITY OF PERFORMANCE

A situation similar to mutual mistake occurs when, unknown to either party, the subject-matter of their contract does not exist at the time they reach agreement. The house which they were buying and selling, or which was being leased, has already burned down. Pretty clearly, in such cases, there is no contract.

Contract performances which become impossible to perform may be excused.

Where a contract specifies a particular item or batch of goods, and those goods are destroyed before the buyer has assumed the risk of their loss, the UCC says the contract is discharged if the goods are totally destroyed. If there is only a partial loss, the buyer has the option of taking the remainder of the goods with an appropriate price reduction or cancelling the contract. The buyer of an antique car which had been damaged in a windstorm might still want the car. Most new car buyers would probably not want a damaged vehicle at all, unless the seller made a very large price reduction.

If a particular source for performance of the contract is specified, such as "the Apex factory in Fostoria, Ohio," and that source is destroyed, the contract is also discharged. In general, when anything occurs which makes the performance of the contract absolutely impossible, the contract is discharged.

◾ Impracticability

The UCC excuses goods contracts which are impracticable.

In contrast to impossibility of performance, performance may be merely "**impracticable**." For sales of goods, the UCC says that where some later event makes the performance "impracticable" the contract is discharged. The basic meaning of this new term is that it is economically unrealistic to require the contract performance. The unforeseen event has made performance much more expensive and the cost greatly disproportionate to any possible benefit the other party would receive.

◾ International Rules

Civil-law legal systems generally recognize the doctrine of *force majeure*, or "*irresistible force*." Derived from the Roman Law, this doctrine excuses performance where an irresistible force, unforeseen by the parties, has substantially changed their situation. The original Latin phrase is *vis major*. It has roughly the same meaning as the common-law phrase "act of God." Events such as hurricanes, floods, or earthquakes would be covered under *force majeure*.

Parties to international transactions frequently include *force majeure* clauses in their contracts. Large U.S. companies, especially those experienced in international trade, may also use such clauses for their contracts within the United States. Since Louisiana law was originally based on the Code Napoleon, the doctrine has special relevance there. The following classic case involving a Louisiana land lease discusses the use of *force majeure*.

VITERBO V. FRIEDLANDER

120 U.S. 707 (1887).

Facts: Viterbo, a French citizen, entered a five-year lease for a Louisiana sugar plantation owned by Friedlander, a Louisiana citizen. Included in the lease were nearly three hundred acres of seed sugar cane growing on the land for the next year's crop. The lease was signed October 27, 1883. In March, 1884, the Mississippi River overflowed its banks, broke through a levee which protected the plantation next door, and flooded Viterbo's leased land as well. Most of the plantation was under water for several months. All the seed sugar cane was destroyed. So were several bridges. The irrigation ditches on Viterbo's plantation were filled with washed-in dirt and not usable without extensive digging and dredging. Viterbo sued to cancel the balance of the lease. The trial judge dismissed the complaint. Viterbo appealed to the U.S. Supreme Court. (At the time there was no U.S. Court of Appeals.)

Issue: Can a lessee cancel a lease when the land is flooded?

Decision: Yes. Trial court judgment is reversed.

Rule: An unforeseen event which wholly or partly destroys the land, or renders it unfit for the intended purpose, entitles the lessee to cancel the lease.

Discussion: *By Justice* GRAY:

"In considering this case it is important to keep in mind that the view of the common law of England and of most of the United States, as to the nature of a lease for years, is not that which is taken by the civil law of Rome, Spain, and France, upon which the Civil Code of Louisiana is based. The common law and the civil law concur in holding that, in the case of an executed sale, a subsequent destruction of the property by any cause is the loss of the buyer.... They also concur in holding that performance of an executory obligation to convey a specific thing is excused by the accidental destruction of the thing, without the fault of the obligor, before the conveyance is made....

"But as to the nature and effect of a lease for years,...the two systems differ materially. The common law regards such a lease as the grant of an estate for years which the lessee takes a title in, and is bound to pay the stipulated rent for, notwithstanding any injury by flood, fire, or external violence, at least unless the injury is such a destruction of the land as to amount to an eviction; and by that law the lessor is under no implied [duty] to repair.... The civil law, on the other hand, regards a lease for years as a mere transfer of the use and enjoyment of the property; and holds the landlord bound, without any express [promise], to keep it in repair...even when the need of repair...is caused by an inevitable accident; and, if he does not do so, the tenant may have the lease annulled, or the rent abated....

[The Court then did an extensive analysis of Louisiana's Civil Code.]

"Upon a comparison of the English text with the French of so much of the Louisiana Code as bears upon this case, the greater uniformity and precision of the French text, and its striking resemblance to the Code Napoleon, make it quite clear that the French is the original, and the English the translation.... In one place *'cas fortuit ou force majeure'* is rendered 'fortuitous event or irresistible force,' and in another, 'accidental and uncontrollable events'; thus treating the two alternative expressions as synonymous.... *'Force majeure'* is also rendered in different places 'unforeseen events,' 'overpowering force,' and 'force,' only; *'evenement de force majeure'* as 'accident'; and *'accidens de force majeure'* as 'inevitable accident.' It cannot be doubted, therefore, that the words 'unforeseen event' and 'accident,' as used in the articles [of the Civil Code] now under consideration, have the meaning of 'fortuitous event' or 'irresistible force.'...

"The breaking of...the Louisiana levees by the waters of the Mississippi River, causing a plantation to be overflowed, must therefore be considered as...a fortuitous or unforeseen event,... entitling the lessee, if thereby the plantation is wholly or partly destroyed, or is rendered unfit for the purpose for which it was leased, to have the lease annulled, although it is not...an extraordinary as well as an unforeseen accident,...so as to justify an abatement of rent if the crop only is destroyed."

Ethical Dimension

Is it fair to force the landlord to bear the entire loss caused by an act of God?

INNOCENT MISREPRESENTATION

If a party misstates a fact by mistake, the contract may be voidable.

In the mutual mistake case discussed previously, each party relied on its own incorrect information. A similar situation arises when one party has mistaken information and communicates it to the other party. The party making the mistaken statement thought it was true and did not intend to deceive anyone, but the other party has been damaged by the incorrect information. What should happen here? If the incorrect information was really important to the formation of the agreement, most courts will say there is no contract. Any performances given will be returned, and the contract based on this innocent misrepresentation will be rescinded.

If the incorrectly stated fact is not all that important, most courts will enforce the contract despite the mistaken communication. The deal stands, in other words, and no dollar damages can be collected because there was no intentional misrepresentation (fraud).

U NCONSCIONABILITY

The UCC provides another escape hatch for sale of goods contracts—**unconscionability**. If the contract, or any clause in it, will produce very unfair results, the courts have a choice under the UCC. A court which finds such gross unfairness can throw out the entire contract, or just the unfair clause, or so interpret the unfair clause as to avoid any unfair result. If one party claims unconscionability, the trial judge—not a jury—makes the decision on this issue after a hearing. Typically, such cases involve the fine print in pre-printed form contracts, where there is little or no chance for real negotiations. Frequently, the case involves a business attempting to impose harsh, standardized terms on an inexperienced, unwary consumer. Although specifically included in the UCC for goods contracts, unconscionability is also part of the general common law rules, as the next case makes clear.

Courts may refuse to enforce grossly unfair contracts.

WILLIAMS V. WALKER-THOMAS FURNITURE CO.

350 F.2d 445 (D.C. Cir. Court of Appeals, 1965)

Facts: Between 1957 and 1962, Ora Lee Williams made a number of installment-sale purchases at Walker-Thomas. In each case, she signed a pre-printed form contract which stated that she was only "leasing" the item and would not own it until she paid for it in full. The form contract also stated that each payment she made would be applied pro rata on all unpaid items and that if she defaulted all items not paid for in full could be repossessed. She missed a payment, and Walker-Thomas threatened to repossess everything. She sued to have these contracts declared invalid. The trial court refused to do so. The UCC, which declares such harsh contracts unconscionable, was not yet in force when these contracts were made.

Issue: Can a court apply unconscionability to a pre-UCC contract?

Decision: Yes. Judgment reversed. The furniture company cannot enforce its repossession clause, if it is shown to be "unconscionable."

Rule: Common law courts have always had the inherent power to refuse to enforce a grossly unfair contract.

Discussion: *By Chief Judge* WRIGHT:

"We do not agree that the court lacked the power to refuse enforcement to contracts found to be unconscionable. In other jurisdictions, it has been held as a matter of common law that unconscionable contracts are not enforceable. While no decision of this court so holding has been found, the notion that an unconscionable bargain should not be given full enforcement is by no means novel....

"In determining reasonableness or fairness, the primary concern must be with the terms of the contract considered in light of the circumstances existing when the contract was made. The test is not simple, nor can it be mechanically applied. The terms are to be considered 'in the light of the general commercial background and the commercial needs of the particular trade or case.' Corbin [the author of a widely-cited treatise on contract law] suggests the test as being whether the terms are 'so extreme as to appear unconscionable according to the mores and business practices of the time and place.' We think this formulation correctly states the test to be applied in those cases where no meaningful choice was exercised upon entering the contract.

"Because the trial court and the appellate court did not feel that enforcement could be refused, no findings were made on the possible unconscionability of the contracts in these cases. Since the record is not sufficient for our deciding the issue as a matter of law, the cases must be remanded to trial court for further proceedings."

Ethical Dimension

Is it ethical to use pre-printed form contracts which contain terms very favorable to the seller in consumer transactions? What alternatives would business have?

F RAUD (INTENTIONAL MISREPRESENTATION)

Persons who commit fraud may be liable for punitive damages.

As opposed to someone who communicates wrong information by mistake, the party committing fraud knows the information is incorrect and intends to deceive the other party. Fraud is an intentional wrong against another. Not only is the contract based on fraud voidable at the option of the person deceived; punitive damages may be awarded, since there has been an intentional tort.

Most courts distinguish between **fraud in the inducement** and **fraud in the execution**. Fraud in the inducement is the more common type. It involves an intentional misrepresentation of some facet of the contract. The person being lied to is aware that a contract is being made, but is induced to make it by the intentional misrepresentation. Fraud in the execution, on the other hand, describes a situation where one party is deceived as to the very nature of the transaction. For example, rock star Michael is in the midst of a mass of screaming fans, who are thrusting programs and other papers at him, trying to get his autograph. Michael is signing quickly as he fights his way through the crowd. One enterprising person puts forward a folded piece of paper which is really a contract to buy a new car. Michael signs the document without reading it, thinking it is just another autograph request. Michael has been deceived as to the nature of the document he signed. This "contract," made on the basis of fraud in the execution, is totally void.

The following discussion focuses on fraud in the inducement, the more usual type of misrepresentation case.

◼ Misrepresentation of Material Fact

The person claiming to have been defrauded must prove that the other party made a false statement of fact which was important to the forming of the agreement. Something was stated to be true which was, in fact, not true. The other party lied.

Statements of opinion are generally not treated as statements of fact, for obvious reasons. If a person says "I think something is thus and so," there is no attempt to guarantee the truth of that assertion; it's only an opinion. There is no fraud in such cases, so long as the person does, in fact, have an honestly held opinion. If you ask me: "What sort of mechanical condition is your used car in?" and I answer that in my opinion it is in good mechanical shape, there is no fraud. Even if the car is in terrible mechanical shape—as long as I honestly and reasonably think that it is in good shape, there is no fraud. But suppose I have been told by a mechanic that the car is in bad shape, and I then make the same response. In this case, my statement is fraudulent.

Statements of opinion are not usually meant to be factual.

For much the same reason, statements as to the value of something are not treated as statements of fact—subject to the same limitation. My opinion of what my car is worth is just that—my opinion. Both of us know that it may be worth more or less in the marketplace. However, courts do treat statements of value or condition by experts as statements of fact. A car mechanic's statement of mechanical condition or an appraiser's estimate of the value of a piece of real estate would be viewed as facts, even if the expert said "in my opinion."

What about the person who actively conceals the facts, or one who simply doesn't say anything? Are these misrepresentations of fact? In the first situation, generally yes; in the second case (silence), usually not. Someone who physically covers up the facts is certainly acting to misrepresent things. But, since we usually do not have any duty to tell each other all we know about the contract, a failure to do so is not a misrepresentation. The securities laws do prohibit trading on "inside (undisclosed) information," and many states now require fuller disclosure in real estate transactions. The *Janinda* case illustrates another exception to the general rule that silence is not fraudulent misrepresentation.

Concealment of the truth is usually treated as a misrepresentation of fact.

JANINDA V. LANNING

390 P.2d 826 (Idaho 1964)

Facts: Harold Janinda's employer transferred him from Denver, Colorado, to Mountain Home, Idaho. Janinda was shown several pieces of real estate by a local realtor, Swearingen. One of these was Mrs. Lanning's property, which had rental spaces for six house trailers and several duplex apartments, as well as a three-bedroom house. She did not disclose that one of the two shallow water wells which supplied the property was contaminated. Janinda bought the property, then discovered the pollution problem. He sued to rescind the purchase contract.

Issue: Was Lanning's failure to tell Janinda about the well a misrepresentation of fact?

Decision: Yes. Janinda gets the contract rescinded, and his money is returned.

Rule: There is a duty to tell the other party about dangerous, life-threatening conditions existing in the subject property.

Discussion: *By Justice SMITH:*

"Particularly, the duty of disclosure is required to be observed 'in cases involving latent dangerous physical conditions of land' Prosser on Torts, § 87 at 535 (2nd ed. 1955). Appellant regarded her property as income producing property and was fully aware, as was her agent, that respondents intended buying it for the same purpose; and admitted on cross examination that if 'I had gone on owning the place and I had had contamination.... I probably would have put in a chlorine system.' Respondents relied upon appellant's representations and were under no duty to make an independent investigation of their own."

Ethical Dimension

Are there any circumstances in which it would be ethical, as well as legal, not to tell someone information you knew that related to the contract you were negotiating?

■ Knowledge and Intent

To prove fraud, it must also be shown that the person making the statement knew at the time that it was false and that it was made with intent to deceive. In most cases, these two aspects can be seen quite clearly. Sometimes, liars try to argue that they did not really know they were lying. If there was an honestly held belief, there is no fraud. But if there was no reasonable basis for the statement, or if there was no knowledge at all, and the speaker said there *was*, there is fraud. A person who says "this document contains X," and has never read the document, *is* lying—about the amount of knowledge the speaker possesses about the contents of the document. That person would not be able to avoid fraud liability by saying, "Well, I really didn't know X wasn't in the document since I had never read the document." By telling you that he or she knew the contents when the person did not know, the person told a *knowing* lie.

Very rarely, the liar will try to argue that "I did it for your own good; I thought you would be benefitted." The courts have rejected this argument, too. What is required for the fraud case is not proof of intent to *injure*, but merely proof of intent to deceive.

■ Reasonable Reliance

The liar will frequently try to argue that there is no fraud case because the other party was not "reasonable" in relying on the lie. "Yes, I lied, and I knew I was lying, and I did it to trick you—but you should not have believed me." Judges and juries are usually not very receptive to this argument. It may be successful if the truth could have been discovered easily—as by checking the odometer to see the actual mileage on the used car. In most cases, since the "reasonableness" of one's conduct is a jury question, the jury vote will be against the liar.

The person relying on the lie must be acting reasonably.

■ Damage

If there is no damage, there is no fraud. If the injured party wants to collect dollars because of the financial loss caused by the fraud, there must be evidence as to what that loss was. If the injured party simply wishes to call off the contract, there must be proof that the misrepresented deal was substantially different from the actual deal.

The following case shows that fraud can also be used as a defense against the defrauder's claim for breach of contract. (Employment law issues found in the case will be discussed more fully in Chapters 13 and 14.)

JOHNSON V. HONEYWELL INFORMATION SYSTEMS, INC.

955 F.2d 409 (U.S. 6th Cir. Court of Appeals, 1992).

Facts: Honeywell placed a help-wanted ad for a person with a college degree and "4 to 6 years combined personnel and industrial relations experience." Mildred Johnson applied for the job. On her application, she indicated that she had a Bachelor of Arts degree from the University of Detroit and the required minimum work experience. The application form she signed stated that the submission of any false information "may be cause for immediate discharge at any time thereafter should I be employed by Honeywell." She was hired in 1976 and performed satisfactorily until mid-1983. In 1983 she was criticized by her supervisors for ineffectiveness, uncooperativeness, and unavailability by telephone. When she refused to make the suggested improvements, she was fired in November, 1984. She sued for breach of contract on the basis that she could be fired only for "just cause." Her lawsuit also claimed that she had been fired in retaliation for being too aggressive in meeting affirmative action goals. [Affirmative action requires employees to attempt to hire and promote minorities, so that their numbers in the work force approximate their numbers in the general population.] A discharge for this reason would violate the Michigan civil rights act. While gathering evidence for the trial, Honeywell discovered that Johnson had lied on her application.

The U.S. District Court denied Honeywell's motion for a summary judgment on each claim. The trial judge felt that "after-acquired" evidence could not be used to justify the firing decision, since the evidence that Johnson had lied on her application was unknown when the decision was made. After a trial, the court did direct a verdict for Honeywell on the civil rights claim, but the jury was permitted to decide for Johnson on the breach of contract claim.

Issue: Can an employee's misrepresentations on a job application be used as a defense against a claim by the employee for breach of contract?

Decision: Yes, they can. Judgment reversed, since the trial judge should have granted Honeywell's pre-trial motions for summary judgment.

Rule: An employee's material misrepresentations of job qualifications, whenever discovered, will normally preclude any claim for wrongful discharge.

Discussion: *By Judge* KEITH:

"Johnson's most glaring misrepresentation involved her education. While she claimed in her employment application to have earned a Bachelor of Arts degree from the University of Detroit, Johnson actually completed only four courses at the University and audited two others.... Johnson similarly submitted false information regarding the nature and extent of her studies at Wayne State University, stating that she had studied Applied Management for one year. Wayne State had no record of her enrollment. Johnson also exaggerated some prior job descriptions and falsely claimed to have been managing some of her properties in the year between her prior job and her hiring at Honeywell....

"We believe the Michigan Supreme Court would hold that just cause for termination of employment may include facts unknown to an employer at the time of dismissal, though obviously such facts would be neither the actual nor inducing cause for the discharge. This result is principally grounded upon the holding of the Michigan Court of Appeals in *Bradley*, but it is also based on the general applicability of this rule, its common sense, and the dearth of Michigan Case Law to the contrary....

"In order to provide a defense to an employer in a wrongful discharge claim, the after-acquired evidence must establish valid and legitimate reasons for the termination of employment. As a general rule, in cases of resume fraud, summary judgment will be appropriate where the misrepresentation or omission was material, directly related to measuring a candidate for employment, and was relied upon by the employer in making the hiring decision....

"We do not hold that any or all misrepresentations on an employment application constitute just cause for dismissal or serve as a complete defense to a wrongful discharge action. We conclude, however, that Johnson's misrepresentations, by virtue of their nature and number, and when viewed in the context of Honeywell's express requirement of a college degree and its warning to applicants that misrepresentations may constitute cause for termination of employment, provide adequate and just cause for her dismissal as a matter of law even though they were unknown to Honeywell at the time of her discharge."

[The court also said that no remedy could be given on the civil rights claim. Someone who is hired as a doctor, but who has falsified credentials, could not later collect damages even though later fired because of race, sex, religion, or age.]

Ethical Dimension

Is it fair to use statements from the application as an after-the-fact justification for discharging an employee?

●

D URESS AND UNDUE INFLUENCE

Sometimes someone takes advantage of a position of trust and confidence to line his or her own pockets. An example might be the lawyer who learns of a pending real estate development and urges a client to sell to the lawyer a piece of property for much less than it will be worth

Contracts made under threats may be void or voidable.

when the development comes. Another example is the friend or relative who convinces the trusting party to transfer assets at much less than their true value. A financial adviser may unload worthless securities on clients. In these **undue influence** situations, a dominant person giving advice has robbed the other party of free will. The law says that these contracts are voidable when the truth is discovered.

A similar problem occurs when one person forces another to make an unwanted contract. Depending on the type of threats used, contracts made under **duress** may be void or voidable. If it is simply economic or similar pressure that was applied, the contract is probably voidable. If death threats are made ("I'll make him an offer he can't refuse"), the contract is totally null and void.

ILLEGALITY

Many contracts involving illegal conduct are void.

What if the agreement requires one or both parties to do something criminal, or to commit an intentional tort? As a rule, these would-be contracts are also null and void. Neither party can get any court relief against the other if both were equally guilty of conspiring to commit a crime. The legal phrase used to describe these equally guilty criminals is **in pari delicto**—in equal wrong. To take the most obvious example, a bank robber could not sue to collect a fair share of the loot. No civil liabilities based on such "contracts" are recognized, but the parties could, of course, be criminally prosecuted. For this latter reason, there are not many such cases recorded in the law books.

Gambling

Gambling is illegal in most states. Several states now run their own lotteries; these are specifically permitted by statute. Some states do permit betting on horse races at the track. Casino gambling is legal in a very few states (and on some Indian reservations). With these few exceptions, the gambling contract is null and void.

Courts do permit the loser of a bet or wager to repudiate the bet and demand the return of the loser's money, up to the point where the money is actually paid over to the winner of the bet. If you paid ten dollars for a chance at a weekly football pool, and your teams did not win, you could (legally) demand the return of your ten dollars from the person who was holding the stakes. You could sue to get your ten dollars, as long as you could prove that you repudiated the bet before the money was paid to the winner.

Sunday Laws

Many states have statutes which prohibit the doing of normal business, or at least some kinds of business, on Sunday. These statutes vary widely in coverage and in interpretation. If a contract is made in violation of the statute, the contract is void (and the parties are *in pari delicto*). Neither can recover anything from the other. In one famous old case, a cow was sold and delivered on a Sunday. The seller could not sue to collect the unpaid contract price, nor could he simply come over to the buyer's farm and take the cow back. With no court remedies, everything should be left exactly as is. In some states, the buyer's retention of the cow on Monday would provide an implied promise—made on a weekday—to pay for the cow. In those states, the buyer who kept the cow would have to pay a fair market price for it. The actual case said that the buyer got a free cow because of the effect of the Sunday law. Businesses need to be aware of these possible limits on their operations.

◼ Licensing Statutes

Businesses also need to be aware that many states, counties, and cities require certain trades and professions to be licensed. What happens if a person performs services without obtaining the required license? Here, the parties are not *in pari delicto*. I don't need a license to be a patient; *you* need a license to perform medical services. These laws (or at least many of them) are designed to protect the patient or client against incompetent practitioners. Such regulatory-type licensing laws require education, experience, examinations, and sometimes the posting of a bond (money) to guarantee proper performance of contracts.

Unlicensed persons who are violating a regulatory statute cannot usually collect payment.

Of course, the violator can be criminally prosecuted. In addition, all money paid has to be refunded to the client or patient (at least if the client or patient was unaware of the violation). The tort of fraud has almost certainly been committed. For the unlicensed M.D., any laying on of hands is the tort of battery. Punitive damages are appropriate.

For revenue-raising licenses, the type anyone can get by paying some money, the results are not nearly as serious. Since the law requiring revenue-raising licenses was not intended as a quality control anyway, the customer owes the contract price. In some states, the unlicensed person can sue without even paying the money and actually getting the license. In other states, even for this revenue-raising licensing statute, the service person must actually get the license before suing. But having done so, the person can then collect the contract price for the services performed.

◼ Usury

Most states (and several of the world's major religions) have rules about charging interest on debts. Here again, the parties are not *in pari delicto*. The aim of these state statutes is to protect the innocent debtor against the greedy creditor. The criminal is the creditor who attempts to charge an illegally high rate of interest.

Unfortunately, however, there is little agreement about usury among the states. The states do not agree on which kinds of credit obligations are subject to usury limitations. Nor do they agree on what rate of interest should be permitted. And they do not agree on what to do with a creditor who has tried to charge an illegally high rate.

Most of the more recent court decisions indicate that any credit contract is subject to usury limits, including charge cards and revolving credit accounts at department stores. Some of the earlier cases held that only an actual loan of money was subject to usury laws. Some states now have special statutes to deal with specific types of credit contracts. In some states, corporations (or any businesses) are not protected by the usury maximums.

Historically, usury laws specified a very low interest rate as the maximum—six percent, seven percent, or perhaps nine percent. If the market price for credit is above these old statutory rates, the creditor business is faced with a no-win decision. Make the loan at the lawful rate, and lose money—or charge the actual (illegal) market rate and run the risk of legal sanctions. Recognizing this dilemma, some states now have separate, higher rates for some of the riskier transactions such as charge cards and department store accounts.

Different results may occur in situations in which a creditor tries to charge excessive interest.

What happens if a creditor tries to charge more than the applicable interest rate? Here, too, there is wide disagreement. There may even be different rules within the same state, depending on the nature of the credit transaction. At the very least, the creditor should not collect the part of the interest that is above the limit. A slightly harsher result says that the creditor collects no interest at all. A third rule would be that the creditor would pay some penalty, perhaps double or triple the illegal interest it tried to charge. The ultimate sanction (used in some states, at least for some transactions) is that the criminal creditor forfeits all principal and all interest (and, conceivably, has to repay all money already received—with interest). Depending on the state, the consequences of trying to charge too much interest may be mild—or disastrous!

■ Other Forms of Illegality

Antitrust violations are a major source of criminal prosecutions of business. So are unfair trade practices. Both of these, and other areas of illegality, will be covered in later chapters, in context.

REVIEW

Our legal/economic system provides maximum freedom to order our own affairs and to make our own contracts as we wish. The legal system does contain limits, however, to make sure that the transaction represents the freely intended—and lawful—agreement of the parties.

Contracts made by persons lacking the capacity to do so are either void or voidable. So are those made under duress. Misrepresentations made by one of the parties to the other may result in a voidable contract. Contracts entered into on the basis of a mistake by one or both parties may also be void or voidable. Finally, contracts which require one or both parties to commit a criminal act will generally be void.

REVIEW QUESTIONS AND PROBLEMS

1. Explain why contracts are not enforced when they are based on mutual mistakes.

2. What does the phrase *in pari delicto* mean? How is it applied in contract situations?

3. Describe a situation where a contract may be discharged due to impossibility.

4. Trace, age seventeen, buys a new Cadillac. As she pulls out of the dealership, she is hit by a large truck and the car is totally wrecked. What are her rights?

5. Why is a person suffering from a mental disability not held liable on contracts she or he makes while so disabled?

6. What is the difference between a "regulatory" licensing statute and a "revenue-raising" licensing statute? Why is this distinction important to businesses?

7. Jerry and Larry had had several alcoholic drinks at their favorite tavern when Jerry claimed that he "could buy you (Larry) out tomorrow." Larry said that his farm was worth $120,000, and that Jerry didn't have that kind of money. Jerry replied, "Write it up, and I'll show you!" Larry grabbed a paper napkin and wrote: "I hereby promise to sell the Larry farm to Jerry for $120,000 cash. (signed) B. Larry." Jerry said that Larry's wife (Nelly) would also have to sign such a document, so Larry changed the "I" to "We" and took the document over to another table where Nelly was talking with some friends. Nelly said, "What's this?" Larry said, "It's only a joke." Nelly signed, and Larry brought to napkin back to his table and tossed it in front of Jerry. Jerry picked it up, and said he would have the money tomorrow. When Jerry tried to enforce the sale of the farm, Larry said that it had only been a joke and that he was too drunk to make a contract. Jerry sues. What result, and why?

8. Juan owned a small auto parts business. He was contacted by his old friend, Cameliard, who was a vice-president of Forge Industries, and who suggested that Juan sell his business to Forge. Cameliard said that Forge's stock would triple in value over the next year. Convinced, Juan sold his business, which had a net value of $55,000, for $70,000 of Forge's stock. The Forge stock did double in value, but then fell to half of its original value. Juan sued for fraud damages of $20,000 ($55,000, less the current $35,000 value of the Forge's stock he received). What result, and why?

9. Repke Builders submitted a bid for $770,000, to do certain work for the city of Los Alamos. The city required that each bidder also post a 10 percent bond, guaranteeing that it would do the work if its bid were selected. Three other bids on the job, for $1 million, $1.2 million, and $1.3 million, were also received. The city accepted Repke's bid. Meanwhile, Repke had discovered that one page of figures had not been added into the final total, and that its bid should have been for $990,000. It said it would do the work for that price or would simply withdraw its bid. The city said it would have to do the job for $770,000 or forfeit its $77,000 bond. How should this dispute be resolved in court?

10. Gwen and Arthur, both medical doctors, shared the rent and overhead expenses on a suite of offices. In November, 1991, they signed a three-year renewal lease on their offices. The lease was drawn up by Gwen's lawyer and included a provision that each would pay half the rent even if "unable to occupy the premises due to incapacity or for any other reason." Beginning in 1990, Arthur had been behaving strangely. He forgot appointments, lost his medical bag, took the bus home instead of driving his car, and climbed over the seats in a movie theater instead of walking down the aisle. In January 1992, Arthur was diagnosed as having an aging disease. He ended his medical practice, but Gwen sued to enforce the half-and-half clause in the office lease. Should the court enforce the lease? Explain.

SUGGESTIONS FOR FURTHER READING

Henkel and Shedd, "Article 2 of the Uniform Commercial Code: Is a Farmer a 'Merchant' or a 'Tiller of the Soil'?," *American Business Law Journal* 18 (Summer 1980): 323.

Highsmith and Havens, "Revocation of Acceptance and the Defective Automobile: The Uniform Commercial Code to the Rescue." *American Business Law Journal* 18 (Summer 1980): 303.

BUSINESS
FUNCTIONS
AND
THE
LAW

PART THREE

Part 3 examines the impact of law and regulation on six major functional areas of business – organization, finance, employment, production, marketing, and international operations. For each functional area, there is a chapter on law and a chapter on regulation. The dichotomy is not perfect. The line between law and regulation is not always clear. The basic idea, however, is to distinguish between the legal frameworks which are provided for these functional areas and the regulatory limitations on their use. In a sense, the law/regulation dichotomy here parallels the coverage given to contract law in Part 2. First, what is the legal framework for the relationship? Second, what limitations are imposed on the use of that framework? Of course, these two questions are inter-related, but the law/regulation approach does provide a useful outline for examining the legal environment within which business must operate.

9
LAW
OF
ORGANIZATIONS

"Drive thy Business, let not that drive thee."
Benjamin Franklin

LEARNING OBJECTIVES: When you have studied this chapter, you should be able to:

DEFINE the various forms of business organizations.

EXPLAIN how each type of organization is created.

DISCUSS the nature of the associates' liabilities to third parties who deal with the firm.

OUTLINE the duties which the associates owe to each other.

EXPLAIN how each type of organization is terminated.

P REVIEW

This chapter is concerned with the first step in the operation of a business—organizing the business. Our legal system provides the would-be business owner with a range of choices which have very different legal characteristics. An entrepreneur may decide to remain a *sole proprietor*, and to use *agents* and/or *independent contractors* to help run the business. To gain additional management expertise, or capital, or both, a new business owner may decide to become a *partner* with one or more co-owners. If she or he wishes to retain management control and simply have investors in the business, the business may be organized as a *limited partnership*. Where there is a serious potential for large liabilities to third parties as the result of business operations, it may be wise to organize the business as a *corporation*.

Each of these relationships is very complex and has been the subject of multi-volume legal treatises. This brief overview will focus on the major features of these relationships and the differences among them. For each form of organization, we will consider five basic questions:

1. Definition—What is it?
2. Creation—How do you form one?
3. Liability—When can third parties sue you?
4. Duties—What do the participants owe each other?
5. Termination—When does it end?

A GENCY LAW

Everyone has occasion to use others to accomplish objectives. All legal systems must provide rules to cover such transactions. The principles of agency law underlie all types of business organizations, but there are some differences in how the rules apply to the various forms. In the United States, the principles of agency law are summarized in the *Restatement of the Law of Agency*.

Definition

An **agent** is a person who has been authorized to conduct one or more business transactions for someone else. Usually the agent is hired by that other person, called the **principal**, and is paid in some way for acting as agent. But there are also situations where no contract between the two is involved. If your friend or roommate agrees to drop off a roll of film at the drugstore for developing, your friend is acting as your agent, even though he or she is not being paid to do the favor for you. Your friend has been authorized by you to enter into a contract for you with the third party (the drugstore) to have your roll of film developed. Your friend is thus an agent, but not your **employee**, since no

An agent acts for the principal.

compensation is being paid. Many employees are not agents, since they have no power to make contracts for their employer. They are simply hired to do a particular job, not to make contracts with third parties.

Most business transactions involve the rules of agency law. You may be representing yourself, as an individual, by buying or selling. But you will nearly always be dealing with an agent representing the business on the other side of the transaction. Only where the business is a sole proprietorship, and you are dealing directly with the owner, would you not be entering into the relationship through an agent. Obviously, knowing the rules of agency law is important both to business organizations and to their customers.

■ Creation/Authorization

One major area of litigation involves the extent of the authority which has been given to the agent. In the typical case, a third party will claim to have made a contract with the principal through the agent. The principal will deny liability on the contract by claiming that the agent was not authorized to make it. If the dispute goes to litigation, the court will have to examine the facts and circumstances to see whether the agent had authority.

An agent may be authorized in one of four ways.

There are four methods by which an agent can be authorized: by express, implied, or apparent authority, and by ratification. **Express authority** is that which was specifically stated in words. Generally, the principal's statements may be oral or written. When you asked your friend to take your film to the drugstore for you, you expressly authorized that agent to make the contract for film developing. Where the agent's authority is stated in a signed writing, the writing is often referred to as a **power of attorney**.

Implied authority has also actually been given to the agent, but it is not stated in so many words. Instead, it is implied, by law, from the actions of the parties and the surrounding facts and circumstances. When you authorized your friend to drop off your film, you implicitly authorized that agent to tell the drugstore whether you wanted the double prints or the free roll of film and to agree on your behalf that next Saturday would be acceptable as the day to pick up your prints. In other words, the agent has the implied authority to take care of whatever details are necessary and appropriate to get the expressly authorized job successfully completed. When a business representative is appointed, it is implied that that agent has all the same authority normally given to agents in that trade or business. However, no authority can be implied contrary to express instructions of the principal.

A principal is liable if he or she has created the appearance of authority.

Even though there is no implied authority, due to the principal's specific instructions, there may still be the appearance of authority. A principal is bound by **apparent authority** if the principal's words or acts have made it appear to a third party that agency authority exists.

For example, if a certain agent has been calling on the principal's customers and making contracts with them for the principal, one of those customers would be justified in continuing to deal with that agent until notified otherwise. If that particular agent left the company, the company would be required to notify all the customers with whom the agent had been dealing that the agent's authority had terminated. Similarly, if a particular company places unusual limits on its agents, the company must communicate those limits to the third parties with whom the agents are dealing. If not, the third party customers would be justified in relying on the appearance of normal agency authority. The latter point was discussed in the *Carl Wagner* case.

CARL WAGNER AND SONS V. APPENDAGEZ, INC.

485 F. Supp. 762 (S.D.N.Y., 1980)

Facts: Carl Wagner and Sons (Wagner) ordered jeans, tops, and sweaters from the "Faded Glory" collection of Appendagez, a manufacturer. Wagner had first seen the line of clothing at a trade show. Later, it had called Appendagez and inquired about ordering for its New York stores. In response, salesman Alan Friedman had come to one of Wagner's stores to take the orders. Friedman said he could take the orders for all four Wagner stores. Out of $25,089 total orders for its four stores in the New York City area, Wagner received only $5,484.50 worth of merchandise. Wagner sued, claiming that Appendagez refused to ship the rest because Wagner refused to sell at fixed retail prices. Fixing prices would have been a violation of New York's antitrust law. Appendagez claimed that its salespeople could not make contracts, but only take orders, and that this was common industry practice. It also said there were credit limits on Wagner's account.

Issue: Did Friedman have apparent authority to make the contract?

Decision: Yes, he did. Plaintiff collects damages, including treble damages for the violation of New York's antitrust law (trying to force Wagner to fix prices).

Rule: Third parties are entitled to rely on the appearance of normal agency authority, unless they are otherwise notified.

Discussion: *By U.S. District Judge* HAIGHT:

"The internal limitations which Appendagez placed upon the authority of its salesmen are irrelevant because such limitations were not communicated to the plaintiffs.... I am mindful of

Appendagez's contention that acceptance of a salesman's orders at the home office, as a condition precedent to a binding contract, is so well known in the industry that plaintiffs must have known of it. To be sure, the terms of an agreement 'may be explained or supplemented by...usage of trade,' UCC § 2–202(a). The 'usage of trade' concept is defined by UCC § 1–205(2).... In the case at bar, Appendagez, seeking by trade usage to avoid contractual obligations which would otherwise arise from the writings and attendant circumstances, bears the burden of proving the 'existence and scope of such a usage.' It has failed to do so. The only witness giving evidence on the point was Nash. While he testified that in his experience with several clothing companies, including Appendagez, comparable order forms were not regarded as binding until approved by the home office, he also acknowledged on cross-examination that other companies specifically provided in their order forms that the orders were 'subject to acceptance at home office.' That concession is fatal to defendant's contention that everyone in the industry should have known that home office acceptance was a condition precedent to a binding contract, even if neither the salesman nor the order form gave notice of the condition to purchasers....

"For comparable reasons, Appendagez's internal credit limitation placed upon plaintiffs' account is of no legal significance. Not only did Appendagez fail to advise plaintiffs of that credit limitation, their salesmen cheerfully wrote up orders which substantially exceeded it. If Appendagez had advised plaintiffs of the credit limitations and given them an opportunity to meet the situation by further economic arrangements, the case would be different. In point of fact, Appendagez did neither; and in the circumstances of the case cannot plead its internal, uncommunicated credit limitation as justification for a refusal to recognize contractual obligations."

Ethical Dimension

Is it ethical for a business to refuse to fill orders that its own sales representatives have solicited from customers?

●

A principal may ratify unauthorized acts of the agent.

Finally, even if there was no actual or apparent authority at all, the principal may decide to ratify what the agent has done. If you did not expressly authorize your friend to order enlargements of some of your photos, you could still decide later on that it was a good idea and **ratify** (approve) that part of the contract with the drugstore. If you decide to ratify, you have to ratify the whole deal. You can't just agree to the part where you get the enlargements and not the part that requires you to pay an extra charge for them. Ratification may be expressly stated or just implied from the facts. If you saw the enlargements and kept them, you would certainly have to pay the charge for them—by repaying your friend who paid cash or paying the bill if your friend used a credit card to pick up the photos.

■ Liability to Third Parties

Where agency power has been created by one of the four methods, the principal is liable on the contract to the third party. The principal could be sued for breach of contract if the contract were not properly performed. Damages could be collected if the third party had to pay a higher price from a second seller or where the third party had lost profits because goods were not delivered. If similar goods are not available from another supplier, the principal might be forced to deliver the promised goods. Normally, the agent would not be liable on the contract unless the agent had personally guaranteed its performance or had signed the contract so that it looked that way. An agent who lied about the extent of the authority that had been given would be liable for fraud. The agent in such a case could be sued for damages sustained by the third party because the principal did not perform the intended contract. In most states, if the agent was not authorized and the contract was not later ratified, there is no contract with anyone.

What about other kinds of torts committed by the agent? The agent—the actual wrongdoer—is, of course, liable for her or his own tort. The third party can sue the agent in tort for actual and punitive damages and other appropriate relief. The main issue in most such cases is whether the principal is also liable for the agent's tort. In other words, are there two possible sources for collecting the damages caused or only one (the agent)? The principal's liability depends on whether the tort was within the scope of the agency authority. Was the agent, at the time the tort was committed, trying to accomplish some business purpose for the principal or engaged in doing something personal? If your friend is careless in driving the car on the way to drop off your film and runs over a pedestrian, you are liable for that negligent tort. Once that errand is finished, your friend is no longer acting as your agent, so you would not be liable for any torts committed after that. There are many, many very close questions of fact which judges and juries will have to decide.

A principal is liable for torts agents commit within the scope of their authority.

■ Mutual Duties of Principal and Agent

Someone who is placed in a position of trust, to manage money or property of another person is designated a **fiduciary** by the law. The

Latin word on which that term is based implies faithfulness, honesty, and fair dealing. An agent is in a fiduciary position to the principal and cannot lawfully use the position to make a personal gain at the principal's expense. The agent may not be the other party in contracts with the principal, at least not without getting the principal's specific approval. The agent cannot serve two principals with conflicting interests without the express permission of both. A principal who has not consented to such a dual agency has an absolute right to disaffirm any such contract made on its behalf. The agent also has a duty to obey all lawful instructions of the principal and can be held liable for any failure to do so (and fired, if the failure is serious enough).

Where the agent has done the job as agreed, the principal owes any compensation called for in their contract. The principal normally also has to reimburse the agent for all reasonable expenses incurred in carrying out the job. Generally, the parties are free to specify any compensation arrangements they wish, since there is no agency relationship unless they create it. If compensation is intended but no amount is specified, a reasonable amount would have to be paid by the principal.

■ Termination

The parties are also free in most cases to work out whatever arrangements they wish with respect to the duration and termination of the agency. Many agency arrangements are **at will**, meaning that either party is free to end the relationship at any time—for any reason or for no reason at all. Where the parties have specified that the agency will last for some definite period of time, either party could still end it at any time but would be liable for breach of the agency contract if there was no legal justification for ending the agency. An agent who quit before the time was up, just to take a better job, for instance, could be liable for the costs of finding and training a replacement. A principal who wrongfully fired an agent might be held liable for the agent's salary until the agent found a similar job at the same or a higher salary.

■ INDEPENDENT CONTRACTOR

Many times, businesses and individuals will have a specific job which needs doing, but for which they do not have sufficient staff, time, or expertise. On these occasions, the person may simply hire an outsider to do this specific work. It is also possible, however, to hire independent representatives on a long-term basis.

■ Definition and Creation

An **independent contractor** is a separate person or business which is hired to do work for someone else. Unlike an agent/employee who is on the principal's payroll and part of the principal's business operation, the independent contractor (IC) has its own organization structure, whether it is one person or a large corporation. It is independent in the sense that it is hired to produce specific results agreed to in the contract, but it decides for itself how those results will be produced. The principal can tell an agent exactly how to do the job; the person who hires an IC leaves all the messy details to the IC.

An independent contractor decides how the job gets done.

One of the major advantages of using ICs rather than employees is that you avoid most of the employment regulations and requirements we will discuss in Chapter 14. For example, you do not have to pay Social Security, Workers' Compensation, Unemployment Compensation, and the like for your independent contractors. (*They* have to pay for their employees.) You don't withhold income tax; the IC pays its own taxes. And there are similar exemptions from other regulatory statutes.

◼ Liability to Third Parties

The other major advantage gained by using ICs rather than agents is that liability to third parties is minimized. As a rule, the employer of an IC is not liable for contracts made with third parties by the IC, nor for torts committed by the IC against third parties. The basic reason for this rule, of course, is that the IC has control over how the work is being done and so is responsible for the contracts it makes and the torts it commits in the process.

The employer of an independent contractor is usually not liable for the IC's torts.

There are several exceptions to this no-liability rule. Persons who are having work done on their real estate by ICs should be aware that an unpaid worker or supplier of the IC can file a **lien** (claim) against the real estate. In some states, the person with such a lien can force a sale of the land if the claim is not paid. Even if there is no provision for such a forced sale of the land, the landowner would not be able to sell the land without paying off the claim first. (A buyer would want to have a clear title to the land.)

A person who hires an IC to do an **extra-hazardous job,** such as one that involves the use of dynamite, can be held liable for damages caused to third parties. The reason for this exception is that the nature of the job itself is exposing members of the public to some risk, even if the IC is carefully chosen and properly licensed to do the work. For similar reasons, there are some liabilities which you can't avoid just by hiring an IC to do a job for you. The law calls them **non-delegable duties.** A store owner owes its customers a reasonably safe place in which to shop. Even if it is an IC that is hired to clean the snow and ice off the parking lot, the store would be liable to a customer who was injured because the job was not done properly.

◼ Mutual Duties and Termination

The relationship with the IC is based on the parties' contract and is subject to its terms. The contract will specify the work to be done and when and how the agreed compensation is to be paid. Usually, the relationship ends when the particular job is finished, although there can certainly be an on-going arrangement. An apartment house owner, for example, could have a standing arrangement with someone to do any necessary repair work whenever notified by a tenant or by the landlord.

◼ SOLE PROPRIETORSHIP

The **sole proprietorship**, or single owner business, is the simplest to organize and to operate. One person has all management authority, so decisions can be reached quickly. That feature may be a plus or a minus, depending on the ability of the sole owner. It may also be more difficult to raise capital, since only one person is responsible for the debts of the business.

◼ Creation

There is no separate organization process for the sole proprietorship, since there is no separate "business" as such. There is simply a single human being conducting a business operation. Some states do require the registration of an assumed name, if the business is going to use one. If, for instance, Irma wishes to operate her restaurant as the "Galleon Galley," she would need to file a disclosure form identifying herself as the owner of the business.

A sole proprietor is responsible for getting all required licenses for the business.

Some types of businesses, such as restaurants, require a special license to operate. Irma, in our example, would need to have a restaurant license, usually issued by a local health department. If the receipts of the business are subject to a state sales tax, a state license to collect the sales tax will be required.

If the business hires employees, other legal requirements must be met. The Internal Revenue Service will need to assign an employer identification number, so income tax can be withheld from employees' wages and social security payments can be collected. State laws require that employees be covered by workers' compensation insurance for on-the-job injuries and by unemployment insurance in the event of layoffs from work. And there are other employer requirements, which are discussed in Chapters 13 and 14. These employer requirements are not specific to sole proprietorships, but apply to all employers regardless of the form of organization of the business.

■ Liability

One primary disadvantage of the sole proprietorship is that the owner has full, unlimited personal liability for all the debts of the business. If the business fails, not only the business assets, but also all the owner's personal assets, may be lost. For this reason alone, businesses which involve a high risk of serious personal injuries to employees or third parties are usually incorporated. (As you will see later in this chapter, the personal assets of the stockholder-owners of a corporation cannot be taken to satisfy claims against the corporate business.)

■ Mutual Duties

Since there is only one owner, there are no "mutual duties" here as there are in other organizational forms. Of course, if the single owner uses agents, employees, or independent contractors to do some of the work, the mutual duties involved in those relationships would apply.

■ Termination

The sole proprietorship ends when the sole owner so decides. The owner might decide to sell the business assets to someone else, who would continue the operation, or to another existing business.

The business would also end on the owner's death, although the owner's heirs might decide to continue the business. In our earlier example, Irma's heirs (her daughter Lucy and her son Alfredo) might want to form a partnership to operate the Galleon Galley. Or one heir might buy out the other and establish a new sole proprietorship. As part of the process of administering Irma's estate when she dies, all her creditors, including creditors of her business, would have to be paid in full before any personal or business assets were turned over to her heirs.

A sole proprietorship could also be terminated by bankruptcy. Bankruptcy will be discussed in more detail in Chapter 12. In simplest terms, bankruptcy occurs when a business is financially unsuccessful. Its assets are turned over to a court administrator, who uses them to pay creditors to the extent possible. Again, in the case of a sole proprietor, most personal assets would have to be turned over to the court, along with the business assets.

The following case illustrates another difference between being organized as a sole proprietor and being organized as a corporation—the tax consequences.

MAXWELL, MAXWELL, AND HI LIFE PRODUCTS, INC. V. COMMISSIONER OF INTERNAL REVENUE

95 TAX CT. 53 (1990)

Facts: Peter Maxwell and his wife Helen were the founders, controlling stockholders, and principal officers of Hi Life Products, Inc. They each owned 47.5 percent of the stock. Helen's sister, Marlene Sadler, and her husband Alan also worked for Hi Life. Marlene and Alan each owned 2.5 percent of Hi Life's stock. Hi Life's board of directors consisted of Peter, Helen, and Alan.

On March 9, 1977, Peter was injured while operating a mixing machine at the Hi Life factory. He suffered a broken arm, cuts, and burns. Surgery was required, and a metal plate was installed in his forearm. State law required employers to have workers' compensation insurance to cover such injuries, but Hi Life had not purchased the required coverage. Peter first consulted with the company's attorney (Brown), who recommended that he retain his own personal lawyer. Peter then hired an outside attorney (Pico), who wrote attorney Brown a letter stating that Peter had a claim for $125,000. Hi Life's directors had a special meeting, from which Peter excused himself. Attorney Brown recommended a settlement of Peter's claim for $122,500. Helen and Alan approved the settlement, and Hi Life paid Peter the $122,500. Hi Life deducted this amount as a business expense in calculating its taxable income for 1977. Peter did not report the $122,500 as income, since section 104(a)(2) of the Internal Revenue Code said that money received as damages for personal injury is not taxable. The Commissioner argued that the payment was really just a disguised dividend, which would not be deductible by the corporation but which would be taxable income to Peter. The Commissioner determined that Peter and Helen owed $64,185 and that Hi Life owed $58,800. Both the Maxwells and Hi Life petitioned the Tax Court for review of the Commissioner's decision.

Issue: Was the payment a valid settlement of a claim for employee injuries?

Decision: Yes, it was. If a similar result had been worked out between unrelated persons acting independently, the transaction would be valid. Judgment for the taxpayers.

Rule: A corporation may settle a valid claim for damages for an employee's injuries, and taxpayers have a legal right to reduce or eliminate taxes by legal means.

Discussion: *By Judge* RUWE:

"Although the points on which [the Commissioner] relies cause us to give close scrutiny to the transaction in issue, the cold hard facts do not lead us in the direction [he] would have us go. [Peter] sustained genuine and serious physical injuries. These injuries were sustained in his employment by Hi Life. The injuries were caused (at least in part) by the improper placement of a bolt in lieu of a setscrew on a mixing machine used at Hi Life. [Peter's] personal injuries were reasonably valued at $122,500. The only remaining question to be resolved is whether [Peter's] legal claim was the reason for Hi Life's payment of $122,500 to [him]. If it was, then the amount paid is deductible by Hi Life and excludable by [Peter].

"In determining whether the form of a transaction between closely related parties has substance, we should compare their actions with what would have occurred between parties who were dealing at arm's length.... One would normally expect unrelated parties who were involved in a claim for damages resulting from serious personal injuries to consult legal counsel in order to get an informed opinion regarding their respective rights and liabilities. [Peter] and Hi Life each retained independent legal counsel. [Peter's] attorney advised him that he had a legal claim against Hi Life and that based upon Hi Life's failure to secure workers' compensation, the traditional defenses... were [not available]. Hi Life's board of directors was advised by its own attorney that payment of damages was reasonable in light of the circumstances and applicable California law. There is nothing in the record to show that this legal advice was given in bad faith or that [the taxpayers] were not entitled to rely upon it in good faith....

"We recognize that tax considerations played a part in [Peter's] claim against Hi Life and in the ultimate settlement of that claim. In that respect, these cases are no different than cases in which we must determine whether corporate payments to an employee-stockholder are compensation for personal services or nondeductible dividends. The question in both instances is whether there was a reasonable basis, independent of tax considerations, for the taxpayer's characterization of the payment. The fact that settlement of [Peter's] claim entitled Hi Life to a deduction and [Peter] to exclude the $122,500 payment, does not vitiate the reasonableness of the underlying transaction.... Taxpayers have the legal right to decrease taxes, or avoid them altogether, by means which the law permits."

Ethical Dimension

Is it ethical to structure your business to minimize taxes?

PARTNERSHIP

Much of partnership law is based on agency law, but there are also some differences. The most important difference is that a partner is acting both as principal *and* as agent for the other partners. Unlike the normal agent, a partner *is* personally liable on the contract for the business. A second major difference is that nearly all states have adopted the Uniform Partnership Act (UPA), which provides the basic rules for this form of business.

Definition

The UPA defines a **partnership** as an association of two or more persons to carry on as co-owners a business for profit. There must be at least two persons; there can be many more. Some large law firms have dozens of partners; the largest C.P.A. firms have hundreds of partners.

These persons are carrying on a business together, which they hope will make a profit. Groups organized for social purposes, or for religious or charitable purposes, are thus not partnerships under this definition. The individual members of such groups are liable for their activities only if they specifically authorize or participate in the liability-producing event.

Partners are not only in business together, they are also co-owners of the business. The principal and the agent are in business together, in the broad sense, but not as co-owners—the principal is the boss and the agent is hired help. Unless otherwise agreed, each partner has an equal voice in running the joint business operation. If there are disagreements on management policy, it's one partner, one vote—unless specifically agreed otherwise. (In the very large partnerships mentioned above, the usual arrangement is to select a smaller management committee to decide policy questions.)

Creation

The partners create their firm by agreement.

You and I create our partnership by agreement. It exists when we say it exists and because we say it exists. No action by the state is necessary, although most states do require us to register our business, particularly if we are using a fictitious name. (The abbreviation **dba** stands for "doing business as" whatever the fictitious name is.) This contrasts sharply with the corporation or the limited partnership, neither of which can come into existence without state approval. The underlying reason for the difference is that some or all of the participants in these other two forms are seeking limited liability for the debts of the business. Only the state can grant limited liability; the participants cannot confer it upon themselves. As long as you and I are willing to assume full personal liability for all the debts of our business, the state lets us form the partnership as we wish.

■ Liability to Third Parties

The major disadvantage to operating as a partnership is the full personal liability which each partner assumes for all the debts of the business. Not only are assets of the partnership business available to its creditors; all the partners' individually-owned property—homes, cars, boats, shares of stock, bank accounts—is also at risk. Normally, the business assets would be used first to pay off business creditors. But if those assets are insufficient, any or all of the partners can be called on to make up the difference. Any partner who pays more than a fair, agreed share of the firm's debts would have a claim against the other partner or partners for the excess amount.

Partners have full personal liability for all debts of the business.

Generally, the personal creditors of individual partners have no direct rights against assets of the partnership. Ralph Able's dentist, for instance, would not be permitted to take any of the assets belonging to the hardware store business in which Ralph was a partner. If Ralph fails to pay his dental bill, a court judgment against Ralph could provide that any profits of the business that would normally be paid to Ralph would instead be paid over to the court to satisfy the judgment against Ralph. Ralph's share of the partnership profits is thus subject to a **charging order** from the court. The hardware store business continues to operate as before; Ralph just doesn't get his share of the profits until the judgment for his dental bill is paid.

Because partnership creditors and personal creditors have different rights against personal assets and business assets, it is important to know which assets are which. Does the building in which the hardware store business is being conducted belong to the business, to Ralph individually, or to Ralph and his partner Ginnie in some other form of co-ownership? It may be necessary to decide this question when there are not enough assets to pay all creditors in full or when the partnership is being terminated. In most cases, the best evidence of who owns an asset will be its treatment on the partnership's books and records. Is the building listed as a business asset? Is the business taking depreciation on the building? Is it paying the taxes and insurance on the building? Positive answers to these questions would usually mean that the partnership owns the building. Conversely, if the business is paying rent to Ralph for using the building, the building probably belongs to Ralph, not to the partnership.

Partners are not liable for each other's personal debts, only for each other's acts within the scope of their business. These "scope" questions are answered essentially the same way that they are in the agency context. What authority was expressly given to the partners? What authority would normally be implied as part of this kind of business? What authority did the acting partner appear to have? Did the firm ratify the otherwise unauthorized act of one partner? If the contract or tort occurred within the scope of the partnership business, the firm and all the other partners are fully liable for it. If not, only the acting partner is liable; only that person's individual assets would be available to the third party.

■ Mutual Duties of Partners

Partners owe each other full disclosure.

Because so much is at stake, the law demands of each partner the highest standards of openness and fair dealing among the partners. Partnership is generally recognized as imposing on partners the highest level of fiduciary duty to each other. Each has a duty to act in the best interest of all and to keep the others fully informed on all business matters. No personal use can be made of firm property without the consent of all. No personal profit can be made at the expense of the firm or the other partners.

This very high fiduciary standard is illustrated by the *Clement* case.

CLEMENT V. CLEMENT

260 A.2d 728 (Pa. 1970)

Facts: Plaintiff Charles Clement and his brother L.W. were partners in a plumbing business for forty years. When Charles began negotiations to sell out to L.W., he discovered that L.W. claimed personal ownership of substantial assets, including real estate and life insurance. L.W. had kept the firm's books and managed its finances. He was unable to explain the source of the funds used to acquire these assets.

The equity chancellor held that L.W. had used partnership funds to purchase these assets. A majority of the appeals court ruled that Charles had not proved any wrongdoing. Charles asked the state supreme court for further review.

Issue: Who has the burden of proof?

Decision: L.W., the partner who kept the books and records, has the burden of proof. Charles owns half the disputed assets. The judgment of the court of appeals is reversed, and the chancellor's decision is reinstated.

Rule: A partner who claims individual ownership of assets must be prepared to prove how he acquired them, especially where he was the partner who managed the finances of the partnership. If he cannot prove individual ownership, the assets belong to the partnership.

Discussion: *By Justice ROBERTS:*

"Our theory is simple. There is a fiduciary relationship between partners. Where such a relationship exists, actual fraud need not be shown. There was ample evidence of self-dealing and diversion of partnership assets on the part of L.W.—more than enough to sustain the chancellor's conclusion that several substantial investments made by L.W. over the years were bankrolled with funds improperly withdrawn from the partnership....

"One should not have to deal with his partner as though he were the opposite party in an arm's-length transaction. One should be allowed to trust his partner, to expect that he is pursuing a common goal and not working at cross-purposes. This concept of the partnership entity was expressed most ably by Mr. Justice, then Judge, Cardozo.... 'Joint adventurers, like co-partners, owe to one another, while the enterprise continues, the duty of the finest loyalty. Many forms of conduct permissible in a workaday world for those acting at arm's length, are forbidden to those bound by fiduciary ties. A trustee is held to something stricter than the morals of the marketplace. Not honesty alone, but the punctilio of an honor the most sensitive, is then the standard of behavior. As to this there has developed a tradition that is unbending and inveterate.... Only thus has the level of conduct for fiduciaries been kept at a level higher than that trodden by the crowd. It will not consciously be lowered by any judgment of this court....'

"It would be unduly harsh to require that one must prove actual fraud before he can recover for a partner's derelictions. Where one partner has so dealt with the partnership as to raise the probability of wrongdoing, it ought to be his responsibility to negate that inference. It has been held that 'where a partner fails to keep a record of partnership transactions, and is unable to account for them, every presumption will be made against him.'... Likewise, where a partner commingles partnership funds with his own and generally deals loosely with partnership assets he ought to have to shoulder the task of demonstrating the probity of his conduct.

"In the instant case L.W. dealt loosely with partnership funds. At various times he made substantial investments in his own name. He was totally unable to explain where he got the funds to make these investments. The court en banc held that Charles had no claim on the fruits of these investments because he could not trace the money that was invested therein dollar for dollar from the partnership. Charles should not have had this burden. He did show that his brother diverted substantial sums from the partnership funds under his control. The inference that these funds provided L.W. with the wherewithal to make investments was a perfectly reasonable one for the chancellor to make, and his decision should have been allowed to stand."

Dissent: *By Justice* EAGEN:

"In 1923 L.W. Clement and his younger brother, Charles, formed a partnership for the purpose of engaging in the plumbing business under the name of Clement Brothers. They agreed to share the profits of the business equally after payment of the debts. L.W. was the more alert and aggressive of the two. He attended special training schools to upgrade his plumbing skills, and became a master plumber. He alone conducted the business here involved, and had complete control of its finances. He frequently worked nights, Sundays, and holidays. Charles, on the other hand, refused to be 'bothered' with the administration of the business or its finances. He insisted also on limiting his work to a regular eight-hour shift and confining his contribution to the business to the performance of various plumbing jobs assigned to him.

"Over the years, L.W. accumulated assets which eventually became quite valuable. For instance, in 1945 he purchased two lots of land for $5,500, and subsequently constructed a commercial building thereon. This construction was financed in most part by money secured through placing a mortgage on the property. In 1951 he purchased another piece of real estate for $3,500, and in 1927, 1936, 1938, 1945, 1947, 1955, and 1965 purchased policies of life insurance on his own life. There are presently existing substantial loans against some of these policies.

"In 1964 Charles for the first time accused his brother, L.W., of misusing partnership funds to gain the assets he had accumulated. Charles did not have any evidence to substantiate the accusation, but surmised something must be wrong since L.W. had so much while he had so little.

"At trial, not a scintilla of evidence was introduced to establish that L.W. diverted any partnership funds to purchase any of his personal assets. In view of this, a majority of the court en banc below ruled that Charles failed to establish that he had any interest or property rights therein. With this I agree. The majority of this Court now rule, in effect, that, because of the fiduciary relationship existing, it is L.W.'s burden to prove that he did not misuse partnership funds. This I cannot accept on the existing record....

"I dissent and would affirm the decree of the court below."

Ethical Dimension

Is it fair to assume that the managing partner is guilty of diverting partnership assets unless he can prove otherwise? Where one partner has worked much harder, both within and without the partnership, is it fair to assume that his "extra" property must have been diverted from the firm at his partner's expense?

TERMINATION

Under the UPA, any change in the membership of the firm causes a **dissolution.** When that happens, the remaining partner or partners have a choice: continue the business or end it. Continuing the business would require a new agreement among all the partners who chose to do so, unless their original agreement already contained a procedure for continuation.

If there is no agreement among the remaining partners to continue the business, it must be terminated. Any net assets must be paid over to the partners according to their agreed shares. The UPA calls the process of finishing up the firm's business, paying off its creditors, and then dividing any remaining assets the **"winding up"** of the partnership. When this process has been completed, the firm is **terminated.**

Large accounting and law partnerships will have lengthy agreements covering these points, since partners will be entering and leaving the firm frequently. The written partnership agreement will provide a method for determining how much will be paid out to a departing partner (or the estate of a deceased partner) and how much capital will be paid in by a new partner. In this way, the large partnership can continue its business operations without interruption, even though there is technically a dissolution every time the membership changes.

The large professional partnership will probably also have provisions for expulsion of a partner for misconduct or breach of agreement. In such cases, damages caused to the firm could normally be deducted from the amount which would otherwise be due to the wrongdoing partner.

A partnership agreement may include a procedure for continuing the business after loss of one partner.

LIMITED PARTNERSHIP

Since one major disadvantage of the partnership is the unlimited personal liability of each partner for all the debts of the business, the limited partnership was developed. It permits some of the owner-partners to enjoy limited personal liability as long as they comply with all legal requirements.

Definition

A **limited partnership** is a business organization in which one or more of the co-owners have limited liability, and one or more have full, unlimited liability. The latter persons are called **general partners**. There must be at least one general partner and at least one **limited partner** in the limited partnership. The basic rules for these organizations are found in the Revised Uniform Limited Partnership Act (RULPA). If a point of law is not covered in RULPA, general partnership rules apply.

Creation

State action is needed to achieve limited liability.

Because one or more of the co-owners are seeking to have limited personal liability for the debts of their business, this form of organization requires state approval for its existence. The approval by the state may be virtually automatic, but it is required. Parties may agree between themselves who will be liable for what business debts, but they cannot insulate themselves from liability to third parties without state action. Usually, the state's approval amounts to nothing more than the filing of required forms with the appropriate state official. Unless and until this is done, however, the co-owners will not have limited liability for the debts of the business they are operating. Dr. Vidricksen learned this lesson the hard way.

VIDRICKSEN V. GROVER

363 F.2d 372 (U.S. 9th Cir. Court of Appeals, 1966).

Facts: Dr. Vidricksen invested $50,000 with his friend Thom on the understanding that Thom would form a limited partnership. The firm would operate a Chevrolet dealership in Dunsmuir, California. There was a written agreement which named Vidricksen as a limited partner, but Thom never filed a limited partnership certificate as required by state law.

When the firm had financial difficulty in March, 1961, the doctor consulted two different lawyers, who told him he had problems. In August, using another lawyer, he filed a lawsuit against Thom. On September 19 (eight days after the business had filed for bankruptcy), he "renounced" his interest in the firm. Both the bankruptcy referee and the U.S. District Court held that his renunciation was too late, and he was therefore liable as a general partner. Dr. Vidricksen asked for review by the U.S. Court of Appeals.

Issue: Did Vidricksen make a "prompt" renunciation of his interest in the business, and so preserve his limited liability for its debts?

Decision: No. Judgment affirmed.

Rule: There can be no limited liability for the debts of a business without conformity with the proper state statute and the required state approval.

Discussion: *By Circuit Judge* CHAMBERS:

"Section 15511 of the Corporations Code of California... reads as follows:

A person who has contributed to the capital of a business conducted by a person or partnership erroneously believing that he has become a limited partner in a limited partnership, is not, by reason of his exercise of the rights of a limited partner, a general partner...provided, that on ascertaining the mistake he promptly renounces his interest in the profits of the business, or other compensation by way of income.

"Was such renunciation timely? We think not.

"[Vidricksen] would count the time on 'promptly' in 'promptly renounces' only from August 7, 1961, to September 19, 1961, or a period of 43 days. We disagree. In our view 'promptly' began to run when he learned in March 1961 that something was wrong with the organizational setup.

"No California case is of help to us in construing the code section, so we must use our best judgment as to what California courts would hold. We do not think Dr. Vidricksen needed a bonded opinion to start the time running. Knowledge that he was probably in trouble was enough. Thus, we conclude that six months from the time he had noticed something was wrong until the actual renunciation is not a prompt renunciation.... Thus, the doctor must be held to the pains of a general partner."

Ethical Dimension

Is it fair to hold unwary "investors" like Dr. Vidricksen fully liable for the debts of their businesses?

◼ Liability to Third Parties

Limited partners are not personally liable for the debts of the business.

If properly formed, the limited partnership does offer protection to those who become limited partners. They may lose the amount of their investment in the business if it is unsuccessful, but their personal assets are not available to the business creditors. As long as one or more of the co-owners has assumed full personal liability, and proper disclosure of which partners are which has been publicly filed, creditors of the business are protected. Creditors can find out who the general partners are and check their credit standing before deciding to extend credit to the limited partnership. If they wish to have additional security for a particular transaction with the firm, RULPA does permit a limited partner to guarantee specific debts of the firm without becoming fully liable for all debts.

Usually, the general partner or partners manage the firm's business, make and perform its contracts, and represent it to third parties. Limited partners who participate in the general operation of the firm's business run the risk of losing their limited liability. RULPA does, however, permit limited partners to be agents or independent contractors for the firm—without losing their limited liability status. They are also allowed to vote on extraordinary business decisions, such as reorganization of the firm, without becoming fully liable for all its debts.

◼ Mutual Duties of General and Limited Partners

As passive investors in the business, the limited partners are relying very heavily on the honesty and competence of the general partners. The same high fiduciary standard applies here as in the general partnership. General partners who violate the terms of the agreement and cause losses to the firm can be held liable by the limited partners.

◼ Termination

In general, the limited partnership is much more durable than the general partnership. Changes in the membership do not necessarily cause dissolution of the limited partnership. Limited partners can change—drop in or drop out—without affecting the continuity of the business. Only if there is *no* limited partner remaining would the business have to be terminated.

A change in the general partners would cause a dissolution of the firm, but the agreement could provide for continuation with a substitute or with the remaining general partners. Amendments to the publicly filed certificate must be made where new general or limited partners are added, or where there is a substantial change in business operations.

LIMITED LIABILITY COMPANY

Part of what lawyers do is to develop new methods of doing business. The limited liability company illustrates this kind of ongoing "new product" development.

Definition

The limited liability company, or LLC, is a new form of business organization in this country. Developed first in Wyoming in 1977, it is recognized in eighteen states as of January, 1993 (Arizona, Colorado, Delaware, Florida, Illinois, Iowa, Kansas, Louisiana, Maryland, Minnesota, Nevada, Oklahoma, Rhode Island, Texas, Utah, Virginia, West Virginia, and Wyoming). The LLC is an attempt to combine the advantages of the partnership and the corporation, while avoiding their disadvantages.

The **LLC** is essentially a partnership with limited liability. All its members can participate in management, unlike the limited partnership, in which limited partners would lose their "limited" status by doing so. All members, not just some, have limited liability for the debts of the business.

The LLC's primary advantage over the corporation is that it pays no separate income tax, as corporations do. (As of early 1993, the U.S. Internal Revenue Service has so ruled only on Colorado, Virginia, and Wyoming LLCs.) Moreover, as a partnership, the members of an LLC are free to allocate profits and losses among themselves as they see fit. With a corporation, profits must be distributed on the basis of the number of shares owned.

The LLC pays no separate income tax.

Formation

Since limited liability is being sought, state approval is necessary. Formation requires the filing of organizational forms with the state. At least two members are necessary, but there is no legal maximum number. Corporations can be members; so can foreign businesses.

Liability to Third Parties

Only the business assets are at risk. None of the personal assets of any of the members are subject to the claims of business creditors. Of course, the personal assets of a member who committed a tort would be available to the injured party, even if the tort were committed in the course of business.

◼ Mutual Duties of Members

Since the LLC is basically a partnership, the same high standard of fiduciary duty among its members should apply. Case law will gradually add more specific rules, as LLCs come into more widespread use.

◼ Termination

One possible disadvantage to the LLC form for large firms is that it follows partnership rules on dissolution. If one member drops out (retires, dies, or just quits), all the others must formally agree to continue the business. This requirement could mean a cumbersome and expensive reorganization, perhaps at an unfavorable time in terms of business operations. It could also involve some negative tax consequences if assets of the old LLC had to be "sold" to a successor LLC because one member didn't want to continue the business. Whether LLC law will develop a rule to avoid these problems is not yet clear.

◼ ORPORATIONS

Corporations are the dominant form of business organization, not only in the United States, but also worldwide. The multi-national corporations have been called the successor to the nation-state. With the end of the Cold War and the lessening of most international tensions, economic concerns become even more important. The multi-national corporations, operating in several nations, exercise an ever-growing economic power.

◼ Definition

A corporation is a separate legal person.

A **corporation** is a separate and distinct legal person, "invisible, intangible, and existing only in the eyes of the Law" (as stated by Chief Justice John Marshall). It is an entity separate from the human beings who represent it and operate it. In contrast, a partnership is merely a collection of persons doing business together.

The corporation owns its own property and pays its own income tax and other taxes. It, in turn, is owned by its stockholders, who pay their own income taxes on any corporate profits which are distributed to them in the form of dividends. This "double taxation"—paying income taxes twice on the same profits—is one of the major disadvantages to the corporate form of organization.

The U.S. Internal Revenue Code contains a special section (Subchapter S) which deals with this double taxation problem. By filing an appropriate form with the IRS, the stockholders can elect to be taxed as if they were partners. The income of this so-called **Subchapter S corporation** is apportioned to the stockholders as if they were partners, and they pay only their own personal income taxes. No corporate income tax is assessed. A Subchapter S corporation can have no more than thirty-five stockholders, none of whom can be another corporation or an alien person.

■ Creation

A corporation is created when the state approves its proposed articles of incorporation. At one time, each corporation was created by a separate statute passed by the state legislature. Now, each state has a general statute which sets out the requirements for incorporation. A standardized form containing these requirements is filled out and filed with the state, together with the required fee. State approval is usually automatic.

Delaware has been and continues to be a very popular place to incorporate. About half of the 500 largest U.S. industrial corporations are incorporated there; so are about one-third of all the corporations listed on the New York Stock Exchange. Why Delaware? Fees and taxes are low. Delaware corporation law is very favorable; generally, we are free to run our Delaware corporation as we wish, with a minimum of state interference. Finally, Delaware still has a separate Chancery Court, staffed with judges who have acquired much specialized knowledge of corporations and their legal problems. Because so many corporations have been formed there, many cases have been litigated there, and so there are known rules for nearly any corporate law question that may arise. Not many other states can say the same. In most other states, corporate managers and their lawyers can only guess how a court would decide a particular question. In Delaware, most of the rules are known, and corporate strategy can be planned with those rules in mind.

Many corporations are formed in Delaware.

■ Liability to Third Parties

As indicated at the beginning of this section, the corporation makes its own contracts. The agents, managers, officers, directors, and stockholders of the corporation are not personally liable on its contracts. Any of these individuals who personally guaranteed performance of one of the corporation's contracts would, of course, be liable if the corporation defaulted. Officers or stockholders in small corporations with limited capital may be required to make such personal guarantees. If they do, they are personally liable for the contracts so guaranteed, but not for any other corporate debts. As is true with any agent, the agent of a corporation who was not authorized to act for it could be held liable by a third party who was damaged by that lack of authority.

A corporate agent or employee who commits a tort against a third party is, of course, personally liable to that third party for any damages caused. If the tort was committed within the scope of the agent or

Agents of a corporation are not personally liable for the torts of other corporate agents.

employee's duties, the corporation is also liable for those tort damages. For the corporation to be held liable for punitive damages, most courts require that the intentional tort have been committed or approved by a managerial-level person. Other individuals within the corporation—employees, agents, managers, officers, directors, stockholders—are not personally liable for a tort they did not commit or sanction. Only the wrongdoer(s) and the corporation itself are liable. The importance of that rule can be seen in the *Birt* case, involving a professional corporation.

BIRT V. MARY MERCY HOSPITAL

370 N.E.2d 379 (Ind. 1978)

Facts: Dr. Valencia and eight other doctors who staffed the hospital's emergency room agreed to incorporate. They had previously been partners. Articles of incorporation were approved on April 9, 1972. Eugene Birt was treated by Dr. Valencia on May 13. At that time, the corporation (Mercy Medical Associates) had not yet received its required certificate of registration from the Medical Board. Birt sued Dr. Valencia and the eight other doctors individually, as well as Mercy Medical and the hospital. Birt claimed that Dr. Valencia had been guilty of malpractice. The trial court gave summary judgment for the eight doctors. The Indiana Medical Professional Corporation Act (IMPCA) permits doctors to incorporate.

Issue: Are the other doctor-stockholders also liable for Dr. Valencia's negligence?

Decision: No—only Dr. Valencia and the corporation itself can be sued.

Rule: Officers, directors, or stockholders are not personally liable for the debts of their corporation.

Discussion: *By Judge* GARRARD:

"Under common law, a corporate stockholder, director, agent, or employee is not personally liable for the torts of the corporation, or of another agent, merely because of his office or holdings; some additional connection with the tort is required....

"Is this general rule contrary to the provisions or purposes of IMPCA? To answer that question it is helpful to review the considerations which spawned the act....

"It is...apparent that our legislature intended that the IMPCA should not destroy the traditional relationship between a professional and his patient through the creation of a corporate shield…. It has been argued that such provisions must be construed to preserve more than the personal liability of a corporate employee for his own negligent tort existing under general corporations law. We agree. However, it does not necessarily follow that the statute imports the vicarious liability of the Uniform Partnership Act to apply to associating physicians….

"Apprehension has also been expressed concerning the ability of an injured patient to collect a damage award without the existence of vicarious liability. Again, however, we believe the fear is overstated. Of course, the malpracticing physician is liable to the extent of his personal assets and such malpractice insurance as he, or the corporation may possess. In addition, it is beyond question that the corporate entity is liable for malpractice committed by one of its members….

"The IMPCA manifests legislative intent that medical professional corporations be imbued with as many of the attributes of general corporations as may be, without destroying the traditional professional relationship between physician and patient. We conclude that neither the express language of the statute, nor the qualification purpose of maintaining strong professional relationships require importation of the partnership doctrine of vicarious liability into the professional corporate arena. Plainly general corporate concepts preclude it. Accordingly we hold that no vicarious liability arises solely from association under the IMPCA."

Ethical Dimension

Is it ethical for professionals to incorporate to achieve limited personal liability for each other's professional malpractice?

●

■ Mutual Duties of Officers, Directors, and Stockholders

While the relationships within corporations, particularly the very large ones, tend to be much more impersonal than those within partnerships, there are still court decisions which require fair dealing among the participants. The officers and directors are clearly fiduciaries, given control of the corporation's assets, with a duty to use them and to manage them for the corporation's benefit. Officers and directors thus owe their corporation and its shareholders duties of honesty and diligence. "Honesty" means that they cannot make a personal profit at the expense of the corporation. As agents, they must be loyal to it, and not subvert its interests to their own. "Diligence" means that they must

Corporate officers and directors owe to the company and its shareholders fiduciary duties.

exercise reasonable care and ability in managing its affairs. They can be held liable for neglecting their corporation's business or for making careless, irrational decisions.

The position of the majority stockholders, with respect to the minority stockholders, is a bit more difficult to assess. There are court cases holding that the majority have a fiduciary duty to the minority, but it is not always clear just what this means. The majority clearly have the right to vote their shares as they see fit, in their own best interests, as they see them. If such a majority vote disadvantages the minority in some way, so be it—that's implicit in the principle of majority rule, either in political elections or in corporate decisions. But there are also some outer limits. Where the majority is using its voting strength to abuse the minority or to deprive it of some agreed benefit, a court may step in. Such situations typically occur within small, closely-held corporations. The courts tend to treat these small corporations as imposing a kind of partnership-like good faith dealing among the members. The *Wilkes* case is one such example.

WILKES V. SPRINGSIDE NURSING HOME, INC.

353 N.E.2d 657 (Mass. 1976)

Facts: Wilkes, Quinn, Riche, and Pipkin formed a partnership in 1951. Later, they decided to incorporate. Each man invested $1,000 for ten shares of $100 par value stock. They agreed that each of them would be a director of Springside and that they would each be an active, paid manager of the corporation. In March, 1967, the other three voted to remove Wilkes as an officer and director and to terminate his salary. Wilkes sued for damages, but was denied relief by the trial court. He appealed.

Issue: Should the majority be permitted to exclude the minority from corporate offices?

Decision: No. Judgment reversed. (Wilkes has stated a case.)

Rule: Stockholders in closely held corporation owe each other the same fiduciary duty that partners owe one another.

Discussion: By Chief Justice HENNESSEY:

"'Freeze outs'...may be accomplished by the use of [various] devices. One such device which has proved to be particularly effective in accomplishing the purpose of the majority is to deprive minority stockholders of corporate offices and of employment with the corporation.... This 'freeze-out' technique has been successful because courts fairly consistently have been disinclined to interfere in those facets of internal corporate operations, such as the selection and retention or dismissal of officers, directors, and employees, which essentially involve management decisions subject to the principle of majority control.... As one authoritative source has said, '[M]any courts apparently feel that there is a legitimate sphere in which the controlling [directors or] shareholders can act in their own interest even if the minority suffers.'...

"The denial of employment to the minority at the hands of the majority is especially pernicious in some instances. A guaranty of employment with the corporation may have been one of the 'basic reason[s] why a minority owner has invested capital in the firm.'... The minority stockholder typically depends on his salary as the principal return on his investment, since the 'earnings of a close corporation...are distributed in major part in salaries, bonuses, and retirement benefits'...Other noneconomic interests of the minority stockholder are likewise injuriously affected by barring him from corporate office.... Such action severely restricts his participation in the management of the enterprise, and he is relegated to enjoying those benefits incident to this status as a stockholder.... In sum, by terminating a minority stockholder's employment or by severing him from a position as an officer or director, the majority effectively frustrate the minority stockholder's purposes in entering on the corporate venture and also deny him an equal return on his investment.

"Therefore, when minority stockholders in a close corporation bring suit against the majority alleging a breach of the strict good faith duty owed to them by the majority, we must carefully analyze the action taken by the controlling stockholders in the individual case. It must be asked whether the controlling group can demonstrate a legitimate business purpose for its action.... In asking this question, we acknowledge the fact that the controlling group in a close corporation must have some room to maneuver in establishing the business policy of the corporation. It must have a large measure of discretion, for example, in declaring or withholding dividends, deciding whether to merge or consolidate, establishing the salaries of corporate officers, dismissing directors with or without cause, and hiring and firing corporate employees.

"When an asserted business purpose for their action is advanced by the majority, however, we think it is open to minority stockholders to demonstrate that the same legitimate objective could have been achieved through an alternative course of action less harmful to the minority's interest.... If called on to settle a dispute, our courts must weigh the legitimate business purpose, if any, against the practicability of a less harmful alternative.

"Applying this approach to the instant case, it is apparent that the majority stockholders in Springside have not shown a legitimate business purpose for severing Wilkes from the payroll of the corporation or for refusing to reelect him as a salaried officer and director.... There was no showing of misconduct on Wilkes's part as a director, officer, or employee of the corporation which would lead us to approve the majority action as a legitimate response to the disruptive nature of an undesirable individual bent on injuring or destroying the corporation. On the contrary, it appears that Wilkes had always accomplished his assigned share of the duties competently, and that he had never indicated an unwillingness to continue to do so.

"It is an inescapable conclusion from all the evidence that the action of the majority stockholders here was a designed 'freeze out' for which no legitimate business purpose has been suggested. Furthermore, we may infer that a design to pressure Wilkes into selling his shares to the corporation at a price below their value well may have been at the heart of the majority's plan."

Ethical Dimension

Why should there be any limits on the principle of majority rule? The minority can always sell out and reinvest elsewhere, can't they?

■ Termination

Corporations normally have perpetual existence. They do not end simply because some of the human beings involved may die or retire. The corporation, as a separate and distinct legal entity, will last until its human managers take some action to terminate it.

A corporation may be terminated by being merged into another existing corporation. Or it may be consolidated with one or more other corporations into a brand-new corporation. Or it may simply be dissolved and go out of business completely. It may be terminated by its state of incorporation for noncompliance with filing and tax requirements. Finally, it may be ended by a bankruptcy liquidation if the business has not been successful.

REVIEW

One of the key decisions which an entrepreneur will make is the form of the new business which is being established. There are several choices, each of which involves advantages and disadvantages. These relative costs and benefits must be weighed carefully. Those forms which provide limited personal liability also require state approval. The corporation, as a separate legal person, requires the payment of taxes on its income, plus a second taxation if the income is distributed to investors as dividends. The various forms also differ in the degree of responsibility which is owed to one's associates and in the duration and termination of the association. All these factors need to be considered in deciding which business organization to use.

REVIEW QUESTIONS AND PROBLEMS

1. What is the difference between "implied authority" and "apparent authority"?

2. When is a company liable for wrongful acts of its agents?

3. What are the advantages a company may gain by using independent contractors, rather than employees, to conduct its business?

4. What is the major disadvantage to operating a business as a partnership?

5. How is the status of a limited partner different from that of a general partner?

6. What is the major disadvantage of operating a business as a corporation?

7. Ned bought eight new fold-up beds for his apartment building. The beds had a powerful spring, which enabled them to be folded up into wall recesses when not in use. Ned had Hank install the beds. Instead of using the large bolts which came with the beds to anchor them to the floor, Hank used ordinary wood screws. Several weeks later, when one of the tenants, Grace, came home from work exhausted and flopped down on her bed, the small wood screws came loose, and the bed folded up with Grace inside. Grace sued both Hank and Ned. What result, and why?

8. Rico owned a barbershop. Rico and his two barbers, Dom and Doris, signed two "partnership" agreements. Rico would handle all the financial affairs of the two partnerships, because he would contribute the existing shop and all its assets. Dom and Doris would contribute their barbering tools and agree to work eight hours on weekdays and a half-day on Saturday. Doris would receive seventy percent of her receipts; Dom would receive sixty percent of his receipts. The state sued Rico for unpaid unemployment compensation premiums due on his two employees. Rico claimed that Dom and Doris were his partners, not his employees, and that he therefore did not owe for unemployment compensation. Who is right, and why?

9. Henry, a medical doctor, was an associate (and also officer, director, and shareholder) in the professional corporation called Meds, Inc. He was forced to resign all these positions (and to sell his stock back to the corporation) by a majority vote of the other members. Since he was fifty-two years old, Henry brought an age discrimination lawsuit under the Age Discrimination in

Employment Act (ADEA). His former associates moved to dismiss the lawsuit on the basis that Henry was "really" a partner and thus not covered by the ADEA. Should the court dismiss the case? Discuss.

10. Mick was employed by Steay Securities as a trainee. He had business cards printed up which identified him as a "portfolio management specialist," and mailed these cards to a list of potential investors. He then telephoned each prospect and made recommendations for securities purchases. Busby and Bertha, who bought large blocks of these "recommended" stocks, sued Mick and Steay when the market price of the securities fell sharply. Steay says it is not liable for Mick's misrepresentations. Is it? Explain.

SUGGESTIONS FOR FURTHER READING

Danos & Danos, "The Fall of the Focal Point Test for Home Office Deductions?" *American Business Law Journal* 29 (Summer 1991): 333.

Nicholson, "The Fiduciary Duty of Close Corporation Shareholders: A Call for Legislation," *American Business Law Journal* 30 (November 1992): 513.

10
REGULATION
OF
ORGANIZATIONS

"Keep thy shop, and thy shop will keep thee."
Benjamin Franklin

LEARNING OBJECTIVES: After you have studied this chapter, you should be able to:

DISCUSS the need for protection of investors in businesses.

EXPLAIN how the national securities acts meet this need.

DEFINE "materiality" and "due diligence" as they relate to securities.

EXPLAIN the liability of corporate officers and directors.

DEFINE the "business judgment rule."

DISTINGUISH the various types of mergers and explain the legality of each.

P REVIEW

In Chapter 9, we examined the legal framework for business organizations. We compared the major forms of associations, in terms of creation, liability, duties, and termination. We now need to take the next step: to see how the government regulates the various forms. Above and beyond the basic framework of the various organizational choices, what additional regulatory requirements are placed on them? Are there significant differences in the way in which the various forms are regulated?

Most government regulation of organizations stems from two characteristics: separation of ownership from control and limited personal liability. As long as the owners are in personal control of the business and are willing to assume full personal liability for all its debts, there is little need for additional government regulation of its operations. Its creditors are protected because the persons with whom they are dealing are fully liable for all debts incurred by the business. Its owners are protected both by their ability to personally control what happens and by the fiduciary duties they owe each other. The basic legal rules, in other words, need little if any supplementing.

When we create an organization in which the operators are not the owners, and in which both operators and owners have limited personal liability, there may be a need for additional regulatory protection. Passive investors in the business may need greater assurance that their investments will be used productively, not siphoned off for the personal benefit of the managers. Creditors certainly need greater assurance that the business assets on which they are relying for payment are available if needed.

We will thus look at the regulation of organizations in three major areas: protection of investors, fiduciary duties of professional managers, and changes in organizational structure or scope.

P ROTECTION OF INVESTORS

In the latter part of the 1800s and the early 1900s, business and industry grew very rapidly in this country. Much of this growth was channeled through the corporate form of organization. Large, impersonal corporations came to dominate most areas of commerce. Inevitably, abuses occurred. Tales of financial manipulators and "robber barons" abound. Fortunes were made, and sometimes lost, almost overnight. Small, unsophisticated investors lost their life savings in all sorts of wild, get-rich-quick schemes.

■ State Regulation

State governments (or at least some of them) recognized the problem and did try to do something about it. State regulation, however, proved to be, at best, limited, and, at worst, ineffective. Promoters could simply move their operation to another, more "liberal," state and continue to fleece the public in the new location. Even within a state determined to regulate, it was difficult to amass the power, expertise, and budget to really do the job. National regulation was required.

State regulation of securities was generally ineffective.

■ Great Depression

The great stock market crash in 1929 traumatized the securities industry and the country as well. The specter of brokers and investors jumping off tall buildings along Wall Street marked the end of the boom years of the 1920s. Business as an institution had lost its credibility. As the Great Depression settled over the land, the search for causes intensified. Blame was fastened on the speculators and wheeler-dealers, who had manipulated the nation's investment markets for their own benefit. The popular belief, shared by many political leaders, was that the stock market had been brought down by a combination of speculation, pyramiding, and self-dealing. Drastic times called for drastic action. The result was comprehensive regulation of the securities and banking industries. Most of the legislation passed during these crisis years has been with us ever since.

■ Securities Act of 1933

One of the first major pieces of New Deal legislation was the Securities Act of 1933. Reform of the securities industry was high on the list of New Deal priorities. Proper operation of this industry is crucial to our free enterprise system. The securities industry provides the means for channeling savings into productive investments, which in turn provide the capital dollars needed by large and small businesses. Malfunctioning of the securities system can have drastic repercussions on the nation's economic, and political, health. It was therefore imperative that reforms occur.

As required first by the Securities Act of 1933, and then in the 1934 Securities Exchange Act and later statutes, the basic national prescription for the ailments of the securities industry was "full disclosure." Companies issuing securities would be required to disclose to investors all material facts relating to the securities. Fraud and manipulation would be prohibited by national law, with national penalties for violation. After that, the investment decision would still be up to the individual investor. The national government would not guarantee that you would win if you played the game; it would just try to guarantee that the wheel wasn't rigged and the deck wasn't marked.

The Federal securities acts aimed at disclosure.

■ Jurisdiction and Definitions

Regulatory jurisdiction for the 1933 act is based on the use of the mails, or of the instrumentalities of interstate commerce, to distribute securities. Before such sales can occur, says the 1933 act, the new issue of securities must be "registered" with the national government. (The 1934 act created the Securities and Exchange Commission [SEC]. For the first year, the 1933 act was enforced by the Federal Trade Commission.)

The major term to be defined, of course, is **security** itself. It is defined in the 1933 act as including "...any note, stock, treasury stock, bond, debenture, evidence of indebtedness, certificate of interest or participation in any profit-sharing agreement, collateral-trust certificate, preorganization certificate or subscription, transferable share, investment contract, voting-trust certificate, certificate of deposit for a security, fractional undivided interest in oil, gas, or other mineral rights, or, in general, any interest or instrument commonly known as a 'security,' or any certificate of interest or participation in, temporary or interim certificate for, receipt for, guarantee of, or warrant or right to subscribe to purchase, any of the foregoing." Since promoters usually wish to avoid the disclosure required by the act, there have been numerous litigations over whether particular schemes involved the sale of "securities."

Securities includes investment contracts.

Those things specifically listed in the statutory definition, such as stocks and bonds, are of course included. Disagreements have arisen over the scope of the phrase "investment contract." In simplest terms, the general rule is that any scheme in which the participants intend to make money based on their passive investment of money, rather than on their own personal efforts, is a security for the purpose of compliance with the 1933 act. Sole proprietors and partners are thus not "investors," under this act, but limited partners and stockholders are. On that basis, the U.S. Supreme Court held that orange grove investments were "securities" and that compliance with the 1933 act was required. The sole owner of a business who was selling half of the business to a new partner who was to be actively involved in the firm would thus not have to comply with the 1933 act. But suppose that same business is incorporated, and the new co-owner is buying half the stock? The "sale of business" doctrine, as applied by some courts, held that the economic reality of the new owner's actual control of the business meant that this was not the sale of a security. Which aspect of the statutory definition should prevail—the letter of the law or the spirit of the law? That question split the U.S. Courts of Appeals until the issue was resolved by the U.S. Supreme Court in the following case.

LANDRETH TIMBER CO. V. LANDRETH

105 S.Ct. 2297 (1985)

Facts: Ivan Landreth and his sons owned all the stock in a lumber business located in Tonasket, Washington. They offered their business for sale through brokers. Before any sale was made, the business was heavily damaged by fire. Potential buyers were then told that the lumber mill would be completely rebuilt and modernized. Samuel Dennis, a Massachusetts tax lawyer, received a letter offering the mill for sale. He had an audit and inspection done and decided to buy the mill by buying the Landreths' stock.

After the sale was made, the mill was not as profitable as expected. Rebuilding costs were more than the estimates, and the new machinery did not match well with the old. Landreth Timber Co. (now Dennis) sued to rescind the sale and to collect $2.5 million in damages because the stock had not been registered under the 1933 act. He also alleged several violations of the 1934 act. The Landreths claimed that the acts did not apply to the sale of a business. The U.S. District Court dismissed the case on that basis, and the Ninth Circuit affirmed. Dennis, in the person of the Landreth Timber Co., asked the Supreme Court to review the case.

Issue: Do the national securities acts apply when all the stock of a corporation is sold to a person who intends to operate it?

Decision: Yes. Judgment reversed. (Dennis wins.)

Rule: There is no "sale of business" exemption from the securities acts if the transaction involves the sale of stock.

Discussion: *By Justice* POWELL:

"The face of the definition shows that 'stock' is considered to be a 'security' within the meaning of the Acts.... [M]ost instruments bearing such a traditional title are likely to be covered by the definition....

"[T]he fact that instruments bear the label 'stock' is not of itself sufficient to invoke the coverage of the Acts...[W]e must also determine whether those instruments possess 'some of the significant characteristics typically associated with' stock,...recognizing that when an instrument is both called 'stock' and bears stock's usual characteristics, 'a purchaser justifiably [may] assume that the federal securities laws apply.'... We identified those characteristics usually associated with common stock as (i) the right to receive dividends contingent upon an apportionment of profits; (ii) negotiability; (iii) the ability to be pledged or hypothecated; (iv) the conferring of voting rights in proportion to the number of shares owned; and (v) the capacity to appreciate in value....

"[I]t is undisputed that the stock involved here possesses all of the characteristics...traditionally associated with common stock. Indeed, the District Court so found.... Moreover,...the context of the transaction involved here—the sale of stock in a corporation—is typical of the kind of context to which the Acts normally apply. It is thus...likely here...that an investor would believe he was covered by the federal securities laws. Under the circumstances of this case, the plain meaning of the statutory definition mandates that the stock be treated as 'securities' subject to the coverage of the Acts.

"Reading the securities laws to apply to the sale of the stock at issue here comports with Congress' remedial purpose in enacting the legislation to protect investors by 'compelling full and fair disclosure relative to the issuance of "the many types of instruments that in our commercial world fall within the ordinary concept of a security".'... Although we recognize that Congress did not intend to provide a comprehensive federal remedy for all fraud,...we think it would improperly narrow Congress' broad definition of 'security' to hold that the traditional stock at issue here falls outside the Acts' coverage....

"[I]f applied to this case, the sale of business doctrine would also have to be applied to cases in which less than 100% of a company's stock was sold. This inevitably would lead to difficult questions of line-drawing. The Acts' coverage would in every case depend not only on the percentage of stock transferred, but also on such factors as the number of purchasers and what provisions for voting and veto rights were agreed upon by the parties.... [C]overage by the Acts would in most cases be unknown and unknowable to the parties at the time the stock was sold. These uncertainties attending the applicability of the Acts would hardly be in the best interests of either party to a transaction.... [Landreths] argue that adopting petitioner's approach will increase the workload of the federal courts by converting state and common law fraud claims into federal claims. We find more daunting, however, the prospect that parties to a transaction may never know whether they are covered by the Acts until they engage in extended discovery and litigation over a concept as often elusive as the passage of control....

"In sum, we conclude that the stock at issue here is a 'security' within the definition of the Acts, and that the sale of business doctrine does not apply. The judgment of the United States Court of Appeals for the Ninth Circuit is therefore reversed."

Ethical Dimension

Should the national securities acts be used to decide a contract dispute between the buyer and the seller of a business, where the buyer has made a personal inspection of the business and its books?

■ Registration of Securities

The essence of the registration requirement is full public disclosure of all material facts relating to the securities being issued. As we saw in Chapter 8, under the common law of contracts, one party generally owes the other no positive duty of disclosure as to facts known to the first about the subject matter of the transaction. A failure to disclose, in other words, does not amount to a misrepresentation, except in special circumstances. A common law fraud case also requires proof that the misstatement was made knowingly and with intent to deceive.

Securities sold in interstate commerce must be registered with the SEC.

The concept of full disclosure found in the national securities acts changes these rules. First, there is a positive duty to make a full and truthful disclosure of all material facts prior to the offer to sell the security. Failure to do so is a violation. And second, a specific intent to deceive need not be proved. Liability for losses sustained by investors may be based on a failure to exercise reasonable care in the preparation and issuance of a registration statement containing false information, i.e., on negligence.

■ Exemptions

The 1933 act contains two sets of exemptions from its registration requirement. Some types of securities are exempt, and some types of transactions are exempt.

TYPES OF EXEMPT SECURITIES

The general theme for the types of securities which are exempt is that they are not such as are susceptible to the sorts of speculative abuses which the act was designed to remedy. This is seen in the exemptions

Some Securities do not have to be registered.

for securities issued by governmental units, by religious and other nonprofit organizations, by savings and loan associations, by carriers of goods regulated by the Interstate Commerce Commission, or by approval of state courts or administrative officials. Certificates of deposit issued by banks and short-term (up to nine months) commercial paper arising out of current transactions are likewise exempt from registration. So are exchanges of securities between the issuer and its existing securities holders, if no commission is paid for making the exchange.

For smaller businesses, the two most important exemptions are the limited-dollar offering and the intrastate offering. Using its rule-making authority, the SEC has adopted a series of regulations which permit simplified procedures for smaller issues of securities. The exemption for intrastate offerings applies where the securities are offered and sold only to residents of one state by a business located there. If the business is a corporation, it must be incorporated in that state and doing business there. The entire issue must be sold to persons who are residents in that state. The securities must be bought for investment, not for resale to persons outside the state. The mails may be used, and there is no dollar maximum. If sales are made to persons outside the state, the exemption is lost, and once lost, it cannot be reinstituted.

TYPES OF EXEMPT TRANSACTIONS

Some transactions in securities do not have to be registered.

Certain types of securities transactions are exempt from the registration requirement even though the securities themselves don't fall into an exempt category. Transactions by persons other than the issuer, securities underwriters (large financial institutions who agree to buy the securities from the issuer and then try to redistribute them at a profit), or securities dealers are exempt. For instance, if there are ten stockholders in a small corporation, and one of those owners sells out, that sale would not require a registration of the stock. That is clearly not the kind of situation that helped cause the bust of 1929 and was intended to be remedied by the 1933 act. Similarly, a sale made through a broker, where the seller-owner took the initiative in ordering the sale, is also exempt.

The most useful, and also the most litigated, of these exempt transactions is the "private offering." The 1933 act does not specifically define this term, so the courts have had to work out its meaning on a case-by-case basis. The basic test here is whether the offerees are the sort of persons who need the protection which would be afforded by registration of the security being offered. Are they a small group of sophisticated professional investors? Or a large group of inexperienced novices? A stock offering to so-called "key employees" at all levels in the company was held to be a public offering by the U.S. Supreme Court. Some of the executive-level personnel might have access to the same kind of information provided by a registration statement, but most of the offeree-employees would not. The public, as this case shows, need not include the whole world. In other cases, courts have approved as private offerings a placement of securities with insurance companies and investment banks and a sale of thirty-two shares in an oil well to thirty-two business associates. In general, thirty-five offerees has been used as a rule-of-thumb maximum number permitted under this exemption. Each case is decided on its own merits, however, and the burden of proof is on the person claiming the exemption. Moreover, exemption from registration only excuses that step; it is not a license to commit fraud. All the other provisions of the 1933 act still apply to the securities being sold.

■ Registration Statement

Full disclosure occurs through the filing of a **registration statement** with the SEC. The registration statement must contain a description of the securities being offered; historical information on the company, its management, and its business; audited financial statements; details and costs of underwriting these securities; the company's major contracts, with copies attached; the company's current management and its salaries and benefit plans; and any material litigation involving the company. Thirteen copies are filed, but only three need contain all the required exhibits. At least one copy must be manually signed by the issuing company, its principal executive officers, its principal financial officer, its principal accounting officer or its comptroller, and a majority of the board of directors. Conforming signatures must be typed on all other copies. The registration fee of 1/50 of one percent (.0002) of the offering price, with a $100 minimum, must be paid in cash or by postal money order or certified check.

The registration statement is the full disclosure document filed with the SEC.

   The registration statement takes effect twenty days after receipt by the SEC, assuming it is in order and the fee has been paid. The SEC may require additional information if it has questions, but it does not, as such, guarantee the accuracy of any information.

■ Prospectus

The primary device for conveying the required information to the investing public is the **prospectus**. The prospectus is in effect the first part of the registration statement, since the first section of the official form is titled "Information Required in Prospectus." It does not have to include all the underwriting and internal accounting details, information on franchises and subsidiaries, nor indemnification agreements with officers and directors. Most important, it does not have to include the certified financial statements which must be filed with the SEC. These

The prospectus is the disclosure document given to investors.

are matters of public record, of course, and available for inspection, but all these exhibits don't have to be distributed to each public offeree. The cover of the prospectus must include the statement that "These Securities Have Not Been Approved Or Disapproved By The Securities And Exchange Commission Nor Has The Commission Passed On The Accuracy Or Adequacy Of This Prospectus. Any Representation To The Contrary Is A Criminal Offense." There are no guarantees that the investment is a good one; there is only a legal requirement that full and accurate information be disclosed.

◼ Materiality

A material fact is one which would be important to the average prudent investor.

The basis for civil liability to investors under the 1933 act is the making of a material misstatement or omission in the registration statement or prospectus. Where is the line to be drawn as to what information is "material"? Unfortunately for potential defendants and their lawyers, there is no hard and fast definition of materiality. In the last analysis, materiality is a fact question, to be decided in each case. The working definition is that a **material fact** is one whose inclusion would have deterred or tended to deter the average prudent investor from buying. That definition is some help, but not much, since the average prudent investor is a hypothetical person, like the reasonably prudent person of negligence law. If this fact question goes to a jury, with injured investors on one side and corporations and bankers on the other, there may be recovery for some misstatements which don't seem very "material" to professionals.

◼ Liability

Liability for misstatement extends to all directors and all underwriters.

Under Section 11 of the 1933 act, all persons who signed the registration statement, including the issuer itself, may be held liable for material omissions or misstatements. Every person who is a director or who agreed to be named as a director is also liable. So is every accountant or other expert who prepared or certified any part of the statement. All the underwriters are also liable. By court interpretation, lawyers are "experts" only as to their opinions on legal matters in the prospectus or registration statement. Lawyers may have put the registration statement together, but that does not mean that it is all "expertised," for the purpose of the due diligence defense.

Civil actions may also be brought under the anti-fraud sections of the 1933 act—Section 12 (2) and 17(a). Here, the plaintiff would have to prove that the particular defendant participated in the fraud, or at least consented to it. Plaintiff would also have to prove a more traditional case, with knowledge, intent to deceive, and reasonable reliance. These cases are harder to prove and easier to defend.

■ Due Diligence

The main statutory defense to a Section 11 case is phrased in terms of "due diligence." A defendant is not liable where, after a "reasonable investigation," either he or she is found to have had reasonable grounds to believe that the statements made were true and complete, or, if he or she relied on statements made by "experts," the defendant had no reasonable grounds for believing that they were not true and complete. This due diligence defense is not available to the issuer itself. Many corporate insiders would not be able to use it successfully either, since they would have had direct access to much corporate information and would therefore have a basis for knowing the truth.

Professionals are not liable if they used "due diligence" in preparing the registration statement.

Accountants, lawyers, and other experts would be required to meet the standards of their respective professions in order to be exercising due diligence. Accountants who certified the financial statements which were included, for example, would have to show that they complied with the firm's own standard audit practice, and that the firm's practice was in conformity with generally accepted accounting standards.

The major application of the due diligence defense concerns the underwriters. What must they do to avoid liability? What is a reasonable investigation to expect of an underwriter of the new securities issue? As to the portions of the registration statement prepared by experts, the underwriters can rely on the expert without making their own independent investigation to verify the experts' statements. The underwriter must correct statements she or he believes, or has reasonable grounds to believe, are false and misleading. In other words, for these portions of the registration statement, the underwriter's only duty is to correct known untruths or half-truths. However, as to the portions not prepared by experts, the underwriter must make an independent investigation. She or he is required to make the investigation which a reasonably prudent person would make before investing. This test would require the underwriter to verify that which was easily verifiable, and, particularly, to verify the crucial facts underlying the securities issue. The underwriter is thus required to ask specific and detailed questions of the issuing corporation's officers and to verify their answers if possible. She or he is also required to examine the issuer's major contracts and other important business records. A reasonably prudent investor would also maintain a continuous check on important and volatile items in the company's business affairs and would have the accountants audit and verify as many of the important matters as possible. Civil liability to investors could result from a failure to do any of these things, any one of which might uncover false or missing information in the registration statement.

Underwriters must correct statements which they should know are false or misleading.

Many of the above points are illustrated by the *Escott* case, one of the leading cases on the meaning of the 1933 act.

ESCOTT V. BAR CHRIS CONSTRUCTION CO.

283 F. Supp. 643 (N.Y. 1968)

Facts: BarChris built bowling alleys. In the late 1950s, there was a surge in demand for these facilities, and by 1960 BarChris was building about 3 percent of the new alleys in the United States. Needing additional working capital to finance this tremendous growth, BarChris decided to issue $5 million in bonds. The 1960 financial statements overstated sales, earnings, and assets by substantial amounts. BarChris did not disclose that over $1 million of the new funds was used to pay off old debts, not for expansion. It did not disclose that it had a contingent liability to its financing agency because its customers were in default on payments for the alleys already built. And it did not disclose that it had been forced to assume operation of some alleys itself because they could not be sold or because the original buyers had defaulted. Escott and other bond-buyers sued BarChris, its directors, some of its officers, the underwriters, and the CPAs who had audited the financial statements. These plaintiffs claimed that the registration statement and the prospectus on the bond issue contained material misstatements and omissions, on which they had relied in buying the bonds. The CPA firm [Peat, Marwick] claimed it had done a reasonable job of reviewing and certifying the financial statements

Issue: Did the CPA firm make a reasonable investigation?

Decision: No. Judgment for plaintiffs.

Rule: An auditing firm is not liable for inaccuracies if it had, after reasonable investigation, a reasonable ground to believe and did believe that the statements were true.

Discussion: *By Judge* MCLEAN:

"Peat, Marwick's work was in general charge of a member of the firm, Cummings, and more immediately in charge of Peat, Marwick's manager, Logan. Most of the actual work was performed by a senior accountant, Berardi, who had junior assistants, one of whom was Kennedy.

"Berardi was then about 30 years old. He was not yet a CPA. He had had no previous experience in the bowling industry. This was his first job as a senior accountant. He could hardly have been given a more difficult assignment.

"It is unnecessary to recount everything that Berardi did in the course of the audit. We are concerned only with the evidence relating to what Berardi did or did not do with respect to those items which I have found to have been incorrectly reported in the 1960 figures in the prospectus. More narrowly, we are directly concerned only with such of those items as I have found to be material.

"First and foremost is Berardi's failure to discover that Capitol Lanes had not been sold. This error affected both the sales figure and the liability side of the balance sheet. Fundamentally, the error stemmed from the fact that Berardi never realized that Heavenly Lanes and Capitol were two different names for the same alley.... Berardi assumed that Heavenly was to be treated like any other completed job....

Berardi testified that he inquired...about Capitol Lanes and [was] told...that Capitol Lanes, Inc., was going to operate an alley some day but as yet it had no alley. Berardi testified that he understood that the alley had not been built and that he believed that the rental payments were on vacant land.

"I am not satisfied with this testimony. If Berardi did hold this belief he should not have held it. The entries as to insurance and as to 'operation of alley' should have alerted him to the fact that an alley existed. He should have made further inquiry on the subject. It is apparent that Berardi did not understand this transaction.

"The burden of proof on this issue is on Peat, Marwick. Although the question is a rather close one, I find that Peat, Marwick has not sustained that burden. Peat, Marwick has not proved that Berardi made a reasonable investigation as far as Capitol Lanes was concerned and that his ignorance of the true facts was justified....

"Berardi made the S-1 review in May 1961. He devoted a little over two days to it, a total of 20 1/2 hours. He did not discover any of the errors or omissions pertaining to the state of affairs in 1961 which I have previously discussed at length, all of which were material. The question is whether, despite his failure to find out anything, his investigation was reasonable within the meaning of the statute.

"What Berardi did was to look at a consolidating trial balance as of March 31, 1961, which had been prepared by BarChris, compare it with the audited December 31, 1960, figures, discuss with Trilling [BarChris' controller] certain unfavorable developments which the comparison disclosed, and read certain minutes. He did not examine any 'important financial records' other than the trial balance.

"In substance, what Berardi did is similar to what...Ballard [the lawyer who prepared the registration statement] did. He asked questions, he got answers which he considered satisfactory, and he did nothing to verify them....

"Berardi had no conception of how tight the cash position was. He did not discover that BarChris was holding up checks in substantial amounts because there was no money in the bank to cover them. He did not know of the loan from Manufacturers Trust Company or of the officers' loans. Since he never read the prospectus, he was not even aware that there had ever been any problem about loans from officers....

"There had been a material change for the worse in BarChris' financial position. That change was sufficiently serious so that the failure to disclose it made the 1960 figures misleading. Berardi did not discover it. As far as results were concerned, his S-1 review was useless.

"Accountants should not be held to a standard higher than that recognized in their profession. I do not do so here. Berardi's review did not come up to that standard. He did not take some of the steps which Peat, Marwick's program prescribed. He did not spend an adequate amount of time on a task of this magnitude. Most important of all, he was too easily satisfied with glib answers to his inquiries.

"This is not to say that he should have made a complete audit. But there were enough danger signals in the materials which he did examine to require some further investigation on his part. Generally accepted accounting standards required such further investigation under these circumstances. It is not always sufficient merely to ask questions.

"Here again, the burden of proof is on Peat, Marwick. I find that that burden has not been satisfied. I conclude that Peat, Marwick has not established its due diligence defense."

ETHICAL DIMENSION

Is it fair to hold a CPA firm liable for the lies told by its client?

●

OFFICERS AND DIRECTORS AS FIDUCIARIES

The second area of increased regulatory concern with corporate operations is less clearly defined. It is derived in part from court decisions and in part from several specific statutory requirements and limitations. It is an attempt to provide some guidelines for the organization's management, which has increasingly become a self-perpetuating elite. Although in the corporate legal structure the stockholders elect the directors who in turn elect the officers, the reality is often quite different. The stockholders in large corporations are widely scattered, infrequently attend even the single regular annual meeting, and generally cast their proxies in support of management. Boards of directors are frequently dominated by the corporation's managers and usually support the existing officer group, to whom they owe their positions on the board. With this kind of relationship, the real question is: who's watching the watchers?

■ Business Judgment Rule

Under the common law, the courts generally took a hands-off approach to matters of corporate policy. This general policy was labelled the **"business judgment rule."** Under this rule, the courts would not try to second-guess corporate management on matters of business policy. If management acted honestly and in good faith, no liability would be imposed for losses which resulted from mistaken judgments. Decisions on products, pricing, dividends, and organizational matters would be left to the discretion of the professional managers. Only when those persons were abusing their position would a court step in, as in the *Wilkes* case in the last chapter.

Corporate managers are not liable if they use reasonable business judgment.

■ Fiduciary Duties of Officers and Directors

Officers and directors of corporations are placed in a position of trust and confidence. They are managing assets which do not belong to them. (Most officers and directors of publicly traded companies own only a very small percentage of the outstanding shares of stock.) Legally, of course, the corporation, not the stockholders, owns the corporate assets. The stockholders are the owners of the corporation, which in turn owns the land, buildings, equipment, inventories and other business assets. Persons who are entrusted with the property of others are, and should be, held to a high standard of fairness and openness.

What all this means in practice is that courts can and will prevent corporate insiders from abusing their positions to gain personal profits. Officers and directors are required to be loyal to their corporation. In one famous case, the chance to buy the trademark and formula for Pepsi-Cola was presented to the CEO of a corporation which had retail and wholesale soft-drink operations. He used his company's assets to develop and market the formula, but then claimed it belonged to him personally, rather than to his corporation. Clearly, he was wrong. The **corporate opportunity doctrine** states that the business opportunity belongs to the corporation, not to the individual manager, if it is presented to the manager in his or her official capacity, if it is within the

Corporate managers must be loyal and diligent.

scope of the company's business, or if it was developed with the company's assets.

Reporting Insider Transactions

Purchases of a company's stock by insiders must be reported.

One way to prevent manipulation of stock prices by corporate insiders is to require that they disclose transactions in their company's stock. The 1934 Securities Exchange Act requires such disclosure. It defines **insiders** as directors, officers, and holders of ten percent or more of the company's stock. These persons are required to report any transactions (purchases or sales) in their company's stock within ten days after the end of the month in which they engaged in such transactions. They are also prohibited from making **short sales** in their company's stock, that is, they cannot make contracts to sell shares which they do not currently own. Others are free to do so, but insiders are prohibited from engaging in this kind of speculation.

While the general regulatory method of preventing insider manipulation is disclosure of such transactions, the 1934 act also provides another remedy. Any profits obtained by these insiders from purchase and sale, or sale and purchase, of their company's equity securities within a six-month period, must be turned over to the company. This is the so-called **short-swing profits rule**, from Section 16(b) of the 1934 act. Unlike the general prohibition against fraud and manipulation, this rule applies only to the defined insiders, and only where less than six months elapses between the buying and selling transactions. Finally, in the fact situation where it applies, the 16(b) rule imposes a kind of strict liability, since it conclusively presumes a misuse of inside information and requires disgorgement of profits without any proof of actual misuse or of intent to defraud. A lawsuit to collect the short-swing profits may be brought by the company itself or by one or more stockholders on its behalf.

Antifraud Provisions

In addition to Section 16b (and other specific prohibitions, rules, and requirements), the 1934 act also contains a general "antifraud" statement. Section 10(b) makes it unlawful for any person "to use or employ, in connection with the purchase or sale of any security,…any manipulative or deceptive device or contrivance in contravention of such rules and regulations as the Commission may prescribe." To implement this section, the SEC adopted its Rule 10b–5.

Under Rule 10b–5, it is illegal "to employ any device, scheme, or artifice to defraud"; "to make any untrue statement of a material fact or to omit to state a material fact necessary in order to make the statements made, in light of the circumstances under which they were made, not misleading"; or "to engage in any act, practice, or course of business which operates or would operate as a fraud or deceit upon any

person"—"in connection with the purchase or sale of any security." *It is illegal to commit fraud in a securities transaction.*
The rule was obviously intended as an all-encompassing prohibition of fraud in securities transactions, and it has clearly served that purpose. Section 10(b) and Rule 10b–5 are the basis for most securities lawsuits. One commentator has noted that this section and rule may be responsible for more litigation than any statutory section except Section 1 of the Sherman Antitrust Act.

It is now well-established that this rule implies a private cause of action in favor of the deceived party. The cases show that *all* securities transactions are covered by this section and rule, not just those which involve securities listed on the exchanges. Unlike Section 16(b), liability under Section 10(b) and Rule 10b–5 can extend to persons outside the corporation, such as dealers, brokers, and tippees (persons who receive "tips," or inside information), as well as to corporate insiders. The corporation and its management may be held liable even though it and they did not themselves engage in the securities transactions involved. Just as is generally true in products liability cases, there need not be a contractual relationship ("privity" of contract) between plaintiff and defendant. It is necessary, however, that the plaintiff actually have bought or sold a security, otherwise, everyone in the world would be a possible plaintiff whenever errors are found in any corporate statement.

The elements of a 10b–5 case are somewhat different from those required to prove common-law fraud. Either a misstatement *or* an omission may be the basis for liability under 10b–5. So may an "act, practice, or course of business." The misstated or omitted fact must be material, but that is a flexible concept, ultimately to be decided by the trier of fact in the lawsuit. The all-purpose definition of a material fact is one "which might have influenced the decision of an average, reasonably prudent investor." That formulation is not terribly helpful to the average juror, and courts have generally been quite liberal in applying it. The elements of reliance by the investor on the misstatement or omission, and causation by the omission of financial damage, have also been glossed over by the courts in many cases.

At least as troublesome as the definitions of "fact," "omission," and "material" is the question of the defendant's state of mind at the time of the alleged wrongful conduct. Common-law fraud requires proof that the defendant knew or ought to have known that the statement was false, and that it was made with the intent to deceive. What sort of "intent" is required for a 10b–5 case? While case decisions have not been totally uniform, some general principles have emerged. At one extreme, knowing and intentional misstatements and omissions are clearly subject to 10b–5. At the other extreme, it is generally agreed *Negligent conduct is not generally defined as fraud.*
that "mere negligence" does not impose liability under Section 10(b) and Rule 10b–5, although parts 2 and 3 of the rule seem to indicate otherwise. As the U.S. Supreme Court has pointed out, however, the

SEC may not, by adopting a rule, extend the coverage of the statutory section on which the rule is based. When Section 10(b) uses the phrase "manipulative or deceptive device or contrivance," it would hardly seem to be applicable to a simple failure to exercise due care. Both adjectives and both nouns imply intentional, willful conduct. Nonetheless, several cases have held defendants liable for "something short of specific intent, and something more than 'mere' negligence." Presumably, by this standard, gross negligence could produce liability, as for example, holding liable for misstatements a director who never showed up for directors' meetings. A reckless disregard for the rights of others would also seem to fall into this middle ground, as conduct which is "intentional" enough to produce 10(b) liability. The closest question would be raised by an allegation that the defendant "ought to have known" that there were material misstatements or omissions. Did that defendant therefore "intend" the adverse consequences which followed? The current answer seems to be no, but the drawing of this line will continue to cause trouble for corporate managements.

Since nearly any form of corporate communication may provide the basis for trading in securities, extreme care must be exercised in making any official corporate pronouncements. At the very least, authority to speak for the corporation should be carefully delineated, and all such communications should probably be reviewed by house counsel. Similarly, all corporate insiders should be made aware of their duty not to disclose confidential information, *and* their duty not to use it for their own benefit by trading in their company's shares.

The *Dirks* case illustrates several of these difficult insider trading questions.

DIRKS V. SECURITIES AND EXCHANGE COMMISSION

452 U.S. 490 (1983)

Facts: Raymond Dirks, an officer in a New York investment firm, specialized in providing investment analysis of insurance company securities to institutional investors. On March 6, 1973, Ronald Secrist, a former officer of Equity Funding of America, told Dirks that Equity's assets were vastly overstated as a result of fraudulent practices. Equity was primarily engaged in selling life insurance/mutual fund packages to individuals. Secrist urged Dirks to verify the fraud and to disclose it publicly.

Dirks visited Equity's Los Angeles headquarters and interviewed officers and employees there. Senior managers denied any wrongdoing, but several employees said the story was true. Neither Dirks nor his firm owned or traded Equity stock, but he did discuss his findings with several clients. Some clients did sell their Equity stock. Dirks was also in touch with William Blundell, the *Wall Street Journal's* Los Angeles bureau chief. Blundell, fearing a libel suit and unwilling to believe that such a massive fraud would not have been detected, refused to publish the story. During this two-week period, Equity's stock fell from $26 per share to $15. The New York Stock Exchange halted trading on March 27; the California insurance regulators seized Equity's records and verified the fraudulent practices; and the SEC finally filed a complaint against Equity. Equity went into receivership, and is now out of business.

The SEC found that Dirks had "aided and abetted" violations of the securities laws by passing along non-public information. The U.S. Court of Appeals affirmed the sanctions against Dirks.

Issue: Did Dirks violate the anti-fraud provisions of the securities laws by passing along non-public information to his clients?

Decision: No. Judgment reversed. (Dirks wins.)

Rule: Communication of non-public information does not violate the securities laws unless there is a breach of duty to the company's stockholders.

Discussion: *By Justice POWELL*

"In the seminal case of *In re Cady, Roberts & Co.,*...the SEC recognized that the common law in some jurisdictions imposes on 'corporate insiders, particularly officers, directors, or controlling stockholders,' an 'affirmative duty of disclosure...when dealing in securities.'... The SEC found that not only did breach of this common-law duty also establish the elements of a Rule 10b–5 violation, but that individuals other than corporate insiders could be obligated either to disclose material nonpublic information before trading or to abstain from trading altogether.... In *Chiarella*, we accepted the two elements set out in Cady, Roberts for establishing a Rule 10b–5 violation: '(i) the existence of a relationship affording access to inside information intended to be available only for a corporate purpose, and (ii) the unfairness of allowing a corporate insider to take advantage of that information by trading without disclosure.'... In examining whether Chiarella had an obligation to disclose or abstain, the Court found that there is no general duty to disclose before trading on material nonpublic information, and held that 'a duty to disclose under §10(b) does not arise from the mere possession of nonpublic market information.'...

"[T]here can be no duty to disclose where the person who has traded on inside information 'was not [the issuing corporation's] agent,...was not a fiduciary, [or] was not a person in whom the [securities] sellers had placed their trust and confidence.'...

"[T]here was no actionable violation by Dirks. It is undisputed that Dirks himself was a stranger to Equity Funding, with no pre-existing fiduciary duty to its shareholders. He took no action, directly or indirectly, that induced the shareholders or officers of Equity Funding to repose trust or confidence in him. There was no expectation by Dirks' sources that he would keep their information in confidence. Nor did Dirks misappropriate or illegally obtain the information about Equity Funding. Unless the insiders breached their...duty to shareholders in disclosing the nonpublic information to Dirks, he breached no duty when he passed it on to investors as well as to the Wall Street Journal.

"It is clear that neither Secrist nor the other Equity Funding employees violated their...duty to the corporation's shareholders by providing information to Dirks. The tippers [the employees who had 'tipped off' Dirks to the illegalities] received no monetary or personal benefit for revealing Equity Funding's secrets, nor was their purpose to make a gift of valuable information to Dirks.... [T]he tippers were motivated by a desire to expose the fraud.... In the absence of a breach of duty by the insiders, there was no derivative breach by Dirks...Dirks therefore could not have been 'a participant after the fact in [an] insider's breach of a fiduciary duty.'...

"We conclude that Dirks, in the circumstances of this case, had no duty to abstain from the use of the inside information that he obtained."

Ethical Dimension

Should the SEC be able to challenge any securities sale in which the parties did not have equal information?

Interlocking Directors

Another major regulatory reinforcement of the fiduciary duties of corporate management stems from antitrust law. Common law agency principles prevent one person from serving as agent for two persons who have conflicting interests. Section 8 of the Clayton Antitrust Act adopts this same basic principle when it prohibits a person from serving on the boards of directors of two or more competing companies at the same time. Section 8 applies where the companies are engaged in interstate commerce, where they do compete with each other in at least one area, and where either of them has more than $1 million in capital, surplus, and undivided profits. Banks and common carriers are not covered by this rule.

It seems clear that the main reason for including this provision in the Clayton Act was to prevent collusion between the competitors—price-fixing, market division, bid-rigging, and similar anti-competitive practices. At the same time, however, this prohibition also means that a board member would not be in a position to disadvantage one company for the benefit of the other. No person should be able to access one company's trade secrets and then disclose them to a competitor. Someone who is serving on the boards of competing companies is in a position to do this; Section 8 prohibits such dual service.

CHANGES IN ORGANIZATIONAL STRUCTURE

A third major area of regulatory concern with organizations relates to decisions which involve extraordinary changes in the structure of the organization or the scope of its operations. Day-to-day decisions, such as pricing a product or hiring a new plant manager, are covered by the business judgment rule, and normally could not be questioned in court. But when a corporate restructuring will change existing rights, or create massive new liabilities, or threaten free competition, state and national government agencies may become involved.

Such regulatory oversight of organizational change comes in a variety of forms. State approval of the organizational change may be required. A particular kind of stockholder approval may be required to ensure that stockholders are not being disadvantaged by the change. And some changes may not be permitted at all, under antitrust law or other regulations.

Doing Business in Other States

By organizing in a particular state, a corporation is of course licensed to conduct its business there. It is also free to engage in interstate commerce, subject only to the specific restrictions which Congress may have imposed on the specific trade or business involved. But if a corporation wishes to engage in local business activities in a second state, it must get that state's permission to do so.

The reason for this additional requirement stems from the U.S. Constitution. As a citizen, each of us enjoys the "privileges and immunities of citizenship" guaranteed by the Fourteenth Amendment. One of these privileges is the freedom to travel to any state we wish and to conduct our personal and business affairs there, free from state interference. Corporations and other artificial ("legal") persons are not

A corporation generally needs permission to do business in another state.

considered citizens for the purposes of this section. Therefore, when a corporation wishes to cross state lines to conduct its business *locally*, it must get that state's approval. The state where it was organized can give it permission to do business in that state, but cannot give it permission to do business in other states. Thus, a corporation must comply with the regulations for **foreign corporations** in every state in which it does local business—other than its own state of incorporation. (Since a partnership is merely a collection of individuals doing business together, the partners are free to travel and to conduct their business anywhere, subject only to general requirements for the trade or profession. The partnership thus enjoys a marked advantage over the corporation in this regard.)

Typically, these regulations are not terribly burdensome. Usually all that is required is the filing of a disclosure form and the payment of a rather minimal fee. The foreign corporation will be required to disclose its place and date of incorporation, the details of its capital structure (number and types of shares authorized and issued), the names and addresses of its officers and directors, the property which it owns within the state, and the estimated amount of business it plans to do there. Nearly always, it will also be required to designate a person located within the state as its authorized agent to receive court process from courts within the state. It will almost certainly have to file an annual report with the state each year, summarizing the prior year's business activity, and pay an annual fee for the privilege of continuing to do local business within the state.

While the annual fee in each state may be rather small, a corporation doing business in a large number of states could face a substantial total each year. Even more than the actual fees, the legal and accounting services required to comply in a large number of states could add up to a sizable annual cost. These extra costs would need to be balanced against the anticipated profits which might be made from the additional business in the other states. Obviously, it is to a company's advantage to avoid such costs if they can do so. That brings us to the basic question: when is registration required?

As noted above, the basic test is the doing of local, as opposed to interstate, business. The line is not always easy to draw, however, and there are frequent litigations on this point. It is unlikely that a corporation which had no personnel, inventories, or office within a state would be asked to register there as a foreign corporation. At the other extreme, a company which had a large number of retail outlets and employees in a state is surely going to have to register. In between these easy cases, there may be a number of close calls. Mail-order companies sending goods into a state normally do not have to register there, but if they have an inventory of goods in the state from which they fill orders, they probably do have to register. Usually, if a company makes sales through independent contractors, rather than through its own employees' activities in a state, it does not have to register. It may also be able to avoid registration by having its sales representatives merely take orders, which then have to be accepted in its home state, as opposed to actually making the sales themselves in the second state. Isolated transactions and incidental activities such as having a bank account normally do not require registration. As with most major business decisions, legal counsel should be involved in the analysis of whether to expand by opening operations in a second state.

Extraordinary Decisions

Since the stockholders have invested their money based on an analysis of the corporation's business and its prospects, it seems only fair to require their approval when a major change in the nature or scope of the business is proposed. The Model Business Corporation Act (MBCA) does exactly that, at least for most such major changes. (The MBCA was developed by the Commissioners on Uniform State Laws, a national organization of law professors and practitioners, as a "model" statute which states could adopt.) The most recent version of the MBCA does permit the directors to make relatively minor changes in the articles of incorporation without stockholder approval. Most substantive amendments, however, do require a shareholder vote. If the rights of a particular class of investors are being diminished, they will probably be entitled to vote separately, as a class, with a veto power over the proposed change.

Companies sometimes wish to cease operations in one line of business and enter a new field. Competitive conditions can change radically, and a company may decide that it can be more profitable in a different type of business. It may thus wish to sell, lease, or exchange all, or almost all, of its existing business assets. Stockholder approval will be required for nearly all such transactions, although the revised MBCA does not require a vote where the transaction occurs in the "usual and regular course of business." An airline's sale of its old fleet of planes to get some cash to buy new ones or its trading in of the old planes as a down payment on a new fleet would thus not require stockholder approval, since this would seem to be in the regular course of business. On the other hand, if the airline sold all its planes, equipment, routes, and other airline assets in order to get out of the airline business altogether, that transaction would not be in the regular course of business and would therefore require stockholder approval.

Extraordinary business decisions may have to be approved by the stockholders.

Most mergers of corporations will have to be submitted to the stockholders of both companies for a vote. The revised MBCA does permit the merger of a subsidiary corporation into the parent corporation, without any shareholder approval, if the parent owns at least 90 percent of each class of stock in the subsidiary.

Minority shareholders are protected by a special section of the MBCA which gives them the right to dissent from any of these extraordinary actions and to demand that the corporation buy back their shares. The corporation must notify the shareholders of these rights. Shareholders who wish to exercise this mandatory buy-back right must in turn notify the corporation of their intent to do so. The MBCA requires payment of the fair value of the shares as of the day before the vote, adjusted for any appreciation or depreciation which occurred because of the proposed action. If these procedures are followed, the dissenting stockholders should be adequately protected. The MBCA says that dissenting stockholders cannot block the majority's decision unless the decision is illegal or fraudulent.

The officers and directors might also decide that the corporation's business is no longer profitable and that the company should be dissolved. Dissolution also requires stockholder approval, usually by a majority of all the shares entitled to vote. A higher majority, such as two-thirds, may be required under some states' statutes or by the directors when they make their recommendation to the stockholders.

The *Anderson* case illustrates several of these points.

ANDERSON V. CLEVELAND-CLIFFS IRON CO.

87 N.E.2d 384 (Ohio 1948)

Facts: Anderson and other preferred stockholders in Cleveland-Cliffs Iron Co. (CCI) sued to prevent a consolidation between it and Cliffs Corporation into a reorganized CCI Co. All of the 408,296 common shares in the old CCI were owned by Cliffs Corporation; each of these common shares would be exchanged for 2 1/2 shares of the new CCI's common stock. The 487,238 preferred shares of the old CCI were owned by various persons; each of these shares would receive one share of preferred and one share of common stock in the new CCI. The same officers managed both Cliffs and the old CCI, but there was only one person who sat on both boards of directors. A special meeting of the stockholders of the old CCI approved the consolidation proposal by a two-thirds majority, as required by state law. Anderson and the others still objected to the consolidation, because they claimed that there was no business necessity for it and that it was really an amendment of the old CCI's charter, with the intent of eliminating the unpaid accumulated dividends on the old CCI's preferred stock. [These unpaid dividends were being eliminated.]

Issue: Does a corporation have to show a specific necessity for its proposed consolidation with another company?

Decision: No, it does not. Judgment for defendant.

Rule: The right of corporations to consolidate is not conditioned upon business or economic necessity.

Discussion: *By Judge* MCNAMEE:

"It is true, as plaintiffs claim, that the defendant corporation had adequate working capital and that there was no real need for the addition of the liquid assets of Cliffs Corporation. Plaintiffs' position in this regard is confirmed by the statements made by officers of Cliffs at the time dissolution of that company was proposed. But the right of corporations to consolidate is not conditioned upon business exigencies or economic necessity. Courts possess no veto power over the purely business judgments of corporate officers or stockholders. Whether the addition of over $20,000,000 of cash and steel stocks was necessary or desirable is a matter peculiarly within the province of the affected interests to determine....

"There is little doubt that one of the important objectives of the consolidation was the elimination of existing preferred dividend arrearages. This matter was the subject of concern and study by the management for many years. While there was no express authorization in Section 67 or any other section of the Corporation Code of 1927 for the elimination of preferred dividend arrearages, that result is the necessary effect of a consolidation. A consolidated corporation comes into being as a result of and at the time of the consolidation agreement. By operation of law all of the property of the constituent corporation is transferred to the new corporation and the debts and liabilities of the constituent companies are assumed by the consolidated company. The rights and interests of consenting shareholders of constituent corporations, in the consolidated corporation, are fixed by the agreement of consolidation which may provide for the issuance of shares in the consolidated company or the distribution of cash, notes, bonds, or property in lieu thereof. If there are existing dividend arrearages on the preferred stock of one of the constituent companies, the consolidation agreement must give effect to the value of the preferred shareholders' rights to such accumulated dividends in determining a fair basis of conversion of shares or distribution of property in lieu of shares in the consolidated corporation. Assuming the plan to be fair, a preferred shareholder's interest in a constituent company, including his right to cumulative dividend arrearages, is fully protected by its conversion into shares or other considerations of the consolidated corporation. In the absence of abuse of discretion by the directors, in failing to pay dividend arrearages, a shareholder in a constituent corporation has no immediate assertable right to collect the full amount of such arrearages. The consolidation of his corporation with another does not confer such right. By the act of consolidation a constituent corporation surrenders its corporate identity. A preferred shareholder no longer can expect payment of dividend arrearages from his corporation and inasmuch as a consolidated corporation can have no existing dividend arrearages at the time of its creation the compromise and adjustment thereof is a necessary incident of consolidation....

"[T]he validity of the plan of consolidation is to be determined by reference to the terms of the shareholders' contracts and the requirement that the plan be free from fraud, actual or constructive, and fair to all the shareholders.

"In considering the issue raised it is to be remembered that the elimination of preferred dividend arrearages was not the only purpose of the consolidation. Wisely or not, the consolidation agreement was intended to and did result in the formation of a corporation of impressively greater financial strength. The view that the consolidation conferred substantial benefits upon the common shareholders is undoubtedly correct. But it has not been demonstrated that this was accomplished by unfair treatment of the preferred shareholders....

"For the reasons hereinbefore indicated, this court is of the opinion and therefore holds that the consolidation agreement was not a perversion of the purposes of [the Corporation Code] and that said agreement was authorized by and executed in conformity with the preferred shareholders' interests."

Ethical Dimension

Is it ethical for majority stockholders to make decisions which benefit themselves but disadvantage the minority?

●

■ Mergers and Acquisitions

Corporate takeovers pose special risks of abuse of investors and competitors. There are, therefore, several regulatory agencies and several bodies of law that may be involved when one company or firm acquires another. State corporation law, national securities law, state takeover law, and national and state antitrust law may all be implicated in a proposed merger or acquisition.

REGULATION THROUGH STATE CORPORATION LAW

State corporation law is involved because a corporation, as a creature of the law, has only those powers which it is given by its state of incorporation. Older corporate charters, or articles of incorporation, tended to list specific and limited powers for the corporation—"buying, developing, and selling real estate," "steel manufacturing," and so on. With this limited grant of powers, it would not be lawful for a corporation to engage in some other, unrelated business. A corporation which engaged in a new line of business not authorized by its articles could be enjoined from continuing, and its officers and directors could be subject to stockholder lawsuits. Fortunately, this problem has been solved for the most part. Modern corporation statutes permit a statement of multiple business purposes. The articles of the Ford Motor Company, for example, list a host of other business operations besides making cars—mining, shipping, agriculture, and many others. Some statutes permit a corporation to state that it may engage in "any lawful business"; there would be no problem when such a company undertook a new line of operations.

REGULATION THROUGH SECURITIES LAW

Since most stockholders in large, widely held companies do not attend their annual meeting, they are permitted to vote by proxy. A **proxy** is a written authorization to vote the owner's shares of stock. It may be issued with specific instructions on how to vote, or the voting decision may be left to the person who holds the proxy. Corporate managements solicit proxies to make sure there is a quorum at the meeting so business can be transacted and to support its positions on issues where there is disagreement. Persons wishing to disagree with management or trying to take control of the corporation by electing directors also solicit proxies. The SEC has established a set of rules for the solicitation and use of proxies. The person soliciting proxies must file an extensive disclosure statement with the SEC. The corporation must provide a statement of the issues to be voted on to each stockholder of record and must include most stockholder proposals in this official proxy statement. Solicitation of proxy votes for or against a merger proposal would thus have to comply with these SEC rules.

The SEC regulates solicitation and voting of shareholder proxies.

REGULATION THROUGH STATE TAKEOVER LAW

With many U.S. industries facing very tough foreign competition, states are also worried about possible job cutbacks after a merger. Local companies provide local jobs and are usually involved in the local community. When a large out-of-state, or alien, conglomerate buys out the local company, it may move operations and eliminate jobs to save costs. To make sure that local businesses and their stockholders are not taken advantage of, states have passed laws requiring that certain procedures be followed in a corporate takeover. Typical of these anti-takeover statutes is the Indiana act involved in the next case.

CTS CORP. V. DYNAMICS CORP. OF AMERICA

107 S. Ct. 1637 (1987)

Facts: The revised Indiana Business Corporation Law, including the "Control Share Acquisitions Chapter," was signed by the Governor on March 4, 1986. A buyer of "control shares" gets the voting rights on those shares only if a majority of the other stockholders approve a resolution to that effect. If they do not, the corporation has the option of buying the "control shares" for their fair market value.

On March 10, Dynamics (which then owned 9.6 percent of CTS) announced an offer to buy another million shares, which would bring its ownership percentage to 27.5, one of the "control" levels specified in the Indiana Act. Dynamics filed suit the same day, claiming that CTS had violated certain parts of the national securities acts. The CTS directors then elected to be covered by the Indiana Act. Dynamics then amended its complaint by alleging that the Indiana Act was preempted by the national act governing hostile takeovers—the Williams Act. The U.S. District Court held for Dynamics, and the Seventh Circuit Court of Appeals affirmed.

Issue: Does the Williams Act preempt state regulation of hostile takeovers?

Decision: No. Judgment reversed. (CTS wins.)

Rule: Unless a national regulation expressly preempts an area, state regulation is permitted so long as it does not frustrate the purpose of the national law.

Discussion: *By Justice POWELL:*

"The Indiana Act operates on the assumption, implicit in the Williams Act, that independent shareholders faced with tender offers often are at a disadvantage. By allowing such shareholders to vote as a group, the Act protects them from the coercive aspects of some tender offers. If, for example, shareholders believe that a successful tender offer will be followed by a purchase of nontendering shares at a depressed price, individual shareholders may tender their shares—even if they doubt the tender offer is in the corporation's best interest—to protect themselves from being forced to sell their shares at a depressed price.... In such a situation under the Indiana Act, the shareholders as a group, acting in the corporation's best interest, could reject the offer, although individual shareholders might be inclined to accept it. The desire of the Indiana legislature to protect shareholders of Indiana corporations from this type of coercive offer does not conflict with the Williams Act. Rather, it furthers the federal policy of investor protection....

"In our view the possibility that the Indiana Act will delay some tender offers is insufficient to require a conclusion that the Williams Act preempts the Act. The longstanding prevalence of state regulation in this area suggests that, if Congress had intended to preempt all state laws that delay the acquisition of voting control following a tender offer, it would have said so explicitly. The regulatory conditions that the Act places on tender offers are consistent with the text and purposes of the Williams Act. Accordingly, we hold that the Williams Act does not preempt the Indiana Act....

[The Court also held that the Indiana Act did not unduly burden interstate commerce.]

"On its face, the Indiana Control Share Acquisitions Chapter evenhandedly determines the voting rights of shares in Indiana Corporations. The Act does not conflict with the provisions of purposes of the Williams Act. To the limited extent that the Act affects interstate commerce, this is justified by the state's interests in defining the attributes of shares of its corporations and in protecting shareholders. Congress has never questioned the need for state regulation of these matters. Nor do we think such regulation offends the Constitution."

Ethical Dimension

Why should one state be able to interfere in a tender offer?

REGULATION THROUGH ANTITRUST LAW

Finally, a merger may be challenged under the national (or state) antitrust laws. Section 7 of the Clayton Antitrust Act prohibits any merger which may have the effect of substantially lessening competition or tending to create a monopoly in any line of business in any section of the country. Both the purchase of stock and the purchase of assets are covered by the amended Section 7. All types of mergers are covered by this section, although they are not all analyzed in the same way or with the same methods. **Horizontal mergers** involve combinations of competing firms. **Vertical mergers** involve combinations of firms in the same industry but at different levels of the production/distribution process, such as the merger of a wholesaler and a retailer, or the merger of a parts supplier into an auto company. **Conglomerate mergers** are combinations of unrelated firms; these are generally considered the least dangerous to the competitive process.

Prior to the 1976 amendments to the Clayton Act, a merger might occur, and then be ruled illegal. When this happened, it was often necessary for a court to figure out how to "un-merge" the companies. Depending on the circumstances, such unscrambling of corporate eggs can quickly become very complicated. The 1976 amendments established a pre-merger notification procedure, so that the Justice Department and the Federal Trade Commission would have a chance to review the merger before it occurred. If either agency believes the proposed merger would be harmful to competition, it has a chance to get a court injunction to prevent it from occurring. If neither has an objection, the merger partners are free to proceed.

The Justice Department uses an index of concentration to evaluate the legality of horizontal mergers.

The Justice Department has also published a set of guidelines for horizontal mergers—the Herfindahl-Hirschmann Index (HHI). The market share of each competitor is squared, and the results are totalled. If the total exceeds 1800, indicating a highly concentrated market, any merger will probably be challenged by the Justice Department. Conversely, if the total is less than 1000, which indicates a fragmented market with many small competitors, a merger will probably not be injurious to competition. Between those figures, the Justice Department will see how much more concentrated the market will be after the proposed merger. The total before the merger will be subtracted from the total after the merger. If the difference is 100 points or more, the merger will probably be challenged; less than 50 extra points, probably not. In between 50 and 100 points, other market factors will be considered—the merger history in the industry, the ease of entry to the business, and similar factors. The FTC has indicated that it will also use the HHI in analyzing mergers. No similar mathematical guidelines exist for vertical or conglomerate mergers; they have to be analyzed individually. One of the leading merger cases involved Procter and Gamble's attempt to take over the Clorox company.

F.T.C. V. PROCTER & GAMBLE COMPANY

386 U.S. 568 (1967)

Facts: P&G and its two largest competitors had over 80 percent of the market for packaged detergent sales. P&G sales in 1957 were over $1 billion; its assets, over a half billion. It was the nation's largest advertiser that year, spending over $80 million on advertising and another $47 million on sales promotions. After it decided not to develop its own laundry bleach, P&G bought all the assets of Clorox, which was the only bleach sold nation-wide and which had nearly half of the industry's sales. Most bleach firms had only one plant and a local market; the top six firms had 80 percent of the market. All bleach is chemically identical; the only difference is in the advertising and promotion. The F.T.C. ordered P&G to divest itself of the Clorox assets, but the U.S. Court of Appeals reversed.

Issue: Is there a substantial probability that this merger will lessen competition?

Decision: Yes. Court of Appeals judgment is reversed; FTC ruling affirmed.

Rule: Mergers which will raise substantial barriers to the entry of new firms and which will eliminate a potential competitor do have the potential for reducing competition.

Discussion: *By Justice* DOUGLAS:

"All mergers are within the reach of § 7 [of the Clayton Act], and all must be tested by the same standard, whether they are classified as horizontal, vertical, conglomerate, or other.... [T]he Commission aptly called this acquisition a 'product-extension merger.'...

"The anticompetitive effects with which this product-extension merger is fraught can easily be seen: (1) the substitution of the powerful acquiring firm for the smaller, but already dominant, firm may substantially reduce the competitive structure of the industry by raising entry barriers and by dissuading the smaller firms from aggressively competing; (2) the acquisition eliminates the potential competition of the acquiring firm....

"There is every reason to assume that the smaller firms would become more cautious in competing due to their fear of retaliation by Procter. It is probable that Procter would become the price leader and that oligopoly would become more rigid.

"The acquisition may also have the tendency of raising the barriers to new entry. The major competitive weapon in the successful marketing of bleach is advertising.... Procter would be able to use its volume discounts to advantage in advertising Clorox. Thus, a new entrant would be much more reluctant to face the giant Procter than it would have been to face the smaller Clorox....

"It is clear that the existence of Procter at the edge of the industry exerted considerable influence on the market. First, the market behavior of the liquid bleach industry was influenced by each firm's predictions of the market behavior of its competitors,

actual and potential. Second, the barriers to entry by a firm of
Procter's size and with its advantages were not insignificant.... Third, the number of potential entrants was not so large
that elimination of one would be insignificant. Few firms would
have the temerity to challenge a firm as solidly entrenched as
Clorox. Fourth, Procter was found by the Commission as the
most likely entrant. These findings of the Commission were
amply supported by the evidence."

Ethical Dimension

Why should the Government be able to object to a merger if
both the companies involved are willing?

●

REVIEW

Regulation of organizations centers on three major problem areas. Investors
are protected under the 1933 Securities Act, the 1934 Securities and Exchange
Act, and, to a lesser extent, under state securities laws.

To protect stockholders and corporate creditors, fiduciary duties are imposed on corporate officers and directors. Restrictions are imposed on certain
trading activities by corporate insiders, and reporting of other transactions is
required.

To protect stockholders, creditors, and competitors, limitations are imposed on mergers and acquisitions. Many states now require special procedures for such decisions by their corporations. Both the Justice Department
and the FTC are prepared to challenge mergers which threaten competition.

In each of these areas, more than one regulatory agency and more than
one body of law may be involved. Management is still given a great deal of
discretion under the business judgment rule, but there are limits.

REVIEW QUESTIONS AND PROBLEMS

1. What is the significance of the business judgment rule?

2. Who are corporate "insiders"?

3. Why are corporate insiders prevented from keeping "short-swing" profits?

4. Why are there limits on corporate mergers? What are those limits?

5. What are the rights of dissenting stockholders when a merger is proposed?

6. Why is SEC Rule 10(b)(5) so important to corporate managers?

7. Ollie Orbit organized Gogo Interstellar as a four-level system to distribute
his new cosmetics. Higher level distributors earned cash finders' fees for bringing

in new distributors. Each new distributor was required to buy an inventory of cosmetics, which could be resold to retail customers or to new distributors who were recruited. Regional groups of distributors held "Go-Go Meetings," run exactly according to Ollie's scripts, to help recruit new distributors. Ollie set all prices and gave higher discounts to the higher level distributors. The SEC sued to enjoin Ollie and Interstellar from selling distributorships because they had not been registered as securities. Should the injunction be granted? Discuss.

8. Luisa owns 2000 shares of $100 par 7 percent cumulative preferred stock in Kola Co. No dividends have been paid on this stock for twelve years. A majority of Kola's stockholders have now voted to amend its articles of incorporation to cancel the old preferred stock and to issue one share of new 9 percent cumulative preferred for every three shares of the old preferred. The amendment also cancelled the accumulated dividends on the old preferred. Although the amendment was adopted according to the procedure specified in the articles and bylaws, Luisa says her rights are violated, and she sues. Does she have a case? Explain.

9. Goods Company made a hostile tender offer for all the common stock of Nocal Nutrition, Inc. Any stockholders who accepted the offer and sold their shares would receive $50 per share in cash. If Goods achieved a majority of the shares, it said it would vote to eliminate the remaining shares by having Nocal exchange "junk bonds" for them. The Nocal stockholders were thus placed under extreme pressure to accept Goods's tender offer. Nocal's current directors responded to the hostile tender offer by having Nocal itself offer its stockholders $57 per share; this offer excluded any shares already owned by Goods. Goods sued, claiming that Nocal's directors violated their fiduciary duty. Is Goods correct? Why or why not?

10. Prudence Porto owned a small catering business. She organized a corporation and transferred the entire business to it, in exchange for $50,000 worth of its $100 par common stock. Two months later, the corporation filed for bankruptcy. One of its suppliers, Fancy Foods, had an unpaid claim for $20,000 worth of goods which had been delivered prior to the corporation's bankruptcy. Fancy sues Prudence on the basis that the net value of her business was only $30,000 when she sold it to the corporation for $50,000 worth of stock. How should the court resolve this case? Explain.

SUGGESTIONS FOR FURTHER READING

Cann, "The New Merger Guidelines: Is the Department of Justice Enforcing the Law?," *American Business Law Journal* 21 (Spring 1983): 1.

Emerson, "Rule 2(a) Revisited: SEC Disciplining of Attorneys since *In Re Carter*," *American Business Law Journal* 29 (Summer 1991): 155.

Kempin, "The Use and Misuse of Inside Information by Corporate Managers and Other Insiders," *American Business Law Journal* 14 (Fall 1976): 139.

Martin, "Insider Trading and Rule 14e–3 after *Chestman*," *American Business Law Journal* 29 (Winter 1992): 665.

McAdams & Tower, "Personal Accountability in the Corporate Sector," *American Business Law Journal* 16 (Spring 1978): 67.

Wang, "Dirks v. Securities and Exchange Commission: An Outsider's Guide to Insider Trading Liability Under Rule 10b–5," *American Business Law Journal* 22 (Winter 1985): 569.

11
LAW
OF
FINANCE

"Creditors have better memories than debtors."
Benjamin Franklin

LEARNING OBJECTIVES: After you have studied this chapter, you should be able to:

EXPLAIN the legal difference between equity financing and debt financing.

IDENTIFY the various types of short-term financing available to a business.

DISCUSS the major problems arising from accounts receivable financing.

OUTLINE the legal technicalities involved in using commercial paper.

DEFINE the requirements for inventory and equipment financing.

EXPLAIN the problems involved in cosigning a company debt.

P REVIEW

The organization of a corporation will necessarily involve the issuance of stock. **Shares of stock** represent the basic ownership interest in the corporation and provide a means of raising capital. In many instances, the promoters of the new corporation will subscribe to the first shares themselves so they can hold the initial meetings necessary to get the corporation officially organized. They may then offer shares to the investing public to raise the capital needed to get operations started.

There are various forms of short-term financing.

There are, of course, various other ways of generating the funds necessary to conduct the company's business. Corporate **bonds**—long-term debt obligations—may be issued. Short-term funds may be generated by selling or pledging the company's **accounts receivable**, that is, money that is due from its customers. The company may be able to borrow short-term funds by issuing commercial paper. Commercial paper is usually in the form of **promissory notes**, which are written promises to pay money at a future date. The other major type of commercial paper is the **draft**—a written order to someone else, usually a bank, to pay money to a third party. Business operations may also be financed through short-term credit purchases of inventory and equipment. Increasingly, companies are also finding it advantageous to lease, rather than buy, some of their equipment. This chapter will examine the legal rules pertaining to each of these financing arrangements.

E QUITY FINANCING (STOCKS)

The basic choice in long-term financing is between (1) **equity financing**—having additional investors as owners of the company, and (2) **debt financing**—borrowing funds from creditors, usually by selling corporate bonds. Issuing additional stock—using equity financing—has the effect of diluting the control exercised by the original group of stockholders. To what extent that occurs depends on the amount already invested and the amount of additional capital that is needed. It may be possible to minimize this effect by issuing a class of preferred stock which does not have voting rights except in very limited circumstances. Bondholders are creditors, and they have no right to vote on any corporate policy matters except in cases of reorganization or bankruptcy.

Directors generally decide on dividend policy.

In addition to the effect on control of corporate policy, there are different financial implications in using equity versus debt financing. Bonds (and other debt financing arrangements) require periodic payments of interest whether the corporation is profitable or not. Stockholders have no legal claim to dividends, as a rule, unless and until they are declared by the board of directors. Just as is the case with other matters of corporate policy, the directors' decisions on dividends are protected by the business judgment rule. Courts are very reluctant to second-guess the directors on decisions as fundamental as dividend policy. Nevertheless, there are some outer limits even here, as Henry Ford learned to his dismay in the following case.

DODGE V. FORD MOTOR CO.

170 N.W. 668 (Mich. 1919)

Facts: The original stockholders of the Ford Motor Company were Henry Ford himself, John and Horace Dodge, Horace Rackham, and James Couzens. The company had been hugely successful. It had been paying 60 percent per year on an original capitalization of $2 million. It had also paid out special dividends of $41 million. It still had a surplus of $112 million, and sales and profits were up. Henry proposed to lower the price of the Model T car from $440 to $360 and to build the River Rouge complex to make iron and steel. "My ambition is to employ still more men, to spread the benefits of the industrial system to the greatest possible number, to help them build up their lives and their homes. To do this, we are putting the greatest share of our profits back in the business." The Dodge brothers sued to enjoin the building of the River Rouge plant and to force payment of an additional special dividend. The trial court found for the plaintiffs. It enjoined the building of the River Rouge plant and ordered a special dividend of over $19 million.

Issue: Did the Ford directors abuse their discretion?

Decision: Yes, as to the payment of dividends. No, as to the River Rouge plant.

Rule: The directors may not act arbitrarily, for personal reasons, in declaring or refusing to declare a dividend.

Discussion: *By Chief Justice* OSTRANDER:

"The discretion of the directors will not be interfered with by the courts, unless there has been bad faith, willful neglect, or abuse of discretion....

"[Ford] had made up his mind in the summer of 1916 that no dividends other than the regular dividends should be paid 'for the present.'...

"The record, and especially the testimony of Mr. Ford, convinces [us] that he has to some extent the attitude towards shareholders of one who has dispensed and distributed to them large gains and that they should be content to take what he chooses to give. His testimony creates the impression, also, that he thinks the Ford Motor Company has made too much money, has had too large profits, and that, although large profits might still be earned, a sharing of them with the public, by reducing the price of the output of the company, ought to be undertaken. We have no doubt that certain sentiments, philanthropic and altruistic, creditable to Mr. Ford, had large influence in determining the policy to be pursued by the Ford Motor Company—the policy which has been herein referred to....

"[I]t is not within the lawful powers of a board of directors to shape and conduct the affairs of a corporation for the merely incidental benefit of the shareholders and for the primary purpose of benefitting others, and no one will contend that, if the avowed purpose of the defendant directors was to sacrifice the interests of shareholders, it would not be the duty of the courts to interfere....

"We are not, however, persuaded that we should interfere with the proposed expansion of the business of the Ford Motor Company.... The Judges are not business experts.... The experience of the Ford Motor Company is evidence of capable management of its affairs."

Ethical Dimension

Is the Michigan court saying that "doing good works in the larger society" is not a proper corporate purpose?

●

L ONG-TERM DEBT FINANCING (BONDS)

Many companies are able to borrow money by issuing bonds, which are simply written promises to repay the money at some future date, usually several years later.

■ Terms and Conditions

Bonds are defined as investment securities.

Bonds are defined as investment securities, both for regulatory purposes, under the national and state securities acts, and for contract law purposes, under the Uniform Commercial Code (UCC). Under both bodies of law, some minimum standards for bond transactions are imposed, but in general the corporation is free to issue its bonds on any terms and conditions it wishes. For investors, these potentially wide variations from company to company mean that close attention must be paid to the terms under which one is purchasing the bond. Since bonds are securities, most bonds will have to be registered with the SEC, and full disclosure will have to be made to potential investors.

(You will recall that a bond issue was involved in the classic *Escott* case in the last chapter.)

Traditionally, both stocks and bonds were represented by pieces of paper. The pieces of paper embodied the owner's rights and were used to transfer or to pledge the security. (A **pledge** is a credit arrangement in which the items being used as collateral for the loan are left in the possession of the creditor.) Under the latest version of the UCC, both stocks and bonds may exist in so-called "uncertificated" form, that is, without a piece of paper. Such securities are simply registered on the books of the issuing corporation. Computerized corporate "books" would presumably make ownership of such securities easy to transfer or to pledge, but it remains to be seen how this new arrangement will work out, given the enormous complexities of the marketplace.

If there is a certificate representing the bond, the UCC says it may be issued either in bearer form or in registered form. (See Figure 11-1.) A bearer certificate could be freely transferred by delivering the certificate to the next owner without notification to the issuing corporation or registration on the corporate books. A registered bond would specify the owner, who could transfer the bond by indorsing it over to the new owner. Until the corporation is notified of the change of ownership (and registers the change), however, the corporation is entitled to treat the person who transferred the bond as the owner of the bond. Interest payments made to the registered owner, for example, would be properly paid. If the registered owner had in fact already transferred the bond, the transferee would have to claim the interest payment from the registered owner/transferor.

Bonds may be in bearer or registered form.

Bonds may also be convertible into preferred stock or common stock. The bond owner may have an option to convert at any time, or conversion may be subject to certain conditions. The conversion privilege might come into existence at some stated time after issuance, for instance. Or the conversion option might arise if there is a default in the payment of interest. Or the conversion right might be based on the existence of a certain financial ratio or formula. Obviously, this conversion feature gives the investor some additional flexibility and usually makes the bond more valuable.

Bonds may be convertible into stock.

Secured or Unsecured

One of the most important variables in the terms of the bond will be whether or not it is secured. Unsecured bonds, generally referred to as **debenture bonds,** or just **debentures,** are issued against the corporation's general net asset values. Typically, only corporations with strong credit ratings and long records of successful performance will be able to borrow money for a long term without specific collateral. If such a loan is made, the terms of the contract (called an **indenture**) will usually restrict the company's management as to future financing arrangements. Debenture holders might have to approve any sale or pledge of the company's major assets, for example.

Bonds may be secured or unsecured.

FIGURE 11–1
A corporate bond in registered form

No. 36 $_____

THE CENTRAL MANUFACTURING CORPORATION
6% BOND
Due_____, 19___

_____, 19___

For Value Received, The Central Manufacturing Corporation, a corporation organized and existing under the laws of the State of _____ (hereinafter called the "Company") hereby promises to pay to [name of owner] or registered assigns on the _____ day of _____, 19___, the sum of _____ ($_____) Dollars, (unless before that date this bond shall have been redeemed [*or converted*]) with interest thereon at the rate of Six Per Cent (6%) per annum, payable semi-annually on the first day of February and August in each year. The principal sum of this bond will be payable at the registered office of the company (or at such other place as may be designated in writing by the Company). Semi-annual interest payments will be mailed to the registered holder of this bond at his address as last furnished the Company in writing.

[Provisions for prepayment, acceleration, conversion, etc., may be added. These provisions can be in the bond itself or may be in another document referred to in the bond.]

These bonds are registered both as to principal and interest and are transferable only on the books of the company by presentation of the bond with an instrument of transfer duly executed by the holder or his duly authorized agent.

IN WITNESS WHEREOF, The Central Manufacturing Corporation has caused its corporate name and seal to be signed and affixed as of the _____ day of _____, 19___.

THE CENTRAL MANUFACTURING CORPORATION

By: _____
                                                   President

_____
                                                   Treasurer

Attest:

_____
Secretary

Most corporations will be required to use specific company assets as collateral for the bonds. Since the bonds are long-term obligations, long-term assets such as land, buildings, and equipment would typically be used as collateral. Mortgages or security agreements against the collateral would be executed by the company as part of the process of borrowing the money and issuing the bonds. When there is a default on the bonds, the specified collateral may be sold and the proceeds used to pay the secured bondholders. Without collateral, the bondholder is simply another general creditor if the corporation files a bankruptcy petition. As we will see in the next chapter, general creditors are the last group to be paid in a bankruptcy proceeding. That is not a desirable position to be in.

SHORT-TERM DEBT FINANCING

While the use of bonds is normally confined to larger corporations, both large and small companies use various forms of short-term financing.

Need for Short-Term Funds

Fluctuations in the business cycle are probably responsible for most businesses' needs for short-term capital, but there are also other reasons. Major purchases of equipment and inventory may also require financing arrangements. Facility expansion or renovation may be done with borrowed funds in the expectation that additional revenues from the new operation will more than cover repayment of the loan. Large, non-recurring expenses may also be covered by temporary funding and be repaid over a period of time from operating revenues. In general, any time the company has a productive use for funds which will produce more net revenue than the funds cost, the company may wish to incur the debt.

Short-term funds may be needed for various reasons.

Alternative Methods

Depending, of course, on its specific circumstances, the company may have several alternatives for raising temporary cash. If its credit standing is good enough, it may simply be able to borrow the funds with an unsecured, short-term loan. If not, it may be able to obtain a loan by having its principal officers, directors, or stockholders personally guarantee the corporate loan. (This is, in fact, a common procedure with small, newly formed corporations.) Collateral owned by the company and/or these individuals may be required as security for the loan. Large corporations with excellent credit issue and sell their own "commercial paper," usually in the form of promissory notes. Promissory notes from customers, given to the company as payment for goods and services, can be sold to a bank or finance company for cash. So can customer accounts receivable, although these would usually have to be sold at a discount due to the greater risk of nonpayment. If the company needs equipment or inventory, these items can often be purchased on credit, using the goods themselves as collateral. For equipment, leasing is another option, and one which would avoid the borrowing of the purchase price.

Different legal devices may be used to obtain short-term funds.

Each of these alternatives involves different legal relationships, as well as different economic relationships. Some of these legal rules are very complicated, in part because the financing arrangements can be very complicated.

■ Accounts Receivable Financing

Customer accounts receivable may be sold or pledged.

Many companies generate customer accounts receivable as a result of their sales operations. The customer has made a promise to pay for goods and services at some future date. The seller company may wait until that date to receive payment and (usually) interest or service charges on the account. But if, in the meantime, the company needs cash for its own purposes, these customer accounts can be used to generate cash flow.

Financing transactions that use accounts receivable are structured in two basic ways. The company may simply use the accounts as collateral for its own loan, continue to collect the accounts itself, and pay off the loan when due. This arrangement may include a requirement for periodic loan payments as the accounts are being collected. The other basic financing method is to simply sell (the legal term is **assign**) the accounts to the lender for cash. The account debtors are notified of this transfer and told to make their payments to the financing agency (the assignee of the accounts).

Clearly, the first method is much simpler—practically, economically, and legally. If everything goes according to plan, and the loan is repaid as required, the account debtors will never know the difference. They will not have been notified that their accounts are being used as collateral and will have continued making payments, as before, to the seller. The lender's only concern here (and it is potentially a big concern) is making sure that it does indeed have first claim to these accounts if there is a default on the loan for which the accounts are being used as collateral. If the loan is not repaid when due, or if the company goes into bankruptcy, the lender wants to be able to access the value which the accounts represent. To do that, the lender needs to comply with the requirements of Article 9 of the UCC.

Public notice should be filed where accounts are being used as collateral.

Where a lender is using personal property, including accounts, as collateral, Article 9 requires the lender to file a public notice to that effect. All other creditors of the debtor company are therefore warned that the specified assets are already subject to the rights of a specific creditor. Standardized, simple forms are used; they can be filled out quickly and easily. The notice form must be filed with the Secretary of State, or another designated official, in the state where the debtor company has its principal executive office. A small filing fee is paid to the state for this service. Lenders are strongly advised to follow this procedure, since it gives them first claim on the assets which they have listed on the form, even against their debtor's trustee in bankruptcy. Creditors are strongly advised to check these public records prior to entering into credit transactions, since most or all of the debtor's assets may already be subject to claims of other creditors.

Account debtors should be notified if accounts are sold.

If the accounts are in fact sold for cash, the lender will normally notify the account debtors to make all future payments to it, rather than to their original seller. As a rule, the account debtors cannot object to this new arrangement. Writing a check to one person should be no different from writing it to another, so the debtor is not really disadvantaged in any way as a result of the sale of the account. The UCC specifically states that a company cannot be prevented from assigning its accounts—money due for goods sold or leased or for services performed—even if there is a provision in the original contract to that effect. An attempt to prohibit the assignment of the account is simply not legally valid. Account debtors who have been properly notified of the transfer have no choice; they must pay the assignee. The account debtor in the next case learned this the hard way.

FIRST NATIONAL BANK OF RIO ARRIBA V. MOUNTAIN STATES TELEPHONE & TELEGRAPH CO.

571 P.2d 118 (N.M. 1977)

Facts: Mountain States Telephone & Telegraph Co. (Mountain Bell) hired Vernon Siler to do certain construction work. Siler borrowed money from First National to get working capital for the job and assigned to them his right to receive payment when he finished the job. This written assignment was delivered to Mountain Bell, but First National made no specific demand for payment, When he finished the job, Siler was paid directly by Mountain Bell. First National sued Mountain Bell to collect the account and was given a summary judgment by the trial court. (Since there was no dispute as to what happened, no trial was necessary. Mountain Bell owed the money on the account.)

Issue: Did Mountain Bell make a proper payment to Siler, since it had received notice of his assignment to First National?

Decision: No, it did not make a proper payment. Judgment affirmed.

Rule: Once properly notified of the assignment, the account debtor must pay the assignee.

Discussion: *By Justice PAYNE:*
"Mountain Bell could readily determine from the assignment form that First National had purchased Siler's right, title, and interest in the contract proceeds and was therefore entitled to payment. There was no reason for the bank to instruct Mountain Bell not to pay Siler because Siler retained no right to payment. The unconditional language of the assignment was notice that 'payment [was] to be made to the assignee.'...

"Mountain Bell takes the position that it was not an account debtor at the time it received notice, as the contract had not been performed and nothing was owed to Siler. Thus it argues that notice of the assignment was untimely since Siler had nothing to assign. [UCC Section] 9–105(1)(a)…defines an account debtor as follows: '"Account debtor" means the person who is obligated on an account, chattel paper, *contract right* or general intangible.' [Emphasis added by the court.]

"Siler had contracted to perform work for Mountain Bell prior to the date of the assignment and the date of acceptance of the assignment by Mountain Bell. At the time of the assignment there was a contract, and Siler had a right to payment upon performance of the contract work."

Ethical Dimension

Why should a person (the account debtor) be forced into a commercial relationship with another party (the assignee) without consenting to that relationship?

■ Assignor's Guarantees

The seller of accounts makes implied warranties to the buyer.

When a company assigns its accounts receivable for return value, it makes three implied warranties, or guarantees, to its assignee. The assignor guarantees that the account is genuine and that it is subject to no limitations or defenses other than those which are apparent or which have been communicated to the assignee. If the account debtor were a minor child, for instance, that fact would have to be communicated to the assignee. If it were not, and the minor disaffirmed the account and refused to pay the balance due, the assignee could sue the assignor for breach of this first implied warranty. The assignor also warrants that any documentation on the account is genuine and what it is supposed to be. Finally, the assignor guarantees that it will do nothing itself to prevent collection of the assigned account. This third warranty would be breached where the assignor transfers the same account to two lending agencies or other creditors. Either assignee would have a claim for breach for any amount not collected. In addition to these normally implied warranties, a particular assignor might make specific, express guarantees to its assignee.

Under what other circumstances could the assignee have recourse against the assignor when the account debtor doesn't pay? Usually, the parties to the assignment will specify the recourse, or buy-back, arrangement they want. They may provide full recourse by the assignee for any uncollected amounts, no recourse at all, or (more likely) something in between. Certainly between themselves their agreement controls, but if the assignor fraudulently assigned the same accounts twice, the assignees have recourse, regardless of what their agreements provide.

Double assignments of accounts have occurred often enough that specific rules have been developed to deal with the problem. Unfortunately, the states give two different answers to the question, Which assignee gets the money from the account debtor? In a majority of states, using the so-called "American rule," the first effective assignment takes priority over the second one. There are several major exceptions under this rule, however, which permit the second assignee to get some or all of the money. Number Two keeps all payments made before Number One notifies the account debtor of Number One's assignment. Number Two gets all the money if it has a specific writing representing ownership of the account, such as a bank passbook. Number Two gets all the money if the first assignment is revocable for any reason. And Number Two gets all the money if it enters into a new contractual arrangement with the account debtor or gets a court judgment against the account debtor. In the minority states, which follow the "English rule," whichever assignee first notifies the account debtor of its assignment gets all the money from the account.

States disagree on which assignee gets paid where an account is double-assigned.

Fortunately for borrowers, lenders, and account debtors, most of these problems are solved by the UCC, *if* at least one lender/assignee does file the required public notice. The rule under the UCC is that the first assignee to file the required notice gets all the money from the account. If nobody is smart enough to file, a court will have to use the old rules to work out the problem, as was done in the next case.

BOULEVARD NATIONAL BANK OF MIAMI V. AIR METALS INDUSTRIES, INC.

176 So. 2d 94 (Fla. 1965)

Facts: Air Metals, a subcontractor for Tompkins-Beckwith Co., made two assignments of its right to receive payment for the job. Air Metals had to post a performance bond to bid on the job. It gave the bonding company, American Fire & Casualty, a conditional assignment "in the event of [Air Metals'] default." Tompkins-Beckwith was not notified of this first assignment. Air Metals then borrowed money from Boulevard, giving them an absolute assignment of moneys due from the job. Again, Tompkins-Beckwith was not notified of the assignment.

Air Metals then defaulted on its performance of the construction job. American Fire notified Tompkins-Beckwith of its assignment from Air Metals, and Tompkins-Beckwith agreed to pay them what it owed Air Metals. Boulevard then notified Tompkins-Beckwith of its assignment, which was actually "first" in time since the one to American Fire had been conditional and had thus not really taken effect until Air Metals defaulted. The trial court ruled for American Fire.

Issue: Does the first assignee to notify the account debtor get paid first?

Decision: Yes (under the English rule). Judgment affirmed.

Rule: Under the English rule, the assignee who first notifies the account debtor gets all the money from the account.

Discussion: *By Justice WILLIS:*

"The American rule for which petitioner contends is based upon the reasoning that an account or other chose in action may be assigned at will by the owner; that the notice to the debtor is not essential to complete the assignment; and that when such assignment is made, the property rights become vested in the assignee so that the assignor no longer has any interest in the account or chose which he may subsequently assign to another....

"It is undoubted that the creditor of an account receivable or other similar chose in action arising out of contract may assign it to another so that the assignee may sue on it in his own name and make recovery....

"It seems to be generally agreed that notice to a debtor of an assignment is necessary to impose on the debtor the duty of payment to the assignee, and that if before receiving such notice he pays the debt to the assignor, or to a subsequent assignee, he will be discharged from the debt.... It would seem to follow that the mere private dealing between the creditor and his assignee unaccompanied by any manifestations discernable to others having or considering the acquiring of an interest in the account would not meet the requirement of delivery and acceptance of possession which is essential to the consummation of the assignment. Proper notice to the debtor of the assignment is a manifestation of such delivery. It fixes the accountability of the debtor to the assignee instead of the assignor and enables all involved to deal more safely....

"We thus find the so-called English rule which the trial and appellate court approved and applied is harmonious with our jurisprudence, whereas the so-called American rule is not."

Ethical Dimension

Could there ever be an ethical justification for a company's double-assigning its accounts?

▨ Commercial Paper Financing

Transactions involving commercial paper arise in two quite different contexts. First, a company's customers may give it a note, draft, or check in payment for goods or services. Second, the company may execute its own commercial paper to its creditors—lenders and suppliers.

Checks, notes, and drafts are types of commercial paper.

A **note** is a promise by the maker to pay money. (See Figures 11–2 and 11–3.) A **draft** is an order by the drawer, directed to a drawee, ordering the drawee to pay money to a named payee. (See Figure 11–4.) A **check** is a draft drawn against a bank at which the drawer presumably has an account, directing the drawee bank to pay money to a named payee. (See Figure 11-5.) There are a number of possible legal consequences arising from each of these commercial paper transactions.

The law on commercial paper has deep historical roots. Such devices were apparently in use even in ancient times to facilitate trade and commerce. Promissory notes provided (and still provide) a way in which payments can be made and values transferred without the need for carrying large sums of cash. Through centuries of use of these instruments, a complex body of law has been developed, although perhaps not all parts of it are equally relevant to today's financial practices.

Under the law of negotiable instruments (now Article 3 of the UCC), commercial paper has several advantages over an ordinary account receivable. First, commercial paper which is in negotiable form carries a presumption that value was given to the person who signed and issued it; that is not true of an account receivable. The business trying to collect an account must prove that it gave value to the person who is claimed to owe the account. The person who signed commercial paper must prove that it in fact received no value—or some other defense—to avoid paying the instrument. Second, negotiable instruments are by definition intended to be freely transferable, although this is also generally true today for accounts receivable (at least for the kinds of accounts covered by the UCC). Finally, certain defenses cannot be used against persons who have bought the negotiable instrument in good faith. By contrast, assignees of accounts step into the legal shoes of their assignors; they have no greater rights to enforce the account than the assignors had. (For consumers, this last rule has been drastically changed, as we will see in the next chapter.)

Most commercial paper is issued in negotiable (transferable) form.

To get these special results, the commercial paper must be in negotiable form. The instrument must be a written promise or order to pay a definite amount of money, either on demand or at a specified future time. The promise must be unconditional, that is, not dependent on some other act or event. Generally, no other promise or order can be contained in the instrument. For notes or drafts, the magic words of negotiability must be used: the instrument must be payable to **bearer** or payable to **order**. A bearer instrument has the same significance here as

An instrument payable to bearer can be transferred by delivery alone.

$ _(Amount in figures)_   __(City)__, __(State)__, __(Date)__

On Demand, the undersigned, for value received, promises to pay to the order of

_____ Bank _____, at its office in _____,

(Amount in words) _____ DOLLARS

with interest thereon from date at the rate of _____ percent per annum until demand and at the
rate of _____ percent per annum after demand, all interest being payable monthly.

(Signature of maker) _____

Address _____   _____

FIGURE 11–2
(above) Note payable on demand

FIGURE 11–3
(right) Installment note

PROMISSORY NOTE

_____(City)_____, _____(State)_____

_____19____

For value received, undersigned makers(s), jointly and severally, promise to pay the order of _____ at the above place _____ dollars ($____) in _____ consecutive monthly payments of $_____each, beginning one month from the date hereof and thereafter on the same date of each subsequent month until paid in full. Any unpaid balance may be paid, at any time, without penalty and any unearned finance charge will be refunded based on the "Rule of 78s." In the event that maker(s) default(s) on any payment, a charge of _____ may be assessed.

1. Proceeds $ _____

2. _____   _____
   (Other charges, itemized)
3. Amount financed (1+2)   _____

4. FINANCE CHARGE   _____

5. Total of payments $ _____

   ANNUAL PERCENTAGE RATE   _____%

   Signed ___(Maker)_____

   _____

   _____

discussed earlier in connection with bonds. Since the instrument is payable to the person in possession of it, ownership can be transferred by delivery alone. An order instrument is also freely transferable, but it requires delivery plus a valid **indorsement** by the current owner/transferor. If the instrument is payable to the order of Jane Smith, for

_____ _(City)_ , _(State)_   _(Date)_
(INDICATE ABOVE WHETHER PAYABLE ON DEMAND, ARRIVAL, OR OTHER TIME LIMIT)

PAY TO THE ORDER OF _____ _(Name of payee)_ _____ $ _(Amount in figures)_

(Amount in words) _____ DOLLARS

_____

_____

VALUE RECEIVED AND CHARGE TO ACCOUNT OF

TO _____ _(Name and address of drawee)_ _____

_____   _(Signature of drawer)_

_____

2120

745-100
724

(Date) 19 ___

PAY
TO THE
ORDER OF _____ _(Payee's name)_ _____ $_ _(Amount in figures)_

(Amount in words) _____DOLLARS

Ann Arbor Bank
and Trust Company   _(Drawee)_
ANN ARBOR MICHIGAN 48107

FOR _____ _____ _(Drawer's name)_ _____

:072112006 :   20 200152 9

FIGURE 11–4
(top) Draft

FIGURE 11–5
(above) Check

example, Jane would indorse it by signing her name on the back of the instrument. If she simply signs "Jane Smith" without indicating the next person to be the owner of the instrument, the instrument is now in bearer form and ownership of it can be transferred by delivery alone. For checks (which are drawn against banks), the latest version of Article 3 does not require the "bearer" or "order" language if the check meets the other requirements.

Since checks are payable on demand, they are nearly always deposited by the payee into the payee's bank account and sent through the banking system to the drawer's bank, where they are presented for payment. Rarely are checks transferred by the payee to other persons, although it is possible to do so. Grocery stores and other retailers will sometimes cash paychecks, as a convenience to their customers, but

Checks are not usually transferred to other persons by the payee of the check.

most checks will follow the normal collection route. Problems can arise if there are insufficient funds in the drawer's account when the check is presented for payment or if the check is altered, lost, or stolen. Out of the billions of checks processed annually, only a tiny fraction will be subject to such irregularities. Where such check problems do arise, many of them will be resolved by reference to the banking rules in Article 4 of the UCC rather than to classic negotiable instruments law. The negotiability rules are therefore not nearly as significant for checks as they are for notes and drafts, which may in fact circulate for some time and through several parties before they are finally presented for payment.

Where the company did receive notes and drafts from its customers and sold them to its bank or finance company to get cash for its operations, it would make implied warranties to its transferee. (*Implied* means that these warranties are automatically assumed to have been made.) The seller of the notes and drafts would guarantee that it owned the instruments and that the transfer was otherwise rightful, that all signatures were genuine or authorized, that the instrument had not been materially altered, that no party liable on it had a valid defense, and that the transferor company had no knowledge of any insolvency of the maker (of a note) or drawer or drawee (of a draft). If it indorsed the instrument when it transferred it, the transferor company would also make these same five warranties to all later owners of the instrument. If the instrument was in bearer form already and was not indorsed by the transferor company, the five warranties would be made only to the immediate transferee.

An HDC can collect the stated amount even though the debtor has a defense.

Where the instrument is transferred by the original payee, and is owned by a good faith purchaser (called a **holder in due course**, or **HDC**), most defenses which the debtor had against the original payee cannot be asserted against the HDC. The HDC, in other words, can enforce the instrument as issued, even though the debtor did not receive the promised value in return. If the services were not performed, or the goods did not perform as promised, the debtor could not use those reasons to avoid payment of the negotiable instrument which it had issued in payment if the instrument is now owned by an HDC. The debtor has to bring her or his own lawsuit for breach of the original contract against the party that failed to perform; meanwhile, the debtor has to pay the HDC. This same "pay anyway" result would follow where a company issued a draft or note in payment for goods or services it was supposed to receive. If the supplier breached, the company must still pay for values is hasn't received. To receive this special HDC status, the transferee must take the instrument in good faith for value and without notice that it is overdue, has been dishonored, or is subject to any third party claim or defense.

An individual promissory note might be given to a bank or insurance company by a company borrowing funds, as evidence of the debt. Negotiability rules are probably not of great significance in many of these cases, since the lender itself would simply hold the note to maturity rather than transferring it to another party. However, large companies issuing batches of commercial paper or trading in the commercial paper markets might be well-advised to be familiar with the negotiability rules. Bankers also need to be on intimate terms with the law of negotiability, as the Arcanum Bank learned in the following case.

ARCANUM NATIONAL BANK V. HESSLER

433 N.E.2d 204 (Ohio 1982)

Facts: Kenneth Hessler was in the business of raising hogs for others. John Smith Grain Company or J&J Farms Inc. would deliver the hogs to him, and he would sign a promissory note for the cost of the hogs and their feed. John Smith Grain then sold the note to Arcanum. (John Smith Grain's president was a director of Arcanum, and Arcanum supplied it with the blank note forms used in these transactions.) J&J usually sold the mature hogs to Producer's Livestock Association and at that point, paid off Hessler's note at Arcanum. Hessler would also receive a flat fee and a share of the profits.

The shipment of hogs Hessler received on January 4, 1977, had already been mortgaged by J&J Farms to Producer's, so Hessler in fact received no value at all in exchange for the note he signed that day. He signed not only his own name but also his wife Carla's name, adding his initials after her name. This note was sold to Arcanum. Producer's took this batch of hogs because of the serious financial problems John Smith Grain was having. Since there were no hogs to sell this time, the note was not paid. The trial court and the appeals court held for Arcanum.

Issue: Was the Arcanum National Bank an HDC?

Decision: No. Judgment for the bank is reversed. Hessler wins.

Rule: A person who takes the instrument with notice of a substantial irregularity cannot be an HDC; neither can a person who does not take the instrument in good faith.

Discussion: *By Justice* KRUPANSKY:

"[T]he trial court...reasoned: 'The defect on the promissory note is that the signature of Carla Hessler was added by Kenneth Hessler and, since the Arcanum National Bank handled the Hesslers' personal finances, it should have noticed that there was a defect on the face of the instrument.... The note also bears the initials "K.H." indicating that Kenneth Hessler had signed Carla Hessler's name.' Accordingly the trial court specifically found 'this "irregularity" does call into question the validity of the note, the terms of the note, the ownership of the note or create an ambiguity as to the party who is to pay the note.' Thus, the trial court, while specifically finding [Arcanum] took the note with notice of a defense, nonetheless erroneously held [the] bank qualified as a holder in due course....

"[Hessler] also contends, in essence, [the] bank failed in its burden of proving holder in due course status because [it] failed to establish it took the note in good faith....

"'Good faith' is defined as 'honesty in fact in the conduct or transaction concerned.'... Under the 'close connectedness' doctrine...a transferee does not take an instrument in good faith when the transferee is so closely connected with the transferor that the transferee may be charged with knowledge of an infirmity in the underlying transaction....

"The facts of this case clearly indicate such close connectedness between [the] bank and John Smith Grain Company as to impute knowledge by [the] bank of infirmities in the underlying transaction. The trial court specifically found, in its separate findings of fact and conclusions of law, the relationship between [the] bank and J&J Farms was not an arm's length transaction. In spite of this finding, the trial court erroneously concluded 'the facts do not permit the court to void the holder in due course protections under these circumstances.'...

"The trial court, however, missed the point. Not only do the facts indicate [the] bank was aware of the impending bankruptcy of John Smith Grain Company, but they also show [the bank] had reason to know of a fatal infirmity in the underlying transaction, [namely], there was no consideration given by John Smith Grain Company for the note. C. North, Jr., an officer and director of both John Smith Grain Company and J&J Farms Inc., obtained [Hessler's] signature and advised [him] to sign his wife's name on the note. As an officer and director of J&J Farms Inc., C. North, Jr., undoubtedly was aware that at the time he obtained [Hessler's] signature, the hogs had already been mortgaged by J&J Farms Inc.... If North...knew there was no consideration for the note, then such knowledge is imputed to both corporations. Thus, H. K. Smith, as president and director of John Smith Grain Company, had ample reason to know of the failure of consideration; and since H. K. Smith was also a director of [the] bank, his knowledge is imputed to [the] bank....

"Under the circumstances of this case, we find the relationship between [the] bank and John Smith Grain Company was so entwined that it was error for the trial court not to apply the doctrine of close connectedness to find [the] bank failed to carry its burden of proving good faith."

Ethical Dimension

Why should the bank be held responsible for Kenneth Hessler's wrongful signing of his wife's name?

■ Inventory Financing

Retailers quite frequently buy inventory for resale on credit. Many small retailers may not have enough capital invested or retained earnings to pay cash for the large amounts they need to buy at the beginning of a selling season. Car dealers typically "floor-plan" their new car inventory, since the cost of each unit may average over $10,000. A dealer with 100 of these units in inventory needs a million dollars of cash or credit just for this one cost of doing business. Manufacturers may need to finance inventories of parts or raw materials.

Car dealers usually "floor-plan" their new car inventory.

The simplest financing arrangement would be an account receivable. The car manufacturer could simply ship the new cars to its dealer, based on the dealer's promise to pay for them. Most car makers are not that gullible. Or the car dealer could go to a local bank, get an unsecured loan, and pay cash for the cars. Most banks aren't that gullible either—although several recent well-publicized cases do make one wonder. A promissory note from the dealer, either to the car manufacturer or to the local bank, would be slightly better than an account receivable, but only slightly.

What a reasonable and prudent creditor wants in these transactions is some greater assurance than the debtor's word that the obligation will be paid. Some debtors will promise anything to get the credit. Their business projections are always rosy; the market will always go up; tomorrow never comes. In business—and in life—there is always a downside risk. The prudent business takes that reality into account, asks the tough "what if" questions, and orders its affairs so it can survive when the wind blows and the river rises. What happens if the owner of the dealership dies, and the successor is incompetent to manage the business? What happens if there is a serious recession, and no one is buying new cars in that area? What happens if the latest Japanese import is getting much better mileage and selling at a lower price? Car dealers, and other businesses, get into financial difficulty—sometimes because of their own decisions, sometimes because of general industry and economic conditions.

What does the prudent creditor do to protect itself? The answer is really quite simple: have the debtor sign a security agreement covering the inventory being bought on credit and a financing statement which describes the inventory collateral; give written notice to any other creditor who is on file as also having a security interest in the debtor's inventory; file the financing statement with the Secretary of State in the state where the debtor has its business; and then—and only then—deliver the new inventory to the debtor. A creditor who has followed these UCC Article 9 procedures will be protected against conflicting claims from the debtor's other creditors, including its bankruptcy trustee. Without this protection, the creditor has no source of payment other than the general net asset value of the debtor, which will have to be shared with all other similarly situated general creditors.

A secured creditor needs a signed security agreement from the debtor.

The document which Article 9 of the UCC describes as the security agreement is simply the credit contract, in which the debtor grants a security interest in the described collateral to the secured creditor. The financing statement is the short form which is publicly filed to give notice to the rest of the world that there is some sort of secured claim against the described collateral. If someone is already on file against the debtor's inventory, including its after-acquired inventory, that prior secured creditor must be notified in writing, prior to the debtor's receipt of the new collateral, that it will be delivered subject to a new security interest. If this notice procedure is not followed, the prior secured party, since it was on record first, will also have first claim to the new inventory, and the seller or financer of that new inventory would have only a secondary claim. The procedure is not terribly difficult or complicated, but it must be done correctly to protect the creditor's interest.

Even with everything done properly, the secured creditor should be aware that some pieces of inventory may slip away. If the inventory is intended for resale by the debtor, some of it may in fact get sold to buyers. Persons who buy goods from a merchant in the ordinary course of the merchant's business operations are protected by the UCC. The buyer in the ordinary course of business (**BIOC**) owns the goods free and clear of the claims of the seller's creditors. A bank which had loaned money to a shoe store to buy inventory would have no claim against persons who had bought some of those shoes out of the store's inventory. In this situation, the secured creditor would (or could) have a priority claim against the proceeds of such sales—whatever the shoe store had received in exchange for the shoes it sold.

■ Equipment Financing

Businesses may also need to finance major equipment purchases. The creditor protection procedure here is basically the same as for inventory, but there are some differences. The credit seller or financing agency needs to have the debtor execute the same two documents—a security agreement and a financing statement. Each must adequately describe the equipment which is being used as collateral. The financing statement must be filed. Unlike the inventory financing transaction, however, a previous secured creditor who is claiming against all the debtor's equipment will not have to be notified that the new equipment is being financed. The prior security interest will still have first priority against the then-existing equipment, but only a secondary claim against the new equipment. The financing statement on the new inventory can be filed either before, or within ten days after, the debtor gets possession of the new equipment.

Usually, creditors need to file a financing statement to protect their interest in the collateral.

If the equipment is a motor vehicle which is required to be licensed by the state, a notation may also have to be made on the vehicle registration certificate, usually called the certificate of title. If the equipment is going to be used in more than one state, but is not required to be licensed as a motor vehicle, the financing statement should be filed in the state where the debtor has its place of business. If the debtor has more than one place of business, then the financing statement should be filed in the state where the debtor has its chief executive office. If the equipment is to be attached to real estate as a fixture, then the financing statement must describe the real estate and must be filed in the county where the real estate is located.

The debtor business will not normally be a dealer in the equipment it is using in its business. Therefore, someone buying the used equipment will not usually qualify as a BIOC. If not a BIOC, even though buying the equipment in good faith, the purchaser of the used equipment will have to give it back to the secured creditor if it is not paid for when it is resold. Alternatively, the used equipment buyer could pay off the balance due on the original purchase price and then sue its seller for a refund.

■ Leasing Equipment

As an alternative to buying equipment, a business may wish to conserve its capital by leasing some of the things required. Particularly where some equipment may be used only on occasion or seasonally, it might make sense to lease those pieces only when needed. Even where there is an ongoing, continuous use of the items, there may be tax benefits or other business reasons for leasing equipment. Recognizing the increased importance of leasing transactions, the UCC added Article 2A, "Leases," to provide uniform rules for these commercial contracts.

There are at least three different kinds of transactions described by the word "lease." There is the temporary lease of equipment for a few days—the same sort of lease that individuals enter into with a car-rental company. There should be no question but that this arrangement is only a lease; the equipment is owned by the leasing company, not by the customer company. No financing statement needs to be filed by the leasing company against the customer company to protect the leasing company against claims of the customer company's creditors. If the customer company doesn't make the rental payments as required, the leasing company simply comes out and picks up its equipment.

Leases intended as security devices are treated like other financing arrangements.

Longer-term equipment leases can create misleading appearances. This equipment is being used by the debtor/customer every day over an extended period of time, perhaps several years. To a casual observer, the equipment appears to belong to the debtor/customer. Even greater ambiguity is created if the lease gives the debtor/customer the option to buy the equipment at the end of the leasing period. Under what circumstances can creditors of the debtor/customer assert claims against the leased equipment? When does the leasing company have to file a financing statement to protect its rights in the leased equipment?

To answer these questions, the UCC distinguishes between a "normal" lease and one which is intended as a security device. The second transaction is really a credit sale, with the "leased" goods being used as collateral for the balance of the contract price; it isn't really a lease at all. The lease which is intended to act as a security device is treated by the UCC as a security device, meaning that the "leasing" company has to file a financing statement to protect its collateral against claims of the other creditors of the debtor/customer. The bankers in the next case did not understand this distinction and lost their bank's collateral as a result.

JAMES TALCOTT, INC. V. FRANKLIN NATIONAL BANK OF MINNEAPOLIS

194 N.W.2d 775 (Minn. 1972)

Facts: Noyes Paving Company bought two dump trucks and some other construction equipment from Northern Contracting Company on February 20, 1968. On the same day, Northern assigned to Talcott its rights under this conditional sale contract. Talcott filed a financing statement the next day, describing the collateral as "Construction Equipment, Motor Vehicles." On May 1, Noyes "leased" a dump truck from Franklin and, on May 31, "leased" two more dump trucks and other construction equipment. Each "lease" stated that Noyes could own the trucks at the end of the lease period by paying $1.00 more if it had complied with all the terms. Franklin filed nothing.

When Noyes had payment problems in late 1968, it asked Talcott for help. Talcott agreed to extend Noyes' payments and to lower the monthly amount due in exchange for a security interest "in all goods (as defined in Article 9 of the Uniform

Commercial Code) whether now owned or hereafter acquired." This extension agreement was signed on January 30, 1969. Talcott did not file a new financing statement. Noyes continued to have difficulties, however, and went into default on all its equipment contracts in 1970. On May 21, 1970, Franklin filed copies of its equipment leases with the Secretary of State. Sometime in May it also repossessed its "leased" trucks and equipment. By agreement of the parties, these items were sold and the proceeds placed in an escrow account, pending the outcome of this lawsuit. Talcott and Franklin both claim these proceeds from the sale of the leased trucks and equipment. The trial court gave summary judgment for Franklin.

Issue: Are Franklin's "leases" really security agreements, so that it lost its priority of payment by failing to file in time?

Decision: Yes, these are really security agreements. Judgment reversed. (Talcott wins.)

Rule: If lessee can become the owner at the end of the lease for no additional money, or for a nominal amount, the lease is one which is intended as security and will be treated as a security agreement.

Discussion: *By Justice HACKEY:*

"The language of the [UCC] specifically determines whether or not a lease creates a security interest in the collateral.... The words of that section are unequivocal. An option given to the lessee to purchase the leased property for a nominal consideration does make the lease one intended for security. Hence, the options to buy the equipment in [this] case for $2, a nominal amount when compared to the total rental of $73,303.32, created security interests. The leases in question were precisely the type that Art. 9 was intended to cover, i.e., transactions in goods which were in substance, although not in form, security agreements....

"[T]he draftsmen of the [UCC] intended that its provisions should not be circumvented by manipulation of the locus of title. For this reason, consignment sales, conditional sales, and other arrangements or devices whereby title is retained by the seller for a period following possession by the debtor are all treated under Art. 9 as though the title had been transferred to the debtor and the creditor-seller had retained only a security interest in the goods. For the purpose of analyzing rights of ownership under Art. 9, we hold, based upon the stipulated facts of this case, that defendant had only a security interest in the equipment despite a purported reservation of title and that

[Noyes] 'owned' the equipment at the time that the extension agreement was executed....

"The description of the collateral in the extension agreement did what it was meant to do—namely, it included all of the goods then owned, or to be owned in the future, by the debtor. The term 'goods' was defined to be those goods as comprehended within the meaning of Art. 9 of the [UCC]. The definition selected is embodied in the statute, a definition that is used and applied frequently. The parties sought to create a security interest in substantially all of the debtor's property. That is what was stated, and that is what was meant. The parties did not particularize any further, and the statute does not require it....

"[W]hen the conflict arose (still assuming it was before [Franklin] had filed), [Talcott] was entitled to priority. Once [Talcott's] priority had been acquired, no subsequent filing by [Franklin] (more than 10 days after [Noyes] received possession) could alter the situation. Moreover, even if...[UCC] 312(5)(a) should apply, [Talcott] would still have priority under the first-to-file rule as its filing preceded [Franklin's] by many months."

Ethical Dimension

Is it fair to award extra value to a party (Talcott) simply because the other party failed to file a small form?

Cosigning Personally

Lenders and sellers dealing with small corporations will usually demand personal guarantees from officers, directors, and principal shareholders before extending credit. Unless the company has an excellent credit rating or has been a good customer over a period of time, the creditor is likely to want to have personal assets available just in case the corporate assets are insufficient. Signing such a personal guarantee will not make the officer or director liable for all the company's unpaid debts, only for the one which has been guaranteed.

Not all cosigners make exactly the same promises. A **surety** cosigns as a full co-debtor, promising "I will pay." When the debt matures, the creditor can take action directly against the surety, without having to try to collect from the principal debtor first. A **guarantor** generally makes a more limited, secondary promise: "I will pay if the principal does not pay." This language means that the creditor must first try to collect from the principal debtor. If that party does not pay, then the creditor can proceed against the guarantor. A **guarantor of collectability** only becomes liable if the creditor gets a judgment against the principal debtor and then is unable to collect it.

Because a surety or guarantor is promising to pay someone else's debt, the law provides a number of special rules for this financial arrangement. Generally, such a promise has to be made in a signed writing in order to be enforceable in court. If the principal debtor is able to pay, but the creditor tries to collect from the surety, the surety can get a court order forcing the principal debtor to pay. This is called the surety's right of **exoneration**. If there is more than one co-signer, any one which has paid more than a fair share of the debt can sue the others to force **contribution** of the others' fair shares. Any surety or guarantor who has paid part of the debt can sue the principal debtor for **reimbursement**, since it was that party's debt in the first place. Finally, any cosigner who has paid part of the debt has the right of **subrogation**, meaning that he or she acquires all the rights which the creditor had against the principal debtor.

Cosigners are given several legal protections.

In addition to all these special rights, the surety/guarantor is also given some special defenses against liability. A cosigner who is not being compensated for acting as such—a friend or relative, for instance—would be discharged from liability if the creditor changed the terms of the credit contract or gave up its rights against collateral. If the creditor releases the principal debtor from liability, the uncompensated surety is also usually released. A professional surety, being paid to act as such, would normally not be discharged unless it could show that its rights were substantially affected by such changes.

Where the underlying credit contract is an Article 9 secured transaction, the cosigner is also entitled to all the protections which the UCC provides for the debtor, as seen in the next case.

CHEMLEASE WORLDWIDE, INC. V. BRACE, INC.

338 N.W.2d 428 (Minn. 1983)

Facts: In October, 1975, Brace, Inc., "leased" certain computer equipment from Chemlease for 62 months for a total price $29,836.26. At the end of the lease, Brace could buy the equipment for an additional $1.00. Charles and Clayton Brace signed personal guarantees of their corporation's performance. Brace, Inc. went out of business in June, 1977, but the lease was taken over by Brace Company, which in turn went out of business that fall. Payments were made to Chemlease through October, 1978. Gamet, the new occupant of the Brace building, then notified Chemlease that the equipment had been abandoned and asked them what to do with it. Chemlease resold the equipment to Chicago Cash Register and told Chicago to pick it up on February 2, 1979.

Chemlease mailed a final demand for payment and a notice of private sale to Brace, Inc., Charles Brace and Clayton Brace on

February 1. Charles signed for his certified letters on February 7 and 8; the other letters were returned as undeliverable. The notices said the private sale would occur on or after February 12. Chicago, in the meantime, had already picked up the equipment, paid the $2,500 agreed price, and received a bill of sale. Chemlease sued Brace, Inc., Charles, and Clayton for the balance still due on the original lease. The trial court gave a directed verdict for $10,406.95, against all three. Charles and Clayton appealed.

Issue: Are these guarantors protected by Article 9's required procedures?

Decision: Yes. Judgment reversed. (Charles and Clayton win.)

Rule: If the lessee can become the owner of leased equipment by paying an additional nominal amount, the lease is really a secured transaction. Guarantors in a secured transaction are "debtors" for Article 9 purposes and are thus entitled to its protective procedures.

Discussion: *By the Court:*

"In [this] case, the computer equipment was moved from Minnesota to Illinois on February 2, 1979. The factual situation here of Gamet delivering the goods to a carrier hired by Chicago Cash Register Company most approximates a shipment contract. Accordingly, we hold that subsection 2 would apply and title would have passed [in the resale of the equipment to Chicago Cash Register] 'at the time and place at which the seller completes his performance with respect to the physical delivery of the goods.'... The last date at which Chemlease can argue that it completed its performance in this shipment contract is the date the goods were handed over to the carrier on February 2, 1979. Because title passed on February 2, 1979, the 'sale' of the equipment, by definition, would have occurred on that date. Because the notices of sale [sent to Brace, Inc., Charles Brace, and Clayton Brace] were not postmarked until February 2, 1979, the date the sale technically occurred, the notification appears to be unreasonable to all appellants because the notices were not sent in sufficient time to enable Brace, Inc. or its guarantors to take protective action....

"The burden of proving its entitlement to the deficiency remained on Chemlease. The trial court's placing of the burden on appellants to show the sale price was commercially unreasonable was misplaced. The reasonableness of the sale price to Chicago Cash Register Company was a close factual question and Chemlease had the burden of proving the commercial reasonableness of the sale, and accepting as true the evidence favorable to appellants, the directed verdict against them was inappropriate."

Ethical Dimension

How fair is it to have a sale of the collateral on the same day the notice of sale of the collateral is delivered to the debtor?

REVIEW

Since financing transactions lie at the heart of business operations, the law has developed a comprehensive set of rules to deal with problems which may arise. Most of these rules are now found in the UCC, Articles 3 and 9. General contract law principles still apply to some of these relationships, however. Long-term investments are regulated under the national securities laws, as was discussed in part in the last chapter. This chapter focused on the use of debt financing, as opposed to equity financing. Rather than getting additional funds from investor-owners, debt financing involves borrowing funds from creditors. Long-term debt instruments, called bonds, are also regulated under the national securities acts. Creditors extending short-term credit will need to comply with the requirements of the UCC and general contract law to protect their interests. Chapter 12 will further elaborate the various regulations which pertain to financing transactions.

REVIEW QUESTIONS AND PROBLEMS

1. What is the difference between transferring an ordinary account receivable and transferring a negotiable draft or note?

2. What extra steps are involved in secured financing of inventory as opposed to secured financing of equipment?

3. What is the difference between a surety and a guarantor?

4. What is the significance of being a BIOC?

5. What is the significance of being an HDC?

6. What are the major differences between stocks and bonds?

7. Mr. and Mrs. Andro decided to go into the tree-nursery business, selling trees, shrubs, and plants. They signed a franchise agreement with Barb's Blossoms, Inc., by the terms of which Barb's was to provide 50,000 small trees for planting, together with fertilizers, equipment, and instructions. Mr. and Mrs. Andro signed a promissory note for $25,000 as payment for the trees and other materials. The note said it was "Payable to Barb's Blossoms, Inc." Barb's sold the note to Investment Company. Barb's failed to perform its part of the franchise contract, so the Andros refused to pay the note when it came due. Investment sued to collect, and the Andros want to use Barb's breach of contract as a reason not to pay. Is Investment the holder in due course of a negotiable instrument? Explain.

8. Ronnie and his wife Rosie (newly married, ages 21 and 19) went shopping for furniture. The pieces they wanted to buy cost $4900 at Racks, Inc.; the salesman told them that the store could not give them that much credit unless they could arrange for a cosigner. Ronnie's mother, Rhonda, agreed to cosign and did so. After about eight months, Ronnie and Rosie were unable to make payments. Racks agreed to lower the monthly payments. Ronnie and Rosie made two of the lower payments and then defaulted again. Racks sued Rhonda for the balance still due. What argument should Rhonda make here to avoid liability?

9. Wylie Wayside owned a hog farm in Purdy County, Texas. He borrowed money from the Springs Bank, using his business assets as collateral. The security agreement and financing statement described the collateral as "all hogs, equipment, crops, and feed." They also contained a description of land in Minie County, but all the items of collateral were located on Wylie's farm in Purdy County. The financing statement was filed in Purdy County. Sometime later, John Jules bought 500 hogs from Wylie (most of his stock). When Wylie defaulted on his bank loan, Springs Bank sued John Jules to recover the hogs. What arguments can John make? Will he have to return the hogs to Springs Bank?

10. Nico bought a $2500 diamond engagement ring from Jewelry Store for his fiance, Ellie. He signed a security agreement on the ring, since he paid only $50 down. Jewelry did not have him sign a financing statement, and nothing was publicly filed. Nico gave the ring to Ellie. Shortly thereafter, he filed for bankruptcy. Ellie then called off the engagement and turned the ring over to the trustee in bankruptcy. Jewelry says it is entitled to priority as a secured creditor. The trustee says Ellie was a consumer who bought the ring in good faith and that the trustee succeeded to her rights when she gave it the ring. Who is right, and why?

SUGGESTIONS FOR FURTHER READING

Ellis, "The New Uniform Payments Code: Highlights of Proposed Changes in the Uniform Commercial Code Articles 3 and 4," *American Business Law Journal* 23 (Winter 1986): 617.

Lloyd, "Loan Guaranty Contracts: How to Make Them Enforceable," *Banking Law Journal* (July/August 1990): 292.

"Report Regarding Legal Opinions in Personal Property Secured Transactions," *Business Lawyer* (May 1989): 791.

Ryan & Wright, "Hazardous Waste Liability and the Surety," *Tort & Insurance Law Journal* (Spring 1990): 663.

Shepard & Scott, "Corporate Dividend Policy: Some Legal and Financial Aspects," *American Business Law Journal* 13 (Fall 1975): 199.

Tillman & Johnson, "Lender Litigation: Variable Interest Rates and Negotiability," *American Business Law Journal* 27 (Spring 1989): 121.

12
REGULATION
OF
FINANCING
TRANSACTIONS

"A pound of that same merchant's flesh is thine: The court awards it, and the law doth give it."
William Shakespeare, *The Merchant of Venice*

LEARNING OBJECTIVES: After you have studied this chapter, you should be able to:

EXPLAIN the applicability of the national securities laws to finance.

DEFINE the major exemptions from the securities acts' coverage.

DISCUSS state regulation of interest rates.

IDENTIFY the regulations dealing with credit disclosure and reporting.

EXPLAIN the significance of FTC Regulation 433.

OUTLINE bankruptcy procedures for liquidation and reorganization.

P REVIEW

As discussed in both Chapter 10 and Chapter 11, stocks and bonds are regulated as investment securities under national and state securities laws. While short-term financing transactions generally escape these comprehensive regulatory systems, several other regulatory packages do apply to short-term credit arrangements. Four major areas have received the most regulatory attention: interest rates, disclosure of terms, collection practices, and consumer protection. In addition, bankruptcy law provides a kind of overall discipline to the whole area of finance.

A PPLICABILITY OF SECURITIES LAWS

The national securities laws do not apply to all types of financing arrangements. Neither do state securities laws. Businesses using the various sources of financing available need to proceed carefully and to make sure that all applicable legal requirements are met. Failure to do so can result in the invalidity of the securities, with the business having to make refunds to the investors. Criminal penalties may be imposed on the managers involved as well. The first thing to be determined is whether the securities acts do apply.

■ Stocks and Bonds

Stocks and bonds are securities under the 1933 and 1934 acts.

Both the 1933 Securities Act and the 1934 Securities and Exchange Act specifically list notes, stocks, bonds, and debentures in their comprehensive definitions of the term *security*. (The 1933 act's definition is quoted in Chapter 10.) Both acts also include the phrase **investment contract**, which the Supreme Court has defined as an investment of money in a common enterprise with an expectation that profits will be derived primarily from the efforts of others. Under this definition, it seems clear that loans and credit sales are not "investment contracts" and therefore are not subject to regulation under the securities laws.

■ Exemptions

Bank CDs are not covered by the federal securities acts.

While certificates for the deposit of securities are also included within the statutory definitions, a bank **certificate of deposit** (CD) is exempt from coverage. (The UCC defines a CD as "an acknowledgement of receipt of money with an engagement to repay it.") So are certain other instruments issued by financial institutions. Financial institutions themselves are already subject to their own set of comprehensive regulations. The 1934 act also exempts short-term notes and drafts (those having a maturity date nine months or less from the date of issue).

Small companies may also avoid the 1934 act's requirements (periodic reports, proxy regulations, insider trading prohibitions). The 1934 act applies if the company has made a registered offering of securities under the 1933 act, or if its equity securities are traded on a national exchange, such as the New York Stock Exchange. The 1934 act also applies if the company has $5 million in assets and 500 or more holders of any class of its equity securities. A company could thus avoid these extra burdens if it made sure that it had no more than 499 stockholders of any class of its shares of stock, made no public offering of securities, and did not have its shares traded on the national exchanges. There is no limit to the number of bondholders which a company can have and still avoid the 1934 act, as long as none of the other jurisdictional tests apply.

◼ Notes

Notes, at least those whose maturity date is over ninety days, are specifically mentioned in the definitions of *security*. Nevertheless, it is generally agreed that some types of notes are not securities. Notes which are given to evidence loans for consumer purchases or for current business operations are almost certainly exempt. Notes given as evidence of mortgage loans are probably also outside the definition in most cases.

In its decisions during the 1980s and 1990s, the Supreme Court developed a four-part test to determine when notes should be considered securities. First, borrowing from the investment contract definition, what are the purposes behind the note transaction? If the seller wants capital for the business and the buyer expects to share in profits, the note sounds like other types of securities. Second, what is the planned distribution of the notes? Are they being offered to the public by the issuing company, much as stocks or bonds would be, or is there but a single note evidencing a one-on-one loan transaction? Third, what are the note buyers' reasonable expectations of being protected by the securities laws? Is this the sort of transaction which the securities laws were intended to regulate? Finally, is the transaction covered by another comprehensive regulatory scheme, such as banking regulations, so that securities laws are probably not needed? Some of these issues are raised in the next case.

Notes may or may not be defined as securities.

MARINE BANK V. WEAVER
102 S. Ct. 1220 (1982)

Facts: Sam and Alice Weaver bought a six-year, $50,000 certificate of deposit from Marine Bank. The CD was insured by the Federal Deposit Insurance Corporation. The Weavers then pledged the CD to Marine as collateral for a $65,000 loan the bank made to Columbus Packing Company. Columbus' owners, Raymond and Barbara Piccirillo, agreed to give the Weavers half of Columbus' profits plus $100 per month, for as long as the

Weavers guaranteed the loan by Marine to Columbus. The Weavers claim that Marine's officers told them that the loan was for working capital. Instead, Marine took $42,800 for its prior claims against Columbus. Back taxes and other old debts took all but $3,800 of the rest of the loan. The Weavers sued, claiming violations of section 10(b) of the 1934 act and of state securities law, as well as common law fraud. The U.S. District Court granted summary judgment for Marine on the 10(b) claim and declined to hear the state claims. The Third Circuit reversed.

Issue: Is either the CD or the business agreement a security?

Decision: No, neither is. The District Court is affirmed on this point, but the case is remanded to the Third Circuit to decide whether the state law claims should be heard in the U.S. courts.

Rule: A certificate of deposit guaranteed by an agency of the U.S. government does not require the protections of the securities acts. Private business agreements are not normally considered to be securities.

Discussion: *By Chief Justice BURGER:*

"The definition of security in the Securities Exchange Act of 1934 is quite broad. The Act was adopted to restore investors' confidence in the financial markets, and the term security was meant to include 'the many types of instruments that in our commercial world fall within the ordinary concept of a security.'... The statutory definition excludes only currency and notes with a maturity of less than nine months. It includes ordinary stocks and bonds, along with the 'countless and variable schemes devised by those who seek the use of the money of others on the promise of profits.'... Thus, the coverage of the antifraud provisions of the securities laws is not limited to instruments traded at securities exchanges and over-the-counter markets, but extends to uncommon and irregular instruments.... We have repeatedly held that the test 'is what character the instrument is given in commerce by the terms of the offer, the plan of distribution, and the economic inducements held out to the prospect.'...

"The broad statutory definition is preceded, however, by the statement that the terms mentioned are not to be considered securities if 'the context otherwise requires.'... Moreover, we are satisfied that Congress, in enacting the securities laws, did not intend to provide a broad federal remedy for all fraud....

"We see...important differences between a certificate of deposit purchased from a federally regulated bank and other long-term debt obligations. The Court of Appeals failed to give appropriate weight to the important fact that the purchaser of a certificate of deposit is virtually guaranteed payment in full, whereas the holder of an ordinary long-term debt obligation assumes the risk of the borrower's insolvency.... We therefore hold that the certificate of deposit purchased by the Weavers is not a security....

"The Court of Appeals also held that a finder of fact could conclude that the separate agreement between the Weavers and the Piccirillos is a security.... [I]n that court's view, the agreement fell within the definition of investment contract..., because 'the scheme involves an investment of money in a common enterprise with profits to come solely from the efforts of others.'...

"Congress intended the securities laws to cover those instruments ordinarily and commonly considered to be securities in the commercial world, but the agreement between the Weavers and the Piccirillos is not the type of instrument that comes to mind when the term security is used and does not fall within 'the ordinary concept of a security.'... The unusual instruments found to constitute securities in prior cases involved offers to a number of potential investors, not a private transaction as in this case....

"Here, in contrast, the Piccirillos distributed no prospectus to the Weavers or to other potential investors, and the unique agreement they negotiated was not designed to be traded publicly. The provision that the Weavers could use the barn and pastures of the slaughterhouse at the discretion of Piccirillos underscores the unique character of the transaction. Similarly, the provision that the Weavers could veto future loans gave them a measure of control over the operation of the slaughterhouse not characteristic of a security. Although the agreement gave the Weavers a share of the Piccirillos' profits, if any, that provision alone is not sufficient to make the agreement a security. Accordingly, we hold that this unique agreement, negotiated one-on-one by the parties, is not a security.

"Whatever may be the consequences of these transactions, they did not occur in connection with the purchase or sale of 'securities'."

Ethical Dimension

How can any party legitimately object to complying with the securities laws?

R EGULATION OF SHORT-TERM FINANCE

Historically, state governments have been the primary source of regulations on short-term financing transactions. State regulation in this area is still significant. Increasingly, however, the national government has become involved here. While there is no comprehensive national regulation corresponding to the national securities laws, there are many specific U.S. statutes dealing with particular problems.

■ Regulation of Interest Rates

States regulate interest rates in various ways.

States have long been concerned with protecting debtors from excessive interest rates. Indeed, this was one of the earliest forms of consumer protection legislation. Many of these early statutes remain on the books, despite the fact that some of their provisions may not be in tune with modern financial realities. The Federal Reserve System exercises considerable control over what the market actually charges for the use of money, but most of the state regulatory statutes are not written to take account of marketplace changes. There have been recent efforts in some states to repeal all the old interest rate limits and to let the market prevail. These efforts are strongly opposed by labor unions and consumer groups. It is generally difficult to mount a popular campaign for increased interest rates, since there are likely to be more debtors voting than creditors. In addition, two of the world's major religions (Islam and Christianity) contain strong condemnations of money lenders who charge excessive interest.

States disagree on all major aspects of this problem. They do not agree on what sorts of transactions involve interest. They do not agree on how much interest can be lawfully charged. And they do not agree on what sanctions should be imposed on a creditor who attempts to charge too much interest.

SOURCES OF CREDIT

Even individual consumers can acquire credit from a variety of sources. Those with strong personal finances may be able to get a bank loan, at simple interest, for sixty or ninety days. They may be given permission by their bank to overdraw their checking accounts, with the bank making automatic loans to cover the shortages. They may be able to get an installment loan from a bank, a credit union, or a small loan company. They may be able to make a major purchase on the installment plan. They have credit accounts at department stores. They have general purpose credit cards and cards issued by large retailers and oil companies. They have mortgages and second mortgages on their homes.

MAXIMUM INTEREST RATE APPLICATION

To which of these types of credit transactions does a state's "maximum" interest rate regulation apply? There is not a uniform answer. Some early court decisions permitted a seller to charge two different prices for its goods—a cash price and a time-payment price. This "time-price differential" can be substantial; over a three-year installment plan, the buyer might pay one-third to one-half more for the same goods. Most recent court cases have held that such differentials are interest, and can be no more than the maximum permitted by state law. Most recent decisions have reached a similar result regarding the service charges on credit card and retail store accounts. Credit sellers and financing agencies have responded by pressuring some state legislatures into passing separate statutes to permit charging higher rates in their particular type of credit sale transactions. Some states thus have several different "maximum" rates, depending on who the lender is, who the borrower is, the purpose of the loan, and the repayment arrangement.

USURY LAWS

Most of the old laws regulating interest rates (called **usury laws**) set very low maximums—typically between five and nine percent per annum. If the market demands more than that for the use of money, it's just too bad. The creditor will have to accept the lower than market rate, or the debtor will have to pay cash and forego the loan. (Or the creditor can make the loan at the market rate and hope that it doesn't get caught.) Loans to corporations are excluded from many of these old statutes, so there may not be a usury issue with business loans. Some statutes do exclude any loan for business purposes, however the borrower is organized.

RESULTS OF VIOLATIONS

What happens to a creditor who attempts to charge an illegally high rate of interest? Here again, the states disagree. The least serious result will be a forfeiture of the excess interest, perhaps accompanied by a small fine. A more serious result would be the forfeiture of all interest; some states also follow that rule. Some states require a penalty deduction of two or three times the interest charged; that way the creditor also loses part of the principal. Finally, in some states, the entire obligation is null and void; the creditor loses all principal as well as all interest. In some states, two or more of these rules may be used, depending on the nature of the transaction. If there are different statutes, they may specify different penalties for violations.

States have different penalties when a creditor charges illegal interest.

In the next case the Washington court is trying to decide whether the transactions involved are subject to the state's usury law.

ROUSE V. PEOPLE'S LEASING CO.

638 P.2d 1245 (Wash. 1982)

Facts: Plaintiffs brought a class action against People's Leasing Co. (PLC), claiming that the car "leases" they had signed were really credit sales of the cars and that PLC was charging an illegally high rate of interest. According to the terms of the leases, PLC retained title to the cars, although the customers were the registered owners. The customer could become the owner by making all payments required by the lease, plus the guaranteed residual value of the car, plus a termination fee. At the end of the lease, the customer was liable for any deficiency if the car was sold for less than the guaranteed residual value. If the car was sold for more, the customer got the surplus. The customer assumed all risks on the car, and paid for insurance, licenses, and maintenance. The trial court granted defendant's motion for summary judgment.

Issue: Are open-end car leases really credit sales?

Decision: Yes, they are. Judgment reversed, and case remanded for trial.

Rule: If payments are made at the end of the lease based on the then market value of the car, the transaction is a sale, not a lease.

Discussion: *By Justice* DOLLIVER:

"The court...seems to be faced with a conflict in the application of its rules: (1) substance should prevail over form to determine whether usury is present and (2) when there is a question of usury, if a contract is susceptible of two constructions, one lawful and the other unlawful, the former will be adopted....

"On a question of usury, the court must first look at the transaction, regardless of what the parties might choose to call it, to see whether it is in fact a loan or forbearance—the first element to be proved where either party claims usury.... In making this initial determination the two-hypotheses rule [the two alternate constructions, as noted in the above paragraph] is not used. It is only after determining the transaction was in fact a loan or forbearance that the court will employ the two-hypotheses test and uphold the lawful construction. To hold as the trial court did that the two-hypotheses test applies to whether the transaction is a loan or forbearance would allow a skillful party to negate the application of the usury laws by characterizing a transaction so that it would not be a loan or forbearance in form but would accomplish the same end and not be susceptible to usury laws. This is not nor should it be the law in Washington.

"The present case revolves on the question of whether a loan or forbearance exists. The trial court, basing its opinion on the two-hypotheses theory, held that, because the parties clearly intended the transaction to be a lease, it must magically be turned into one. As noted previously, this triumph of form over substance, if followed, could have an emasculating effect on the usury laws. While finding intent is important in determining the computation of charges pursuant to a contract, it is irrelevant as it pertains to the determination of the transaction being a loan or forbearance as opposed to a lease....

"We hold as a matter of law that the open-end motor vehicle lease is the functional equivalent of a loan and that it is a 'loan or forbearance, express or implied' for the purpose of the usury statutes. The case is remanded to the trial court to determine whether these transactions which are loans for the purpose of the usury statute are usurious."

Ethical Dimension

Why is the company attempting to disguise these transactions as leases?

◾ Disclosure Requirements

Companies generating accounts receivable as a result of consumer transactions are now subject to a host of regulations. Congress was very active in this area during the late 1960s and throughout the 1970s. Several major statutes were passed, and extensive administrative regulations were adopted, dealing with topics which had not previously been regulated by the national government at all.

TRUTH IN LENDING ACT

The first of these major statutes was the Truth In Lending Act of 1968. The basic purpose of TILA was the same as that of the national securities acts: full disclosure. Borrowers and credit buyers should know the terms of the proposed credit contract, both so they are aware of what they are agreeing to and so they can compare alternatives. Credit for business use, including farming, is not covered; only that for personal, family, or household purposes. Not even all consumer credit transactions are covered—only those for $25,000 or less. (Congress evidently felt that a consumer entering into contracts for over $25,000 is smart enough not to need the protection of TILA.)

TILA requires disclosure of credit terms.

What sorts of disclosures are required? There are some differences, based on the type of credit contract involved. (See Figure 12–1 for an example of a disclosure statement.) In most cases, the creditor will be required to disclose the annual percentage rate or cost of credit, the method of determining the balance on which finance charges will be calculated, the time at which finance charges will be added, and any other charges and how they are calculated. The debtor's rights to dispute charges must also be stated. If the creditor is claiming a security interest in any of the debtor's assets, that too must be disclosed. For installment purchases, the total finance charge must be stated, along with the total number of installment payments and their amounts and due dates, the total contract amount, and any possible late charges.

EXPANSION OF COVERAGE

Consumer leases and home equity loans are regulated by national statutes.

As new consumer credit arrangements have become popular, Congress has expanded TILA's coverage to include them. In 1976, the Consumer Leasing Act was adopted to more completely regulate such transactions. Its definitions are similar to those in the original act: personal use; $25,000 or less. The Consumer Leasing Act applies to personal property leases for terms longer than four months. This latter requirement obviously excludes rental car contracts and similar temporary leases of equipment. Disclosures of the financial details of the lease are required, along with a statement of any warranties made by the lessor to the customer. Home equity loans are now also covered as a result of 1988 amendments to TILA. For these transactions, the $25,000 maximum does not apply. Advertisements for home equity loans, consumer leases, and consumer credit generally are also regulated by TILA.

■ Regulation of Collection and Reporting Practices

Another area in which considerable abuse occurred was debt collection and credit reporting. Occasionally, major creditors themselves would resort to strong-arm tactics and deception in efforts to collect debts. More frequently, it was collection agencies and credit bureaus who were the real offenders. In addition to force and fraud, collection and reporting processes suffered from bureaucratic inertia, arrogance, and numerous instances of "computer error." Some states have responded to these problems by passing privacy statutes and other restrictions on collection agencies and credit bureaus. Congress responded with a wave of new national legislation.

FAIR CREDIT REPORTING ACT

Consumer credit reporting agencies are regulated by the Fair Credit Reporting Act of 1970. Such agencies are required to have reasonable

Seller _(Corporate, Firm or Trade Name)_   __(Business Address)__

Buyer(s) _____(Name)_____   __(Residence Address)__

1. Cash Price......................$ ____

2. Less: Cash Down
                   Payment....$ ____
3.   Trade-In ...$ ____
4. Total Down
                   Payment ....$ ____
5. Unpaid Balance of Cash
           Price ....$ ____
6. Other Charges:
           Official Fees...................$ ____
           Physical Damage
                   Insurance ....$ ____
           Credit Life Insurance ....$ ____
           Credit Disability
                   Insurance ....$ ____
           Other _____$ ____
7. Amount Financed ....$ ____
8. FINANCE CHARGE ......$ ____
9. Total of Payments.........$ ____
10. Deferred Payment Price
           (1+6+8)......................$ ____
11. ANNUAL PERCENTAGE
           RATE ....___%

The "TOTAL OF PAYMENTS" shown herein is payable in_____ installments of $_____ each and a final installment of $_____, beginning on _____, 19__ and continuing on the same day of each successive month thereafter until paid in full.

Finance charge begins to accrue _____, 19__ (If different from date of transaction)

Delinquency charge on each installment in default for a period of not less than 10 days is 5% of the installment or $5, whichever is less. In addition, Buyer is obligated to pay reasonable attorneys' fees incurred by Seller in the collection or enforcement of the debt.

In the event of prepayment in full at any time before maturity, the rebate of unearned finance charge is computed on the Rule of 78s after first deducting an acquisition charge of $25.

FIGURE 12–1

Front side of a motor vehicle installment sale contract

procedures for assuring that they send credit information only for proper purposes—use by prospective employers, credit sellers, insurance companies, and other concerned businesses. Obsolete information (more than seven years old or bankruptcies more than ten years ago) must be removed from the credit file. The agency's "reasonable procedures" must also assure the maximum possible accuracy of information in the credit file. Businesses using these reports are required to disclose that fact to the person who is the subject of the report. The business must also disclose that the person has the right to further information about the scope of the credit investigation if a request is made by the subject person. If a business rejects the consumer's credit application or charges a higher rate for credit or insurance on the basis of the credit report, it must so advise the consumer and provide the name and address of the reporting agency. If the business uses information from sources other than reporting agencies, it must likewise disclose that fact if it rejects the consumer's application. FTC administrative

Consumer credit reporting agencies are subject to FCRA.

proceedings are available to enforce this act, and criminal charges are possible, as well. Injured consumers can bring private lawsuits for damages, including punitive damages for willful violations.

The *Millstone* case involves a claim under the FCRA.

MILLSTONE V. O'HANLON REPORTS, INC.

528 F.2d 829 (U.S. 8th Cir. Court of Appeals, 1976)

Facts: After Fireman's Fund Insurance issued a policy covering James Millstone's Volkswagen bus, they asked O'Hanlon Reports, Inc., for a credit report on Millstone. O'Hanlon used information gathered in Washington, D.C., where Millstone had lived before moving to St. Louis. The credit report described Millstone as "a hippie-type person, with shoulder-length hair and with a beard on one occasion, who participated in many demonstrations in the Capitol, carried demonstrators back and forth to his home, where he housed them in his basement and wherever else there was room." Further, the report said he "was strongly suspected of being a drug user, was rumored by neighbors to have been evicted from three previous residences in Washington, D.C., and was very much disliked by his neighbors there." Fireman's then told its agent to cancel Millstone's insurance. When the agent told them that Millstone was in fact a highly respected assistant managing editor at the St. Louis *Post-Dispatch* and had been a White House reporter in D.C., Fireman's rescinded the cancellation order. Millstone sued O'Hanlon when they refused to give him an adequate explanation of what had happened. The trial court awarded $2,500 actual damages, $25,000 punitive damages, and $12,500 attorney fees.

Issue: Did the reporting agency violate the act's requirements?

Decision: Yes, it did. Judgment for Millstone affirmed.

Rule: Credit investigators are required to take reasonable steps to verify information in credit reports.

Discussion: *By Justice* CLARK:

"The...contention is that O'Hanlon did not violate the accuracy or disclosure provisions of the Act...and that even if it did, Millstone was not damaged. Given the detailed account of the facts found in the record, we believe this contention merits a short answer.

"To us it seems amazing that O'Hanlon makes the claim that its agent followed reasonable procedures promulgated by it to attain the maximum possible accuracy. Everything in the record is to the contrary. It shows that O'Hanlon's agent devoted at most 30 minutes in preparing his report. His report was rife with innuendo, misstatement, and slander. Indeed, the recheck of his investigation shows that he depended solely on one biased informant; made no verification of the same despite O'Hanlon's requirement that there must be verification; and, finally, it took three days to recheck the original investigation, and every allegation therein was found untrue.

"O'Hanlon further asserts that its disclosures to Millstone completely revealed the nature and substance of the derogatory matters in its report. Again, the report proves otherwise. O'Hanlon sought at every step to block Millstone in his attempt to secure the rights given to him by the Act. Not only did O'Hanlon delay and mislead Millstone on the occasion of his first request, but it even did so on a second and third occasion. Not until Millstone brought pressure to bear, through the Federal Trade Commission, and, ultimately, through this lawsuit, did O'Hanlon make the disclosure required [by the Act]."

Ethical Dimension

How can a credit investigator know that the information being received is biased?

EQUAL CREDIT OPPORTUNITY ACT

To prevent discrimination in credit transactions on the basis of sex or marital status, the Equal Credit Opportunity Act (ECOA) was passed in 1974. Other prohibited bases for denial of credit were added in 1976: age, race, color, national origin, religion, and receipt of public assistance income. Each individual applicant for credit is now entitled to be judged on financial criteria, not on the basis of the lender's stereotypes. ECOA and its implementing regulations limit the kinds of information which may be requested on credit applications and the way in which it can be used. If credit is denied, the lender must notify the applicant of the reasons for the denial. ECOA is enforced by FTC proceedings and by private lawsuits for damages.

Creditors may not discriminate under ECOA regulations.

FAIR CREDIT BILLING ACT

Credit card companies are targeted by the Fair Credit Billing Act of 1974, another set of amendments to TILA. A customer has sixty days

Credit disputes are regulated by FCBA.

after a billing is sent within which to notify the credit card company, in writing, of any alleged error in the statement. The company must then reply within ninety days or two full billing cycles, whichever period is less. It must either correct the error, or if it believes the bill is correct, send a written statement which justifies the billing. Meanwhile, it cannot try to collect the disputed amount, close or limit the account, or report or threaten to report the failure to pay to a credit agency. After it complies with the act, the company must give the customer ten days in which to pay the account. If the customer still disputes the billing after receiving the company's written explanation, the company can make a report to a credit agency only if it indicates that the amount is disputed, and also notifies the customer of the agency's name and address. If it does file a report, it must also report the final settlement of the dispute. A company forfeits the first $50 of the account balance if it fails to follow any of these regulations. Customers may also file private civil lawsuits for violation of the FCBA.

FAIR DEBT COLLECTION PRACTICES ACT

FDCPA regulates collection procedures.

To deal with the abuses inflicted on consumers by debt collection agencies, Congress passed the Fair Debt Collection Practices Act in 1977. Threats, force, and fraud were widespread. Aggressive collection tactics included harassment and embarrassment of debtors and various kinds of trickery. The act's prohibitions are a catalog of the agencies' wrongdoing: harassment, oppression, threats, obscene language, repeated telephone calls, false statements, and unfair practices such as collect telephone calls. All such conduct is now prohibited. Collection agency contacting of third parties is generally illegal; it is permitted only when done in an attempt to locate the debtor. The agency cannot contact the debtor at unusual or inconvenient times or places (between 9 p.m. and 8 a.m. or at a friend's dinner party) without the debtor's consent. If the debtor is known to have an attorney handling the matter, the debtor cannot be contacted at all, unless the attorney agrees or fails to reply to the agency's communications. The agency must give the debtor the basic information about the claim within five days after first contacting the debtor. If the debtor responds within thirty days with a written notice that the debt is disputed, the agency can take no further collection steps until it sends verification of the claim to the debtor. FDCPA rules are enforced by the FTC, and private lawsuits are also permitted for collection agency violations.

■ Consumer Protection

All the disclosure requirements and reporting and collection limitations are also contained in the broad category called "consumer protection."

But there are also other specific regulations which do not fit neatly into either of those two sub-categories.

TILA gives a consumer debtor a three-day cancellation privilege where the debtor's principal residence is being used as collateral for the credit transaction. This privilege is not available for the transaction in which the debtor first acquires ownership of the home and enters into a mortgage agreement to finance the purchase. The cancellation privilege is only available for second mortgages and other transactions using the home as collateral, such as a home improvement loan. If the creditor does not make all the required disclosures, the three-day period does not commence until the required disclosures are made; otherwise, the three days are counted from the date the transaction was completed.

Consumers have a three-day cancellation privilege for second mortgages on homes.

In a drastic change from prior law, TILA sets an absolute limit of $50 on a credit card holder's liability for unauthorized charges. Previously, a card holder who did not notify the issuing company of a lost or stolen card could be held liable for the full amount of the unauthorized charges.

As discussed in the last chapter, the holder in due course doctrine prevents a person who has signed a negotiable instrument from asserting most defenses against a holder in due course of that instrument. In the consumer context, this meant that consumers who had been victimized by shoddy merchandise or sloppy services still had to pay the agreed contract price in full if they had signed such an instrument (they usually had to) and if it had been sold to a bank or finance company (it nearly always was). Many consumers were thus being substantially harmed by the HDC rule.

Some states took action to limit or to repeal the rule, but the major action was the FTC's adoption of Regulation 433. The regulation requires a notice in consumer credit contracts to the effect that any holder of the contract will be subject to all the consumer's defenses. The regulation covers credit sales in which the consumer signs a promissory note, those in which the contract itself contains an express waiver-of-defenses clause, and those in which the seller refers the consumer to a lending agency to get the financing for the sale. Checks, since they will typically be deposited and processed right away, are not covered by this regulation. Nor are situations in which the consumer obtains a loan first and then negotiates with a seller and pays cash for the merchandise. In that case, the loan will have to be repaid as promised, regardless of what happens with the merchandise. Failure to include the required notice will subject the lender or seller to a fine of up to $10,000 for each offense, in an FTC administrative proceeding. In the *Woffard* case the reverse happened; the seller used the notice when it didn't have to.

Under FTC Regulation 433, consumers cannot waive defenses.

FIRST NEW ENGLAND FINANCIAL CORP. V. WOFFARD

421 So.2d 590 (Fla. 1982)

Facts: Woffard bought a 36-foot sailing yacht from a yacht broker, who had suggested that he contact First New England Financial Corp. (FNEFC) to finance the deal. FNEFC represented out-of-state banks that wanted to make marine loans. The printed form that Woffard signed stated that the contract was automatically assigned by the seller to FNEFC. FNEFC in turn reassigned the contract to City Trust, a Connecticut bank whose name, address, and telephone number were also stated on the contract. The form contained the FTC statement prohibiting waivers of defenses in consumer contracts, but indicated that the rule did not apply if the purchase price of the consumer good was over $25,000. The price of the yacht was well over $50,000, so a waiver of defenses contract signed by Woffard would have been effective.

When Woffard first took the boat to sea, he found several manufacturing defects. He notified the manufacturer, the broker, FNEFC, and City Trust. He kept making his monthly payments for eight months, but finally stopped when no one would agree to fix the defects. City Trust and FNEFC sued for the $42,054.25 balance due. Woffard counterclaimed for return of the $12,349.56 down payment, plus his monthly payments and costs for docking and maintenance. The trial court found for Woffard.

Issue: Can the buyer assert his breach of warranty defenses?

Decision: Yes. Judgment for Woffard affirmed.

Rule: A buyer can assert all defenses against an assignee of the account unless the buyer has signed a negotiable instrument or an express waiver of defenses, and the assignee has purchased the account in good faith.

Discussion: *By Judge* DAUKSCH:

"As the amount financed in this consumer transaction exceeds $25,000, we look to applicable state law to determine whether appellant is subject to [Woffard's] claims/defenses. Under [UCC section] 9.206(1), an agreement by a buyer waiving any claims/defenses against the seller is enforceable by an assignee who takes his assignment for value, in good faith and without notice of any claim/defense. Such an agreement waiving claims/defenses often appears in the form of a waiver of defenses clause in a contract. There is no such clause in this contract. Section 679.206(1) also provides that a buyer who, as part of one transaction, signs both a negotiable instrument and a security agreement makes such an agreement waiving claims/defenses. The contract does not meet the requisites of negotiability and does not appear to be a negotiable instrument. Thus, [UCC section] 9.206 (1) is inapplicable....

"An assignee has traditionally been subject to defenses or setoffs existing before an account debtor is notified of the assignment. When the account debtor's defenses on an assigned claim arise from the contract between him and the assignor, it makes no difference whether the breach giving rise to the defense occurs before or after the account debtor is notified of the assignment. The account debtor may also have claims against the assignor which arise independently of that contract: an assignee is subject to all such claims which accrue before, and free of all those which accrue after, the account debtor is notified. The account debtor may waive his right to assert claims or defenses against the assignee to the extent provided in [UCC section] 9.206(1).... This is in accord with the general rule in sales transactions that the assignee takes his assignment subject to the purchaser's defenses, set-offs and counterclaims against the seller....

"Just as an assignee is subject to defenses and claims accruing before the obligor receives notification, so a sub-assignee is subject to defenses and claims accruing between the assignee and obligor before the obligor receives notice of the sub-assignment. Defenses and claims arising from the terms of the contract creating the right are available to the obligor regardless of when they accrue....

"[Woffard's] claim of breach of warranty arose out of the terms of the contract and also accrued before receipt of notification of assignment. Testimony during trial proved that [Woffard] told the seller that he specifically wanted to buy a sailing yacht that he could live aboard full time and also use for pleasure sailing. [Woffard] told the seller the yacht must be suitable for 'blue water' sailing (i.e., ocean sailing). Thus, if there was breach of warranty, it arose out of the terms of the contract (as incorporating the sale agreement) and accrued before [Woffard] received notification of assignment, in this case by receipt of the coupon payment books....

"To be effective, a seller's disclaimer of warranties in the sale of consumer goods must be part of the basis of the bargain between the parties.... The evidence indicates that

[Woffard] and seller entered into the sales agreement on the premise that the yacht was suitable for [his] purposes. Circumstances indicate that seller's disclaimer of warranty of fitness for particular purpose was not made a part of the bargain; to the contrary, seller's warranty of fitness for the particular purpose was an essential factor in the initial agreement between the parties.

"Appellant has not convinced this court that the lower court erred in ruling in [Woffard's] favor on the damages claim."

Ethical Dimension

Is it fair to permit Woffard to use his defense just because the seller had him sign the wrong credit contract?

Article 9 of the UCC regulates repossession of collateral.

Some debtor protection provisions are also included in the UCC. Article 9 does regulate the procedures for repossessing collateral and selling it after the debtor goes into default in a secured transaction. The creditor cannot "breach the peace" in repossessing the goods; this means no force can be used and, generally, that no door or gate can be opened without the debtor's permission. The creditor is given considerable flexibility in disposing of the repossessed goods, but all aspects of the disposition, including the price received, must be reasonable. As an alternative to disposition of the goods, the creditor can propose to keep the goods in satisfaction of the balance of the debt. The creditor must sell the goods if the debtor or any other creditor with an interest in them objects. If a consumer debtor has paid at least 60 percent of the contract price, the creditor must resell the goods unless the debtor signs a written waiver of these rights after default occurs. Unless otherwise agreed, the debtor is liable for any deficiency if the resale doesn't bring enough to pay off the balance, but is entitled to any surplus. At any time before there is a final disposition of the goods, the debtor has a right to redeem them by paying all sums due. If the creditor fails to comply with these requirements, some states prevent it from collecting any claimed deficiency. In all states, the creditor is liable for any damage the debtor sustains because of the noncompliance. In all states, a consumer debtor can collect a penalty for the creditor's noncompliance: 10 percent of the principal amount of the debt and 100 percent of the finance charges. In some states, the debtor may also be able to collect punitive damages. Whether punitive damages can be collected is the issue in the following case.

DAVIDSON V. FIRST BANK & TRUST CO., YALE

609 P.2d 1259 (Okla. 1976)

Facts: Davidson owned a marble-making business which was having some difficulty. First Bank held a security interest on the business's equipment. At First Bank's suggestion, Davidson hired Sneed to assist in the business. When differences arose between Davidson and Sneed, the bank tried to enforce its security interest although the loan was not yet in default. This problem was worked out, and the bank refinanced the loan. When the two men had another argument several months later, Sneed took the two major pieces of business equipment to a location across the street, where he opened his own competing business. Davidson went out of business and defaulted on his last loan payment. Sneed let the bank's agents into Davidson's store, where they repossessed the rest of the equipment. The bank posted only three notices of its public sale, even though much of the equipment was unique. It kept the front door locked on the day of the sale. The bank sold the items to Sneed four months later, for one-fourth of their value. The jury awarded $20,000 punitive damages. The Court of Appeals affirmed the award.

Issue: Can a secured party be held liable for punitive damages where its violation of UCC procedures amounts to common-law conversion?

Decision: Yes. Punitive damages award is affirmed.

Rule: Any illegal taking of another's rights in personal property is conversion. A secured party may be guilty of conversion where it acts in disregard of the debtor's rights.

Discussion: *By Justice DOOLIN:*

"Bank has tacitly conceded it failed to dispose of the collateral in a commercially reasonable manner.... It bases its right to rehearing on lack of authority of a jury to award punitive damages (1) where there is no determination of actual damages and (2) where the repossession itself is not wrongful.

"It is settled in Oklahoma that for a jury to award punitive damages, actual damages must first be shown. The trial court and the parties stipulated [agreed] the value of the collateral equaled the debt, consequently if punitive damages are awarded the requisite actual damages are present by stipulation. Bank may not extricate itself from liability for punitive damages by admitting the amount of actual damages sustained and then claiming because it made this concession there are no actual damages on which to base a punitive award.

"Bank's second point is more complex. Although Davidson elected to sue in conversion, petition for rehearing is based on the idea that under the U.C.C. punitive damages should not be awarded because the U.C.C. does not specifically provide for them. §1–106 provides exemplary [punitive] damages may not be had except as specifically provided in the Code or by other rule of law. Although the U.C.C. does not explicitly allow punitive damages for [a] commercially unreasonable sale, if that right does exist outside the Code, it is retained and permitted through §1–106.

"Numerous cases, not decided under the U.C.C., have awarded punitive damages for actions involved in repossession of collateral where aspects of malice, fraud, or oppression are shown. Although the U.C.C. does not favor punitive damages, these jurisdictions have applied rules of damages, including punitive, in proper cases under aggravated circumstances....

"A secured party who repossesses (and sells) without judicial action subjects himself to liability for any tortious conduct. A bank taking possession of collateral for a defaulted loan cannot be permitted to ignore completely the rights and interests of the debtor. The U.C.C. provides the Bank a right to minimize its losses by conducting a commercially reasonable sale; it affords the defaulting borrower fair value or credit for the repossessed chattel.

"Submitting the question of punitive damages to the jury in the circumstances of this case was proper."

Ethical Dimension

Could First Bank claim to have acted ethically in this case?

B ANKRUPTCY

The national bankruptcy laws provide a different kind of regulation for credit transactions. Rather than focusing on the details of the particular credit arrangement, bankruptcy law provides a mechanism for dealing with the debtor who is experiencing financial difficulties. Congress adopted a new bankruptcy code in 1978 and passed major amendments to it in 1984.

■ Purposes and Policy

Bankruptcy law has two major purposes: to give the debtor a fresh start, and to provide equal treatment to creditors with the same types of claims. Reality, however, may be a bit different than these two ideals would indicate. A prior bankruptcy may make creditors somewhat reluctant to extend credit, even though an individual is only permitted to go through bankruptcy every six years. The debtor is not discharged of all obligations; some debts survive bankruptcy. The bankruptcy statute does classify creditors so that some categories of debts are paid before other categories get anything. And creditors who have been prudent enough to create secured debts will have preferences to the extent of their collateral.

Despite these limitations, bankruptcy is an increasingly popular solution to various kinds of financial difficulties. Hundreds of thousands of businesses and individuals go through bankruptcy every year in this country. Bankruptcy of a customer-debtor is thus a very real risk to every lender, credit seller, and financing agency.

■ Types of Bankruptcy Proceedings

There are actually two possible approaches in the bankruptcy act for dealing with financial problems. The basic approach is the one most people probably think of when the word "bankruptcy" is mentioned: a **liquidation** proceeding. A trustee is appointed to collect the debtor's assets, sell them, and pay off the creditors. But there is also another, more creative possibility: a **reorganization** proceeding. The business or individual debtor is given a chance to modify existing obligations and to develop a repayment plan.

Bankruptcy provides for either liquidation or reorganization.

Liquidation proceedings are covered in Chapter 7 of the bankruptcy act. Most business reorganizations are regulated under Chapter 11. Reorganizations of family farming businesses are now governed by a new section, Chapter 12, which was added to the statute in 1986. Chapter 13 deals with individual repayment plans for personal debts. These Chapter 13 repayment plans represent a kind of personal financial reorganization.

■ Chapter 7 Procedure

The bankruptcy proceeding is begun by filing a petition with the appropriate U.S. District Court. Special bankruptcy judges are appointed by the president for fourteen-year terms. The bankruptcy judge to whom the case is referred will be in charge, to interpret the bankruptcy act and to ensure that it is being followed. If state law issues arise which are not properly decided by a bankruptcy court, those parts of the case may have to be referred to an appropriate state court for decision. For some special situations relating to interstate commerce, any interested party may request that the U.S. District Court itself decide the issue. Most issues will be decided by the bankruptcy judge, whose rulings can then be appealed to the U.S. District Court, the U.S. Court of Appeals, and ultimately, the U.S. Supreme Court.

FILING A BANKRUPTCY PETITION

Liquidation may be commenced voluntarily or involuntarily.

The liquidation may be filed voluntarily by the individual or business debtor. Creditors may also file an involuntary petition against the debtor. If the debtor has twelve or more creditors, at least three of them must sign the petition. If there are fewer than twelve, any one of them can file an involuntary petition. The creditor(s) who file must have claims of $5000 or more, over and above any collateral they have. The creditor(s) filing must allege that the debtor is unable to pay debts as they become due, or that within the 120 days prior to the filing, the debtor made a general transfer of assets to a trustee for the benefit of creditors. In other words, a person cannot be forced into bankruptcy unless one of these two things is proved.

The filing of the petition prevents creditors from taking any further independent steps to collect their claims against the debtor. If they want their money, they will have to participate in the bankruptcy proceeding. If the debtor is a business, an interim trustee may be appointed to take control and to prevent waste or transfer of its assets. Otherwise, the debtor will remain in possession for the time being.

ORDER FOR RELIEF

If the debtor has filed a voluntary petition or does not contest an involuntary one, the bankruptcy court will automatically enter an "order for relief." This means that the debtor will go through bankruptcy. If the debtor contests an involuntary petition, no such order will be issued unless the creditors prove one of the two conditions noted above. Once the order is entered, the debtor will need to prepare and file lists of assets, liabilities, creditors, and any claimed exemptions.

CREDITORS' MEETING

The trustee manages the debtor's affairs.

The judge will hold a meeting of the creditors, at which they normally select a trustee to take over the debtor's financial affairs. The judge must officially appoint the trustee. The trustee's job is to collect all the debtor's property and to use it to pay off the creditors in accordance with the statutory rules. Obviously, if the debtor has made fraudulent transfers of assets to friends and relatives for less than fair market value, those assets will have to be turned over to the trustee. Even payments to favored creditors within the 90 days prior to the filing of the petition will have to be returned (if the payment was more than $650). Those creditors which the debtor tried to favor will have to wait for their proper turn in the bankruptcy proceeding. The debtor cannot change the statutory priorities by paying some creditors and then filing for bankruptcy.

EXEMPT PROPERTY

Not all the debtor's property has to be turned over, however. The bankruptcy statute provides a long list of exemptions. States may choose to have their own lists of exemptions used for their citizens; some states are even more generous than the national act. The bankruptcy act's list includes up to $7,500 for the debtor's interest in a home; up to $1,200 for the debtor's interest in a motor vehicle; up to $200 per item, with a maximum total of $4,000, for personal items—household goods and furnishings, appliances, clothing, books, animals, crops, and the like; up to $500 in jewelry; up to $400 in any other property, plus up to $3,750 of unused home equity may be applied to any other property; up to $750 for tools of the debtor's trade; life insurance contracts; up to $4,000 in interest and dividends from certain kinds of life insurance policies; health aids prescribed by a doctor; payments from Social Security, disability, alimony, and the like, which are reasonably necessary to support the debtor or dependents; future receipts of some insurance and liability payments. The statutory dollar limits indicate that this is not exactly "the lifestyles of the rich and famous;" nevertheless, an individual debtor can come out of the process with enough for a fresh start.

Some of the debtor's property is exempt from bankruptcy.

CREDITORS' CLAIMS

Unsecured creditors (those who have no collateral securing the debt) must file a "proof of claim" with the court. A **proof of claim** is a written, signed statement indicating the nature and amount of the debt. If a secured creditor's claim exceeds the amount of its collateral, and it wishes to participate in the proceeding, it must also file a proof of claim. The trustee may not allow some claims, where the debtor had a defense against liability. The trustee must be satisfied, in other words, that the claim is a valid one. The bankruptcy judge may have to make a ruling on some of these disputed claims. The trustee may also question whether a particular creditor in fact does have a secured claim; those disputes, too, may require rulings from the bankruptcy judge.

Not all claims which are allowed will be paid at the same time, or to the same extent. Creditors who have valid secured claims will of course have the first right to payment from the sale proceeds of their pieces of collateral. But not all creditors with claims against the general asset values in the debtor's estate are treated the same, either. The bankruptcy act establishes seven categories of claims which are given priority of payment, ahead of "general" creditors. All expenses of administering the estate are paid first. What this means in plain English is that all the lawyers and accountants who have been advising the

Some creditor's claims are given priority.

various parties during the proceeding are paid before other creditors. As with any claim, these fees will have to be allowed by the trustee. The trustee's own compensation also falls in this first category. Next to be paid are persons who extended credit to a debtor business during the period between the filing of an involuntary petition and the court's order for relief or appointment of a trustee. Persons who kept the debtor business going by supplying goods, services, and credit should not be disadvantaged by their helpfulness. The next two categories protect employees. Wage claims up to $2,000 per person, for earnings from the 90 days prior to the filing of the petition or cessation of business, are given third priority. Fourth in line are claims for payments to benefit plans, earned within the prior 180 days, up to $2,000 per person, less any wages paid under the third priority. (No employee will receive more than $2,000 combined wages and benefits under these two priorities.) Grain growers and U.S. commercial fishermen now have a fifth priority claim against a debtor who has stored their products. Consumers who made advance payments for goods or services not delivered have sixth priority, against their bankrupt seller, for up to $900 per claim. Government tax claims have seventh priority. Creditors in each category are entitled to be paid in full before any payments are made to creditors in lower priority categories. Only after each of these seven groups has been paid in full will the general unsecured creditors receive any payments on their claims. Of course, not all priority categories will apply to all debtors, but any that do will have to be recognized and those creditors paid in the specified order.

DISCHARGE

Generally, at the conclusion of the proceeding, an individual will receive a discharge from any further liability for any of the listed debts. Corporations wishing to stay in business are not eligible to receive such discharges from any of their debts which remain unpaid. During or after the bankruptcy proceeding, however, the corporation's existence might be terminated by a separate procedure under its state's corporation law. Discharges will not be given to debtors who have withheld or destroyed property or financial records, failed to obey proper court orders, or committed bribery or other crimes during the process. A debtor may waive the right to be discharged. Once the discharge is given, the creditors are prevented from doing anything to try to collect any unpaid amounts on the discharged debts.

Not all debts are discharged in bankruptcy.

Not all debts can be discharged. The bankruptcy act lists as nondischargable: taxes and fines due to governments; alimony and child support obligations; amounts owing because of the debtor's fraud or embezzlement while acting as a fiduciary; liability for money obtained by false pretenses; liability for willful or malicious injury to person or property; injuries caused by the debtor's driving while intoxicated; educational loans which became due within the seven years prior to the filing of the petition. Claims of creditors who were not notified of the proceeding in time to participate, even though the debtor knew of the claim, are also not discharged. Where a debtor has purchased more than $500 worth of luxury goods and services from a single creditor during the forty days prior to the petition or has received cash advances of more than $1,000 during the twenty days prior to the petition, such creditors may ask the court to decide that their claims are not discharged. Similarly, if the debts are primarily consumer debts, the court may dismiss a voluntary petition altogether if it finds that a bankruptcy discharge would be a "substantial abuse" of the statute. Substantial abuse of the bankruptcy process means that the debtor was able to pay existing debts and is trying to avoid paying them.

■ Business Reorganization Under Chapter 11

A business faced with what it believes is a temporary and curable financial problem may use a Chapter 11 reorganization to gain some breathing room. Creditors may feel they will be better off by working out a rehabilitation of the debtor rather than forcing it into a Chapter 7 liquidation. A Chapter 11 petition may thus be voluntary or involuntary, following the same basic procedure outlined above.

Chapter 11 governs corporate reorganizations.

The court enters an order for relief and appoints a creditors' committee, usually the seven largest unsecured creditors. A committee to represent the interests of the stockholders is also appointed. The creditors' committee, after examining the status of the debtor business, will decide whether to proceed with a reorganization or ask the court to convert the proceeding to Chapter 7. The creditors' committee may also recommend that the court appoint a trustee to run the business rather than leave company management in control. The debtor has the exclusive right to propose a reorganization plan for the first 120 days following the filing and then has another 60 days to try to convince the creditors to accept the plan. After the 120 days, the trustee or any creditor can propose a plan.

The reorganization plan must classify creditor claims and ownership interests and indicate which classes will be adversely affected by the plan. Normally the court will not approve a plan unless it has been accepted by each such class. Two-thirds of the dollar value of each affected ownership class must vote in favor. Two-thirds of the dollar value and a majority in number of each such creditor class must vote in favor. The consent of owners and creditors whose rights were not impaired is not required. The court may also approve a plan that did not receive the required vote if the members of the affected class are treated in a "fair and equitable manner" by the plan. Any persons voting against the plan can insist that they receive at least what they would have received from a Chapter 7 liquidation of the debtor.

These procedures are at issue in the *White* case.

IN RE WHITE

41 B.R. 227 (Bankr. S.D. Tenn. 1984)

Facts: Thomas C. White had owned a small land-surveying business for over eleven years. He employed his wife (a co-debtor), his two sons, and three other employees. Depressed economic conditions in the Waverly area led to financial problems in 1981, and the Whites defaulted on several mortgage payments. They filed a Chapter 11 petition in 1983.

Midland Bank held mortgages on four parcels of real estate and was the Whites' largest creditor with a $146,000 total claim. Midland was permitted to foreclose on three parcels, and wanted to do the same on the fourth parcel, an 87-acre family farm. The Whites' proposed plan would have paid its creditors $2,800 per month from the surveying business, plus the proceeds received by subdividing part of the family farm. Under the proposed plan, Midland's $12,000 claim would be secured by the business's accounts receivable and be paid off at $270 per month with interest at 12 percent until paid in full. Midland's other claim for $88,200 would be secured by the farm, would accrue interest at the FMHA rate, and would be paid off in ten years. Any proceeds from subdividing the farm would go to Midland.

Midland was the only creditor who objected to the plan. Its objections were based on its belief that (1) White had not had enough income in the prior two years to fund the plan as proposed; (2) the local real estate market was depressed; (3) needed road improvement for development would cost at least $30,000 rather than the $1,500 estimated by the Whites; and (4) the interest rates were too low.

Issue: Does the proposed plan meet Chapter 11's requirements?

Decision: Yes. The plan is confirmed.

Rule: To be confirmed, a reorganization plan must be proposed in good faith, be feasible, and be fair and equitable.

Discussion: *By Judge* PAINE:

"In order for a plan of reorganization to be approved by this court, the plan must comply with all the requirements of Chapter 11.... The court has a duty to examine the plan and determine whether or not the plan conforms to the requirements of 11 U.S.C. §1129, regardless of whether objections are filed.... In fulfilling this duty, the court concludes that the specific objections raised by Midland are without merit.

"First, Midland asserts that the plan was not proposed in good faith.... Essentially, a reorganization plan is proposed in good faith when there is 'a reasonable likelihood that the plan will achieve a result consistent with the objectives and purposes of the Bankruptcy Code.'... Herein, the debtors have proposed a plan which provides for payments to both secured and unsecured creditors. The secured creditors will receive the value of their collateral plus interest while the unsecured creditors will receive payment contingent upon both the surveying business and the subdivision of the debtor's property. The court finds that the financial assumptions underlying the debtors' plan are reasonable and there is a likelihood of success. Thus, the requisite good faith has been established by the debtors.

"Midland also claims that the proposed plan...is not feasible and will most likely be followed by liquidation. Courts have held that in order to determine whether a plan is feasible, the court must examine '...the adequacy of the capital structures; the business's earning power; economic conditions; management's ability; the probability of the present management's continuation; and any other factors related to the successful performance of the plan.'... The court need not find that the plan is guaranteed of success, but only that a reasonable expectation of success exists.... At trial, the court heard testimony concerning the present earning power of the surveying business and the projected earning power of the business based on work in progress. The court also heard testimony concerning prospective purchasers of the subdivided farmland. Based on this evidence, as well as the debtors' demonstrated expertise in the surveying business, the court has determined that the plan is feasible within the meaning of §1129(a)(11).

"Finally, Midland alleges that the debtors' plan does not meet the fair and equitable requirements of §1129(b)(2) and thus, may not be confirmed over its objection. The court finds that the debtors' plan allows Midland to retain its lien on the property securing its claims, provides Midland with deferred cash payments totaling the allowed amount of its claims plus appropriate interest, and provides that Midland receive any proceeds obtained from the sale of its collateral. With respect to Midland, the court finds that the debtors' plan meets both the fair and equitable requirement of §1129(b)(2) and the requirement that the plan not discriminate unfairly pursuant to §1129(b)(1).... The plan proposed by the debtor not only conforms to all of the applicable requirements of §1129(a), but also conforms to the requirements of §1129(b) with respect to each class of dissenting creditors. Therefore, the court hereby orders that the plan proposed by the debtor is confirmed.

Ethical Dimension

Why should one creditor be able to prevent the adoption of the debtor's reorganization plan? Is that fair?

■ Family Farm Reorganization Under Chapter 12

Family farm reorganizations are governed by Chapter 12.

Responding to the serious economic problems which smaller farmers were facing in the 1980s, Congress added Chapter 12 to the bankruptcy act in 1986. Chapter 12 is designed to give small family farming operations a chance to work their way out of financial difficulties. To prevent the use of its more favorable procedures by the giant agribusinesses which exist in many areas, Chapter 12 has several specific qualifications which the farmer-debtor must meet.

The farmer must have regular income. At least half of the farmer's income (or combined incomes of farmer and spouse) during the year preceding the filing must have come from farming operations. This requirement thus excludes the part-time farmer. The total debt must be less than $1.5 million, and at least 80 percent of the fixed, certain ("noncontingent") debts must arise out of the farming operations. A family corporation or partnership may be able to use Chapter 12, if the business is more than half owned by the family, if the family actually operates the farm, and if it meets the dollar and percentage limits noted above.

The farmer usually stays in possession and operates the farm, but a trustee is appointed by the court to oversee the operation. The trustee has the power to sell unneeded land or equipment without creditors' consent and prior to the adoption of a reorganization plan. The farmer has ninety days to develop a plan. The court will hold a hearing on the plan and may confirm it over the objections of creditors. Here again, the unsecured creditors must receive at least what they would have under a Chapter 7 liquidation. If the plan is approved by the court and fulfilled by the debtor, the debtor is entitled to a discharge from further liability. The debtor may also receive a discharge if the debtor is prevented from fulfilling the plan because of subsequent "hardship."

■ Individual Debt Adjustments Under Chapter 13

Individuals may also wish to work their way out of financial difficulty rather than give up most of their assets and go through liquidation. Chapter 13 gives persons with regular incomes that choice. Creditors cannot force a person into Chapter 13; only voluntary petitions are permitted. Only persons with regular incomes can use Chapter 13; self-employed persons are included. The debtor (or debtor and spouse) must owe less than $100,000 in fixed, unsecured debts and less than $350,000 in secured debts.

Individual debt adjustments are covered by Chapter 13.

The debtor's petition indicates either insolvency (that is, an excess of debts over assets), or an inability to pay debts as they mature. The petition requests a composition, in which each creditor receives a portion of what is due, or an extension, in which the debtor makes smaller payments over a longer period of time. The debtor prepares a payment plan and submits it to the secured creditors. If they accept it, and the court feels that it is proposed in good faith and meets legal requirements, the court approves the plan and appoints a trustee to carry it out. The act requires completion of a plan in three years or less, but the court may approve a plan for up to five years for good cause shown. The plan will not be approved if the trustee or an unsecured creditor objects unless the objecting creditor will in fact get the full value of its claim or unless the debtor has committed all expected disposable income to pay off creditors. The plan may be modified by the court subsequently, if the debtor's situation changes materially.

REVIEW

Long-term financing transactions involving stocks and bonds are generally regulated under the national securities acts. While short-term financing transactions will usually not be subject to those regulations, they are controlled and limited by a host of other national and state regulations. Most states have statutory limits on the amount of interest that can be charged and impose penalties for violation of these limits. National and state laws now require full disclosure in many credit transactions, particularly those where the debtor is a consumer. Debt collection and exchange of credit data are now also regulated by both state and national governments. Criminal penalties, administrative fines, actual damages, and punitive damages may be incurred for violations of these regulations. Both levels of government have also been very active participants in the consumer protection movement, and many new regulations have been adopted. Finally, overall discipline to the financial system is provided by the national bankruptcy act, which provides for a liquidation of the debtor's assets, reorganization of the insolvent debtor, or an extended time payment plan for individuals with regular income. In any case, the rights of secured creditors will be given preferential treatment to the extent of their collateral security.

REVIEW QUESTIONS AND PROBLEMS

1. What is the difference between a Chapter 7 and a Chapter 11 proceeding in bankruptcy?

2. What protections are given to a debtor who defaults on a secured transaction?

3. What is the significance of FTC Regulation 433?

4. Why are state "usury laws" important to business?

5. What creditor claims are given priority in a bankruptcy liquidation?

6. What property may a debtor exclude from a bankruptcy liquidation?

7. Harlan Stumbo married Lynn Meere in December, 1989. He was then a captain in the U.S. Navy. Anticipating retirement from the service, Harlan and his wife bought a cosmetics boutique in April, 1990; they borrowed $8000 from a local bank to finance the purchase. Harlan retired in October, 1990; the local Navy base also closed that month. Business at the boutique fell off sharply after the base closed. Harlan hoped to make a profit on a real estate development, but the base closing also ended demand for new homes and offices. Despite these financial reverses, the couple spent over $30,000 on new credit purchases during the next five months—a new car, a fur coat, new furniture, and travel. Their creditors objected to their being discharged in bankruptcy, claiming that they had been engaged in a scheme to defraud by buying on credit with no intent to pay. Should Harlan and Lynn be discharged by the bankruptcy court? Explain.

8. In 1987 Richard Henry Hatfield defaulted on his car payments and had his car repossessed. Bluster Bank turned in his name to the local area credit agency, but did not include his social security number. In 1989 Richard Homer Hatfield applied for credit at a Super Store located in the same city. Super Store ran a credit check on Richard Homer Hatfield, and the credit agency reported the bad information it had on file against Richard Henry Hatfield. Super Store denied the credit application of Richard Homer Hatfield. When he discovered that a mistake had been made, he contacted the credit agency to have them correct the mistake. They failed to do so, and replied to his inquiries by sending him letters addressed to Richard Henry Hatfield. Richard Homer Hatfield sued the credit agency for damages and attorney fees. Should he collect? Why or why not?

9. Maxie and Jackie Elmer called Mortgage Company to ask about refinancing their house. When they met with the Mortgage Company representative, he asked them to sign some preliminary documents so their credit could be checked and the necessary paperwork could be processed. He said they would sign the final loan papers when they actually received the money. He gave them one copy of a "Notice of Right to Cancel." (TILA requires that each debtor be given a copy of this form.) One of the forms that the Elmers signed was actually a negotiable promissory note for $80,000, the amount they had requested. They never received the money from Mortgage Company, which sold the note to Bessed Bank. Mortgage Company is now in bankruptcy. Bessed Bank sues to collect the note, claiming it is a holder in due course. The

Elmers assert the TILA violation as a defense. Which party should win this lawsuit? Explain.

10. Mickey filed a voluntary petition in bankruptcy, seeking a discharge of his debts, including $6,800 in educational loans. Mickey has completed three years towards his BBA degree. He was recently divorced and moved back into his parents' home. He has less than $100 in the bank, no car, and no job. He receives about $100 per week in unemployment benefits. His total debts are just over $15,000. Mickey claims that he will be subjected to "undue hardship" if the educational loans are not discharged, too. Is he correct? Discuss.

SUGGESTIONS FOR FURTHER READING

Bowers, "Cash Tender Offers and Mandated Disclosure," *American Business Law Journal* 20 (Spring 1982): 59.

Fox, "New Hope for the Harassed Consumer: The Federal Fair Debt Collection Practices Act," *American Business Law Journal* 18 (Spring 1980): 19.

Graml, "Bondholder Rights in Leveraged Buyouts in the Aftermath of Metropolitan Life Insurance Co. v. RJR Nabisco, Inc.," *American Business Law Journal* 29 (Spring 1991): 1.

Hiller, "Good Faith Lending," *American Business Law Journal* 26 (Winter 1989): 783.

13
LAW
OF
EMPLOYMENT

"He that hath a Trade, hath an Estate."
Benjamin Franklin

LEARNING OBJECTIVES: After you have studied this chapter, you should be able to:

EXPLAIN the contract basis of the employment relationship.

DISCUSS the various theories of "wrongful discharge."

DEFINE the limits on employees' privacy rights off the job.

IDENTIFY potential conflicts relating to employees' privacy rights on the job.

EXPLAIN an employee's duty of loyalty, including the post-employment duty.

P REVIEW

The foundation of employment law is the contract of hire, in which the employee promises to perform certain services and the employer promises to pay compensation in return. However, this relationship is heavily regulated by government, not only in the U.S., but in many other countries as well. This chapter focuses on the employment contract, and on four major problem areas: the "at-will" rule, the employee's right to privacy, the ownership of intellectual property, and post-employment obligations.

T HE EMPLOYMENT CONTRACT

General rules of contract law apply to the formation of the employment contract. One of the parties will make an offer, which the other will accept. Of course, there may be several counter-proposals before the parties finally reach an agreement. Value is promised each way— services for compensation. If the term of employment is specified as lasting over one year from the date the contract is made, it must be in writing to be enforceable in court. If a complete written contract is signed, its terms cannot be changed by proof of alleged "extra" promises made before it is signed.

■ Later Modifications

As a rule, to be enforceable, any later modifications of the employment contract must provide new value to both sides. That is, a one-way promise which benefits only one party is not enforceable as part of the contract. This is another example of the pre-existing duty rule, discussed in Chapter 7. If the employment contract is for an indefinite period, or "at-will," as many are, this problem is solved. In the at-will employment contract, neither party is bound to continue the relationship for any specific period. In effect, therefore, the parties make a new contract each day, so they are free to agree to any new terms at any time.

New value must be given in exchange for new promises to be binding.

■ Enforcement

Equity courts normally did not issue specific performance orders for employment contracts. First, most services could be performed by others and were thus not "unique." Money damages for any difference would thus be a full remedy for the injured party if the substitute performance cost more than the original contract which had been breached. Second, services contracts would be much too hard to supervise, to see whether the court's decree was being followed. With land or unique goods, either the subject-matter was given to the buyer or it wasn't. With services, it's often hard to tell whether the work is being

Employees are not usually ordered to continue working for an employer.

done as promised. In the U.S., there is also a third reason for not giving specific performance of services contracts—the Thirteenth Amendment. Forcing one party to work for another would seem to be "involuntary servitude," which is directly prohibited by the Thirteenth Amendment.

Some regulatory statutes, such as the civil rights laws and the labor laws, do provide for forced hiring or rehiring of employees. These statutes are exceptions to the general rule. These regulations will be covered more fully in the next chapter.

TERMINATION OF THE CONTRACT

Many disputes arise when employees are terminated. Sometimes the employer has valid reasons for doing so, but sometimes improper motives enter into the decision. As many U.S. industries went through a down-sizing process in the 1980s and early 1990s, courts were increasingly called on to resolve these disputes.

Discharge of Employee

Most employees are at will.

Where an employee has a binding contract to work for a specific period of time, discharge of that person by the employer would be a breach of the contract unless the employer could show just cause for the early termination. The vast majority of employees, however, are not hired for a specific period, but are rather "at-will" employees. They are free to leave at any time, without liability to the employer for breach of contract. Likewise, the employer is completely free to discharge them at any time, for any reason or for no reason at all. The regulatory statutes discussed in the next chapter also make exceptions to this rule. A discharge cannot be based on race, sex, religion, union membership, and other specified reasons.

The general rule still prevails for cases not covered by these special regulatory exceptions. A business owner who fired an at-will employee in order to hire one of the owner's relatives would not seem to be violating any of these regulations and would be protected against a breach of contract lawsuit by the general rule on at-will employees. No regulatory statute prevents an employer from firing employees for this sort of random, arbitrary reason.

Union contracts, tenure, and civil service protect some employees.

Union collective bargaining agreements generally require an employer to prove cause for discharge of an employee who is a member of the bargaining unit covered by the contract. However, only about 15 percent of nonfarm workers are union members. Government workers are given similar protection under civil service rules, and professors and teachers are usually protected by tenure. For these employees, cause for termination must be proven at a hearing. Again, these government workers may represent 10 to 15 percent of the nation's employees. Most workers, perhaps as many as two-thirds of the total, are thus still subject to dismissal at the whim of the employer. They do not have the protection of a specific term of employment, and they are not protected by a union, civil service, or tenure.

For most workers, then—and for their employers—the at-will employment rules are of vital importance. Both sides need to know what the outer limits to this doctrine are, or indeed if there are any outer limits. During the 1980s, the courts struggled to draw the line between lawful and unlawful dismissals as more and more lawsuits were brought against employers for "wrongful discharge." Figure 13-1 shows some of the personal characteristics of the plaintiffs bringing these lawsuits.

■ Theories of Wrongful Discharge

Few would question an employer's right to discharge an employee for cause. An employee caught stealing money or other property *should* be fired, in most cases. One committing other criminal acts or intentional torts *should* be subject to discipline up to and including termination, depending on the circumstances. Such cases are not really the issue.

EXERCISE OF RIGHTS THEORY

The problem cases are those in which the employee has done nothing wrong, or at least has committed no crime or tort, and has been doing a proper job and complying with all normal job requirements. Examples include firings for failing to contribute to a political fund favored by the employer, for filing a worker's compensation claim after an on-the-job injury, or for serving on a jury. Forced political contributions violate the employee's First Amendment rights. Worker's compensation is a right given to injured employees by state statute. Jury service is a duty imposed on the employee as a citizen. Should we permit

Discharge because an employee exercised legal rights is probably wrongful.

FIGURE 13–1
Plaintiffs in Wrongful Discharge Suits

Male	Female
68.6%	31.4%

Executive	Middle Mgmt.	Other
13.6%	39.8%	46.6%

Years of Service

< 1 Year	1–5 Years	6–10 Years	11–15 Yrs	> 15 Years
15%	35%	20%	10%	20%

discharge of an employee simply for exercising constitutional or statutory rights? Some states have said no and limited the at-will doctrine under the "exercise of rights" theory.

EXPRESS OR IMPLIED CONTRACT THEORIES

Other courts have constructed a limitation based on the theory of express or implied contract.

Companies may make promises of continued employment.

Promise of Continuing Employment Theory. If there was, in fact, an agreement that the employee would not be discharged except for cause, that in effect there would be a job "for life," then any firing other than for cause would be a breach of contract. How does an employer make such a promise of lifetime employment? Courts have been quite creative in defining these promises. They have been found in such seemingly innocent statements as "your career here at X Company." The word *career* is read as implying that one can stay with X Company as long as performance is satisfactory. Statements in employee handbooks or personnel manuals providing for discharge hearings might be interpreted as meaning that no one will be discharged unless there is a hearing and cause for the discharge is proven at the hearing. Assurances by recruiters or supervisors might be taken as meaning that one's future with the company is secure. Placing an employee in special training programs could be seen as a promise of future promotion to the company position in which the special training could be used. And so on.

The *Toussaint* case is one of the leading precedents in this area.

TOUSSAINT V. BLUE CROSS/BLUE SHIELD OF MICHIGAN

292 N.W.2d 880 (Mich. 1980)

Facts: Charles Toussaint claims he was wrongfully discharged by Blue Cross/Blue Shield of Michigan. A second plaintiff, Walter Ebling, claims wrongful discharge by Masco Corporation. When he was hired in 1967, Toussaint was given a "Supervisory Manual" and a pamphlet of "Guidelines." These documents contained the Blue Cross personnel procedures for discipline and termination. Toussaint claimed that these documents indicated that he could be discharged "for just cause only," and only after warnings, notice, hearing, and other specified procedures. He claimed that he was fired without being given all these protections. Ebling made similar claims against Masco. Toussaint was awarded $73,000 by a jury, but the Court of Appeals reversed. Ebling was awarded $300,000 by a jury; his award was affirmed by a different three-judge panel of the Court of Appeals. The Michigan Supreme Court granted review of both cases.

Issue: Can employer documents create limitations on the at-will contract?

Decision: Yes. Both jury awards are affirmed.

Rule: There is no legal reason why an employer cannot agree to limit its right to discharge an employee at will.

Discussion: *By Justice* LEVIN:

"We see no reason why an employment contract which does not have a definite term—the term is 'indefinite'—cannot legally provide job security. When a prospective employee inquires about job security and the employer agrees that the employee shall be employed as long as he does the job, a fair construction is that the employer has agreed to give up his right to discharge at will without assigning cause and may discharge only for cause (good or just cause). The result is that the employee, if discharged without good or just cause, may maintain an action for wrongful discharge.

"Suppose the contracts here were written, not oral, and had provided in so many words that the employment was to continue for the life of the employee who could not be discharged except for cause (including as a cause, if you will, his attaining the company's mandatory retirement age). To construe such an agreement as terminable at the will of the employer would be tantamount to saying...that a contract of indefinite duration '*cannot* be made other than terminable at will by a provision that states that an employee will not be discharged except for cause'...and that only in exceptional circumstances, where there are 'distinguishing features or provisions or a consideration in addition to the services to be rendered,' would an employee be permitted to bargain for a legally enforceable agreement providing job security.

"Where the employment is for a definite term—a year, five years, ten years—it is implied, if not expressed, that the employee can be discharged only for good cause, and collective bargaining agreements often provide that discharge shall only be for good or just cause. There is, thus, no public policy against providing job security or prohibiting an employer from agreeing not to discharge except for good or just cause. That being the case, we can see no reason why such a provision in a contract having no definite term of employment with a single employee should necessarily be unenforceable and regarded, in effect, as against public policy and beyond the power of the employer to contract.

"Toussaint and Ebling were hired for responsible positions. They negotiated specifically regarding job security with the persons who interviewed and hired them. If Blue Cross or Masco had desired, they could have established a company policy of requiring prospective employees to acknowledge that they served at the will or the pleasure of the company and, thus, have avoided the misunderstandings that generated this litigation."

Ethical Dimension

Is it fair to hold an employer liable for statements made in recruiting brochures or employee handbooks?

In response to decisions such as Toussaint, employers have examined their personnel materials and tried to remove language which could be interpreted by courts as implying continuous employment. In addition, many have inserted a specific statement to the effect that employment is at-will and that there is no guarantee of continued employment. The employer would then argue that there could be no ambiguity about the nature of the employment relationship. Any new employee would be very clear about the terms of the contract. Any prior employee who continued on the job after being notified that the clarifying language had been added to the personnel manual or employee handbook would be agreeing to the new language by staying with the company. Such clear language would seem to eliminate the "promise of continuing employment" theory.

Some courts imply a promise to deal with employees in good faith.

Implied Good Faith Theory. Quite apart from the "continuing employment" theory, there is another contract argument which some courts have adopted as a limitation on the at-will doctrine. Some courts have held that every contract imposes on the parties a duty to deal with each other in good faith, as to the subject-matter of that contract. Thus, even though there is no guarantee of employment for a specific period, there is at least an implied obligation to deal fairly with the employee. Firing an able and willing worker to make room for a relative of the employer would seem to violate that implied promise of "fair dealing." So would the "retaliatory" firings suggested earlier (political contribution, worker's compensation claim, jury duty).

If there is such a duty of good faith imposed by the courts in a particular state, it is hard to imagine how it would be disclaimed successfully. Would an employer state "we reserve the right to deal with our employees in bad faith"? Or, "we reserve the right to discharge our employees arbitrarily"? It's hard to believe that such a company could recruit the personnel they wanted with such language in a personnel manual. A statement providing that employment is at-will might be some help in marginal cases, but does not really seem to disclaim all the good faith requirement.

STATE VARIATIONS

Some states have refused to create a new tort of "wrongful discharge," and have also rejected the two contract theories discussed above. New York is a notable example. In states such as New York, the general rule on at-will employment still prevails. To have a case in these states, an employee must prove discrimination under one of the regulatory statutes discussed in the next chapter.

The *Patton* case shows that some courts are also reluctant to go too far with the exceptions to the at-will doctrine, even though they might recognize an exception in the right sort of case.

PATTON V. J.C. PENNEY CO.

719 P.2d 854 (Or. 1986)

Facts: David Patton was hired by J.C. Penney Co. in 1969. In 1980 he was transferred to the Portland store as a merchandising manager. In 1981, the store manager (McKay) told him to stop dating a female co-employee. Patton refused to do so because he was not socializing with the woman at work and because the company had no written policy on such matters. Despite Patton's having received several awards as "Merchant of the Month" and "Merchant of the Year," McKay told Patton his job performance was unsatisfactory. Patton was fired in February 1982. He sued for wrongful discharge and intentional infliction of emotional distress. The trial court dismissed both claims, but the Court of Appeals reinstated the claim for emotional distress.

Issue: Does a discharge for failure to follow a supervisor's order not to date other co-workers provide a basis for either claim here?

Decision: No. Both claims should be dismissed.

Rule: Generally an employer may discharge an employee at any time and for any reason unless there is a specific contractual, statutory, or constitutional requirement that says otherwise.

Discussion: *By Judge* JONES:

"Plaintiff does not allege that his discharge was for pursuing statutory rights related to his status as an employee. Nor does plaintiff allege interference with an interest of public importance equal or analogous to serving on a jury or avoiding false, defamatory remarks. Plaintiff claims that certain of his 'fundamental, inalienable human rights were compromised, put on the auction block, and made the subject of an illicit barter in that he was forced to forego these rights or to purchase them with his job.' He claims that the employer invaded his personal right of privacy and that the employer could not fire him for pursuing a private right. But these claims blur 'rights' against governmental infringement with 'rights' against a private employer. Plaintiff's acts were voluntary, and no state or federal law mandates or prohibits discrimination on that account. It may seem harsh that an employer can fire an employee because of dislike of the employee's personal lifestyle, but because the plaintiff cannot show that the actions fit under an exception to the general rule, plaintiff is subject to the traditional doctrine of 'fire at will.'

"Count II of plaintiff's allegations demonstrates that he is attempting to plead the emerging tort of intentional infliction of severe emotional distress, which consists of several elements. First, ordinarily a plaintiff must allege that a defendant intended to inflict severe mental or emotional distress. It is not enough that he intentionally acted in a way that causes such distress. Second, a defendant's act must in fact cause a plaintiff severe mental or emotional distress. Third, a defendant's actions must consist of 'some extraordinary transgression of the bounds of socially tolerable conduct' or the actions must exceed 'any reasonable limit of social toleration.'...

"In the case at bar, the alleged manner in which plaintiff was discharged does not reach the level of intolerable conduct described in the [precedent] cases. We agree with the Court of Appeals dissent that McKay's alleged behavior was 'rude, boorish, tyrannical, churlish and mean—and those are its best points,' but that it was not 'outrageous in the extreme,' and that the allegations do not support plaintiff's claim for intentional infliction of severe emotional distress.... The Court of Appeals is affirmed as to the wrongful discharge claim and reversed as to the intentional infliction of severe emotional distress claim."

Ethical Dimension

Are any ethical issues raised when a supervisor or manager dates a co-worker?

●

The *Patton* case also illustrates a second major problem area in employment law: the employee's right to privacy. Specifically, what kinds of employee conduct off the job can result in sanctions by the employer?

E MPLOYEES' RIGHT TO PRIVACY

Stories from the early years of the Industrial Revolution describe some situations where employees lived in company housing subject to detailed company rules. Similar "life-style" restrictions existed in many of the so-called company towns which existed in this country in the late 1800s and early 1900s. Today, much of the motivation for employers' conduct rules arises from the high cost of health care. Use of tobacco, alcohol, and drugs has adverse effects on the health of employees. (Second-hand smoke in the workplace may also injure the health of other, non-smoking employees.) Increased absenteeism costs the employer money. So do higher premiums for a company health-care plan. For these and other reasons, employers are more and more concerned with employees' life-styles.

■ Employees' Conduct Off the Job

Certainly, while the employee is on the job, and representing the employer, the employer can specify codes of conduct. But what about the employee's conduct after work? How far can an employer lawfully go in telling you what to do on your own time?

The courts have barely begun to deal with this problem. There has been a rule for many years that employer sanctions could be imposed where the employee's off-the-job conduct reflected adversely on the employer's business. The example given in the *Restatement of the Law of Agency, Second,* is the bank teller who becomes known as a "patron of the horse races." A bank teller who was seen gambling large sums of cash at the race track might lead the bank's customers to feel insecure about the safety of their deposits. This sort of "job-related" conduct could be sanctioned by the employer. That also seems to be a major concern in the *Patton* case. The supervisor who dates a subordinate employee after hours might create an appearance of favoritism or sexual harassment which reflects unfavorably on the employer's business.

Some employee conduct away from the workplace impacts on the employer.

The most recent development in this area of employment law has to do with what some authorities are calling "lifestyle discrimination." Health-care costs are continuing to increase rapidly. Many employers provide health insurance plans, for which they pay part or all of the premiums. As claims go up, so do premiums. Healthier employees cost the employer less, in terms of health insurance premiums and in terms of time lost from work. Healthier employees are also more productive. Faced with these economic realities, some employers have tried to turn "health habits" into job requirements. While a recent survey found that only 2 percent of employers absolutely refused to hire smokers, another 15 percent gave preference to nonsmokers. At one point, a city in Georgia required its employees to score satisfactorily on blood cholesterol tests, but political opposition forced the city to rescind the policy. Over twenty states now prohibit employer discrimination against employees who smoke on their own time. A few of these states extend the same protection for any lawful activity by employees on their own time. Without such a statute, it would hardly seem to be a violation of "public policy" or "outrageous" conduct to fire an at-will employee who presented clear health risks. As employers continue to cut costs to try to remain competitive, these points will be increasingly litigated.

■ Employees' Rights to Privacy on the Job

A related, but quite different, problem concerns the employee's privacy rights while on the job. Can your employer control what you put on your desk? How about the wall area behind your desk? If you have a private office, can you post signs and messages on your door? Or your office walls?

FREE SPEECH ON THE JOB

Employees of private companies have limited free speech rights in the workplace.

There are two problems with employee-originated messages in the workplace. First, the premises belongs to the employer, not to the employees. That means that the employer should exercise primary control over what happens there. Second, messages on the job site could be construed as originating from the employer rather than from the individual employees. The employer should thus be able to control the content of such "messages," to prevent an adverse impact on its business. As you will see in the next chapter, employers have been held liable for sexual harassment in the workplace on the basis of posters and graffiti placed there by employees.

WORKPLACE SECURITY

In addition to these "free speech on the job" issues, there are also many difficult problems related to the employer's control of workplace security and supervision. The employer clearly has the right (and the duty) to control workplace conditions. Courts generally have no difficulty upholding nondiscriminatory rules on such matters as required hair length, dress, safety equipment, identification badges, and the like. Restrictions can certainly be imposed on access to cash, business records, and the premises in general. However, employers do need to be careful about searching the employees' "private" areas, as seen in the *Trotti* case.

K MART STORE NO. 7441 V. TROTTI

677 S.W.2d 632 (Tex. 1984)

Facts: When Trotti arrived for work at K Mart, she put her purse in her locker in the area which the store provided for its employees. She testified that she had snapped the lock and pulled on it to make sure that it was closed. When she returned on her afternoon break, she saw that the lock was hanging open. Although nothing was missing, when she checked her purse she saw that it was in considerable disorder. When she confronted the store manager later that day, he denied searching her locker or her purse. About a month later, he admitted having done so. He said that the store's security personnel suspected that some employee had stolen a watch and that several price-marking "guns" were missing. He and several assistant managers had then conducted the search. Ms. Trotti was awarded $8,000 actual damages and $100,000 punitive damages by a jury. K Mart appeals.

Issue: Was this search an invasion of the employee's privacy?

Decision: Yes. Judgment affirmed.

Rule: Neither an employee's personal effects nor her "personal space" can be searched by the employer without her consent.

Discussion: *By Justice* BULLOCK:

"The appellants intentionally intruded upon an area where [Trotti] had a legitimate expectation of privacy. The evidence supports a further finding that the appellants wrongfully intruded upon [her] personal property. The conduct of this inspection, and the appellants' subsequent denial and ultimate admission support the conclusion that they were aware that their actions constituted a covert intrusion. The appellants clearly made the wrongful intrusion with neither [her] permission nor justifiable suspicion that [she] had stolen any store inventory. Sufficient factors exist to enable this court to conclude that the jury's award of exemplary damages was the result of proper motivations. We disagree with the appellant that any set ratio of exemplary damages to actual damages constitutes a ceiling beyond which a greater award would be excessive, and even were we to agree with appellants, we do not find that the exemplary damages in [this] case exceed that ceiling.

"The evidence supports the jury's award of exemplary damages from the factors cited. There is no evidence to support a conclusion that the jury acted as a result of passion or prejudice."

ELECTRONIC SPYING

New technologies and new social concerns have led to new "privacy" issues in the workplace. With the greatly increased use of electronic communications via computer has come a renewed fear of employer monitoring. To what extent should an employer be able to use unannounced electronic snooping as a means of ensuring employee productivity? Here, too, the courts may analyze these cases under the "expectation of privacy" used for Ms. Trotti's personal locker. If the computer system belongs to the employer and is to be used only for business purposes some sort of reasonable monitoring may be allowed. Similarly, if the employees' jobs are to utilize the employer's facilities to deal with the public (telephone operators, order takers, stock brokers), courts may be sympathetic to the employer's need to monitor operations, both to ensure productivity and to avoid improper use. More litigation should be anticipated in this area, too.

DRUG TESTING

Increased use of alcohol and legal and illegal drugs in our society has given rise to another "privacy" issue: can employers require random drug testing as a condition of employment? This deceptively simple question also raises a number of related legal problems. Would the firing of an employee who failed such a test constitute a wrongful discharge? (Probably not, since there would be a non-arbitrary reason for the discharge, but there are few cases so far.) Would failing a drug test be "good cause" for discharge where a union contract so required? (Most arbitrators have sided with the employees unless the presence of drugs was interfering with the employee's job performance.) Could a worker discharged for failing a drug test collect unemployment compensation, or is this "misconduct," which bars collection of such benefits? (The few cases to date are split.) With alcoholism and drug addiction being defined as "handicaps" in some new pieces of legislation, would discharging an employee who tested positive constitute illegal handicap discrimination? (Probably it would, if the employee is truly so "handicapped." This topic will be covered more fully in the next chapter.)

States have various statutory rules on drug testing.

Some states have tried to answer the main question—the legality of such testing—with a statute. These statutes are of three general types. Some give the employer a general permission to require such tests and protect the employee only by providing that any positive test results must be confirmed by a reliable testing method before any disciplinary action can be taken. A second group permit random testing of employees in "safety-sensitive" jobs and testing of other employees who are reasonably believed to be under the influence or who have been involved in a workplace accident. The third group of laws prohibit random testing and require the employer to have reasonable grounds to believe, based on objective facts, that a particular employee's job performance is being impaired by drugs or alcohol. Under this third type, employer violation of the act is a crime, and the employee can sue for actual and punitive damages plus attorney fees. Without a statute, most cases involving public employers or heavily regulated industries have been analyzed under the employer's need for such testing. Airline pilots, train engineers, and bus drivers—because of public safety concerns—would seem to be legitimate candidates for such testing. Testing of prison guards was upheld, due to the need for a high level of security in the prison. On the other hand, several state courts have held that random drug/alcohol testing of other classes of public employees (teachers, for example) violated the state's constitution. With or without a statute, this area will remain a fertile field for litigation. The following case is one recent example of this growing problem.

RITCHIE V. WALKER MFG. CO.

963 F.2d 1119 (U.S. 8th Cir. Court of Appeals, 1992)

Facts: Jim Ritchie and several other employees were terminated by Walker after they failed a drug test. Walker had hired an investigator to detect drug abuse by its employees. Walker's actions were based on the investigator's report. Ritchie was identified as being under drug influence while on company property. He was then required to take the test, in accordance with the company's established policy.

Ritchie sued in Nebraska state court. He alleged that Walker had breached his contract; that Walker had violated public policy by conducting an unreasonable search and seizure; that the test violated his Nebraska statutory right to privacy; that Walker had violated his rights under the U.S. Constitution; and that it had also violated his rights under the state constitution. After the case was removed to U.S. District Court, it was dismissed.

Issue: Did the drug test violate Ritchie's right to privacy?

Decision: No. Judgment of dismissal is affirmed.

Rule: An employer may require a drug test where there is probable cause to believe an employee is under the influence of drugs on company time.

Decision: *By Judge* HEANEY:

[The court said there was no breach of contract in firing Ritchie, since he had violated the company's drug abuse policy. There was no search and seizure violation, since those constitutional provisions only apply to public bodies. There was no indication that any specific provision of the national or state constitutions had been violated. The court then turned to the privacy issue.]

"[B]efore requiring Ritchie to take a drug test, Walker reasonably believed that he was violating its drug policy. This approach conformed with Walker's drug-testing policy which specifically limits drug-testing to employees who are 'suspected of using or being under the influence of a drug.'

"Walker's drug-testing policy and its actions to discharge employees who are using or under the influence of drugs on company property or company time reflect Nebraska law, which expressly permits the dismissal of an employee who fails a drug test and of '[a]ny employee who refuses the lawful directive of an employer to provide a bodily fluid.'... Indeed, [the statute] details the drug-testing procedures which an employer must follow before disciplining an employee for drug use. Ritchie does not contend that Walker violated these procedures. Thus, not only did Walker's drug-testing policy incorporate the probable cause typically required to justify an invasion of an individual's liberty, it also conformed with Nebraska's statutorily-imposed drug-testing procedures. Given these facts, Walker's drug-testing of Ritchie cannot be considered unreasonable. Therefore, Ritchie's claim that Walker violated his right of privacy cannot survive...review.

"Accordingly, we affirm the district court's dismissal of Ritchie's claims."

Ethical Dimension

Should an employee be required to provide "bodily fluids" in order to keep his job?

POLYGRAPH TESTING

State rules differ on polygraph testing.

Searching one's body is offensive enough for most of us. But how about a "search" of one's *mind*? Can an employer legally require a person to take a polygraph ("lie detector") test as a condition of employment?

The states (at least half of them) have responded aggressively to this new threat to the dignity of the individual employee. Several states, recognizing the inherent unreliability of such "tests," prohibit them entirely. Most of the other statutes permit tests where the employee has consented to them. Prior to the statutes, or in those states which still do not have statutes, courts have ruled that tests cannot be required, and/or that refusal to take one cannot be used as the basis for discharge, even of an at-will employee. At least on this point, a national consensus does seem to be emerging. The Federal Employee Polygraph Protection Act prohibits most nongovernment employers from using lie detector tests on prospective or current employees. This act does not preempt stricter state laws.

COMPETITION BY PRESENT AND FORMER EMPLOYEES

Another area of major significance in modern employment law is the use of information and technology by former employees in competition with the ex-employer. As intellectual property (patents, trade secrets, copyrights, trademarks) becomes increasingly important to business operations, it also becomes more important to know who "owns" what. Specifically, what intellectual property belongs to the employer and what belongs to the employee (or ex-employee)?

Employee's Duty of Loyalty

An employee owes the employer a duty of loyalty as part of the employment relationship. An employee who competes with the employer during the existence of the relationship is breaching this contract duty. As a remedy, the employer could ask for any damages proved and for an injunction to prevent further improper competition. Such a breach of duty would probably be cause for firing the employee in most cases.

Rights to Inventions

In our increasingly high-tech world, new and improved products are the key to business success. When an employee comes up with an idea which results in a patentable invention, to whom does it belong? Can the employee get a personal patent on the invention and sell it to someone or develop it outside the employer's business?

To answer these questions, the courts generally start with the employment contract. If the contract specifies the ownership of inventions, the contract provision usually controls. A typical contract provision would give the employer the ownership of all inventions, wherever developed, during the term of employment. Individual employees may be able to negotiate for some modification of this contract term.

An employer has the right to use patents developed on the job.

If there is no express contract clause regarding the ownership of inventions, a court would consider the circumstances of the case if a dispute arose. An employee who was hired specifically to do research and development work will probably have to turn over all inventions to the employer, even without an express contract provision to that effect. By implication, this person is being paid for precisely that activity—the development of inventions. At the other extreme, a non-R&D employee who developed an idea on personal time would probably own the invention which resulted. Where a non-R&D employee has developed an idea by using the employer's facilities or personnel, the employee may own the resulting patent, but the employer is given a non-exclusive right to use the patent. This right to use is called a **shop right**.

■ Former Employee's Duties

What about competition by an ex-employee? Phrased another way, how long does this duty of loyalty last? Does it survive the end of the employment relationship? In answering these questions, the courts are usually careful to distinguish two aspects of the duty of loyalty—the duty not to compete, and the duty not to use confidential information.

Non-compete agreements must be reasonable in area and time.

Once the employment relationship is ended, the ex-employee is generally free to engage in the same line of business as the former employer. Increasingly, employees with access to customer lists, product formulas, marketing plans, and other confidential business information are being asked to sign **non-compete agreements**. Such agreements restrict the former employee from competing, usually within a designated area and for a specified period of time. The courts' general analysis of such provisions is that they are permissible, and enforceable, under certain conditions. First, there must be a need for such protection. If the ex-employee is not carrying away any prospective competitive advantage, such as names of customers, there is no need for such restrictions. Second, the restrictions themselves must be reasonable—both in geographic area and in time duration. Finally, the employee must not be prevented from earning a living by using the personal training and skills which have been developed. Some courts take a dim view of non-compete agreements, and invalidate nearly all of them. These rules are also subject to statutory modification where a state legislature thinks that employers are abusing these rules. Unless there is an enforceable contract not to compete, however, the ex-employee is generally free to do so.

Trade secrets may not be used by former employees.

Competing in the same line of business and stealing the ex-employer's trade secrets, however, are two different things. The former employee has no right to use confidential business information which is the property of the ex-employer. Clients and customers don't really "belong" to anyone. Subject to any agreed period of service in an existing contract, they are free to hire whomever they wish. *Lists* of clients and customers, however, can be a trade secret and thus entitled to protection against theft by former employees. An ex-employee could probably send simple announcements to the clients and customers that a new firm had been formed and then let them make the decision to stay or move. Active solicitation of the former customers could be improper conduct by the ex-employee. It is so defined by lawyers' codes of ethics and may also be improper for other professionals. Clearly, stealing and using the former employer's formulas, business plans, and similar business information would be illegal conduct.

Wohlgemuth, one of the early cases drawing this distinction, involved an engineer who had had access to highly confidential information concerning the space-suit technology developed by Goodrich Company.

B.F. GOODRICH CO. V. WOHLGEMUTH

192 N.E.2d 99 (Ohio 1963)

Facts: Donald W. Wohlgemuth graduated from the University of Michigan in 1954 with a Bachelor of Science in Chemistry. Soon after, he was hired by Goodrich. Following a short period in the U.S. Army, he returned to Goodrich in 1956 and was assigned to their spacesuit department. He received several promotions and was finally named department manager. In 1962, dissatisfied with his treatment by Goodrich, he accepted an offer to work for a competitor, International Latex, on its spacesuit program. When he returned from the Army, he had signed a confidentiality agreement which required him to keep secret all company information. Goodrich sought an injunction to prevent him from going to work for International Latex and from disclosing to them any information related to spacesuits or other trade secrets. The trial court denied an injunction.

Issue: Should Wohlgemuth be enjoined from working for a competitor of his former employer?

Decision: No. He should not be prevented from supporting himself by using his general professional knowledge, but he will be enjoined from using trade secrets.

Rule: Agreements not to compete should not be interpreted to prevent an ex-employee from earning a living.

Discussion: *By Judge* DOYLE:

"There is no evidence before this court that Goodrich trade secrets have been revealed by Wohlgemuth; however, the circumstances surrounding his employment by Latex, and his own attitude as revealed by statements to fellow Goodrich employees, are sufficient to satisfy this court that a substantial threat of disclosure exists. We have no doubt that an injunction may issue in a court of equity to prevent a future wrong, although the right has not yet been violated.

"In cases of this character the law does not require an agreement between an employer and employee restricting the employee from securing employment with a competitor before an injunction may issue.

"It is a rule of equity jurisprudence that, if an employee gains knowledge of his employer's trade secrets as a result of the confidential relationship existing between employer and employee, and, in violation of the confidence, discloses such secrets to competitors after the termination of his employment, such abuse of confidence may be enjoined. The basis for equitable intervention is the employee's wrongful conduct in violating the confidence. Equitable intervention is sanctioned when it appears, as it does in the instant case, that there exists a present real threat of disclosure, even without actual disclosure....

"We have no doubt that Wohlgemuth had the right to take employment in a competing business, and to use his knowledge (other than trade secrets) and experience, for the benefit of his new employer; but a public policy demands commercial morality, and courts of equity are empowered to enforce it by enjoining improper disclosure of trade secrets known to Wohlgemuth by virtue of his employment. Under the American doctrine of free enterprise, Goodrich is entitled to this protection."

Ethical Dimension

What information can Wohlgemuth legally and ethically use for the benefit of his new employer? Is it possible to sort out those things which he can use from those which he cannot?

AGREEMENTS FOR POST-EMPLOYMENT DUTIES

Normally, when a contract is ended, the contractual obligations of the parties to each other are also ended. That would also usually be true for employment contracts and is the reason why the ex-employee is generally free to compete with the former employer. But here, as in other contracting situations, the parties may change the usual rules by provisions in their own contract.

Particularly where an employee's termination has occurred as the result of some personality dispute, the ex-employee may wish to bargain for a good recommendation to later prospective employers. An employee may agree to leave without bringing litigation in return for the employer's promise that the employee will receive an honest and fair recommendation if one is requested by a prospective new employer. The court in the next case saw no reason why such agreements should not be enforceable, since the employee only wants the ex-employer to tell the truth.

STEUMPGES V. PARKE DAVIS & COMPANY

297 N.W.2d 252 (Minn. 1980)

Facts: Neil Steumpges had been a sales representative for Parke Davis for about fifteen years and had won sales awards for his outstanding record, when Robert Jones became his district sales manager in 1973. Jones did not agree with Steumpges' approach to selling. About seven months later, Jones presented Steumpges with an ultimatum: resign, or be fired and be black-balled in the industry. If he resigned "voluntarily," Steumpges was promised a good recommendation. Faced with this choice, he did resign.

About ten days later, he went to an employment agency, Sales Consultants, to find a new job. He was interviewed by Robert Hammer and listed Parke Davis as his most recent job. When Hammer called Jones, Jones said that Steumpges was a poor salesman, was hard to motivate, was not industrious, could not sell, and had been fired. Hammer refused to try to place Steumpges because of this "recommendation." Steumpges sued for defamation and was awarded $27,750 in actual damages and $10,000 in punitive damages. Defendants appealed.

Issue: Were the defendant's comments privileged?

Decision: No. Judgment for Steumpges affirmed.

Rule: A former employer's privilege to answer inquiries about an ex-employee does not include the freedom to tell lies.

Discussion: *By Chief Justice* SHERAN:

"Although Jones's words to Hammer clearly related to Steumpges' reputation in his profession, Parke Davis contends that they were not slanderous because substantially true.... There are indications in the record that Jones himself acknowledged the falsity or at least distortion of his statements to Hammer. The jury accepted Steumpges' version and found the statements made by Jones to Hammer to be false....

"Parke Davis also argues that Jones's statements to Hammer are not defamatory because they were conditionally privileged. Thus, even if the statements were slanders per se, by pleading and proving the existence of a conditional privilege, it has re-butted the presumption of common law malice....

"We agree with Parke Davis that an employer called upon to give information about a former employee should be protected so that he can give an accurate assessment of the employee's qualifications. It is certainly in the public interest that this kind of information be readily available to prospective employers, and we are concerned that, unless a significant privilege is recog-nized by the courts, employers will decline to evaluate honestly their former employees' work records. We believe, however, that the falsity of the statements made by Jones to Hammer, after he had on February 25 indicated that he had a favorable impres-sion of Steumpges' capabilities as a salesperson and would give a good recommendation to prospective employers, takes this case out of the realm of privilege. Thus, Parke Davis cannot be relieved of responsibility on the basis of this theory....

"Since the evidence supports a jury finding that Jones acted with malice in making the statement to Hammer, it was reason-able for the jury to have determined that the conditional privi-lege of fair comment concerning the character of a past em-ployee had been abused....

"Since media self-censorship is not involved in this case and since 'the imposition of liability for private defamation does not abridge the freedom of public speech or any other freedom pro-tected by the First Amendment,'...we are free to permit juries to award punitive damages to punish defendants for this type of unsanctioned behavior."

Ethical Dimension

Why should there be any limits at all on what a former em-ployer says about an ex-employee?

REVIEW

What was once a relatively simple contract between employer and employee has been radically transformed by conditions in modern society. Courts and legisla-tures are making substantial changes in this relationship to meet these new con-ditions. The traditional rule of at-will employment is now significantly limited in many states. New challenges to employee privacy are resulting in new legal rules to cover these situations. New importance is attached to the rules regarding ownership and use of intellectual property. On all of these points litigation is increasing and will undoubtedly continue to do so throughout the 1990s.

REVIEW QUESTIONS AND PROBLEMS

1. When can an ex-employee compete with the former employer?

2. What is the significance of the "employment at will" doctrine?

3. When is an employer liable to a former employee for intentional infliction of emotional distress?

4. What is the scope of an employer's privilege to provide information about a former employee when asked to do so?

5. Why can't an ex-employee use the trade secrets of a former employer after the employment relationship is ended?

6. To what extent are agreements not to compete with a former employer valid and enforceable?

7. Barry was president of the state teachers college union. In that role, he was often asked to testify on education issues by the state legislature. On one occasion, he told the legislature that he thought that the junior college where he taught should become a four-year state university. The college's board of trustees, which was opposed to its becoming a four-year school, did not renew Barry's teaching contract. Barry was not tenured, so the board said he could be let go at any time. Barry sued for wrongful discharge. What should happen here, and why?

8. Armando signed an employment contract in which he promised to turn over to the employer, Solly-Rant Company, any invention which he developed within one year after leaving the company. About two months after he left, Armando came up with an idea for an improved surgical clamp. Solly-Rant sued to force him to turn over the invention. Does he have to do so? Explain.

9. Bessie was hired to manage Ski Shop. The owner told her that she would have a job "as long as the shop was profitable," and promised her ten percent of the profits. Bessie was a very good manager, and the shop was very profitable, but Ski Shop fired her anyway. Bessie sued for breach of contract. Does she have a case? Discuss.

10. The state passed a statute regulating the use of polygraph ("lie detector") tests by employers. Such tests could be given only with an employee's permission and could only be given by a police department. Octo Bank adopted a policy which required all its employees who worked as bank tellers to undergo a polygraph test, in which they were asked whether they had taken any money from the bank, every three months. Rennie and Stan refused to take the test and were fired. They sued for wrongful discharge. What result, and why?

SUGGESTIONS FOR FURTHER READING

Ballam, "Intentional Torts in the Workplace: Expanding Employee Remedies," *American Business Law Journal* 25 (Spring 1987): 63.

Callaghan, "Employment at Will: The Relationship Between Societal Expectations and the Law," *American Business Law Journal* 28 (1990): 455.

Callaghan, "The Public Policy Exception to the Employment at Will Rule Comes of Age: A Proposed Framework for Analysis," *American Business Law Journal* 29 (1991): 481.

Callaghan and Dworkin, "Internal Whistleblowing: Protecting the Interest of the Employee, the Organization, and Society," *American Business Law Journal* 29 (1991): 267.

Doughtrey, "Another Exception Under the Employment-At-Will Doctrine: Bowman v. State Bank," *American Business Law Journal* 24 (Summer 1986): 243.

Lansing & Regnetter, "Fair Dismissal Procedures for Non-Union Employees," *American Business Law Journal* 20 (Spring 1982): 75.

Phillips, "Toward a Middle Way in the Polarized Debate over Employment at Will," *American Business Law Journal* 30 (1992): 441.

Stevens, "'Insult and Outrage' in the Employer-Employee Relationship," *American Business Law Journal* 16 (Spring 1978): 103.

Stevens, "The Legality of Discharging Employees for Insubordination," *American Business Law Journal* 18 (Fall 1980): 371.

14
REGULATION OF THE EMPLOYMENT RELATIONSHIP

"One of the eternal conflicts out of which life is made up is that between the efforts of every man to get the most he can for his services, and that of society, disguised under the name of capital, to get his services for the least possible return."

Oliver W. Holmes, Jr.,
dissenting in *Vegalahn v. Guntner*

LEARNING OBJECTIVES: After you have studied this chapter, you should be able to:

SUMMARIZE the major limitations on the parties' freedom to set their own terms for the employment contract.

EXPLAIN the need for unemployment compensation laws.

DISTINGUISH workers' compensation from OSHA requirements.

OUTLINE the requirements for dealing with employee unions.

DESCRIBE the major areas covered by national anti-discrimination laws.

413

P REVIEW

The employment relationship is probably the most heavily regulated area of business operations. Some of the terms of the employment contract are specified, or at least limited, by wage and hour (and other) regulations. Persons temporarily laid off from their jobs are entitled to unemployment compensation. Workers have the right to be compensated for on-the-job injuries. Employers are required to provide a reasonably safe workplace. Employees have the right to join unions if they wish to do so, and the employer is obligated to bargain with the employees' chosen representative. Discrimination in employment, including sexual harassment, is prohibited. Various state and national administrative agencies, as well as both court systems, are involved in protecting these rights.

T ERMS OF EMPLOYMENT

In the usual contracting situation, the parties negotiate their own arrangement. They decide whether they wish to enter into the relationship, and, if so, on what terms. While the parties to an employment contract are generally still in control of the first decision, they have lost some control over the second. National and state laws now impose regulations on the terms of the employment contract.

Wages and Hours

In the 1800s, with a surplus of workers capable of performing relatively simple industrial jobs and with a legal doctrine which said a worker could be fired at will, there were strong legal and economic incentives for paying laborers as little as possible. In some mines and factories, women and children were used extensively and paid even less than adult men. Long hours were usually required; twelve- and fourteen-hour workdays were common. Beginning in the early 1900s, both Congress and the state legislatures became concerned about the effect of these employment conditions on the workers' health, safety, and well-being. At first, the statutes which imposed wage and hour standards were held unconstitutional, as an infringement on the parties' freedom to make any contract they wished on whatever terms they accepted. It was not until the late 1930s, after the advent of the New Deal, that the U.S. Supreme Court finally upheld such legislation.

The FLSA requires minimum wages and overtime pay.

The Fair Labor Standards Act of 1938 (FLSA) is the major national statute regulating wages and hours. It covers almost all employees, including those working for governmental agencies. It does not, however, cover professionals—an important exclusion. Workers on small farms, in amusement parks, in the fishing industry, and babysitters are likewise exempt. Car salespersons, cab drivers, and live-in domestics are not covered by the required overtime sections of the law. Special rules also apply to hospital workers, firefighters, retail salespersons receiving commissions, and seasonal workers.

The original required minimum wage was twenty-five cents an hour—an unbelievably low figure by today's economic standards. Even today, with the figure over $4.00 an hour, fast-food restaurants are finding it difficult to hire help. Only for the most menial, lowest status jobs is the minimum wage a real "floor." Although there are lengthy debates and seemingly fierce battles every time Congress raises the minimum wage, market demands have increased wages more than legislative demands, for most businesses.

Of greater importance for most firms is the law's requirement for overtime pay. For each hour in excess of forty per week, the employee is entitled to be paid one and one-half times the normal hourly rate. A person with a base pay rate of eight dollars an hour who worked fifty hours in a given week would be entitled to $440. For the first forty hours, the regular $8.00 an hour would equal $320; for the extra ten hours, the required rate would be $12.00 an hour, for another $120. Without the law, the employer could pay the regular rate for all fifty hours, or a total of $400.

Faced with these economic results, one would imagine that employers who had extra work would hire more workers at the regular hourly rate, thus avoiding the necessity of paying the overtime premium. Indeed, that was one of the New Deal's objectives in adopting the act in the first place. Other economic factors, however, have operated to limit this "spreading of employment" effect of the act. Employees today typically receive a number of fringe benefits in addition to their regular wages. It may therefore be more cost efficient, in some cases much more cost efficient, to simply have the existing workers do the extra work at the higher overtime wage. Many jobs today involve complex, often computerized, machinery and other technology. As a result, a new employee typically requires extensive training for which the employer normally pays. This factor, too, may make it much more cost effective to pay the overtime premium to existing employees rather than hire new ones.

■ Child Labor

Another long and fierce battle was fought in the state legislatures and in Congress over the use of child labor in mines and factories. The FLSA prohibits the use of children under the age of eighteen in types of jobs classified as "hazardous"—mining, meat processing, excavation, building demolition, and the like. For most jobs, there is a minimum age of sixteen. Children between fourteen and sixteen may be hired for nonmanufacturing, nonmining jobs, provided the job does not interfere with school. Work on a family's farm, newspaper delivery, and a few other jobs are exempt from these age restrictions. Penalties for

Child labor is limited by law.

violation include up to six months in jail, and/or a fine up to $10,000, plus forfeiture of any goods produced by the illegal child labor. The states are permitted to enact laws which are more strict, and some states have done so.

■ Social Security

One of the centerpieces of the New Deal was the Social Security Act of 1935. Creating several new programs, it represented a massive readjustment in the employer-employee relationship. Social Security today includes five major programs: retirement, life insurance, disability, medical insurance, and welfare. These programs constitute the major "safety net" for most working people. Funding for the programs comes from contributions by both employers and employees (and self-employed persons). The employer and the employee each pay in a percentage of the wages earned (7.65 percent each in 1993). The self-employed pay in the entire amount, but have been given a tax credit for such payments, which has the effect of reducing the actual rate. No tax is paid on wages above a certain figure ($57,600 in 1993), or on income from dividends, interest, pensions, or (most) rentals.

RETIREMENT BENEFITS

Social Security provides retirement benefits.

Retirement benefits are paid at age sixty-five to someone who has earned minimum amounts (on which Social Security taxes have been paid) during each of forty quarter-years. Payments at a reduced rate (now 80 percent of the normal payment) can begin at age sixty-two, if one wishes to retire early. A person who delays retirement past sixty-five can receive slightly higher than normal payments. The weekly retirement payment for a worker who had earned only minimum wages would be 60 percent of the minimum wages earned for a normal forty hour week. The higher the career earnings, the lower the percentage paid as Social Security retirement would be. For a person who had earned the maximum salary subject to Social Security taxes, the retirement benefit would be less than one-fourth of that maximum amount.

LIFE INSURANCE

Since surviving dependents of a deceased worker also receive benefits, Social Security also functions as a kind of life insurance program. Dependent children and dependent parents usually qualify for these benefits. A surviving spouse will qualify if sixty years old, or if fifty and disabled, or if he or she has minor children living at home.

DISABILITY BENEFITS

Disability payments are also based on prior wages earned and calculated under a complex formula. The law does provide a cap on the amount of these payments. When they are added to any workers' compensation payments, the total cannot be more than 80 percent of the prior wages. During recent years, the average disabled (single) worker got about $500 a month; for those with dependents, the average figure was just over $900 per month.

MEDICAL INSURANCE

The medical insurance part of Social Security consists of Medicaid and Medicare. Medicaid helps poor persons pay for medical care. There are qualifying tests using both income received and assets owned. The amounts used for these qualifying tests vary from state to state because the program is funded and administered jointly by the states and the national government. Medicare helps pay the doctor and hospital bills of persons who are over sixty-five and receiving Social Security payments. Persons wishing this coverage at age sixty-five pay a small monthly premium which can be deducted from the monthly Social Security check. The individual does have to pay a once-a-year deductible amount for hospital charges; Medicare pays the balance. There is also a deductible amount for doctor bills, but doctors are permitted to charge higher fees than the standardized ones set by the government. Thus, in addition to the deductible amount for doctor bills, the individual would have to pay any excess amounts where the doctor charged a fee above the "allowable" one set by Medicare.

Medicaid and Medicare help pay medical bills.

WELFARE

Finally, there is Supplemental Security Income (SSI), a welfare program administered through Social Security. It does not use Social Security funds, however, but is funded out of the national government's general tax revenues. Here again, there are both asset and income tests to qualify. A single person can own no more than $2,000, although the value of one's home is not counted. Nor are certain personal and household goods, a car valued at under $4,500, a burial plot, burial funds up to $1,500, and certain life insurance policies. Minimal earnings, support from charities, food stamps, and certain other payments do not disqualify one from receiving SSI payments. For a single person, the maximum total of such payments which one could receive during 1993, without being disqualified, was $448 per month. For a couple, the corresponding figure was $656 a month. These figures are adjusted each year. In addition, to qualify for SSI, one must be over sixty-five, or blind, disabled, or retarded.

SSI is a welfare program.

■ Other Requirements

The terms of the employment contract may also be affected, either directly or indirectly, by numerous other national and state statutory requirements. Many states regulate the frequency with which wages must be paid and also the procedure for authorizing deductions from the employee's paycheck. Declaring a particular day as an official holiday usually has the effect of increasing labor costs. Either that day is a day's lost business output or the employer will have to pay a premium to convince employees to work on the holiday. Where there is a union contract, and in many other employment situations as well, major holidays are usually paid vacation days.

A national statute now requires an employer to give employees advance notice of a plant closing. Most recently, legislation requiring "family leave time" has become a popular cause. These statutes require the employer to give a certain number of unpaid days off after the birth of a child or in the event of serious illness within the family. The national statute passed early in 1993 requires that the employee be permitted such family leave time, but does not require that wages be paid during the leave.

◼ UNEMPLOYMENT COMPENSATION

Part of the New Deal recovery program was the establishment of a system which would provide some weekly income to temporarily laid-off workers. The unemployment compensation system was established in 1935 as part of the Social Security Act. Minimum national standards were established, but the program is administered primarily by the states. Weekly benefit levels for the unemployed, and premiums paid by employers to fund the program, can vary considerably from state to state.

◼ Benefit Payments

Benefits are paid to persons who have lost their jobs.

Benefits are typically paid for twenty-five weeks, but may be extended through various special programs or emergency legislation. The worker receives, spread over these twenty-five weeks, the amount earned during the best quarter-year of the four quarters immediately preceding the last full quarter-year prior to the layoff. For example, if Emmy is laid off on November 29, 1991, her last full quarter-year would be July–September 1991. To calculate her weekly benefits, we would use her best quarter of earnings between July 1, 1990, and June 30, 1991, and divide that quarter's earnings by twenty-five.

States have varying provisions for maximum and minimum amounts. For example, many states will pay no more than 27 percent of the total earned during the entire four-quarter "Base Period." Unemployed workers with dependent children or a nonworking spouse are entitled to extra benefits in about one-fourth of the states.

■ Eligibility for Benefits

Workers are required to be available for work and to actively seek work. They must be ready, willing, and able to work if a job is found. Disabled persons who are unable to work are not eligible for unemployment compensation, although they may be eligible for disability payments under some other program or insurance. Generally, the unemployed worker does not have to accept much lower-paying or different types of jobs. For instance, teachers can wait for teaching jobs; they don't have to take jobs as bus drivers or custodians if no teaching jobs are available. (Of course, after their unemployment compensation runs out, they may very well want to accept any job they can find.)

Generally, persons who are unemployed due to a labor dispute cannot collect unemployment compensation. The reason for this rule is simple: the employer should not be required to pay benefits to persons who are trying to injure its business by going out on strike. That is not the sort of situation which the system was designed to cover, nor would that seem to be a very logical, or fair, result. Obviously, there are many interpretation questions as to when employees are unemployed due to a labor dispute.

Likewise, employees who voluntarily quit their jobs do not normally receive unemployment compensation. Again, this is not the kind of problem with which the system is concerned. However, even here, there are exceptions and interpretation questions. What if the employee is in effect forced to resign because of harassment, dangerous working conditions, or substantial adverse changes in the job? Where the resignation is due to these (and perhaps other) reasons, some states will still permit collection of benefits. Even where the reason for quitting is "compelling personal reasons," some states will pay benefits anyway.

Persons who quit or who are fired for misconduct usually cannot collect unemployment.

Finally, employees who are lawfully fired for misconduct usually do not qualify for unemployment compensation benefits. Here, too, it would not seem fair or logical to charge benefit payments against an employer who had a legal basis for discharging the worker. The major problem in these cases is the definition of "misconduct" which is sufficient to deny unemployment benefits. Usually, an isolated incident is not a sufficient basis, unless it involved serious criminal conduct, such as theft or assault. Use of drugs or alcohol may or may not be misconduct; courts may be lenient with addicts and alcoholics who are unable to modify their behavior. Negligence on the job might justify discharge, but it would not normally be "misconduct" for benefit purposes. An isolated outburst of temper—throwing a tool or using obscene language—is probably not a disqualification. That is the issue in the Kowal case.

KOWAL V. UNEMPLOYMENT COMPENSATION BOARD

512 A.2d 812 (Pa. 1986)

Facts: Sara Kowal was employed as a monitor of government-funded programs. Kowal's supervisor put her and two other co-workers in a room, closed the door, and began criticizing their job performance. He claimed they did not smile enough on the job. He yelled at them for about forty-five minutes. He then asked Sara if she "liked her job." She threw a writing tablet at him and told him in obscene language what he could do with it. When she came to work the next day, she was fired. A hearing officer denied benefits, and the Board affirmed.

Issue: Is the employee's violent reaction "misconduct"?

Decision: No. Kowal gets her unemployment compensation.

Rule: Isolated incidents, especially when provoked by a supervisor, are not misconduct which disqualifies the employee from receiving unemployment compensation.

Discussion: *By Judge* BARRY:

"The Board's conclusion...was premised on its view that, because the other employees present at the meeting did not react in the same way, claimant's own behavior was *necessarily* unjustified.... This conclusion, however, ignores the Board's own finding that, directly before the outburst, claimant had *personally* borne the brunt of the executive director's loud and aggressive meeting oratory.... Testimony from the other meeting attendees supports this finding, as it does the claimant's assertion that this additional directed abuse was carried out in the same intimidating fashion as was the meeting in general....

"We think that this individually-targeted aggression, coming as it did after forty-five minutes of harassment, constitutes justifiable provocation for claimant's reaction. We are, likewise, of the view that this harmless conduct, considered in context, was of a de minimus nature. The record is replete with evidence that animated behavior on the part of the executive director occurred with frequency, ostensibly as part of some sort of misconceived management technique. In light of that occupational environment, the throwing of a tablet and uttering of an expletive must be considered innocuous....

"We find the Board's reasoning unpersuasive that justifiable provocation can be measured in the present case on an objective basis, when the immediately provocative conduct was directed personally at the claimant."

W ORKERS' COMPENSATION

For at least 150 years, English and American courts have recognized a
duty on the part of the employer to provide a reasonably safe workplace for its employees. This duty would include having reasonably
safe machines and equipment, enforcing safety rules, providing necessary training to ensure employee competence, and warning of any
known dangerous conditions. Employees who were injured on the job
because of the employer's violation of this duty had a claim for damages covering lost wages and medical expenses.

■ Common Law Defenses

The employer could of course defend a lawsuit by denying that it had
breached any part of its duty of care, or that, even if it had, the breach
did not cause the employee's injury. In addition to these usual arguments in a personal injury action, the courts also accepted three other
defenses which the employer could use. **Contributory negligence**, as applied in this context, meant that if an employee had also been partially
at fault, and if that personal negligence had contributed to help cause
the injury, the employee could collect nothing. **Assumption of risk**, another standard tort defense, could be used to prevent recovery by an
employee who knew there was a danger, and yet continued to do the
work anyway. (Coal mining, for instance, is dangerous work, and
everyone knows that. Thus, someone who goes down into the mine
"assumes the risk" of cave-ins, fires, explosions, gas, and all the other
"normal hazards" of mine operations.) The third defense held that the
employer was not liable if the injury had been caused, at least in part,
by the actions of a **"fellow servant."** In combination, these three defenses meant that most employees recovered nothing for their on-the-
job injuries. On the other hand, in the rare case in which none of these
defenses applied, a large award might be made. An injured worker's
seeking compensation was thus a game of chance under this system,
with the employee standing about as much chance of winning as a
roulette-wheel player in Las Vegas.

*At common law, the
employer had three
defenses against claims
for employees' injuries.*

■ Statutory Change

The English Parliament led the way to reform in 1897 by passing a
statute which provided compensation for most employee injuries,

although in limited amounts. The three common-law defenses would not apply. The objectives of the statute were to provide a real incentive to have a safe workplace, to pay for injuries which did occur, and to include these costs as part of the final price of the product. State legislatures in this country adopted similar legislation.

■ Persons Covered

Independent contractors are not covered by workers' compensation.

Most U.S. employees are now covered by state workers' compensation statutes. However, owners working in their own businesses, including partners, are usually not covered. Employee-stockholders, working for their small closely-held corporation, would be covered, since the corporation is the "employer." Independent contractors are by definition not "employees," since they are working for themselves and are not under the control of the person hiring them as to how the work is done. They are therefore not covered under the hiring company's workers' compensation. Many statutes contain specific exemptions; farm workers may not be covered, for example. A few states give employees the right to elect not to be covered and to sue under the traditional common law rules. National laws provide a form of workers' compensation coverage for sailors, dock and harbor workers, and railroad workers.

■ Nature of Claim

To be covered, an injury must arise out of and in the course of employment.

Employees are injured in all kinds of situations. Not every injury will be covered by workers' compensation. Typically, the statute will require that the injury (1) be accidental; (2) "arise out of" the work; and (3) "arise in the course of" the job. Most courts originally required a sudden and unexpected occurrence, causing injury, as opposed to an injury which gradually developed as a result of doing normal work. Many courts have dropped this definition, but there is still some uncertainty over whether chronic illnesses such as back strain, heart conditions, mental stress, and miners' "black lung" disease are covered. Compensation claims for mental illness are especially troublesome. Physical injury may cause mental pain and stress, or mental illness may cause a physical injury. Courts generally agree that compensation should be paid in these two cases. The third situation, where there is no accompanying physical injury at all, causes much disagreement. Some state courts interpret their statutes as not covering strictly mental illness. Some will permit recovery if the employee can show that the mental illness was caused by "abnormal" working conditions. Others permit recovery if the mental illness arose out of and in the course of the job.

The general interpretation of the statutory phrase "arising out of" is that the work itself must in some way cause the injury. The purpose of this requirement is to distinguish those injuries which are truly job-related, and for which the employer ought therefore to pay compensation, from those which merely occur on the job-site by happenstance. For example, can outside workers collect for weather-caused injuries such as frostbite or sunburn? A strict interpretation (and some older cases) would say no; most courts today would probably say yes. Injuries caused by physical assaults on the job-site may or may not be job-related, depending on the wrongdoer's motivation and connection with the employer's business.

The final test or requirement is that the injury occur "in the course of" employment. Most simply put, this means that the employee has to be acting as an employee when the injury occurs. Injuries sustained while commuting to work are usually not covered because of this third requirement. There are, however, several possible exceptions to this rule. Commuting injuries may be compensated if there is no specific workplace, if transportation expenses are paid by the employer, or if the employee is doing something for the employer's business at the time of the injury. For instance, an employee who was on the way to the Post Office to mail something for the employer would be engaged in the employer's business (at least on the way there), and would thus be covered by workers' compensation while doing so. Recreational activities are another area where difficulty arises. Injuries sustained while playing for company-sponsored teams are generally compensated. Physical activities on breaks, on the company premises, or in company-provided facilities may or may not be covered. "Horseplay" and "fun and games" on the job also create an ambiguous situation. Some courts have held that the employer should expect such conduct, and, since the statute eliminates the "fellow servant" defense, injuries which arise from such conduct should be covered. Under a stricter interpretation, conduct which directly violates employer rules and instructions and which does not benefit the employer in any way would hardly seem to be "in the course of" employment.

■ Benefits Payable

Workers' compensation statutes typically provide three types of benefits: death benefits for dependents, medical expenses, and weekly payments for disabilities. Family members who were dependent on the deceased employee for support are usually entitled to receive death benefits for a work-related fatality. A few states, recognizing modern social customs, extend this coverage to dependents "cohabiting" with the employee. Most states, however, require the dependent claimant to be related by blood or marriage to the deceased employee. The amount of the death benefit varies, but is usually the maximum amount which the employee would have received for a total disability. Medical expenses include doctor and hospital bills due to the injury and, in some states, the cost of rehabilitation training.

Most statutes provide for limited weekly payments for permanent disability. A typical statute might say that the employee is entitled to

Limited payments are made for limited periods.

two-thirds of the average weekly wage for the quarter-year immediately preceding the injury. The number of payments would depend on the nature of the disabling injury. Loss of a little finger might require 30 weeks of payment, for example; loss of a thumb, 80 weeks; loss of a hand, 200 weeks; loss of an eye, 300 weeks; and so on. Most statutes do not give compensation for "pain and suffering," which could be awarded in a tort lawsuit. Workers' compensation awards thus tend to be smaller.

■ Alternative Lawsuits

Employees injured on equipment may sue its manufacturer.

Under most statutes, the workers' compensation award is the employee's exclusive remedy against the employer. As noted above, only a few states permit the employee to "opt out" of the system and bring a tort lawsuit. There are, however, some other possible alternatives which may provide further recovery. The most popular alternative is to file a product liability action against the manufacturer of the machinery or equipment which the employee was using at the time of the accident. Such lawsuits account for about 60 percent of all product liability cases filed. In addition, if the injury was caused by a motor vehicle accident, the driver of the other vehicle could be sued. If the business was operating in leased premises, the owner/landlord might be liable for the injury. In some states, if the insurance company providing workers' compensation coverage for the employer refuses, in bad faith, to pay a legitimate claim, it can be sued and may even be liable for punitive damages because it acted in bad faith. Finally, many states permit lawsuits against an employer for *intentional* wrongful conduct which causes injury.

The *Luddie* case illustrates the difficulty of defining what activities are "in the course of" employment.

LUDDIE V. FOREMOST INSURANCE COMPANY
97 A.2d 435 (Conn. 1985)

Facts: Caryn Luddie was a claims adjuster for Foremost. She worked out of her home in Marlborough, Connecticut. About 5:30 p.m., she received a telephone call from a client who was unable to find a $12,000 check that Foremost had sent to cover his fire loss claim. She drove her car to New London to meet the client. After finishing their business, she agreed to drive him to Hartford so he could catch a train there. They stopped along the way at the Plainfield dog track to watch the races and stayed until 11:30. While on the way to Hartford and looking for a restaurant, Luddie got lost. When she found she was close to home, she decided to go there, get something to eat, take a shower, and then drive the client on to Hartford. They had a car accident about 3:00 a.m. while still on the way to her house. When Luddie swerved to miss a deer, she hit a bridge. Luddie was injured and filed a claim for workers' compensation. The hearing officer awarded compensation, but the review division reversed.

Issue: Was this accident "in the course of" employment?

Decision: No. No compensation should be paid.

Rule: Only those activities which are intended to benefit the employer's business are "in the course of" employment.

Discussion: *By Judge* DALY:

"The determinative question is whether the plaintiff, at the time of her injury, was engaged in the line of her duty in the business or affairs of her employer.... The general rule is that '[a]n injury sustained on a public highway while going to or from work is ordinarily not compensable.'... The exceptions to the general rule 'arise in situations where the contract of employment itself involves, in its actual performance, or as an incident annexed to it with the knowledge and consent of the employer, the use of the public highways';...or that the employer contracts to furnish transportation to and from work....

"In determining whether an unauthorized deviation from the employment is so slight as not to relieve the employer from liability, or of such a character as to constitute a temporary abandonment of the employment, '[t]he true test is analogous to that applied to determine whether a deviation in agency terminates that relationship.'... '[T]he trier must take into account, not only the mere fact of deviation, but its extent and nature relative to time and place and circumstances, and all the other detailed facts which form a part of and truly characterize the deviation, including often the real intent and purpose of the servant making it.'...

"Even if we assume that the plaintiff's meeting with the insured in New London was within the scope of her authority to placate policy holders, the review division's findings are still devoid of any facts which would support a conclusion that the subsequent junket to the Plainfield dog track was within the scope of her employment, or in any way related to that employment.... Under the plaintiff's theory, if she had driven her automobile to any point in or out of the state that evening, the moment she started toward Hartford with the intention of bringing the insured to a transportation center, she would have brought herself back into the course of an employment which had long since terminated for the day.... In taking her course for the purpose intended (to take a shower), the plaintiff was doing nothing incidental to her employment. Her injury did not arise in the course of her employment."

Ethical Dimension

Is this case saying that employees should not try to be "good Samaritans"?

WORKPLACE SAFETY

Workers' compensation statutes at least provide some minimal payments to injured employees. However, precisely because the payments are "minimal," the statutes do not, in many cases, provide any real incentive to the employer to correct dangerous workplace conditions. If correction would require extensive physical changes, or expensive new technology, a straight cost/benefit analysis might indicate that the correction should not be made.

OSHA regulates workplace safety.

To change this equation, Congress passed the Occupational Safety and Health Act in 1970. A new agency, the Occupational Safety and Health Administration (OSHA), would establish workplace safety standards, inspect workplaces, and assess fines for violations. Intentional, repeated violations can result in fines of up to $10,000 per violation. If a worker's death results, the employer (or agent) can be imprisoned for six months; repeat offenders can be jailed for up to one year. The intent of these criminal penalties is to change the cost/benefit analysis. However, most of the fines assessed thus far have been quite small and are thus a limited deterrent.

OSHA has also lost some credibility because it has seemed to focus mainly on trivia, such as the number of inches a fire extinguisher is mounted from the floor, rather than on the real poisons and perils in our workplaces. Only a very few standards have been adopted, and there are only some 1,000 inspectors for the hundreds of thousands of workplaces in our country.

One major problem which has come to the attention of the U.S. Supreme Court is the conflict between workplace safety and the prohibition against discrimination in employment. If the workplace is hazardous to an unborn fetus, may women of child-bearing age be prevented from holding a job there? That was the question in the *Johnson Controls* case.

UNITED AUTOWORKERS V. JOHNSON CONTROLS

111 S. Ct. 1196 (1991)

Facts: Johnson Controls manufactures batteries; lead is a primary ingredient in the process. Lead is a toxic element, especially harmful to the unborn. When eight of its female employees with blood lead levels exceeding the OSHA standard became pregnant, Johnson adopted a policy which prevented fertile women from working on jobs where they would be exposed to lead. The UAW filed a class action in U.S. District Court alleging sex discrimination. The District Court granted summary judgment for Johnson, based on "business necessity," and the Court of Appeals affirmed.

Issue: Can an employer exclude fertile females from certain jobs because of its concern for the fetuses which the women employees might conceive?

Decision: No. Judgment reversed.

Rule: Employers cannot discriminate against women on the basis of their capacity to become pregnant unless the employer can show that women are unable to perform the duties of the job.

Discussion: *By Justice* BLACKMUN:

"The bias in Johnson Controls' policy is obvious. Fertile men, but not fertile women, are given a choice as to whether they wish to risk their reproductive health for a particular job.... [Johnson's] fetal-protection policy explicitly discriminates against women on the basis of their sex. The policy excludes women with childbearing capacity from lead-exposed jobs and so creates a facial classification based on gender....

"Our conclusion is bolstered by the Pregnancy Discrimination Act of 1978..., in which Congress explicitly provided that, for purposes of Title VII, discrimination 'on the basis of sex' includes discrimination 'because of or on the basis of pregnancy, childbirth, or related medical conditions.' 'The Pregnancy Discrimination Act has now made clear that, for all Title VII purposes, discrimination based on a woman's pregnancy is, on its face, discrimination because of her sex.'... In its use of the words 'capable of bearing children' in the 1982 policy statement as the criteria for exclusion, Johnson Controls explicitly classifies on the basis of potential for pregnancy. Under the PDA, such a classification must be regarded, for Title VII purposes, in the same light as explicit sex discrimination. [Johnson] has chosen to treat all its female employees as potentially pregnant; that choice evinces discrimination on the basis of sex....

"[T]he absence of a malevolent motive does not convert a facially discriminatory policy into a neutral policy with a discriminatory effect. Whether an employment practice involves disparate treatment through explicit facial discrimination does not depend on why the employer discriminates but rather on the explicit terms of the discrimination.... The beneficence of an employer's purpose does not undermine the conclusion that an explicit gender-based policy is sex discrimination...and thus may be defended only as a BFOQ [bona fide occupational qualification]....

"The wording of the BFOQ defense contains several terms of restriction that indicate the exception reaches only special situations. The statute thus limits the situations in which discrimination is permissible to 'certain instances' where sex discrimination is 'reasonably necessary' to the 'normal operation' of the 'particular' business. Each one of these terms—certain, normal, particular—prevents the use of general subjective standards and favors an objective, verifiable requirement. But the most telling term is 'occupational'; this indicates that these objective, verifiable requirements must concern job-related skills and aptitudes....

"Johnson Controls argues that its fetal-protection policy falls within the so-called safety exception to the BFOQ. Our cases have stressed that discrimination on the basis of sex because of safety concerns is allowed only in narrow circumstances....

"Our case law...makes clear that the safety exception is limited to instances in which sex or pregnancy actually interferes with the employee's ability to perform the job. This approach is consistent with the language of the BFOQ provision itself, for it suggests that permissible distinctions based on sex must relate to ability to perform the duties of the job. Johnson Controls suggests, however, that we expand the exception to allow fetal-protection policies that mandate particular standards for pregnant or fertile women. We decline to do so. Such an expansion contradicts not only the language of the BFOQ and the narrowness of its exception but the plain language and history of the Pregnancy Discrimination Act."

Ethical Dimension

Is this decision telling employers that they don't need to care about the health of their pregnant workers or those who might become pregnant?

LABOR RELATIONS

Although the percentage of the workforce belonging to unions has declined to less than 15 percent, some important basic industries are still dominated by union collective bargaining contracts. Production workers in the transportation, steel, and auto industries are largely governed by unions. Even for companies who are not unionized, the right of the employees to unionize whenever they wish acts as a significant check against arbitrary actions by management.

New Deal Legislation

If the Social Security Act was one centerpiece of the New Deal, so also was the National Labor Relations Act of 1935. There had, of course, been organized craft unions—plumbers, carpenters, and the like—prior to the New Deal. But general industrial workers were largely unorganized. The Industrial Workers of the World (IWW, called the "Wobblies") had been largely discredited, due to their association with bombings and other acts of sabotage. The National Labor Relations Act (NLRA, also known as the Wagner Act) legitimized the formation of industrial unions. The Committee on Industrial Organization (later the Congress of Industrial Organizations, or CIO) provided a general framework for organizing the large, mass-production industries—autos, steel, mining, and others.

The NLRA recognized the right of employees to organize and to select an agent (the union) to bargain with the employer about wages, hours, and terms and conditions of employment. The basic premise of the act was that collective bargaining would provide a mechanism for resolving labor disputes and for protecting the employees against arbitrary employer decisions. The National Labor Relations Board was established to administer the statute. It would conduct representation elections and handle complaints about employer "unfair labor practices," which were defined in the act. The employer could not interfere with the employees' right to organize, prefer one union over another, or discriminate on the basis of union membership. Once a union had been selected, the employer had a duty to bargain with it in good faith and committed an unfair labor practice by not doing so.

The NLRA gave employees the right to organize and bargain collectively.

Selection of Bargaining Agent

When a political election is held, the voting unit (city, county, state) has already been defined, and the qualifications for voting (residence and registration) have already been set. Occasionally a particular person's qualification to vote may be challenged, but usually there are few if any such questions. In a union election, on the other hand, both of these definitional questions—what is the unit and who can vote—can quickly become very complicated. Does each of the employer's plants, stores, or offices vote separately for its own union representation, or are all the votes counted together and all locations bound by the outcome? Do persons doing specialized work, such as plumbing and carpentry, vote separately—in which case they might choose a craft union, even though they are working in an auto plant or a steel mill? If some members of a university faculty want to organize, and an election is called, who gets to vote? Teaching assistants? Part-time lecturers? Adjunct faculty? Visiting faculty? Librarians? Researchers? Department heads? Deans? (Many administrators are drawn from the faculty, retain their faculty appointments and tenure, and return to the classroom after serving as administrators.)

The NLRB supervises elections to choose bargaining agents.

An NLRB regional office (there are several, located throughout the country) makes these determinations when it receives a petition requesting an election. If employees or a union files the petition, it must claim support of a "substantial" part (meaning at least 30 percent) of the workforce. If the employer files, it need not allege any "support," unless it is claiming that the existing union should be de-certified because it no longer enjoys majority support. Thus, even to make an initial evaluation of the employee or union petition, the NLRB's regional office must decide what is the appropriate bargaining unit, within which the proposed election would be held. The Board has generally favored larger units over smaller ones and has generally been reluctant to hold separate elections for small groups claiming "special interests." If there are, in fact, substantial differences among various groups of employees, separate elections would probably be held. Within the university context, for instance, separate elections would almost certainly be held for secretarial staff, maintenance personnel, and faculty.

Having decided on the appropriate bargaining unit, the NLRB regional office then has to resolve any questions about who can vote in the election. Family members who are in fact employees of a small family business will probably be permitted to vote, even though they are strongly motivated to vote "no union." Managers and supervisors, on the other hand, are not permitted to vote. The vote is by secret ballot, supervised by the regional office. The "no union" choice will appear on the ballot. If no choice receives a majority, a run-off election is held between the top two choices. The majority result is then certified. If the "no union" choice receives a majority, no new election can be held for a year. If a union is the winner, the employer must now bargain with it.

■ Scope of the Duty to Bargain

Union shops or agency shops give unions protection by requiring dues payment.

The employer is required to bargain with the certified union about "wages, hours, and other terms and conditions of employment." Matters covered by this phrase are classified as "mandatory" subjects of collective bargaining because the parties are required by law to discuss them if the other party wishes to do so. Nearly all other topics are called "permissive" subjects; that is, the parties may discuss them if they both wish to do so, but one party cannot insist that the other do so. (Such insistence, in fact, could itself be a violation of the duty to bargain in good faith.) A few topics are "prohibited" subjects, made illegal by the act: closed shop, "hot cargo," and secondary boycott agreements. **Closed shops**, which prevent the employer from hiring any nonunion employees, were outlawed by the Taft-Hartley Act of 1947, which amended the original NLRA. (The union can demand that all employees become members of the union after a probationary period. This is a **union shop**. Alternatively, the union can at least require that all employees pay dues to the union which represents them. This creates an **agency shop**. Some states do not permit union shops. Some do not even permit agency shops.) **"Hot cargo" agreements**, by which the employer agrees not to handle non-union produced goods, are likewise illegal. So are **secondary boycotts**, in which the union requires an employer not to do business with another employer with whom the union has a labor dispute.

Many topics are easily categorized as "wages, hours, and working conditions." Bonuses, pensions, break times, holidays, seniority, promotion policy, and disciplinary procedures are all quite clearly mandatory topics. Other matters are just as clearly permissive—management's decisions on product pricing and advertising, for example. Lying somewhere between these obvious cases are several very difficult topics, which involve management's right to operate the business, but which also impact on the availability of jobs. Strong international competition and economic downturns have forced many companies to look for ways to cut costs and to improve productivity. As part of that process, management may decide to move some work from one existing plant to another, to relocate a plant, to contract out some operations, or to discontinue some part of the business. Each of these four decisions will have a significant impact on the employees who are currently doing the work in question. Does management have a duty to bargain with the union in these cases? The answer is clearly yes—at least as to the "effects" of the management decision on the existing workforce. Assuming that management is making the decision for legitimate economic reasons and not just to punish the union the decision itself would be lawful.

Employers must bargain about most subjects that impact on working conditions.

The Board and the courts have generally been very careful to distinguish between the statutory duty to *bargain* and a requirement that the parties *agree* (there is none). All the act requires—and it's actually quite a lot, in comparison to the situation before the 1935—is that the parties bargain with each other over the mandatory topics. Good faith bargaining normally requires meeting with each other, exchanging proposals, and discussing alternatives. When a GE officer (Boulware) told its union that it was making its final offer at the beginning of the

Neither party has a duty to agree to bargaining demands.

negotiations and that it could not do better than that initial offer no matter what the union said, the U.S. Court of Appeals said that GE had violated its duty to bargain in good faith. Some "process" of bargaining is required, in other words.

■ Use of Economic Weapons

Either party can insist that the other agree on a proposal relating to a mandatory subject, as the price of an overall contract. Such insistence is not an unfair labor practice. Neither is the other party's refusal to agree. Once they have bargained to this kind of "impasse," each is free to unholster its economic weapons. The union is free to call a strike, to establish picket lines at the place of business, or to ask that its members and others not buy the employer's product or service (a **boycott**). The employer is free to suspend operations (a **lockout** of the employees). If the employees are on strike, the employer is (legally) free to hire replacements and continue operations, if it wishes to do so. (Organized labor has been trying to get legislation passed which would change this last rule.)

Picketing must be peaceful.

Picketing must be "peaceful," and must not interfere unduly with normal traffic flows. Picketing can be enjoined where it violates these basic requirements, and persons injured by violent acts could of course bring tort lawsuits for damages. Picketers committing extreme violent acts need not be rehired when the strike ends. On the other side of the coin, the employer cannot lock out its employees or relocate work as a tactic to discourage union membership or to punish the union. Doing so would be an unfair labor practice and would subject it to back pay, rehiring, and other NLRB remedies.

The following case shows a UAW challenge to an employer's attempts to cut costs by moving work from a unionized plant to a nonunionized one.

INTERNATIONAL UNION, UNITED AUTOWORKERS V. NLRB

765 F.2d 175 (D.C. Cir. Court of Appeals, 1985)

Facts: To save on its labor costs, Illinois Coil Spring Company decided to move certain work from its Milwaukee Division to its McHenry Division. Workers at the unionized Milwaukee plant received hourly pay of $8 in wages and $2 in fringe benefits. At the nonunion McHenry plant, the workers got $4.50 in wages and $1.35 in fringes. Illinois Coil asked the union for changes in the Milwaukee contract rates, but the union refused to permit any changes. Illinois Coil then began to move work to the McHenry plant. The UAW filed unfair labor practices charges. The NLRB at first found a violation of Section 8(d) of the act, since the company had made "changes" in an existing contract without the union's consent. After the case had been appealed, but before it had been heard by the Court of Appeals, the NLRB asked that the case be returned to it for a rehearing. The NLRB then decided there had been no violation. This time, the UAW appealed.

Issue: Is the employer's relocation of work from the bargaining unit an illegal "change" in the terms of contract?

Decision: No. NLRB decision affirmed.

Rule: The existence of a collective bargaining contract does not guarantee the existence of jobs in the bargaining unit unless it so provides.

Discussion: *By Judge* EDWARDS:

"The stipulated facts indicate that the employer acted without antiunion animus, that the relocation was prompted by purely economic considerations, and that the employer satisfied all contractual and legal obligations to bargain over the proposed relocation. The employer further asserts, without challenge from the union, that the relocation was fully consistent with the terms of the parties' collective bargaining agreement. We hold that, under these circumstances, Section 8(d) proscribes neither the announcement of a tentative intention to relocate nor the final decision to relocate, and we therefore affirm the decision of the National Labor Relations Board....

"We think the Board correctly held there to be no Section 8(d) violation here. Milwaukee Spring apparently possessed the contractual right to make the relocation decision. As the union seems to concede on appeal, no provision of the collective bargaining agreement was modified by that decision. In addition, no antiunion animus tainted the company's decision. Under these circumstances, we can discover nothing in Section 8(d) that proscribes Milwaukee Spring's actions. Furthermore, we find no merit to the union's argument that the announcement of the tentative intention to relocate violated Section 8(d). The value of the company's contractual right to relocate would be undermined—not to mention the strain it would put on logic—if we were to hold that although Milwaukee Spring had the right to decide unilaterally to relocate, the act prohibited it from declaring in advance the intention to do so....

"Given that Milwaukee Spring acted without antiunion animus for purely economic reasons and fulfilled any statutory obligation to bargain that it might have had, we hold that the company did not violate Section 8(d) of the act, either by offering to exchange its right to relocate for a midterm modification of the contract or by deciding to relocate when the union rejected its modification proposals."

Ethical Dimension

Is it "ethical" for a company to agree to the terms of a collective bargaining contract and then move work out of the plant covered by the contract?

D ISCRIMINATION IN EMPLOYMENT

Historically, private employers were free to hire whomever they wished to hire, without limitation. Likewise, the at-will doctrine permitted them to fire whomever they wished at any time for any reason. Thus, in hiring and firing, in promotion and salary, and in all other aspects of the job, blatant discrimination was legally permissible. The NLRA did prohibit discrimination against union members, and was amended by the 1947 Taft-Hartley Act to also prohibit discrimination against nonmembers of a union, but otherwise the historical rule prevailed until 1964. Prior to that date, some states had laws which prohibited certain types of employment discrimination, but there was no national statute.

Public Employers Versus Private Employers

Governments, on the other hand, when acting as employers as in all of their other activities have been bound by the U.S. Constitution to give all affected persons "equal protection of the laws." While the Fourteenth Amendment only applied to the states and their agencies, a similar "equal protection" requirement for the national government and its agencies was found by the U.S. Supreme Court to be implied in the Fifth Amendment "due process" clause. Discrimination by a governmental employer on the basis of race, sex, religion, and similar bases would therefore be a constitutional violation, while the same sort of employment practice by a private employer was perfectly lawful.

Title VII of the 1964 Civil Rights Act

Private employers may not discriminate based on race, sex, religion, or national origin.

All this finally changed in 1964, with the passage of the Civil Rights Act. Title VII of the act dealt with discrimination in employment. Private employers with fifteen or more employees were prohibited from discriminating on the basis of race, color, religion, sex, or national origin. Equal treatment was required in hiring, promotion, and discharge, and in compensation and other terms and conditions of employment. (In contrast, the statute passed one year earlier—the Equal Pay Act—had prohibited only *pay* differentials, and only on the basis of the employee's sex.) Unions and employment agencies are likewise prohibited from discriminating on any of these grounds. In 1972, the law was amended to cover most state and local government employees, as well.

■ Bona Fide Occupational Qualification

An employer is permitted to use religion, sex, or national origin as the basis for a hiring decision if the employer can prove there is a reasonable business necessity for doing so. A religious organization can certainly require religious training for the clergy it hires. A closer question would be presented if church doctrine permits members of only one sex to be clergy. Even this discrimination would usually be permitted by the BFOQ exception. (If the BFOQ exception were not so interpreted, the constitutionality of Title VII might be in question under the First Amendment freedom of religion clause.) The employer bears the burden of proving that the discriminatory requirement is reasonably necessary to its normal business operations, and that may not be so easy. The operation of a "French" restaurant, for example, might not really require that only persons of French nationality be hired; the ability to speak French to the customers might be enough of a qualification for "normal operation" of the restaurant. Similarly, the BFOQ exception applies only to the *hiring* decision. If the French restaurant decides to hire a German woman who speaks French, it cannot pay her less due to her "non-French" national origin—or because of her sex. Finally, the law does not recognize any BFOQ based on race or color. As far as Title VII is concerned, there can be no valid business necessity based on race or color.

Employers must use BFOQs to disqualify job applicants.

Similarly, the employer is not committing a violation by complying with the terms of a bona fide collective bargaining agreement which requires seniority as the basis for employment decisions. The use of seniority as a protection against favoritism is so well established in labor relations law that there is a specific exemption written into Title VII. This exemption is so strong that the U.S. Supreme Court has held that it even overrides a court decree requiring affirmative action by the employer (*Firefighters Local 1784 v. Stotts* [1984]).

■ Procedure

To enforce Title VII, the Equal Employment Opportunity Commission was established. The EEOC receives and investigates complaints of employment discrimination and first tries to resolve the problem between the parties. Such complaints must be filed within 180 days after the

The EEOC enforces the national civil rights laws.

alleged act of discrimination; this time period is extended to 300 days if the state where the alleged act occurred has its own employment commission and requires such charges to be filed with it. If its efforts at conciliation are unsuccessful, the EEOC can then bring a lawsuit itself on behalf of the complainant or on behalf of a whole class of employees, if it believes that there is a "pattern" of illegal discrimination. If it decides not to bring its own lawsuit, the EEOC can issue a "right to sue letter" to the claimants, who can then bring their own lawsuit (at their own expense) in U.S. District Court. The act specifies that such private lawsuits must be filed within 90 days after receipt of the right to sue letter.

If it finds that there has been illegal discrimination, the court may issue an injunction to prevent future wrongs and order "affirmative action" to make up for the prior acts of discrimination. The employer may also be required to reinstate specific persons who were wrongfully discharged. Back pay awards can be made, but only for a maximum of two years prior to the date when the complaint was filed with the EEOC. Other damages were not permitted by the act prior to its amendment in 1991.

The Civil Rights Act of 1991 substantially amended the remedy provisions of Title VII. If intentional discrimination is proved, the plaintiff may collect damages to compensate for any injury caused, as well as punitive damages. A successful plaintiff may be awarded attorney fees whether the discrimination was intentional or unintentional. The 1991 act thus raises the stakes for wrongful discrimination and encourages the injured party to bring a lawsuit.

■ Disparate Impact

The obvious civil rights violation occurs when a specific person is treated differently because of race, color, religion, sex, or national origin. This type of case is described as **disparate treatment.**

Disparate impact occurs when a job requirement disqualifies large numbers of a protected class.

A much more difficult problem concerns the use of seemingly neutral job qualifications which have a **disparate impact** on one of the protected groups. An employer's requirement that applicants for jobs as security guards must be six feet tall, for instance, would disqualify disproportionate numbers of women and Asians. Unless the employer could demonstrate that the height requirement was necessary for the proper performance of the job, Title VII would be violated. In the leading precedent case, *Griggs v. Duke Power Company* (1961), the U.S. Supreme Court held that there had been such a violation where the company was using a standardized test and a high school diploma as job requirements. Because the company could not show that either was related to successful job performance, there was unlawful—though unintended—discrimination.

From the employer's viewpoint, the problem with this approach is that it casts the burden of proof of job-relatedness on the company.

This can be a very tough burden to meet; just the fact that the more educated employees will probably be more efficient will not satisfy this standard. In 1989, this burden of proof was substantially lightened by the Supreme Court's decision in *Ward's Cove Packing v. Atonio*, excerpted below. However, in 1991, new amendments to the Civil Rights Act restored the *Griggs* standard. The 1991 legislation also specifically prohibits the use of quotas as a basis for hiring decisions. The employer is now caught between a rock and a hard place. If it uses any requirement as a basis for hiring and any protected class is not hired in proportionate numbers as a result, it must show that the requirement is necessary to do the job properly. On the other hand, if it seeks to avoid litigation by hiring the "right" percentage of each protected class, it is violating the new act by doing so. Every indication is that this problem will intensify in the coming years.

WARD'S COVE PACKING CO., INC. V. ATONIO

109 S. Ct. 2115 (1989)

Facts: Atonio and others brought a class action lawsuit alleging that certain hiring and promotion practices had a disparate impact on nonwhite employees and prospective employees. Workers doing the actual cannery jobs (cleaning and packing salmon) were primarily nonwhite—Filipinos and Alaska Natives. The Filipinos were hired primarily through a union hiring hall; the Alaska Natives were primarily local residents, who lived near the remote cannery locations. The non-cannery jobs, both skilled and unskilled, were predominantly held by white workers, hired at the companies' offices in Oregon and Washington. Plaintiffs claimed that the companies' preference for rehiring prior employees, their failure to post non-cannery openings, the English language requirement, and alleged nepotism in hiring—and other practices—resulted in a racial imbalance in the work force.

The U.S. District Court made 172 separate findings of fact. It rejected all claims of disparate treatment and of disparate impact based on "subjective" criteria. It further held that disparate impact due to "objective" criteria had not been proven by the statistical differences in the racial makeup of the two categories of employees. The Court of Appeals three-judge panel affirmed, but after a hearing by the entire Court, the ruling on "subjective" criteria was reversed and the case remanded to the three-judge panel. The panel then held that the statistics showed a prima facie case of disparate impact, which would require the employer to prove that its practices were justified by "business necessity." The employers asked for Supreme Court review.

Issue: Does a statistical disparity in the racial makeup of two categories of workers prove a prima facie case of discrimination?

Decision: No. Judgment of the Court of Appeals is reversed.

Rule: Disparate impact may be shown where there is a statistical disproportion between the racial makeup of the at-issue job category and that of the qualified population in the relevant labor market.

Discussion: *By Justice* WHITE:

"It is clear to us that the Court of Appeals' acceptance of the comparison between the racial composition of the cannery work force and that of the noncannery work force, as probative of a prima facie case of disparate impact in the selection of the later group of workers, was flawed for several reasons. Most obviously, with respect to the skilled noncannery jobs at issue here, the cannery work force in no way reflected 'the pool of *qualified* job applicants' or the '*qualified* population in the labor force.' Measuring alleged discrimination in the selection of accountants, managers, boat captains, electricians, doctors, and engineers—and the long list of other 'skilled' noncannery positions found to exist by the District Court...—by comparing the number of nonwhites occupying these jobs to the number of nonwhites filling cannery worker positions is nonsensical. If the absence of minorities holding such skilled positions is due to a dearth of qualified nonwhite applicants (for reasons that are not petitioners' fault), petitioners' selection methods or employment practices cannot be said to have had a 'disparate impact' on nonwhites.

"One example illustrates why this must be so. [Plaintiffs'] own statistics concerning the noncannery work force at one of the canneries at issue here indicate that approximately 17% of the new hires for medical jobs, and 15% of the new hires for [office] worker positions, were nonwhite.... If it were the case that less than 15–17% of the applicants for these jobs were nonwhite and that the nonwhites made up a lower percentage of the relevant qualified labor market, it is hard to see how [plaintiffs], without more,...would have made out a prima facie case of disparate impact. Yet, under the Court of Appeals' theory, simply because nonwhites comprise 52% of the cannery workers at the cannery in question,...[plaintiffs] would be successful in establishing a prima facie case of racial discrimination under Title VII.

"Such a result cannot be squared with our cases or with the goals behind the statute. The Court of Appeals' theory, at the very least, would mean that any employer who had a segment of his work force that was—for some reason—racially imbalanced, could be haled into court and forced to engage in the expensive and time-consuming task of defending the 'business necessity' of the methods used to select the other members of his work force. The only practicable option for many employers will be to adopt racial quotas, insuring that no portion of his work force deviates in racial composition from the other portions thereof; this is a result that Congress expressly rejected in drafting Title VII."

Ethical Dimension

Confronted with a labor pool in the relevant market that does not contain the same skill levels among all racial groups, what is the employer to do?

■ COMPARABLE WORTH DOCTRINE

Another area of potentially great difficulty involves the concept of "comparable worth." The 1963 Equal Pay Act did require that persons of different sexes be paid the same wage for the same work. If women doing the same job were receiving lower pay than men, the women's wages would have to raised to equal those of the men. Such sex-based pay differentials would of course also violate Title VII. **Comparable worth,** however, goes far beyond these basic requirements. It would require equal pay for doing *similar* work; that is, for two different jobs which had similar value to the employer, similar skill levels, similar responsibilities, and so on. The comparable worth doctrine has not yet been widely adopted, in large part because of the difficulty in deciding which jobs are "comparable."

Comparable worth requires equal pay for similar work.

■ Age Discrimination

Age was not included as one of the prohibited factors in Title VII. The Age Discrimination in Employment Act (ADEA) was passed in 1967 as an amendment to the Fair Labor Standards Act. It prohibits employer discrimination against persons over age forty. Like Title VII, it contains a BFOQ exception; the employer would need to show that age was a requirement for the particular job. Even if age as such is not a job requirement, the employer can still show that there is no violation of the ADEA because the employment decision was based on "reasonable factors other than age" (RFOTA). It would clearly be lawful to discharge a professional athlete who could no longer run and throw as well as competing employees. The physical skill level would be a RFOTA, and thus be permitted by the ADEA.

The ADEA prohibits age discrimination.

■ Pregnancy Discrimination

Pregnancy discrimination is now illegal.

Title VII was amended in 1978 to specifically include pregnancy and childbirth as part of its prohibition against sex-based discrimination. Pregnant women who are no longer able to perform some part of their jobs must be treated the same as men who are temporarily disabled. No employer is required to establish a medical benefits plan but, if it does have one, pregnancy must be given the same coverage as other medical conditions. Abortion expenses, however, need not be covered by such plans, unless necessary to save the mother's life. Figure 14–1 compares the filings of pregnancy discrimination cases with those alleging sexual harassment.

■ Sexual Harassment

Sexual harassment includes actions which create a hostile work environment.

Under Title VII, sexual harassment of an employee is discrimination based on sex. Sexual harassment occurs when a supervisor conditions a favorable job decision on receipt of sexual favors from the employee. This is called *quid pro quo* harassment ("I will do that for you, if you will do this for me.") This kind of blatant abuse by a supervisor is clearly improper and should result in discharge, demotion, or severe

FIGURE 14–1
EEOC Complaints Filed –Pregnancy/Maternity (P) vs. Sexual harassment (S)

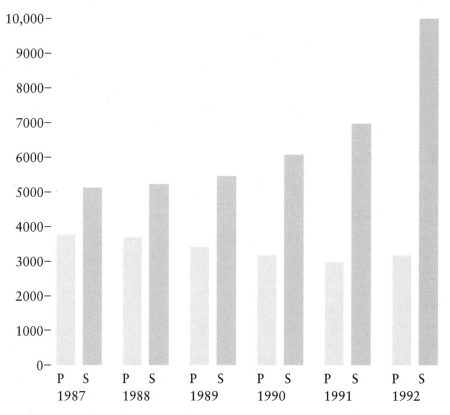

Source: Equal Employment Opportunity Commission

discipline. Much more subtle is conduct by co-workers which creates a **"hostile work environment."**

Employees can be insensitive to each other's feelings. Sometimes, they can be outright cruel to each other. Mean pranks and tricks, off-color jokes, nasty notes, unwanted physical contact—all can be used to create a very unpleasant atmosphere in the workplace. No one should have to work under such conditions, or could be expected to be very productive where they exist. Where such obnoxious behavior is sex-based, Title VII has been violated, at least if the employer is liable under agency principles for the wrongs of the co-workers. The *Meritor* case is the leading precedent on this problem.

MERITOR SAVINGS BANK V. VINSON

477 U.S. 57 (1986)

Facts: Mechelle Vinson was hired in 1974 by Sidney Taylor, a branch manager and vice-president of the bank. She started in his branch as a teller-trainee, and was later promoted to teller, head teller, and assistant branch manager. In September, 1978, she told Taylor she was going to take sick leave for an indefinite period of time. On November 1, 1978, she was fired—for "excessive use of sick leave."

Vinson then filed a lawsuit, claiming that Taylor had forced her to have sex with him some forty or fifty times, usually at the bank, both during and after business hours. She claimed that she had never reported him because she was afraid of losing her job. Taylor denied everything. The bank denied liability for any actions by Taylor because it had no knowledge of them. The U.S. District Court said the claim had not been proved and that the bank could not be liable if it was not told of the problem. The U.S. Court of Appeals reversed and remanded for further proceedings. The bank asked the Supreme Court for further review.

Issue: Can an employer be held liable for a hostile work environment, even if it has not received a complaint?

Decision: Yes, it can. Judgment of the Court of Appeals is affirmed.

Rule: Employers can be held liable under agency law principles for the wrongful acts of supervisory employees.

Discussion: *By Justice REHNQUIST:*

"Since the [EEOC] guidelines were issued, courts have uniformly held, and we agree, that a plaintiff may establish a violation of

Title VII by proving that discrimination based on sex has created a hostile or abusive work environment....

"Of course...not all workplace conduct that may be described as 'harassment' affects a 'term, condition, or privilege' of employment within the meaning of Title VII.... [F]or sexual harassment to be actionable, it must be sufficiently severe or pervasive 'to alter the conditions of...employment and create an abusive working environment'.... [Vinson's] allegations in this case—which include not only harassment but also criminal conduct of the most serious nature—are plainly sufficient to state a claim for 'hostile environment' sexual harassment....

"Although the District Court concluded that [Vinson] had not proved a violation of Title VII, it nevertheless went on to consider the question of the bank's liability. Finding that 'the bank was without notice' of Taylor's alleged conduct, and that notice to Taylor was not the equivalent of notice to the bank, the court concluded that the bank therefore could not be held liable for Taylor's alleged actions. The Court of Appeals took the opposite view, holding that an employer is strictly liable for a hostile environment created by a supervisor's sexual advances, even though the employer neither knew nor reasonably could have known of the alleged misconduct. The court held that a supervisor, whether or not he possesses the authority to hire, fire, or promote, is necessarily an 'agent' of his employer for all Title VII purposes, since 'even the appearance' of such authority may enable him to impose himself on his subordinates....

"The EEOC, in its brief as *amicus curiae* ['friend of the court'], contends that courts formulating employer liability rules should draw from traditional agency principles. Examination of those principles has led the EEOC to the view that where a supervisor exercises the authority actually delegated to him by his employer by making or threatening to make decisions affecting the employment status of his subordinates, such actions are properly imputed to the employer whose delegation of authority empowered the supervisor to undertake them. Thus, the courts have consistently held employers liable for discriminatory discharges of employees by supervisory personnel, whether or not the employer knew, should have known, or approved of the supervisor's actions."

Ethical Dimension

How can an employer prevent such unethical and illegal conduct by its supervisors?

Handicap Discrimination

In 1973, Congress passed the Vocational Rehabilitation Act, designed to end discrimination against handicapped persons. Its coverage, however, was limited to agencies of the national government and to private companies which had government contracts valued at $2,500 or more. It thus did cover most major U.S. companies, which do deal with one or more executive branch agencies. Covered firms were required to implement an affirmative action plan for hiring and promoting qualified handicapped persons.

An important new statute was adopted in 1990: the Americans with Disabilities Act. This new act extends the prohibition against handicap discrimination to all private employers with fifteen or more employees (twenty-five or more for the first two years after the act took effect in 1992) and to public employers other than the United States itself. As is true under Title VII, labor unions and employment agencies are also covered. There are also provisions guaranteeing nondiscriminatory access to public facilities and to privately operated places of public accommodation.

The ADA now prohibits discrimination against handicapped persons.

Employers covered by the ADA not only may not discriminate against persons with disabilities, employers are required to make "**reasonable accommodations**" to enable such persons to perform a job for which they are otherwise qualified. Accommodations which would impose an "undue hardship" on the employer are not required. Moreover, the handicapped person must meet the criteria actually required for the job. An employer who was hiring a CPA could not refuse to hire a paraplegic because of the physical disability, but could refuse if the person was not a qualified CPA.

The ADA's definition of **disability** includes physical or mental impairments, a past history of such impairments, or being regarded as having such impairments. It does not, however, include such conditions as homosexuality, transsexualism, sexual behavior or gender identity disorders, kleptomania, pyromania, or substance abuse disorders resulting from current use of illegal drugs. Prior use of illegal drugs does not exclude a person from coverage by the ADA so long as the person is not currently using illegal drugs. The employer can adopt reasonable procedures for making sure that such former drug users are no longer doing so.

Government Contractors

Most firms contracting with the U.S. Government are required to adopt affirmative action plans if their work force does not approximate the pool of potential employees, with respect to race, color, sex, and national origin. Contractors are not required to hire unqualified persons, nor are they required to fire existing employees in order to make positions available. They are required to develop and to implement

Government contractors must have an affirmative action plan.

a plan to make up any statistical imbalance by finding and hiring qualified members of the underrepresented groups as positions become available. Disabled veterans of the Vietnam War are covered by a special statute, which requires firms with government contracts of $10,000 or more to list all available jobs with the local employment service. Referral preference is then given to the disabled Vietnam veterans in the area. The Office of Federal Contract Compliance Programs enforces these administrative requirements for doing business with the national government. Many states have similar programs for their contractors.

REVIEW

Employment law has been substantially modified; many national and state statutes now apply to various aspects of the employer/employee relationship. Some benefits and overtime pay are mandated by government. Workplace safety is regulated, and employee injuries must be compensated. Employees have the right to join unions, and if they do so, the employer is required to bargain with their chosen representative. Finally, and perhaps most important, employer discrimination is now illegal.

Each of these areas may produce lawsuits and administrative proceedings against the employer. Charges of discrimination are especially likely to be made if employer policies are not carefully thought out and tightly administered. These areas of employment law are clearly of vital importance to successful business operation in today's social environment.

REVIEW QUESTIONS AND PROBLEMS

1. What is the difference between a discrimination case based on disparate treatment and one based on disparate impact?

2. Why does workers' compensation only cover injuries "arising out of and in the course of employment"?

3. When is an employer liable for sexual harassment of one employee by another employee?

4. What is the nature of an employer's "duty to bargain"?

5. How does the BFOQ defense differ from the RFOTA defense?

6. Why is pregnancy discrimination illegal?

7. Engine Employees United represented the production workers at Massive Machinery Company. Massive and the EEU were unable to agree on the terms of a new collective bargaining contract, so the EEU members went on strike. After about one month, Massive announced that it would begin hiring replacements for any workers who did not report for work the following Monday. Only a few of the EEU members crossed the picket lines and went back to work. Massive hired replacements for the rest. When the strike was finally settled, Massive refused to fire the replacements in order to put the other union members back to work. The EEU filed unfair labor practice charges. How should the NLRB rule, and why?

8. Condo College adopted a voluntary affirmative action plan to increase the number of women and minorities in supervisory positions. The plan permitted race and sex to be considered as factors when hiring or promotion decisions were made until the numbers of women and minorities in the various job categories approximated the percentages in the available labor pool.

When a position as maintenance supervisor was posted, nine college employees applied and were interviewed. Jonah, a white man, tied for second on the scoring of the interviews. Jill had the fourth highest score, but received the job. (There were no other women among the forty-two maintenance supervisors at the college.) Jonah sues under Title VII. Will he collect? Why or why not?

9. Hilow Builders had a contract to do remodeling work on a retail store owned by BookWell Company. The store was located in Mega Mall, a large regional shopping plaza owned by Barre Developers. Nailers United, the union representing construction workers in the area, is handing out leaflets which ask shoppers not to buy at any of the stores in the mall because Hilow is paying its nonunion workers lower wages and fringe benefits than the area's standards for union workers. Barre sues for an injunction to stop the handbilling of mall customers. Should the court grant an injunction? Explain.

10. Keep-Kleen Inc. operates a cleaning and maintenance service for owners of commercial buildings. It had a contract to clean a large office building for $1500 per week. When its costs for supplies and equipment increased, it told the building's owner, Pluto Motors, that it would have to receive $2000 per week for its service. Pluto did not respond, so Keep-Kleen told its forty-five employees who had worked on cleaning the Pluto building that they were laid off. Meanwhile, Keep-Kleen's employees had voted to be represented by a union. The union demanded that Keep-Kleen bargain with it before deciding not to continue with the cleaning contract on the Pluto building. Keep-Kleen refused, and the union filed unfair labor practice charges. How should the NLRB rule here? Discuss.

SUGGESTIONS FOR FURTHER READING

Ballam, "The Worker's Compensation Exclusivity Doctrine: A Threat to Workers' Rights Under State Employment Discrimination," *American Business Law Journal* 27 (1989): 95.

Boehmer. "The Age Discrimination in Employment Act—Reductions in Force as America Grays," *American Business Law Journal* 28 (1990): 379.

Brankey, "Prohibited Discrimination in the Replacement and Reinstatement of Strikers Under Section 8(a)(3) of the National Labor Relations Act," *American Business Law Journal* 23 (Winter 1986): 583.

Brockhoeft, "AIDS in the Workplace: Legal Limitations on Employer Action," *American Business Law Journal* 26 (Summer 1988): 255.

Donohue & Siegelman, "The Changing Nature of Employment Discrimination Litigation," *Stanford Law Review* (May 1991): 983.

Dumaine, "Illegal Child Labor Comes Back." *Fortune* 127 (April 5, 1993): 86.

Scheibal, "Title VII and Comparable Worth: A Post-AFSCME Review," *American Business Law Journal* 25 (Summer 1987): 265.

15
LAW
OF
PRODUCTION

"Work as if you were to live 100 years, Pray as if you were to die Tomorrow."
Benjamin Franklin

LEARNING OBJECTIVES: After you have studied this chapter, you should be able to:

DISCUSS the legal process involved in acquiring ownership of land.

EXPLAIN the limits on the landowner's rights imposed by the law of nuisance.

DIFFERENTIATE between trade secrets and patent rights.

DEFINE the three major theories of product liability.

EXPLAIN "market share" liability.

P REVIEW

Of the "four factors of production"—land, labor, capital, management—we have already covered three. Management of the business is provided in part by the owner/organizers discussed in Chapters 9 and 10. Additional managers and the rest of the workforce are hired as employees under the legal and regulatory rules covered in Chapters 13 and 14. Capital for the business is the result of the financial transactions outlined in Chapters 11 and 12.

Production requires a location and technology.

This chapter begins with the legal rules governing the acquisition and use of the fourth factor—land. It then covers a major concern of today's business manager: the acquisition and protection of intellectual property. Since patents and trade secrets are the types of intellectual property most closely associated with production, they are covered in this chapter. (Copyright and trademark law, being more concerned generally with the advertising and promotion of the product, are covered in the chapter on the Law of Marketing.) This chapter concludes by showing how the law also impacts on the result of the production process—the product. This last section of the chapter thus provides an overview of a major problem area for manufacturers—product liability. Product liability under state case law and the UCC are covered here. The special national regulations imposed on the manufacturers of particular types of products are covered in the next chapter.

L AND OWNERSHIP

Every business enterprise needs a location for its operations. Even a sole proprietor providing financial advice to clients and carrying most of the "business" in a lap-top computer will probably want to have an office somewhere. An office would at least provide a place for the receipt of mail, telephone, and fax messages and for the storage of hard-copy records. Personal service firms usually seek a location close to their customers or potential customers. For firms manufacturing a tangible product, location decisions typically involve such factors as low taxes, availability of raw materials, and skilled workers. For a retail business, because location can be so important, a commitment on the land may be made even before the business is organized. For some retail businesses, the availability of the particular location may itself be the business opportunity seen by the organizers. The first item on the agenda is thus securing the location; then the firm can be organized and capital raised.

Several factors affect the location of production.

■ Acquisition of Ownership

In many cases, the first legal document involved in acquisition of the land will be an option. The typical **option** is an irrevocable offer to sell

A buyer may want an option to buy a location for production.

the land for a certain price and on certain terms. It could also be an option for the lease (rental) of the land, rather than for a sale. The prospective buyer pays the seller/owner for the time—usually thirty, sixty, or ninety days—to consider the offer. During this time period, the would-be buyer can look at alternative business locations and compare them with the offered property. The seller is legally bound to keep the property available for the time period specified in the option. The buyer can form a contract to buy the land by accepting the offer any time within the option period.

◼ Offer and Acceptance

If no option is used, the first document is usually an **offer to purchase** (or lease), signed by the would-be buyer and presented to the seller/owner. If the seller/owner has employed a real estate **broker** to assist in making the sale, the broker will usually conduct the initial negotiations with the prospective buyers and present their offers to the seller. It is then up to the seller/owner to decide whether to accept an offer to purchase. The usual offer form has signature lines for the seller and witnesses to the seller's signature at the bottom of the form. If the seller accepts and signs the offer, each party receives a copy of this now complete written contract.

◼ Closing

At the time specified in the contract, the parties will meet for the final exchange of documents and money. This meeting is called the **closing**. The broker's office or the seller's office may be the site for this meeting. If a financing agency such as a mortgage company or bank is involved, however, their office is normally the site for the closing.

Documents and funds are exchanged at the closing on the location purchase.

At this meeting, the seller will give the buyer a **deed** (a document transferring title to the land), the keys to any buildings, and a bill of sale for any personal property included in the deal. The buyer will pay the seller, usually with a **certified check** (one on which the bank has guaranteed payment). If the buyer is financing the purchase with a mortgage, the buyer will sign the loan contract, a promissory note for the amount of the loan, and a mortgage on the land in favor of the mortgage company or bank making the loan. The **mortgage** is a contract giving the lender a claim against the property as security for the amount of the loan. If necessary, the lender can have the property sold and use the proceeds of the sale to pay off the balance due on the loan. As an alternative to the mortgage, a **land contract** may be used. Under this arrangement, the buyer gets possession and use of the land, but does not actually get a deed until the balance due on the purchase price is paid in full. Some states use a **deed of trust** as the financing document. Under this arrangement, title to the land is deeded to a trust company or bank, which holds legal ownership until the buyer has paid the full purchase price. The land is then deeded to the buyer. Meanwhile, as long as there is no payment default, the buyer has the full use of the land.

■ Types of Deeds

In a **warranty deed,** the seller (the "grantor" of the land) makes certain promises or guarantees. The primary warranties are that the title is clear and that the buyer (the "grantee" in the deed) will be able to use and enjoy the land. In a **quitclaim deed,** the seller/grantor makes no guarantees as to its title to the land. The grantor is transferring whatever claim it may have to the land—if any.

■ Buyer Protection

Usually, a buyer will want more protection than just the seller's personal promise that the title to the land is clear. There are two ways to provide this extra protection. The traditional method is to prepare a complete history of all documents which have been publicly recorded and which relate to the subject property. This history of the public record is called an **abstract.** It will trace the property back to the original owner—the U.S. Government or a colonial proprietor through some original land grant. This packet containing copies of the documents from the public record is then given to the buyer's attorney. The attorney gives an opinion as to whether the seller does or does not have clear title to the land. If the buyer's attorney says there are defects in the title, these must be corrected or the buyer must agree to go through with the deal despite them. Usually, if the seller cannot or will not correct the title defects, the deal is off.

The land buyer may receive an abstract of title or title insurance.

The second method of protection is to buy **title insurance** from a title insurance company. For a fee, the title insurance company agrees to defend the buyer's title to the land. The insurance company also agrees to reimburse the buyer for the purchase price of the land if another party proves to have a better title, causing the buyer to lose the land. The title insurance policy will also cover other types of claims against the land which would interfere with the buyer's ownership and enjoyment.

■ Rights of Owner of Land

Once lawfully acquired, the land and the things on or in it are subject to the will of the owner. The owner is generally free to remove or erect structures on the land, subject to zoning and other regulations. (These will be considered in the next chapter.) The owner is also free to remove or to plant trees, shrubs, and other vegetation on the land. Persons who only lease, rather than buy, land usually have to get the landlord's

The land buyer is generally free to change structures on the land.

Landowner's airspace rights are now limited.

permission to make any structural changes in the premises. Assuming that our business owns the land, we are free to tear down the old house on it and to build our new car wash, factory, or other structure.

Historically, the common law said that the landowner owned "from the center of the Earth to the Sky." As a practical matter, this means that the owner of the land is also the owner of any minerals beneath it. In some cases, however, mineral rights have been reserved in the deed and sold separately to someone else. With the advent of air (and space) travel, the old rule has had to be modified. Now, the owner's rights to the airspace above the land are limited. The Federal Aviation Administration regulates the height at which planes may fly over one's land.

The law continues to recognize a landowner's right to lateral support of the adjoining parcels of land. A next-door neighbor who was excavating a large hole on its property would have to make sure that it did not weaken the support for a building on your property. On the other hand, in most states there is no right to free passage of light and air across the neighbor's property, as the next case shows.

FOUNTAINEBLEAU HOTEL CORP. V. FORTY FIVE TWENTY-FIVE, INC.

114 So.2d 357 (Fla. 1959)

Facts: The parties operate competing luxury resort hotels in Miami Beach, Florida. The Fontainebleau was built in 1954; the Eden Roc (Forty Five Twenty-Five, Inc.) about a year later. Fontainebleau started construction on a 14-story addition 20 feet from its north property line; the Eden Roc is located immediately to the north of Fontainebleau's property. The tower would be 160 feet high and 416 feet long from east to west. Eden Roc claims that during the winter months the tower will block the sun from two p.m. on, and that its cabana, swimming pool, and sunbathing areas will not be useable as intended. No city zoning ordinance was violated by the tower. The trial court granted an injunction to prevent completion of the tower, and Fontainebleau appealed.

Issue: Have Eden Roc's rights been violated by the tower construction?

Decision: No. Judgment reversed.

Rule: A landowner has the right to make any lawful use of its property, so long as it does not deprive others of their lawful rights. A landowner has no right to free passage of light and air across neighboring property.

Discussion: *By the State Supreme Court:*

"[The chancellor's decision] is indeed a novel application of the maxim sic utere tuo ut alienum non laedas. This maxim does not mean that one must never use his own property in such a way as to do any injury to his neighbor.... It means only that one must use his property so as not to injure the lawful rights of another.... [U]nder this maxim, it was stated that 'it is well settled that a property owner may put his own property to any reasonable and lawful use, so long as he does not thereby deprive the adjoining landowner of any right of enjoyment of his property which is recognized and protected by law, and so long as his use is not such a one as the law will pronounce a nuisance.'

"No American decision has been cited, and independent research has revealed none, in which it has been held that—in the absence of some contractual or statutory obligation—a landowner has a legal right to the free flow of light and air across the adjoining land of his neighbor. Even at common law, the landowner had no legal right, in the absence of an easement or uninterrupted use and enjoyment for a period of 20 years, to unobstructed light and air from the adjoining land....

"There being then no legal right to the free flow of light and air from the adjoining land, it is universally held that where a structure serves a useful and beneficial purpose, it does not give rise to a cause of action, either for damages or for an injunction...even though it causes injury to another by cutting off the light and air and interfering with the view that would otherwise be available over adjoining land in its natural state, regardless of the fact that the structure may have been erected partly for spite....

"The construction of the 14-story addition is proceeding under a permit issued by the city pursuant to the mandate of this court...which permit authorized completion of the 14-story addition according to a plan showing a 76-foot setback from the ocean bulkhead line. Moreover, the plaintiff's objection to the distance of the structure from the ocean appears to have been made for the first time in the instant suit, which was filed almost a year after the beginning of the construction of the addition, at a time when it was roughly eight stories in height, representing the expenditure by defendants of several million dollars. In these circumstances, it is our view that the plaintiff has stated no cause of action for equitable relief based on the violation of the ordinance—assuming, arguendo, that there has been a violation.

"Since it affirmatively appears that the plaintiff has not established a cause of action against the defendants by reason of the structure here in question, the order granting a temporary injunction should be and it is hereby reversed with the directions to dismiss the complaint."

Ethical Dimension

Is it ethical to block sunlight to the resort competitor's location?

⬤

■ Nuisance Law

Long before cities and counties enacted zoning regulations, the common law recognized that one person's use of land could interfere with the rights of others to use and enjoy their land. Such interference is called a **nuisance**. The injured parties may be able to get damages for any actual financial losses and a court injunction to stop the wrongful conduct. Even before environmental protection statutes, a business which was polluting a stream could be sued under the nuisance theory and sanctions could be imposed.

One landowner's use cannot prevent others' enjoyment of nearby lands.

More and more of us live and work closer and closer together. Most of us are no longer separated by 160 acre farms. Most of us are crowded together in apartments, stores, factories, offices, restaurants, and theaters. If one of us lights a cigarette, dozens of others smell (and inhale) the smoke. Part of the price we have to pay for living in such close contract with others is a limitation on our freedom to do as we please, even on our own property. Where there are two conflicting land uses, a court may have a very difficult job balancing one against the other. The following case is one example of this balancing.

SPUR INDUSTRIES V. DEL E. WEBB DEVELOPMENT CO.

494 P.2d 700 (Ariz. 1972)

Facts: In 1954, Youngtown, located about fifteen miles west of Phoenix, was founded as a retirement community. The area had been a farming area since 1911. A feedlot company had started operating two and a half miles south of Youngtown in 1956. Spur Industries later took over this feedlot business. By 1959, there were twenty-five such cattle feeding operations in the area. At that time, Del Webb began work on its large retirement development, Sun City, and by 1960 had 450 to 500 homes completed or under construction. In 1962, Spur enlarged its operation to 114 acres and by 1967 came within 500 feet of the Sun

City property. Del Webb's manager testified that homes in the southwestern part of Sun City, nearest the feedlots, could not be sold. By 1967, Spur had 20,000 to 30,000 cattle on the lots, producing over one million pounds of wet manure per day. Del Webb sued to prevent continued operation of the feedlots, due to the flies and the smell. The trial court granted the injunction, and Spur appeals.

Issue: Can the feedlots be enjoined as a public nuisance?

Decision: Yes. Judgment is affirmed, but the case is remanded to decide how much in damages Del Webb should pay to Spur, since Spur was the prior user.

Rule: A landowner's use of its property which substantially and continuously interferes with the rights of others in the community can be enjoined.

Discussion: *By Vice Chief Justice CAMERON:*

"[D]espite the admittedly good feedlot management and good housekeeping practices by Spur, the resulting odor and flies produced an annoying if not unhealthy situation as far as the senior citizens of southern Sun City were concerned. There is no doubt that some of the citizens of Sun City were unable to enjoy the outdoor living which Del Webb had advertised and that Del Webb was faced with sales resistance from prospective purchasers as well as strong and persistent complaints from the people who had purchased homes in that area....

"The difference between a private nuisance and a public nuisance is generally one of degree. A private nuisance is one affecting a single individual or a definite small number of persons in the enjoyment of private rights not common to the public, while a public nuisance is one affecting the rights enjoyed by citizens as a part of the public. To constitute a public nuisance, the nuisance must affect a considerable number of people or an entire community or neighborhood....

"It is clear that as to the citizens of Sun City, the operation of Spur's feedlot was both a public and a private nuisance....

"In addition to protecting the public interest, however, courts of equity are concerned with protecting the operator of a lawful, albeit obnoxious, business from the result of a knowing and willful encroachment by others near his business....

"It does not equitably or legally follow...that Webb, being entitled to the injunction, is then free of any liability to Spur if Webb has in fact been the cause of the damage Spur has sustained. It does not seem harsh to require a developer, who has taken advantage of the lesser land values in a rural area as well as the availability of large tracts of land on which to build and develop a new town or city in the area, to indemnify those who are forced to leave as a result."

Ethical Dimension

Why should Spur have to move its operations, since it was there first?

INTELLECTUAL PROPERTY

Production requires ideas and know-how.

In addition to acquiring a physical location for its operation, the business will also need to acquire other equipment. Depending on its nature, the business may need office furniture and equipment, production machinery, computers, motor vehicles, and many other tangible items. For many firms, the key assets are those which are the product of human ingenuity—technology, or as the law describes it, **intellectual property**. In popular terminology, intellectual property might be defined as business know-how. In technical terms, intellectual property includes trade secrets, patents, copyrights, and trademarks.

Even this simple listing conveys the crucial importance of intellectual property to modern business. Patents and trade secrets are most important in manufacturing businesses and will be considered here. Copyrights and trademarks have primary significance in marketing operations and will thus be discussed in Chapters 17 and 18.

Trade Secrets

Secret business information is protected by law.

Any piece of non-public information which has commercial value can qualify as a **trade secret**. It will enjoy legal protection so long as it is in fact secret. Examples of trade secrets would include a specific cola formula and a chicken colonel's "eleven herbs and spices." Customer lists, formulas, and business plans could also qualify for protection as trade secrets.

Former employees, managers, and partners can be enjoined from disclosing trade secrets to business competitors. Competitors who gain knowledge of the trade secret by spying or other improper means can be enjoined from using or disclosing the trade secret. Common law protection is available even though the trade secret is not subject to patent or copyright.

Patents

There are no property rights in an idea, as such. However. inventions which are expressed in tangible form can be patented. A **patent**, issued by the U.S. Patent Office, gives the patent owner the exclusive right to manufacture the item for seventeen years. To be patentable, the invention must be "useful," new ("novel"), and "unobvious." The patentability issue is decided initially by the Patent Office, but is subject to court review. The U.S. Supreme Court has held that a computer program, since it is simply a mathematical formula, is not patentable—as a rule. However, in the *Diehr* case, excerpted below, a majority of the Supreme Court approved the patentability of a "process" for operating a rubber molding press with the aid of a computer. Further litigation of the patentability of computer software seems inevitable unless the patent statute is amended one way or the other.

A patent gives the holder the exclusive right to make and use an invention.

Once granted, the patent is valid for seventeen years. During that period, only the patent-holder can make and sell the patented device. However, at the end of the seventeen-year period, anyone can produce and market the product. For this reason, companies such as the cola company and the chicken colonel may wish to keep their secret formulas as trade secrets rather than patent them. The other disadvantage to patenting is the fact that the patent is a public document. A competitor can study the patent and then try to design a comparable product without copying anything covered by the patent. The danger of *not* having a patent is, of course, that a competitor may come up with a similar formula on its own, or by reverse-engineering from your product. (Reverse engineering involves an analysis of the end product and a logical working-backwards to see how it must have been produced.) If your formula is not patented, anyone who comes up with it independently can use it in the marketplace.

DIAMOND V. DIEHR

101 S. Ct. 1048 (1981)

Facts: The patent application at issue was filed by Diehr and Lutton on August 6, 1975. The claimed invention is a process for molding raw, uncured synthetic rubber into cured precision products. The process uses a mold for precisely shaping the uncured material under heat and pressure and then curing the synthetic rubber in the mold so that the product will retain its shape and be functionally operative after the molding is completed.

Diehr and Lutton claim that their process ensures the production of molded articles which are properly cured. Achieving the perfect cure depends upon several factors including the thickness of the article to be molded, the temperature of the molding process, and the amount of time that the article is allowed to remain in the press. It is possible, using well-known time, temperature, and cure relationships, to calculate by means of the Arrhenius equation when to open the press and remove the cured product. Nonetheless, according to Diehr and Lutton, the industry has not been able to obtain uniformly accurate cures because the temperature of the molding press could not be precisely measured. This made it difficult to do the necessary computations to determine cure time. The conventional industry practice has been to calculate the cure time as the shortest time in which all parts of the product will definitely be cured. The shortcoming of this practice is that it inevitably led in some instances to overestimating the mold-opening time and overcuring the rubber and in other instances to underestimating that time and undercuring the product.

Diehr and Lutton characterize their contribution to the art as residing in the process of constantly measuring the actual temperature inside the mold. These temperature measurements are then automatically fed into a computer which repeatedly recalculates the cure time by use of the Arrhenius equation. When the recalculated time equals the actual time that has elapsed since the press was closed, the computer signals a device to open the press. According to the applicants, the continuous measuring of the temperature inside the mold cavity, the feeding of this information to a digital computer which constantly recalculates the cure time, and the signaling by the computer to open the press are all new in the art.

A patent examiner and the Patent Office Board of Appeals both denied the patent, but the Court of Customs and Patent Appeals upheld its validity. Sydney Diamond, the Commissioner of Patents, asked for U.S. Supreme Court review.

Issue: Is a process for curing synthetic rubber which includes in several of its steps the use of a mathematical formula and a programmed digital computer patentable subject matter?

Decision: Yes. Judgment for Diehr and Lutton is affirmed.

Rule: "Whoever invents or discovers any new and useful process, machine manufacture, or composition of matter, or any new and useful improvement thereof, may obtain a patent thereof, subject to the conditions and requirements of this Title." 35 U.S.Code § 101.

Discussion: *By Justice* REHNQUIST:

"The Patent Act of 1793 defined statutory subject matter as 'any new and useful art, machine, manufacture or composition of matter, or any new or useful improvement thereof.'... Not until the patent laws were recodified in 1952 did Congress replace the word 'art' with the word 'process.' It is that latter word which we confront today, and in order to determine its meaning we may not be unmindful of the Committee Reports accompanying the 1952 Act which inform us that Congress intended statutory subject matter to 'include anything under the sun that is made by man.'...

"Analyzing [applicants'] claims according to the...statements from our cases, we think that a physical and chemical process for molding precision synthetic rubber products falls within the §101 categories of possibly patentable subject matter. That [applicants'] claims involve the transformation of an article, in this case raw uncured synthetic rubber, into a different state or thing cannot be disputed. The [applicants'] claims describe in detail a step-by-step method for accomplishing such beginning with the loading of a mold with raw uncured rubber and ending with the eventual opening of the press at the conclusion of the cure. Industrial processes such as this are the type which have historically been eligible to receive the protection of our patent laws.

"Our conclusion regarding [applicants'] claims is not altered by the fact that in several steps of the process a mathematical equation and a programmed digital computer are used. This Court has undoubtedly recognized limits to §101 and every discovery is not embraced within the statutory terms. Excluded from such patent protection are laws of nature, physical phenomena and abstract ideas.... 'A principle, in the abstract, is a fundamental truth; an original cause; a motive; these cannot be patented, as no one can claim in either of them an exclusive right.'...

"The [applicants] here do not seek to patent a mathematical formula. Instead, they seek patent protection for a process of curing synthetic rubber. Their process admittedly employs a well known mathematical equation, but they do not seek to pre-empt the use of that equation. Rather, they seek only to foreclose from others the use of that equation in conjunction with all of the other steps in their claimed process. These include installing rubber in a press, closing the mold, constantly determining the temperature of the mold, constantly recalculating the appropriate cure time through the use of the formula and digital computer, and automatically opening the press at the proper time. Obviously, one does not need a 'computer' to cure natural or synthetic rubber, but if the computer use incorporated in the process patent significantly lessens the possibility of 'overcuring' or 'undercuring,' the process as a whole does not thereby become unpatentable subject matter....

"Because we do not view [applicants'] claims as an attempt to patent a mathematical formula, but rather to be drawn to an industrial process for the molding of rubber products, we affirm the judgment of the Court of Customs and Patent Appeals."

Ethical Dimension

Why shouldn't someone who develops a new mathematical formula be able to patent it?

P RODUCT LIABILITY

Traditionally, the liability of sellers for defective goods was not a matter for government regulation, but was rather left to the parties themselves and the specific provisions of their contract. The government might provide uniform standards for weights and measures and might regulate the selling of certain products like drugs and alcohol, but otherwise private contract law prevailed. The rule was **caveat emptor**—let the buyer beware. The seller was liable only for breach of specific provisions of the sales contract or for fraudulent misrepresentations about the character or quality of the goods. The buyer was generally expected to ask the right questions and to make personal investigations and then to decide whether or not to enter into the contract. If things didn't work out as expected, that was too bad; there was generally no remedy against the seller, absent breach or fraud.

Producers of goods are today generally liable for any injury caused by a defect in the product.

Today the rules have been reversed almost completely; the rule might more accurately be described as **caveat vendor**—let the seller beware! It is clear by this time that the area of product liability has mutated into something far different from the traditional private law of contracts. Liability has changed from its basis in the parties' contract to a set of social rules imposed by the courts and the legislatures. Most recently, there has been a strong movement for legislative modification and clarification of some of the most stringent product liability rules. (These new legislative regulations on product liability rules will be discussed in the next chapter.) While it originated as a private law topic, product liability today is being increasingly drawn into the public law area.

Negligence

As part of the general development of the tort of negligence, the courts applied the standard of reasonable care first to the seller and then to the manufacturer of the product. As discussed in Chapter 6, society requires every person to exercise ordinary care in conducting all his or her activities. If this duty to others is breached and an injury results, the injured party can sue the person whose lack of care caused the harm. The remedy is monetary damages. Courts began to hold sellers to this same duty, and also manufacturers. Social policy requires that persons be held liable for the results of their carelessness and disregard of the health and safety of others. The manufacturer's liability for negligence which causes harm to the ultimate buyer has been recognized in this country at least since the famous MacPherson case in New York in 1916. MacPherson was injured when a defective wheel on his new Buick collapsed. Justice Cardozo said that retail buyers should be able to sue the manufacturer for negligence, even though the car was bought from an independent dealer.

Negligence is still a valid theory of product liability, and, on the right set of facts, may be the sole basis for recovery. If the defect is one that must have been apparent or that would have been discovered with any sort of reasonable inspection of the product, the negligence of the seller and/or manufacturer may be established without too much difficulty. Where the alleged defect is the failure of an internal part or component, however, proof of negligence may be very difficult. This is particularly true if large numbers of the same product have been manufactured, sold, and used without incident. If the product was sold at the retail level in a closed container, it would also be very difficult to establish a negligence case against the seller. However, if it could be proved that the seller had dropped or crushed the container and that the mishandling caused the defect, liability could be imposed.

A goods producer is liable for its carelessness in design or production of the product.

Traditionally, any negligence by an injured plaintiff which contributed to help cause the injury prevented recovery against the defendant. In many product liability suits, the plaintiff was misusing or abusing the product when the injury occurred. For example, in the Moran case in Chapter 4, two young girls poured a highly flammable perfume into a flame to see how their home-made candles would smell when they burned it. Under the traditional rule of **contributory negligence**, such persons could not recover for their injuries. Today, however, many states have adopted the rule of **comparative negligence**, in which the negligent plaintiff is still entitled to recover at least part of the damages if the defendant was more at fault than the plaintiff.

Warranties

While liability for negligence is imposed under a tort theory as a general social responsibility, **warranty** liability originated as a contract law theory. Clearly, a seller who has not fulfilled specific guarantees should be held liable to the buyer for all damages resulting from this breach of the contract. Gradually, by court decision and by statute, warranty liability has become more and more socially imposed and less and less the result of bargaining between the parties. This change has occurred in several ways: by expansion of the circumstances under which warranties are made, by the imposition of implied warranties, and by the courts' refusals to recognize disclaimers of liability.

Producers may be held liable for breach of promises made about the goods.

The obvious express warranty case occurs where a specific guarantee is made to the buyer. In addition, the Uniform Commercial Code (UCC) says that any affirmation of fact or promise which relates to the goods and which becomes part of the basis of the bargain creates an **express warranty** that the goods will conform to the statement or promise. No specific reliance has to be proved by the buyer. The reliance is assumed by the UCC, unless there is a clear indication otherwise. The UCC also states that express warranties arise where the seller furnishes the buyer with any sample, model, or description of the goods. Under prior law, these situations gave rise to implied warranties of conformity. Now, as express warranties, they are almost impossible to disclaim without renegotiating the whole contract.

Producers make an implied guarantee that their goods are reasonably fit for normal use.

The UCC recognizes two major implied warranties—the **implied warranty of merchantability** and the **implied warranty of fitness** for the buyer's particular purpose. Merchantability is defined in the UCC as meaning that the goods are of fair, average quality and that they are reasonably fit for their normal use. In addition, merchantability implies that the goods are properly packaged and labelled, that they conform to any promises made on the package or label, and that they will pass without objection in the trade under the contract description. This implied warranty of merchantability arises only if the seller is a **merchant** with respect to goods of that kind—a dealer, or one whose occupation makes the person an expert on that sort of goods, or one who employs an agent or broker whose occupation makes the agent an expert on the goods. Under the UCC, the serving for value of food or drink to be consumed either on or off the seller's premises is a sale for the purposes of the implied warranty of merchantability. Under special statutes in most states, giving a blood transfusion to a patient as part of a course of medical treatment is *not* a sale. This means that the patient must prove negligence against the doctor or hospital to recover for any injuries caused by the transfusion. Courts may differ as to whether implied warranties arise in other "combined" transactions, where services are being performed and goods are being transferred. Examples include medicines administered in a hospital or parts installed in a car by a service garage. In such cases, the courts usually try to determine which aspect of the contract is the major part. If the contract is basically a sale of goods with some incidental services also provided, the rules for goods will be applied.

The implied warranty of fitness does not automatically arise every time goods are sold by a merchant. It arises only when the buyer somehow makes known to the seller the buyer's *special* needs. Also, the buyer must let the seller know that the buyer is relying on the seller to select the proper goods to do that *specific* job. This contrasts with the warranty of merchantability, by which the merchant guarantees only that the goods are reasonably suitable for the normal uses to which they are put. Stated another way, the merchantability warranty is general; the fitness warranty is specific. If the warranty of fitness for a particular purpose has been made, it is breached if the goods do not take care of this buyer's special needs. The fitness warranty is not satisfied just because the goods are merchantable. The fitness warranty may arise, under the UCC, even though the goods are brand name goods, so long as the seller did the selecting at the buyer's request.

CUMULATIVE WARRANTIES

Under the UCC, there is a presumption that all warranties made on the facts apply, that they are consistent with each other, and that they are cumulative. Unless all the warranties that were made are satisfied, the buyer has a case for damages caused by the breach. The UCC also extends all warranties made by the seller to the buyer to certain third parties. Originally, warranty protection was extended to members of the buyer's family, household, and guests in the buyer's home. The UCC provides two alternate versions of this section which states may adopt. Under the most liberal version, the seller is liable to "any person who may reasonably be expected to use, consume or be affected by the goods." The UCC did not extend liability back up the chain of distribution to the manufacturer. There was no need to do so, since the courts in nearly every state were imposing such liability on a case-by-case basis. In the vast majority of states, recovery for breach of warranty no longer requires proof of a contractual relationship ("**privity**" of con**tract**) between the plaintiff and the defendant.

Producers are liable for breach of any express or implied guarantee that was made.

DISCLAIMERS

Just as dramatic as the extension of warranty liability up and down the chain of distribution has been the courts' refusal to recognize the validity of contractual **disclaimers** of warranty liability. The UCC does recognize the validity of such disclaimers, within limits, provided that they are stated in the manner required by the applicable UCC sections. To disclaim merchantability, the disclaimer must mention the word "merchantability." If part of a writing, the disclaimer must be stated conspicuously—as by using different size, style, or color of type, or by underlining or shading the disclaimer. To disclaim fitness, the disclaimer need not mention "fitness" specifically, but the disclaimer must be made in writing and must be conspicuous as a part of the writing. It is also possible to disclaim both implied warranties by stating that the

To be valid, product disclaimers must be stated in a certain way.

goods are sold "as is" or "with all faults." The UCC provides that where an express warranty and an express disclaimer conflict, the disclaimer is ineffective. This means that it is very difficult to remove an express warranty, once made, without renegotiating the whole contract.

UNCONSCIONABILITY

Product disclaimers may not be valid if they are grossly unfair.

Even though a disclaimer is stated in the manner specified by the UCC, it may still be held ineffective under other UCC provisions. The most widely applied section is that dealing with **unconscionability**, meaning gross unfairness. Where the court finds that the contract, or a particular provision of the contract such as a disclaimer clause, is unconscionable, the court has three choices. It may refuse to enforce the contract, refuse to enforce the offending clause, or interpret that clause to avoid any grossly unfair result. Cases where the court so rules typically involve form contracts that are signed on a take-it-or-leave-it basis by unsophisticated consumers with little knowledge of their rights. Under such circumstances, the disclaimer may very well produce a grossly unfair result if enforced as written. The UCC further states that a disclaimer which limits a consumer's right to recover for personal injury is presumed to be unconscionable. The seller or manufacturer has the burden of convincing the court otherwise. The UCC also states that a contracting party's basic duties of good faith, diligence, reasonableness, and care may not be disclaimed by agreement. This section, too, can be used to prevent the enforcement of disclaimers of warranties.

In sum, warranty liability is no longer controlled by the contract between the seller and the buyer, but is rather another area where social standards have been and are being imposed.

The *Henningsen* case is generally recognized as the most important precedent in product liability. It represents the beginning of the "product liability revolution." It abolished the privity of contract requirement for a suit against the manufacturer and refused to uphold a form disclaimer clause in the retail sale contract. This case is thus perhaps the most important commercial law decision in our history.

HENNINGSEN V. BLOOMFIELD MOTORS, INC.

161 A.2d 69 (N.J. 1960)

Facts: Mrs. Henningsen was driving her new Plymouth when she heard a loud noise from under the hood. She said it "felt as if something had cracked." The steering wheel spun in her hands, and the car veered to the right and crashed into a brick wall. Her husband, Claus, had purchased the car ten days before as a Mother's Day present. When the Henningsens sued the dealer (Bloomfield) and Chrysler, the defendants said that they had disclaimed all liability in the sale contract, except for a promise to replace any defective part at the factory. The trial court refused to enforce the contract disclaimer, so the defendants appealed.

Issue: Can the manufacturer and seller disclaim all liability for defects in consumer goods which are purchased new from an authorized dealer?

Decision: No. Judgment for plaintiffs affirmed.

Rule: Warranties are imposed by law to protect the buyer, not to exempt the seller from any responsibility.

Discussion: *By Justice FRANCIS:*

"[A]utomobile manufacturers, including Chrysler Corporation, undertake large scale advertising programs over television, radio, in newspapers, magazines and all media of communication in order to persuade the public to buy their products.... [A] number of jurisdictions, conscious of modern marketing practices, have declared that when a manufacturer engages in advertising in order to bring his goods and their quality to the attention of the public and thus to create consumer demand, the representations made constitute an express warranty running directly to a buyer who purchases in reliance thereon. The fact that the sale is consummated with an independent dealer does not obviate that warranty....

"[W]arranties originated in the law to safeguard the buyer and not to limit the liability of the seller or manufacturer. It seems obvious in this instance that the motive was to avoid the warranty obligations which are normally incident to such sales. The language gave little and withdrew much. In return for the delusive remedy of replacement of defective parts at the factory, the buyer is said to have accepted the exclusion of the maker's liability for personal injuries arising from the breach of the warranty. An instinctively felt sense of justice cries out against such a sharp bargain....

"The warranty before us is a standardized form designed for mass use. It is imposed upon the automobile consumer. He takes it or leaves it, and he must take it to buy an automobile. No bargaining is engaged in with respect to it. In fact, the dealer through whom it comes to the buyer is without authority to alter it; his function is ministerial—simply to deliver it....

"The gross inequality for bargaining position occupied by the consumer in the automobile industry is thus apparent. There is no competition among the car makers in the area of express warranty....

"In the area of sale of goods, the legislative will has imposed an implied warranty of merchantability as a general incident of sale of an automobile by description. The warranty does not depend upon the affirmative intention of the parties. It is a child of the law; it annexes itself to the contract because of the very nature of the transaction.... The disclaimer of the implied warranty and exclusion of all obligations except those specifically assumed by the express warranty signify a studied effort to frustrate that protection.... Chrysler's attempted disclaimer of an implied warranty of merchantability and of the obligations arising therefrom is so inimical to the public good as to compel an adjudication of its invalidity."

Ethical Dimension

Why shouldn't a manufacturer be able to disclaim all its responsibility for the goods it advertises and sells?

Strict Liability in Tort

From earliest times, legal systems have recognized that a person could be held liable for injuries to others by that person's agents or servants. The principal or employer might not really be at fault in the sense of having done anything wrong. However, there was fault—either intentional or negligent wrong—on the part of the agent or employee. The imposition of liability for injury to others where there was no proof of fault at all, even by circumstantial evidence, occurred only in very limited categories of cases. The owner of a dangerous wild animal was held strictly liable for any injury caused by the animal. This liability existed no matter how the injury occurred or who was at fault, or even if no one was at fault. Likewise, a person engaged in an extra-hazardous activity, such as blasting, was held strictly liable for injuries to others. Liability was imposed even though all reasonable care had been taken to avoid such injury. There may be some marginal definitional questions as to what is a wild animal or an extra-hazardous activity. In general, however, these are very limited classes of business risks and are therefore quite manageable.

Producers are usually liable where a defect in the product causes personal injury.

As part of the general expansion of warranty liability, courts gradually began to create a third category of **strict liability**. The first cases involved food products intended for human consumption. The processor or manufacturer was held liable to the ultimate consumer where the food product created an unreasonable risk to the consumer's health, even without proof of negligence. Some of these cases could, perhaps, be explained on the basis of a presumption of negligence. However, the courts came to impose liability even where the processor could show that all reasonable steps to avoid a harmful product had in fact been taken. This new liability without fault was then extended, by analogy, to drugs and cosmetics. Both types of products were also used in or on the human body. If the drug or cosmetic was defective in any way, and injury resulted, the manufacturer and the seller could be held liable even though no amount of reasonable care could have prevented the injury. The courts then began to talk about strict liability for any product that was inherently dangerous if negligently made. For example, an automobile would be subject to the strict liability rule.

There are still some differences from state to state in the exact limits of this newer theory of product liability. Most courts, though, now agree that anyone who is caused an injury by a defective product can sue anyone responsible for the defect. The product must be shown to have been defective when it left the defendant's control. The defect must be shown to have caused the injury, and the amount of damages which result must be proved. This new theory is thus very favorable from a plaintiff's point of view. It cannot be successfully defended simply by showing a statistically high success rate for the product. It would be theoretically possible, but extremely difficult, to disclaim this new strict liability in tort.

The traditional defenses against a negligence case—contributory negligence and assumption of risk—do not apply in the same way in a strict liability case. A defense exists only where it is shown that the plaintiff's own conduct, rather than the defect, caused the injury. For example, a defense exists where the plaintiff discovered the defect, had a chance to fix the product, but then decided to use the defective product in its dangerous condition. Similarly, the fact that the "defect" was not known, or even knowable, at the time the product was made does not prevent the imposition of liability. For products made with asbestos, which was not known to be dangerous in the 1930s and 1940s, most courts have rejected this **state of the art defense**.

Producers may be liable even if they were not aware of the defect when the product was made and sold.

The Illinois court in the next case discussed the state of the art defense. However, its major focus was on two other issues: a manufacturer's liability for property damage caused by its product and the application of the statute of limitations to governmental agencies.

BOARD OF EDUCATION OF CHICAGO V. A.C. AND S, INC.

546 N.E.2d 580 (Ill. 1989)

Facts: The Chicago board of education and thirty-three other school districts sued A, C and S along with seventy-seven other named defendants, ranging from local lumber yards and builders to multinational corporations. The various defendants had made, sold, or installed asbestos products which had been used in the various school districts' buildings. Most of the construction had been done many years before. Because of the health hazards caused by asbestos, Illinois had passed a statute in 1987 which required all school districts to remove all asbestos which posed a significant health risk and to repair or contain all other asbestos sources. The costs of such removal or repair would be enormous.

The school districts' complaints included thirteen different theories of liability, including negligence, breach of warranty, strict liability, consumer fraud, intentional misrepresentation, negligent misrepresentation, and restitution. The trial court dismissed all thirteen theories. Plaintiffs appealed as to nine theories (including those listed above). The Illinois court of appeals reversed as to the seven listed theories of liability and affirmed the trial court's dismissal of the other two theories. The defendants appeal from the reinstatement of these seven claims.

Issues: Is strict liability applicable where the "defective" product is installed in a building? Is the statute of limitations applicable to governmental bodies?

Decision: Yes to the first issue. No to the second issue. The appeals court is affirmed as to claims for strict liability, negligence, and negligent misrepresentation. All other claims are dismissed.

Rules: Strict liability does not apply to "commercial" or "economic" losses, but it does apply where a defective product causes damage to other property.

Statutes of limitations do not apply to "public rights" unless expressly so stated in the statute.

Discussion: *By Justice* RYAN:

"The demarcation between tort recovery for physical harm and a contract recovery for economic losses usually depends on (1)the nature of the defect and (2)the manner in which the damage occurred.... As stated, the defect in a tort claim results in either personal injury or property damage.... Whereas, in the economic loss doctrine, the defect results in damages for the inadequate value of the product, costs of repair and replacement of the defective product, loss of profits, as well as diminution in the value of the product because of its inferior quality and failure to work for the general purposes for which it was manufactured and sold....

"Perhaps it is difficult, and may appear somewhat artificial, to fit a claim for asbestos damage within the framework which has been established for more traditional tort and contract actions. Indeed, the nature of the 'defect' and the 'damage' caused by asbestos is unique from most of the cases we have addressed. Nonetheless, we do believe that this complaint has alleged sufficient facts to establish a tort action...."

"The nature of the defect...is the asbestos fibers, which are toxic and which, it has been determined, may, in certain circumstances, be harmful.... It is alleged in these complaints that friable asbestos exists in plaintiffs' buildings and asbestos has been released throughout the schools. We need not, in ruling on this motion to dismiss, determine whether the amounts of friable asbestos which exist in the buildings are harmful. Our focus is to take as true the facts alleged in the complaints and determine whether they sufficiently state a claim.

"We conclude that it would be incongruous to argue there is no damage to other property when a harmful element exists throughout a building or an area of a building which by law must be corrected and at trial may be proven to exist at unacceptably dangerous levels. The view that asbestos fibers may contaminate a building sufficiently to allege damage to property has been recently adopted in a number of cases....

"[T]he public should not suffer as a result of the negligence of its officers and agents in failing to properly assert causes of action which belong to the public...

"This complaint has alleged...an interest in the safety of these public buildings and in the safety of a large segment of this State's population which attends the public schools and for the children who will in the future attend these schools. There is also the interest of the parents, faculty, staff and other people who use or will use our public school system. Moreover, unlike 'any other property owner,' these buildings are owned by the government, maintained with tax revenue, and used for mandatory classroom attendance as well as for other public functions."

Ethical Dimension

Is it fair to impose liability for a condition which was not known to be dangerous when the product was made and sold? Is it fair to exempt governmental bodies from the requirement of filing their claims within a certain number of years?

■ Market Share Liability

The theory of strict liability is based on the fact that a manufacturer's defective product has caused personal injury or property damage. The person sustaining the injury or loss sues the manufacturer whose defective product is responsible. But what happens when there are several

A few states have held all producers liable for market share percentages where a generic product has caused injury.

manufacturers of the same chemically identical product, and it is impossible to prove which one caused the injury to a particular plaintiff? One possibility would be to permit no recovery at all, since the responsible party could not be identified. That result would preserve the legal niceties of the "burden of proof," since a plaintiff generally cannot collect without proving the particular defendant's responsibility for the injury.

Confronted with this proof difficulty, several states have taken a different approach. Each of the several defendants which manufactured some of the product which caused the plaintiff's harm is held liable for a proportionate part of the plaintiff's damages. This is the so-called **market share liability** theory. The liability is imposed because each of the defendants did make and sell some of the harmful product. Each of them thus did expose the public to an unreasonable risk, even though the plaintiff in the particular case cannot prove which of them caused the plaintiff's injury.

In the following case, the New York court also had to answer a related question—can a producer avoid liability by showing that it could not have been its product which was used by the plaintiff? The courts have not answered that question uniformly.

HYMOWITZ V. ELI LILLY AND CO.

539 N.E.2d 1069 (N.Y. 1989)

Facts: Mindy Hymowitz and several other plaintiffs filed lawsuits against Eli Lilly and several other drug companies. Plaintiffs claimed that they had been injured when their mothers took the drug diethylstilbestrol (DES) during pregnancy. The Food and Drug Administration had originally approved use of DES in 1941, for non-pregnancy illnesses. In 1947, the FDA approved use of DES to prevent miscarriages. In 1971, however, the FDA banned further use of the drug for this latter purpose when studies showed it had harmful effects on the children of the mothers who took it during pregnancy. About 300 companies made the drug during the period in which it was used to prevent miscarriages. All DES was of identical chemical composition. Because of the long time lapse between use of the drug and the occurrence of illness in the children, nearly all records of distribution are gone. As a result, there is generally no proof of which plaintiff took which defendant's drug. The trial court nevertheless refused to dismiss these cases. The appellate court affirmed. The defendants asked the New York Court of Appeals (the state's highest court) for further review.

Issue: Can manufacturers of a generic product be held liable for a share of plaintiff's damages, even if plaintiff cannot prove which one made the product that harmed?

Decision: Yes, each manufacturer is liable for its market share of the generic product.

Rule: Each manufacturer whose products caused risk of harm to the public should be held liable according to the proportion of the risk it created.

Discussion: *By Chief Judge* WACHTLER:

"In a products liability action, identification of the exact defendant whose product injured the plaintiff is, of course, generally required.... In DES cases in which such identification is possible, actions may proceed under established principles of products liability.... The record now before us, however, presents the question of whether a DES plaintiff may recover against a DES manufacturer when identification of the producer of the specific drug that caused the injury is impossible....

"The past decade of DES litigation has produced a number of alternative approaches to resolve this question. Thus, in a sense, we are now in an enviable position; the efforts of other courts provided examples for contending with this difficult issue, and enough time has passed so that the actual administration and real effects of these solutions now can be observed. With these useful guides in hand, a path may be struck for our own conclusion....

"[F]or essentially practical reasons, we adopt a market share theory using a national market. We are aware that the adoption of a national market will likely result in a disproportion between the liability of individual manufacturers and the actual injuries each manufacturer caused in this State. Thus our market share theory cannot be founded on the belief that, over the run of cases, liability will approximate causation in this State.... Nor does the use of a national market provide a reasonable link between liability and the risk created by a defendant to a particular plaintiff.... Instead, we choose to apportion liability so as to correspond to the over-all culpability of each defendant, measured by the amount of risk of injury each defendant created to the public-at-large. Use of a national market is a fair method, we believe, of apportioning defendants' liabilities according to their total culpability in marketing DES for use during pregnancy. Under the circumstances, this is an equitable way to provide plaintiffs with the relief they deserve, while also rationally distributing the responsibility for plaintiffs' injuries among defendants.

"To be sure, a defendant cannot be held liable if it did not participate in the marketing of DES for pregnancy use; if a DES producer satisfies us that it was not a member of the market for DES sold for pregnancy use, disallowing exculpation would be unfair and unjust. Nevertheless, because liability here is based on the over-all risk produced, and not causation in a single case, there should be no exculpation of a defendant who, although a member of the market producing DES for pregnancy use, appears not to have caused a particular plaintiff's injury. It is merely a windfall for a producer to escape liability solely because it manufactured a more identifiable pill, or sold only to certain drugstores. These fortuities in no way diminish the culpability of a defendant for marketing the product, which is the basis of liability here....

"Accordingly, in each case the order of the Appellate Division should be affirmed."

Ethical Dimension

Is it fair and just to force a company to pay damages to a person it can prove that it did not injure? Is a company "culpable" when it sells a product which the government has approved for sale, and which all current tests indicate is safe for use?

■ Other Types of Transactions

Lessors of goods are usually held to the same liabilities as sellers of goods.

The three major theories of liability discussed above (negligence, warranty, strict liability) were developed in the context of a contract for the sale of goods. What about a seller of land or services? What about non-sales transactions? The liability rules for these other types of transactions vary from state to state. Most states now agree that a professional lessor of goods—for example, a car rental agency—is subject to the same three theories of liability as a merchant-seller of goods. In other words, a car rental agency could be held liable for any proven negligence, for any warranties not met (including express statements in brochures and advertisements, and the implied warranties of merchantability and fitness), or for any defect in the leased car which caused injury. On the other hand, where there is simply a free loan of a car or some other item, the lender's only obligation is to disclose to the borrower any known defects in the goods. (The technical legal term for these temporary transfers of possession of personal property is **bailment**. The lessor or lender is the bailor. The person renting or borrowing the item is the bailee.)

A new section on leases of goods, Article 2A, has been added to the UCC. It has not yet been adopted by all states, but probably will be in the near future. The warranty provisions of Article 2A are very similar to those in Article 2 for the sale of goods.

Traditionally, *caveat emptor* has applied to the sale or lease of real estate. The land is there; it can be inspected by the buyer or tenant; questions can be asked. Many states, however, have now passed statutes which impose an implied warranty of habitability on the landlord. In such states, the tenant may sue for damages or withhold rentals if the warranty is breached. Likewise, about half the states now impose a kind of implied merchantability warranty on the seller of new homes. Some of these states have thus far imposed the warranty only for machinery and equipment, such as an air conditioner or a furnace, in the new home.

Real estate sellers may make quality guarantees as to structures on the land.

For services contracts, the states still generally agree that there are no implied quality warranties. To recover for "defects" in the job, the customer must generally prove a breach of specific contract clauses, or a breach of ordinary professional standards of care and competence, i.e., malpractice or professional negligence. An accountant, for example, only guarantees to do what is specified in the contract and to exercise reasonable professional care.

REVIEW

This chapter examined three areas of the law closely related to the production function of business. First, since nearly every business needs a fixed base of operations, you read about the legal rules covering the acquisition and use of land. Second, since ideas are a crucial part of many of today's high-tech businesses, you covered two aspects of intellectual property—trade secrets and patents. Third, since producers of tangible products face a whole new set of liabilities, you studied the major theories of product liability. In the next chapter, you will see how the production process is increasingly subject to regulation by national, state, and local governments.

REVIEW QUESTIONS AND PROBLEMS

1. What is the difference between an option and a purchase agreement?

2. What is the difference between a warranty deed and a quitclaim deed?

3. Why is the law of nuisance important to business operations?

4. What are the relative advantages and disadvantages of patent protection and trade secret protection of business ideas?

5. Why is caveat emptor not a viable rule for product buyers in modern society?

6. What is the difference between product liability based on negligence and product liability based on strict liability?

7. Grape Computers manufacturers a popular line of computers known as "the Grapes." Makurown, Inc., a retailer of electronic parts, began selling a computer kit called "Grapefruit," which the buyer could assemble into a computer. To make sure that its kit could use all the application programs available for "the Grapes," Makurown used semiconductor chips which contained operating instructions (to the computer) which were essentially the same as the ones Grape had copyrighted for its computers. When Grape sued for patent, copyright, and trademark infringement, Makurown claimed that these internal operating instructions were only "ideas" which themselves cannot be patented or copyrighted. Is this a valid argument? Explain.

8. Weathermen Company provides weather modification services, using chemicals and other means. It was hired by a group of farmers to "seed" rain clouds in the area with chemicals to prevent hailstorms, which had been damaging the farmers' crops. After several weeks of these "seeding" operations, several nearby landowners sued for an injunction, claiming that the cloud-seeding was depriving their properties of normal rainfall. Do they have a case? Discuss.

9. Tessie was driving her new Gazelle sedan when she had to swerve suddenly to avoid colliding with another vehicle. She lost control of the car, and it ran off the road and rolled over, landing upside down. Tessie was seriously injured when the roof supports buckled under the weight of the car. Claiming that the car was "defective," she sued the manufacturer, Major Motors. Major can prove that the car met all U.S. government safety standards and that the roof support system was similar to those used by all other carmakers. Tessie's lawyer has found an engineer, Jamie, who used to work for Major. In Jamie's opinion, every car made during this period was "defective" because none of them had a built-in roll-bar system to support the roof. Should Tessie collect? Why or why not?

10. Myron and Myrna Mild sued the Shore Sand Company, which operates a large sand and gravel quarry. Shore digs large pits in the ground to extract the sand and gravel which it sells. Periodically it pumps water from the bottom of its pits, emptying the water into a nearby creek. As a result of these operations, ground water flowed from underneath the Milds' land, leaving large cavities. Heavy spring rains seeped through the ground and rushed through these cavities. The earth above, and the Milds' house, then collapsed into these holes. Shore said that it was only making "reasonable use" of its own land, and is therefore not liable. How should the court rule? Explain.

SUGGESTIONS FOR FURTHER READING

Leibman, "The Manufacturer's Responsibility to Warn Product Users of Unknowable Dangers," *American Business Law Journal* 21 (Winter 1984): 403.

Razook, "The Ultimate Purchaser's and Remote Seller's Guide Through the Code Defenses in Product Economic Loss Cases," *American Business Law Journal* 23 (Spring 1985): 85.

16
REGULATION
OF
THE
PRODUCTION
PROCESS

"Love your Neighbor; yet don't pull down your hedge."
Benjamin Franklin

LEARNING OBJECTIVES: After you have studied this chapter, you should be able to:

IDENTIFY two major restrictions on land ownership.

DISTINGUISH between private land use restrictions and zoning laws.

EXPLAIN how environmental and safety regulations affect the production process.

DISCUSS the special regulations which apply to manufacturers of three major product categories.

SUMMARIZE the states' recent reforms of product liability laws.

P REVIEW

Production facilities have social pluses and social minuses.

To some extent, there is a kind of "love/hate" relationship between manufacturers and the rest of society. As individuals and as communities we like the jobs, the income, and the tax revenues that these production facilities bring us. At the same time, as homeowners and nature lovers, we are concerned about possible adverse impacts on the environment—noise, traffic, pollution. We also worry about safety, since some of these large, complex facilities are potentially very dangerous. While we enjoy the products that are the output of these facilities, we want those products to be safe and effective. The result of these dual feelings is regulation. Our society gives the widest possible scope to the development and production of new and improved products. At the same time, we impose certain protective limits on where and how those products are made and demand certain standards of product safety and performance.

R EGULATION OF LAND OWNERSHIP

Ownership of land, or the right to occupy it to the exclusion of others, represents an important component of modern society. The exercise of dominion over a piece of the planet enables you to carve out a personal space within which you can be yourself. Likewise, control of land ownership is the ultimate expression of sovereignty—governmental authority.

◼ Aliens as Landowners

Many nations impose restrictions on land ownership by non-citizens, or aliens. Under the feudal system, all land was held by grant from the king. The king made large land grants to a few trusted nobles, in exchange for their vows of loyalty and service. The nobles did the same with their supporters. In such a system, there was no room for aliens as landowners.

Some state restrictions on land ownership by aliens are unconstitutional.

Many states in this country carried on the rule that aliens could not own land within the state. Gradually, however, the U.S. Supreme Court has extended to aliens nearly all the same rights enjoyed by citizens. Aliens do not have the right to vote, to run for public office, or (in some states) to serve on juries. In nearly all other respects, they are protected by the Constitution. Under more recent constitutional interpretations, therefore, most state restrictions on land ownership by aliens would probably be ruled invalid today. It is possible, however, that restrictions against alien corporations as landowners might be validated by the Supreme Court. The Oklahoma rules are at issue in the following case. Notice how the appeals court avoided deciding the constitutional validity of the restrictions on aliens by deciding that an alien corporation which registered with the state was "domesticated."

STATE V. HILLCREST INVESTMENTS, LTD.

630 P.2d 1253 (Okla. 1981)

Facts: Jan Eric Cartwright, the Oklahoma Attorney General, filed suit to declare a forfeiture to the state of several parcels of land. These parcels were owned by alien corporations. The Oklahoma constitution and statutes restricted land ownership by aliens. Hillcrest, the owner of one parcel, was a Canadian corporation. It had registered with the state and had been given a state certificate of authority to do business there. The trial court held for Hillcrest, on the basis that alien corporations were not covered by the prohibition and that, in any case, Hillcrest had become "domesticated" by registering to do business. The state appealed.

Issue: Do these prohibitions apply to an alien corporation that has registered to do business in the state?

Decision: No, they do not apply. Judgment affirmed.

Rule: Registration with the state does entitle the alien corporation to own land there, since the corporation is then "domesticated."

Discussion: *By Justice BARNES:*

"After an examination of the territorial statutory law which existed at the time the Constitution was adopted, and the propositions introduced at the Constitutional Convention, we conclude that the drafters of our constitution did intend to include corporations within the terms person and alien, as they were used in Section 1 of Article 22 of the Oklahoma Constitution....

"Having determined that the restrictions on alien land ownership provided by Article 22, Section 1, of the Oklahoma Constitution apply to corporations, as well as natural persons, we must now determine whether the defendant corporation comes within the restrictions of that constitutional provision. A resolution of this issue requires this court to answer two questions: first, whether the defendant corporation is an alien corporation, and, second, whether the defendant corporation is a nonresident.

"An answer to the first inquiry is easily ascertained. The defendant admitted in its answer that it was a corporation which was formed under the laws of Alberta, Canada, and which exists by virtue of the laws of that country. It is well settled that corporations formed under the laws of foreign nations are alien corporations...."

"Because the defendant is an alien corporation and because the restrictions of Article 22, Section 1, apply to alien corporations which are nonresidents, the determinative question then becomes whether the defendant corporation, for the purposes of restriction on alien land ownership, is a resident. If the defendant is a resident, the restrictions on alien ownership are not applicable, as the provisions of Article 22, Section 1 specifically provide that the restrictions do not apply to aliens or persons who become bona fide residents of this state....

"After examining the constitutional and statutory provisions dealing with the treatment of domesticated corporations, we conclude that a foreign corporation, once it has complied with the domestication procedures established under Oklahoma law, is for the purposes of restrictions on alien land ownership a resident of the state—and thus no longer subject to the restrictions of Article 22, Section 1, of the Oklahoma Constitution....

"For the above stated reasons, we hold that the trial court was correct in ruling that the defendant below, Hillcrest Investments, Ltd., could, by virtue of its domestication, own real property within the state of Oklahoma, located within an incorporated town or city."

Ethical Dimension

Why would a state try to challenge such land ownership by alien corporations?

●

■ Eminent Domain

Governments have the power to take land for public use.

Another very significant limitation on the rights of all landowners is the power of the government to take land for public purposes, even against the owner's wishes. As noted in Chapter 3, the U.S. Constitution says for public use, but the U.S. Supreme Court has ruled that any public purpose for taking the land is a public "use." In any event, the Constitution does require that the landowner receive "just compensation" for the land. The scope of this phrase is also subject to interpretation. Many states permit a jury trial on this compensation question, but there is still a basic question of what factors a jury may properly consider.

Urban renewal/redevelopment projects have been particularly difficult to deal with under the compensation requirement. As part of the redevelopment, the existing buildings are torn down and new ones are constructed. The new buildings are then made available for business relocation. A major problem has been that the amount of compensation received by a small business for an old building will not be enough to buy or lease space in the new, much higher priced buildings. Many small businesses have just closed their doors as a result. Quite apart from these compensation issues, there is also the question of whether it is proper for government to use its power to take land from one private owner and transfer it to another private owner.

■ Regulatory Takings

A different, but equally difficult, problem is presented when government wishes to regulate the use to which property is put. In the classical sense, there is no "taking," since the government does not actually become the owner of the land. The government does, however, limit what the owner can do with the land.

Regulation of use may be so complete as to constitute a taking of the land.

As will be discussed in the next two sections of this chapter, government does restrict land use in various ways. Most such restrictions are not viewed as "takings" which require compensation to the landowner. The basic reason for the "no payment required" result is that the landowner may still make other uses of the property. Suppose, however, that the government regulation, in effect, prevents any use of the land. That was the issue confronting the Supreme Court in the next case.

LUCAS V. SOUTH CAROLINA COASTAL COUNCIL

112 S. Ct. 2886 (1992)

Facts: In 1986, David Lucas paid $975,000 for two lots on the Isle of Palms, an island east of Charleston, South Carolina. He intended to build single-family homes on the lots and hired an architect to draw up plans. In 1988, South Carolina adopted the Beachfront Management Act. The act prohibited building any "occupiable improvements" within twenty feet of any point along the cost where erosion had occurred during the prior forty years. That area included both the Lucas lots, so he could not build any type of habitable structure on either one.

Lucas sued in state court for compensation. He did not challenge the state's power to enact the statute. The trial court judge agreed that a taking had occurred which had rendered the property valueless. It set just compensation at $1,232,387.50. The state supreme court reversed, holding that no compensation was due when the state acted to prevent "serious public harm" (to save the state's beaches). Lucas asked the U.S. Supreme Court for further review.

Issue: Must government pay compensation when its regulation deprives a landowner of any reasonable economic use of the land?

Decision: Yes. Case is remanded to the trial court for further proceedings.

Rule: A state may prohibit a landowner's activities which constitute a public nuisance without paying compensation. It may not prohibit all economic use of the land unless it pays compensation.

Discussion: *By Justice SCALIA:*

"Justice Holmes recognized...that if the protection against physical appropriations of private property was to be meaningfully enforced, the government's power to redefine the range of interests included in the ownership of property was necessarily constrained by constitutional limits.... If, instead, the uses of private property were subject to unbridled, uncompensated qualification under the police power, 'the natural tendency of human nature [would be] to extend the qualification more and more until at last private property disappear[ed].'... '[W]hile property may be regulated to a certain extent, if regulation goes too far it will be recognized as a taking.'...

"In 70-odd years of...'regulatory takings' jurisprudence, we have generally eschewed any 'set formula' for determining how far is too far, preferring to 'engag[e] in...essentially ad hoc, factual inquiries.'... We have, however, described at least two discrete categories of regulatory action as compensable without case-specific inquiry into the public interest advanced in support of the restraint. The first encompasses regulations that compel the property owner to suffer a physical 'invasion' of his property....

"The second situation in which we have found categorical treatment appropriate is where regulation denies all economically beneficial or productive use of land....

"We have never set forth the justification for this rule. Perhaps it is simply, as Justice Brennan suggested, that total deprivation of beneficial use is, from the landowner's point of view, the equivalent of a physical appropriation....

"It seems unlikely that common-law principles would have prevented the erection of any habitable or productive improvements on [the] land; they rarely support prohibition of the 'essential use' of land.... [T]o win its case...South Carolina must identify background principles of nuisance and property law that prohibit the uses [Lucas] now intends in the circumstances in which the property is presently found. Only on this showing can the State fairly claim that, in proscribing all such beneficial uses, the Beachfront Management Act is taking nothing."

Ethical Dimension

Is it ethical for a landowner to demand compensation when the state is simply trying to protect its beachfront environment?

●

R EGULATION OF PLANT LOCATION

Businesses normally do complicated site analyses before deciding where to locate new facilities. In addition to the economic factors involved, there are legal restrictions which must be considered.

■ Private Land Use Restrictions

Quite apart from governmental regulation of land use, private parties may also agree that certain use restrictions will apply. Such private restrictions may be contained in individual deeds for specific parcels of land or may be included by a real estate developer for an entire neighborhood or other large area. Once so established, these limitations will normally bind all future owners of the land. In an area of expensive homes, for instance, there might be prohibitions against outdoor clotheslines, tents, sheds, and similar unsightly structures.

Land use may be restricted by private agreements.

■ Zoning

As more and more people crowded into large urban areas, and more large manufacturing plants were built, conflicts over land use increased. Some manufacturing operations involve noise, smoke, and various waste products. Such businesses are not good neighbors in residential areas. Persons who can afford to do so may move to another location, but some people can't afford to or think that they should not have to.

People turned to government for an answer to this social problem. The result was **zoning**. Government at the local level divided the city or county into use zones and specified what kinds of activities could be conducted on the land in each zone. For example, there might be zones for heavy industry (steel mills and auto plants), light industry (computer assembly), commercial (stores and offices), multi-family (apartments and condominiums), and single-family homes. The basic idea is that one owner won't bother another if they are making similar uses of their properties. The steel mill probably won't care that there is an auto

Cities restrict land use through zoning.

plant next door. The stores won't bother the offices, and vice versa. Homeowners will be able to enjoy a cleaner and quieter neighborhood. The Supreme Court upheld the constitutionality of zoning laws in an early case involving Euclid, Ohio. Although they are legal, zoning laws still have to be interpreted, as the next case shows.

TALCOTT V. CITY OF MIDLAND

387 N.W.2d 845 (Mich. 1985)

Facts: Thomas Reer asked for a building permit so he could remodel a building for his "Good Times Pizza" business. The city building inspector told him he could not operate a carryout restaurant in the "Business A" zoning district. The zoning board of appeals overruled the building inspector. The city attorney asked the board to reconsider, but the board took no action. Reer got his building permit and began extensive renovations; he also signed a ten-year lease on the building. Thayre Talcott and other citizens then sued the city, claiming that there had not been proper notice of the first board hearing. In a new hearing, the board reversed its prior decision.

The trial court upheld the board's reversal. It also said that the city was estopped from preventing Reer from continuing with his plans, since he had already made substantial commitments in reliance on the zoning board's decision. The trial court then granted Talcott and his group an injunction against Reer's operation of his business. Talcott's group had not done anything on which Reer had relied. Reer appealed.

Issue: Is the carryout pizza business a permissible use under the zoning ordinance?

Decision: Yes. Judgment reversed and injunction vacated.

Rule: Where a zoning ordinance is ambiguous, it should be interpreted in favor of the property owner.

Discussion: *By the Court:*

"When construing provisions of a zoning ordinance, the court seeks to discover and give effect to the lawmaker's intent.... The interpretation problem at issue arises when one attempts to reconcile the definitions in Article II of the ordinance with Article XIV, which regulates land uses within business districts. Section 14.1(a)(12) of Article XIV of the city zoning ordinance provides that 'restaurants, excluding drive-ins' are permitted uses in Business A districts. Section 2.0 of Article II defines in subsecs (50), (51), and (52), respectively, 'restaurant,' 'restaurant, carry-out,' and 'restaurant, drive-in.'...

"The city and plaintiffs-appellees contend, and the zoning board of appeals and circuit court held, that the word restaurants in Section 14.1(a)(12) should be limited to the definition of Section 2.0(50), '[a]n establishment where food and drink is served to sit-down customers.' Reer contends that the language in Section 14.1(a)(12), 'restaurants, excluding drive-ins' requires an inference that Section 2.0(51) carryout restaurants are a permissible use since carryout restaurants were not expressly excluded.

"When interpreting the language of an ordinance to determine the extent of a restriction upon the use of property, the language must be interpreted, where doubt exists regarding legislative intent, in favor of the property owner.... Applying this principle of interpretation to Midland's zoning ordinance, we hold that a carryout pizzeria is a permissible use in a Business A district....

"Finally, the interpretation advanced by Reer is consistent with the statement of intent found in Section 14.0. The primary intent of the Business A district is to serve the surrounding residential neighborhood with goods and services of day-to-day needs.

"Because we find that appellant Reer's proposed use is a permissible use, we need not consider the other issues raised by appellants Reer and City of Midland."

Ethical Dimension

Why should individual citizens be able to bring lawsuits to enforce the city's zoning ordinance?

R EGULATION OF POLLUTION

Zoning may prevent the location of a production facility in the middle of a residential area, but zoning by itself is by no means a complete solution to all "quality of life" problems in modern society. Restricting manufacturing to one side of a city may help with noise and traffic, but not with other forms of pollution. Pollution travels. Coal-fired electric plants in the Midwest produce pollutants which cause acid rain in the Northeast and in Canada. If the wind and weather combine in the right way, the entire Los Angeles area may be choked with smog. Wastes discharged into the Ohio River at Pittsburgh and Wheeling have adverse effects hundreds of miles downstream. Air and water pollution are

Governments may wish to regulate pollution.

problems far beyond the scope of the zoning law in a single city. Clearly, action at the national level was required.

■ Environmental Protection Agency

The EPA is the main agency regulating pollution.

The EPA was set up to coordinate the national government's efforts to protect the environment. It grew enormously during the 1970s and early 1980s, as new areas of concern developed. The EPA is now one of the largest regulatory agencies. It sets the standards in a wide variety of areas and issues permits and licenses which are required for certain business operations. It has jurisdiction over the water we drink and the air we breathe. It regulates hazardous and harmful substances and conditions—pesticides, poisons, nuclear radiation, excessive noise, even garbage disposal. In addition to the original National Environmental Policy Act of 1969 (NEPA), the EPA has been given regulatory authority under the Clean Air Act, the Clean Water Act, and other statutes.

■ Environmental Impact Statement

All national agencies must file an EIS for any project significantly affecting the environment.

The 1969 NEPA requires all agencies of the national government to consider the "environmental impact" of their operational decisions. Prior to beginning any project which would significantly affect the environment, the agency must prepare an Environmental Impact Statement (EIS). The EIS must specifically present any harmful effects of the project and must weigh the project's short-term benefits against long-term costs and problems. The EIS must also identify any irreversible effects on the environment. The EIS must present alternatives to the proposed project, together with their environmental impacts. If the facts simply cannot be obtained at all, or only at great cost, the agency must present a "worst-case scenario." This requirement means that the agency must imagine the worst that could happen as a result of the project and the likelihood that the worst result would occur. The objective of NEPA is to make sure that power dams, airports, nuclear plants, and the like are not built without taking into account their impact on the environment.

CERCLA created a superfund to clean up polluted sites.

Comprehensive Environmental Response, Compensation, and Liability Act Passed in 1980, CERCLA created a $1.6 billion "Superfund" to begin the process of cleaning up existing hazardous waste sites. These sites include abandoned industrial plants which had used or produced hazardous chemicals or wastes, landfills in which hazardous materials had been dumped, gasoline stations with leaking storage tanks, and other similar public and private operations. Taxes on chemical and petroleum products provide the funds for the clean-up program. However, the costs of the clean-up can be recovered from the owner/operator who caused the problem or from the landowner. Since these costs can be very large, many of these cases end up in court to establish who is liable and for what.

ANSPEC COMPANY, INC. V. JOHNSON CONTROLS, INC.

922 F.2d 1240 (U.S. 6th Cir. Court of Appeals, 1992)

Facts: Anspec purchased a parcel of land with improvements in Washtenaw County, Michigan, from the defendant Ultraspherics in 1978. Anspec later sold the property to the plaintiff Montgomery and now leases it from him. Ultraspherics went through a series of mergers after the sale of the property to Anspec. On December 31, 1987, Ultraspherics merged into Hoover Group, which was designated as the surviving corporation. As the surviving corporation, Hoover Group assumed all assets and liabilities of Ultraspherics. Johnson Controls is the sole shareholder of Hoover Group and of Hoover Universal, which was the sole shareholder of Ultraspherics as the result of an earlier merger.

Prior to the sale of the property to Anspec, Ultraspherics buried an underground storage tank on the site "into which was disposed hazardous sludge and liquids from the grinding process of metal and plastic balls and degreaser…" used by Ultraspherics in its business of manufacturing metal and plastic precision balls. After the underground tank was filled to capacity, two above-ground storage tanks were placed on the property and filled with the same hazardous substances. Ultraspherics' disposal of hazardous sludge and liquids caused these materials "to be routinely released into the soil and groundwater" at the site. Ultraspherics further contaminated the soil and groundwater through leaks and spills of toxic cleaning solvents used at the site.

The plaintiffs notified Ultraspherics that they were required to clean up the site and requested Ultraspherics to pay the costs associated with the cleanup. When Ultraspherics refused this request, the plaintiffs filed the present action, which the District Court dismissed.

Issue: Is a successor corporation resulting from a merger with a corporation that had released hazardous waste materials on a previously owned site liable for cleanup costs incurred by the present owner?

Decision: Yes. Judgment reversed, and case remanded for trial.

Rule: The word "corporation," as used in CERCLA, includes a successor corporation.

Discussion: *By Judge* LIVELY:

"At oral argument, counsel for the defendants agreed that so far as he knew, all jurisdictions recognize the doctrine of successor corporate liability. The universal acceptance of this rule cannot be gainsaid. Judge Weis discussed the venerable nature and present vitality of this rule in Smith Land.

Corporate successor liability is neither completely novel nor of recent vintage. Blackstone described the continuing vitality of a corporation. '[A]ll the individual members that have existed from the foundation to the present time, or that shall ever hereafter exist, are but one person in law, a person that never dies; in like manner as the river Thames is still the same river, though the parts which compose it are changing every instant'...Changes in ownership of a corporation's stock will not affect the rights and obligations of the company itself. The corporation survives as an entity separate and distinct from its shareholders even if all the stock is purchased by another corporation. 'In general, when two corporations merge pursuant to statutory provisions, liabilities become the responsibility of the surviving company. In the case of merger of one corporation into another, where one of the corporations ceases to exist, the other corporation is liable for the debts, contracts and torts of the former, at least to the extent of the property and assets received, and this liability is often expressly imposed by statute.

"We are not creating or fashioning federal common law when we adopt an interpretation of a statute that is in harmony with a universally accepted rule of law. Rather, we are merely saying that the drafters of CERCLA were not blind to the universal rule that 'corporation' includes a successor corporation resulting from a merger and that the drafters intended 'corporation' to be given its usual meaning....

"CERCLA does not define either 'corporation' or 'association,' and to this extent is incomplete. Nevertheless, the United States Code contains rules of construction that apply to all federal statutes unless the context indicates otherwise.... One of these rules of construction states that when the word 'company' or 'association' is used in reference to a corporation, it 'shall be deemed to embrace the words "successors and assigns of such company or association," in like manner as if the last-named words, or words of similar import were expressed.'... It seems clear that the listing of the various terms applied to business entities within the meaning of 'person' in §9601(21)—'firm, corporation, association, partnership, consortium, joint venture, commercial entity...'—was intended to include all known forms of business and commercial enterprises. Congress would have failed to carry out its purpose of reaching all such entities if successor corporations were exempted from liability....

"The allegations of the complaint are sufficient to state a claim against Hoover Group as the successor to Ultraspherics. The exact relationship of Johnson Controls and Hoover Universal to Ultraspherics is not clear. If they are parent corporations rather than successors, there are legal issues not presented in this appeal which the district court must address after the exact relationship of these two corporations to Ultraspherics is determined on the basis of evidence not yet produced.

"The dismissal of Ultraspherics on the ground that it no longer exists is somewhat anomalous in light of the record. Ultraspherics appeared without raising an issue as to its existence. It was the most active of the four defendants, filing an answer and initiating discovery while the others rested solely on their motion to dismiss. The complaint alleges that Ultraspherics was the actual polluter—the person who owned and operated the facility at the time of disposal of the hazardous substances. If Ultraspherics is to be dismissed, it is only because its corporate successor or successors stand in its shoes as the person or persons described in §9607(a)(2)."

Ethical Dimension

How can a corporation claim to be the "successor" of a previous firm and yet deny liability for the prior firm's debts?

PLANT SAFETY REQUIREMENTS

Government's concern does not stop with the plant's location. Various regulations also exist to try to ensure its safe operation. Dangers exist in the form of large machines (and small ones), hazardous chemicals, and toxic byproducts of the production process. Both the plant's workers and its neighbors need protection from as many of these hazards as possible.

Worker Safety

As discussed in Chapter 14, both national and state governments are concerned with worker safety. When liability for worker's injuries did not prove to be enough incentive for plant safety, both levels of government attacked the problem directly. The occupational safety and health statutes were the result. Workplaces must now meet governmental safety standards and are subject to inspection by state and/or national agencies to ensure compliance. Large fines can be imposed for serious violations.

■ Area Safety

Location of nuclear plants may create safety concerns.

Some types of manufacturing operations also raise concerns about the safety of the neighborhood surrounding the plant. The most notable example is the nuclear power plant. A nuclear accident could have consequences not only for the workers in the facility, but also for persons anywhere within hundreds of miles. (Or thousands of miles, as we saw at Chernobyl.) Clearly, extra precautions need to be taken when locating and constructing these power plants. Again, both national and state governments are involved in these operations, although the U.S. Nuclear Regulatory Commission has primary responsibility.

Nuclear facilities also present another special problem. Many types of nuclear wastes are hazardous for hundreds, or thousands, of years. Proper disposal and storage of these radioactive waste materials has been an ongoing problem since the beginning of the nuclear age. Nobody wants a radioactive waste dump in the back yard. Until a long-term solution for this problem can be agreed on, nuclear power will continue to have a serious drawback. Safety concerns and massive regulation have combined to prevent construction of any new nuclear generating plants in the United States for more than a decade. "Safety" has essentially put this industry out of business, at least as far as new construction is concerned.

▉ PRODUCT SAFETY: THE FDA, THE DOT, AND THE CPSC

The national government has a long-standing interest in the area of product safety, dating back at least to the passage of the Pure Food and Drug Act of 1906. Regulation of this field occurs under the commerce clause. The relation of products such as food and drugs to the public health, safety, and welfare seems fairly clear. The Food and Drug Administration (FDA), the Department of Transportation (DOT), and the newer Consumer Product Safety Commission (CPSC) are not the only agencies of the national government involved in product safety. Specific products may be subject to the jurisdiction of other specialized agencies. Pesticides, for example, may be regulated by the EPA, OSHA, and the Department of Agriculture. Boating safety regulation is delegated to the U.S. Coast Guard, and there are other similar specific delegations. In addition, there may be several product safety agencies operating in a particular state. There seems to be general agreement that product safety is a legitimate area of governmental concern. However, one might ask whether a more effective job might be done by one centralized agency.

F OOD AND DRUG SAFETY

Food and drug safety was one of the first major areas of governmental regulation in the United States. No one who has read *The Jungle* by Upton Sinclair can forget his description of the brutal working conditions and the horribly unsanitary methods in Chicago's meat-packing industry. Stories like these, regardless of how generally true they were, gave considerable impetus to passage of the Pure Food and Drug Act of 1906. Anyone who has worked in the industry is aware of the many opportunities for impurities to be introduced during the processing operation. The need for close regulation and continuous testing is obvious.

The national government regulates the safety of food and drug products.

National regulation in this area is now over 100 years old. The government started inspecting interstate shipments of meat in 1880. Early emphasis of the Department of Agriculture's administration of the 1906 act was also on food rather than drugs. The main job initially was to prevent the sale of misbranded or adulterated foodstuffs. Legislation established standards for canned goods in 1930, and set up the FDA in 1931. By 1938, with the passage of the Food, Drug, and Cosmetic Act, the emphasis had shifted from foods to drugs. Jurisdiction to regulate food additives and colorings was given to the FDA in 1958, including a proviso which prohibited the use of any additive which was carcinogenic to humans or animals at any dosage level. The European experience with the drug thalidomide, which caused horrible deformities in unborn children when taken by their mothers, brought a sharp reaction in this country in 1962. Under the leadership of Senator Estes Kefauver, an amendment was added which required proof that a new drug was effective as well as safe before it could be approved by the FDA. Largely as a result of this amendment and the greatly increased testing costs it required, the introduction of new drugs decreased markedly after 1962. With tens of millions of dollars in costs involved for periods ranging up to several years there are substantial economic disincentives to the introduction of new drugs.

Scope of the Food, Drug, and Cosmetic Act

The Food, Drug, and Cosmetic Act, as amended, provides the basis for a comprehensive regulatory scheme for these three very large industries. Manufacturing, labelling, and distribution are all regulated and monitored. The primary objective, of course, is the prevention of the manufacture and sale of adulterated or misbranded food, drugs, cosmetics, and health devices. The act also contains other specific prohibitions, such as those against simulating labels and altering or removing labels. The act specifies permitted tolerances for any harmful substances necessary in food processing and for pesticides. It regulates the distribution of toxic and otherwise potentially harmful drugs and

Cosmetic products are also regulated for safety.

habit-forming drugs and requires specific certification for any drug product containing insulin or certain antibiotics. Broad authority is given to the FDA to enforce the act.

■ Food and Drug Administration

The FDA is the main agency regulating foods, drugs, and cosmetics.

The FDA monitors the manufacture of products by inspecting facilities and by examining samples taken from interstate shipments. For antibiotic drugs and insulin, it tests every batch for safety and effectiveness. It establishes standards for food products, and approves and monitors the use of food additives. It establishes limits for pesticide residues on food products and inspects shipments to ensure compliance. It approves the use of coloring agents for food, drugs, and cosmetics and monitors the products for compliance. It ensures the safety and accurate labelling of therapeutic devices. It approves the manufacture and sale of all new drugs for safety and effectiveness. It also enforces the Hazardous Substance Labelling Act, which requires warning labels for household products that are toxic, corrosive, flammable, that may generate dangerous pressure, or that may be an irritant to human tissue. Imports of any of the products regulated under the act are also checked to make sure that they comply with its provisions.

■ New Drug Application

For the would-be manufacturer of a proposed new drug, the FDA is the gatekeeper. The act prohibits the sale in interstate commerce of any new drug without FDA approval. The application procedure is designed to ensure, through FDA investigation of all aspects of production and marketing of the proposed new drug, that it is safe and effective. Along with samples of the drug, its components, and the proposed labelling, the applicant must submit a full statement of the drug's composition, a full list of all components used, a full description of the facilities and methods to be used in manufacturing and packing the drug, and full reports of all testing for safety and effectiveness.

TIME LIMITS

Applications for permits on new drugs must be processed in a timely fashion.

The act and the regulations provide time limits for action. These limits are designed to permit a thorough, yet expeditious, examination of the application. Within 180 days after the application is filed, the Secretary of Health and Human Services (through the FDA) must either approve the application or give notice to the applicant that it can request a hearing on approval of the application. The applicant may file a written request for a hearing within 30 days after the notice. If it does so, the hearing must commence within 90 days thereafter, unless the parties agree otherwise. The hearing is to be conducted "on an expedited basis," and the secretary's final order is to be issued within 90 days after the date for filing final briefs. Appeals are filed with a Court of Appeals within 60 days after the final order.

REJECTION OF AN APPLICATION

The application may be rejected for a number of reasons: Inadequate safety tests; test results indicating lack of safety; inadequate manufacturing methods; inadequate evidence of effectiveness; or false or misleading labelling. Labelling defects can perhaps be corrected without too much difficulty or expense, but the other listed defects might be difficult and expensive to correct. Manufacturing processes might have to be altered substantially, and new quality control procedures might have to be instituted. In most cases, if the FDA is not convinced of the new drug's safety and effectiveness, the applicant has little choice but to withdraw the drug or to engage in extended new testing. Since matters of expert scientific judgment are at issue, the courts would normally give great deference to the FDA's administrative expertise.

◼ Enforcement of the Act

Three principal weapons are at the Government's disposal for enforcement of the act: injunction, seizure, and criminal prosecution. A manufacturer or distributor can be prevented from introducing adulterated or misbranded products into interstate commerce by means of a U.S. District Court injunction. If the product has already been distributed, or becomes contaminated or adulterated during distribution, a seizure action may be commenced in the U.S. District Court where the offending product is located. This action is a direct proceeding against the product itself. The owner is not a necessary party but may intervene if it so chooses.

The Secretary of Health and Human Services also has the discretionary power to refer a case to the U.S. Attorney for possible criminal prosecution. In such cases, no specific intent to misbrand or to adulterate need be proved. In a sense, a type of strict liability exists where a violation of the act is proved. Persons working in these industries obviously need to be aware of this potential for criminal liability.

◼ TRANSPORTATION SAFETY

Transportation is another area with a long history of governmental involvement, at both the national and state levels. Government has played varying and sometimes conflicting roles in the transportation industry—promoter, licensor, regulator, and even operator. *Gibbons v. Ogden*, 9 Wheat. 1 (1824)—one of Chief Justice John Marshall's great dissertations on the meaning of the Constitution—was a transportation case. In that case the U.S. Supreme Court held that New York's grant of a steamboat service monopoly to Robert Fulton and Robert

The national government also regulates transportation safety.

Livingston was an unconstitutional interference by the state with the power granted to the national government to regulate interstate commerce. First canals and then railroads were built with government subsidies and assistance. As other means of transporting goods and people were developed, such as pipelines, trucks, and airplanes, these methods of transportation were also regulated.

Over the years, various attempts have been made to coordinate national transportation policy, such as the Transportation Act of 1940. So long as several independent agencies—the Interstate Commerce Commission, the Civil Aeronautics Board, the Federal Maritime Commission, and the like—were trying to administer separate parts of the transportation industry, coordination was difficult. A Department of Transportation (DOT) was created in 1966. A movement to deregulate much of the industry began in the late 1970s, with the airlines and the trucking industry as the first candidates.

■ National Transportation Safety Board

While there is strong current sentiment for deregulation of such operating details as routes, schedules, and fares, there are few people who believe that the government should also terminate its concern for safety. Passengers, shippers, and the public at large are subjected to the risk of catastrophic injuries if vehicles are unsafe, if precautions are not taken for shipments of hazardous substances, or if adequate safety procedures are not followed. The stakes are too high and the public interest is too great for the elimination of all safety regulation in the industry.

The NTSB regulates the safety of carriers of passengers.

The major administrative agency in the industry is now the National Transportation Safety Board, created in 1966 within the DOT, to coordinate transportation safety. The Board became an independent agency under a 1974 act. It was charged with investigating railroad accidents involving a fatality, substantial damage, or a passenger train; pipeline accidents involving a fatality, substantial property damage; selected highway accidents; and major water transport casualties. The Board had already been given the authority to investigate airplane accidents by the 1966 statute. The Board has delegated to the Federal Aviation Administration the power to investigate most small plane crashes and may delegate other investigations to the Department of Transportation.

■ Auto Safety

By far, the area which has generated the most controversy, and which continues to do so, is regulation of auto safety. This issue is very highly charged emotionally for at least two reasons. First, many jobs are at stake; any government action which threatens the industry also threatens the millions of workers who make, sell, and service cars, components and supplies, including gasoline. Second, for many people the personal car is the symbol of our freedom to go where we want, when we want. When Henry Ford and his contemporaries put the nation on wheels, they not only revolutionized the economy; they also revolutionized society. Any government action which makes the ownership of a personal vehicle prohibitively costly will encounter resistance.

For most of automotive history, safety features were added as they were developed and as economics and popular demand dictated. Common sense surely indicates that headlights are required for night driving; no government decree is necessary for that. Improved brakes, turn signals, and the like were added to vehicles in much the same way. Specific defects in individual vehicles were taken care of under manufacturers' warranties or, if necessary, by product liability lawsuits under general theories of liability.

While those private remedies still exist, a whole new area of massive national regulation has been developed to deal with automotive safety. As Sinclair's *Jungle* was to the food industry, Ralph Nader's *Unsafe at Any Speed* has been to the auto industry. Nader and his book struck the industry like a thunderbolt. It is no coincidence that Congress passed the National Traffic and Motor Vehicle Act and the Highway Safety Act in 1966, one year after the book's publication.

The National Highway Traffic Safety Administration (NHTSA) now establishes standards for safe operation of motor vehicles and their equipment. Not only must there be headlights, for example, but they must meet standards for brightness, distance, durability, and control. New safety equipment such as seat belts and head rests has been required on all vehicles. "Crashworthiness" standards have been established for bumpers and fuel tanks. Added weight means added cost, both in terms of the initial purchase price of the car and in terms of lower fuel economy. The desirability of many adopted and proposed auto safety standards continues to be a matter of controversy.

The NHTSA regulates car and truck safety.

The nature of this debate over objectives and methods can be illustrated by the continuing battle over the need for a "passive restraint system." After some eight years of study, NHTSA adopted Standard 208 in 1977. It required the installation of one of two types of passive restraint system on each new car, commencing in 1983 for some models and by 1984 for all new cars. Each car would have to have either an automatic seat belt system or an automatically inflated air bag system. The NHTSA believed that most manufacturers would probably pick the automatic belt, since it would cost about $90 per car, as opposed to $200-$330 for the air bag. In addition, reports indicated that air bags provide no protection against side or rear collisions, since the triggering device for inflation of the bag is at the front of the car. Moreover, air bags can cause injuries of their own to any passenger who is "out of position."

After the election of President Reagan, who had adopted deregulation as one of his main campaign themes, NHTSA decided in October, 1981, to scrap Standard 208. The Agency said that since automatic belts were the probable choice, and since only eleven percent of motorists use the belts they now have in their cars, it would be logical to assume that many of them would find ways to disconnect the belts. In this light, the added costs did not seem justified. A group of insurance companies challenged the withdrawal of Standard 208. The U.S. Supreme Court ultimately decided that, while the NHTSA did have the power to change its mind and to revoke a safety standard, it had to provide a "reasoned analysis" for doing so. Since NHTSA had not provided that kind of reasoning for its revocation of Standard 208, the case was sent back to the agency for still further proceedings. (The case is Motor Vehicle Manufacturers Assn. v. State Farm Mutual Insurance Co., 103 S. Ct. 2856 [1983].)

■ Mileage and Pollution Standards

The lives of automakers are further complicated by two other kinds of manufacturing requirements—fuel economy and pollution control standards. The internal combustion engine used in most motor vehicles is a major source of air pollution. Manufacturers are now required to include certain kinds of pollution-control devices on their vehicles. These devices add substantial costs and weight to the car or truck.

CAFE standards have been set for car manufacturers.

While requiring auto manufacturers to add safety features and pollution-control devices, the government also told them to improve fuel economy. Standards were adopted for required "corporate average fuel economy" (CAFE). These CAFE standards have been raised over time, so car-makers have had to improve their vehicles' average performance. Smaller, lighter cars must be made and sold to balance sales of large luxury cars. Meeting all these conflicting government requirements presents automotive engineers with a continuing challenge.

C ONSUMER PRODUCT SAFETY

Another area where sharp controversy continues is that of consumer product safety. Just as the main danger in the operation of a motor vehicle is the person behind the wheel, many of the injuries which result from other consumer products are caused by the operator's inattention, recklessness, or lack of skill. One of the key questions for this whole area of regulation is the extent to which products such as chain saws and power lawnmowers can, or should, be made "idiot-proof." How many fail-safe devices should all users of a consumer product have to pay for, in the hope of avoiding injury to a few careless or unskilled users? Are there some products which are simply unavoidably dangerous when improperly used? Is there a difference, requiring a different regulatory standard, between such products and those which are really poorly and dangerously designed and manufactured? Are the taxpayers being well-served when thousands of dollars are spent on a study which concluded that the main reason for children's bicycle injuries was that children lose their balance and "fall off"? Congress' solution to these policy questions was the Consumer Product Safety Act of 1972, which created the Consumer Product Safety Commission (CPSC).

■ Consumer Product Safety Commission

The CPSC was established by Congress in 1972 as an independent regulatory agency. Its mission is to protect consumers from unreasonable risk of injury from dangerous products. It is governed by five commissioners appointed for staggered seven-year terms. Appointments are made by the president with the consent of the Senate. No more than three commissioners may be from one political party. Also created by the 1972 act was the Product Safety Advisory Council, which has members from business, consumer groups, and various government agencies.

The CPSC regulates the safety of consumer products.

■ Jurisdiction

Consumer products, other than those already regulated under another statute and agency, are subject to the jurisdiction of the CPSC. Consumer products are defined by the act to include those things used in or around a residence or a school, in recreation or otherwise. The key is use or consumption of the product by a consumer. Administrative rulings, though, have stretched the act to cover traffic control signals, fire alarm equipment (sold to a city), elevators to be used by the public, and copying machines which are coin-operated. Components of products which fall within the definition are also covered. Both manufacturing and distribution of such products are subject to regulation. Among those products which are excluded from CPSC control are motor vehicles and equipment, firearms, aircraft and components, boats, food, drugs and health devices, cosmetics, and tobacco products.

The CPSC is empowered to make investigations, to educate distributors and consumers on safety awareness, and to set product standards. If necessary, the CPSC may ban further distribution of a hazardous product and ask for a court order of seizure of existing supplies of the product.

■ Procedure

The CPSC may learn about a dangerous product from its own investigations, through its consumer hotline, or even from a manufacturer (who is required by the act to notify the CPSC when it learns of such dangers). When the CPSC is alerted to a dangerous product in the stream of commerce, it has a variety of procedures available. Which alternative it uses depends primarily on the nature of the risk of harm involved.

The CPSC may ask a court to seize dangerous consumer products.

Where there is an imminent and unreasonable risk of death, serious illness, or severe injury, the CPSC may apply to U.S. District Court for a seizure order and a ban against further distribution of the product. On the other hand, if it finds that there is a substantial risk of injury, but of a lesser nature, it may simply require that notices be sent to purchasers of the defective product. Alternatively, the CPSC may require the distributors recall the product for repair, replacement, or refund.

Most proceedings are brought under sections 8 and 9 of the act for a ban on the hazardous product. These sections require notice and a full-scale administrative hearing in accordance with the Administrative Procedure Act. The CPSC, based on the hearing, must make findings as to the nature and seriousness of the potential injury involved, the number of products involved, the need for the product, and the available alternative means of compliance, if any. If the ban is to be implemented, the CPSC must also find that the ban is necessary to eliminate the risk—that a safety standard under the act would not adequately protect the public.

The CPSC also has the power to promulgate product standards, again after notice and hearing. It may investigate to determine whether standards are necessary. Its investigative powers include the power to subpoena witnesses and to compel production of documents. The manufacturer and distributor are required by the act to notify the CPSC when a "substantial product hazard" is discovered. The Commission may also require that it receive advance notice, with a product description, prior to distribution of a new consumer product.

Generally, information disclosed to the CPSC will be available to the public because of the Freedom of Information Act.

■ Enforcement

The CPSC may ask for civil and/or criminal penalties.

Where violations of the act are alleged and no voluntary compliance arrangement can be worked out, civil or criminal enforcement proceedings may be brought against the offending company or individual. For committing violations specified in the act, a civil fine of $2,000 for each offense may be imposed, up to a maximum of $500,000 for a series of related violations. The acts specified include such things as manufacturing, importing, or distributing a banned product or one which fails to comply with a safety standard; refusing access to records or inspection of products or premises; failing to comply with a CPSC order for repair, refund or replacement; falsifying or failing to furnish compliance certificates; and stockpiling a product to avoid a safety rule.

Each act and each day is a separate violation, up to the $500,000 maximum.

Criminal penalties are provided for willful and knowing violations of these provisions—fines up to $50,000 or imprisonment for up to one year, or both. All corporate agents, officers, and directors who authorize or order such violations are subject to these criminal penalties. Once again, persons involved in the manufacture or distribution of consumer products need to be aware of the serious criminal consequences, in addition to possible civil liability, for violations of the CPS Act.

The CPS Act was designed to supplement, not to supplant, private civil lawsuits for damages under product liability theories. In addition to the civil lawsuits for damages based on the tort and contract theories discussed in the last chapter, the act authorizes lawsuits by private parties damaged by a product distributed in violation of the act's provisions. In such actions, attorneys' fees, as well as damages, may be recovered. Even where no actual damage has been sustained by an individual, he or she may bring a civil action to enforce the act's provisions. The individual must first give notice to the CPSC and the Attorney General. The provision authorizing suits by private parties is designed to encourage the "private attorney general" approach to enforcement.

The following case discusses the CPSC's power to file a lawsuit directly in court without first having held hearings to declare the product dangerous.

X-TRA ART V. CONSUMER PRODUCT SAFETY COMMISSION

969 F.2d 793 (U.S. 8th Cir. Court of Appeals, 1992)

Facts: Linda Weill, an elementary school teacher, invented and patented "Rainbow Foam Paint." Intended for use as fingerpaint by grade school children, the product is a mixture of shaving cream and food colors, contained in pressurized cans. CPSC tests showed that the hydrocarbon propellant used in the cans was highly flammable. All hydrocarbon propellants are highly flammable, but are also necessary to create the "foam" effect of the product. CPSC sent Weill a letter stating that, due to the test results, her product had been classified as a "banned hazardous substance" under the Federal Hazardous Substance Act (FHSA). Additional nasty letters were exchanged between Weill and the CPSC staff.

The CPSC staff referred the matter to the U.S. Attorney's office in Connecticut. The U.S. Attorney filed a lawsuit in U.S. District Court to seize the product inventory located there. Weill and her company then filed this lawsuit in U.S. District Court in California, asking for review of the CPSC decision and for injunctive relief against any further action by the CPSC. The U.S. District Court in California dismissed Weill's lawsuit, stating that the proper place to resolve the issues was in the first case, filed in Connecticut.

Issue: Must the CPSC take formal agency action to declare a product "hazardous" before it can ask a court to ban (and seize) the product?

Decision: No, prior agency action is not necessary. Dismissal affirmed.

Rule: The CPSC has the option of making an agency determination that a product is hazardous or of proceeding directly to court and letting the court make the determination.

Discussion: *By Judge* SCHROEDER:

"Under the FHSA, any substance, or mixture of substances, that is flammable or combustible is a 'hazardous substance' if it may cause substantial illness or injury as a proximate result of foreseeable use.... A toy, or other article intended for use by children, is a 'banned hazardous substance' if it 'is a hazardous substance, or bears or contains a hazardous substance in such manner as to be susceptible of access by a child.'... This subsection, applicable to products intended for children, defines a 'banned hazardous substance' in terms that do not require a formal classification by regulation, if the product contains a hazardous substance accessible to children....

"Here the Commission is accountable for instituting the condemnation proceeding. Under the statutory scheme established, where the Commission opts to proceed in court on an allegation that the substance is a banned hazardous substance, the issue should be litigated by the manufacturer in that forum. As the Fourth Circuit explained, 'where the Commission elects to [go directly to court]..., the issue of whether the [product] is, in fact, a "banned hazardous substance" is a question to be later determined in a hearing on the merits in the condemnation proceeding.'... Such procedure does not violate the requirements of due process."

Ethical Dimension

Is it ethical to manufacture a product intended for use by children which contains a flammable substance?

P RODUCT LIABILITY REFORM

As outlined in Chapter 15, the law of product liability developed as part of tort law and contract law. Article 2 of the Uniform Commercial Code provides rather detailed regulation of sales of goods, including the seller's liability for warranties. Manufacturers and other sellers of goods may be held liable for any negligence occurring during the production and distribution of the goods. Most recently, as noted, the state courts have extended the concept of strict liability in tort to manufacturers and sellers of defective products.

National Warranty Legislation

One might assume that the state courts' creativity would have been enough to protect the buyers of goods, but the U.S. Congress felt otherwise. In 1975 Congress passed the Magnuson-Moss Warranty Act (MMWA) as an amendment to the FTC Act. The MMWA empowers the FTC to implement the provisions of the MMWA by appropriate regulations. The goals of the act are noble: to make warranties more understandable and to encourage competition among sellers.

The act does not require sellers to make warranties. It only requires that when an express warranty is made on a consumer product the warranty must comply with the new national standards for availability, clarity, and content. Sellers are required to make warranty information available prior to purchase and to display it conspicuously with the product. The terms of the warranty must be stated in easily understood language. If the product costs over $15, the express warranty must be labelled as a "full" warranty or a "limited" warranty. Under the MMWA, a full warranty means that the seller must repair or replace the defective product at no cost to the buyer and within a reasonable time. If repairs cannot be made, the buyer is entitled to a cash refund or replacement merchandise. A full warranty extends for the full time period specified, even if the product is resold. Any other warranty is, under the act, a limited warranty and must be so labelled, regardless of how extensive it is otherwise. The warranty must include specific statements as to its coverage, the procedures the customer is to follow, the times for performance, and any available dispute-resolution mechanism. The seller cannot make the warranty's existence contingent on the return of a warranty card or registration, or on service only by authorized dealers.

The MMWA regulates consumer product warranties.

There have been only a very few enforcement proceedings under the Magnuson-Moss Warranty Act. Rather than engage in extended jousting with the FTC, some sellers have simply eliminated their warranties completely. Other sellers have substantially reduced their warranties, since they have to be called limited warranties anyway.

■ New State Legislation

Many states have tried to limit product liability.

The most recent developments in product liability reform are occurring in the state legislatures. Confronted by the specter of tens of thousands of product liability lawsuits, many of them frivolous or filed in bad faith, manufacturers and distributors have turned to the legislatures for relief. Several kinds of statutory changes are being proposed. One piece of legislation would create a strong presumption that a product was not "defective" where it had been used for a certain period of time without incident—ten years is a likely period. After ten years, damages which arose from an injury occurring from the use of the product could normally not be collected under the strict liability theory. Another proposed remedy would codify the contributory negligence and assumption of risk defenses so that the kind of case described earlier involving misuse of the product could not be successfully litigated under strict liability. Manufacturers would also like legislative sanction for compliance with all industry standards and the existing "state of the art" when the allegedly defective product was manufactured and sold. They do not like decisions which hold them liable for not having later improvements on items previously sold. These are some of the suggested changes; there will be others. Business organizations are lobbying hard for such changes, and some further legislative changes in product liability doctrines seem very likely.

The next case indicates the state courts' reluctance to permit legislative reform of the product liability rules. Statutes on this topic have to be very carefully drafted.

HEATH V. SEARS, ROEBUCK & CO.

464 A.2d 288 (N.H. 1983)

Facts: Clifford Heath was using a Sears tool when it snapped, sending a piece into his eye. He lost almost all sight in that eye. Strict liability in tort for defective products was adopted by the New Hampshire Supreme Court in 1969. The state legislature passed a reform statute in 1978. Heath and several other injured parties who had filed similar product liability suits challenged the constitutionality of several sections of the reform act. The challenges were based on the equal protection clause and other requirements.

Issue: Can the state legislature establish separate rules for product liability cases?

Decision: No. The classification is arbitrary, thus the statute is invalid.

Rule: Persons in substantially similar situations cannot be treated differently by the state.

Discussion: *By Judge* DOUGLAS:

"[T]he 12-year 'statute of repose,' requires a products liability action to be brought not 'later than 12 years after the manufacturer of the final product parted with its possession and control or sold it, whichever occurred last.' The effect of this absolute limitation on suits against manufacturers is to nullify some causes of action before they even arise. As compared with nonproducts liability causes of action, which generally must be brought within 6 years after they accrue, whenever that may be,...we hold that the 12-year bar...is neither reasonable nor substantially related to the object of the legislation....

'The 12-year limit is unreasonable because the mere purchase of pills produced by a drug manufacturer in California, or of a defective automobile made in Michigan, does not place the consumer on notice of a hidden defect injurious to his health or safety. When product defects lead to injury, our law has long provided for recovery without regard to when the substance or object was made or placed into the national or international stream of commerce. This is particularly important in cases where the injuries may not clearly manifest themselves until years later, such as the clear-cell adenocarcinomas found in the daughters of mothers who 20 or more years previously took a female estrogen pill commonly known as DES (diethylstilbestrol).... The unreasonableness inherent in a statute which eliminates a plaintiff's cause of action before the wrong may reasonably be discovered was noted by Judge Frank...: 'Except in topsy-turvy land, you can't die before you are conceived, or be divorced before ever you marry, or harvest a crop never planted, or burn down a house never built, or miss a train running on a non-existent railroad. For substantially similar reasons, it has always heretofore been accepted, as a sort of logical "axiom," that a statute of limitations does not begin to run against a cause of action before that cause of action exists.'...

"The plaintiffs also challenge the three-year statute of limitations.... This three-year period begins to run from the 'time the injury is, or should, in the exercise of reasonable diligence, have been discovered by the plaintiff.' As previously mentioned, personal actions generally must be brought within six years of the time they accrue, with the exception of libel or slander actions, to which a three-year limit applies.... We do not think that merely because a manufactured product causes the injury, or because the cause of action is legislatively defined as a 'product liability action'..., a plaintiff's injury is therefore different from any other injury....

"This is not to say that the legislature could not constitutionally establish a statute of limitations of three years for all personal injury actions, if it so desired. However, it may not constitutionally discriminate against one class of plaintiffs for the purpose of protecting manufacturers by means of a statute of limitations which is neither reasonable nor substantially related to a legitimate legislative object....

"[The statute] distinguishes impermissibly between plaintiffs injured by modified products and plaintiffs injured by misused products. Under current New Hampshire law, a plaintiff may recover some percentage of his damages where his misuse of a product did not contribute more to the accident than did the manufacturer's conduct, and the misuse is found to have been foreseeable to the manufacturer. This holds true whether the product is misused by the plaintiff...or by a third party.... In contrast, [the statute] by its own terms bars recovery altogether by plaintiffs whose 'misconduct' takes the form of modification or alteration not in accordance with the manufacturer's specifications or instructions, irrespective of how foreseeable such a modification may have been....

"[W]e are not sure whether the legislature would have enacted a 'state of the art' defense in the absence of all of the unconstitutional provisions of the products liability statute. We must therefore leave that question to the legislature. Because we have stricken the remainder of the substantive sections of the statute, we void the entire chapter."

Ethical Dimension

Why shouldn't the state legislature be able to change product liability rules if it wants to?

REVIEW

Any production process for tangible items requires a location. Society favors these activities yet at the same time wishes to avoid their adverse impacts on the community. As a result, regulations of various kinds are imposed on the manufacturing process. Land ownership by non-citizens may be restricted. Private land may be taken for public use if compensation is paid. Private landowners may agree among themselves to restrict certain uses of their property. Cities and other local agencies may restrict land uses through zoning. Activities causing pollution may be regulated. Plant safety requirements may be imposed to protect both workers and neighbors.

The general tort and contract theories of product liability discussed in the last chapter are applicable to all products and to all manufacturers and distributors. Obviously, some products are more likely targets for such lawsuits than others. A defective car is more likely to cause serious injury than an improperly bound textbook. While there is thus a varying impact of the product liability rules, it is due to the facts and circumstances of the cases, including the nature of the product itself, rather than to any discrimination in the rules themselves.

For the products and industries discussed in this chapter, however, very substantial additional special requirements have been imposed by statute. Food, drug, and cosmetic products are regulated by the FDA. Auto safety is regulated by the DOT. The safety of most consumer products is under the jurisdiction of the CPSC. For these products, avoidance of product liability under the general theories is not enough. The manufacturer and distributor must also make sure that the product is in compliance with all the requirements of the special regulatory statute. These are large, important industries—foods, drugs, cosmetics, motor vehicles, consumer products. The stakes are high—for both distributors and consumers. Regulation of product safety seems likely to remain a key aspect of the relationship between government and business for the foreseeable future.

Finally, dissatisfaction with the courts' development of general legal rules of tort and contract for products cases has led to legislative changes. The major national statute, the MMWA, has gone in the direction of imposing further regulation on manufacturers' warranties. Most state regulatory laws have gone in the other direction. Most states' laws on product liability reform have limited, rather than expanded, liability of sellers and manufacturers. Similar limitations have been proposed at the national level, but passage of a national reform law seems unlikely at this time.

REVIEW QUESTIONS AND PROBLEMS

1. What are the limitations on the government's power of eminent domain?

2. What are the legal restrictions on a landowner's right to use the property as it wishes?

3. Why was it necessary to pass new statutes to deal with the problem of pollution?

4. Why is it necessary for the government to regulate the safety of food and drugs?

5. What are some of the major exclusions from coverage of the Consumer Product Safety Act?

6. Why might state product liability reform legislation be declared unconstitutional?

7. Dan was admitted to Hover Hospital for a routine surgical procedure. At 8:00 a.m. on the morning of his scheduled surgery, Dan was given several drugs to sedate him for the procedure. When he was taken to the operating room, the anesthesiologist decided that Dan had not been properly sedated and injected Dan with a drug called Novar. As the surgery began, Dan said he could still feel what was happening, so he was given a second shot of Novar. About fifteen minutes later, Dan turned blue and went into cardiac arrest. He was revived, but he suffered severe brain damage and is now comatose. His legal guardian has sued the Mell Drug Company, the maker of Novar. Mell had FDA approval to sell Novar, had disclosed all known risks connected with the drug, and had properly manufactured the drug. What result, and why?

8. A state legislature passed a statute which required a ten-cent deposit on all beverage bottles and cans. Cola Company, which makes soft drinks, sued in U.S. District Court to have the law declared unconstitutional. Cola Company claimed that the law imposed an undue burden on interstate commerce in beverages. The state's attorney general argues that the law is an attempt to deal with pollution, which is an important state concern. Who will win this case, and why?

9. Nearly 80,000 people are injured every year in the United States by power lawn mowers. After hearings, the CPSC adopted a product safety standard for walk-behind mowers. Main Mowers, a manufacturer, asked a U.S. District Court to invalidate the standard because it included special types of mowers which did not need such regulation. Specifically, Main said that three-wheel, five-wheel, and air-cushion mowers operated differently and did not present the same dangers as the usual consumer mower. How should the court decide this case, and why?

10. Jan owns an apartment building in Metroplis. The state legislature passed a statute which prohibits a landlord from interfering with the installation of cable television lines on the property. The law says that that landlord will be paid $1.00 when cable lines are installed on her property. Cable TV lines were installed on Jan's building. She claims that this is a "taking" by the state for which she must receive "just compensation" (not just $1.00). Does she have a valid claim? Explain.

SUGGESTIONS FOR FURTHER READING

Bixby, "Judicial Interpretations of the Magnuson-Moss Warranty Act," *American Business Law Journal* 22 (Summer 1984): 125.

Kegley and Hiller, "Emerging Lemon Car Laws," *American Business Law Journal* 24 (Spring 1986): 87.

Zollers, "The Power of the Consumer Product Safety Commission to Levy Civil Penalties," *American Business Law Journal* 22 (Winter 1985): 4.

17
LAW
OF
MARKETING

"Capitalism is the uneven distribution of wealth, and socialism the even distribution of poverty."
Winston Churchill

LEARNING OBJECTIVES: After you have studied this chapter, you should be able to:

EXPLAIN the legalities involved in the physical distribution of goods.

DEFINE the terms "warehouse receipt" and "bill of lading."

IDENTIFY the six ownership interests which can exist in goods.

SUMMARIZE the remedies available to the parties in a goods contract.

DESCRIBE the warranties which may be made by the seller of goods.

DISTINGUISH the quality guarantees made by sellers and renters in other types of transactions.

503

P REVIEW

Marketing has been described as the process of defining the "4 Ps"—product, place, price, and promotion. This chapter focuses on the first two points—the law concerning the product itself and the process of physical distribution (moving the product to the place where it will be delivered to the customer). Since pricing and promotion of products are heavily regulated by both state and national governments, those matters are discussed in the next chapter.

Historically, the law's concern in distribution transactions was for the formation and enforcement of the parties' agreement. We examined many of these specific legal rules in Chapters 7 and 8. Our focus here will be a bit different. Since most of the complexities involved in marketing and distribution have to do with tangible products ("goods," in legal terms), we begin with the legal rules covering sales of goods: When does ownership of the goods pass from the seller to the buyer? What are the performance obligations of the parties? What remedies do they have for a failure of performance by the other party? What are the seller's responsibilities for the quality and performance of the goods? Most of these legal rules are contained in Article 2 of the Uniform Commercial Code.

Different legal rules apply to sales of goods, as opposed to other types of business transactions.

Somewhat different rules exist for other commercial transactions—leases of goods, sales of services, sales of intangibles, sales of real estate, and leases of real estate. We therefore need to make some comparisons and distinctions between the marketing of goods and the selling of services, intangibles, and real estate. There is now a new Article 2A in the Uniform Commercial Code covering leases of goods. This article has been adopted in a majority, but not all, of the states. The law relating to the various other marketing transactions is found in cases and in special national and state statutes. As a result, there may be a much greater variation from state to state in the legal rules applicable to these other commercial transactions than is true for sales of goods.

S ALES OF GOODS

It has been said recently that the U.S. economy is changing from one which concentrates on the production of goods to one which concentrates on the production of services. In the broadest sense, of course, this observation is correct. The traditional production-line blue-collar worker is being displaced by white collars—the information generators and processors. What is often overlooked in this "big picture," however, is the fact that the information industry itself relies on a host of tangible products to generate, process, store, retrieve, and transmit that information. Without computers and all their related electronic equipment, the information industry would not be such a dominant force in our economy.

The distribution structure for goods, particularly consumer goods, can be quite complex. In contrast, distribution of services is usually quite simple—a provider and a customer. Components for the finished goods may be manufactured by one firm and sold to the assembler of the finished product. Components may be subassemblies, such as electrical equipment for a car, or may be the sheet steel that the car manufacturer will shape into the body of the car. Tools of various kinds may be needed by the manufacturer of the finished product—robots to weld the car together; "hi-lo" trucks to move crates of parts; drills, screwdrivers, wrenches; stamping presses—the list could be continued indefinitely. All these industrial products need to be made and marketed in order for the finished good to get to the consumer. After the finished product is ready at the factory, it must still be sent through distribution channels to locations where consumers will be able to buy it. Several other companies may be involved in this process—a transportation firm, one or more independent wholesalers or intermediate distributors, and a separate retailer. By the time Kathleen picks up her new car from her local dealer, several dozen companies may have had a hand in the process. Much of the complexity in the law of sales of goods is a direct reflection of the complexity in the marketplace. We need legal rules to deal with all the various situations.

◼ Uniform Commercial Code

Most of the legal rules governing the transfer of ownership of products from one person to another are found in Article 2 of the UCC. The UCC provides fairly detailed rules concerning the formation of the agreement, the performance obligations of the parties, and the remedies for any nonperformance. We discussed the agreement rules earlier, in Chapters 7 and 8. We will concentrate here on the parties' duties to each other and their remedies if things go wrong.

The UCC contains the basic legal rules for the sale of goods in the U.S.

Since many contracts involve the movement or storage of goods, we also need to review the legal rules which govern those activities. Article 7 of the UCC covers those topics. Where the goods are moved through interstate commerce (as most are), regulations of the Interstate Commerce Commission may also be involved.

◼ Storage of Goods

There are many reasons why goods may be stored temporarily. A manufacturer may wish to assure itself of a future supply of raw materials or parts and so may buy in excess of its current needs. If its production exceeds the demands of the current market, it may continue to produce anyway and store the excess finished goods in anticipation of future sales. A retailer may also buy and store inventory in advance of the selling season. A mid-level distributor may buy and store goods while it attempts to find buyers for them. In all these situations, the time-utility of the goods is being enhanced. The goods exist now, but the need or demand for them is (hopefully) in the future. Therefore they must be cared for until that future time.

The owner of the goods may itself have sufficient storage facilities and keep the "extra" goods on its own premises. In many cases, however, another firm—usually a commercial warehouse—will be paid to store the goods. This situation in which one person has lawful possession of goods which are owned by another person is called a **bailment**. The owner of the goods is called the **bailor**, and the person in possession (the warehouse) is called the **bailee**.

A bailee in possession of another's goods owes a duty of reasonable care.

The law imposes on the bailee a duty to take reasonable care of the goods in its possession. It is liable to the bailor/owner for any loss or damage to the goods caused by its failure to exercise reasonable care, and it usually has the burden of proving that it has exercised such care. Whether a particular bailee exercised reasonable care is a fact question. The nature of the goods themselves is a key factor in making this determination. Obviously, a bailee of gems or precious metals would be expected to take greater care than a bailee of bulk, low-value goods such as wheat or cotton. If the bailee has exercised reasonable care, any loss or damage to the goods falls on the bailor/owner. Businesses are generally free to change these rules in their own contract and to specify the value of the goods being stored.

■ Warehouse Receipts

A warehouse receipt is evidence of ownership of the goods it describes.

Typically, a warehouse will issue a receipt to the bailor for the goods. The **warehouse receipt** acknowledges the transfer of the goods to the warehouse, and sets the terms of the storage contract—how long, how much, what services, and the like. The warehouse receipt also acts as what the law calls a **document of title**; that is, it is evidence of ownership of the goods it represents. As such, it is used as a symbol for the goods themselves. The owner can sell the goods or pledge the goods as collateral for a loan by transferring the document. It is not necessary to physically handle the goods themselves in the sale or pledge transaction. The goods stay in the warehouse, but they are sold or pledged to someone else simply by handing over the document. The document of title is thus a very useful commercial device.

Documents of title are issued in two different forms (plus some other variations). A document issued in **negotiable** form is intended to be freely and fully transferable—to anyone. (See Figure 17–1 for an example of a negotiable warehouse receipt.) The warehouse promises that it will redeliver the goods to the bailor or "its order." The bailor may still wish to come back to the warehouse and pick up its goods. But it is also possible that the bailor may wish to sell or pledge the

FIGURE 17–1
Negotiable Warehouse Receipt (Front only)

Consecutive Number __1286__

National Warehouse Co.
2121 Northland Avenue
Detroit, Michigan   __September 25__, 19__

This is to certify that we have received in Storage Warehouse, __Unit "B", 2125 Northland Avenue__ for th account of __Evergreen Canning Company__ Ex __Car__ in apparent good order, except as noted hereon (contents, condition and quality unknown) the following described property, subject to all the terms and conditions contained herein and on the reverse hereof, such property to be delivered to __its__ order, upon the payment of all storage, handling and other charges and the surrender of this Warehouse Receipt properly endorsed.

NUMBER	PACKAGES	SAID TO BE OR CONTAIN	MARKS
1,000	Cartons	Baby Lima Beans in tin - 24/#2½'s	Evergreen Brand

THIS RECEIPT IS ISSUED FOR EXACTLY ONE THOUSAND CARTONS.

NEGOTIABLE
(Specimen Copy)

Storage __5¢__ per carton per month from __9/25__ 19__ Handling __7¢__ per __carton__ in and out inclusive.
Lot No. __5852__ Frt. Bill No. __Q-4576__
Car Initial No. __P.R.R. 562343__
Advances have been made and liability incurred on such goods as follows
This Receipt _____
Coopering _____
Cartage _____
Freight _____
Weighing _____
Misc'l Advances _____
Shipped from __Canningtown, Wisc.__

The National Warehouse Co. claims a lien for all lawful charges for storage and preservation of the goods, also for all lawful claims for money advanced, interest, insurance, transportation, labor, weighing, coopering, and other charges and expenses, in relation to such goods.

The National Warehouse Co.
By ___Ileana Garza___

THIS RECEIPT IS VALID WHEN SIGNED BY ONE OF THE FOLLOWING OFFICERS, Harold Jackson, Pres.; Ileana Garza, Secy.–Treas.

goods to someone else. If the bailor wishes to sell or pledge the goods, it simply indorses the document to the buyer or creditor. That indorsement is the "order" to the bailee to redeliver the goods to that buyer or creditor. Some negotiable documents are issued in **bearer** form, in which the warehouse simply promises to redeliver the goods to "the Bearer." Whoever shows up with the document is entitled to receive the goods it represents.

Warehouse receipts and similar documents may be issued in negotiable or nonnegotiable form.

A **nonnegotiable** document indicates that the goods are to be redelivered only to the bailor. (See Figure 17–2 for an example of a nonnegotiable warehouse receipt.) The bailor can still sell or pledge these goods by using the nonnegotiable document, but the process is a bit more complicated. The nonnegotiable document itself will usually be indorsed over to the buyer. In addition, the seller/bailor will usually have to execute a separate bill of sale for the goods and will probably want to notify the warehouse that the sale transaction has occurred. When the buyer presents the bill of sale and the indorsed nonnegotiable document of title, it should be able to take possession of the

FIGURE 17–2
Nonnegotiable Warehouse Receipt (Front only)

Consecutive Number __3462__

National Warehouse Co.
2121 Northland Avenue
Detroit, Michigan __September 25__, 19__

This is to certify that we have received in Storage Warehouse, __Unit "B", 2125 Northland Avenue__ for th account of __Evergreen Canning Company__ Ex __Car__ in apparent good order, except as noted hereon (contents, condition and quality unknown) the following described property, subject to all the terms and conditions contained herein and on the reverse hereof, such property to be delivered to__it__, upon the payment of all storage, handling and other charges.

NUMBER	PACKAGES	SAID TO BE OR CONTAIN	MARKS
1,000	Cartons	Baby Lima Beans in tin - 24/#2½'s	Evergreen Brand

NON-NEGOTIABLE
(Specimen Copy)

Storage __5¢__ per carton per month from __9/25__ 19__ Handling __7¢__ per carton in and out inclusive.
Lot No.__5852__ Frt. Bill No. __Q-4576__
Car Initial No. __P.R.R. 562343__
Advances have been made and liability incurred on such goods as follows
Coopering _____
Cartage_____
Freight _____
Weighing_____
Misc'l Advances _____
Shipped from__Canningtown, Wisc.__

The National Warehouse Co. claims a lien for all lawful charges for storage and preservation of the goods, also for all lawful claims for money advanced, interest, insurance, transportation, labor, weighing, coopering, and other charges and expenses, in relation to such goods.

The National Warehouse Co.
By __Ileana Garza__

THIS RECEIPT IS VALID WHEN SIGNED BY ONE OF THE FOLLOWING OFFICERS, Harold Jackson, Pres.; Ileana Garza, Secy.-Treas.

goods from the warehouse. The need for these extra procedures is significant in deciding when ownership of the goods passes to the buyer, as we will see in the discussion of that topic.

Shipment of Goods

In many cases, the goods will need to be transported from the seller's location to the buyer. The UCC assumes that the place of delivery of the goods is the seller's place of business. Therefore, a buyer who wishes to have the seller send the goods will have to make sure that requirement is included in the contract. The parties are generally free to negotiate any delivery arrangement they wish, including who pays the delivery charges.

Common shipping terms include COD, CIF, C&F, FOB, and FAS. Many consumers have ordered merchandise through the mail and agreed to pay for the merchandise when it arrives. That is the meaning of COD—cash on delivery, or collect on delivery. The buyer must pay for the goods in order to receive them from the transportation company. Usually the buyer is paying for the shipping costs, too. In the CIF contract, the seller prepays the shipping charges and the cost of insuring the goods while they are in transit and sends the buyer one bill for cost of the goods, insurance, and freight—CIF. The C&F contract covers only the cost of the goods and the freight charges. The FOB contract requires the seller to transfer the goods to a designated carrier at a specific location, such as "FOB Columbus, Ohio." FOB (Free On Board) indicates that it is the seller's job to get the goods to the carrier at the FOB point. The buyer will presumably pay the shipping costs from the specified location to the place where the buyer will take possession. The seller's duty ends when it delivers goods to the named carrier in the specified location. Free AlongSide is used when the goods are being transported by ship, as for example, "FAS USS WATERTITE." The seller is required to get the goods "alongside" the named boat, according to the custom used in the particular port named in the contract. The seller gets a receipt for the goods and delivers it to the buyer, who then finalizes the transport arrangements with the operator of the ship.

Abbreviations are used to indicate common shipping terms.

Bills of Lading

Companies which transport goods also issue documents of title; in this context, they are called **bills of lading**. (See Figure 17–3 for a negotiable railway bill of lading.) The bill of lading serves the same basic functions as the warehouse receipt: it is the contract for the services involved, a receipt for the goods, and a means of transferring rights in the goods without physically handling the goods themselves. Bills of lading may also be issued in negotiable or nonnegotiable form. If the goods are to be transported by air, the document is called an **airbill**. (See Figure 17–4 for a nonnegotiable airbill form.)

The bill of lading is a contract for transportation of goods.

FIGURE 17–3
*Railway Order, or
Negotiable, Bill of
Lading (Front only)*

UNIFORM ORDER BILL OF LADING

Shipper's No. _____
Agent's No. _____

[name of] RAILWAY COMPANY

RECEIVED, subject to the classifications and tariffs in effect on the date of the issue of this Bill of Lading.

At _____ 19 ____ *From* _____

the property described below, in apparent good order, except as noted (contents and condition of contents of packages unknown), marked, consigned, and destined as indicated below, which said company (the word company being understood throughout this contract as meaning any person or corporation in possession of the property under the contract) agrees to carry to its usual place of delivery at said destination, if on its own road or its own water line, otherwise to deliver to another carrier on the route to said destination. It is mutually agreed, as to each carrier of all or any of said route to destination, and as to each party at any time interested in all or any of said property, that every service to be performed hereunder shall be subject to all the conditions not prohibited by law, whether printed or written, herein contained, including the conditions on back hereof, which are hereby agreed to by the shipper and accepted for himself and his assigns.

The surrender of this original ORDER Bill of Lading properly indorsed shall be required before the delivery of the property. Inspection of property covered by this Bill of Lading will not be permitted unless provided by law or unless permission is indorsed on this Original Bill of Lading or given in writing by the shipper.

Consigned to ORDER OF _____

Destination _____ State of _____ County of _____

Notify _____

At _____ State of _____ County of _____

Route _____

Delivering Carrier _____ Car Initial _____ Car No. _____

No. Pkgs.	DESCRIPTION OF ARTICLES, SPECIAL MARKS, AND EXCEPTIONS	*Weight (Subject to Correction)	Class or Rate	Check Col.	
					Subject to Section 7 of conditions, if this shipment is to be discovered to the consignee without recourse on the consignor, the consignor shall sign the following statement:
					The carrier shall not make delivery of this shipment without payment of freight and other lawful charges.
					(Signature of Consignor)
					If charges are to be prepaid, write or stamp here, "To be Prepaid."
					Received $_____ to apply in prepayment of the charges on the property described hereon.
					(Agent or Cashier)
					Per _____ (The signature here acknowledges only the amount prepaid.)

*If the shipment moves between two ports by a carrier by water, the law requires that the bill of lading shall state whether it is "carrier's or shipper's weight."

NOTE—Where the rate is dependent on value, shippers are required to state specifically in writing the agreed or declared value of the property. The agreed or declared value of the property is hereby specifically stated by the shipper to be not exceeding...............per...............

Charges Advanced:

$ _____

_____ **Shipper.**   _____ **Agent.**

Per _____   Per _____

Permanent Post-Office Address of Shipper _____

FIGURE 17–4
*Nonnegotiable Uniform
Airbill (Front only)*

(Name of Airline)

UNIFORM AIRBILL NONNEGOTIABLE

AIRBILL NUMBER (INSERTED BY CARRIER)
01-   -   788447

FROM (CONSIGNOR)   TO (CONSIGNEE)

CONSIGNOR'S STREET ADDRESS   CONSIGNEE'S STREET ADDRESS

CITY   ZONE   STATE   CITY   ZONE   STATE

BY
X   CONSIGNOR'S NO.   DESTINATION AIRPORT CITY   COSIGNEE'S NO.

Declared Value   Routing: Airline routing applies unless shipper
                                                    inserts *specific* routing here

Received by carrier at (check one)   Delivery   Charges
☐ CONSIGNOR'S   ☐ CITY   ☐ AIRPORT   ☐ CITY   ☐ AIRPORT   ☐ PREPAID   ☐ COLLECT
   DOOR   TERMINAL   TERMINAL   TERMINAL   TERMINAL

NO. OF PIECES	DESCRIPTION OF PIECES AND CONTENTS PACKING – MARKS – NUMBERS	WEIGHT	AIRLINE ROUTING TO	VIA	RATE	CHARGES
	Instructions To Carrier					

IMPORTANT: Write or print clearly. Weights are subject to correction. Carrier will complete all items below bold line except Consignor's C.O.D.

Dimensions   Dimensional Weight
_____ X _____ X _____ cu. in.

$_____ received to apply in prepayment of the charges on the property described hereon.

by_____ agent

It is mutually agreed that the goods herein described are accepted in apparent good order (except as noted) for transportation as specified herein, subject to governing classifications and tariffs in effect as of the date hereof which are filed in accordance with law. Said classifications and tariffs, copies of which are available for inspection by the parties hereto, are hereby incorporated into and made part of this contract.

Carriage hereunder is subject to the rules relating to liability established by the Convention for the Unification of Certain Rules relating to International Carriage by Air, signed at Warsaw, October, 12, 1929, unless such carriage is not "International Carriage" as defined by the convention.

RECEIVED BY

Agent   (NAME OF AIR CARRIER)

At   (SIGNATURE OF AGENT)

Date   Time   AM PM

CONSIGNOR'S RECEIPT – NOT AN INVOICE

SUMMARY OF CHARGES	PREPAID CHARGES	COLLECT CHARGES
Weight – Rate charges		
Pick up Charge		
Delivery Charge		
Excess Value Transportation Charge		
Transportation Charges Advanced		
Other Charges Advanced		
➤ CONSIGNOR'S C.O.D X X X		
C.O.D. Fee		
Insurance Charge		
TOTAL CHARGES		

☐ CASH   ☐ CHARGE

■ Special Liability of Common Carriers

Common carriers of goods are liable for loss unless they can prove one of five exceptions applies.

As noted above, bailees are generally required to exercise reasonable care of the goods entrusted to them. **Common carriers** (those who hold themselves out to the public as being willing to transport goods for anyone) are held to a much higher standard of care than ordinary bailees. They are presumed to be liable for any loss or damage to the goods while in transit. The common carrier can avoid liability only by proving that the loss was due to one of the five recognized exceptions: (1) act of God, (2) act of the government, (3) act of an enemy government, (4) act of the person making the shipment, or (5) the inherent nature of the goods themselves. The act of God exception refers to natural disasters, such as lightning, hurricanes, and floods. If an agency of the national or state government seizes or detains the goods, the common carrier is not liable for any loss involved. If the ship carrying the goods is attacked and sunk by warships of a foreign government during wartime (an oil tanker during the Persian Gulf War, for instance), the common carrier is excused from liability. If the loss occurs because the goods were not properly packed by the person making the shipment, the carrier is not liable. Finally, a carrier which has taken all proper precautions is not liable for naturally occurring deterioration of the goods. In each of these cases, the carrier has the burden of showing that the loss was caused by one of the five exceptions and that its own conduct did not contribute to the problem. That point is made in the *Southern Pacific* case.

SOUTHERN PACIFIC CO. V. LODEN

508 P.2d 347 (Ariz. 1973)

Facts: Lou Loden was a produce broker in Nogales, Arizona. About 1:30 p.m. on January 24, 1969, he gave Southern Pacific two refrigerated vans, each containing 725 crates of cucumbers, for delivery to two of his customers in Los Angeles. The train with this shipment left Nogales at 4:15 a.m. on January 25 and should have arrived that same evening. The train stopped at Yuma, Arizona, from 8:55 p.m. January 25 until 5:30 p.m. January 28 because heavy rains had washed out the railroad bridges at Thermal, California. It had been raining for about a week prior to January 25, when Southern Pacific first sent out its local bridge inspector to check the railroad line. The cucumbers did not arrive until 6:40 p.m. on the 29th. The trial court awarded Loden $10,047.68 for spoilage. The railroad appealed.

Issue: Had the railroad proved that the loss was caused by an "act of God"?

Decision: No, Judgment for Loden affirmed.

Rule: A common carrier, to claim the "act of God" defense, must prove that there is no way that the loss could have been avoided.

Discussion: *By Judge* HOWARD:

"[C]ommon carriers undertaking to carry perishable goods are held to a higher standard of care than when engaged in the shipment of other articles not inherently perishable, and a failure to comply with this duty which results in a loss or injury to the shipper renders the carrier liable for the loss sustained, unless a proper defense is alleged and proved....

"In addition, common carriers undertaking to transport property must, in the absence of an express contract providing for the time of delivery, carry and deliver within a reasonable time....

"The law recognizes various fact situations as an excuse for delay which constitutes a good defense.... The delay, however, must have been due to an occurrence such as could not have been anticipated in the exercise by the carrier of reasonable prudence, diligence and care....

"[E]very strong wind, snowstorm, or rainstorm cannot be termed an act of God merely because it is of unusual or more than average intensity.... Ordinary, expectable, and gradual weather conditions are not regarded as acts of God even though they may have produced a disaster, because man had the opportunity to control their effects....

"[Southern Pacific] did not offer any evidence of the condition of the Bridge at Thermal on or before January 25, 1969.... [T]here was no evidence shown of a causal connection between the rainfall and the destruction of the bridge....

"The rainfall in the instant case was not shown to be totally unforeseeable or of greater intensity than other rainfalls in the region so as to justify being called an 'act of God' and, therefore, the judgment of the trial court is affirmed."

Ethical Dimension

Is it fair to hold the railroad liable because heavy rains washed out one of its bridges?

●

■ Transfer of Ownership Interests

The basic definition of a **sale** is a transaction in which the ownership of the goods is transferred from the seller to the the buyer, in exchange for a consideration called the price. It is not a gift, because the buyer is

A sale of goods is the transfer of ownership for value in return.

paying a price for the goods. It is not a bailment, because ownership, not just possession, of the goods is being transferred. (Of course, bailments may be involved in the overall process of getting the goods to the buyer, as we have just seen.)

The definition sounds simple enough, and some sales are that simple. The seller and the buyer negotiate, agree, and make the exchange. Sale transactions can also be much more complicated. Not only may there be storage and transportation arrangements, but credit may also be required by the buyer. Prudent sellers will want to take steps to protect their interest in the goods until the price is paid in full. In some cases, the goods will not even be in existence and may have to be produced to the buyer's exact specifications. Legal rules cover the various fact combinations which can occur in the marketplace.

The UCC recognizes six different interests which can exist in goods.

The UCC recognizes six different property rights which can exist in the same goods at the same time: special property, insurable interest, title, risk of loss, right to possession, and security interest. The parties are generally free to agree on when these property interests will pass from the seller to the buyer (or third parties), with two exceptions. The UCC says that no interest can pass to anyone, regardless of what the contract states, until the goods are both existing and identified. This first exception is simply common sense. The parties cannot transfer rights in things which do not yet exist or which have not been identified in some way as the goods which are for this particular buyer. The other exception represents a big change from pre-UCC law: the seller cannot retain title to goods which have been delivered to the buyer. Prior to the UCC, the "conditional sale" was a very popular security device. The seller retained title to the goods until the buyer paid the last installment of the contract price. The conditional sale is no more. Under the UCC, an attempt by the seller to retain title is limited in effect to giving the seller a security interest. If the buyer defaults on a payment, the seller can repossess and resell the goods, but, meanwhile, the buyer is the owner of the goods.

Because the parties may not specify their intentions on all these points, Article 2 of the UCC contains a set of presumptions as to when the six ownership interests pass. These rules apply unless the parties agree otherwise.

SPECIAL PROPERTY AND INSURABLE INTEREST

Special property interest gives the buyer certain rights against the goods prior to delivery.

The policy of the UCC is to give the buyer some protections at the earliest possible moment, that is, when the goods come into existence and are in some way designated as being for the particular buyer. At that point, unless otherwise agreed, the buyer is presumed to have a special property interest and an insurable interest in the goods. As defined by the UCC, the buyer's **special property interest** includes a right to inspect the goods, a right to recover damages caused by a third party's injury to the goods, and a right to recover the goods from the seller in two special situations. If the seller refuses to deliver the goods after they have been identified to the contract, and if the buyer is unable to get similar goods elsewhere, the buyer can get a court order forcing the seller to deliver. Similarly, the buyer can force delivery if the seller becomes insolvent (bankrupt) within ten days after receiving the first payment on the contract price.

The **insurable interest** merely means that the buyer has a sufficient interest in the identified goods to sustain insurance coverage in its favor. Once the goods are identified, the buyer can get an insurance policy on them to protect it against losses it sustains due to damage to the goods. The seller also has an insurable interest in the goods as long as the seller has title to the goods or a security interest in them. If a third party were financing the sale, and the third party had a security interest in the goods, it would also have an insurable interest in them, since damage to the collateral might damage its chances of collecting the balance of the contract price. Warehouses, carriers, and other bailees also have insurable interests in goods which are in their possession, since they may be held liable for damages to the goods. Any of these persons can buy property insurance covering its interest in the goods.

PASSING OF TITLE

Title is the basic ownership interest. Who is the "owner" of the goods? The person who has title to the goods is the owner. The titleholder is normally the person who is responsible for registering the goods with the appropriate government official, where that is required. The titleholder is normally liable for damages caused while the goods are being used with its permission. And the titleholder's creditors have rights against the goods in a bankruptcy proceeding or other court process. For all these reasons, it is important in many cases to know whether title to certain goods has passed from seller to buyer as of a particular point in time. For example, at the time of an accident involving the subject car, which party had title to it—seller or buyer? Or, as of the date of bankruptcy, did the goods still belong to the bankrupt seller, or had title already passed to the buyer (who would thus be able to claim the goods against the seller's creditors)?

Title is the basic ownership interest in the goods.

Article 2 of the UCC provides a general presumption as to when title passes and then elaborates this general rule by stating four presumptions for specific fact situations. In general, unless otherwise agreed, title is presumed to pass when the seller completes its performance with respect to the physical delivery of the goods. That is, when the seller gets the goods to the location where its responsibility for moving them ends, the assumption is that the buyer becomes the owner at that time and place. The UCC notes that the goods need not necessarily be in final deliverable condition in order for title to pass. If, for instance, Maybelle orders a new car from her local dealer, but the car is

The UCC contains several presumptions as to when title passes to the buyer.

to be manufactured to her specifications, title to the car would be presumed to pass to Maybelle when the dealer got her car to the dealership where she was to pick it up. Even though the car had not been finally "dealer-prepped" (washed, waxed, final dealer accessories installed), it would be her car, for title purposes. When the car gets to the dealership, the dealer/seller has completed its performance with respect to the physical delivery of the goods. Most courts apply these UCC rules even though the transfer of title has not yet been registered with the state and a new title certificate issued to the buyer.

If the contract requires that the goods are to be transported to the buyer's location, the seller has some additional obligations "with respect to the physical delivery of the goods." Just what those obligations are depends on whether the contract simply authorizes the seller to ship, or actually requires it to make delivery to the buyer. In a **shipment contract**, title is presumed to pass to the buyer when the seller delivers the goods to the carrier for shipment in accordance with the contract. En route, then, the goods would belong to the buyer. If the seller is required to deliver the goods to the buyer, then the seller's obligations would not be completed until the carrier got the goods to the buyer's city and made an attempt to physically transfer them to the buyer. The UCC says that a sale contract which involves transportation of the goods is presumed to be a shipment contract, since this is the normal practice. "To send" the goods means "to ship" them rather than to deliver them. A buyer who wants the goods delivered has to specify that in the contract.

If the goods are already at the location where the buyer is to pick them up, passing of title depends on whether the seller is required to deliver a document of title to complete its performance. Where the goods are in a warehouse under a warehouse receipt or have been shipped under a bill of lading and are still in the carrier's possession, delivery of the document to the buyer would be necessary. Title would not pass until the buyer received the document. If there is no document involved, and the contract does not require that the goods be moved further, title passes at the same instant the parties make the sale contract. When the buyer says "I'll take it," the buyer gets title.

PASSING OF RISK OF LOSS

The UCC separates the title interest from the **risk of loss** on the goods. Sometimes these two interests pass together, but in many cases they do not. The risk of loss in the two "movement" cases described above passes at the same time as the title interest. In a shipment contract, risk of loss is presumed to pass to the buyer at the time and place where the seller gives the goods to the carrier for shipment. These goods will be travelling at the buyer's risk. If anything happens to them *en route*, it will be the buyer's loss. Depending on the terms of the contract, it might also be necessary for the seller to notify the buyer that the goods have been turned over to the carrier. In the delivery contract, risk of loss does not pass to the buyer until the carrier makes a **tender** (offer) of delivery to the buyer in the buyer's city.

If the goods are in the possession of a bailee and already at the location where the buyer is to pick them up, there are three different presumptions on the passing of risk to deal with three different fact situations. If no document of title (warehouse receipt or bill of lading) has been issued by the bailee, the goods are at the buyer's risk when the bailee acknowledges the buyer's right to them. This would be the situation where the seller agreed to have the car's engine oil changed at a service station, and the buyer would take possession of the car when it was ready. As soon as the service station (bailee) acknowledged the buyer's right to possession of the car, the buyer would have risk of loss on the car. If the service station was not aware that the car was being sold and that there was a buyer, the seller would still have the risk of loss on the car.

The UCC contains several presumptions as to when risk of loss passes to the buyer.

If a document of title has been issued by the bailee (usually a warehouse or carrier), and the seller's only delivery obligation is to give the document to the buyer, risk of loss passes under one of two presumptions. As previously discussed in this chapter, documents of title may be issued in negotiable or nonnegotiable form. If the document is negotiable, the buyer takes the risk of loss when it gets the negotiable document. If the document is nonnegotiable, the buyer does not take over risk until it gets the document and has had a reasonable time in which to present it to the bailee. The reason for the delay period in the second case is the nature of the expectations of the bailee, as discussed earlier. With a negotiable document, the bailee is automatically alerted to the possibility that someone other than the person who left the goods may come back for them, so there is no need to explain what has happened. The nonnegotiable document does not automatically notify the bailee of that possibility, so the buyer of the goods must be given a reasonable time to prove its right to the goods.

In the "no move, no bailee" case, risk of loss depends on the identity of the seller. If the seller is a merchant with respect to the goods being sold, risk of loss does not pass to the buyer until the buyer actually receives possession of them. In the Maybelle example above, she would have title to the new car when it arrived at the dealership, but she would not have risk of loss until she actually went out to the dealership and took possession of her car. If the seller is a nonmerchant (Maybelle selling her old car through the classified ads), risk of loss passes to the buyer when the seller tenders delivery. For example, Maybelle calls her buyer, Ned, and tells him he can come over and pick up the car that afternoon. The old car is now at Ned's risk.

Out of fairness to the buyer, if the goods do not substantially conform to the contract, risk does not pass until the seller cures the nonconformity or the buyer indicates that it will take them despite the

Risk of loss is not presumed to pass if the goods are nonconforming.

nonconformity. Out of fairness to the seller, if the buyer breaches the contract by refusing to take delivery, the seller can treat the risk of loss as being with the buyer for a reasonable time to the extent of any deficiency in the seller's own insurance coverage on the goods. In other words, if the loss or damage were not covered by the seller's insurance, the seller could hold the buyer liable for the loss for a reasonable time after the buyer's breach.

The risk of loss rules and the use of shipping documents are involved in the next case.

RHEINBERG-KELLEREI G.M.B.H. V. VINEYARD WINE CO.

281 S.E.2d 425 (N.C. 1981)

Facts: Rheinberg-Kellerei is a West German wine producer and exporter. Sutton was its authorized agent for the U.S.; Sutton in turn employed Switzer in Raleigh, North Carolina, on a commission basis. Vineyard gave Switzer an order for 620 cases of Rheinberg's wine. The "Special Instructions" which Sutton sent with the order said: "Insurance to be covered by purchaser"; "Send a 'Notice of Arrival' to both the customer and to Frank Sutton & Company"; and "Payment may be deferred until the merchandise has arrived at the port of entry." Rheinberg was to send the bill of lading and the invoice, through its bank, to the Wachovia Bank in North Carolina. Vineyard would then pay the invoice, get the bill of lading, and pick up the goods when they arrived.

Rheinberg included these 620 cases in a larger container of wine which it delivered to a shipping company. It notified Sutton of the date of shipment, port of origin, name of ship, and port of arrival. Sutton, however, never notified Switzer or Vineyard of anything. The container was loaded on board the MS Munchen in Rotterdam. The ship left port in early December and was lost at sea with all hands and cargo sometime between December 12 and December 22, 1978. Vineyard first learned that the shipment had been made on or about January 24, 1979. It refused to pay the invoice which had been sent to the Wachovia Bank. Rheinberg sued. The trial court dismissed the case.

Issue: Had risk of loss already passed to the buyer when the goods were lost at sea?

Decision: No. Judgment for Vineyard affirmed.

Rule: In a shipment contract, the seller is required to give the buyer prompt notice that the goods have been delivered to a carrier for shipment.

Discussion: *By Judge* WELLS:

"All parties agree that the contract in question was a 'shipment' contract, i.e., one not requiring delivery of the wine at any particular destination.... The Uniform Commercial Code, as adopted in North Carolina, dictates when the transfer of risk of loss occurs in this situation....

"Before a seller will be deemed to have 'duly delivered' the goods to the carrier,...he must fulfill certain duties owed to the buyer. In the absence of any agreement to the contrary, these responsibilities [are] set out in [UCC] 2–504....

"The trial court concluded that the plaintiff's notification of the defendant of the shipment after the sailing of the ship and the ensuing loss was not 'prompt notice' within the meaning of...2–504, and therefore, the risk of loss did not pass to defendant upon the delivery of wine to the carrier pursuant to the provisions of [UCC] 2–509(1)(a). We hold that the conclusions of the trial court were correct. The seller is burdened with special responsibilities under a shipment contract because of the nature of the risk of loss being transferred.... Where the buyer, upon shipment by seller, assumes the perils involved in carriage, he must have a reasonable opportunity to guard against these risks by independent arrangements with the carrier. The requirement of prompt notification by the seller...must be construed as taking into consideration the need of a buyer to be informed of the shipment in sufficient time for him to take action to protect himself from the risk of damage to or loss of the goods while in transit.... It would not be practical or desirable, however, for the courts to attempt to engraft onto...2–504 of the UCC a rigid definition of prompt notice. Given the myriad factual situations which arise in business dealings, and keeping in mind the commercial realities, whether notification has been 'prompt' within the meaning of the UCC will have to be determined on a case-by-case basis, under all the circumstances....

"In the case at hand, the shipment of wine was lost at sea sometime between December 12 and December 22, 1978. Although plaintiff did notify its agent, Frank Sutton, regarding pertinent details of the shipment on or about November 27, 1978, this information was not passed along to defendant. The shipping documents were not received by defendant's bank for forwarding to defendant until December 27, 1978, days after the loss had already been incurred. Since the defendant was never notified directly or by the forwarding of shipping documents within the time in which its interest could have been protected by insurance or otherwise, defendant was entitled to reject the shipment pursuant to the terms of [UCC] 2–504(c)."

Ethical Dimension

Is the result in this case fair? Why or why not? Who was "at fault" here?

RIGHT TO POSSESSION OF THE GOODS

In the COD situation, as noted above, the buyer does not have the right to possession of the goods until it pays for them. Even though it almost certainly has special property and insurable interest, title, and risk of loss, it does not have the right to possess its goods until it pays for them in full. The carrier has the right to withhold delivery, pending full payment, because that is what the seller and the buyer have agreed.

Carriers and warehouses may keep possession of goods until they have been paid for their services.

Even without the COD term, the carrier is given the right to withhold possession of the goods until it has been paid for its services. The warehouse is also given this right, called a **lien** against the goods. The common law also gives a similar lien to other bailees for the value of their services. In many states there are now special statutes covering these points. The repair garage, for example, would not have to return your car until the repair bill is paid. Thus, bailees may have the right to possession of the goods even though they do not have title or risk.

SECURITY INTEREST

Finally, where the buyer's purchase of the goods has been financed by a bank or other lender, that creditor may want to use the goods as collateral for the loan obligation. This "secured transaction" was discussed in Chapter 11 as one of the typical business financing arrangements. The **security interest** gives the creditor the right to repossess the collateral, to resell it, and to apply the sale proceeds to pay off the loan.

■ Performance Obligations of the Parties

Stated most simply, the seller's obligation is to deliver conforming goods at the time and place specified in the contract, and the buyer's duty is to take them and pay for them as agreed. The assumption is that these performances are to occur simultaneously and that neither party is obliged to perform if the other is not also ready and willing to do so. Advance payments required of the buyer or deliveries on credit by the seller would need to be stated specifically in their agreement.

Unless otherwise agreed (as in the COD contract, for example), the buyer has the right to make a reasonable inspection of the goods before accepting them or paying for them. The buyer accepts the goods by inspecting them and agreeing that they conform to the contract or that it will take them despite some nonconformity. Acceptance also occurs when the goods are delivered to the buyer and the buyer gives no indication that it wishes to reject them. Rejection of the goods occurs when the buyer simply refuses to receive them or when it takes possession to make an inspection, does so, and then indicates that it is rejecting the goods. If the buyer initially accepted the goods, it can revoke that acceptance when it later discovers a hidden nonconformity in them. The buyer can also revoke acceptance when the seller fails to cure a known nonconformity which the buyer called to the seller's attention and which it promised to fix.

The buyer generally has the right to inspect the goods.

Where the buyer rejects tendered goods for nonconformity, the seller is given a chance to "cure" the problem in two situations. First, if the contract time for delivery has not yet expired, the seller should be given the remaining time to correct the problem and to make a second tender. The UCC says the seller should also have a reasonable time after the contract deadline within which to make a conforming tender, if the seller reasonably believed that its first tender would be acceptable. If the first tender was 297 units, and the buyer rejected it because the contract called for 300 units, the seller should be given a reasonable chance to get the other 3 units and to re-tender the entire lot of 300. In most commercial situations, such minor quantity discrepancies probably make no difference, and sellers are probably reasonable in believing that their buyers will not reject solely for that reason. Clearly, if there are substantial nonconformities which the seller can't or won't fix, the buyer should not have to take and pay for the goods. That point is made rather forcefully by the Ohio court in the next case.

McCULLOUGH V. BILL SWAD CHRYSLER-PLYMOUTH, INC.

449 N.E.2d 1289 (Ohio 1983)

Facts: The car which Ms. McCullough bought from the Bill Swad dealership turned out to be the proverbial "lemon." Defects occurred in its steering, transmission, and brakes. She brought the car back for repairs several times, each time being assured that the problems were fixed. Not only did the dealer not fix the original problems; others developed. After several months, she finally told the dealer she wanted her money back. When the dealer refused, she sued. The trial court held in her favor, and Bill Swad appealed.

Issue: Can the buyer revoke her acceptance of defective goods after having used them for several months, knowing they were defective?

Decision: Yes, she can still revoke. Judgment affirmed.

Rule: If the buyer's continued use of the goods after revocation of her acceptance was reasonable, that use is not an implied waiver of her right to revoke.

Discussion: *By Justice* LOCHER:

"The genesis of the 'reasonable use' test lies in the recognition that frequently a buyer, after revoking [an] earlier acceptance of a good, is constrained by exogenous circumstances—many of which the seller controls—to continue using the good until a suitable replacement may realistically be secured. Clearly, to penalize the buyer for a predicament not of his own creation would be patently unjust....

"In ascertaining whether a buyer's continued use of an item after [her] acceptance was reasonable, the trier of fact should pose and divine the answers to the following queries: (1) Upon being apprised of the buyer's revocation of [her] acceptance, what instructions, if any, did the seller tender the buyer concerning return of the now rejected goods? (2) Did the buyer's business needs or personal circumstances compel the continued use? (3) During the period of such use, did the seller persist in assuring the buyer that all nonconformities would be cured or that provisions would otherwise be made to recompense the latter for the dissatisfaction and inconvenience which the defects caused [her]? (4) Did the seller act in good faith? (5) Was the seller unduly prejudiced by the buyer's continued use?...

"It is manifest that, upon consideration of the aforementioned criteria, [McCullough] acted reasonably in continuing to operate her motor vehicle even after revocation of acceptance. First, the failure of the seller to advise the buyer, after the latter has revoked [her] acceptance of the goods, how the goods were to be returned entitles the buyer to retain possession of them....

"[The dealer]...did not respond to [her] request for instructions regarding the disposition of the vehicle. Failing to have done so, [it] can hardly be heard now to complain of [her] continued use of the automobile.

"Secondly, [McCullough], a young clerical secretary of limited financial resources, was scarcely in a position to return the defective automobile and obtain a second in order to meet her business and personal needs. A most unreasonable obligation would be imposed upon [her] were she to be required, in effect, to secure a loan to purchase a second car while remaining liable for repayment of the first car loan....

"Additionally, [the dealer's] successor, by attempting to repair [her] vehicle even after she tendered her notice of revocation, provided both express and tacit assurances that the automobile's defects were remediable, thereby, inducing her to retain possession. Moreover, whether [the dealer] acted in good faith throughout this episode is highly problematic, especially given the fact that whenever repair of the car was undertaken, new defects miraculously arose while previous ones frequently went uncorrected. [Their] refusal to honor the warranties before their expiration also evidences less than fair dealing....

"It is beyond reasonable dispute that the warranties furnished [her] failed of their essential purpose. The automobile was severally and severely flawed, and [the dealer] proved incapable of curing its defects....

"'[A]t some point after the purchase of a new automobile, the same should be put in good running condition, that is, the seller does not have an unlimited time for the performance of the obligation to replace and repair parts.' Clearly, the hour glass has run on [the dealer's] efforts to place the car in good running order. Thus, notwithstanding [her] continued operation of the vehicle, the instant action is plainly one which permits the buyer to resort to remedies [beyond] the warranties."

Ethical Dimension

Is it fair to keep reassuring the customer that the car's problems will be fixed and then say that she can't return the car because she has waited too long?

■ Remedies of the Parties

Where the buyer breaches by failing to take and pay for the goods, the seller's basic remedy is to resell them and sue the buyer for the difference, if any. The seller could also collect any incidental expenses involved in the resale, such as advertising, storing, or modifying the goods. If the buyer has the goods, but has defaulted on payment, the seller simply sues for the balance due on the agreed contract price. If credit problems arise prior to delivery of the goods, the seller can generally send the buyer a written notice which demands that the buyer provide adequate assurance of its willingness and ability to pay. Having done so, the seller could then withhold delivery of the goods until it got such assurance of payment (an escrow account at a bank, for instance, with the bank directed to pay the seller from the account when the seller delivered the goods).

REPOSSESSION

Generally, an unpaid seller has no right to retake "its" goods from a buyer who defaults on payment unless the seller has a security interest in the goods. There is one special situation, however, in which the unpaid but unsecured seller can get the goods back. If the seller discovers that the buyer was insolvent when the goods were delivered, the seller can demand their return if it does so within ten days after delivery. The ten-day limit does not apply if the buyer, within the three months prior to delivery of the goods, gave the seller a written credit statement which showed the buyer to be solvent. Where the seller had received such a written statement, it could repossess its goods at any time prior to their resale to a third party good faith purchaser. The seller's right of repossession under this special rule is also subject to the rights of the buyer's lien creditors, such as a bank or finance company which had a blanket security interest on all the buyer's inventory.

COVER

If the seller breaches by refusing to deliver the goods, the normal remedy for the buyer is to get the goods elsewhere (to **cover**) and sue the seller for any damages caused. A buyer unable to get substitute goods in the marketplace may be able to get a court order forcing the seller to deliver goods which have already been identified to the contract. In the most extreme situation—if there are no other suppliers—the buyer may be able to get a court order which forces the seller to continue to deliver for the rest of the contract period.

CANCELLATION

If the seller is guilty of a material breach, either by not delivering at all or by delivering goods with a substantial nonconformity, the buyer has the right to cancel the contract. Where the goods have already been delivered, the buyer may return them and demand a refund of any payment made, as well as any damages caused by having to buy substitute goods. Alternatively, if the goods can be fixed, the seller would be liable for the cost of repair or modification. Where the seller has breached one of its warranties and personal injury has occurred, the seller is liable to the person injured.

CONTRACTUAL REMEDIES

The UCC generally permits the parties to negotiate their own remedies for their own contract. They may agree to limit the kinds of remedies which will be available, and/or the kinds of damages which will be collectible. Within reason, such limitations are valid. When a breach occurs, however, the injured party must have a real remedy available. If the agreed remedy package "fails of its essential purpose," all the normal UCC remedies apply. Likewise, the parties may agree that the seller will not be liable for certain secondary, or **consequential**, damages. A buyer may agree to assume the risk of business losses caused by defects in the goods; if it does, it is generally bound by that agreement. On the other hand, the UCC presumes that any attempt to disclaim liability for personal injuries caused by the goods is unconscionable and therefore not valid. These points are at issue in the *Chatlos* case.

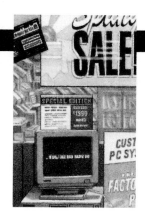

CHATLOS SYSTEMS V. NATIONAL CASH REGISTER CORP.

635 F.2d 1081 (U.S. 3rd Cir. Court of Appeals, 1980)

Facts: Chatlos designs and manufactures cable pressurization equipment for the telecommunications industry. Early in 1974, it decided to buy some new computer equipment. NCR was one of the suppliers contacted. NCR proposed its 399/656 disc system, which it said would perform six functions for Chatlos—accounts receivable, payroll, order entry, inventory deletion, state income tax, and cash receipts. NCR said it could have the system "up and running" in six months. An agreement was signed on July 24, and the hardware was delivered in December. NCR would not itself make the sale on credit, so it sold the computer equipment to Midlantic Bank, which in turn leased it to Chatlos for $870,162.09, payable in monthly rentals.

Chatlos expected the system to be operational by March, 1975, but only the payroll function was working by then. The NCR programmer could not get the order entry and inventory deletion programs to run successfully. When NCR tried to demonstrate the order entry and accounts receivable programs a year later, there were still serious problems in each. Chatlos tried to cancel the lease in June, 1976, but agreed to give NCR another chance. On August 31, problems developed in the payroll system, the only one that had been running properly. The state income tax program was installed on September 1, but when the NCR agent came back the next day to install the order entry system, Chatlos refused to allow further work and demanded to cancel the lease. When NCR refused, saying that it no longer owned the computer, Chatlos sued for damages and was awarded $57,152.76 as difference in value damages and $63,558.16 for lost profits, extra labor costs, and similar damages. NCR argued that its contract limited its liability to "correction of defects" and that liability for consequential damages had been expressly excluded.

Issue: Is the exclusive "repair" remedy legally effective for eliminating liability for difference-money damages? Is the exclusion of consequential damages legally effective?

Decision: No to the first issue. Yes to the second. Trial court is affirmed on the first point, but reversed on the second point.

Rule: A contract clause limiting the buyer to a single remedy is not effective where that remedy "fails of its essential purpose," that is, where it does not provide an effective remedy for the problem.

A disclaimer of consequential damages is effective unless it is "unconscionable," that is, grossly unfair under the particular facts of the case.

Discussion: *By Judge WEIS:*

"To be effective, the repair remedy must be provided within a reasonable time after discovery of the defect....

"When presented with the question whether an exclusive repair remedy fails of its essential purpose, courts generally have concluded that so long as the buyer has the use of substantially defect free goods, the limited remedy should be given effect. But when the seller is either unwilling or unable to conform the goods to the contract, the remedy does not suffice....

"In this case we consider a product programmed specifically to meet the customer's individual needs. Time was of substantial importance. Chatlos realized that the increasing scale of its operations required computerization and undertook the investment in 1974 because added efficiency was needed at that time. NCR represented to Chatlos that a six-function system would be up and running by March 1975. Yet, more than a year later, only one of the functions was in operation, and by September 1976, less than half of the desired capability of the system was available to Chatlos.

"NCR repeatedly attempted to correct the deficiencies in the system, but nevertheless still had not provided the product warranted a year and a half after Chatlos had reasonably expected a fully operational computer. In these circumstances, the delay made the correction remedy ineffective, and it therefore failed of its essential purpose. Consequently, the contractual limitation was unenforceable and did not preclude recovery of damages for the breach of warranty.

"This conclusion, however, does not dispose of the contractual clause excluding consequential damages....

"The limited remedy of repair and a consequential damages exclusion are two discrete ways of attempting to limit recovery for breach of warranty.... The Code, moreover, tests each by a different standard. The former survives unless it fails of its essential purpose, while the latter is valid unless it is unconscionable. We therefore see no reason to hold, as a general proposition, that the failure of the limited remedy provided in the contract, without more, invalidates a wholly distinct term in the agreement excluding consequential damages. The two are not mutually exclusive....

"One fact in this case that becomes significant under the Code is that the claim is not for personal injury but for property damage. Limitations on damages for personal injuries are not favored, but no such prejudice applies to property losses. It is also important that the claim is for commercial loss and the adversaries are substantial business concerns. We find no great disparity in the parties' bargaining power or sophistication. Apparently, Chatlos, a manufacturer of complex electronic equipment, had some appreciation of the problems that might be encountered with a computer system. Nor is there a 'surprise' element present here. The limitation was clearly expressed in a short, easily understandable sales contract. This is not an instance of an ordinary consumer being misled by a disclaimer hidden in a 'linguistic maze.'...

"Thus, at the time the contract was signed there was no reason to conclude that the parties could not competently agree upon the allocation of risk involved in the installation of the computer system....

"In short, there is nothing in the formation of the contract of the circumstances resulting in failure of performance that makes it unconscionable to enforce the parties' allocation of risk. We conclude, therefore, that the provision of the agreement excluding consequential damages should be enforced, and the district court erred in making an award for such losses."

Ethical Dimension

Should the law enforce any damage limitations? Why shouldn't the seller be fully liable for all damages caused?

●

THEORIES OF SELLERS' LIABILITY FOR DEFECTIVE GOODS

We have already seen in Chapter 15 that a manufacturer of goods may be held liable for personal injuries caused by its negligence in manufacturing a product. The manufacturer may also be held liable on the basis of strict liability in tort where a defect in its product causes personal injury. Those same two theories are also available against the seller of the product.

■ Product Liability Theories

Strict liability applies to sellers in much the same way it does to manufacturers.

Strict liability applies to the seller in much the same way as it does to the manufacturer. Strict liability applies if the product was defective when sold, personal injury was sustained, and the defect caused the injury. Negligence may be a bit harder to prove against the retail seller, especially if the product is sold in a closed carton or container. The retail seller has no reasonable way of knowing about many of the defects which may occur in the products it sells. If it cannot be expected to inspect them, it can hardly be said to be negligent when it fails to do so. A car dealer can be expected to see a flat tire and to fix it before delivering the car. The dealer would almost certainly be negligent if it failed to do so. An internal engine part, however, is another matter. Unless it caused some obvious malfunction, the dealer would have no reasonable way of knowing that it was defective.

■ Warranties of Sellers of Goods

The buyer's main case against the seller of defective goods is based on breach of warranty. The seller made certain guarantees about the goods when it sold them, and those guarantees have not been met. The guarantees are the essence of the seller's obligation under the UCC and are defined in some detail in Article 2. While the UCC does extend warranty liability down the chain of distribution to at least some third parties beyond the buyer, it does not extend warranty up the chain of distribution to the manufacturer and others. In nearly all states, however, the courts have extended warranty liability up the distribution chain to all parties involved.

EXPRESS WARRANTIES

Express warranties include any statement of fact relating to the goods.

Any statements of fact by the seller about the goods are defined by the UCC as express warranties if they are part of the basis of the bargain. In most cases, it would be assumed that the buyer did rely on such statements, at least partially, in entering into the sale contract. It is not necessary to show that the seller intended to make a warranty or that the factual statement was called a warranty or a guarantee. There are now many cases indicating that the manufacturer's statements in advertising can become express warranties, binding also the dealer who is the manufacturer's authorized representative.

In addition, the UCC says that express warranties are created every time the seller sends or shows a sample, model, or description of the goods to the buyer. In these cases, the express warranty is that the goods will conform to the sample, model, or description.

Once express warranties are made, they are virtually impossible to disclaim without a renegotiation of the entire contract. The warranty disclaimer section of the UCC says that where an express warranty and an express disclaimer are in conflict, the disclaimer gives way. An express warranty overrides an attempted disclaimer.

The warranties involved in the sale of a new car are at issue in the next case.

WARNER V. REAGAN BUICK, INC.

483 N.W2d 764 (Neb. 1992)

Facts: George and Virginia Warner sued to recover damages from the dealer-seller, Reagan Buick, for breach of contract, breach of express and implied warranties, and violation of the Nebraska Uniform Deceptive Trade Practices Act. Reagan in turn sued the dealer from whom it had purchased the car, Superior Buick-Pontiac-GMC. Reagan claimed that Superior should reimburse any damages Reagan had to pay to the Warners.

Reagan's salesman had told the Warners that the car was a "one-owner" vehicle which had been acquired through a trade-in. On February 5, 1986, the Warners signed a purchase contract which described the car as a 1983 Buick Riviera. The price of the car was $12,647.17. When interest, credit life insurance, and a maintenance agreement were added on, the total contract price was $17,120.97. A sticker prominently displayed in the window of the car said that it was sold "as is," without any express or implied warranties.

Problems developed shortly after the Warners took possession of the car. The power windows did not operate properly. When they did operate, they caused the interior lights to go on. The transmission did not function properly. The car leaked if it was left out in the rain. Sometime in late March or early April the Warners asked Reagan to take the car back, but Reagan refused to do so. The Warners continued to drive the vehicle, adding another 15,000 miles to the 26,761 on the odometer when they bought the car.

The Warners had not originally been given a title certificate when they bought the car. The title certificate was being held by General Motors Acceptance Corporation, which financed the purchase for the Warners. Investigation showed that the car had first been sold by a dealer to a Michael Stevens in Illinois. The car had been stolen from Stevens, stripped, and burned. Stevens' insurer sold the burned-out frame to an auto parts store in

Illinois, which rebuilt the car with scrap parts and sold it to Mitchell Used Cars in Missouri. Mitchell sold the rebuilt car to Martz Auto in Iowa, which sold the car at an auction to Superior.

The trial court awarded $7,734 in damages to the Warners from Reagan. Reagan was awarded one-half of this amount from Superior. Reagan and Superior were assessed $1,000 each as attorney fees for the Warners. Reagan and Superior both appealed.

Issue: Did Reagan Buick breach its express warranties?

Decision: Yes. Judgment for plaintiffs is affirmed.

Rule: Any affirmation of fact creates an express warranty that the goods shall conform to the affirmation. Any description of the goods creates an express warranty that the goods shall conform to the description.

Discussion: *By Justice* WHITE:

"In all the documents of sale, financing, and repair, the automobile is described as a 1983 Buick Riviera. The overwhelming evidence that the car was in fact only the skeleton of a 1983 Buick Riviera and a mishmash of assorted parts is sufficient evidence of a breach of an express warranty.... The outright misrepresentations made by Reagan's salesmen regarding the history of the car strengthens our conclusion that Reagan breached an express warranty.

"The measure of damages for breach of an express warranty is the difference between the value of the goods at acceptance and their value as warranted.... The automobile appraisers who testified at trial generally agreed that the value of the car at the time of acceptance was between $3,000 and $5,000. Assuming the actual purchase price represents the market value of the vehicle as warranted, we cannot say that the trial court's award was clearly erroneous....

"Superior argues that the Warners' failure to effectively revoke acceptance of the vehicle and continued use thereof after Reagan rejected the tendered return of the car precludes their suit.... Superior is correct that continued use of an automobile after discovery of defects may result in a waiver of the right to revoke acceptance.... However, it is well established...that the right to revoke acceptance, cancel the contract, and recover any amounts paid is a separate, independent, and alternative cause of action from one for breach of warranty with regard to accepted goods.... The Warners brought this case under theories of breach of contract and express and implied warranties.

Revocation of acceptance is not a prerequisite to such a suit, and thus Superior's argument is without merit....

"Reagan contends that the trial court erred in failing to award Reagan [as against Superior] the full amount of damages awarded the Warners....

"The trial court obviously concluded that Reagan and Superior are equally to blame for the Warners' mistreatment. With this conclusion, we agree. There is evidence that Superior knew that car was a salvaged wreck, yet affirmatively misrepresented the car's history to Reagan's representative. There is also evidence that Reagan should have known the true nature of the vehicle by the time it was sold to the Warners.... The judgment entered on Reagan's third-party petition is within the equitable powers of the court and is therefore affirmed."

Ethical Dimension

What ethical violations did Reagan and Superior commit?

IMPLIED WARRANTY OF MERCHANTABILITY

If the seller is a merchant with respect to the goods involved in the sale, the seller makes an implied warranty that the goods are merchantable. This is not a guarantee that the goods are perfect or that they will do anything and everything. As defined in Article 2, **merchantability** means that the goods are of fair, average quality, and that they are reasonably suitable for the normal purposes to which such goods are put. Merchantability, in other words, is a general guarantee of normal quality in the product. Merchantability has also been applied to used goods, but the guarantee in such cases would be fair, average quality as used goods of the kind—not brand-new units.

Merchantability means that the goods are reasonably fit for normal use.

Under the UCC, restaurants are bound by the merchantability warranty when they serve food or drink. The serving for value of food or drink to be consumed on the seller's premises or elsewhere is a sale for the purposes of the merchantability warranty. The restaurant patron who is served unmerchantable food or drink thus has a case for breach of warranty.

There is, however, a disagreement among the states which is not solved by the UCC. That is the test to be used to determine the merchantability of the food product. Merchantability is, of course, a fact question, but what is the test to be applied? In some states, the merchantability of the food product is determined by the natural-foreign test. Was the objectionable item part of the food product at some stage of preparation? Under this test, a cherry pit in a cherry pie or in cherry ice cream would not breach the implied warranty of merchantability, since cherries do have pits. Other states use the reasonable-expectations test: what would a reasonable consumer expect to find in the food product as presented. A person buying fresh cherries knows, or should know, that there are pits inside. A person being served cherry pie in a restaurant probably does not expect to find cherry pits still in the product. At least this second test gives the jury a chance to decide what one would normally anticipate as being included in the food product in question.

IMPLIED WARRANTY OF FITNESS

Fitness refers to a product's suitability for the buyer's particular purpose.

The implied warranty of fitness for the buyer's particular purpose arises only in a very specific context. The buyer must make known to the seller some special need or use for the goods and a reliance on the seller to select the proper goods to satisfy that special need or use. The seller may or may not be a merchant, but would be in most cases. The implied warranty of merchantability thus might or might not also be made. The difference is that the warranty of merchantability only guarantees that the goods are suitable for the normal uses to which they are put by most people. The fitness warranty guarantees that the goods will be suitable for the buyer's special use.

IMPLIED WARRANTIES OF TITLE AND AGAINST INFRINGEMENT

The seller also warrants that a clear title to the goods is being conveyed. This warranty includes a guarantee that the transfer of goods is rightful and that there are no undisclosed security interests or other liens against the goods.

If the seller is a merchant who regularly deals in goods of the kind being sold, there is also a warranty against rightful claims by third parties for infringement. This warranty would protect the buyer against third party claims for infringement of patents, copyrights, and the like. This "non-infringement" warranty is subject to the parties' specific agreement. Also, if the seller is manufacturing the goods to the buyer's specifications, the buyer must bear the cost of such third party claims if the seller complies with the buyer's specifications.

DISCLAIMERS OF WARRANTIES

Product warranties may be disclaimed unless an unconscionable result would occur.

The basic rules on warranty disclaimers are summarized in the *Henningsen* case included in Chapter 15. The UCC permits the seller to disclaim warranties, if the provisions of the UCC are followed. To disclaim merchantability, the disclaimer must mention the word "merchantability." If in a writing, the merchantability disclaimer must be stated conspicuously. "Conspicuously" is defined as being in a different style of type, in a different color, being underlined, or having some other quality which calls attention to the disclaimer. To disclaim fitness, that exact word need not be used, but the disclaimer must be in writing and must be conspicuous. As an alternative, all implied warranties may be excluded by words such as "with all faults" or "as is." The use of such phrases is not effective, however, where the circumstances indicate that the goods are not really being sold "as is." That point was made earlier by the *Warner* case. Even if the disclaimer is in the precise form specified in the UCC, it can still be challenged as unconscionable, as it was in the *Henningsen* case. Attempts to disclaim liability for personal injuries caused by the goods will nearly always be ruled ineffective.

LIABILITY OF LESSORS AND OF SELLERS OF SERVICES OR INTANGIBLES

Historically, implied quality warranties were imposed only on sellers of goods. Courts and legislatures are gradually extending implied warranty liability to sellers and lessors in other types of transactions.

Liability of Lessors of Goods

The customer in a lease transaction relies on the lessor even more than a buyer of goods relies on the seller. A person buying a car will at least usually take it for a test drive and may also drive other vehicles for comparison. The customer leasing a car will usually simply get in and drive away, trusting completely in the rent-a-car company. Largely because of this commercial reality, nearly every court has held the professional lessor of goods to the same standards as the professional seller of goods. Professional bailors, such as the rent-a-car company, will thus be held liable for negligence, breach of warranty, and strict liability. The lessor's warranty obligations are now codified in Article 2A of the UCC. Those sections are similar to the warranty sections in Article 2 for the sale of goods. The *Cucchi* case discusses the applicability of Article 2 warranties to a lease of goods prior to the adoption of Article 2A. The same results should occur under Article 2A's warranty provisions.

Lessors of goods are also liable for express and implied warranties.

CUCCHI V. ROLLINS PROTECTIVE SERVICES CO.

574 A.2d 565 (Pa. 1990)

Facts: In July, 1973, Anthony and Grace Cucchi leased a burglar alarm system for their home. The Rollins salesman told Anthony that the system was "state of the art" and "almost unbeatable." The written contract signed by the Cucchis contained a clause which limited Rollins' liability to $250 for any loss caused by the system's failure to operate. However, this contract also stated that it would not become effective until signed by Rollins' home office, and it was never so signed.

The Cucchis' house was burglarized in 1984. The alarm system did not work, and some $36,000 worth of property was taken. The Cucchis sued, alleging negligence, breach of warranty, and strict liability. The trial court held that strict liability did not apply to this case. After trial, the trial judge directed a verdict for Rollins on the negligence count, but permitted the jury to consider the Cucchis' claims for express and implied warranty. The jury awarded Grace Cucchi $20,000 and Anthony $10,000. On appeal, the Superior Court reversed on the basis that the UCC's four-year statute of limitations applied and that the lawsuit had been filed more than four years after the lease commenced. The Cucchis appealed to the state supreme court.

Issues: Does a professional lessor of goods make implied warranties?

Does the four-year limitations period begin when the lease starts?

Decision: Yes, on the first issue. No, on the second issue. (The Cucchis had four years after the system failed within which to start their lawsuit, which they did.) Judgment of the Superior Court is reversed; the jury verdict is reinstated.

Rule: Professional lessors of goods are held to the same warranty standards as professional sellers of goods.

The statute of limitations period begins when the breach of warranty occurs.

Discussion: *By Justice LARSEN:*

"[M]ost (but not all) courts that have considered the issue have concluded that Article 2 of the UCC...should be judicially extended to other sorts of transactions in goods, including various forms of leases,...because...there are sufficient economic and practical similarities between sales and leases of goods to apply at least some of the provisions of Article 2...to lease transactions....

"Many consumers and businesses are leasing goods rather than buying them.... By leasing goods, parties achieve substantially the same result as by buying and selling. The essence of both transactions is that the lessee/buyer seeks to acquire the right to use goods and the lessor/seller seeks to sell the right to use the goods.... Considering that a large volume of commercial transactions is being cast in the form of a lease instead of a sale, and that leases reach the same economic result as sales, it would be illogical to apply a different set of rules to leases than to sales where there is no justification for doing so....

"[L]essees rely upon implied and express representations of lessors as to the quality, merchantability and fitness of goods to the same extent and in the same manner as buyers rely upon similar representations by sellers.... Accordingly, we hold...that the express and implied warranty provisions of Article 2...apply to transactions involving the lease of goods....

"Considering the nature of the transaction involved in this case, and the respective interests of the lessor and lessee, we have no difficulty finding that the express and implied warranties made by Rollins explicitly extended to future performance of the burglar alarm system and that discovery of the breach had to await the time of performance....

"[T]he very nature of a conventional lease of goods with monthly payments by the lessee and the continuous obligation of the lessor to service and repair, especially where (as here) the goods are to be returned in working order to the lessor at the end of the lease, supports a finding that the future performance of the goods has been warranted, and that the goods will continue to operate and remain fit for their ordinary and intended use."

Ethical Dimension

Why should an equipment lessor be held liable for losses to the lessee which occur more than ten years after the start of the lease?

■ Liability of Sellers of Services

As noted originally in Chapter 6, sellers of services are required to exercise reasonable professional care and to comply with the specific promises made in their contracts with customers. They are not, however, held to the same automatic quality guarantees as the sellers of goods. The implied warranty of merchantability does not apply to sales of services (at least not in most states). Likewise, there is no strict liability in tort against sellers of services whose "product" is in some way "defective." To collect for damages caused by allegedly improper services, the customer must prove professional malpractice (negligence), or prove the failure to perform a specific contract promise.

■ Liability of Sellers of Intangibles

What about sellers of intangibles, such as patents, accounts receivable, or shares of stock? What quality guarantees do these distributors make about the products they are selling? While there are some variations for particular types of intangibles, most of these sellers will also escape liability for implied warranties and for strict liability in tort.

The implied warranties made by sellers of intangibles are quite limited.

The seller of intellectual property such as a patent or a copyright would normally be held to an implied guarantee that the patent or copyright was valid. But just because a valid patent has been granted, there is no assurance that it will prove to be commercially successful. The seller could not be expected to know that or to guarantee it. Commercial success would depend on a host of factors, all of which would be beyond the control, or even knowledge, of the seller. The only implied warranty in this sale transaction would be the very limited one that the transaction itself is valid. That is, the seller does own the patent or copyright and does have the right to transfer it.

The implied warranties of the seller (assignor) of accounts receivable, as discussed in Chapter 11, are likewise quite limited. Here again, the seller/assignor warrants that the assigned account actually exists and is subject to no limitations except those which have been stated or which are apparent. If documentary or other physical evidence of the account has been shown to the buyer, there is a warranty that those things are genuine and what they purport to be. Finally, the seller/assignor warrants that it will do nothing to defeat or impair the value of the assigned account. Significantly, there is no implied guarantee that the account debtor is solvent or collectible. To take recourse against the seller of a "defective" account, in other words, the buyer must normally show that the seller committed fraud or that the assignment contract contains a specific recourse provision for uncollectible accounts.

Sellers of stocks are not held to any implied warranty of performance because there are too many independent variables that may affect the price of a particular stock. Any market condition which affects the company's business can have a positive or negative effect on the price of its stock. General economic conditions can depress or enhance the stock market as a whole, an entire industry, or only selected companies. There is no way that the seller of stocks (or bonds) can guarantee the investment's performance in the future. Securities issuers do have to register with the SEC, as we saw in Chapter 10, and are required to provide full and accurate information about their company as part of that process. The issuing company and its agents who are responsible for the registration process can be sued for filing false or incomplete information. A seller of the securities who defrauds the buyer can, of course, be sued on that basis. But here, too, there are no implied quality warranties on the securities themselves and no strict liability theory against the securities seller for "defective" stocks or bonds.

■ Liability of Seller or Lessor of Land

States are gradually imposing implied warranties on sellers of buildings.

Perhaps the strongest "no warranties" rules were developed for real estate transactions. Historically, the rule of **caveat emptor** (let the buyer beware) was applied very strictly in real estate transactions. The seller of land and buildings made no guarantees as to the condition of the property and was not even required to make a full disclosure of known defects. The same basic approach was used for leases of real estate; the landlord's obligations were absolutely minimal.

Gradually, by statute and court decision, these rules are being modified. Nondisclosure of hidden conditions which pose a serious threat to the occupant's health and safety would probably be classified as fraud by most courts today. Statutes in many states now require the landlord to furnish premises that are at least "habitable," that is, livable. Most states now do impose a similar implied warranty of habitability on the builder of new residences. This warranty roughly equates to the warranty of merchantability on goods. Construction or equipment defects in the new house or apartment would thus subject the builder/seller to liability in most states today. The builder/seller would have to pay the cost of repairs or the loss in value of the house due to the defect. Most states are probably willing to extend this habitability warranty to later buyers of the house, but not all courts are willing to change the rules that much. Disclaimers or limitations of this new implied warranty are possible if carefully drafted and clearly bargained for as part of the sale transaction.

REVIEW

From earliest times, legal rules have been provided for distribution transactions—sales or leases of goods, sales of services and intangibles, sales or leases of real estate. Unfortunately, the rules applied to these various commercial transactions have not been uniform, particularly as to the seller's quality guarantees. Sellers and lessors of goods have generally been held to higher standards than distributors in other types of transactions. While some of these rules are being changed, there are still significant variations based on the subject matter of the contract and, to some extent, on the identity of the seller.

The physical distribution process for goods is quite complex in many industries. There is thus a parallel complexity to the legal rules covering such transactions. Article 7 of the UCC contains detailed rules for the storage and shipment of goods. Article 2 covers the actual sale of the goods, including the rules for the transfer of the various ownership interests in the goods, the performance obligations of the parties, and the remedies available for breach of the sale contract.

In general, the parties control their contract, but the UCC does provide some required minimal standards for performance.

REVIEW QUESTIONS AND PROBLEMS

1. When is a carrier liable for damage to goods which have been given to it for transportation?

2. Why is it important to know when title to goods passes from a seller to a buyer?

3. How is the liability of a seller of goods different from that of a seller of services?

4. What is "identification" in a sale of goods contract, when does it occur, and why is it important?

5. What remedies are available to a buyer who receives defective goods?

6. When does risk of loss pass to the buyer in a sale of goods in which the buyer is to pick up the goods at the seller's place of business?

7. Norah was admitted to the hospital for surgery. As part of the surgical procedure, she received a blood transfusion from which she contracted serum hepatitis. At the time, there was no test available to detect serum hepatitis virus in whole blood. Since there was no evidence that the hospital had been negligent in any way, it moved to dismiss the case. It had not sold goods, but rather provided services, and therefore implied warranty and strict liability did not apply. How should the court rule, and why?

8. Argonaut Foods contracted to sell 50,000 pounds of pork spareribs to Miracle Markets. Since both companies stored products in Warmer Warehouse, the contract provided that Argonaut would simply notify Warmer to transfer the goods from Argonaut's account to Miracle's account. Argonaut told Miracle that it would have the transfer made between May 3 and May 7. On May 6, Argonaut telephoned Warmer and told it to make the transfer to Miracle's account. Warmer immediately entered the transfer on its books, but did not send notice to Miracle until May 10 or 11. Miracle received the notice (that the ribs had been transferred to its account and were being held for it) on May 18. Meanwhile, Warmer's warehouse had been completely destroyed by fire, which was not its fault, on May 12. Argonaut sues for the contract price of the (now "barbecued") ribs. Which party had the risk of loss? Explain.

9. On Saturday, April 25, 1959, about 1 p.m., the plaintiff, accompanied by her sister and her aunt, entered the Blue Ship Tea Room operated by the defendant. The group was seated at a table and supplied with menus.

This restaurant, which the plaintiff characterized as "quaint," was located in Boston "on the third floor of an old building on T Wharf, which overlooks the ocean."

The plaintiff, who had been born and brought up in New England, ordered clam chowder and crabmeat salad. Within a few minutes she received word that "there was no more clam chowder." Presently, there was set before her a "small bowl of fish chowder." "The fish chowder contained haddock, potatoes, milk, water, and seasoning. The chowder was milky in color and not clear. The haddock and potatoes were in chunks." "She agitated it a little with the spoon and observed that it was a fairly full bowl.... After three or four spoonfuls she was aware that something had lodged in her throat because she couldn't swallow and couldn't clear her throat by gulping and she could feel it." This misadventure led to two esophagoscopies at the Massachusetts General Hospital, in the second of which, on April 27, 1959, a fish bone was found and removed. Plaintiff sued the restaurant. How should the court rule? Discuss.

10. Airevans Limited converted standard automotive vans into travel vehicles by installing sleeping and cooking facilities. The glue which Airevans was using to install carpeting in the vans did not work well in hotter climates; carpets came loose and Airevans had to reinstall them. Airevans' chief engineer, Emma Redmon, contacted Gluepot Company and asked if Gluepot had a product which would do the job. Gluepot sent several samples of its product, Stadown, which Emma tested in Airevans' air-conditioned plant. Stadown worked very well. Emma suggested that the tests should also be made in hotter temperatures, but Airevans' president said he was satisfied. Airevans subsequently had to re-glue the carpeting in 700 vans, when Stadown also failed to hold up under hotter temperatures. Airevans sued Gluepot for breach of an implied warranty of fitness. Do they have a case? Why or why not?

SUGGESTIONS FOR FURTHER READING

Cherry, "Negligence: An Expanded Cause of Action Against Builders for Used Home Defects," *American Business Law Journal* 26 (Spring 1988): 167.

Elfin, "The Changing Philosophy of Products Liability and the Proposed Model Uniform Product Liability Act," *American Business Law Journal* 19 (Fall 1981): 267.

Henderson, "Coping with the Time Dimension in Products Liability," *California Law Review* 69 (July 1981): 919.

Hurd & Zollers, "Desperately Seeking Harmony: The European Community's Search for Uniformity in Product Liability Law," *American Business Law Journal* 30 (May 1992): 35.

Leete, "Marketing of Musical Performance Rights and Antitrust: the Clash Continues," *American Business Law Journal* 21 (Fall 1983): 335.

Mislow, "Reducing the High Risk of High Tech: Legal Planning for the Marketing of Computer Systems," *American Business Law Journal* 23 (Spring 1985): 123.

Priest, "A Theory of the Consumer Product Warranty," *Yale Law Journal* 90 (May 1981): 1297.

Razook, Horrell, & Roblyer, "A Descriptive and Analytical Matrix for Product Liability Defenses," *American Business Law Journal* 30 (May 1992): 69.

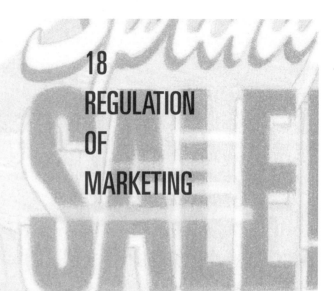

18
REGULATION
OF
MARKETING

"Old Boys have their Playthings as well as young
Ones; the Difference is only in the Price."
Benjamin Franklin

LEARNING OBJECTIVES: After you have studied this chapter, you should be able to:

EXPLAIN the major regulations dealing with advertising and packaging.

DISTINGUISH predatory pricing, resale price maintenance, and price discrimination.

DISCUSS the chief regulations dealing with choice of distribution channels.

DEFINE tying contracts and exclusive dealing agreements.

IDENTIFY the situations when a refusal to deal may be illegal.

DISCUSS the rules on unfair methods of competition.

P REVIEW

If, as we noted in Chapter 14, the employment relationship is the most heavily regulated part of business operations, the marketing function is at least a close second. Today, the proper question is not "What's regulated?" but rather, "Is there any aspect of marketing which isn't regulated?" The answer, of course, is that nearly every aspect is regulated— advertising, packaging, labeling, trademarks, pricing, selection of distribution channels, trade practices. Both national and state governments are actively involved in policing the marketplace to protect consumers and to make sure that the process of free competition is allowed to function.

Marketing is heavily regulated.

Most of our attention will be given to national regulations, since most products are distributed through interstate commerce. Even with these products, however, some state regulation can be involved. States are sovereign political entities and can regulate what happens within their territory. Part of the problem which business faces is the necessity to comply with all these various state regulations. For example: the stricter air pollution regulations in California mean that some cars cannot be sold there and that those which are must be specially designed to comply. One state is thus specifying the characteristics which a product must have to be lawfully sold there.

R EGULATION OF PRODUCT PRESENTATION

To make rational purchasing decisions, buyers need accurate information about the available choices of products and services. One major group of regulations is those requiring accuracy in seller to buyer communications. Included in this general grouping are the requirements for use of trademarks and trade names. More recently, the public has become concerned with the environmental impact of packaging materials. New regulations are being developed to deal with that problem.

■ Regulation of Advertising

State authorities have been concerned with false advertising for many years. Most states now have some kind of statutory prohibition against false advertising, although there are specific variations from state to state. These statutes typically make it a crime (a misdemeanor) to publish ads containing statements which are untrue, deceptive, or misleading. Some states also require proof of an intent to deceive, a requirement which makes a criminal conviction unlikely. In some states, the prohibition against false advertising is part of a comprehensive statute directed against all forms of deceptive trade practices.

Both state and national governments provide penalties for false advertising.

The Federal Trade Commission also has a long history of involvement with this problem. Section 5 of the FTC Act forbids "unfair or deceptive acts or practices." This phrase was intended to be interpreted with flexibility, to meet new forms of marketplace deception and trickery. It is clearly a much broader concept than common law fraud. A statement in an ad may be technically true and still be labeled by the FTC as "unfair" or "deceptive." Intent to deceive does not have to be proved. Actual reliance on the ad statement by a specific buyer does not have to be shown, either, nor does actual injury to a buyer.

What is necessary, then, for an FTC prosecution under Section 5? As summarized in the FTC's 1983 policy statement, the ad or other practice must make a material misrepresentation or omission which is likely to mislead a reasonable consumer. Defining materiality in this context involves many of the same uncertainties as it does in securities regulation. Here, the basic meaning is "information which would be important to a reasonable person in making a decision to buy the advertised good or service." Points which are stated specifically in the ad are at least material in the sense that the seller thought they would be important in making the buy/no-buy decision.

Not all statements in ads are meant to be taken as factual.

Advertisements, almost by definition, include a great deal of high-powered language, wild claims, and hearty endorsements. Sellers generally try to "accentuate the positive and eliminate the negative." Reasonable persons don't necessarily believe everything they read and hear, especially when the source is someone who is trying to get them to buy something. Most people are naturally skeptical of advertising claims. Some advertisers also use clever parodies in their ads. Most reasonable people can probably tell when an ad is "only kidding," and not intended to be taken seriously. Historically, such non-specific, non-factual language as "the best deal in town," or "it looks great on you," has been taken for what it is—harmless "puffery" of the product by the seller. What the law is concerned with are significant factual misrepresentations of the performance characteristics of the product or service. The *Colgate-Palmolive* case is one of the key precedents in trying to draw this subtle distinction.

FEDERAL TRADE COMMISSION V. COLGATE PALMOLIVE CO.

380 U.S. 374 (1965)

Facts: Ted Bates & Co., a well-known advertising agency, prepared three one-minute commercials using different sports personalities to show the superior performance of Rapid Shave, a Colgate product. "Who's the man behind the sandpaper mask?" asked the announcer. The sports hero would then proceed to "shave sandpaper," using Rapid Shave, while the announcer said, "It was apply—soak—and off in a stroke." The "sandpaper" appeared to be shaved clean. What was really used was a "mock-up," a piece of plexiglass to which some sand had been applied.

The FTC filed a complaint, charging that the commercials were false and deceptive. At the hearing, it was proved that real sandpaper could indeed be "shaved" after soaking for eighty minutes, but that if real sandpaper had been used it would have appeared to the TV viewer to be nothing more than colored paper. The trial examiner dismissed the complaint, holding that there had been no material misrepresentation. On appeal, the FTC overruled the trial examiner and issued a cease and desist order. The U.S. Court of Appeals refused to enforce the order, so the FTC appealed.

Issue: Was the use of the plexiglass mock-up "false and misleading"?

Decision: Yes. The FTC order will be enforced.

Rule: Undisclosed mock-ups can not be used in TV commercials to prove the truth of claims about the performance or quality of the product itself.

Discussion: *By Chief Justice* WARREN:

"We are not concerned in this case with the clear misrepresentation in the commercials concerning the speed with which Rapid Shave could shave sandpaper, since the Court of Appeals upheld the Commission's finding on that matter and the respondents have not challenged the finding here. We granted [review] to consider the Commission's conclusion that even if an advertiser has himself conducted a test, experiment, or demonstration which he honestly believes will prove a certain product claim, he may not convey to television viewers the false impression that they are seeing the test, experiment, or demonstration for themselves, when they are not because of the undisclosed use of mock-ups.

"We accept the Commission's determination that the commercials involved in this case contained three representations to the public: (1) that sandpaper could be shaved by Rapid Shave; (2) that an experiment had been conducted which verified this claim; and (3) that the viewer was seeing this experiment for himself. Respondents admit that the first two were made, but deny the third was. The Commission, however, found to the contrary, and, since this is a matter of fact resting on an inference that could reasonably be drawn from the commercials themselves, the Commission's finding should be sustained. For the purposes of our review, we can assume that the first two representations were true; the focus of our consideration is on the third which was clearly false. The parties agree that Section 5 prohibits the intentional misrepresentation of any fact which would constitute a material factor in a purchaser's decision whether to buy. They differ, however, in their conception of what 'facts' constitute a 'material factor' in a purchaser's decision to buy. Respondents submit, in effect that the only material facts are those which deal with the substantive qualities of a product. The Commission, on the other hand, submits that the misrepresentation of any fact so long as it materially induces a purchaser's decision to buy is a deception prohibited by Section 5....

"We agree with the Commission...that the undisclosed use of plexiglass in the present commercials was a material deceptive practice, independent and separate from the other misrepresentation found. We find unpersuasive respondents' other objections to this conclusion. Respondents claim that it will be impractical to inform the viewing public that it is not seeing an actual test, experiment, or demonstration, but we think it inconceivable that the ingenious advertising world will be unable, if it so desires, to conform to the Commission's insistence that the public be not misinformed. If, however, it becomes impossible or impractical to show simulated demonstrations on television in a truthful manner, this indicates that television is not a medium that lends itself to this type of commercial, not that the commercial must survive at all costs. Similarly unpersuasive is respondents' objection that the Commission's decision discriminates against sellers whose product claims cannot be 'verified' on television without the use of simulations. All methods of advertising do not equally favor every seller. If the inherent limitations of a method do not permit its use in the way a seller desires, the seller cannot by material misrepresentation compensate for those limitations."

Ethical Dimension

Why should a TV advertiser be required to disclose specifically its use of "mock-ups" to sell its products? Don't reasonable consumers understand that they are seeing simulations, rather than the real thing?

●

Misleading simulations on TV can be banned.

A ban on all simulations in TV commercials would probably go too far. Much of the potential for misleading consumers might be removed by an express statement in the ad that the demonstration was a simulation. Even with such a statement, outright deception is still unlawful. In a recent example, a car manufacturer had a "monster truck" run over a line of five parked cars. The roofs of all but the advertised car collapsed as the heavy truck passed over. What the ad did not disclose was that the roof supports of the other cars had been weakened and that extra supports had been added to the advertised car. That commercial was stopped after state officials complained.

■ Regulation of Packaging and Labeling

Both state and national governments are also concerned with the packaging and labeling of products. These concerns take several distinct forms. For some types of products, there are very specific labeling requirements. For many consumer products, the use of certain language ("giant economy size") may be misleading. The vast number of unusual package sizes makes price comparison difficult for the average shopper, even with a pocket calculator. Most recently, the public's increased awareness of environmental pollution has led to restrictions—some voluntary, some imposed—on the use of certain packaging materials.

LABELING REQUIREMENTS

Several national statutes require specific labeling for clothing products. The Wool Products Labeling Act of 1939 specifies disclosure of the percentage of wool and other fibers in the product, and the name of the manufacturer/distributor. There is a similar percentage-disclosure requirement for fur products under the Fur Products Labeling Act of 1951. As synthetic fibers such as rayon and orlon came into greater use, there was potential for consumer confusion over the type of clothing product being purchased. The result was another statute—the Textile Fiber Products Identification Act of 1958, which again required disclosure of percentages of fibers in the product, the manufacturer/distributor's name, and the country of origin, for imported textile products. The FTC is charged with administering these labeling statutes.

Some products are required to have certain labeling.

Tobacco products are required to carry health warnings. So are advertisements for these products. More recently, most alcoholic beverages have been subjected to similar labeling. Given consumers' increased health-consciousness, requirements for this kind of labeling could increase dramatically. In 1990, Congress passed the Nutrition Labeling and Education Act. In November 1991, to implement the provisions of the act, the Food and Drug Administration proposed 400 pages of new regulations for food labeling. Food labels are required to disclose amounts of vitamins and minerals contained in the product. The use of certain terms such as "low fat," "high fiber," and "light" is restricted. Such terms are now defined by law, and the terms can be used only on food products which meet the definitions.

Using an excessively large but only partially filled package would certainly seem to qualify as a deceptive marketing practice. Clear rules are difficult to develop in this area, however, because many products "settle" or compact themselves during shipment to the retailer. The box or package may be filled to the top at the factory and the correct weight placed on the label, but it may appear to be only partially filled by the time the consumer opens it. At least equally confusing to most consumers is the array of different package sizes. A thrifty consumer who wishes to make price comparisons will have difficulty doing so with a variety of odd-sized packages. Which is the better buy: 3 and 7/8 ounces at 39 cents or 6 and 1/3 ounces at 79 cents? Even for a math major, that is not an easy calculation. Multiply that difficulty for one product by the 10,000 or so different products in a large supermarket, and the "rational economic person" is in trouble. The Fair Packaging and Labeling Act has imposed some limitations, but this problem is still a long way from being solved.

PACKAGING

States and cities are beginning to impose regulations on packaging materials.

Increasingly, pollution of the environment has become a major problem for modern industrial society. The sheer volume of waste is enormous. Landfill space is being used up. Trash from Long Island is being bailed in Brooklyn and trucked to a landfill in Illinois. Product packaging—boxes, cans, bottles, wrappings—contributes to this waste disposal problem. Public policy has only just begun to deal with this looming crisis. A few states, led by Oregon, have passed laws requiring deposits on most beverage bottles and cans; the can or bottle must be returned to the distributor to redeem the deposit. Consumers may resent the hassle involved at first, but there are few cans or bottles lying along the roadsides in these states. A few cities have begun mandatory recycling programs for trash by requiring residents to separate glass bottles, cans, and newspapers from the rest of their household waste. Here, too, a bit of extra effort on the part of the individual is required, but the long-range benefits could be very great. Product sellers may want to capitalize on this movement by adopting more easily recyclable packaging. The Minnesota law that was in force in the next case represents a more drastic approach to the problem—simply banning one particular type of product packaging.

MINNESOTA V. CLOVER LEAF CREAMERY CO.

419 U.S. 456 (1981)

Facts: A 1977 Minnesota statute banned the retail sale of milk in plastic nonreturnable, nonrefillable containers, but allowed such containers made from other materials, such as waxed paperboard. Clover Leaf wanted to use the plastic jugs and challenged the constitutionality of the statute under the Commerce Clause and the Equal Protection Clause. Clover Leaf agreed that the state's objective—protecting the environment—was proper.

However, Clover Leaf did not feel that the classification used (plastic vs. nonplastic) was "rationally related" to that legitimate objective. The Minnesota courts held the statute unconstitutional, and the state appealed.

Issues: Was the statutory classification system reasonably related to proper state purposes? Does the statute unduly interfere with interstate commerce?

Decision: Yes, the classification system was reasonably related to a proper state purpose. No, the statute does not unduly interfere with interstate commerce. The statute is valid.

Rule: If there is any reasonable basis for the legislature's decision on a policy question, the court must defer to it.

A nondiscriminatory statute is invalid under the Commerce Clause only if the burden imposed on commerce is clearly excessive in relation to the benefits sought by the state.

Discussion: *By Justice BRENNAN:*
"The state identified four reasons why the classification between plastic and nonplastic nonreturnables is rationally related to the articulated statutory purposes. If any one of the four substantiates the state's claim, we must reverse the Minnesota Supreme Court and sustain the Act....

"The Minnesota Supreme Court found that plastic milk jugs in fact take up less space in landfills and present fewer solid waste disposal problems than do paperboard containers.... But its ruling on this point must be rejected for the same reason we rejected its ruling concerning energy conservation: it is not the function of the courts to substitute their evaluation of legislative facts for that of the legislature.

"We therefore conclude that the ban on plastic nonreturnable milk containers bears a rational relation to the state's objectives, and must be sustained under the Equal Protection Clause.

"The District Court also held that the Minnesota statute is unconstitutional under the Commerce Clause because it imposes an unreasonable burden on interstate commerce. We cannot agree.

"When legislating in areas of legitimate local concern, such as environmental protection and resource conservation, states are nonetheless limited by the Commerce Clause.... Even if a statute regulates 'even-handedly,' and imposes only 'incidental' burdens on interstate commerce, the courts must nevertheless strike it down if 'the burden imposed on such commerce is clearly excessive in relation to the putative local benefits.'... Moreover, 'the extent of the burden that will be tolerated will of course depend on the nature of the local interest involved, and on whether it could be promoted as well with a lesser impact on interstate activities.'...

"Since the statute does not discriminate between interstate and intrastate commerce, the controlling question is whether the incidental burden imposed on interstate commerce by the Minnesota Act is 'clearly excessive in relation to the putative local benefits.'... We conclude that it is not....

"A nondiscriminatory regulation serving substantial state purposes is not invalid simply because it causes some business to shift from a predominantly out-of-state industry to a predominantly in-state industry. Only if the burden on interstate commerce clearly outweighs the state's legitimate purposes does such a regulation violate the Commerce Clause."

Ethical Dimension

Why should a state be able to tell a manufacturer how to package (or how it cannot package) its lawful products?

◼ Trademarks and Trade Names

Companies use trademarks to identify their products.

Advertisers spend billions of dollars each year in this country to establish identities for their companies and their products. A well-established trade name for the company, or trademark for its products, is therefore a very valuable piece of property. A **trademark** is any word (or words), symbol, or device which a company has adopted to identify its product. A **service mark** performs a similar function in identifying services. Obviously, the more distinctive the trademark, the more effective it is. Fanciful or arbitrary words (those which have no other meaning but are simply created by the advertiser) can be very effective in identifying a particular product and/or its distributor. Kodak, Polaroid, and Xerox are well-known examples of such fanciful product names. Even such trademarks as these can be lost, however, if the fanciful word comes into general public use as the name of a type of product, rather than just that of the one producer. Xerox has been fighting this battle for years, trying to distinguish its Xerox copying machines from improper uses of its trademark as a noun or a verb ("I'll xerox it"; "Make a xerox of that"). The words aspirin and linoleum have already been lost as protected trademarks in this country, in precisely that way—public use of the term as having a generic rather than a specific meaning.

Trademarks can be registered with the national government.

The main legal protection for the trademark owner is the Lanham Act of 1946. Under that act's authority, the U.S. Patent and Trademark Office (PTO) has established a procedure for registering trademarks. A company which has used a distinctive mark on its products in interstate commerce files an application to register the mark. A company may also apply for advance registration (up to three years prior to use of the trademark). The PTO, if it agrees that the mark is distinctive, lists it in the "Principal Register" of trademarks. This listing creates a presumption that the company is the owner of the trademark and also provides notice to other companies of the owner's exclusive right to use the mark. Five years after such listing, the validity of the trademark becomes incontestable, so third parties can no longer challenge its validity. Registration is now valid for only ten years, but may be renewed. Nonuse of the mark can result in cancellation of the trademark. Fraudulent use or certain other misuses of the trademark can also cause cancellation.

The trademark owner's rights are violated when another company uses a deceptively similar mark on its products. If the infringement case is proved, the trademark owner can get a court injunction preventing further sales of the infringing product. In some cases, the trademark owner can also collect its lost profits or the wrongful profits made by the infringer.

The common law rules on unfair competition provide similar protections against the practice known as **"passing off"**—copying the look of the competitor's product and passing your product off as theirs. Both the competitor and the buyer are injured by this unfair marketing tactic. The buyers are not receiving what they wanted, and the competitor is losing sales which it should have made. Passing off can occur by use of a word or symbol which is deceptively similar to a registered trademark, or it can occur where the targeted product is not identified by a registered trademark at all. In the latter case, the copycat uses the same color, size, shape, and lettering on its product or package. The **"trade dress"** (package size, shape, color) of the targeted product is copied to such an extent that a buyer can't tell the difference without very close examination. In these cases, too, some difficult line-drawing has to be done by the courts, particularly if the targeted product's trade dress has not been protected by trademark or copyright. The *Nutra-Sweet* case is a recent example of this problem.

Passing off occurs when a competitor imitates a product's packaging to try to deceive buyers.

NUTRA-SWEET CORP. V. STADT CORP.

(917 F.2d 1024, U.S. 7th Cir. Court of Appeals, 1990)

Facts: Nutra-Sweet, Stadt, and Cumberland all manufacture and distribute sugar substitute products in single-serving packets which are sold to restaurants and other food service establishments. Since 1948, real sugar has been distributed for these uses in white single-serving packets. Until 1958, sugar was the customer's only choice. In 1958, Cumberland began selling its sugar substitute, Sweet 'N Low, in pink packets. In 1981, Nutra-

Sweet first sold its sugar substitute, Equal, in a white packet, but changed to a blue packet the next year. In 1988, Stadt and Cumberland started selling their new sugar substitute, Sweet One, in blue packets. The packets were a different shade of blue from the blue packets used by Nutra-Sweet.

Nutra-Sweet sued for an injunction claiming that the "trade dress" of its product had been infringed, and that the defendants (Stadt and Cumberland) were guilty of unfair competition. The trial court granted the defendants' motion for summary judgment, and Nutra-Sweet appealed.

Issue: Can a manufacturer prevent a competitor from using a similar, nonfunctional color for its product?

Decision: (Generally) No. Judgment affirmed.

Rule: A product's "trade dress" is the overall image used to present it to purchasers and can include its size, shape, color, graphics, packaging, and label. A manufacturer cannot normally appropriate a color for its own exclusive product use.

Discussion: *By Judge* REYNOLDS:
"As a rule color cannot be monopolized to distinguish a product.... Color is not subject to trade-mark monopoly except in connection with some definite arbitrary symbol or design.... This court believes that should continue to be the law in this circuit....

"Nutra-Sweet urges this court to adopt the position of the United States Court of Appeals, Federal Circuit, which has declined to establish a per se prohibition against registering colors as trademarks.... Confronted with an unusual set of facts, the court in Owens-Corning established a limited rule that in certain situations a particular color could itself be registered as a trademark.... Using a two-step analysis, the Federal Circuit Court determined first that there was no competitive need in the insulation industry for the color pink to remain available to all insulation producers and, second, that pink insulation had acquired a secondary meaning....

"Judge Jean Galloway Bissel dissented and proposed adherence to the traditional rule that the overall color of a product cannot be a trade identity designation, nor is it entitled to registration.... This court finds Judge Bissel's reasoning persuasive, and especially so in this circuit, for the following reasons:

"First, lawyers have advised clients, clients have conducted their affairs, and litigants have won, lost, and settled, all based on the prevailing law in this circuit. Consistency and pre-dictability of the law are compelling reasons for not lightly setting aside a settled principle of law.

"Second, there is no need to change the law. This court's interpretation of the Lanham Act adequately protects the use of color as an element of a trademark. Although color alone cannot be protected as a trademark, it may be protected if it is used in connection with some symbol of design or impressed in a particular design, as a circle, square, triangle, a cross, or a star....

"The third reason for the general rule that defines the appropriation of a particular color is that infringement actions could soon degenerate into questions of shade confusion.... The case before the court provides a vivid example of the problems with shade confusion. Nutra-Sweet does not contend that the color blue of the 'Sweet One' packet is identical to the color blue of the 'Equal' packet, but rather, based upon market research, that the shades of blue are confusingly similar. How different do the colors have to be? Under Nutra-Sweet's proposed test, the only way to answer that question is through litigation.

"Lastly, changing the law based on the facts in this case might create a barrier to otherwise lawful competition in the tabletop sweetener market."

Ethical Dimension

Is it fair for a competitor to use the same color for its product as one already being marketed?

R EGULATION OF PRODUCT PRICING

Determining the price at which the product will be sold is clearly one of the most crucial marketing decisions which the distributor will make. Not only the setting of a final price for specific items, but also the company's overall pricing strategy will demand careful attention by top-level management. Set the price too high, and the product may not sell in sufficient quantities. Set the price too low, and the product may not be sufficiently profitable. Pricing decisions impact on market share, profitability—even the life of the company. Even though so much is at stake for the company in these decisions, state and national regulatory agencies are involved in the pricing process at several points.

◼ Price Advertising

Just as is true with other product information, pricing statements in a company's advertising can be stated in a deceptive manner. Probably the most troublesome ads are those which use the word *free*, as in "buy one, get one free." The FTC has insisted that such language is false and misleading unless the buyer is in fact able to buy one item for the regular, usual price and receive a second unit at no cost. In one famous case involving a paint company, the quoted price was really the price for two cans of paint, not one, so there was no "free" second can at all. *Cents-off* or *X percent off* is another frequently misused term. Just before the *40 percent off* sale, the prices are raised substantially, so the alleged discount price is really about the same as the regular retail price. Pricing is also involved in the classic "bait-and-switch" ads. An incredibly low price is advertised, but when the customer attempts to buy one of these items, the clerk tries to switch the sale to a high-priced alternative. The clerk may point out all the negatives of the lower priced unit, claim it's temporarily out of stock, or use other excuses to avoid selling at the low price. Deceptions of this kind are also disapproved.

◼ Unit Pricing

States may also be involved in the mechanics of communicating retail prices to the customer, particularly with food items. Many supermarkets and department stores now use electronic pricing mechanisms which permit the check-out clerks to simply pass the product over a scanner built into the counter. The price, electronically coded into a tag or label on the product, is read by the scanner and signalled into the cash register. These systems are generally accurate and efficient, but there are some drawbacks. If the products do not also contain a regular price label, it is difficult to make price comparisons while shopping. Much of the cost savings of the electronic system may be lost, however, if clerks are still required to hand-mark each item with a traditional price tag.

A related problem is the common retail pricing practice of stating a price for multiple units, such as "3 for $1.09." Math majors can calculate the price per item readily enough, but many of us cannot, or don't want to have to take the time to do so. Many of us want to be able to look at a can of brand A and see what it costs, then look at a can of brand B, make the price comparison, and decide which to buy. The problem here is similar to the one discussed earlier, which involved making price comparisons with odd-sized packages. If enough consumers feel strongly enough about having this sort of price information, and if the retailers aren't providing it voluntarily, a state legislature may require it. Some states have already done so.

■ Predatory Pricing

Price is, of course, a primary competitive weapon and one that can be used offensively as well as defensively. A political and economic system committed to competitive free enterprise should favor price competition and price flexibility. But regulatory agencies are also aware that large, aggressive competitors can use the price weapon to destroy competition. Large companies with multiple product lines and multiple markets can drive out smaller competitors by lowering prices on products where they face competition and subsidizing losses there by raising prices on other products or in other markets.

State governments responded to this problem by passing statutes which prohibit sales below cost as a specific type of unfair trade practice. On the national level, this practice is usually referred to a "predatory pricing," and is prosecuted as an attempt to monopolize, in violation of Section 2 of the Sherman Act. Historically, the courts said that the price charged the customer had to cover all costs of production, both fixed costs and variable costs. As a result of newer economic analysis of this problem, several of the U.S. Courts of Appeals now require that the price charged only has to cover the variable costs of producing that unit. With this new approach, management's decision-making is less likely to be successfully challenged.

Pricing below cost may violate state or national law.

■ Resale Price Maintenance

One of the most controversial pricing strategies involves the manufacturer's attempt to maintain the "quality" image of its product by preventing it from being price-discounted. Throughout the 1930s, 1940s, and 1950s, virtually continuous battles were waged in the state legislatures, and in Congress, on this issue. At the national level, manufacturers wanted assurance that the antitrust laws could not be used against such arrangements. They were successful in convincing Congress to pass the Miller-Tydings Act in 1937 and the McGuire Act in 1952. These amendments authorized such "no discounts" agreements, first, only to those retailers who did agree, and later, to all retailers in a state in which one retailer had so agreed. At the state level, the manufacturers wanted laws which enforced such "fair trade" agreements. By 1963, forty states had such laws, and in twenty-three of them, "nonsigners" were bound if any retailer in the state agreed to the set retail price. With the 1975 repeal of the fair trade amendments to the national antitrust acts, agreements for resale price maintenance are almost certain to be held unlawful. Here again, new economic analysis of the problem may produce further changes in the law. The following case is one indication of the current reexamination of these antitrust problems.

Resale price maintenance is probably an antitrust violation.

ATLANTIC RICHFIELD CO. V. USA PETROLEUM CO.

110 S. Ct. 1184 (1990)

Facts: Atlantic Richfield Co. (ARCO), a large integrated oil company, operates company-owned retail stations and franchises stations to dealers. ARCO urged its dealers to match the retail prices of independents like USA. ARCO gave its dealers temporary allowances and also reduced their costs by eliminating credit card sales. As a result, ARCO and its dealers increased market share to the detriment of USA and similar independents. USA sued, alleging a conspiracy to set maximum retail prices, a *per se* violation of Section 1 of the Sherman Act. The District Court granted summary judgment for ARCO, but the Ninth Circuit reversed.

Issue: Has a competitor who lost market share because of an agreement to set maximum prices sustained an antitrust injury?

Decision: No. Court of Appeals judgment reversed. (ARCO wins.)

Rule: Loss of business due to a competitor's lower prices is not an antitrust injury. An antitrust injury is damage caused by lack of competition, not because of it.

Discussion: *By Justice* BRENNAN:

"A private plaintiff may not recover damages under §4 of the Clayton Act merely by showing 'injury causally linked to an illegal presence in the market.' Instead, a plaintiff must prove the existence of 'antitrust injury, which is to say injury of the type the antitrust laws were intended to prevent and that flows from that which makes defendants' acts unlawful.'... [I]njury, although causally related to an antitrust violation, nevertheless will not qualify as 'antitrust injury' unless it is attributable to an anti-competitive aspect of the practice under scrutiny, 'since [i]t is inimical to [the antitrust] laws to award damages for losses stemming from continued competition.'...

"When a firm, or even a group of firms adhering to a vertical agreement, lowers prices but maintains them above predatory levels, the business lost by rivals cannot be viewed as an 'anti-competitive' consequence of the claimed violation. A firm complaining about the harm it suffers from nonpredatory price competition 'is really claiming that it [is] unable to raise prices.'... This is not antitrust injury; indeed, 'cutting prices in order to increase business often is the very essence of competition.'... 'The antitrust laws were enacted for the protection of competition, not competitors.'... 'To hold that the antitrust laws protect competitors from the loss of profits would, in effect, render illegal any decision by a firm to cut prices in order to increase market share.'...

"We also reject [USA's] suggestion that no antitrust injury need be shown where a per se violation is involved. The per se rule is a method of determining whether §1 of the Sherman Act has been violated, but it does not indicate whether a private plaintiff has suffered antitrust injury and thus whether he may recover damages under §4 of the Clayton Act....

"The purpose of the antitrust injury requirement is different. It ensures that the harm claimed by the plaintiff corresponds to the rationale for finding a violation of the antitrust laws in the first place, and it prevents losses that stem from competition from supporting suits by private plaintiffs for either damages or equitable relief. Actions per se unlawful under the antitrust laws may nonetheless have some procompetitive effects, and private parties might suffer losses therefrom....

"We decline to dilute the antitrust injury requirement here because we find that there is no need to encourage private enforcement by competitors of the rule against vertical, maximum price-fixing. If such a scheme causes...anticompetitive consequences..., consumers and the manufacturer's own dealers may bring suit....

"[USA] has failed to demonstrate that it has suffered any antitrust injury."

Ethical Dimension

Why should the government care if a manufacturer imposes a maximum retail price for its product on its distributors? Isn't the ultimate consumer being benefitted by such a restriction?

■ Price Discrimination

The major source of government interference in management's pricing decisions is the Robinson-Patman Act of 1936. Passed at the height of the Great Depression, it is often referred to as the anti-chain store act. It was passed at the insistence of the organizations representing small independent retailers. The independents objected to the very substantial quantity discounts which the chain stores were able to extract from manufacturers. In one famous case, it was shown that the quantity discounts which A&P received from Morton's Salt enabled it to sell the salt at retail for a lower price than that at which independent whole-

Price discrimination violates the Robinson-Patman Act.

salers could buy it from Morton's. The independent wholesalers, dealing directly with the manufacturer, were paying more than individual retail customers at the local A&P store.

The Robinson-Patman Act amended Section 2 of the Clayton Act by outlawing price discrimination between two buyers. Price differentials which substantially lessen competition, or tend to create a monopoly, are illegal. So are those which injure or prevent competition with the persons giving or receiving the price break or with the customers of either of them.

There are, however, some very significant limitations to this section of the antitrust laws. Only sales in interstate commerce are covered, not local sales and not international sales. Only "commodities" (goods) are covered, not services, real estate, or intangibles. The goods sold for different prices must be "of like grade and quality" (that is, the same goods). Only price variations which have the specified adverse effects on competition are prohibited—a very important qualification. In 1966, in the *Borden* case, the U.S. Supreme Court held that brand name and private label products were goods of "like grade and quality" for purposes of the act. However, the U.S. Court of Appeals to which the case was remanded held that Borden's price differentials had not caused any competitive injury. The Court of Appeals felt there was no likelihood of injury to competition if the price variations were no more than those reflected by the market's perception of the differences between the "premium" product and the "generic" one. The goods were legally the same, but competition was not being injured so long as the price variation reflected only the market's perception of the differences between the products.

■ Defenses against Price Discrimination Charges

Lower prices can be charged to non-profit agencies.

In addition to the arguments presented above, a defendant charged with price discrimination can also try to show any one of several specific justifications for the alleged price discrimination. Lower prices can be charged to non-profit institutions for goods for their own use. Lower prices can be charged for goods which are deteriorating or which are nearing the end of a seasonal selling period. Surely there should be no violation of Robinson-Patman if a Christmas tree seller marked down its remaining trees on the day before Christmas. (It's also hard to see that there would be any injury to competition on the basis of that kind of discount.)

Lower prices to one buyer are legal if they can be cost-justified.

The act specifically permits differential prices which can be cost-justified. If the lower price to one customer merely reflects cost savings as a result of larger orders or other distribution short-cuts, the lower price is legal. While the statute specifically establishes this defense, it has proved to be very difficult to use the defense in actual cases. The courts have tended to demand exact and positive proof of the cost savings and their relationship to the price differentials involved. In one famous case, the "voluminous" cost studies prepared by the Borden Company were rejected because they were based on customer categories which the court felt had not been properly defined. In practice, as several commentators have noted, the cost justification defense has been largely illusory.

Companies have had much better success arguing another statutory defense—meeting competition. The act permits the charging of a lower price to one buyer where it is done "in good faith to meet an equally low price of a competitor." The competitor referred to here is the seller's competitor, not a competitor of the buyer/customer. As interpreted, this section permits a seller to meet, but not to beat, its competition, but does permit a lowering of prices to gain new customers as well as to retain old ones. Of course, the underlying assumption is that the goods are of the same quality. Lowering the price of a "premium" product to the same level as that of a non-premium product would not merely be meeting the competitor's price, but beating the competitor's price. A 1979 case involving A&P and Borden presented an interesting twist on the problem—how does this defense apply when the buyer is charged with receiving an illegal price discrimination (also a violation)? The Supreme Court decided that since Borden had been "meeting competition" by offering the lower price, Borden had committed no violation and the lower price was legal. If it was legal on the seller's end of the transaction, it was also legal on the other end when the buyer received it. The Supreme Court held there had been no violation. The next case is a more recent version of this continuing problem.

Lower prices may be charged to meet competition from other sellers.

TEXACO, INC. V. HASBROUCK

110 S. Ct. 2535 (1990)

Facts: Texaco is a large integrated oil company. Between 1972 and 1981, it sold gasoline at its retail tank wagon prices to Hasbrouck and eleven other independent Texaco retailers, but gave large discounts to Gull and Dompier. Gull resold the gas under its own name. Dompier resold the gas to retailers as Texaco gas. Both distributors picked up the gasoline from Texaco and delivered it to their retail outlets; neither had any large storage facilities. Texaco also paid Dompier for delivering the gasoline to retailers. Texaco had refused a request by two of the plaintiffs to pick up their own gasoline. The shares of Gull and Dompier in the Spokane market increased dramatically, while the plaintiffs' shares declined. Plaintiffs sued in 1976,

alleging violations of the Robinson-Patman Act. Texaco argued that, since Gull and Dompier were performing some wholesaler functions, they could be given a "wholesaler discount." The trial court, after a jury trial, awarded treble damages of $449,900, and the Court of Appeals affirmed.

Issue: Are the "functional discounts" given to wholesalers Gull and Dompier permitted by the Robinson-Patman Act?

Decision: No. Judgment for plaintiffs affirmed.

Rule: There is no specific statutory exemption for functional discounts; to be legal, they must be cost-justified.

Discussion: *By Justice STEVENS:*

"The [Robinson-Patman] Act contains no express reference to functional discounts. It does contain two affirmative defenses that provide protection for two categories of discounts—those that are justified by savings in the seller's cost of manufacture, delivery or sale, and those that represent a good faith response to the equally low prices of a competitor.... As the case comes to us, neither of those defenses is available to Texaco....

"Texaco's first argument would create a blanket exemption for all functional discounts. Indeed, carried to its logical conclusion, it would exempt all price differentials except those given to competing purchasers. The primary basis for Texaco's argument is the following comment by Congressman Utterback, an active sponsor of the Act: '...[W]here the goods are sold in different markets and the conditions affecting those markets set different price levels for them, the sale to different customers at those different prices would not constitute a discrimination within the meaning of this bill.'...

"We have previously considered this excerpt from the legislative history, and have refused to draw from it the conclusion which Texaco proposes.... Although the excerpt does support Texaco's argument, we remain persuaded that the argument is foreclosed by the text of the Act itself. In the context of a statute that plainly reveals a concern with competitive consequences at different levels of distribution, and carefully defines specific affirmative defenses, it would be anomalous to assume that the Congress intended the term 'discriminate' to have such a limited meaning....

"Since we have already decided that a price discrimination within the meaning of §2(a) 'is merely a price difference,' we must reject Texaco's first argument....

"[A]n injury to competition may be inferred from evidence that some purchasers had to pay their supplier 'substantially

more for their goods than their competitors had to pay.'...
Texaco...argues that this presumption should not apply to differences between prices charged to wholesalers and those charged to retailers.... [T]his argument endorses the position advocated 35 years ago in the Report of the Attorney General's National Committee to Study the Antitrust Laws....

"The hypothetical predicate for the Committee's entire discussion of functional discounts is a price differential 'that merely accords due recognition and reimbursement for actual marketing functions.' Such a discount is not illegal. In this case, however, both the District Court and the Court of Appeals concluded that even without viewing the evidence in the light most favorable to [plaintiffs], there was no substantial evidence indicating that the discounts to Gull and Dompier constituted a reasonable reimbursement for their actual marketing functions.... Indeed, Dompier was separately compensated for its hauling function, and neither Gull nor Dompier maintained any significant storage facilities....

"The evidence indicates, moreover, that Texaco affirmatively encouraged Dompier to expand its retail business and that Texaco was fully informed about the persistent and marketwide consequences of its own pricing policies. Indeed, its own executives recognized that the dramatic impact on the market was almost entirely attributable to the magnitude of the distributor discount and the hauling allowance.... The special facts of this case thus make it peculiarly difficult for Texaco to claim that it is being held liable for the independent pricing decision of Gull and Dompier."

Ethical Dimension

Why shouldn't the parties be permitted to bargain out their own contract, without government interference?

REGULATION OF DISTRIBUTION CHANNELS

Historically, regulation of distribution channels has occurred for two reasons. The primary objective has been to prevent monopolization. Some judges and regulators have also been concerned with protecting smaller distributors against unfair practices by large marketers. Both of these objectives continue to be reflected in the statutes, regulations, and cases.

■ Choice of Distribution Channels

In general, of course, the choice of distribution channels is left up to each company. Management is free to establish whatever distribution structure it feels will best suit the company and its products. It may decide on full vertical integration and control all aspects of product distribution itself. It may wish to use independent wholesalers and jobbers or perform those functions itself and merely use independent retailers. It may establish franchise or licensing arrangements. It may wish to sell on consignment, both to control the terms of the ultimate sale and to help convince small retailers to handle its products. All of these are perfectly legal and proper distribution channels.

What, then, are the problems? Problems arise when a large distributor uses its market power to take unfair advantage of the other parties in the relationship. As in other areas, government regulation of distribution practices exists because abuses exist. What sort of abuses are we concerned with here? Typical problems include refusals to deal, territorial restrictions on distributors, forcing distributors to buy unwanted products or to buy exclusively from the particular seller, and arbitrary termination of distributors. The regulatory response may be an outright prohibition of the challenged marketing practice or an evaluation of its impact on competition in the particular case.

■ Abuse of Independent Dealers

One widely used method of distribution involves independent retail dealers. The dealer is a separate business which enters into a franchise or licensing agreement to distribute the name-brand products (or services) of the manufacturer/licensor. New car dealers, branded gasoline stations, and restaurant chains are all examples of this sort of distribution structure.

Statutes offer small dealers some protection from unfair termination.

Over the years, many disputes have arisen from the termination of these independent dealers. Car dealers are infrequently terminated by the manufacturer, since they are usually carefully selected to begin with and usually own their own buildings and facilities, Even so, by statute, car dealers are now guaranteed a "day in court" if they feel they have been wrongfully terminated.

Retail gasoline stations typically involve a very modest investment, the dealers are not as carefully selected, and there is thus considerable turnover. Here too, abuses can occur, especially since many stations are owned by the large oil companies and simply leased to the independent dealer. There is tremendous potential for abuse of these small businesses, which are operating almost totally at the mercy of the large oil company/franchisor. Some oil companies also own and operate their own retail stations to better control the retail market. Over the last two decades, many small independent stations have been closed in favor of large self-serve locations or convenience store combinations. The independent dealer can try to bring a lawsuit for breach of contract but probably needs more protection than that. A national statute now regulates at least some aspects of this relationship. One state has attacked the problem head-on by prohibiting large oil-refining companies from owning retail outlets. That sort of drastic approach deals with one aspect, but does not do much to protect the dealer in the typical relationship.

As a result of a wave of deceptive franchising schemes that swept the country in the late 1960s and early 1970s, most states now have statutes regulating the selling of franchises. The franchisor is now generally required to provide the same sort of information as the seller of securities. Indeed, since some these schemes required little or no personal effort on the part of the "franchisee" (other than the payment of substantial sums of money), they were in fact held to be investments under the national acts. Some states have gone farther and actually outlawed "pyramid" schemes which consist of selling franchises to sell franchises, with no real effort to market an actual product or service.

■ Tying Contracts

One of the clearest cases of abuse of market power is the **tying contract**. A supplier company is the exclusive source for product X, either because it has a patent or for some other reason. A customer wants to buy product X, but the supplier refuses to sell unless the customer also buys product Y. The customer has to buy Y in order to get X. This type of economic coercion is also called **full-line forcing**.

Historically, tying contracts were all but universally condemned by the courts, as a *per se* violation of the antitrust laws. Today, in this area too, some economic justifications for tying contracts are gradually beginning to emerge. One early case recognized the validity of a requirement that a buyer of equipment must have it serviced by the seller's personnel. The technology was new and untried; it was unfamiliar to most outside service persons; and the seller had a strong interest in ensuring that the equipment functioned properly, since its new business would fail if the equipment was perceived as unreliable. In that particular context, the tying-in of the service aspect was considered reasonable.

Tying contracts are usually illegal.

Courts have also generally recognized that a sale-and-financing package is not really a tying contract. If a car manufacturer wishes to stimulate sales of its cars by offering a very low financing rate for car loans, there should be no antitrust violation just because it insists that you buy one of its cars if you get one of its loans. Courts have also accepted the validity of some kinds of franchisor operational controls as necessary to ensure quality standards and uniform business practices. Some judges and economists reject the application of the *per se* rule altogether, and are prepared to analyze tying contracts under a rule of reason.

■ Geographic and Customer Limitations

Territorial restraints may have reasonable business purposes.

On one very important point of marketing law, the U.S. Supreme Court has already changed its ruling (twice, in fact). The question is how to analyze territorial and customer-class restraints which a manufacturer places on its independent distributors. Can a manufacturer legally require that one distributor sell only in Florida and not in Georgia and Alabama, or only sell to government agencies? The Supreme Court originally used the rule of reason to decide these cases. Under the **rule of reason** analysis, the Court examined the actual marketplace effect of the restraint in question. Was competition being harmed or enhanced by the restraint? Then, in the 1967, in the *Schwinn* case, the Court held that such restraints were *per se* illegal if the products had been sold to the distributors. The rule of reason analysis would be used only if the products had been consigned to the distributors. In 1977, in the *GTE Sylvania* case, the Supreme Court returned to its prior position, by overruling the *Schwinn* decision. This 1977 reversal marked the beginning of the Supreme Court's reworking of much antitrust doctrine.

■ Exclusive Dealing Agreements

There does seem to be a general consensus today on the rule to be applied to exclusive dealing agreements. They can and do serve useful functions for both sellers and buyers. Sellers have an assured market, and buyers have an assured supply. Such long-term distribution agreements can thus have beneficial marketplace effects. Under the rule of reason analysis, these benefits can be considered and the contracts would not be held invalid unless there were clear evidence of substantial anticompetitive effects.

■ Refusals to Deal

One person can usually refuse to deal with another.

Businesses ordinarily have no duty to deal with each other. They are free to make contracts, or not, as they see fit. They are free to reject offers to make contracts for any reason, or for no reason at all. As a rule, therefore, a manufacturer's refusal to do business with a retailer who wishes to distribute its products is perfectly lawful. Actual marketplace situations are rarely that simple, however, particularly when an antitrust violation is alleged.

Based on the Supreme Court's decision in the *Colgate* case in 1919, courts have generally permitted refusals to deal which were the manufacturer's sole decision. On the other hand, where two or more businesses conspired to deny products to a third, the denial was usually held to be illegal *per se*. Under this analysis, a conspiracy among manufacturers to deny products to a price-cutting retailer would be a violation. So would a termination of the price-cutter in response to complaints from other retailers, as happened with Los Angeles Chevrolet dealers in 1966.

A series of more recent Supreme Court decisions indicates some rethinking of these rules on group boycotts. The *GTE Sylvania* case, noted earlier, seems to validate sanctions against retailers who violate the manufacturer's distribution rules. Presumably, knowledge of such violations would in most cases come from other distributors—a situation very similar to the one which the Court held illegal in the Chevrolet case in 1966. In two very recent decisions, the Court has said that there is no violation simply because the manufacturer terminated the offending dealer in response to complaints from its other retailers, and that there would have to be proof of an actual price-fixing conspiracy in order for the termination to be a violation. In another decision from the 1980s, the Court indicated that it might even be prepared to accept some group boycotts by manufacturers. All of these changes mean that the U.S. Supreme Court is now willing to give businesses a much greater degree of control over their distribution systems. The next case is one of these recent "change" decisions.

BUSINESS ELECTRONICS CORP. V. SHARP ELECTRONICS CORP.

108 S. Ct. 1515 (1988)

Facts: Business Electronics Corp. (BEC) was the exclusive dealer for Sharp electronic calculators in the Houston, Texas, area from 1968 to 1972. In 1972, Hartwell was appointed as a second dealer for the area. Sharp published a list of suggested retail prices, but did not require the dealers to comply with them. Hartwell complained to Sharp a number of times about BEC's price-cutting and also felt that BEC was free-riding on Hartwell's presale educational and promotional services, rather than also doing these things for its own customers. In June, 1973, Hartwell told Sharp he would cease selling their calculators unless Sharp terminated BEC as a dealer. BEC was terminated the next month.

BEC filed suit, claiming an illegal conspiracy in violation of Section 1 of the Sherman Act. The jury found that there was an agreement to terminate BEC because of its price-cutting. The trial judge entered a treble damage award of $1,800,000, plus attorney fees. The Fifth Circuit Court of Appeals reversed.

Issue: Is this vertical agreement (between manufacturer and retailer) a *per se* violation of the Sherman Act, even without proof that it included an agreement on prices to be charged?

Decision: No. Judgment of the Court of Appeals affirmed.

Rule: A vertical restraint of trade is not a *per se* violation of Section 1 of the Sherman Act unless it contains an agreement on prices or price levels.

Discussion: *By Justice* SCALIA:

"Since the earliest decisions of this Court interpreting [Section 1 of the Sherman Act], we have recognized that it was intended to prohibit only unreasonable restraints of trade.... Ordinarily, whether particular concerted action violates §1 of the Sherman Act is determined through case-by-case application of the so-called rule of reason—that is, 'the factfinder weighs all of the circumstances of a case in deciding whether a restrictive practice should be prohibited as imposing an unreasonable restraint on competition.'... Certain categories of agreements, however, have been held to be per se illegal, dispensing with the need for case-by-case evaluation. We have said that *per se* rules are appropriate only for 'conduct that is manifestly anticompetitive.'...

"Although vertical agreements on resale prices have been illegal per se since [1911], we have recognized that the scope of *per se* illegality should be narrow in the context of vertical restraints....

"There has been no showing here that an agreement between a manufacturer and a dealer to terminate a 'price cutter,' without a further agreement on the price or price levels to be charged by the remaining dealer, almost always tends to restrict competition and reduce output. Any assistance to cartelizing that such an agreement might provide cannot be distinguished from the sort of minimal assistance that might be provided by vertical nonprice agreements like the exclusive territory agreement in *GTE Sylvania*, and is insufficient to justify a *per se* rule....

"Any agreement between a manufacturer and a dealer to terminate another dealer who happens to have charged lower prices can be alleged to have been directed against the terminated dealer's 'price cutting.' In the vast majority of cases, it will be extremely difficult for the manufacturer to convince a jury that its motivation was to ensure adequate services, since price cutting and service cutting usually go hand in hand. Accordingly, a manufacturer that agrees to give one dealer an exclusive territory and terminates another pursuant to that agreement, or even a manufacturer that agrees with one dealer to terminate another for failure to provide contractually-obligated services, exposes itself to the highly plausible claim that its real motivation was to terminate a price cutter. Moreover, even vertical restraints that do not result in dealer termination, such as the initial granting of an exclusive territory or the requirement that certain services be provided, can be attacked as designed to allow existing dealers to charge higher prices. Manufacturers would be likely to forgo legitimate and competitively useful conduct rather than risk treble damages and perhaps even criminal penalties....

"In sum, economic analysis supports the view, and no precedent opposes it, that a vertical restraint is not illegal *per se* unless it includes some agreement on price or price levels."

Ethical Dimension

Is it fair for a manufacturer to terminate one dealer in order to keep another dealer?

REGULATION OF TRADE PRACTICES

Nearly any of the marketing practices discussed above can be used to injure competition, competitors, and consumers. Unscrupulous persons continue to devise ways to gain an unfair advantage and make a dishonest dollar. State and national regulators know that they have to keep up with new fraudulent schemes and deceptive tactics. Both levels of government are concerned with protecting honest businesses, as well as consumers, from commercial predators.

State Laws on Unfair Competition

As noted in the earlier discussion of false advertising, some states have comprehensive laws against unfair competition. Some states have statutes similar to the Federal Trade Commission Act, with a general prohibition against unfair or deceptive acts or practices. Other states have tried to construct a laundry list of deceptive practices in the statute. The best solution is a combination of these two approaches. The general prohibition requires a court decision that a particular practice is in fact prohibited by the general language. Some courts may be unwilling to interpret a criminal statute broadly. The list of specific wrongful practices simply challenges the predators to come up with a new deception that is not on the list. Both kinds of prohibition need to be included.

State laws prohibit unfair or deceptive business practices.

■ Section 5 of the FTC Act

The language of Section 5 ("unfair or deceptive acts or practices") is broad enough to reach any form of commercial wrongdoing. The section has been so interpreted by the FTC itself and by the courts. It prohibits both unfair methods of competition and unfair or deceptive acts or practices. Using its rule-making authority, the FTC has adopted regulations covering a wide variety of problems: bait and switch advertising, deceptive guarantees, deceptive pricing, use of the word *free*, games of chance, and home study programs, among others. It has also issued advisory opinions on the legality of specific marketing methods, in response to inquiries.

Section 5 of the FTC Act also prohibits unfair methods of competition.

Using its powers under Section 5, the FTC can reach "unfair" commercial practices which are not prohibited under any of the antitrust acts. To cite just one very significant example, the FTC decided that it was unfair to require consumers to sign negotiable instruments or express contracts which waived their defenses. Thus the Commission adopted a rule which said that such contracts would not be effective against consumers; consumers would be able to use any defense they could prove to defeat or to reduce the amount they owed on the credit contract. This one FTC rule has thus resulted in a massive change in the legal position of the consumer debtor and thus of marketplace realities.

REVIEW

Nearly all aspects of the marketing function are subject to some form of legal regulation. Advertising, packaging, labeling, trademarks, pricing, distribution channels, and trade practices are all subject to government restrictions of one kind or another. Both state and national governments are actively involved in this policing of the marketplace. Both honest businesses and consumers need to be protected against frauds, cheats, and tricksters.

Some practices are so inherently unfair or destructive of competition that they are almost always considered illegal. Most practices which have the capacity to do harm are judged on a case-by-case basis under the rule of reason. Using its rule-making powers, the Federal Trade Commission has become increasingly active in overseeing marketing activities.

REVIEW QUESTIONS AND PROBLEMS

1. What is the difference between a tying contract and an exclusive dealing agreement?

2. What difference does it make whether a business practice is judged under the rule of reason or under the *per se* rule?

3. Why is "passing off" one's product as that of a competitor an illegal trade practice?

4. When is the use of "mock-ups" in TV commercials prohibited?

5. Explain the difference between "predatory pricing" and price discrimination.

6. When is it illegal for one company to refuse to deal with another?

7. *Jukebox Journal* is published monthly as a specialized magazine for music lovers. It competes for readers and advertisers with several larger circulation music magazines. *Jukebox Journal* entered into a printing contract with Pressly Press; *Jukebox* supplies the text, pictures, and ads, and Pressly actually prints the copies. Pressly is the only printer using the less expensive "letter-press" method of printing. *Jukebox* thought it was being charged the same price per copy as its larger competitors but discovered after about six months that it was paying eleven cents per copy and its larger competitors were paying Pressly only seven cents per copy. *Jukebox* sued Pressly, alleging illegal price discrimination. What result, and why?

8. New Knob, Montana, is a world-famous ski resort with four different locations for downhill skiing—Bighill, Hihill, Steephill, and Massnow. The Massnow facility is owned by Snowy Company; the other three locations are owned by Hilly Corporation. Skiers like to be able to use all four facilities, so Snowy and Hilly agreed to let customers buy an "all-facilities" ticket. This option was very popular, but Hilly decided it should have a larger share of the ticket sales. Snowy refused to agree to give Hilly more than 75 percent of the joint ticket sales, so Hilly terminated the "all-facilities" agreement. Hilly customers could ski on all three of its hills with only one ticket, but Snowy customers had to buy a separate ticket if they wished to ski one of the Hilly facilities. As a result of the termination of the joint ticket agreement, Snowy's share of the market fell from 20 percent to 12 percent. Snowy sued, claiming an antitrust violation. Does it have a case? Explain.

9. Assume legal practice in a certain state is regulated by the Professional Attorneys Association (PAA), under the supervision of the state supreme court. The PAA published a list of "recommended" minimum prices for common legal services and told attorneys that it would be unethical to "habitually" charge clients less than these suggested minimums. Lawyers engaging in unethical conduct can be disciplined by the PAA and, ultimately, be barred from practicing law. Barry and Irene Golden paid a legal fee of one percent of the property's total value when they bought their new house. They had contacted seventeen lawyers, but none would do the legal work for less than the one percent "recommended" in the PAA's fee schedule. The Goldens sued the PAA. Is there a legal violation here? Discuss.

10. Saltsellers, Inc. produces about 70 percent of the salt used for industrial and commercial purposes. It also holds patents on several machines which use salt in their processes. One of its machines, the Saltab, injects salt tablets into canned food products during the canning process. Saltab machines are leased to food processors, and each lease requires the Saltab user to buy all its salt from Saltsellers. When the U.S. Justice Department learned of this lease provision, it filed a lawsuit asking that Saltsellers be prevented from enforcing this clause in the leases of the Saltab machines. Should the court issue an injunction against Saltsellers? Why or why not?

SUGGESTIONS FOR FURTHER READING

Allison, "Complaining Dealers, the Terminated Price-Cutter, and Sherman Act Conspiracy Doctrine," *American Business Law Journal* 22 (Winter 1985): 467.

Behringer & Otte, "Liability and the Trademark Licensor: Advice for the Franchisor of Goods or Services," *American Business Law Journal* 19 (Summer 1981): 109.

Burgunder, "Trademark Protection of Smells: Sense or Nonsense," *American Business Law Journal* 29 (Fall 1991): 459.

Donegan, "Section 43(a) of the Lanham Trademark Act as a Private Remedy for False Advertising," *Food, Drug, & Cosmetic Law Journal* 37 (July 1982): 264.

Easterbrook, "Maximum Price Fixing," *University Of Chicago Law Review* 48 (Fall 1981): 886.

Frederickson, "Recovery for False Advertising Under the Revised Lanham Act: A Methodology for the Computation of Damages," *American Business Law Journal* 29 (Winter 1992): 585.

Handler, "The Self-Regulatory System—An Advertiser's Viewpoint," *Food, Drug, & Cosmetic Law Journal* 37 (July 1982): 257.

Leete, "Betamax and Sound Recordings: Is Copyright in Trouble?" *American Business Law Journal* 23 (Winter 1986): 551.

Ordover & Willig, "An Economic Definition of Predation: Pricing and Product Innovation," *Yale Law Journal* 91 (November 1981): 8.

Petty, "FTC Advertising Regulation: Survivor or Casualty of the Reagan Revolution?" *American Business Law Journal* 30 (May 1992): 1.

Petty, "Predatory Promotion: A Theory of Antitrust Liability Whose Time Has Come?" *American Business Law Journal* 27 (Summer 1989): 215.

Reitzel, "The Exploding Bottle Situation: Is There a Better Basis for Shopper Protection?" *American Business Law Journal* 15 (Fall 1977): 187.

19
LAW
OF
INTERNATIONAL
BUSINESS

"[T]he law of nations may be deduced, first, from the general principles of right and justice, applied to the concerns of individuals, and thence to the relations and duties of nations..."

Justice Joseph Story, U.S. v. The Schooner *La Jeune Eugenie*.

LEARNING OBJECTIVES: After you have studied this chapter, you should be able to:

IDENTIFY the various sources of international law.

DISCUSS the problems involved in selecting a forum to hear an international dispute.

DISTINGUISH between the sovereign immunity doctrine and the act of state doctrine.

EXPLAIN the structure of an international sale of goods.

DEFINE the phrase *letter of credit*.

DIFFERENTIATE between joint ventures and foreign subsidiaries as methods of doing business overseas.

569

P REVIEW

Most U.S. businesses are "involved" in international trade, whether they want to be or not. There's simply no choice, given the realities of today's world. Our "Big Three" auto makers have felt the effects of foreign competition. Late in 1991, its U.S. market share fallen from around 50 percent to around 35 percent, General Motors announced a plan to cut 70,000 jobs and to close 21 of its North American plants over the next several years. The major "fast-food" chains are heavily involved in international operations; one can eat U.S.-style hamburgers in London and fried chicken in Beijing. Even service companies are expanding overseas; U.S. law firms are opening branches in other countries, often as joint ventures with local firms. International competitiveness is the watchword. Under these circumstances, international law is no longer just an esoteric elective for the senior year of law school, but rather a subject of direct relevance to the ongoing operations of many business firms, both here and overseas.

S OURCES OF INTERNATIONAL LAW

As is true of the U.S. legal system, international law is drawn from a variety of sources. Custom, cases, texts, and treaties can all be used as evidence of what international rules have been. Treaties also serve as the primary vehicle of change. Nations can enter into specific agreements which establish binding rules between themselves, thus in effect "legislating" international law. Various bodies of the United Nations have certain rule-making powers. Such rules also develop and extend international law.

■ Custom

Custom is a major source of international law.

Much of international law is derived from the centuries of customary practice of international relations. The "three-mile limit" on a nation's sovereignty over its coastal waters was apparently derived from the range of a coastal cannon; the nation's guns indicated its ability to control within their range. Gradually, as nations dealt with each other, customary practice developed and became accepted as the standard which must be met in such international dealings. The sanctity of a nation's embassy and its diplomatic personnel is another outgrowth of customary practice.

■ Cases

While there is no official doctrine of precedent in international law, as there is in the United States and the United Kingdom, cases are an important source of international practice. The decisions of national and international bodies in disputes illustrate the accepted doctrines in many areas. They are not completely binding on a future body hearing a new dispute, but they are generally persuasive evidence of what international practice has been.

■ Texts

Similarly, textbooks and treatises on general and specialized international law topics are not binding in specific disputes. They are, however, frequently used as source materials to indicate what practice has been, what specific decisions have been made, and what customs have been recognized. Some commentators' works are generally recognized as authoritative statements of the international rules of the game. Hugo Grotius, the great Dutch jurist, is generally recognized as the "father of international Law." His major work on the subject was *De Jure Bellis ac Pacis (Of the Law of War and Peace)*, published in 1625. Charles Hackworth's *Digest of International Law* has been a very influential modern text.

■ Treaties

Nations can also establish the relationships which they want to exist between them by specific agreements. Such agreements may be only bilateral, may be agreed to by nations in a geographic region, or may be open for signature by all the nations of the world. These agreements are typically called **treaties**.

Nations can agree by treaty what obligations they owe each other.

The word "treaty" also has a special meaning within the United States constitutional system. Treaties are specifically included in our Constitution as part of the "supreme law of the land," and are therefore binding on all state governmental agencies. But our president also enters into various international agreements which are not submitted to the Senate for ratification as are treaties. The U.S. Supreme Court has ruled that these other international agreements are also part of the supreme law of the land, even without Senate ratification. Both types of arrangements would be treaties in the international sense.

Many multilateral agreements are referred to as **conventions**. The Warsaw Convention, for example, is a multinational agreement on international air travel. More recently negotiated is the United Nations Convention on Contracts for the International Sale of Goods (CISG). The CISG has been adopted by about twenty countries thus far, including the U.S., France, and China. The CISG applies to international sales transactions in which both the contracting parties are located in nations which have ratified the CISG, unless the parties themselves specify otherwise in their sale contract. Since, as noted in Chapter 7, CISG does contain several major differences from U.S. law, U.S. businesses do need to be aware of its existence and to take it into account during international negotiations.

■ Interpretation of Treaties

Just as is true with a country's domestic legislation, treaties also need to be interpreted when it comes time to apply them to specific disputes. If the dispute arises between nations, it will probably be heard by an international tribunal rather than the courts of one of the nations involved in the dispute. If the dispute arises between private parties, and the treaty is invoked as the applicable law, a national court may very well be called on to interpret the meaning of the treaty. That is what happened to Ms. Avagliano's claim of sex discrimination in the following case.

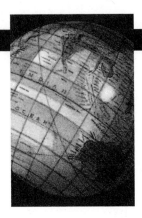

SUMITOMO SHOJI AMERICA, INC. V. AVAGLIANO

457 U.S. 176 (1982)

Facts: Ms. Avagliano and other past and present female secretarial employees brought a class action, alleging employment discrimination on the basis of race and sex. All but one of the plaintiffs were U.S. citizens; the single exception is a Japanese citizen living here. Plaintiffs claimed that Sumitomo hired only male Japanese for executive, managerial, and sales positions, in violation of Title VII of the Civil Rights Act of 1964. Sumitomo Shoji America is a New York corporation which is a wholly owned subsidiary of Sumitomo Shoji Kabushiki Kaisha, a large Japanese trading company. Sumitomo Shoji America claimed it was exempt from Title VII and other U.S. employment law because the treaty between the U.S. and Japan permits the companies of each to follow their own nation's employment practices. The U.S. District Court refused to dismiss the complaint, but the Court of Appeals reversed.

Issue: Does the treaty apply to a wholly owned U.S. subsidiary of a Japanese corporation?

Decision: No. Court of Appeals judgment is reversed, and case remanded for trial.

Rule: The nationality of a corporation is determined by its place of incorporation, not by the nationality of its stockholders.

Discussion: *By Chief Justice* BURGER:

"Interpretation of the Friendship, Commerce and Navigation Treaty between Japan and the United States must, of course, begin with the language of the Treaty itself....

"Article VIII(1) of the Treaty provides in pertinent part: '[C]ompanies of either Party* shall be permitted to engage, within the territories of the other Party, accountants and other technical experts, executive personnel, attorneys, agents, and other specialists of their choice....' Clearly, Article VIII(1) only applies to companies of one of the Treaty countries operating in the other country. Sumitomo contends that it is a company of Japan, and that Article VIII(1) of the Treaty grants it very broad discretion to fill its executive, managerial, and sales positions exclusively with male Japanese citizens....

"Article VIII(1) does not define any of its terms; the definitional section of the Treaty is contained in Article XXII. Article XXII(3) provides: 'As used in the present Treaty, the term "companies" means corporations, partnerships. companies, and other associations, whether or not with limited liability and whether or not for pecuniary profit. Companies constituted under the applicable laws and regulations within the territories of either Party *shall be deemed companies thereof* and shall have their juridical status recognized within the territories of the other Party...'

"Sumitomo is 'constituted under the applicable laws and regulations' of New York; based on Article XXII(3), it is a company of the United States, not a company of Japan. As a company of the United States operating in the United States, under the literal language of Article XXII(3) of the Treaty, Sumitomo cannot invoke the rights provided in Article VIII(1), which are available only to companies of Japan operating in the United States and to companies of the United States operating in Japan.

"The governments of Japan and the United States support this interpretation of the Treaty. Both the Ministry of Foreign Affairs of Japan and the United States Department of State agree that a United States corporation, even when wholly owned by a Japanese company is not a company of Japan under the Treaty and is therefore not covered by Article VIII(1)."

Ethical Dimension

Is it proper for a company to try to claim it has special rights under a treaty which its local competitors do not have?

●

The *Sumitomo* case involved the wholly-owned U.S. subsidiary of a Japanese parent corporation. Managers of foreign subsidiaries of U.S. parent corporations need to be aware of the reverse side of the problem. The potential for the application of the foreign nation's law needs to be considered carefully as part of the strategic decision to incorporate a subsidiary overseas.

RESOLUTION OF INTERNATIONAL DISPUTES

Nations have historically been very reluctant to surrender any of their sovereign powers to an international body. Whereas within a nation the courts can be given power to adjudicate claims between litigants, international courts have only the powers conferred on them by agreement of the litigants. Governments may grant power to an international body to hear a certain type of dispute, or may agree to have only a particular case heard. Arbitrations are also frequently used to settle international disputes.

International Courts

The ICJ hears disputes between nations.

Established under the U.N. Charter, the International Court of Justice (ICJ) hears cases and claims between nations. Investors and companies who have claims against a host nation for violations of international law must have their claims submitted to the court by their home country; they cannot themselves file a claim. The home country's government decides whether to pursue the claim and what to do with any monetary settlement.

There are fifteen judges on the ICJ; no more than two can be from the same nation. Five are elected by the U.N. General Assembly and the Security Council every third year for nine-year terms. The General Assembly has now over 150 members. The Security Council is made up of the U.S., the U.K., Russia, China, and France as permanent members; ten other nations are elected for terms. These two bodies hold independent elections. A person chosen by both bodies is automatically elected to the ICJ. Two additional separate ballots may be cast. If there are still not five persons agreed on, the selection will be made by a committee consisting of three members from each body.

Under the provisions of the 1958 Treaty of Rome, a supranational court—the Court of Justice—was also established for the European Economic Community (EEC). Most of Western Europe, including its largest economies, is included in the EEC: Belgium, Denmark, France, Germany, Greece, Ireland, Italy, Luxembourg, the Netherlands, Portugal, Spain, United Kingdom. Other nations, including several of the former Soviet satellites in Eastern Europe, have applied for or have already been granted a kind of associate membership. 1992 was designated as the year in which full and free economic exchanges among the members would finally be implemented and a "single Europe" would finally exist. The members have also recently agreed to move towards a common currency, but a single Europe has not yet been achieved.

The European Court of Justice hears cases involving the law of the European Economic Community.

The Court of Justice is the court of last resort on matters of Community law; it hears appeals in cases in which a party alleges that national courts did not follow Community law. Community law supersedes national law to the extent of any conflict, in much the same way as a treaty supersedes the law of a state in this country. New regulations for the Community are proposed by its executive body, the Commission. Such proposals are then referred to the elected legislature, the EEC Assembly, for discussion and comment. Regulations are finally adopted by the EEC Council of Ministers and at that point become binding on the member-nations. Since the EEC is now by far the largest trading bloc in the world, its economic policies are a very important part of international law.

In the following case, the European Court of Justice is asked to decide what legal force a provision of the EEC Treaty has within one of the member-nations. The specific issue is sex discrimination in employment.

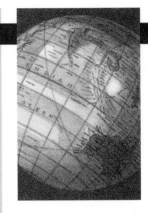

DEFRENNE V. SOCIETE ANONYME BELGE DE NAVIGATION ARIENNE

[1976] E.C.R. 455, [1976]2 C.M.L.R. 98 (1976)

Facts: Gabrielle Defrenne was hired by Sabena as a "trainee air hostess" in 1951. In 1963 she was promoted to "Cabin Steward and Air Hostess—Principal Cabin Attendant." In 1968, she was fired in accordance with a collective bargaining agreement which required termination of female cabin staff at age forty. Defrenne sued for the difference between the wages she received from 1963 to 1968 and those which a male cabin attendant of similar seniority would have received, and also for additional severance pay and lost pension rights.

Article 119 of the Treaty of Rome requires equal pay for equal work. The *Tribunal du Travail* in Brussels, however, dismissed all her claims. She appealed to the *Cour du Travail*, which affirmed the claims for severance pay and pension rights, but referred the issuance on the equal pay for equal work to the European Court of Justice (the EEC Court).

Issue: Is Article 119 of the Rome Treaty legally effective within a member-nation, even without implementing legislation?

Decision: Yes. Judgment for Defrenne on her equal pay claim.

Rule: No implementing national legislation is necessary to confirm the rights of employees stated in Article 119.

Discussion: *By the Court:*
"The question of the direct effect of Article 119 must be considered in the light of the nature of the principle of equal pay, the aim of this provision and its place in the scheme of the Treaty. Article 119 pursues a double aim. First, in the light of the different stages of the development of social legislation in the various member-States, the aim of Article 119 is to avoid a situation in

which undertakings established in States which have actually implemented the principle of equal pay suffer a competitive disadvantage in intra-Community competition as compared with undertakings established in States which have not yet eliminated discrimination against women workers as regards pay. Secondly, this provision forms part of the social objectives of the Community, which is not merely an economic union but is at the same time intended, by common action, to ensure social progress and seek the constant improvement of the living and working conditions of their peoples, as is emphasized by the Preamble to the Treaty. This aim is accentuated by the insertion of Article 119 into the body of a chapter devoted to social policy whose preliminary provisions, Article 117, marks 'the need to promote improved working conditions and an improved standard of living for workers, so as to make possible their harmonisation while the improvement is being maintained.' This double aim, which is at once economic and social, shows that the principle of equal pay forms part of the foundations of the Community. Furthermore, this explains why the Treaty has provided for the complete implementation of this principle by the end of the first stage of the transitional period. Therefore, in interpreting this provision, it is impossible to base any argument on the dilatoriness and resistance which have delayed the actual implementation of this basic principle in certain member-States. In particular, since Article 119 appears in the context of the harmonisation of working conditions while the improvement is being maintained, the objection that the terms of this Article may be observed in other ways than by raising the lowest salaries may be set aside.

"Under the terms of the first paragraph of Article 119, the member-States are bound to ensure and maintain 'the application of the principle that men and women should receive equal pay for equal work.'...

"The second question asks whether Article 119 has become 'applicable internal law of the member-States by virtue of measures adopted by the authorities of the European Economic Community' or whether the national legislature must 'be regarded as alone competent in this matter.'...

"Article 119 itself provides that the application of the principle of equal pay was to be uniformly ensured by the end of the first stage of the transitional period at the latest....

"The reply to the second question should therefore be that the application of Article 119 was to have been fully secured by the original member-States as from 1 January 1962, the beginning of the second stage of the transitional period....

"The Governments of Ireland and the United Kingdom have drawn the Court's attention to the possible economic consequences of attributing direct effect to the provisions of Article 119, on the ground that such a decision might, in many branches of economic life, result in the introduction of claims dating back to the time at which such effect came into existence.... Therefore, the direct effect of Article 119 cannot be relied on in order to support claims concerning pay periods prior to the date of this judgment, except as regards those workers who have already brought legal proceedings or made an equivalent claim."

Ethical Dimension

Why did the Court of Justice restrict its holding to pay periods after the date of its judgment in this case? Is this restriction fair?

■ National Courts and Jurisdictional Questions

Since there are no international trial courts in which private parties can directly file lawsuits, they are forced to use national courts when disputes arise. The plaintiff will naturally try to select a court where it thinks it can receive a fair hearing, at least. Often, the plaintiff will try to bring the litigation in its home country, feeling that it may have some advantage there over the alien defendant. A plaintiff seeking damages will probably try to select a court where larger awards are possible. If the claim is based on a new or unestablished theory of liability, the plaintiff will try for a sympathetic or innovative court.

The defendant, wishing to avoid liability, will in many cases object to plaintiff's choice of **forum** (the court where the case has been filed). The defendant may also object to the use of the body of law which plaintiff says applies to the case. These two issues arise with considerable frequency in international disputes.

FORUM

On the first issue, the forum court will have to decide if it does have jurisdiction over the defendant and, if so, whether there are other factors which would prevent it from hearing the case. We saw the Illinois courts grappling with this issue in the case in Chapter 4 which involved Morita Iron Works, a Japanese corporation. The basic test is whether

A company must have some connection with another country in order to be sued there.

the defendant has had sufficient contacts with the forum nation to justify its being sued there. Modern rules are generally quite liberal on this point, even though the *Morita* case held there was no jurisdiction in Illinois. Commission of a tort within the forum nation is generally considered a sufficient basis for a lawsuit based on that wrong. Entering into or performing a contract in the forum state would normally also be a sufficient basis for claims arising out of that contract. Ownership of property within the forum state is clearly enough basis for a lawsuit related to that property; under German law, it is a sufficient basis for suing the owner there for any claim, regardless of amount. Organization of a business in the forum state would certainly give it jurisdiction to hear any claims related to the operation of the business or to its internal management.

APPLICABLE LAW

Rules exist for deciding which nation's law applies to an international dispute.

The second issue—choice of the applicable law—is even more complicated. Much of private international law is still concerned with this basic question: whose law applies to the dispute? Over the centuries, some general rules have become widely accepted, but the development of modern commercial practices has required some updating of these rules. It is generally agreed that the validity of a contract is determined according to the law of the country where it was made. Contract performance will normally be judged according to the law of the nation where performance was to occur. Questions relating to the internal management of an organization are nearly always determined by the law of the place of organization. Tort liability may be based on the law of the place where the alleged wrongful act occurred or where its effects were felt. Using a newer "grouping of contacts" approach, some courts use the law of the country which, overall, has the major relationship to the alleged wrong and the parties involved. Since the forum court uses its own nation's procedural law, there are many tough questions as to whether a particular point is "procedural" or "substantive" (and thus subject to some other law under the above tests). Much time, effort, and money can be expended just in deciding these two preliminary issues before the court ever gets to merits of the dispute. Meanwhile, the attention of the involved companies' managers may be diverted from ongoing business operations.

■ Arbitration of International Disputes

Parties may agree to arbitrate contract disputes.

To avoid these extended preliminary wrangles, many international contracts contain **arbitration clauses**. As noted in Chapter 4, an arbitration clause permits the parties to select a person or panel of persons who are experienced in the type of problem at issue and who are trusted by both sides. Quite often, a nation respected for its impartiality, such as

Sweden or Switzerland, will be selected as the site for the hearing. Arbitrators and established procedures are available in such locations. Either party is thus able to refer any problem to a specific place for hearing and resolution.

As pointed out in Chapter 4, arbitration also has the great advantage of being private, as opposed to having the publicity associated with a court trial. The parties can make concessions and work out a compromise settlement without having to worry about playing to the press and the public. Arbitrators are also selected for their expertise in dealing with commercial problems. In contrast. litigants take the luck of the draw with judges and juries.

Arbitration awards are today generally enforceable in court in the event the parties do not voluntarily comply. The lawsuit in court does not retry the whole case on the merits, but only makes sure that the dispute was properly subject to arbitration and that the arbitrator followed the rules.

◼ Disputes with Governments and Their Agencies

In developing countries, the government is likely to be responsible for a large share of the nation's economic activity. This means that the government and its various agencies will be parties in international transactions. Governmental agencies will be buying goods and services and selling them. It is not at all unusual for a third-world government to contract with a foreign partner for the development of natural resources, with the foreign partner agreeing to be paid "in kind," that is, with some share of the minerals or timber extracted. Government officials will typically be actively involved in any establishment of new production operations or infrastructure construction within their country. Even though many nations have renounced socialism as their official doctrine, they still provide substantial direction, guidance, and promotion to their economies.

Making government one of the players in international commerce creates some added difficulties when disputes arise. A government will not want to appear to its people as having surrendered its sovereignty, or the nation's resources, to some foreign corporation. It may insist on having its own courts adjudicate any dispute and refuse to be bound by any judgment from the courts of another country. These factors probably indicate the inclusion of an arbitration clause, if possible, in most government contracts. In the following case, the governments involved were in fact quite willing to use the U.S. courts and U.S. law to establish their claims for damages. In response to this decision, Congress amended the Clayton Act in 1982; a foreign government, for its "governmental" purchases, may now recover only its actual damages, plus costs and attorney fees in such cases—the same remedy given to the U.S. Government as an injured purchaser.

Many governments are involved directly in international commerce.

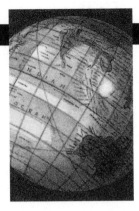

PFIZER, INC. V. GOVERNMENT OF INDIA

434 U.S. 308 (1978)

Facts: The governments of India, Iran, and the Philippines filed antitrust lawsuits against Pfizer and several other U.S. drug manufacturers, claiming damages as a result of price-fixing and market-splitting by the defendants. The governments asked for treble damages for themselves and for several classes of buyers within each of their countries. Pfizer and the other drug makers argued that the plaintiffs were not "persons" who had the right to sue for treble damages under Section 4 of the Clayton Antitrust Act. The U.S. District Court refused to dismiss the case, and the Court of Appeals affirmed that decision. The drug companies asked for certiorari.

Issue: Is a foreign government a "person" within the meaning of the Clayton Act?

Decision: Yes. Judgment affirmed. The case must go to trial.

Rule: The word "person" as used in Section 4 of the Clayton Act covers foreign governments as well as other foreign plaintiffs.

Discussion: *By Justice STEWART:*

"[W]hether a foreign nation is entitled to sue for treble damages depends upon whether it is a 'person' as that word is used in §4. There is no clear statutory provision or legislative history that provides a clear answer; it seems apparent that the question was never considered at the time the Sherman and Clayton Acts were enacted.

"The Court has previously noted the broad scope of the remedies provided by the antitrust laws. 'The Act is comprehensive in its terms and coverage, protecting all who are made victims of the forbidden practices by whomever they may be perpetrated.'... And the legislative history of the Sherman Act demonstrates that Congress used the phrase 'any person' intending it to have its naturally broad and inclusive meaning. There was no mention in the floor debates of any more restrictive definition. Indeed, during the course of those debates the word 'person' was used interchangeably with other terms even broader in connotation. For example, Senator Sherman said that the treble-damages remedy was being given to 'any party,' and Senator Edmunds, one of the principal draftsmen of the final bill, said that it established 'the right of anybody to sue who chooses to sue.'...

"The [plaintiffs] possess two attributes that could arguably exclude them from the scope of the sweeping phrase 'any person.' They are foreign, and they are sovereign nations...

"Yet it is clear that a foreign *corporation* is entitled to sue for treble damages, since the definition of 'person' contained in the Sherman and Clayton Acts explicitly includes 'corporations and associations existing under or authorized by...the laws of any foreign country.'... Moreover the antitrust laws extend to trade 'with foreign nations' as well as among the several States of the Union.... Clearly, therefore, Congress did not intend to make the treble-damages remedy available only to consumers in our own country....

"Moreover, an exclusion of all foreign plaintiffs would lessen the deterrent effect of treble damages. The conspiracy alleged...in this case operated domestically as well as internationally. If foreign plaintiffs were not permitted to seek a remedy for their antitrust injuries, persons doing business both in this country and abroad might be tempted to enter into anticompetitive conspiracies affecting American consumers in the expectation that the illegal profits they could safely extort abroad would offset any liability to plaintiffs at home. If, on the other hand, potential antitrust violators must take into account the full costs of their conduct, American consumers are benefitted by the maximum deterrent effect of treble damages upon all potential violators....

"On the two previous occasions that the Court has considered whether a sovereign government is a 'person' under the antitrust laws, the mechanical rule urged by the [defendants] has been rejected....

"It is clear that in *Georgia v. Evans* the Court rejected the proposition that the word *person* as used in the antitrust laws excludes all sovereign states. And the reasoning of that case leads to the conclusion that a foreign nation, like a domestic State, is entitled to pursue the remedy of treble damages when it has been injured in its business or property by antitrust violations. When a foreign nation enters our commercial markets as a purchaser of goods or services, it can be victimized by anticompetitive practices just as surely as a private person or a domestic State. The antitrust laws provide no alternative remedies for foreign nations as they do for the United States."

Ethical Dimension

Should a government and its agencies have the same rights as any other buyer of goods or services?

■ Sovereign Immunity and Act of State Doctrines

There is disagreement as to the suability of governments who engage in commerce.

Governments are protected by two international law rules which prevent certain of their activities from being challenged in court. **Sovereign immunity** means that a government cannot be sued without its consent. This immunity can be waived by the government for a particular case or for a class of cases. Some nations claim that there is no sovereign immunity for a government's commercial activities; socialist nations and many developing countries reject that idea and claim immunity for all their activities. The U.S. officially adopted the no-commercial-immunity rule in 1976 with the passage of the Foreign Sovereign Immunities Act.

Sovereign governments' acts usually cannot be challenged in the courts of other countries.

The **"act of state" doctrine** operates a bit differently. Governmental actions within a country cannot be challenged in the courts of another country, even if the litigation is between two private parties. Company A's claim that its property was wrongfully taken by Country X and transferred to Company B should be heard only in the courts of Country X. Since each nation is sovereign within its own borders, its decisions there should not be second-guessed by the courts in other countries. The international system could not function well if this were permitted. These points are discussed in the *OPEC* case.

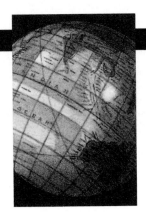

INTERNATIONAL ASSOCIATION OF MACHINISTS V. OPEC

649 F.2d 1354 (U.S. 9th Cir. Court of Appeals, 1981)

Facts: The Organization of Petroleum Exporting Countries (OPEC) was formed to coordinate the oil producing and pricing activities of its thirteen member-nations. Some of the members nationalized private production facilities; others substantially raised the royalty payments which private oil companies were required to pay. Partly as a result of OPEC's efforts, the world price of oil rose sharply during the 1970s.

The International Association of Machinists (IAM) filed suit in U.S. District Court, claiming that OPEC was violating the U.S. antitrust laws and asking for damages and injunctive relief. The District Court dismissed the case, saying it had no jurisdiction over the defendants and that the IAM had no valid antitrust claim.

Issue: Is this private antitrust lawsuit barred by the doctrine of sovereign immunity? By the act of state doctrine?

Decision: Perhaps the suit would be barred by the doctrine of sovereign immunity, but the court does not decide on this basis. Yes, the suit is barred by the act of state doctrine. Judgment affirmed.

Rule: Some nations do not recognize sovereign immunity for the commercial activities of other governments.

Courts of one nation may not judge the legality of the acts of another nation within the other's territory.

Discussion: *By Judge* CHOY:

"The District Court was understandably troubled by the broader implications of an antitrust action against the OPEC nations. The importance of the alleged price-fixing activity to the OPEC nations cannot be ignored. Oil revenues represent their only significant source of income. Consideration of their sovereignty cannot be separated from their near total dependence upon oil. We find that these concerns are appropriately addressed by application of the act of state doctrine. While we do not apply the doctrine of sovereign immunity, its elements remain relevant to our discussion of the act of state doctrine....

"The remedy IAM seeks is an injunction against the OPEC nations. The possibility of insult to the OPEC states and of interference with the efforts of the political branches to seek favorable relations with them is apparent from the very nature of this action and the remedy sought. While the case is formulated as an antitrust action, the granting of any relief would in effect amount to an order from a domestic court instructing a foreign sovereign to alter its chosen means of allocating and profiting from its own valuable natural resources. On the other hand, should the court hold that OPEC's actions are legal, this 'would greatly strengthen the bargaining hand' of the OPEC nations in the event that Congress or the executive chooses to condemn OPEC's actions....

"While conspiracies in restraint of trade are clearly illegal under domestic law, the record reveals no international consensus condemning cartels, royalties, and production agreements. The United States and other nations have supported the principle of supreme state sovereignty over natural resources. The OPEC nations themselves obviously will not agree that their actions are illegal. We are reluctant to allow judicial interference in an area so void of international consensus. An injunction against OPEC's alleged price-fixing activity would require condemnation of a cartel system which the community of nations has thus far been unwilling to denounce. The admonition...that the courts should consider the degree of codification and consensus in the area of law is another indication that judicial action is inappropriate here...."

"The act of state doctrine is applicable in this case. The courts should not enter at the will of litigants into a delicate area of foreign policy which the executive and legislative branches have chosen to approach with restraint. The issue of whether the [Foreign Sovereign Immunity Act] allows jurisdiction in this case need not be decided, since a judicial remedy is inappropriate regardless of whether jurisdiction exists. Similarly, we need not reach the issues regarding the indirect-purchaser rule, the extraterritorial application of the Sherman Act, the definition of 'person' under the Sherman Act, and the propriety of injunctive relief."

Ethical Dimension

Is it fair to have a class of persons whose actions cannot be challenged in court?

■NTERNATIONAL BUSINESS TRANSACTIONS

International business is conducted in a wide variety of forms. Any sort of commercial transaction which occurs within the United States can also take place in international commerce. U.S. companies sell to foreign customers and buy from foreign suppliers. U.S. companies license their technology and intellectual property to overseas companies and also receive similar licenses. Foreign companies set up subsidiaries here, and our companies do the same overseas. Increasingly, securities of our corporations are being marketed overseas, and foreign companies' stocks and bonds are being sold here. As business operations have become more and more internationalized, new treaties (such as CISG) have been negotiated to modernize and clarify international law.

■ International Sales of Goods

Many international sales of goods involve letters of credit.

An international sale of goods usually requires the services of two banks, one in the seller's country and one in the buyer's country. The transfer of funds to pay for the goods is accomplished by a device called a "letter of credit." Security for payment is achieved by maintaining control of the bill of lading issued by the carrier who is transporting the goods to the buyer.

Figure 19–1 shows how this sales transaction fits together. (1) The seller and the buyer enter into a sales contract. (2) The buyer makes arrangements with its bank, the "issuing bank," for enough credit to cover the purchase price. (3) The issuing bank notifies the seller's bank,

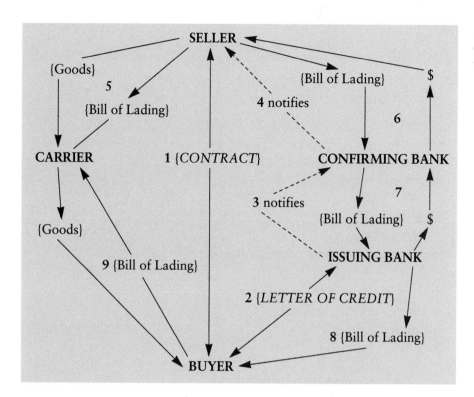

FIGURE 19–1
*Structure of an
International Sale*

the "confirming bank," that the buyer does have a line of credit for the specified amount. (4) The confirming bank notifies the seller that the credit arrangements have been made. (5) The seller delivers the goods to the carrier for shipment, and receives a bill of lading from the carrier. (6) The seller presents the bill of lading to the confirming bank and receives payment of the purchase price. (7) The confirming bank sends the bill of lading to the issuing bank, which in turn pays the confirming bank. (8) The issuing bank gives the bill of lading to the buyer (who has promised to repay the issuing bank according to the terms of the credit arrangement). (9) The buyer presents the bill of lading to the carrier and gets the goods.

■ Letters of Credit

Letters of credit are frequently used in international sales in the manner described above. They can also be used within the United States, for the same purposes—establishing a fund for payment while at the same time permitting the seller to maintain control of the goods until it gets payment. Article 5 of the UCC governs letters of credit within the United States. Article 5 defines a **letter of credit** as a promise by a bank that it "will honor drafts or other demands for payment upon compliance with the condition specified in the credit." The condition usually is the presentation of a bill of lading showing that the specified goods have been sent to the buyer. (See Figure 19–2.)

The letter of credit is a contract to honor drafts up to an agreed amount.

FIGURE 19–2
Letter of Credit

Confirmed Irrevocable Straight Credit

_____ *Bank*

_____ Street, _____, ____

CABLE ADDRESS_____

CONFIRMED IRREVOCABLE STRAIGHT CREDIT   DATE
OUR CREDIT NO._____

DEAR SIRS:

　　WE ARE INSTRUCTED BY
TO ADVISE YOU THAT IT HAS OPENED ITS IRREVOCABLE CREDIT NO.

　　　　　　　　　　　　　　　　　　　　　　　　　　　　IN YOUR FAVOR

FOR ACCOUNT OF

FOR A SUM OR SUMS NOT EXCEEDING A TOTAL OF

AVAILABLE BY YOUR DRAFT(S) AT   ON US TO BE ACCOMPANIED

BY

　　ALL DRAFTS DRAWN UNDER THE CREDIT MUST BE MARKED:
　　" DRAWN UNDER [name of confirming bank] CREDIT NO._____."

　　EXCEPT AS OTHERWISE EXPRESSLY STATED HEREIN, THIS ADVICE IS SUBJECT TO THE UNIFORM CUSTOMS AND PRACTICE FOR COMMERCIAL DOCUMENTARY CREDITS AS SET FORTH IN THE INTERNATIONAL CHAMBER OF COMMERCE BROCHURE NO. 222.

　　THE ABOVE NAMED ISSUER OF THE CREDIT ENGAGES WITH YOU THAT EACH DRAFT DRAWN UNDER AND IN COMPLIANCE WITH THE TERMS OF THE CREDIT WILL BE DULY HONORED ON DELIVERY OF DOCUMENTS AS SPECIFIED IF PRESENTED AT THIS OFFICE ON OR BEFORE
WE CONFIRM THE CREDIT AND THEREBY UNDERTAKE TO HONOR EACH DRAFT AND PRESENTED AS ABOVE SPECIFIED.

　　　　　　　　　　　　　　　　　　　　　　　　YOURS VERY TRULY,

　　　　　　　　　　　　　　　　　　　　　　　　ASSISTANT CASHIER

With goods, documents, and funds flowing across international boundaries, questions of which country's law applies can arise very quickly. If the parties fail to specify, courts will use normal "conflict-of-laws" principles to try to solve the problem. Disputes between the buyer and its issuing bank should clearly be governed by the law of the country where the bank is located, since that's where the letter of credit was issued. On the other end of the transaction, disputes between the seller and its confirming bank should be governed by the law of the country where that bank is located, since that's where the confirming bank is performing its obligations. Disputes between the buyer and the seller may be governed by the national law of either party, depending on the nature of the dispute. The following case raises the question of the enforceability of a letter of credit after the government-customer cancels the underlying contract.

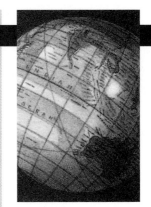

AMERICAN BELL INTERNATIONAL, INC. V. ISLAMIC REPUBLIC OF IRAN

474 F. Supp. 420 (S.D.N.Y. 1979)

Facts: American Bell International (ABI), a wholly owned subsidiary of AT&T, made a contract with the Imperial Government of Iran in 1978 to provide communications equipment and consulting services. The total contract price was about $280 million, with $38 million to be paid in advance. Iran could demand return of this advance payment at any time, but the amount refundable was to be reduced by 20 percent of the invoices filed by ABI and accepted by Iran. As ABI did the work, it got to keep more of the advance. About $30 million was still refundable at the time of trial.

Iran required a guarantee that it would get a refund if demanded, so ABI had Bank Iranshahr sign an irrevocable letter of guaranty in favor of the Iranian government. To protect Bank Iranshahr, ABI got a letter of credit from Manufacturers Hanover Trust in favor of Bank Iranshahr.

When the Shah of Iran was overthrown in 1979, ABI was left with large unpaid claims, so it stopped work under the contract. The new Islamic Republic placed a refund demand with Bank Iranshahr, which in turn demanded $30,220,724 from Manufacturers Hanover. Bank Iranshahr's first demand was not in proper form and was refused. ABI then brought this lawsuit to enjoin payment by Manufacturers Hanover, which had now received a proper demand for payment on the letter of credit.

Issue: Should the court enjoin payment of the letter of credit?

Decision: No. Injunction denied, but a delay in payment is ordered to permit an appeal of this decision.

Rule: On proper demand, a letter of credit must be paid unless there is fraud in the transaction.

Discussion: *By Judge* MACMAHON:

"There is credible evidence that the Islamic Republic is xenophobic and anti-American and that it has no regard for consulting service contracts such as the one here. Although Bell has made no effort to invoke the aid of the Iranian courts, we think the current situation in Iran, as shown by the evidence, warrants the conclusion that an attempt by Bell to resort to those courts would be futile.... However, Bell has not demonstrated that it is without adequate remedy in this court against the Iranian defendants under the Sovereign Immunity Act which it invokes in this very case....

"In order to succeed on the merits, Bell must prove, by a preponderance of the evidence, that either (1) demand for payment of the Manufacturers Letter of Credit conforming to the terms of the Letter has not yet been made...or (2) a demand, even though in conformity, should not be honored because of fraud in the transaction....

"[T]he United States now recognizes the present Government of Iran as the legal successor to the Imperial Government of Iran. That recognition is binding on American courts.... Though we may decide for ourselves the consequences of such recognition upon the litigants in this case..., we point out that American courts have traditionally viewed contract rights as vesting not in any particular government but in the state of which that government is an agent....

"Plaintiff's argument requires us to presume bad faith on the part of the Iranian government.... On the evidence before us, fraud is not more inferable than an economically rational decision by the government to recoup its down payment, as it is entitled to do under the consulting contract, and still dispute its liabilities under that contract."

Ethical Dimension

Is it fair and reasonable to permit the enforcement of a letter of credit in favor of the party who has cancelled the underlying contract?

■ Licensing

Many companies license others to use their technology.

Another very frequently used mechanism for increasing the firm's business operations is the licensing of the firm's technology to other companies. The firm owning a patent licenses a foreign company to use the patent, for a fee—usually a percentage of sales. Similar licensing may occur using trade secrets or popular trademarks or trade names. In all these arrangements, one firm is permitting another to use the business "know-how" which the first firm has developed. Both parties benefit, one in the form of increased sales, the other in the form of royalty payments for the use of the technology. Obviously, a U.S. firm could be on either end of this transaction. (Licensing is by no means confined to international transactions; it is also frequently used inside the United States and in other countries.)

■ Joint Ventures

Another very popular form of international business transaction is the joint venture. It is similar to a partnership, but it is usually limited in scope to a specific project. Perhaps the best-known joint venture in the United States is the auto plant set up in California by General Motors and Toyota. Each partner receives part of the plant's production.

Joint ventures are also very popular with the governments in developing countries. The host government provides the land and the labor, and the foreign company provides the capital, the technology, and the management (or at least some of it). The host government will normally insist that its law govern these transactions, but some negotiation may be possible.

■ Foreign Subsidiaries

Where extensive operations within another country are anticipated, it may be necessary or desirable to form a foreign subsidiary company. Doing so will obviously require compliance with the local law, which will specify the types of organizations which may be formed and the requirements for each.

The subsidiary company is clearly subject to the jurisdiction of the courts in the nation where it is organized. The parent company's ownership of shares in a subsidiary corporation, in and of itself, would not usually be a sufficient basis for asserting jurisdiction over the parent corporation except as to claims relating to the stock ownership. Likewise, under general principles of corporate law, mere ownership of stock does not make the parent liable for the actions of the subsidiary. Parent corporations may be held liable for the subsidiary's actions, however, if the parent supervised the activity or was otherwise actively involved in it. That point was at issue in the next case, which involved one of the worst chemical disasters of all time.

Parent corporations are not usually liable for actions of their foreign subsidiaries.

IN RE UNION CARBIDE CORP. GAS PLANT DISASTER

809 F.2d 195 (U.S. 2nd Cir. Court of Appeals, 1987)

Facts: On the night of December 2–3, 1984, winds blew a cloud of deadly methyl isocyanate gas, which had leaked out of facilities at a chemical plant, into densely populated parts of the city of Bhopal, India. Over 2,000 people died, and more than 200,000 were injured. The plant was owned and operated by an Indian corporation, Union Carbide India Limited (UCIL). Fifty and nine-tenths percent of UCIL's stock is owned by Union Carbide Corporation, a New York corporation; 22 percent is

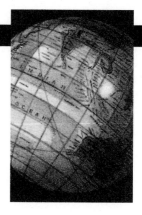

owned or controlled by the government of India, and the balance is owned by about 23,500 individual Indian citizens. UCIL operates fourteen chemical and plastics plants in India. UCIL employs over 9,000 Indian citizens.

Four days after the disaster, the first of some 145 purported class actions was filed in a U.S. District Court. These actions were consolidated in the U.S. District Court for the southern district of New York. India passed a statute authorizing its government to file lawsuits on behalf of all the victims. The government then filed such a lawsuit in the southern district. On motion, the District Court dismissed the actions on the basis of *forum non conveniens*, as long as Union Carbide consented to jurisdiction in India, agreed to pay any judgment given there, and agreed to be subject to U.S. rules on discovery of evidence. The individual plaintiffs appealed the dismissal. Union Carbide objects to the discovery condition.

Issue: Should the doctrine of *forum non conveniens* be applied?

Decision: Yes. Judgment affirmed (as modified).

Rule: Where nearly all plaintiffs, witnesses, and evidence are located in one country, and that country's courts provide an adequate legal process, the trial should normally be held there.

Discussion: *By Judge* MANSFIELD:

"Little or no deference can be paid to the plaintiffs' choice of a United States forum when all but a few of the 200,000 plaintiffs are Indian citizens located in India who, according to [their government], have revoked the authorizations of American counsel to represent them here and have substantiated the [government], which now prefers Indian courts. The finding of our district court, after exhaustive analysis of the evidence, that the Indian courts provide a reasonably adequate alternative forum cannot be labelled clearly erroneous or an abuse of discretion.

"The emphasis placed by plaintiffs on [Union Carbide's] having its domicile here, where personal jurisdiction over it exists, is robbed of significance by its consent to Indian jurisdiction. Plaintiffs' contention that the most crucial and probative evidence is located in the United States is simply not in accord with the record or the district court's findings. Although basic design programs were prepared in the United States and some assistance furnished to UCIL at the outset of the 10-year period during which the Bhopal plant was constructed, the proof bearing on the issues to be tried is almost entirely located in India. This includes the principal witnesses and documents bearing on the development and construction of the plant, the detailed designs, the implementation of plans, the operation and regulation of the plant, its safety precautions, the facts with respect to the accident itself, and the deaths and injuries attributable to the accident....

"We are concerned, however, that as written the district court's requirement that [Union Carbide] consent to the enforcement of a final Indian judgment, which was imposed on the erroneous assumption that such a judgment might not otherwise be enforceable in the United States, may create misunderstandings and problems of construction. Although the order's provision that the judgment 'comport with the minimal requirements of due process'...probably is intended to refer to 'due process' as used in the New York Foreign Country Money Judgments Law and others like it, there is the risk that it may also be interpreted as providing for a lesser standard than we would otherwise require. Since the court's condition with respect to enforceability of any final Indian judgment is predicated on an erroneous legal assumption and its 'due process' language is ambiguous, and since the district court's purpose is fully served by New York's statute providing for recognition of foreign-country money judgments, it was error to impose this condition upon the parties.

"We also believe that the district court erred in requiring [Union Carbide] to consent (which [Union Carbide] did under protest and subject to its right of appeal) to broad discovery of it by the plaintiffs under the Federal Rules of Civil Procedure when [Union Carbide] is confined to the more limited discovery authorized under Indian law.... Basic justice dictates that both sides be treated equally, with each having equal access to the evidence in the possession or under the control of the other. Application of this fundamental principle in the present case is especially appropriate since the [Indian government], as the sovereign government of India, is expected to be a party to the Indian litigation, possibly on both sides."

Ethical Dimension

How can a company justifiably deny liability when thousands of people have been injured?

REVIEW

International law has been developing over many centuries, virtually from the beginning of recorded history. Despite its ancient origins, it is very much a part of modern business operations. International business transactions are increasing, as is international competition. The poet John Donne said, "No man is an island." American business has learned, in part to its dismay, that no nation is—or can be—an economic island. International competition is no longer an option; it is a requirement for economic survival.

International business law, derived from custom, cases, textbooks, and treaties, provides the rules for international transactions. There are many different business methods in use: direct sales, licensing, joint ventures, and foreign subsidiaries—to name several of the most popular. Each of these various methods involves different legal relationships and different combinations of national and international law.

REVIEW QUESTIONS AND PROBLEMS

1. What is the difference between organizing a foreign subsidiary and participating in a joint venture?

2. Why is it that the International Court of Justice has only a relatively minor impact on international business operations?

3. What is the difference between the sovereign immunity doctrine and the act of state doctrine?

4. Why is the letter of credit important to international business operations?

5. What is CISG? Why is it important?

6. What is the Treaty of Rome? Why is it important?

7. Pizzata Oil Company, a Texas corporation, hired a German company, Unterzee Boats Ltd., to tow a deep-sea oil drilling rig from Houston, Texas, to a new location in the North Sea. The contract specified that any disputes between the parties would be resolved in Switzerland's courts. Unterzee assigned one of its ocean-going tugs, the Hamburg, to do the job. There was a severe storm off the coast of North Carolina, and the oil drilling rig was seriously damaged. The Hamburg made port in North Carolina. Pizzata immediately filed an admiralty suit there, asking that the tug and its owners be held liable for the damage to the oil rig. Unterzee moved to dismiss the lawsuit. How should the U.S. District Court rule? Why?

8. Autopart, an Ohio corporation, exchanged a series of letters with Sterko, a Greek corporation, concerning a possible purchase from Sterko. At a London meeting, Autopart's president, Rogie Smythe, signed an agreement stating that it would buy "up to 500,000 spark plugs" from Sterko. The plugs were to be made at Sterko's plant in Madrid, but Autopart never sent any orders, so none of these plugs were ever made. Because no definite amount was ever agreed on, there is probably no contract at all under U.S. law. Sterko nevertheless filed a lawsuit in Athens, claiming damages. When Autopart did not appear and defend the case, the Greek court awarded a default judgment for

$55,000. Sterko then filed a lawsuit in U.S. District Court in Cleveland, asking enforcement of its Greek court judgment against Autopart's assets in Ohio. How should the U.S. District Court handle this request? Explain.

9. Alaska has a statute in force which prohibits nonresident aliens, including any corporation in which more than 25 percent of the stock in owned by nonresident aliens, from owning more than 600 acres of land. Lucky Lumber, Inc., is a Delaware corporation which is wholly owned by a British parent corporation. Lucky has acquired a purchase option on 20,000 acres of timberland in Alaska. Lucky brought a lawsuit in the Alaska courts, claiming that the statute violated international law and should thus be declared null and void. What is the correct decision in this case? Discuss.

10. Commo Company, a South Carolina corporation, contracted to buy 700 tons of pineapples from Bwana Ltd., which had extensive operations in the nation of Tarzania. (Bwana was a wholly owned subsidiary of a Dutch corporation.) The pineapples were loaded on a ship, the *S.S. Smedley*. Before the ship could sail, there was a revolution in Tarzania, and the ship and its cargo were seized by the new government as part of its nationalization program. When it was notified of the seizure, Commo agreed to pay the new Tarzania government for the pineapples when they were delivered in Charleston, South Carolina. Bwana filed suit in South Carolina, claiming that it still owned the pineapples and asking the court to order Commo to pay it the purchase price. What should the court do here, and why?

SUGGESTIONS FOR FURTHER READING

Cameron, "The Development of Individual Property Rights Under Soviet Law," *American Business Law Journal* 14 (Winter 1977): 333.

Chandra, "International Licensing," *American Business Law Journal* 17 (Spring 1979): 117.

D'Amato, "The Concept of Human Rights in International Law," *Columbia Law Review* 82 (October 1982): 1110.

Franke and Whittaker, "The Extraterritoriality Issue: A Title VII Case Study," *American Business Law Journal* 30 (May 1992): 1.

Johnson, "The Japanese Legal Milieu and Its Relationship to Business," *American Business Law Journal* 13 (Winter 1976): 335.

Turner, "International Harmonization: A Professional Goal," *Journal Of Accountancy* 155 (January 1983): 58.

Watson, "Business Law in the People's Republic of China: 1978–1988," *American Business Law Journal* 27 (Fall 1989): 315.

20
REGULATION
OF
INTERNATIONAL
COMMERCE

*"The noblest question in the world is: 'What good
may I do in it?'"*
Benjamin Franklin

LEARNING OBJECTIVES: After you have studied this chapter, you
should be able to:

EXPLAIN how governments both promote and restrict
international trade.

DISCUSS the impact of various kinds of tax policies on
international trade.

SUMMARIZE the liability rules for international carriers of goods.

DISTINGUISH nationalization of assets from limitation of profit
repatriation.

EVALUATE the application of the Sherman Act to transactions
overseas.

P REVIEW

From earliest times, governments have been concerned with developing and protecting their national economies. This chapter explores some of the major regulatory devices currently in use and shows how they impact on international trade and commerce.

Governments generally try to promote exports and often place various kinds of restrictions on imports. Post-World War II Japan is a classic example of a national trade policy in action. As of the early 1990s, all foreign companies combined sold only 3 percent of the cars and trucks in Japan, while Japanese companies had 15 percent of the European market and a hefty 35 percent of the rich North American market. **Tariffs** (taxes on imported goods) can be, and are, used to discourage imports. There are now a variety of international agreements to deal with tariff barriers. International rules have also been established to govern carrier liability for goods being transported. The objective of these international carrier rules, however, is simply to provide some uniformity of treatment and thus to facilitate, rather than impede, international trade.

National governments are very much aware of multinational companies' operations within their countries. Standards of required local participation may be set. Removal of profits and capital investments may be restricted. At the extreme, foreign assets may be nationalized. In addition to the various kinds of specific restrictions, national law enforcement agencies will be on the alert for possible antitrust or trade practice violations. International business operations may thus require steering a careful course through bureaucratic mazes and legal minefields. For most firms, however, the potential addition to the "bottom line" is worth it.

G OVERNMENT TRADE POLICIES

At one extreme, governments may attempt to protect their home market and home manufacturers from foreign competition. At the other end of the spectrum are those who favor free worldwide competition. Most governments try to compromise somewhere in between those two positions.

■ Mercantilism, 1500–1800

Early on, the great trading nations of Western Europe adopted economic policies intended to strengthen themselves politically and militarily. The major economic objective was the acquisition of precious metals—gold and silver—which could be used to buy or build armaments and to pay the rising costs of government. The approach of Spain and Portugal was to simply extract these precious metals from

Several western nations adopted a policy called mercantilism.

their colonial empires, primarily in the New World. For a time, they were reasonably successful.

Over the longer term, the policy followed by Holland, France, and England proved to be more durable. The leaders of these nations used foreign trade as a means of acquiring large monetary surpluses for their national purposes. This trading policy was generally referred to as **mercantilism**. It required the production of high-quality, low-cost goods, and the domination of foreign markets. (In this respect, its resemblance to Japanese trade policy after World War II is remarkable.) One problem with mercantilism is the internal inflationary effect of the large money surpluses which it produced. In any event, mercantilist policies were effectively ended by the Industrial Revolution. After the Industrial Revolution, national strength was proportionate to industrial strength, not to gold and silver reserves.

■ Adam Smith and The Wealth of Nations

Although "An Inquiry into the Nature and Causes of the Wealth of Nations" was published in 1776, well before the Industrial Revolution was fully developed, Smith's famous text provided the ethical and theoretical basis for capitalism. Smith was generally opposed to mercantilism and to other forms of monopoly. He felt that each individual's pursuit of personal goals would produce an overall social well-being. He thought that the best government policy was summed up in the French phrase: *laissez faire*—let people do as they please; leave the economy alone. In the international sphere, Smith in general favored free trade among nations. ("It is the maxim of every prudent master of a family, never to attempt to make at home what it will cost him more to make than to buy.... What is prudence in the conduct of every private family can scarce be folly in that of a great kingdom.") This belief grew out of Smith's basic ideas about the division of labor and free exchanges in the domestic economy. He did recognize, however, that some trade regulations might be necessary in an imperfect world.

■ Government Promotion of Exports

The U.S. has been reluctant to adopt a national economic strategy.

Many modern governments do recognize the need to promote their nation's exports, although some do so much more aggressively than others. The United States has been reluctant to adopt a national industrial strategy, in part because there is a strong current of opinion that still believes that *laissez faire* is the best government policy. Only reluctantly have we realized that even our largest industries are unable to compete in a world market against companies with government sponsorship and government subsidies. Early in 1992, President Bush and the heads of twenty large U.S. corporations, including the Big Three auto companies, toured the Far East in an attempt to work out new agreements to deal with our huge trade deficit. The United States trades with some 200 countries, yet 60 percent of our trade deficit in 1990 (over $40 billion) resulted from trade with one nation—Japan. The mission was a partial success, at best, in terms of specific, substantive gains. But symbolically, the unity of U.S. government and U.S. business on trade issues sent an important message to the world, and especially to Japan.

One of the earliest official recognitions by the U.S. government that international trade presented our companies with special problems was the Webb-Pomerene Act of 1918. Much of international trade in the period following the First World War was dominated by giant "cartels," large combinations of companies which attempted to regulate production, divide markets, and fix prices. U.S. companies were prevented by our antitrust laws from forming similar combinations in order to compete more effectively. The Webb-Pomerene Act created a special exemption from the U.S. antitrust laws for U.S. exporters who wished to engage in joint marketing activities overseas. They are permitted to do so, free from antitrust liability, as long as their joint operations do not "artificially or intentionally enhance or depress prices within the United States."

A more recent example of our government's export promotion policies is the creation of the Overseas Private Investment Corporation in 1979. OPIC is an agency of the national government, charged with promoting overseas investment by U.S. companies. One major incentive is the Investment Insurance Program (IIP), by which our government promises to reimburse private companies who lose overseas assets because of expropriation, revolution, or war. The IIP thus removes one of the major uncertainties involved in overseas investment, but it is available only for approved projects in developing nations.

OPIC reimburses companies who lose overseas investments through actions of foreign governments.

International trade is also facilitated by the International Monetary Fund (IMF) and the International Bank for Reconstruction and Development (IBRD). The U.S. government participates in both the IMF and the IBRD. The IMF, using funds paid in by the member-nations, purchases currencies on the world market. It thus helps to stabilize foreign exchange rates. More stable exchange rates are clearly important in assisting international credit transactions. The IBRD, also called the World Bank, is another specialized agency of the United Nations. The IBRD makes loans to member governments and, with government guarantees, to private companies. These loan funds are used for trade and investment purposes. A closely related agency, the International Finance Corporation, is authorized to invest in private projects without government guarantees. U.S. government funding is an important resource for all of these trade promotion agencies.

■ Government Restriction of Export Activity

Our government does not only promote exports, however; it also imposes restrictions. Exports to some countries are prohibited. Exports of some products are prohibited. And certain sales practices are prohibited.

While most products and services may be sold to most countries, there are a few nations with which U.S. trade is restricted by the government. The political wounds from the Korean War and the Vietnam War have not yet healed, so nearly all exports to North Korea, Vietnam, and Cambodia are prohibited. Due to its attempts to export revolution throughout Latin America, Cuba is given similar treatment. Sponsorship of international terrorism has earned Libya its place on our national blacklist.

The OEA controls U.S. exports in the interest of national security.

The Department of Commerce's Office of Export Administration (OEA) exercises general control over U.S. exports under the authority of the Export Administration Act. The OEA's charge is to control exports to maintain our national security and assist our foreign policy. Specifically, OEA is to ensure that we retain the goods and technology necessary for the strength of our own economy. Using its licensing authority under these statutory directions, OEA banned exports of certain "high-tech" products to the Communist Bloc nations. Similar restrictions are imposed on military hardware by the State Department, and on nuclear materials and technology by the Nuclear Regulatory Commission. Some of these restrictions, such as those on computers, will need to be reexamined now that Eastern Europe has renounced Communism, and the Soviet Union has disintegrated. Some restrictions have already been removed.

The *Elkins* case involves restrictions on trade with Libya.

U.S. V. ELKINS

885 F.2d 775 (U.S. 2nd Cir. Court of Appeals, 1989)

Facts: Edward Elkins was convicted of criminal conspiracy to defraud and of engaging in or aiding and abetting illegal export activity in violation of the Export Administration Act, the Arms Export Control Act, and the International Emergency Economic Powers Act. The U.S. Government had investigated his participation in a complex scheme to sell two Lockheed L-100-30 jet airplanes to Libya. Libya was then (and still is) subject to strict export controls. Export licenses for these two jets would not have been given by the U.S. Government, so Elkins and other persons set up dummy transactions. The planes were purchased by a West German company which was owned by Libyans. The planes were flown first to Bordeaux, France, then to the small African nation of Benin, and finally to Libya. Elkins told Lockheed that Badir, who controlled the West German company, had no connection with the Libyan Government; this was untrue. Elkins did not tell Lockheed that the planes were to be modified to allow air-to-air refueling. Based on Elkins' assurances that the planes were for Benin, the U.S. Department of Commerce issued an export license on April 18, 1985. One of the planes was found at the Cairo airport on March 7, 1987; its radio signal and operations manual indicated that it had been used by the Libyan air force. Elkins appealed his fraud conviction on several bases, including the government's failure to prove violation of the mail fraud or wire fraud statutes.

Issue: Was Edwards guilty of "fraud" against the U.S. government?

Decision: Yes. Convictions affirmed.

Rule: One need not be guilty of mail fraud or wire fraud to be guilty of an attempt to defraud the government.

Discussion: *By Judge JOHNSON:*

"Defendant was charged with conspiring to commit, among other things, the substantive offense of wire fraud against the United States.... That statute prohibits the use of wire transmission services in furtherance of any scheme or artifice to defraud. The object of the scheme alleged was to defraud the United States of the right to implement its foreign policy free from stealth, false statement, and fraud....

"[T]he...statute applies only to schemes to defraud others of property rights. [A] scheme to defraud citizens of their interest in fair and effective government does not violate [the] section.... Thus, the wire and mail fraud statutes are limited to schemes to deprive others of property rights, although the object of the scheme to defraud may be intangible property rights....

"An individual may also violate section 371 [the conspiracy statute], however, by conspiring to defraud the United States in any manner or for any purpose. The scope of 'defraud' in section 371 is broader than 'defraud' as used in section 1343 [the wire fraud statute].... [T]o 'defraud' the government within the meaning of section 371 'also means to interfere with or obstruct one of its lawful governmental functions by deceit, craft or trickery, or at least by some means that are dishonest.'... Therefore, although the object of the scheme alleged in the indictment, to defraud the government of its right to implement its foreign policy, would not support a wire fraud conviction..., it would support a conviction under section 371 of conspiracy to defraud the government....

"The jury could not have convicted defendant of conspiracy in this case without having found an unlawful object of the conspiracy. The indictment adequately charged defendant with conspiracy to defraud the United States, and the jury was adequately charged on this object of the conspiracy....

"The government introduced into evidence two documents used to show that the Libyan military had purchased these aircraft. The documents were found in West Germany in a briefcase allegedly owned by Badir. One was a letter by Jabir, purportedly the head of the Libyan military, to Badi, Badir's superior, authorizing the purchase of two L-100-30 jet aircraft with air-to-air refueling capability. The other was a progress report written by Badir to 'Chief of Staff Colonel Ahmad Mahmoud' about the purchase of the jets. Defendant challenges the admission into evidence of these letters....

"We conclude that the district court correctly found that the government satisfied the elements required for admission of the Jabir letter.... The presence of corroborating evidence that these planes were destined for use in Libya by the Libyan armed forces provides circumstantial guarantees of the trustworthiness of the letter.... The official stationery and its presence in Badir's briefcase also constitute circumstantial guarantees of trustworthiness. The letter is clearly material, indicating as it does the direct involvement of high Libyan officials in the purchase of the planes. The letter, authored by Jabir, was more probative than any other information reasonably available to indicate that the Libyan military participated in the purchase of these planes. We conclude that the district court did not err in admitting this letter. Even if this letter had been erroneously admitted, however, we would not reverse defendant's conviction, because we conclude that the admission would have constituted harmless error."

Ethical Dimension

Why shouldn't someone be able to sell products—airplanes or whatever—to whomever is willing to buy them?

●

▪ Regulation of International Sales Practices

Bribing a purchasing agent in order to make a sale is generally illegal in this country, whether the agent represents a private company or a public body. In many other nations, however, payments to public officials in return for favorable business actions are an accepted way of commercial life. When the sales representatives of U.S. companies are selling in overseas markets, whose law should apply—ours or theirs?

Under general conflict of laws rules, an action which is lawful where done cannot be made illegal elsewhere. Congress, however, did not see the problem that way.

Another generally accepted conflicts rule says that regulation of a corporation's internal management is governed by its place of incorporation. Using that rule as its primary justification, Congress enacted the Foreign Corrupt Practices Act (FCPA) in 1977 to govern the overseas conduct of U.S. businesses. Payments to a foreign official to influence a discretionary decision, such as purchase of goods or services by a government agency, are now illegal under U.S. law. A corporation violating the law is subject to a fine of up to $2 million; the individual agent, a fine up to $100,000 and imprisonment up to five years. It is still permissible to make small payments to foreign officials to assure proper performance of their already assigned duties, such as clearing the U.S. company's goods through customs. The FCPA also requires that U.S. companies keep adequate records and maintain adequate internal controls to assure that such illegal payments are not being made. Since the FCPA is an amendment to the 1934 Securities Act, the record-keeping and internal-control requirements apply to all companies required to register with the SEC under the 1934 act. The act is intended to make sure that similar illegal payments to officials in this country do not occur.

The FCPA prohibits bribery of foreign officials by U.S. companies.

Restrictions on Imports

The other side of a nation's trade equation is the amount of goods and services it imports. Countries try to control imports in various ways—**quotas** (quantity limits), product standards, tariffs, and other methods.

QUOTAS

The United States finally persuaded the Japanese to agree on a "voluntary" quota for car imports. However, the Japanese then built seven new assembly plants in this country. Overall, the sales and market share of Japanese cars and trucks in the North American market increased substantially during the 1980s. These "transplant" factories produce vehicles which have a U.S. content of less than 50 percent. The similar figure for Big Three auto plants is nearly 90 percent. As a result, each new transplant job costs about two "old" jobs, so the Big Three closed nine assembly plants during this same period.

Governments may set quotas on imports.

Mandatory import quotas are in force, however, for a wide variety of products, from many different countries. Jamaican producers can sell to U.S. importers no more than 970 gallons of ice cream annually. Poland is limited to sending us an annual maximum of 350 tons of alloy tool steel. Haiti can sell us no more than 7730 tons of sugar. There are similar quotas for table linens, tapestries, tents, ties, twine, typing ribbons, and other products. U.S. producers of all these goods are protected from foreign competition, but U.S. consumers and industrial buyers are paying more than they would otherwise.

PRODUCT STANDARDS

Product standards can also be used to discourage foreign entry into a market. The Japanese have been very skillful at using this method. A Jeep Cherokee costs a Japanese buyer about $12,000 more than a U.S. buyer, primarily because everything needs to be "recertified." (One of the Japanese "concessions" to President Bush was that the number of Jeep dealers in Japan would be expanded from 100 to 300, with total annual sales to rise to 1200; that means that each Japanese dealer would sell ONE Jeep every three months!)

COUNTERFEIT GOODS

Many U.S. firms are being damaged by the importation of counterfeit goods, illegally produced by companies using trademarks, copyrights, or patents without the owner's permission. Importation of such counterfeit goods can be enjoined, and damages can be collected. Such goods already in the country can be seized and destroyed. For trademark violations, the 1984 Trademark Counterfeiting Act permits treble damages and provides criminal penalties.

"GRAY MARKET" GOODS

Licensee companies may try to sell their goods in the licensor's home market.

Equally as troublesome for some U.S. firms are so-called "gray market" goods. The producer of these goods was lawfully licensed to use the U.S. company's patent, copyright, or trademark—but only to produce and sell the goods overseas. Someone has purchased the goods overseas, imported them into the United States, and is now selling them here—usually at a lower price. The foreign producer may have breached the licensing agreement, but even if it has, the U.S. licensor company may not be able to prevent the sales in the United States, as shown in the *K Mart* case.

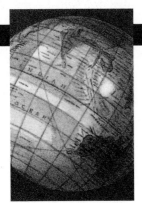

K MART CORP. V. CARTIER, INC.

108 S. Ct. 1811 (1988)

Facts: So-called "gray-market" goods have been legally manufactured and trademarked in one country. They are then imported into another country and sold there in competition with goods made in that country by another company which has the rights to use the trademark there. In what the Court calls a Case 1 fact pattern, a foreign company owns the trademark and licenses a U.S. company to use it here. Trademarked goods are then imported to the United States, either by the foreign company which owns the trademark, or by another company which has bought goods from it. In Case 2, the U.S. manufacturer is a subsidiary of the foreign firm holding the trademark, its parent, or just one of its divisions. In Case 3, the U.S. company owns the trademark and licenses an independent foreign firm to use it in a particular country overseas. The goods manufactured overseas are then imported into the United States, either by the trademark licensee itself or by one of its buyers. The Trademark Act of 1930 prevents importation into the United States of foreign-made goods bearing a U.S. registered trademark which is owned by a U.S. citizen or corporation unless the U.S. trademark owner gives written consent. The U.S. Customs Service's implementing regulation permits importation of goods made overseas by the "same person" that holds the U.S. trademark, by another person subject to "common control," or by a foreign company which has authorization to use the trademark. The regulation, in other words, permits the goods to be imported in Case 2 and Case 3. This regulation was challenged by an association of holders of U.S. trademarks. The U.S. District Court for the District of Columbia upheld the regulation, but the U.S. Court of Appeals reversed. The U.S. Supreme Court split five to four on both parts 2 and 3, with a different group of judges in each majority.

Issue: Is the Customs Service regulation consistent with the statute?

Decision: Yes, as to the Case 2 part of the regulation.

   No, as to the Case 3 part of the regulation.

Rule: It is logical to permit importation by the "same person" who owns the U.S. trademark or by a firm subject to "common control" with the owner of the U.S. trademark. It is not logical to permit importation by a foreign licensee in violation of the licensing contract restrictions.

Discussion: *By Justice* KENNEDY, *who was on both majorities:*
"Until 1922, the Federal Government did not regulate the importation of gray market goods, not even to protect the investment of an independent purchaser of a foreign trademark, and not even in the extreme case where the independent foreign manufacturer breached its agreement to refrain from direct competition with the purchaser. That year, however, Congress was spurred to action by a Court of Appeals decision declining to enjoin the parallel importation of goods bearing a trademark that (as in Case 1) a domestic company had purchased from an independent foreign manufacturer at a premium....

   "In an immediate response...Congress enacted §526 of the Tariff Act of 1922.... That provision [was] later reenacted in identical form as §526 of the 1930 Tariff Act....

"The regulations implementing §526 for the past 50 years have not applied the prohibition to all gray-market goods. The Customs Service regulation now in force...establishes a 'common-control' exception from the ban, permitting the entry of gray-market goods manufactured abroad by the trademark owner or its affiliate.... The Customs Service regulation further provides an 'authorized-use' exception....

"Subsection (c)(3)...of the regulation...cannot stand.... This subsection of the regulation denies a domestic trademark holder the power to prohibit the importation of goods made by an independent foreign manufacturer where the domestic trademark holder has authorized the foreign manufacturer to use the trademark. Under no reasonable construction of the statutory language can goods made in a foreign country by an independent foreign manufacturer be removed from the purview of the statute."

(Justice BRENNAN, *discussing the section of the regulation dealing with Case 2)* "The most blatant hint that Congress did not intend to extend §526's protection to affiliates of foreign manufacturers (Case 2) is the provision's protectionist, almost jingoist, flavor. Its structure bespeaks an intent, characteristic of the times, to protect only domestic interests. A foreign manufacturer that imports its trademarked products into the United States cannot invoke §526 to prevent third parties from competing in the domestic market by buying the trademarked goods abroad and importing them here: The trademark is not 'registered in the Patent and Trademark Office.' The same manufacturer cannot protect itself against parallel importation merely by registering its trademark in the United States: It is not 'a person domiciled in the United States.' Nor can the manufacturer insulate itself by hiring a United States domiciliary to register the trademark: The owner is not 'organized withi[n] the United States.' For the same reason, it will not even suffice for the foreign manufacturer to incorporate a subsidiary here to register the trademark on the parent's behalf, if the foreign parent still owns the trademark."

Ethical Dimension

Has the Court worked out a proper result in this case? If I permit you to use my property for sales in country X, should you be able to violate that agreement and send the goods back into my own country to compete with my goods? Should there be any restrictions on foreign competition?

INTERNATIONAL TAXATION ISSUES

Taxes represent a government-imposed cost, which must be added to the price of the product and passed along to the consumer. Governments use taxes not only to raise revenues but also to promote social policies. Higher taxes on some activities tend to discourage persons from engaging in those activities. Taxes are used that way internationally, too.

Taxation as a Deterrent

Foreign firms should not enjoy any special immunity from local taxes. If a company from country *A* makes sales in country *B*, there is no reason why it should not have to pay sales taxes imposed by country *B*, the same as local firms. That's not really the problem. Difficulties arise when the foreign firm is subjected to discriminatory taxation, or double taxation.

This problem is not unique to international commerce. As we saw in Chapter 10, because of our federal system, with states and national government both having authority to tax, the same kind of situation can arise when a company does business in more than one of our states. Within the United States, the Supreme Court can act as an umpire when disputes arise as to which state has the power to tax which transactions. Unfortunately, there is as yet no similar body for international trade. Multinational operations must rely on the fairness and good sense of the national courts where they are doing business. Japan Line successfully argued this point in the next case.

Multiple taxation is a problem for firms doing international business.

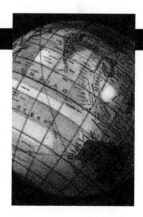

JAPAN LINE, LTD. V. COUNTY OF LOS ANGELES

441 U.S 434 (1979)

Facts: Japan Line and five other Japanese shipping corporations sued for a refund of personal property taxes paid under protest. Los Angeles County (and other political subdivisions in California) were taxing the large cargo containers which were used to transport goods in international trade. The containers were all registered in a Japanese "home port," just as were the ships in which the containers were carried, and fully taxed in Japan. Japan does not impose its personal property taxes on U.S. ships and containers which happen to come to Japan as part of international trade. The California political subdivisions were "apportioning" their taxes and were not discriminating against international commerce. Taxes for the three years in question totalled over $550,000. The trial court held for Japan Line, but the California Appeals Court reversed, and the State Supreme Court affirmed that latter decision.

Issue: Does this local property tax violate the Commerce Clause of the U.S. Constitution?

Decision: Yes. Judgment of California Supreme Court is reversed.

Rule: A tax on the instrumentalities of international commerce must be examined more closely by the courts than one applied only to property used in interstate commerce.

Discussion: *By Justice* BLACKMUN:

"First, California's tax results in multiple taxation of the instrumentalities of foreign commerce. By stipulation, [plaintiffs'] containers are owned, based and registered in Japan; they are used exclusively in international commerce; and they remain outside Japan only so long as needed to complete their international missions. Under these circumstances, Japan has the right and the power to tax the containers in full. California's tax, however, creates more than the risk of multiple taxation; it produces multiple taxation in fact. [Plaintiffs'] containers not only 'are subject to property tax...in Japan,'...but, as the trial court found, 'are, in fact, taxed in Japan.'... Thus, if [the taxes] were sustained, [plaintiffs] 'would be paying a double tax.'...

"Second, California's tax prevents this nation from 'speaking with one voice' in regulating foreign trade. The desirability of uniform treatment of containers used exclusively in foreign commerce is evidenced by the Customs Convention on Containers, which the United States and Japan have signed.... Under this Convention, containers temporarily imported are admitted free of 'all duties and taxes whatsoever chargeable by reason of importation.'... The Convention reflects a national policy to remove impediments to the use of containers as 'instruments of international traffic.'... California's tax, however, will frustrate attainment of federal uniformity. It is stipulated that American-owned containers are not taxed in Japan.... California's tax thus creates an asymmetry in international maritime taxation operating to Japan's disadvantage. The risk of retaliation by Japan, under these circumstances, is acute, and such retaliation of necessity would be felt by the Nation as a whole.... California, by its unilateral act, cannot be permitted to place these impediments before this Nation's conduct of its foreign relations and its foreign trade.

"Because California's...tax, as applied to [plaintiffs'] containers, results in multiple taxation of the instrumentalities of foreign commerce, and because it prevents the Federal Government from 'speaking with one voice' in international trade, the tax is inconsistent with Congress' power to 'regulate Commerce with foreign Nations.' We hold the tax, as applied, unconstitutional under the Commerce Clause."

Ethical Dimension

Would it make sense for every "home state" to tax property of its companies at full value, so the companies could then make the same argument as Japan Line did?

●

■ Constitutional Limitations on U.S. States' Taxing Power

In order to provide a national trading market, the U.S. Constitution places several restrictions on the states' power to tax commerce from outside their own borders. Ships from one state cannot be required to pay duties (tariffs) to another. No state may, without the consent of Congress, impose any duties on imports or exports "except what may be absolutely necessary for executing its inspection laws." Any such revenues "shall be for the use of the Treasury of the United States; and all such laws shall be subject to the revision and control of the Congress." Similarly, no state can impose any "duty of tonnage" (on ships) without the consent of Congress. These constitutional limitations can be seen operating in the following case.

Limits are placed on states' power to tax foreign companies.

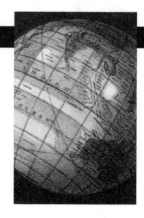

XEROX CORP. V. COUNTY OF HARRIS, TEXAS

103 S. Ct. 523 (1982)

Facts: Xerox, a New York corporation, manufactures and sells business machines on a worldwide basis. It has several foreign sales affiliates and owns assembly plants and production facilities in Mexico. It manufactured parts for copying machines in Colorado and New York and then shipped them to Mexico City for assembly. The copiers assembled in Mexico were intended for sale in Latin America; all operating instructions were in Spanish and Portuguese. These machines could not operate on U.S. electrical current without being modified and did not meet the certification standards required for sale in the United States.

After assembly in Mexico, the copiers were taken back to the Customs Service Warehouse in Houston, Texas, where they were stored until orders from Latin America were received. Transportation from Mexico City to Houston and from the Houston Customs Warehouse to the Port of Houston or the Port of Miami were by bonded carrier. Because the copiers were all sold overseas and were under the complete control of the U.S. Customs Service while they were in the United States, Xerox was not required to pay national import duties on them. However, both the city of Houston and the county of Harris, Texas, notified Xerox that it owed personal property taxes. Xerox sued to enjoin collection of the taxes. The trial court held for Xerox. The Texas Appeals Court reversed, and the Texas Supreme Court refused to review that decision.

Issue: Do these local property taxes violate the Commerce Clause?

Decision: Yes. Judgment of Texas Appeals Courts is reversed.

Rule: State and local taxes which conflict with Congress' regulatory plan are preempted by the national law.

Discussion: *By Chief Justice* BURGER:

"Pursuant to its powers under the Commerce Clause, Congress established a comprehensive customs system which includes provisions for government-supervised bonded warehouses where imports may be stored duty-free for prescribed periods. At any time during that period the goods may be withdrawn and re-exported without payment of duty. Only if the goods are withdrawn for domestic sale or stored beyond the prescribed period does any duty become due.... While the goods are in the bonded warehouses they are in the joint custody of the United States Customs Service and the warehouse proprietor and under the continuous control and supervision of the local customs officers.... Detailed regulations control every aspect of the manner in which the warehouses are to be operated....

"In short, Congress created secure and duty free enclaves under federal control in order to encourage merchants here and abroad to make use of American ports. The question is whether it would be compatible with the comprehensive scheme Congress enacted to effect these goals if the states were free to tax such goods while they were lodged temporarily in government regulated bonded storage in this country....

"First, Congress sought...to benefit American industry by remitting taxes otherwise due.... Here, the remission of duties benefitted those shippers using American ports as transshipment centers. Second, the system of customs regulation is...pervasive.... [T]he imported goods were segregated in warehouses under continual federal custody and supervision. Finally, the state tax was large enough...to offset substantially the very benefits Congress intended to confer by remitting the duty. In short, freedom from state taxation is...necessary to the Congressional scheme here....

"Accordingly, we hold that state property taxes on goods stored under bond in a customs warehouse are preempted by Congress' comprehensive regulation of customs duties."

Ethical Dimension

Is it fair that the companies who are selling such goods are avoiding paying local taxes, while sellers who are selling goods within the country are carrying the whole tax burden?

■ Tariff Policies

The tariff is usually a percentage of the value of the imported goods. Historically, nations have used high tariffs to protect their newly developing industries against foreign competition. U.S. tariffs have been raised and lowered over the years, as the national government has changed its international trading policies. Congress establishes our basic tariff policy and rates, but day-to-day administration is delegated to the Customs Service. Appeals from their determination of the appropriate rate may be made to the U.S. Court of International Trade and then to the Court of Appeals for the Federal Circuit and the U.S. Supreme Court.

■ General Agreement on Tariffs and Trade (GATT)

GATT is a multilateral treaty, now signed by some 80 countries, providing for the reduction or elimination of tariffs. It generally requires that all countries' products be given treatment equal to that of the "most favored nation" under a country's trade policies. Exceptions are permitted for developing countries and also for regional organizations such as the European Community.

GATT attempts to reduce tariff barriers.

The tariff reductions required by GATT do not apply, however, if the country of origin subsidizes exports of its companies. Countries to which such goods are exported can impose **"countervailing duties"** on the preferred goods. Tariffs are imposed to equalize the amount of the government subsidy. The Trade Agreements Act of 1979 authorizes such countervailing duties where a foreign government's trade subsidy materially injures a U.S. industry, threatens to do so, or impedes establishment of one.

The 1979 Act also deals with another unfair international practice—**dumping**. The foreign producer "dumps" goods on the U.S. market by selling them here at unfairly low prices, below the price charged in the home market, or perhaps even below the cost of production. The reason for doing so is to gain market share in the United States, and, often, to drive out or to injure U.S. competitors. The Department of Commerce's International Trade Commission (ITC) hears and decides such complaints. If the dumping charge is proved to have injured a U.S. industry, the ITC can impose an antidumping duty on the imports involved.

INTERNATIONAL CARRIER LIABILITY RULES

To facilitate international trade, various treaties and conventions governing the liability of carriers of goods have been agreed to by most of the major trading nations. These international rules may of course vary considerably from the carrier liability rules in force within a particular country.

Ground Carrier Rules

The international ground carrier rules of most concern to U.S. shippers are those in force in Europe for trucks and railroads. In this case, the carriers' liabilities are in fact similar to those imposed by U.S. law. Both types of ground carriers are liable for loss or damage to goods, with only limited exceptions—such as damage caused by improper packing by the shipper or caused by government actions or natural disasters. The European conventions for both types of ground carriers limit the amount of the carrier's liability, but the shipper may declare and pay for a higher amount. These European rules are thus similar in overall effect to the U.S. rules discussed in Chapter 17.

Water Carrier Rules

There are some very different international rules for carriage of goods by sea. Most of these are contained in a treaty entered into at the Hague, Netherlands, and amended in 1968 by a further agreement negotiated at Visby, Sweden. The United States officially adopted the Hague rules in the Carriage of Goods by Sea Act (COGSA), but has not ratified the relatively minor 1968 amendments.

Under international rules, carriers of goods are not liable for losses beyond their control.

Under the Hague rules, just as is true for land carriers, sea carriers are not liable for cargo losses which are beyond their control—war, piracy, government seizure, storms, and the like. The sea carrier must furnish a "seaworthy" ship, must stow the cargo carefully on the ship, and must exercise reasonable care in operating the ship. The sea carrier would be liable for losses caused by a breach of any of those duties, but generally not otherwise. The U.S. COGSA limits the amount of liability to $500 for each package unless the shipper declares and pays for a higher value. The Hague rules limit the sea carrier's liability to the value specified in the contract for shipment.

The owner of cargo being transported by ship may be held liable to the owners of other cargo on the ship in several situations. If one batch of cargo somehow causes damage to other cargo, the first owner will have to reimburse the others. Sea law recognizes a doctrine called **general average**, which views the voyage as a kind of joint sharing of the hazards of the sea. If the cargo of one owner is sacrificed to save the ship, each other owner must contribute a proportionate part of the loss. Each cargo owner's share is calculated by dividing the value of its cargo by the total at risk on the voyage: the value of all cargo, plus the value of the ship, plus the total shipping fees. Since the U.S. Supreme Court validated such clauses in the New Jason case, many shipment contracts provide that the rule of general average will be applied to any losses of cargo for which the carrier is not at fault.

Each cargo owner must bear a part of any loss at sea.

■ Air Carrier Rules

The Warsaw Convention, mentioned in the last chapter, governs carriage of goods, as well as passengers, by air. Like the rules for ground and water carriers, it too makes the carrier liable for the loss of goods, subject to similar limited exceptions. The Warsaw Convention, however, limits the air carrier's liability on the basis of the weight of the cargo. The shipper can declare and pay for a higher value if it wishes to do so.

R ESTRICTIONS ON INTERNATIONAL FIRMS

Governments may also impose various other types of restrictions on foreign firms. Particularly where local production operations are being conducted, the host country may try to ensure fair treatment for local workers and local investors.

■ Local Participation Requirements

Every nation wishes to avoid being exploited by foreign investors. Canada objects to domination by U.S. corporations. The United States is concerned about purchases of its land and businesses by Japanese and Arab investors. How much more danger, then, would there be where the target country is small, weak, and economically undeveloped. The typical antidote for foreign domination is a requirement for local participation in the investment. This may take several forms. The host country may require that a local subsidiary have majority local ownership. A certain percentage of local managers may be required.

Another option is required training for local workers to qualify them for management positions. If products are to be made and sold within the host country, it may require that they contain a minimum percentage of locally added value (parts and labor). Foreign firms may be completely prohibited from competing in some key industries, such as mining, electric power, transportation, and communication. Foreign technology may be purchased and used, and foreign experts employed, but actual operations run exclusively by local companies or by the government itself.

■ Repatriation of Profits

Some countries limit the amount of profits which can be sent out of the country by a foreign firm.

Another frequently used limitation on foreign firms is a restriction on taking the local profits out of the country. Restrictions can be imposed on converting the local funds earned into one of the major international currencies. Limits could be set on how much could be transferred out of the country each year. Higher income taxes can be imposed if the earnings are to be taken out of the host country rather than being reinvested there. Removal of capital investments can also be subject to restrictions.

As a possible alternative to restricting the removal of profits from local sales, the arrangement with the host country may provide for "payment" in goods produced with the foreign technology. The foreign firm that supplied the technology for the battery factory simply takes part of the batteries made there as payment. Alternatively, the foreign firm may use the money it received for its technology to buy the goods produced by its technology. These goods are then exported by the foreign firm to wherever there is a market, and the foreign firm receives the price for the goods at the place specified in the sale contract. The profits resulting from this "buy-back" arrangement are thus already outside the host country. In another variation, the foreign firm sells its technology to the host country and then uses the local currency in which it is paid to buy the goods of other local producers, which it exports and sells at a profit. In the simplest arrangement, the foreign firm simply exchanges its goods for local goods which it can export and sell. These various types of "**countertrade**" have been used frequently with socialist and other nonmarket economies.

■ Nationalization

Some countries have nationalized private business assets.

Since the Bolshevik Revolution in Russia in 1917, there has been one additional serious threat to foreign investors. In countries accepting the socialist theory which requires state ownership of the means of production, nationalization of private property could occur at any time. Under Marxist theory, all means of production should be owned by the state, held in common for all. The Bolsheviks proceeded to implement this theory vigorously, seizing land, factories, equipment, and bank accounts. As socialist governments were established in other countries, similar nationalization programs were adopted. In nations such as Great Britain, with strong traditions of the rule of law, compensation was paid when businesses were taken over by the government. Communist governments in such nations as Cuba might or might not provide prompt and adequate compensation.

A foreign firm suffering such seizure of its assets will probably not have an adequate court remedy. Both the act of state doctrine and the sovereign immunity doctrine will operate to prevent court challenges to the government policy of nationalization of industries. In fact, in the landmark *Sabbatino* case in which the U.S. Supreme Court upheld the validity of Cuba's nationalization scheme, the U.S. Department of State filed a brief in support of the Cuban government.

Where there is a treaty between the United States and the other nation which requires payment of compensation for expropriated property, U.S. courts may have a basis for recognizing the company's claim. If the other nation has property in this country, a U.S. court judgment could then be enforced against it. If that nation has property in another country, for instance a bank account in London, the U.S. company would have to convince the courts there to enforce the judgment of the U.S. court. The next case illustrates some of these issues.

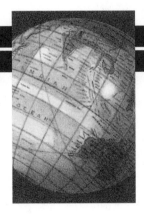

KALAMAZOO SPICE EXTRACTION CO. V. PROVISIONAL MILITARY GOVERNMENT OF SOCIALIST ETHIOPIA

729 F.2d 422 (U.S. 6th Cir. Court of Appeals, 1984)

Facts: Kalamazoo Spice is a U.S. corporation which established Ethiopian Spice Extraction Company (ESESCO) as a joint venture with Ethiopian citizens in 1966. ESESCO was organized as an Ethiopian corporation with Kalamazoo Spice Extraction Co. (KZOO) owning 80 percent of the stock. KZOO provided capital and training. Spice production began in 1970. In 1974, a revolution resulted in the Provisional Military Government of Socialist Ethiopia (PMGSE), which proceeded to nationalize much of the country's industry. KZOO's interest in ESESCO was reduced from 80 percent to about 39 percent. PMGSE's Compensation Commission offered to pay $450,000 in local currency for KZOO's claim of $11 million. KZOO refused the offer. Meanwhile, ESESCO had been shipping spices to KZOO—some $1.9 million worth. KZOO kept making payments for the spices until it saw that PMGSE did not really intend to pay for the expropriated property. ESESCO sued for payment for the spices delivered. KZOO counterclaimed for the value of its seized assets. The U.S. District Court in Michigan held for ESESCO and PMGSE, and KZOO appealed.

Issue: Does the act of state doctrine prevent a court from considering claims based on a nationalization of property?

Decision: No. Judgment reversed; case remanded.

Rule: Expropriation claims may be heard as "set-offs" against the foreign government's claims in certain exceptional cases.

Discussion: *By Judge KEITH:*

"'The judicial branch will not examine the validity of a taking of property within its own territory by a foreign sovereign government, extant and recognized by this country at the time of suit, in the absence of a treaty of other unambiguous agreement regarding controlling legal principles, even if the complaint alleges that the taking violates customary international law.'...

"[KZOO asserts that this rule] and the existence of a treaty between the United States and Ethiopia...requires a 'treaty' exception to the rule that a United States court will not exercis jurisdiction over a foreign sovereign for an act done by that sovereign within its borders. The treaty in existence between the United States and Ethiopia is the 1953 Treaty of Amity and Economic Relations.... Article VIII, paragraph two of that treaty provides: 'Property of nationals and companies of either High Contracting Party, including interests in property, shall receive the most constant protection and security within the territories of the other High Contracting Party. Such property shall not be taken without prompt payment of just and effective compensation.'...

"The 1953...Treaty...is one of a series of treaties, also known as the FCN [Friendship, Commerce, and Navigation] Treaties, between the United States and foreign nations negotiated after World War II. As the legislative history of these treaties indicates, they were adopted to protect American citizens and their interests abroad.... Almost all of these treaties contain sections which provide for 'prompt, adequate, and effective compensation,' 'just compensation,' or similar language regarding compensation for expropriated property....

"It should be apparent that the greater the degree of codification or consensus concerning a particular area of international law, the more appropriate it is for the judiciary to render decisions regarding it, since the courts can then focus on the application of an agreed principle to circumstances of fact rather than on the sensitive task of establishing a principle not inconsistent with the national interest or with international justice....

"Numerous treaties employ the standard of compensation used in the 1953 Treaty.... Undoubtedly, the widespread use of this compensation standard is evidence that it is an agreed upon principle in international law.

"Nor will adjudication in this matter interfere with any efforts by the Executive Branch to resolve this matter. In fact, the Executive Branch has also intervened in this matter through the Departments of State, Treasury, and Justice who have filed a joint amicus ["friend of the court"] brief urging that the 1953 Treaty of Amity makes the act of state doctrine inapplicable. Obviously, the Executive Branch feels that an adjudication in this matter is appropriate. Thus, the Supreme Court's concern...for judicial interference with foreign policy activity by the Executive Branch is not a consideration in this case.

"Additionally, there is a great national interest to be served in this case, i.e., the recognition and execution of treaties that we enter into with foreign nations. Article VI of the Constitution provides that treaties made under the authority of the United States shall be the supreme law of the land. Accordingly, the Supreme Court has recognized that treaties, in certain circumstances, have the 'force and effect of a legislative enactment.'... The failure to recognize a properly executed treaty would indeed be an egregious error because of the position that treaties occupy in our body of laws."

Ethical Dimension

Why should a U.S. court be able to judge the government policies of another nation? Why should a treaty make any difference?

●

INTERNATIONAL ANTITRUST CONCERNS

Not all nations take the same view of competition as does the United States. Practices which we may condemn as restrictive and anticompetitive may be tolerated, or even encouraged, elsewhere. Nations in different stages of economic development may wish to promote large business combinations to better compete on the world market. Nations adopting different economic theories may have different views of certain business practices. These differences are brought into sharp focus when the United States attempts to enforce its antitrust policies against conduct outside its borders.

◼ Uniqueness of the Sherman Act

The U.S. sometimes applies the Sherman Act to activities outside the United States.

Commercial transactions involving more than one country always present the possibility of a conflict between the laws of the nations concerned. For the first half of its 100-year existence, the Sherman Act provided the U.S. economy with a body of law which set it apart from other nations. In most of the world, businesses were free to combine and to contract as they saw fit. Governments in many cases encouraged and sponsored cartels and combinations of businesses, so they could better compete internationally. Virtually alone among the world's economies, the United States prohibited cooperation among competitors and outlawed a wide range of distribution arrangements. Foreign firms marketing their products and services here might find that they needed to adapt their distribution practices to comply with U.S. law. Contrariwise, U.S. firms selling overseas found that local law permitted them to do many things which would be illegal at home.

◼ Extraterritorial Jurisdiction

As long as each country applies its own law only to acts which occur within its own borders, conflicts of law are minimized. But when one nation says that its laws also apply to actions taken in other countries, there are obviously going to be problems. Beginning in 1945, U.S. courts have applied our antitrust laws to the overseas activities of both U.S. and foreign firms when those activities have substantial effects within the U.S.

Judge Learned Hand's opinion for the Second Circuit in the 1945 *Alcoa* case indicated that conduct which was intended to have an effect within the United States could be subject to prosecution under U.S. law. In the intervening decades, our courts have been trying to define just how substantial these effects have to be to justify the application of U.S. law. The 1977 Guidelines issued by the Justice Department's Antitrust Division state that there is no U.S. jurisdiction unless the overseas activity has a "substantial and foreseeable effect" here. The U.S. Courts of Appeal do not agree on what the test should be. Three other Circuits have approved the "jurisdictional rule of reason" test announced by the Ninth Circuit in the *Timberlane* case in 1976. Under that test, the court should look at the actual effect on the U.S. market of the challenged conduct. Two Circuits have doubts that the Ninth Circuit has stated the proper standards. The American Law Institute recommended the test in its 1985 revision of the Restatement of Foreign Relations Law. The Supreme Court does not quite resolve the issue in the following case.

MATSUSHITA ELECTRIC INDUS. CO. V. ZENITH RADIO CORP.

106 S. CT. 1348 (1986)

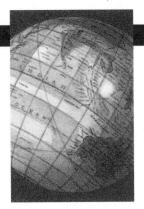

Facts: Zenith and other U.S. manufacturers of television sets sued twenty-one Japanese and Japanese-controlled TV makers, alleging a conspiracy to restrain trade in violation of the Sherman Act, price discrimination in violation of the Robinson-Patman Act, and other illegal activities. There was proof of an agreement in Japan that each Japanese manufacturer would sell to only five U.S. distributors, and that the Japanese Ministry of International Trade and Industry (MITI) had established, or helped establish, minimum prices for consumer goods exports to the United States. The U.S. District Court granted defendants' motion for summary judgment, but the Court of Appeals reversed, holding that there was a material issue of fact that required a trial. According to Justice Powell, the Court of Appeals' main opinion was 69 pages long, that of the District Court over 200 pages, and the total opinions in this case would fill an entire volume. In support of their arguments to the Supreme Court, the parties filed a 40-*volume* "appendix" of evidence, produced by "several years of detailed discovery." The courts thus had plenty of "raw material" to work with.

Issue: Is there sufficient evidence to infer an antitrust conspiracy which caused antitrust harm to plaintiffs?

Decision: No. Court of Appeals reversed; case remanded for dismissal.

Rule: To sustain a private antitrust lawsuit against a motion for summary judgment, there must be some indication in the evidence that a conspiracy existed and caused harm to the plaintiff.

Discussion: *By Justice* POWELL:
"We begin by emphasizing what [plaintiffs'] claim is *not*. [Plaintiffs] cannot recover antitrust damages based solely on an alleged cartelization of the Japanese market, because American antitrust laws do not regulate the competitive conditions of other nations' economies.... Nor can [plaintiffs] recover damages for any conspiracy by [defendants] to charge higher than competitive prices in the American market. Such conduct would indeed violate the Sherman Act..., but it would not injure [plaintiffs]: as [defendants'] competitors, [plaintiffs] stand to gain from any conspiracy to raise the market price.... Finally, for the same reason, [plaintiffs] cannot recover for a conspiracy to impose nonprice restraints that have the effect of either

raising market price or limiting output. Such restrictions, though harmful to competition, actually *benefit* competitors by making supracompetitive pricing more attractive. Thus, neither [defendants'] alleged supracompetitive pricing in Japan, nor the five-company rule that limited distribution in this country, nor the check prices insofar as they established minimum prices in this country, can by themselves give [plaintiffs] a cognizable claim against [defendants] for antitrust damages. The Court of Appeals therefore erred to the extent that it found evidence of these alleged conspiracies to be 'direct evidence' of a conspiracy that injured [plaintiffs]....

"The alleged conspiracy's failure to achieve its ends in the two decades of its asserted operation is strong evidence that the conspiracy does not in fact exist. Since the losses in such a conspiracy [to engage in predatory pricing] accrue before its gains, they must be repaid with interest....

"Nor does the possibility that [defendants] have obtained supracompetitive profits in the Japanese market change this calculation. Whether or not [defendants] have the *means* to sustain substantial losses in this country over a long period of time, they have no *motive* to sustain such losses absent some strong likelihood that the alleged conspiracy in this country will eventually pay off. The courts below found no evidence of any such success—the facts are actually to the contrary.... More important, there is nothing to suggest any relationship between [defendants'] profits in Japan and the amount [defendants] could expect to gain from a conspiracy to monopolize the American market. In the absence of any such evidence, the possible existence of supracompetitive profits in Japan simply cannot overcome the economic obstacles to the ultimate success of this alleged predatory conspiracy."

Ethical Dimension

Should U.S. courts be prevented from acting when overseas firms conspire to destroy their U.S. competitors?

●

■ Blocking Laws and Clawback Laws

Some countries have passed statutes to prevent enforcement of U.S. courts' orders.

Some foreign governments have tried to prevent our efforts to apply our law to the whole world by enacting statutes. **Blocking statutes** prevent the enforcement of U.S. courts' orders in that other country. These laws are typically concerned with U.S. court orders for pretrial discovery of documents. Australia, Canada, France, Germany, and the United Kingdom, among others, have such blocking laws. Even where such a law is in force, the (U.S.) Restatement says it will not necessarily control the U.S. court proceedings. A party can be required to make a good faith effort to get the foreign government's permission to produce the evidence. If permission is not granted, normal sanctions for contempt of court should (usually) not be applied, but the court can decide fact questions against the party who failed to produce. There is a 1972 Hague Convention which establishes procedures for gathering evidence overseas, but our Justice Department says that these procedures are optional, not exclusive.

The Protection of Trading Interests Act passed by the U.K. in 1980 goes beyond merely blocking U.S. court orders; it also contains a so-called "clawback" provision. U.K. companies can sue in the British courts to recover any treble damages they have had to pay under U.S. antitrust law; the U.K. subsidiaries of the successful U.S. plaintiff will be the defendants in the British lawsuit. Not only U.K. companies, but also the companies of any other nation with a similar clawback provision can use the British courts to sue U.S. subsidiaries operating in the U.K. The clawback provision represents an aggressive effort (by a close friend and ally) to stop the U.S. from applying its laws to conduct outside its borders.

■ Foreign Antitrust Law after 1945

Many German industrialists had supported Hitler. After suffering horrendous losses in two world wars against the German military-industrial complex, within less than thirty years, the Russians in particular wanted to make sure that it would not happen again—at least not soon. They favored a complete dismantling of German industry and did in fact move large quantities of equipment and machinery from East Germany to the Soviet Union.

While there was also some similar sentiment in the western nations, U.S. leaders soon realized that we would have to help rebuild Western Europe if it was to resist Communism. While post-war Germany did adopt an antitrust law aimed at preventing the rebuilding of the giant pre-war cartels, most effort was directed at reviving the European economies, including Germany's. Europe's industries needed to be encouraged and nurtured, not regulated; indeed, there was very little to "regulate."

In 1958, the Treaty of Rome established the European Economic Community, consisting then of Belgium, France, Italy, Luxembourg, the Netherlands, and West Germany. Article 85 of the Rome Treaty prevents a firm from abusing its "dominant position" in an industry to injure competition. Article 86 forbids mergers which would injure competition within the Community. These articles reflect the spirit of

The Treaty of Rome does have antitrust rules for the European Community.

the Sherman Act and the Clayton Act, although they obviously will be applied differently. They do not completely preempt national antitrust laws in the EEC nations, although the treaty prevails over national law to the extent of any conflict. Each of the other six member-nations who have joined the EEC since 1958 is also subject to these antitrust sections of the Rome Treaty. As a result, the largest trading bloc in the world is governed by competition rules similar in objective, if not in detail, to the U.S. antitrust laws.

The U.K. is the other European nation (along with Germany) which has a strong domestic antitrust law. It even has an enforcement body similar to the U.S. Federal Trade Commission—the Office of Fair Trading. The OFT was established in 1973 to protect British consumers against unfair trade practices. It provides consumers with information and advice. It consults with the EEC's competition commission and enforces the EEC's rulings in the U.K. It is headed by a Director-General, who has the power to investigate proposed mergers and to refer those which may have anti-competitive effects to the Monopolies and Mergers Commission for further action. A merger of British and German firms would thus have to pass review by three sets of enforcers—British, German, and EEC.

Large Japanese conglomerates were broken up immediately after World War II.

Many of the same dynamics were at work in postwar Japan. As the primary occupying power, our initial policy was aimed at breaking up the *zaibatsu*—the giant trading companies. The *zaibatsu* had combined banking, manufacturing, and marketing units into huge trusts, which totally dominated the Japanese economy between the wars. As was true in Germany, many Japanese industrialists supported the warlords; some actively collaborated during the Second World War. There was thus strong U.S. sentiment against permitting them to reassert their strength. When the Communists took control of China in 1948/49, and the Cold War came to the Far East, our Japanese policy changed radically. The U.S. Government moved forcefully to assist Japan's economic and social recovery. Thus, after an initial "importation" of antitrust policies, the emphasis changed to one of industrial development. Today, Japanese law and policy clearly permit much more "cooperation" between firms than would be lawful within the U.S.

▌NTO THE 21ST CENTURY

With the passing of the Cold War, international trade issues are clearly a major concern of those of us who inhabit this small, fragile planet. It is true that there are still thousands of nuclear missiles in place, but their use becomes increasingly less likely. The U.S. is unloading its nuclear arsenal and is ceasing manufacture of these weapons of mass destruction. "Conventional" forces are being substantially reduced. People are still shooting at each other, and innocents are still dying.

Perhaps we will always suffer such individual wrongs, and even civil wars and international wars. But at least the likelihood of the "doomsday," "end-of-the-world," all-out nuclear war has substantially receded.

Our task now is a positive one, perhaps even more difficult than the negative one of the past forty-plus years—not just to avoid mutual destruction, but to provide a rich and meaningful life for all the world's citizens. International trade is clearly one of the key parts in this new world order. The challenge is to provide each person with the opportunity to develop fully and to receive a fair return for individual contributions of time and effort.

With the renunciation of communism by the nations of Eastern Europe and the end of the Soviet Union, it seems clear that Marxism is not the answer to the problem of world poverty. Some third world nations do continue to mouth Marxist slogans, and China—the world's largest nation—is still officially Communist. But even in China, the state-owned enterprises stagnate, while its (capitalist) Special Economic Zones are booming, and its incentives to private farming have greatly increased agricultural output. Surely to have any chance of success, whatever international system is developed must provide individual incentives and individual rewards.

Socialism failed for precisely this reason. Most people are willing to make some sacrifices for the common good—for a while. When the "common good" takes on a life of its own, however, and is corrupted to mean the "good" of a select few, people are bound to become disillusioned. A system based on envy of those better off, and offering only the "hope" of shared poverty, soon becomes less appealing when the leaders are not really sharing the poverty of the masses.

In contrast, an international system based on free exchange offers real hope for the future. There is no need to assume an international "pie" of a given size, such that an increase in the size of one slice necessarily means a decrease in the size of someone else's slice. The size of the pie is unlimited; at least, the only limits are our own imaginations and willingness to work. We have shown we can do anything we wish—conquer space, land on the moon, mine the depths of the oceans. "Job One" as we prepare to enter the new century is the development of an international trading system which provides for the needs of all the world's people.

REVIEW

Just as is true for business within this country, international trade is subject to many governmental regulations. Nations have historically attempted to establish trade policies which would maximize their own national wealth. Governments usually try to encourage exports, but there may also be restrictions on exports of certain technology. A nation's foreign policy may also dictate restrictions on imports to protect domestic producers.

International taxation also poses problems for business firms. There are many troublesome questions having to do with which nation can tax which activities. There are also tariff barriers to trade. Governments may try to impose tariffs to protect their local market from foreign competition. The General Agreement on Tariffs and Trade is an international effort to minimize these tariff barriers.

To try to facilitate international shipments of goods, rules have been developed for water, sea, and air carriers. While not all nations have agreed to all these rules, efforts to promote uniformity are continuing.

Nations may impose various requirements on foreign firms doing business there. Local personnel and ownership may be required. There may be restrictions on the removal of profits from the country. In extreme cases, assets may be nationalized by the host country.

The Sherman Act has been interpreted by U.S. courts as being applicable to international trade. Other countries generally do not believe that acts within their borders should be judged by U.S. courts according to U.S. law. Such conflicts have been difficult to resolve. Germany and the United Kingdom also have strong antitrust laws, as does the European Community. International firms may thus be subject to several such laws when doing business in Western Europe.

REVIEW QUESTIONS AND PROBLEMS

1. What are "gray market" goods? How are they different from counterfeit goods?

2. What is "dumping"? Why is it an international trade problem?

3. What is the rule of "general average"? Why is it significant to firms making international shipments of goods?

4. Why does the Foreign Corrupt Practices Act permit making small payments to foreign officials to do their assigned duties, but prohibit payments to them as a bribe for making contracts?

5. What restrictions does the U.S. place on exports?

6. Why does the U.S. try to impose antitrust sanctions on firms for their actions outside the U.S.?

7. By treaty (the North American Free Trade Agreement), the U.S. and Canada have agreed to permit certain products manufactured in either country to be imported into the other without paying normal tariffs. To be eligible for this exemption, the product must contain more than 50 percent "North American" content. Rondo Motors, the wholly owned subsidiary of a Spanish company, has a large car assembly plant in Quebec, Canada. It sends large numbers of cars into the U.S. In calculating the 50 percent content to qualify for the tariff exemption, Rondo counted major sub-assemblies such as the cars' engines as "North American" if their values were over half "North American." In fact, substantial portions of the engines, drive trains, and other major components were parts imported from Europe or Asia. The U.S.

government claims the value of each small part needs to be considered in deciding whether the car as a whole is more than 50 percent North American. Which "valuation" approach is correct? Explain.

8. Deepsix Inc. holds the U.S. patent rights on a certain fish-cleaning machine. It thus has the exclusive rights to "make" or "sell" the machines in the U.S. Trammel Corporation, located in Texas, is now making the component parts for a very similar machine. It does not assemble the machine or sell the components in the U.S., but rather ships the components, in three separate crates, to customers outside the U.S. Deepsix sues for an injunction to prevent violation of its patent rights. How should a U.S. District Court rule in this case, and why?

9. As part of a massive economic development plan, the national government of Crotonia contracted with various suppliers around the world for the purchase of a total of 20 million metric tons of cement. The cement was to be delivered and unloaded at Crotonia's only ocean port, Nowaygone, over the course of the next year. The contracts provided for daily fees of up to $4000 per boat for any delays at Nowaygone in unloading the cargoes of cement. In fact, the limited facilities at the port could unload only 1,000,000 metric tons of cement a year. When boats began to stack up outside the port and the daily fees began to add up, the Crotonian government passed an embargo. No ships would be permitted to unload at Nowaygone without the government's specific permission, and the cement contracts would have to be renegotiated to make allowance for the inevitable delays in deliveries. Cementors, Inc., one of the sellers, sued in U.S. District Court to enforce the terms of its original contract with Crotonia. What result in this case, and why?

10. Foodland Industries, a U.S. company, bought a Swiss cheese business from OLC, an Italian corporation. The contract was signed in Berlin, and provided that any disputes between the parties would be arbitrated in Stockholm under Swedish rules. Foodland alleges that OLC made certain misrepresentations which violate the U.S. securities laws and files a lawsuit in U.S. District Court in New York. OLC moves to dismiss the case. How should the court rule? Discuss.

SUGGESTIONS FOR FURTHER READING

Davidow, "U.S. Antitrust, Free Trade, and Nonmarket Economics," *Journal Of World Trade Law* (November–December 1978): 473.

Dick, "Learning by Doing and Dumping in the Semi-Conductor Industry," *Journal Of Law & Economics* (April 1991): 133.

Leinster, "Vietnam: Business Rushes to Get In," *Fortune* 127 (April 5, 1993): 98.

Mahaney, "The Foreign Corrupt Practices Act: Curse or Cure?" *American Business Law Journal* 19 (Spring 1981): 73.

Pomeranz, "Toward a New International Order in Government Procurement," *Public Contract Law Journal* 12 (March 1982): 129.

APPENDIX A
THE CONSTITUTION OF THE UNITED STATES

PREAMBLE

We the People of the United States, in Order to form a more perfect Union, establish Justice, insure domestic Tranquility, provide for the common Defence, promote the general Welfare, and secure the Blessings of Liberty to ourselves and our Posterity, do ordain and establish this Constitution for the United States of America.

ARTICLE I

Section 1. All legislative Powers herein granted shall be vested in a Congress of the United States, which shall consist of a Senate and a House of Representatives.

Section 2. [1] The House of Representatives shall be composed of Members chosen every second Year by the People of the several States, and the Electors in each State shall have the Qualifications requisite for Electors of the most numerous Branch of the State Legislature.

[2] No Person shall be a Representative who shall not have attained to the Age of twenty five Years, and been seven Years a Citizen of the United States, and who shall not, when elected, be an Inhabitant of that State in which he shall be chosen.

[3] Representatives and direct Taxes shall be apportioned among the several States which may be included within this Union, according to their respective Numbers, which shall be determined by adding to the whole Number of free Persons, including those bound to Service for a Term of Years, and excluding Indians not taxed, three fifths of all other Persons. The actual Enumeration shall be made within three Years after the first Meeting of the Congress of the United States, and within every subsequent Term

of ten Years, in such Manner as they shall by Law direct. The Number of Representatives shall not exceed one for every thirty Thousand, but each State shall have at Least one Representative; and until such enumeration shall be made, the State of New Hampshire shall be entitled to chuse three, Massachusetts eight, Rhode Island and Providence Plantations one, Connecticut five, New York six, New Jersey four, Pennsylvania eight, Delaware one, Maryland six, Virginia ten, North Carolina five, South Carolina five, and Georgia three.

[4] When vacancies happen in the Representation from any State, the Executive Authority thereof shall issue Writs of Election to fill such Vacancies.

[5] The House of Representatives shall chuse their Speaker and other Officers; and shall have the sole Power of Impeachment.

Section 3. [1] The Senate of the United States shall be composed of two Senators from each State, chosen by the Legislature thereof, for six Years; and each Senator shall have one Vote.

[2] Immediately after they shall be assembled in Consequence of the first Election, they shall be divided as equally as may be into three Classes. The Seats of the Senators of the first Class shall be vacated at the Expiration of the Second Year, of the second Class at the Expiration of the fourth Year, and of the third Class at the Expiration of the sixth Year, so that one third may be chosen every second Year; and if Vacancies happen by Resignation, or otherwise, during the Recess of the Legislature of any State, the Executive thereof may make temporary Appointments until the next Meeting of the Legislature, which shall then fill such Vacancies.

[3] No Person shall be a Senator who shall not have attained to the Age of thirty Years, and been nine Years a Citizen of the United States, and who shall not, when elected, be an Inhabitant of that State for which he shall be chosen.

[4] The Vice President of the United States shall be President of the Senate, but shall have no Vote, unless they be equally divided.

[5] The Senate shall chuse their other Officers, and also a President pro tempore, in the Absence of the Vice President, or when he shall exercise the Office of President of the United States.

[6] The Senate shall have the sole Power to try all Impeachments. When sitting for that Purpose, they shall be on Oath or Affirmation. When the President of the United States is tried, the Chief Justice shall preside: And no Person shall be convicted without the Concurrence of two thirds of the Members present.

[7] Judgment in Cases of Impeachment shall not extend further than to removal from Office, and disqualification to hold and enjoy any Office of Honor, Trust, or Profit under the United States: but the Party convicted shall nevertheless be liable and subject to Indictment, Trial, Judgment, and Punishment, according to Law.

Section 4. [1] The Times, Places and Manner of holding elections for Senators and Representatives, shall be prescribed in each State by the Legislature thereof; but the Congress may at any time by Law make or alter such Regulations, except as to the Places of chusing Senators.

[2] The Congress shall assemble at least once in every Year, and such Meeting shall be on the first Monday in December, unless they shall by Law appoint a different Day.

Section 5. [1] Each House shall be the Judge of the Elections, Returns, and Qualifications of its own Members, and a Majority of each shall constitute a Quorum to do Business; but a smaller Number may adjourn from day to day, and may be authorized to compel the Attendance of absent Members, in such Manner, and under such Penalties as each House may provide.

[2] Each House may determine the Rules of its Proceedings, punish its Members for disorderly Behavior, and, with the Concurrence of two thirds, expel a Member.

[3] Each House shall keep a Journal of its Proceedings, and from time to time publish the same, excepting such Parts as may in their Judgment require Secrecy; and the Yeas and Nays of the Members of either House on any question shall, at the Desire of one fifth of those Present, be entered on the Journal.

[4] Neither House, during the Session of Congress, shall, without the Consent of the other, adjourn for more than three days, nor to any other Place than that in which the two Houses shall be sitting.

Section 6. [1] The Senators and Representatives shall receive a Compensation for their Services, to be ascertained by Law, and paid out of the Treasury of the United States. They shall in all Cases, except Treason, Felony and Breach of the Peace, be privileged from Arrest during their Attendance at the Session of their respective Houses, and in going to and returning from the same; and for any Speech or Debate in either House, they shall not be questioned in any other Place.

[2] No Senator or Representative shall, during the Time for which he was elected, be appointed to any civil Office under the Authority of the United States, which shall have been created, or the Emoluments whereof shall have been increased during such time; and no Person holding any Office under the United States, shall be a Member of either House during his Continuance in Office.

Section 7. [1] All Bills for raising Revenue shall originate in the House of Representatives; but the Senate may propose or concur with Amendments as on other Bills.

[2] Every Bill which shall have passed the House of Representatives and the Senate, shall, before it becomes a Law, be presented to the President of the United States; If he approve he shall sign it, but if not he shall return it, with his Objections to the House in which it shall have originated, who shall enter the Objections at large on their Journal, and proceed to reconsider it. If after each Reconsideration two thirds of that House shall agree to pass the Bill, it shall be sent together with the Objections, to the other House, by which it shall likewise be reconsidered, and if approved by two thirds of that House, it shall become a Law. But in all such Cases the Votes of both Houses shall be determined by Yeas and Nays, and the Names of the Persons voting for and against the Bill shall be entered on the Journal of each House respectively. If any Bill shall not be returned by the President within ten Days (Sundays excepted) after it shall have been presented to him, the Same shall be a Law, in like Manner as if he had signed it, unless the Congress by their Adjournment prevent its Return in which Case it shall not be a Law.

[3] Every Order, Resolution, or Vote, to Which the Concurrence of the Senate and House of Representatives may be necessary (except on a question of Adjournment) shall be presented to the President of the United States; and before the Same shall take Effect, shall be approved by him, or being disapproved by him, shall be repassed by two thirds of the Senate and House of Representatives, according to the Rules and Limitations prescribed in the Case of a Bill.

Section 8. [1] The Congress shall have Power To lay and collect Taxes, Duties, Imposts and Excises, to pay the Debts and provide for the common Defence and general Welfare of the United States; but all Duties, Imposts and Excises shall be uniform throughout the United States;

[2] To borrow money on the credit of the United States;

[3] To regulate Commerce with foreign Nations, and among the several States, and with the Indian Tribes;

[4] To establish an Uniform Rule of Naturalization, and uniform Laws on the subject of Bankruptcies throughout the United States;

[5] To coin Money, regulate the Value thereof, and of foreign Coin, and fix the Standard of Weights and Measures;

[6] To provide for the Punishment of counterfeiting the Securities and current Coin of the United States;

[7] To Establish Post Offices and Post Roads;

[8] To promote the Progress of Science and useful Arts, by securing for limited Times to Authors and Inventors the exclusive Right to their respective Writings and Discoveries;

[9] To constitute Tribunals inferior to the supreme Court;

[10] To define and punish Piracies and Felonies committed on the high Seas, and Offenses against the Law of Nations;

[11] To declare War, grant Letters of Marque and Reprisal, and make Rules concerning Captures on Land and Water;

[12] To raise and support Armies, but no Appropriation of Money to that Use shall be for a longer Term than two Years;

[13] To provide and maintain a Navy;

[14] To make Rules for the Government and Regulation of the land and naval Forces;

[15] To provide for calling forth the Militia to execute the Laws of the Union, suppress Insurrections and repel Invasions;

[16] To provide for organizing, arming, and disciplining, the Militia, and for governing such Part of them as may be employed in the Service of the United States, reserving to the States respectively, the Appointment of the Officers, and the

Authority of training the Militia according to the discipline prescribed by Congress;

[17] To exercise exclusive Legislation in all Cases whatsoever, over such District (not exceeding then Miles square) as may, by Cession of particular States, and the Acceptance of Congress, become the Seat of the Government of the United States, and to exercise like Authority over all Places purchased by the Consent of the Legislature of the State in which the Same shall be, for the Erection of Forts, Magazines, Arsenals, dock-Yards and other needful Buildings;—And

[18] To make all Laws which shall be necessary and proper for carrying into Execution the foregoing Powers, and all other Powers vested by this Constitution in the Government of the United States, or in any Department or Officer thereof.

Section 9. [1] The Migration or Importation of Such Persons as any of the States now existing shall think proper to admit, shall not be prohibited by the Congress prior to the Year one thousand eight hundred and eight, but a Tax or duty may be imposed on such Importation, not exceeding ten dollars for each Person.

[2] The privilege of the Writ of Habeas Corpus shall not be suspended, unless when in Cases of Rebellion or Invasion the public Safety may require it.

[3] No Bill of Attainder or ex post facto Law shall be passed.

[4] No Capitation, or other direct, Tax shall be laid, unless in Proportion to the Census or Enumeration herein before directed to be taken.

[5] No Tax or Duty shall be laid on Articles exported from any State.

[6] No Preference shall be given by any Regulation of Commerce or Revenue to the Ports of one State over those of another: nor shall Vessels bound to, or from, one State be obliged to enter, clear, or pay Duties in another.

[7] No money shall be drawn from the Treasury, but in Consequence of Appropriations made by Law; and a regular Statement and Account of the Receipts and Expenditures of all public Money shall be published from time to time.

[8] No Title of Nobility shall be granted by the United States: And no Person holding any Office of Profit or Trust under them, shall, without the Consent of the Congress, accept of any present, Emolument, Office, or Title, of any kind whatever, from any King, Prince, or foreign State.

Section 10. [1] No State shall enter into any Treaty, Alliance, or Confederation; grant Letters of Marque and Reprisal; coin Money; emit Bills of Credit; make any Thing but gold and silver Coin a Tender in Payment of Debts; pass any Bill of Attainder, ex post facto Law, or Law impairing the Obligation of Contracts, or grant any Title of Nobility.

[2] No State shall, without the Consent of the Congress, lay any Imposts or Duties on Imports or Exports, except what may be absolutely necessary for executing its inspection Laws: and the net Produce of all Duties and Imposts, laid by any State on Imports or Exports, shall be for the Use of the Treasury of the United States; and all such Laws shall be subject to the Revision and Control of the Congress.

[3] No State shall, without the Consent of Congress, lay any Duty of Tonnage, keep Troops, or Ships of War in time of Peace, enter into any Agreement or Compact with another State, or with a foreign Power, or engage in War, unless actually invaded, or in such imminent Danger as will not admit of delay.

ARTICLE II

Section 1. [1] The executive Power shall be vested in a President of the United States of America. He shall hold his Office during the Term of four Years, and, together with the Vice President, chosen for the same Term, be elected, as follows:

[2] Each State shall appoint, in such Manner as the Legislature thereof may direct, a Number of Electors, equal to the whole Number of Senators and Representatives to which the State may be entitled in the Congress; but no Senator or Representative, or Person holding an Office of Trust or Profit under the United States, shall be appointed an Elector.

[3] The Electors shall meet in their respective States, and vote by Ballot for two Persons, of whom one at least shall not be an Inhabitant of the same State with themselves. And they shall make a List of all the Persons voted for, and of the Number of Votes for each; which List they shall sign and certify, and transmit sealed to the Seat of

the Government of the United States, directed to the President of the Senate. The President of the Senate shall, in the Presence of the Senate and House of Representatives, open all the Certificates, and the Votes shall then be counted. The Person having the greatest Number of Votes shall be the President, if such Number be a Majority of the whole Number of Electors appointed; and if there be more than one who have such Majority, and have an equal Number of Votes, then the House of Representatives shall immediately chuse by Ballot one of them for President; and if no Person have a Majority, then from the five highest on the List the said House shall in like Manner chuse the President. But in chusing the President, the Votes shall be taken by States, the Representation from each State having one Vote; A quorum for this Purpose shall consist of a Member or Members from two thirds of the States, and a Majority of all the States shall be necessary to a Choice. In every Case, after the Choice of the President, the Person having the greater Number of Votes of the Electors shall be the Vice President. But if there shall remain two or more who have equal Votes, the Senate shall chuse from them by Ballot the Vice President.

[4] The Congress may determine the Time of chusing the Electors, and the Day on which they shall give their Votes; which Day shall be the same throughout the United States.

[5] No Person except a natural born Citizen, or a Citizen of the United States, at the time of the Adoption of this Constitution, shall be eligible to the Office of President; neither shall any Person be eligible to that Office who shall not have attained to the Age of thirty-five Years, and been fourteen Years a Resident within the United States.

[6] In Case of the Removal of the President from Office, or of his Death, Resignation, or Inability to discharge the Powers and Duties of the said Office, the Same shall devolve on the Vice President, and the Congress may by Law provide for the Case of Removal, Death, Resignation or Inability, both of the President and Vice President, declaring what Officer shall then act as President, and such Officer shall act accordingly, until the Disability be removed, or a President shall be elected.

[7] The President shall, at stated Times, receive for his Services, a Compensation, which shall neither be increased no diminished during the Period for which he shall have been elected, and he shall not receive within that Period any other Emolument from the United States, or any of them.

[8] Before he enter on the Execution of his Office, he shall take the following Oath or Affirmation: "I do solemnly swear (or affirm) that I will faithfully execute the Office of President of the United States, and will to the best of my Ability, preserve, protect and defend the Constitution of the United States."

Section 2. [1] The President shall be Commander in Chief of the Army and Navy of the United States, and of the militia of the several States, when called into the actual Service of the United States; he may require the Opinion, in writing, of the principal Officer in each of the Executive Departments, upon any Subject relating to the Duties of their respective Offices, and he shall have Power to grant Reprieves and Pardons for Offenses against the United States, except in Cases of Impeachment.

[2] He shall have Power, by and with the Advice and Consent of the Senate to make Treaties, provided two thirds of the Senators present concur; and he shall nominate, and by and with the Advice and Consent of the Senate, shall appoint Ambassadors, other public Ministers and Consuls, Judges of the supreme Court, and all other Officers of the United States, whose Appointments are not herein otherwise provided for, and which shall be established by Law; but the Congress may by Law vest the Appointment of such inferior Officers, as they think proper, in the President alone, in the Courts of Law, or in the Heads of Departments.

[3] The President shall have Power to fill up all Vacancies that may happen during the Recess of the Senate, by granting Commissions which shall expire at the End of their next Session.

Section 3. He shall from time to time give to the Congress Information of the State of the Union, and recommend to their Consideration such Measures as he shall judge necessary and expedient; he may, on extraordinary Occasions, convene both Houses, or either of them, and in Case of Disagreement between them, with Respect to the Time of Adjournment, he may adjourn them to such Time as he shall think proper;

he shall receive Ambassadors and other public Ministers; he shall take Care that the Laws be faithfully executed, and shall Commission all the Officers of the United States.

Section 4. The President, Vice President and all civil Officers of the United States, shall be removed from Office on Impeachment for, and Conviction of, Treason, Bribery, or other high Crimes and Misdemeanors.

ARTICLE III

Section 1. The judicial Power of the United States, shall be vested in one supreme Court, and in such inferior Courts as the Congress may from time to time ordain and establish. The Judges, both of the supreme and inferior Courts, shall hold their Offices during good Behaviour, and shall, at stated Times, receive for their Services a Compensation, which shall not be diminished during their Continuance in Office.

Section 2. [1] The judicial Power shall extend to all Cases, in Law and Equity, arising under this Constitution, the Laws of the United States, and Treaties made, or which shall be made, under their Authority;—to all Cases affecting Ambassadors, other public Ministers and Consuls;—to all Cases of admiralty and maritime Jurisdiction;—to Controversies to which the United States shall be a Party;—to Controversies between two or more States;—between a State and Citizens of another State;—between Citizens of different States;—between Citizens of the same State claiming Lands under the Grants of different States, and between a State, or the Citizens thereof, and foreign States, Citizens or Subjects.

[2] In all Cases affecting Ambassadors, other public Ministers and Consuls, and those in which a State shall be a Party, the supreme Court shall have original Jurisdiction. In all the other Cases before mentioned, the supreme Court shall have appellate Jurisdiction, both as to Law and Fact, with such Exceptions, and under such Regulations as the Congress shall make.

[3] The trial of all Crimes, except in Cases of Impeachment, shall be by Jury; and such Trial shall be held in the State where the said Crimes shall have been committed; but when not committed within any State, the Trial shall be at such Place or Places as the Congress may by Law have directed.

Section 3. [1] Treason against the United States, shall consist only in levying War against them, or, in adhering to their Enemies, giving them Aid and Comfort. No Person shall be convicted of Treason unless on the testimony of two Witnesses to the same overt Act, or on Confession in open Court.

[2] The Congress shall have Power to declare the Punishment of Treason, but no Attainder of Treason shall work Corruption of Blood, or Forfeiture except during the Life of the Person attainted.

ARTICLE IV

Section 1. Full Faith and Credit shall be given in each State to the public Acts, Records, and judicial Proceedings of every other State. And the Congress may by general Laws prescribe the Manner in which such Acts, Records and Proceedings shall be proved, and the Effect thereof.

Section 2. [1] The Citizens of each State shall be entitled to all Privileges and Immunities of Citizens in the several States.

[2] A Person charged in any State with Treason, Felony, or other Crime, who shall flee from Justice, and be found in another State, shall on demand of the executive Authority of the State from which he fled, be delivered up, to be removed to the State having Jurisdiction of the Crime.

[3] No Person held to Service or Labour in one State, under the Laws thereof, escaping into another, shall, in Consequence of any Law or Regulation therein, be discharged from such Service or Labour, but shall be delivered up on Claim of the Party to whom such Service or Labour may be due.

Section 3. [1] New States may be admitted by the Congress into this Union; but no new State shall be formed or erected within the Jurisdiction of any other State; nor any State be formed by the Junction of two or more States, or Parts of States, without the Consent of the Legislatures of the States concerned as well as of the Congress.

[2] The Congress shall have Power to dispose of and make all needful Rules and Regulations respecting the Territory or other Property belonging

to the United States; and nothing in this Constitution shall be so construed as to Prejudice any Claims of the United States, or of any particular State.

Section 4. The United States shall guarantee to every State in this Union a Republican Form of Government, and shall protect each of them against Invasion; and on Application of the Legislature, or of the Executive (when the Legislature cannot be convened) against domestic Violence.

ARTICLE V

The Congress, whenever two thirds of both Houses shall deem it necessary, shall propose Amendments to this Constitution, or, on the Application of the Legislatures of two thirds of the several States, shall call a Convention for proposing Amendments, which, in either case, shall be valid to all Intents and Purposes, as part of this Constitution, when ratified by the Legislatures of three fourths of the several States, or by Conventions in three fourths thereof, as the one or the other Mode of Ratification may be proposed by the Congress; Provided that no Amendment which may be made prior to the Year One thousand eight hundred and eight shall in any Manner affect the first and fourth Clauses in the Ninth Section of the first Article; and that no State, without its Consent, shall be deprived of its equal Suffrage in the Senate.

ARTICLE VI

[1] All Debts contracted and Engagements entered into, before the Adoption of this Constitution shall be as valid against the United States under this Constitution, as under the Confederation.

[2] This Constitution, and the Laws of the United States which shall be made in Pursuance thereof; and all Treaties made, or which shall be made, under the Authority of the United States, shall be the supreme Law of the Land; and the Judges in every State shall be bound thereby, any Thing in the Constitution or Laws of any State to the Contrary notwithstanding.

[3] The Senators and Representatives before mentioned, and the Members of the several State Legislature, and all executive and judicial Officers, both of the United States and of the several States, shall be bound by Oath or Affirmation, to support this Constitution; but no religious test shall ever be required as a Qualification to any Office or public Trust under the United States.

ARTICLE VII

The Ratification of the Conventions of nine States shall be sufficient for the Establishment of this constitution between the States so ratifying the Same.

Articles in addition to, and amendment of, the Constitution of the United States of America, proposed by Congress, and ratified by the Legislatures of the several States pursuant to the Fifth Article of the original Constitution.

AMENDMENT I (1791)

Congress shall make no law respecting an establishment of religion, or prohibiting the free exercise thereof; or abridging the freedom of speech, or of the press; or the right of the people peaceably to assemble, and to petition the Government for a redress of grievances.

AMENDMENT II (1791)

A well regulated Militia, being necessary to the security of a free State, the right of the people to keep and bear Arms, shall not be infringed.

AMENDMENT III (1791)

No Soldier shall, in time of peace be quartered in any house, without the consent of the Owner, nor in time of war, but in a manner to be prescribed by law.

Appendix A

AMENDMENT IV (1791)

The right of the people to be secure in their persons, houses, papers, and effects, against unreasonable searches and seizures, shall not be violated, and no Warrants shall issue, but upon probable cause, supported by Oath or affirmation, and particularly describing the place to be searched, and the persons or things to be seized.

AMENDMENT V (1791)

No person shall be held to answer for a capital, or otherwise infamous crime, unless on a presentment or indictment of a Grand Jury, except in cases arising in the land or naval forces, or in the Militia, when in actual service in time of War or public danger; nor shall any person be subject for the same offence to be twice put in jeopardy of life or limb; nor shall be compelled in any criminal case to be a witness against himself, nor be deprived of life, liberty, or property, without due process of law; nor shall private property be taken for public use, without just compensation.

AMENDMENT VI (1791)

In all criminal prosecutions, the accused shall enjoy the right to a speedy and public trial, by an impartial jury of the State and district wherein the crime shall have been committed, which district shall have been previously ascertained by law, and to be informed of the nature and cause of the accusation; to be confronted with the witnesses against him; to have compulsory process for obtaining witnesses in his favor, and to have the Assistance of Counsel for his defence.

AMENDMENT VII (1791)

In Suits at common law, where the value in controversy shall exceed twenty dollars, the right of trial by jury shall be preserved, and no fact tried by jury, shall be otherwise reexamined in any Court of the United States, than according to the rules of common law.

AMENDMENT VIII (1791)

Excessive bail shall not be required, nor excessive fines imposed, nor cruel and unusual punishments inflicted.

AMENDMENT IX (1791)

The enumeration in the Constitution, of certain rights, shall not be construed to deny or disparage others retained by the people.

AMENDMENT X (1791)

The powers not delegated to the United States by the Constitution, nor prohibited by it to the States, are reserved to the States respectively, or to the people.

AMENDMENT XI (1798)

The Judicial power in the United States shall not be construed to extend to any suit in law or equity, commenced or prosecuted against one of the United States by Citizens of another State, or by Citizens or Subjects of any Foreign State.

AMENDMENT XII (1804)

The Electors shall meet in their respective states and vote by ballot for President and Vice-President, one of whom, at least, shall not be an inhabitant of the same state with themselves; they shall name in their ballots the person voted for as President, and in distinct ballots the person voted for as Vice-President, and they shall make distinct lists of all persons voted for as President, and of all persons voted for as Vice-President, and of the number of votes for each, which lists they shall sign and certify, and transmit sealed to the seat of the government of the United States, directed to the President of the Senate;—The President of the Senate shall, in the presence of the Senate and House of Representatives, open all the certificates and the votes shall then be counted;—

The person having the greatest number of votes for President, shall be the President, if such number be a majority of the whole number of Electors appointed; and if no person have such majority, then from the persons having the highest numbers not exceeding three on the list of those voted for as President, the House of Representatives shall choose immediately, by ballot, the President. But in choosing the President, the votes shall be taken by states, the representation from each state having one vote; a quorum for this purpose shall consist of a member or members from two-thirds of the states, and a majority of all states shall be necessary to a choice. And if the House of Representatives shall not choose a President whenever the right of choice shall devolve upon them before the fourth day of March next following, then the Vice-President shall act as President, as in the case of the death or other constitutional disability of the President.—The person having the greatest number of votes as Vice-President, shall be the Vice-President, if such number be a majority of the whole number of Electors appointed, and if no person have a majority, then from the two highest numbers on the list, the Senate shall choose the Vice-President; a quorum for the purpose shall consist of two-thirds of the whole number of Senators, and a majority of the whole number shall be necessary to a choice. But no person constitutionally ineligible to the office of President shall be eligible to that of Vice-President of the United States.

AMENDMENT XIII (1865)

Section 1. Neither slavery nor involuntary servitude, except as a punishment for crime whereof the party shall have been duly convicted, shall exist within the United States, or any place subject to their jurisdiction.

Section 2. Congress shall have power to enforce this article by appropriate legislation.

AMENDMENT XIV (1868)

Section 1. All persons born or naturalized in the United States, and subject to the jurisdiction thereof, are citizens of the United States and of the State wherein they reside. No State shall make or enforce any law which shall abridge the privileges or immunities of citizens of the United States; nor shall any State deprive any person of life, liberty, or property, without due process of law; nor deny to any person within its jurisdiction the equal protection of the laws.

Section 2. Representatives shall be apportioned among the several States according to their respective numbers, counting the whole number of persons in each State, excluding Indians not taxed. But when the right to vote at any election for the choice of electors for President and Vice President of the United States, Representatives in Congress, the Executive and Judicial officers of a State, or the members of the Legislature thereof, is denied to any of the male inhabitants of such State, being twenty-one years of age, and citizens of the United States, or in any way abridged, except for participation in rebellion, or other crime, the basis of representation therein shall be reduced in the proportion which the number of such male citizens shall bear to the whole number of male citizens twenty-one years of age in such State.

Section 3. No person shall be a Senator or Representative in Congress, or elector of President and Vice President, or hold any office, civil or military, under the United States, or under any State, who having previously taken an oath, as a member of Congress, or as an officer of the United States, or as a member of any State legislature, or as an executive or judicial officer of any State, to support the Constitution of the United States, shall have engaged in insurrection or rebellion against the same, or given aid or comfort to the enemies thereof. But Congress may by a vote of two-thirds of each House, remove such disability.

Section 4. The validity of the public debt of the United States, authorized by law, including debts incurred for payment of pensions and bounties for services in suppressing insurrection or rebellion, shall not be questioned. But neither the United States nor any State shall assume or pay any debt or obligation incurred in aid of insurrection or rebellion against the United States, or any claim for the loss or emancipation of any slave; but all such debts, obligations and claims shall be held illegal and void.

Section 5. The Congress shall have power to enforce, by appropriate legislation, the provisions of this article.

A MENDMENT XV (1870)

Section 1. The right of citizens of the United States to vote shall not be denied or abridged by the United States or by any State on account of race, color, or previous condition of servitude.

Section 2. The Congress shall have power to enforce this article by appropriate legislation.

A MENDMENT XVI (1913)

The Congress shall have power to lay and collect taxes on incomes, from whatever source derived, without apportionment among the several States, and without regard to any census or enumeration.

A MENDMENT XVII (1913)

[1] The Senate of the United States shall be composed of two Senators from each State, elected by the people thereof, for six years; and each Senator shall have one vote. The electors in each State shall have the qualifications requisite for electors of the most numerous branch of the State legislature.

[2] When vacancies happen in the representation of any State in the Senate, the executive authority of such State shall issue writs of election to fill such vacancies; *Provided*, That the legislature of any State may empower the executive thereof to make temporary appointments until the people fill the vacancies by election as the legislature may direct.

[3] This amendment shall not be so construed as to affect the election or term of any Senator chosen before it becomes valid as part of the Constitution.

A MENDMENT XVIII (1919)

Section 1. After one year from the ratification of this article the manufacture, sale, or transportation of intoxicating liquors within, the importation thereof into, or the exportation thereof from the United States and all territory subject to the jurisdiction thereof for beverage purposes is hereby prohibited.

Section 2. The Congress and the several States shall have concurrent power to enforce this article by appropriate legislation.

Section 3. This article shall be inoperative unless it shall have been ratified as an amendment to the Constitution by the legislatures of the several States, as provided in the Constitution, within seven years from the date of the submission hereof to the States by the Congress.

A MENDMENT XIX (1920)

[1] The right of citizens of the United States to vote shall not be denied or abridged by the United States or by any State on account of sex.

[2] Congress shall have power to enforce this article by appropriate legislation.

A MENDMENT XX (1933)

Section 1. The terms of the President and Vice President shall end at noon on the 20th day of January, and the terms of Senators and Representatives at noon on the 3d day of January, of the years in which such terms would have ended if this article had not been ratified; and the terms of their successors shall then begin.

Section 2. The Congress shall assemble at least once in every year, and such meeting shall begin at noon on the 3d day of January, unless they shall by law appoint a different day.

Section 3. If, at the time fixed for the beginning of the term of the President, the President elect shall have died, the Vice President elect shall become President. If the President shall not have been chosen before the time fixed for the beginning of his term, or if the President elect shall have failed to qualify, then the Vice President elect shall act as President until a President shall have qualified; and the Congress may by law provide for the case wherein neither a President elect nor a Vice President elect shall have qualified, declaring who shall then act as President, or the manner in which one who is to act shall be selected, and such person shall act accordingly until a President or Vice President shall have qualified.

Section 4. The Congress may by law provide for the case of the death of any of the persons from whom the House of Representatives may choose a President whenever the right of choice shall have devolved upon them, and for the case of the death of any of the persons from whom the Senate may choose a Vice President whenever the right of choice shall have devolved upon them.

Section 5. Sections 1 and 2 shall take effect on the 15th day of October following the ratification of this article.

Section 6. This article shall be inoperative unless it shall have been ratified as an amendment to the Constitution by the legislatures of three-fourths of the several States within seven years from the date of its submission.

AMENDMENT XXI (1933)

Section 1. The eighteenth article of amendment to the Constitution of the United States is hereby repealed.

Section 2. The transportation or importation into any State, Territory, or possession of the United States for delivery or use therein of intoxicating liquors, in violation of the laws thereof, is hereby prohibited.

Section 3. This article shall be inoperative unless it shall have been ratified as an amendment to the Constitution by conventions in the several States, as provided in the Constitution, within seven years from the date of the submission hereof to the States by the Congress.

AMENDMENT XXII (1951)

Section 1. No person shall be elected to the office of the President more than twice, and no person who has held the office of President, or acted as President, for more than two years of a term to which some other person was elected President shall be elected to the office of President more than once. But this Article shall not apply to any person holding the office of President when this Article was proposed by the Congress, and shall not prevent any person who may be holding the office of President, or acting as President, during the term within which this Article becomes operative from holding the office of President or acting as President during the remainder of such term.

Section 2. This article shall be inoperative unless it shall have been ratified as an amendment to the Constitution by the legislatures of three-fourths of the several States within seven years from the date of its submission to the States by the Congress.

AMENDMENT XXIII (1961)

Section 1. The District constituting the seat of Government of the United States shall appoint in such manner as the Congress may direct:

A number of electors of President and Vice President equal to the whole number of Senators and Representatives in Congress to which the District would be entitled if it were a State, but in no event more than the least populous state; they shall be in addition to those appointed by the states, but they shall be considered, for the purposes of the election of President and Vice President, to be electors appointed by a state; and they shall meet in the District and perform such duties as provided by the twelfth article of amendment.

Section 2. The Congress shall have power to enforce this article by appropriate legislation.

AMENDMENT XXIV (1964)

Section 1. The right of citizens of the United States to vote in any primary or other election for President or Vice President, for electors for President or Vice President or for Senator or Representative in Congress, shall not be denied or abridged by the United States, or any State by reason of failure to pay any poll tax or other tax.

Section 2. The Congress shall have power to enforce this article by appropriate legislation.

A MENDMENT XXV (1967)

Section 1. In case of the removal of the President from office or of his death or resignation, the Vice President shall become President.

Section 2. Whenever there is a vacancy in the office of the Vice President, the President shall nominate a Vice President who shall take office upon confirmation by a majority vote of both Houses of Congress.

Section 3. Whenever the President transmits to the President pro tempore of the Senate and the Speaker of the House of Representatives his written declaration that he is unable to discharge the powers and duties of his office, and until he transmits to them a written declaration to the contrary, such powers and duties shall be discharged by the Vice President as Acting President.

Section 4. Whenever the Vice President and a majority of either the principal officers of the executive departments or of such other body as Congress may by law provide, transmit to the President pro tempore of the Senate and the Speaker of the House of Representatives their written declaration that the President is unable to discharge the powers and duties of his office, the Vice President shall immediately assume the powers and duties of the office as Acting President.

Thereafter, when the President transmits to the President pro tempore of the Senate and the Speaker of the House of Representatives his written declaration that no inability exists, he shall resume the powers and duties of his office unless the Vice President and a majority of either the principal officers of the executive department or of such

other body as Congress may by law provide, transmit within four days to the President pro tempore of the Senate and the Speaker of the House of Representatives their written declaration and the President is unable to discharge the powers and duties of his office. Thereupon Congress shall decide the issue, assembling within forty-eight hours for that purpose if not in session. If the Congress, within twenty-one days after receipt of the latter written declaration, or, if Congress is not in session, within twenty-one days after Congress is required to assemble, determines by two-thirds vote of both Houses that the President is unable to discharge the powers and duties of his office, the Vice President shall continue to discharge the same as Acting President; otherwise, the President shall resume the powers and duties of his office.

A MENDMENT XXVI (1971)

Section 1. The right of citizens of the United States, who are eighteen years of age or older, to vote shall not be denied or abridged by the United States or by any State on account of age.

Section 2. The Congress shall have power to enforce this article by appropriate legislation.

A MENDMENT XXVII (1992)

No law, varying the compensation for the services of the Senators and Representatives, shall take effect, until an election of Representatives shall have intervened.

APPENDIX B
PROCEDURAL STATUTES (EXCERPTS)
Revised Judicature Act (Michigan)

600.711 CORPORATIONS; GENERAL PERSONAL JURISDICTION

Sec. 711. The existence of any of the following relationships between a corporation and the state shall constitute a sufficient basis of jurisdiction to enable the courts of record of this state to exercise general personal jurisdiction over the corporation and to enable such courts to render personal judgments against the corporation.

(1) Incorporation under the laws of this state.

(2) Consent, to the extent authorized by the consent and subject to the limitations provided in section 745.

(3) The carrying on of a continuous and systematic part of its general business within the state.

600.715 CORPORATIONS; LIMITED PERSONAL JURISDICTION

Sec. 715. The existence of any of the following relationships between a corporation or its agent and the state shall constitute a sufficient basis of jurisdiction to enable the courts of record of this state to exercise limited personal jurisdiction over such corporation and to enable such courts to render personal judgments against such corporation arising out of the act or acts which create any of the following relationships:

(1) The transaction of any business within the state.

(2) The doing or causing any act to be done, or consequences to occur, in the state resulting in an action for tort.

(3) The ownership, use, or possession of any real or tangible personal property situated within the state.

(4) Contracting to insure any person, property, or risk located within this state at the time of contracting.

(5) Entering into a contract for services to be performed or for materials to be furnished in the state by the defendant.

Administrative Procedure Act

PUBLIC INFORMATION

Sec. 3. Except to the extent that there is involved (1) any function of the United States requiring secrecy in the public interest or (2) any matter relating solely to the internal management of an agency—

(a) *Rules.*—Every agency shall separately state and currently publish in the Federal Register (1) descriptions of its central and field organization including delegations by the agency of final authority and the established places at which, and methods whereby, the public may secure information or make submittals or requests; (2) statements of the general course and method by which its functions are channeled and determined, including the nature and requirements of all formal or informal procedures available as well as forms and instructions as to the scope and contents of all papers, reports, or examinations; and (3) substantive rules adopted as authorized by law and statements of general policy or interpretations formulated and adopted by the agency for the guidance of the public, but not rules addressed to and served upon named persons in accordance with law. No person shall in any manner be required to resort to organization or procedure not so published.

(b) *Opinions and Orders.*—Every agency shall publish or, in accordance with published rule, make available to public inspection all final opinions or orders in the adjudication of cases (except those required for good cause to be held confidential and not cited as precedents) and all rules.

(c) *Public Records.*—Save as otherwise required by statute, matters of official record shall in accordance with published rule be made available to persons properly and directly concerned except information held confidential for good cause found.

RULE MAKING

Sec. 4. Except to the extent that there is involved (1) any military, naval, or foreign affairs function of the United States or (2) any matter relating to agency management or personnel or to public property, loans, grants, benefits, or contracts—

(a) *Notice.*—General notice of proposed rule making shall be published in the Federal Register (unless all persons subject thereto are named and either personally served or otherwise have actual notice thereof in accordance with law) and shall include (1) a statement of the time, place, and nature of public rule making proceedings; (2) reference to the authority under which the rule is proposed; and (3) either the terms or substance of the proposed rule or a description of the subjects and issues involved. Except where notice or hearing is required by statute, this subsection shall not apply to interpretative rules, general statements of policy, rules of agency organization, procedure, or practice, or in any situation in which the agency for good cause finds (and incorporates the finding and a brief statement of the reasons therefor in the rules issued) that notice and public procedure thereon are impracticable, unnecessary, or contrary to the public interest.

(b) *Procedures.*—After notice by this section, the agency shall afford interested persons an opportunity to participate in the rule making through submission of written data, views, or arguments with or without opportunity to present the same orally in any manner; and, after consideration of all relevant matter presented, the agency shall incorporate in any rules adopted a concise general statement of their basis and purpose. Where rules are required by statute to be made on the record after opportunity for an agency hearing, the requirements of sections 7 and 8 shall apply in place of the provisions of this subsection.

(c) *Effective Dates.*—The required publication or service of any substantive rule (other than one granting or recognizing exemption or relieving restriction or interpretative rules and statements of policy) shall be made not less than thirty days prior to the effective date thereof except as otherwise provided by the agency upon good cause found and published with the rule.

(d) *Petitions.*—Every agency shall accord any interested person the right to petition for the issuance, amendment, or repeal of a rule.

A DJUDICATION

Sec. 5. In every case of adjudication required by statute to be determined on the record after opportunity for an agency hearing, except to the extent that there is involved (1) any matter subject to a subsequent trial of the law and the facts de novo in any court; (2) the selection or tenure of an officer or employee of the United States other than examiners appointed pursuant to section 11; (3) proceedings in which decisions rest solely on inspections, tests, or elections; (4) the conduct of military, naval, or foreign affairs functions; (5) cases in which an agency is acting as an agent for a court; and (6) the certification of employee representatives—

(a) *Notice.*—Persons entitled to notice of an agency hearing shall be timely informed of (1) the time, place, and nature thereof; (2) the legal authority and jurisdiction under which the hearing is to be held; and (3) the matters of fact and law asserted. In instances in which private persons are the moving parties, other parties to the proceeding shall give prompt notice of issues controverted in fact or law; and in other instances agencies may by rule require responsive pleading. In fixing the times and places for hearings, due regard shall be had for the convenience and necessity of the parties or their representatives.

(b) *Procedure.*—The agency shall afford all interested parties opportunity for (1) the submission and consideration of facts, arguments, offers of settlement, or proposals of adjustment where time, the nature of the proceeding, and the public interest permit, and (2) to the extent that the parties are unable so to determine any controversy by consent, hearing, and decision upon notice and in conformity with sections 7 and 8.

(c) *Separation of Functions.*—The same officers who preside at the reception of evidence pursuant to section 7 shall make the recommended decision or initial decision required by section 8 except where such officers become unavailable to the agency. Save to the extent required for the disposition of ex parte matters as authorized by law, no such officer shall consult any person or party on any fact in issue unless upon notice and opportunity for all parties to participate; nor shall such officer be responsible to or subject to the supervision or direction of any officer, employee, or agent engaged in the performance of investigative or prosecuting functions for any agency. No officer, employee, or agent engaged in the performance of investigative or prosecuting functions for any agency in any case shall, in that or a factually related case, participate or advise in the decision, recommended decision, or agency review pursuant to section 8 except as witness or counsel in public proceedings. This subsection shall not apply in determining applications for initial licenses or to proceedings involving the validity or application of rates, facilities, or practices of public utilities or carriers; nor shall it be applicable in any manner to the agency or any members or members of the body comprising the agency.

(d) *Declaratory Orders.*—The agency is authorized in its sound discretion, with like effect as in the case of other orders, to issue a declaratory order to terminate a controversy or remove uncertainty.

APPENDIX C
UNIFORM COMMERCIAL CODE (EXCERPTS)

SECTION 1–102. PURPOSES; RULES OF CONSTRUCTION; VARIATION BY AGREEMENT

(1) This Act shall be liberally construed and applied to promote its underlying purposes and policies.

(2) Underlying purposes and policies of this Act are

    (a) to simplify, clarify and modernize the law governing commercial transactions;

    (b) to permit the continued expansion of commercial practices through custom, usage and agreement of the parties;

    (c) to make uniform the law among the various jurisdictions.

(3) The effect of provisions of this Act may be varied by agreement, except as otherwise provided in this Act and except that the obligations of good faith, diligence, reasonableness and care prescribed by this Act may not be disclaimed by agreement, but the parties may by agreement determine the standards by which the performance of such obligations is to be measured if such standards are not manifestly unreasonable.

SECTION 1–107. WAIVER OR RENUNCIATION OF CLAIM OR RIGHT AFTER BREACH

Any claim or right arising out of an alleged breach can be discharged in whole or in part without consideration by a written waiver or renunciation signed and delivered by the aggrieved party.

SECTION 1–203. OBLIGATION OF GOOD FAITH

Every contract or duty within this Act imposes an obligation of good faith in its performance or enforcement.

SECTION 2–104. DEFINITIONS: "MERCHANT"; "BETWEEN MERCHANTS"

(1) "Merchant" means a person who deals in goods of the kind or otherwise by his occupation holds himself out as having knowledge or skill peculiar to the practices or goods involved in the transaction or to whom such knowledge or skill may be attributed by his employment of an agent or broker or other intermediary who by his occupation holds himself out as having such knowledge or skill....

(3) "Between merchants" means in any transaction with respect to which both parties are chargeable with the knowledge or skill of merchants.

SECTION 2–105. DEFINITIONS: "GOODS"

(1) "Goods" means all things (including special manufactured goods) which are movable at the time of identification of the contract for sale other than the money in which the price is to be paid, investment securities (Article 8) and things in action. "Goods" also includes the unborn young of animals and growing crops and other identified things attached to realty as described in the section on goods to be severed from realty.

SECTION 2–201. FORMAL REQUIREMENTS; STATUTE OF FRAUDS

(1) Except as otherwise provided in this section, a contract for the sale of goods for the price of $500 or more is not enforceable by way of action or defense unless there is some writing sufficient to indicate that a contract for sale has been made between the parties and signed by the party against whom enforcement is sought or by his authorized agent or broker. A writing is not insufficient because it omits or incorrectly states a term agreed upon but the contract is not enforceable under this paragraph beyond the quantity of goods shown in such writing.

(2) Between merchants if within a reasonable time a writing in confirmation of the contract and sufficient against the sender is received and the party receiving it has reason to know its contents, it satisfies the requirements of subsection (1) against such party unless written notice of objection to its contents is given within 10 days after it is received.

(3) A contract which does not satisfy the requirements of subsection (1) but which is valid in other respects is enforceable

(a) if the goods are to be specially manufactured for the buyer and are not suitable for sale to others in the ordinary course of the seller's business and the seller, before notice of repudiation is received and under circumstances which reasonably indicate that the goods are for the buyer, has made either a substantial beginning of their manufacture or commitments for their procurement; or

(b) if the party against whom enforcement is sought admits in his pleading, testimony or otherwise in court that a contract for sale was made, but the contract is not enforceable under this provision beyond the quantity of goods admitted; or

(c) with respect to goods for which payment has been made and accepted or which have been received and accepted (Section 2–606).

SECTION 2–202. FINAL WRITTEN EXPRESSION: PAROL OR EXTRINSIC EVIDENCE

Terms with respect to which the confirmatory memoranda of the parties agree or which are otherwise set forth in a writing intended by the parties as a final expression of their agreement with respect to such terms as are included therein may not be contradicted by evidence of any prior agreement or of a contemporaneous oral agreement but may be explained or supplemented

(a) by course of dealing or usage of trade (Section 1–205) or by course of performance (Section 2–208); and

(b) by evidence of consistent additional terms unless the court finds the writing to have been intended also as a complete and exclusive statement of the terms of the agreement.

SECTION 2–204. FORMATION IN GENERAL

(1) A contract for sale of goods may be made in any manner sufficient to show agreement, including conduct by both parties which recognizes the existence of such a contract.

(2) An agreement sufficient to constitute a contract for sale may be found even though the moment of its making is undetermined.

(3) Even though one or more terms are left open a contract for sale does not fail for indefiniteness if the parties have intended to make a contract and there is a reasonably certain basis for giving an appropriate remedy.

SECTION 2–205. FIRM OFFERS

An offer by a merchant to buy or sell goods in a signed writing which by its terms gives assurance that it will be held open is not revocable, for lack of consideration, during the time stated or if no time is stated for a reasonable time, but in no event may such period of irrevocability exceed three months; but any such term of assurance on a form supplied by the offeree must be separately signed by the offeror.

SECTION 2–206. OFFER AND ACCEPTANCE IN FORMATION OF CONTRACT

(1) Unless otherwise unambiguously indicated by the language or circumstances

    (a) an offer to make a contract shall be construed as inviting acceptance in any manner and by any medium reasonable in the circumstances;

    (b) an order or other offer to buy goods for prompt or current shipment shall be construed as inviting acceptance either by a prompt promise to ship or by the prompt or current shipment of conforming or non-conforming goods, but such a shipment of non-conforming goods does not constitute an acceptance if the seller seasonably notifies the buyer that the shipment is offered only as an accommodation to the buyer.

(2) Where the beginning of a requested performance is a reasonable mode of acceptance, an offeror who is not notified of acceptance within a reasonable time may treat the offer as having lapsed before acceptance.

SECTION 2–207. ADDITIONAL TERMS IN ACCEPTANCE OR CONFIRMATION

(1) A definite and seasonable expression of acceptance or a written confirmation which is sent within a reasonable time operates as an acceptance even though it states terms additional to or different from those offered or agreed upon, unless acceptance is expressly made conditional on assent to the additional or different terms.

(2) The additional terms are to be construed as proposals for addition to the contract. Between merchants such terms become part of the contract unless:

    (a) the offer expressly limits acceptance to the terms of the offer;

    (b) they materially alter it; or

    (c) notification of objection to them has already been given or is given within a reasonable time after notice of them is received.

(3) Conduct by both parties which recognizes the existence of a contract is sufficient to establish a contract for sale although the writings of the parties do not otherwise establish a contract. In such case the terms of the particular contract consist of those terms on which the writings of the parties agree, together with any supplementary terms incorporated under any other provisions of this Act.

SECTION 2–302. UNCONSCIONABLE CONTRACT OR CLAUSE

(1) If the court as a matter of law finds the contract or any clause of the contract to have been unconscionable at the time it was made the court may refuse to enforce the contract, or it may enforce the remainder of the contract without the

unconscionable clause, or it may so limit the application of any unconscionable clause as to avoid any unconscionable result.

(2) When it is claimed or appears to the court that the contract or any clause thereof may be unconscionable the parties shall be afforded a reasonable opportunity to present evidence as to its commercial setting, purpose and effect to aid the court in making the determination.

SECTION 2–313. EXPRESS WARRANTIES BY AFFIRMATION, PROMISE, DESCRIPTION, SAMPLE

(1) Express warranties by the seller are created as follows:

(a) Any affirmation of fact or promise made by the seller to the buyer which relates to the goods and becomes part of the basis of the bargain creates an express warranty that the goods shall conform to the affirmation or promise.

(b) Any description of the goods which is made part of the basis of the bargain creates an express warranty that the goods shall conform to the description.

(c) Any sample or model which is made part of the basis of the bargain creates an express warranty that the whole of the goods shall conform to the sample or model.

(2) It is not necessary to the creation of an express warranty that the seller use formal words such as "warrant" or "guarantee" or that he have a specific intention to make a warranty, but an affirmation merely of the value of the goods or a statement purporting to be merely the seller's opinion or commendation of the goods does not create a warranty.

SECTION 2–314. IMPLIED WARRANTY: MERCHANTABILITY; USAGE OF TRADE

(1) Unless excluded or modified (Section 2–316), a warranty that the goods shall be merchantable is implied in a contract for their sale if the seller is a merchant with respect to goods of that kind. Under this section the serving for value

of food or drink to be consumed either on the premises or elsewhere is a sale.

(2) Goods to be merchantable must be at least such as

(a) pass without objection in the trade under the contract description; and

(b) in the case of fungible goods, are of fair average quality within the description; and

(c) are fit for the ordinary purposes for which such goods are used; and

(d) run, within the variations permitted by the agreement, of even kind, quality and quantity within each unit and among all units involved; and

(e) are adequately contained, packaged, and labeled as the agreement may require; and

(f) conform to the promises or affirmations of fact made on the container or label if any.

(3) Unless excluded or modified (Section 2–316) other implied warranties may arise from course of dealing or usage of trade.

SECTION 2–315. IMPLIED WARRANTY: FITNESS FOR PARTICULAR PURPOSE

Where the seller at the time of contracting has reason to know any particular purpose for which the goods are required and that the buyer is relying on the seller's skill of judgment to select or furnish suitable goods, there is unless excluded or modified under the next section an implied warranty that the goods shall be fit for such purpose.

SECTION 2–316. EXCLUSION OR MODIFICATION OF WARRANTIES

(1) Words or conduct relevant to the creation of an express warranty and words or conduct tending to negate or limit warranty shall be construed wherever reasonable as consistent with each other; but subject to the provisions of this Article on parol or extrinsic evidence (Section 2–202) negation or limitation is inoperative to the extent that such construction is unreasonable.

(2) Subject to subsection (3), to exclude or modify the implied warranty of merchantability or any part of it in the language must mention merchantability and in case of a writing must be conspicuous, and to exclude or modify any implied warranty of fitness the exclusion must be by a writing and conspicuous. Language to exclude all implied warranties of fitness is sufficient if it states, for example, that "There are no warranties which extend beyond the description on the face hereof."

(3) Notwithstanding subsection (2)

(a) unless the circumstances indicate otherwise, all implied warranties are excluded by expressions like "as is," "with all faults" or other language which in common understanding calls the buyer's attention to the exclusion of warranties and makes plain that there is no implied warranty; and

(b) when the buyer before entering into the contract has examined goods or the sample or model as fully as he desired or has refused to examine the goods there is no implied warranty with regard to defects which an examination ought in the circumstances to have revealed to him; and

(c) an implied warranty can also be excluded or modified by course of dealing or course of performance or usage of trade.

(4) Remedies for breach of warranty can be limited in accordance with the provisions of this Article on liquidation or limitation of damages and on contractual modification of remedy.

SECTION 9–101. SHORT TITLE

This Article shall be known and may be cited as Uniform Commercial Code—Secured Transactions.

SECTION 9–102. POLICY AND SUBJECT MATTER OF ARTICLE

(1) Except as otherwise provided in Section 9–104 on excluded transactions, this Article applies

(a) to any transaction (regardless of its form) which is intended to create a security interest in personal property or fixtures including goods, documents, instruments, general intangibles, chattel paper or accounts; and also

(b) to any sale of accounts or chattel paper.

(2) This Article applies to security interests created by contract including pledge, assignment, chattel mortgage, chattel trust, trust deed, factor's lien, equipment trust, conditional sale, trust receipt, other lien or title retention contract and lease or consignment intended as security. This Article does not apply to statutory liens except as provided in Section 9–310.

(3) The application of this Article to a security interest in a secured obligation is not affected by the fact that the obligation is itself secured by a transaction or interest to which this Article does not apply.

SECTION 9–301. PERSONS WHO TAKE PRIORITY OVER UNPERFECTED SECURITY INTERESTS; RIGHTS OF "LIEN CREDITOR"

(1) Except as otherwise provided in subsection (2), an unperfected security interest is subordinate to the rights of

(a) persons entitled to priority under Section 9–312;

(b) a person who becomes a lien creditor before the security interest is perfected;

(c) in the case of goods, instruments, document and chattel paper, a person who is not a secured party and who is a transferee in bulk or other buyer no in ordinary course of business or is a buyer of farm products in ordinary course of business, to the extent that he gives value and receives delivery of the collateral without knowledge of the security interest and before it is perfected;

(d) in the case of accounts and general intangibles, a person who is not a secured party and who is a transferee to the extent that he gives value without knowledge of the security interest and before it is perfected.

* * * *

(2) If the secured party files with respect to a purchase money security interest before or within ten days after the debtor receives possession of the collateral, he takes priority over the rights of a transferee in bulk or of a lien creditor which arise between the time the security interest attaches and the time of filing.

(3) A "lien creditor" means a creditor who has acquired a lien on the property involved by attachment, levy or the like and includes an assignee for the benefit of creditors from the time of assignment, and as trustee in bankruptcy from the date of the filing of the petition or a receiver in equity from the time of appointment.

(4) A person who becomes a lien creditor while a security interest is perfected takes subject to the security interest only to the extent that it secures advances made before he becomes a lien creditor or within 45 days thereafter or made without knowledge of the lien or pursuant to a commitment entered into without knowledge of the lien.

SECTION 9-307. PROTECTION OF BUYERS OF GOODS

(1) A buyer in ordinary course of business (subsection (9) of Section 1–201) other than a person buying farm products from a person engaged in farming operations takes free of a security interest created by his seller even though the security interest is perfected and even though the buyer knows of its existence.

(2) In the case of consumer goods, a buyer takes free of a security interest even though perfected if he buys without knowledge of the security interest, for value and for his own personal, family or household purposes unless prior to the purchase the secured party has filed a financing statement covering such goods.

(3) A buyer other than a buyer in ordinary course of business (subsection (1) of this section) takes free of a security interest to the extent that it secures future advances made after the secured party acquires knowledge of the purchase, or more than 45 days after the purchase, whichever first occurs, unless made pursuant to a commitment entered into without knowledge of the purchase and before the expiration of the 45-day period.

APPENDIX D
NATIONAL REGULATORY STATUTES (EXCERPTS)
Securities Act of 1933

D EFINITIONS

Section 2. When used in this title, unless the context requires—

(1) The term "security" means any note, stock, treasury stock, bond, debenture, evidence of indebtedness, certificate of interest or participation in any profit-sharing agreement, collateral-trust certificate, preorganization certificate or subscription, transferable share, investment contract, voting-trust certificate, certificate of deposit for a security, fractional undivided interest in oil, gas, or other mineral rights, any put, call, straddle, option, or privilege on any security, certificate of deposit, or group or index of securities (including any interest therein or based on the value thereof), or any put, call, straddle, option, or privilege entered into in a national securities exchange relating to foreign currency, or, in general, any interest or instrument commonly known as a "security,"

or any certificate of interest or participation in, temporary or interim certificate for, receipt for, guarantee of, or warrant or right to subscribe to or purchase, any of the foregoing.

E XEMPTED SECURITIES

Section 3. (a) Except as hereinafter expressly provided the provisions of this title shall not apply to any of the following classes of securities:

* * * * *

(2) Any security issued or guaranteed by the United States or any territory thereof, or by the District of Columbia, or by any State of the United States, or by any political subdivision of a State or Territory, or by any public instrumentality of one or more States or Territories, or by any person controlled or supervised by and acting as an instrumentality of the Government of the

United States pursuant to authority granted by the Congress of the United States; or any certificate of deposit for any of the foregoing; or any security issued or guaranteed by any bank; or any security issued by or representing an interest in or a direct obligation of a Federal Reserve bank....

(3) Any note, draft, bill of exchange, or banker's acceptance which arises out of a current transaction or the proceeds of which have been or are to be used for current transactions, and which has a maturity at the time of issuance of not exceeding nine months, exclusive of days of grace, or any renewal thereof the maturity of which is likewise limited;

(4) Any security issued by a person organized and operated exclusively for religious, educational, benevolent, fraternal, charitable, or reformatory purposes and not for pecuniary profit, and no part of the net earnings of which insures to the benefit of any person, private stockholder, or individual;

* * * * *

(11) Any security which is a part of an issue offered and sold only to persons resident within a single State or Territory, where the issuer of such security is a person resident and doing business within, or, if a corporation, incorporated by and doing business within, such State or Territory.

(b) The Commission may from time to time by its rules and regulations and subject to such terms and conditions as may be described therein, add any class of securities to the securities exempted as provided in this section, if it finds that the enforcement of this title with respect to such securities is not necessary in the public interest and for the protection of investors by reason of the small amount involved or the limited character of the public offering; but no issue of securities shall be exempted under this subsection where the aggregate amount at which such issue is offered to the public exceeds $5,000,000.

E XEMPTED TRANSACTIONS

Section 4. The provisions of section 5 shall not apply to—

(1) transactions by any person other than an issuer, underwriter, or dealer.

(2) transactions by an issuer not involving any public offering.

(3) transactions by a dealer (including an underwriter no longer acting as an underwriter in respect of the security involved in such transactions), except—

(A) transactions taking place prior to the expiration of forty days after the first date upon which the security was bona fide offered to the public by the issuer or by or through an underwriter,

(B) transactions in a security as to which a registration statement has been filed taking place prior to the expiration of forty days after the effective date of such registration statement or prior to the expiration of forty days after the first date upon which the security was bona fide offered to the public by the issuer or by or through an underwriter after such effective date, whichever is later (excluding in the computation of such forty days any time during which a stop order issued under section 8 is in effect as to the security), or such shorter period as the Commission may specify by rules and regulations or order, and

(C) transactions as to securities constituting the whole or a part of an unsold allotment to or subscription by such dealer as a participant in the distribution of such securities by the issuer or by or through an underwriter.

With respect to transactions referred to in clause (B), if securities of the issuer have not previously been sold pursuant to an earlier effective registration statement the applicable period, instead of forty days, shall be ninety days, or such shorter period as the Commission may specify by rules and regulations or order.

(4) brokers' transactions, executed upon customers' orders on any exchange or in the over-the-counter market but not the solicitation of such orders.

* * * * *

(6) transactions involving offers or sales by an issuer solely to one of more accredited investors, if the aggregate offering price of an issue of securities offered in reliance on this paragraph does not exceed the amount allowed under section 3(b) of this title, if there is no advertising or public

solicitation in connection with the transaction by the issuer or anyone acting on the issuer's behalf, and if the issuer files such notice with the Commission as the Commission shall prescribe.

Section 5. (a) Unless a registration statement is in effect as to a security, it shall be unlawful for any person, directly or indirectly—

(1) to make use of any means or instruments of transportation or communication in interstate commerce or of the mails to sell such security through the use or medium of any prospectus or otherwise; or

(2) to carry or cause to be carried through the mails or in interstate commerce, by any means or instruments of transportation, any such security for the purpose of sale of for delivery after sale.

(b) It shall be unlawful for any person, directly or indirectly—

(1) to make use of any means or instruments of transportation or communication in interstate commerce or of the mails to carry or transmit any prospectus relating to any security with respect to which a registration statement has been filed under this title, unless such prospectus meets the requirements of section 10, or

(2) to carry or to cause to be carried though the mails or in interstate commerce any such security for the purpose of sale or for delivery after sale, unless accompanied or preceded by a prospectus that meets the requirements of subsection (a) of section 10.

(c) It shall be unlawful for any person, directly or indirectly, to make use of any means or instruments of transportation or communication in interstate commerce or of the mails to offer to sell or offer to buy through the use or medium of any prospectus or otherwise any security, unless a registration statement has been filed as to such security, or while the registration statement is the subject of a refusal order or stop order or (prior to the effective date of the registration statement) any public proceeding of examination under section 8.

Securities Exchange Act of 1934

D EFINITIONS

Section 3. (a) When used in this title, unless the context otherwise requires—

* * * * *

(4) The term "broker" means any person engaged in the business of effecting transactions in securities for the account of others, but does not include a bank.

(5) The term "dealer" means any person engaged in the business of buying and selling securities for his own account, through a broker or otherwise, but does not include a bank, or any person insofar as he buys or sells securities for his own account, either individually or in some fiduciary capacity, but not as part of a regular business.

* * * * *

(7) The term "director" means any director of a corporation or any person performing similar functions with respect to any organization, whether incorporated or unincorporated.

(8) The term "issuer" means any person who issues or proposes to issue any security; except that with respect to certificates of deposit for securities, voting-trust certificates, or collateral-trust certificates, or with respect to certificates of interest or shares in an unincorporated investment trust not having a board of directors or the fixed, restricted management, or unit type, the term "issuer" means the person or persons performing the acts and assuming the duties of depositor or manager pursuant to the provisions of the trust or other agreement or instrument under which such securities are issued; and except that with respect to equipment-trust certificates or like securities, the term "issuer" means the person by whom the equipment or property is, or is to be, used.

(9) The term "person" means a natural person, company, government, or political subdivision, agency, or instrumentality of a government.

SECURITIES AND EXCHANGE COMMISSION

Section 4. (a) There is hereby established a Securities and Exchange Commission (hereinafter referred to as the "Commission") to be composed of five commissioners to be appointed by the President by and with the advice and consent of the Senate. Not more than three of such commissioners shall be members of the same political party, and in making appointments members of different political parties shall be appointed alternately as nearly as may be practicable.

* * * * *

TRANSACTIONS ON UNREGISTERED EXCHANGES

Section 5. It shall be unlawful for any broker, dealer, or exchange, directly or indirectly, to make use of the mails or any means or instrumentality of interstate commerce for the purpose of using any facility of an exchange within or subject to the jurisdiction of the United States to effect any transaction in a security, or to report any such transaction, unless such exchange (1) is registered as a national securities exchange under…this title, or (2) is exempted from such registration upon application by the exchange because, in the opinion of the Commission, by reason of the limited volume of transactions effected on such exchange, it is not practicable and not necessary or appropriate in the public interest or for the protection of investors to require such registration.

REGULATION OF THE USE OF MANIPULATIVE AND DECEPTIVE DEVICES

Section 10. It shall be unlawful for any person, directly or indirectly, by the use of any means or instrumentality of interstate commerce or of the mails, or of any facility of any national securities exchange—

(a) To effect a short sale, or to use or employ any stop-loss order in connection with the purchase or sale, of any security registered on a national securities exchange, in contravention of such rules and regulations as the Commission may prescribe as necessary or appropriate in the public interest or for the protection of investors.

(b) To use or employ, in connection with the purchase or sale of any security registered on a national securities exchange or any security not so registered, any manipulative or deceptive device or contrivance in contravention of such rules and regulations as the Commission may prescribe as necessary or appropriate in the public interest for the protection of investors.

REGISTRATION REQUIREMENTS FOR SECURITIES

Section 12. (a) It shall be unlawful for any member, broker, or dealer to effect any transaction in any security (other than an exempted security) on a national securities exchange unless a registration is effective as to such security for such exchange in accordance with the provisions of this title and the rules and regulations thereunder.

National Labor Relations Act

RIGHTS OF EMPLOYEES

Section 7. Employees shall have the right to self-organization, to form, join, or assist labor organizations, to bargain collectively through representatives of their own choosing, and to engage in other concerted activities for the purpose of collective bargaining or other mutual aid or protection, and shall also have the right to refrain from any or all such activities except to the extent that such right may be affected by an agreement requiring membership in a labor organization as a condition of employment as authorized in section 8(a)(3).

UNFAIR LABOR PRACTICES

Section 8. (a) It shall be an unfair labor practice for an employer—

(1) to interfere with, restrain, or coerce employees in the exercise of the rights guaranteed in section 7;

(2) to dominate or interfere with the formation or administration of any labor organization or contribute financial or other support to it: *Provided,* That subject to rules and regulations made and published by the Board pursuant to section 6, an employer shall not be prohibited from permitting employees to confer with him during working hours without loss of time or pay;

(3) by discrimination in regard to hire or tenure of employment or any term or condition of employment to encourage or discourage membership in any labor organization: *Provided,* That nothing in this Act, or in any other statute of the United States, shall preclude an employer from making an agreement with a labor organization (not established, maintained, or assisted by any action defined in section 8(a) of this Act as an unfair labor practice) to require as a condition of employment membership therein on or after the thirtieth day following the beginning of such employment or the effective date of such an agreement, whichever is the later, (i) if such labor organization is the representative of the employees as provided in section 9(a), in the appropriate collective-bargaining unit covered by such agreement when made, and (ii) unless following an election held as provided in section 9(e) within one year preceding the effective date of such agreement, the Board shall have certified that at least a majority of the employees eligible to vote in such election have voted to rescind the authority of such labor organization to make such an agreement: *Provided further,* That no employer shall justify any discrimination against an employee for nonmembership in a labor organization (A) if he has reasonable grounds for believing that such membership was not available to the employee on the same terms and conditions generally applicable to other members, or (B) if he has reasonable grounds for believing that membership was denied or terminated for reasons other than the failure of the employee to tender the periodic dues and the initiation fees uniformly required as a condition of acquiring or retaining membership;

(4) to discharge or otherwise discriminate against an employee because he has filed charges or given testimony under this Act;

(5) to refuse to bargain collectively with the representatives of his employees, subject to the provisions of section 9(a).

(b) It shall be an unfair labor practice for a labor organization or its agents—

(1) to restrain or coerce (A) employees in the exercise of the rights guaranteed in section 7: *Provided,* That this paragraph shall not impair the right of a labor organization to prescribe its own rules with respect to the acquisition or retention of membership therein; or (B) an employer in the selection of his representatives for the purpose of collective bargaining or the adjustment of grievances;

(2) to cause or attempt to cause an employer to discriminate against an employee in violation of subsection (a)(3) or to discriminate against an employee with respect to whom membership in such organization has been denied or terminated on some ground other than his failure to tender the periodic dues and the initiation fees uniformly required as a condition of acquiring or retaining membership;

(3) to refuse to bargain collectively with an employer, provided it is the representative of his employees subject to the provisions of section 9(a);

(4) (i) to engage in, or to induce or encourage any individual employed by any person engaged in commerce or in an industry affecting commerce to engage in, a strike or a refusal in the course of his employment to use, manufacture, process, transport, or otherwise handle or work on any goods, articles, materials, or commodities or to perform any services; or (ii) to threaten, coerce, or restrain any person engaged in commerce or in an industry affecting commerce, where in either case an object thereof is:

(A) forcing or requiring any employer or self-employed person to join any labor or employer organization or to enter into any agreement which is prohibited by section 8(e);

(B) forcing or requiring any person to cease using, selling, handling, transporting, or otherwise dealing in the products of any other producer, processor, or manufacturer, or to cease doing business with any other person, or forcing or requiring any other employer to recognize or bargain with a labor organization as the representative of his employees unless such labor organization has been certified as the representative of such employees under the provisions of section 9: *Provided*, That nothing contained in this clause (B) shall be construed to make unlawful, where not otherwise unlawful, any primary strike or primary picketing;

(C) forcing or requiring any employer to recognize or bargain with a particular labor organization as the representative of his employees if another labor organization has been certified as the representative of such employees under the provisions of section 9;

(D) forcing or requiring any employer to assign particular work to employees in a particular labor organization or in a particular trade, craft, or class rather than to employees in another labor organization or in another trade, craft, or class, unless such employer is failing to conform to an order or certification of the Board determining the bargaining representative for employees performing such work: *Provided*, That nothing contained in this subsection (b) shall be construed to make unlawful a refusal by any person to enter upon the premises of any employer (other than his own employer), if the employees of such employer are engaged in a strike ratified or approved by a representative of such employees whom such employer is required to recognize under this Act: *Provided further*, That for the purposes of this paragraph (4) only, nothing contained in such paragraph shall be construed to prohibit publicity, other than picketing, for the purpose of truthfully advising the public, including consumers and members of a labor organization, that a product or products are produced by an employer with whom the labor organization has a primary dispute and are distributed by another employer, as long as such publicity does not have an effect of inducing any individual employed by any person other than the primary employer in the course of his employment to refuse to pick up, deliver, or transport any goods, or not to perform any services, at the establishment of the employer engaged in such distribution;

(5) to require of employees covered by an agreement authorized under subsection (a)(3) the payment, as a condition precedent to becoming a member of such organization, of a fee in an amount which the Board finds excessive or discriminatory under all the circumstances. In making such a finding, the Board shall consider, among relevant factors, the practices and customs of labor organizations in the particular industry, and the wages currently paid to the employees affected;

(6) to cause or attempt to cause an employer to pay or deliver or agree to pay or deliver any money or other thing of value, in the nature of an exaction for services which are not performed or not to be performed; and

(7) to picket or cause to be picketed, or threaten to picket or cause to be picketed, any employer where an object thereof is forcing or requiring an employer to recognize or bargain with a labor organization as the representative of his employees, or forcing or requiring the employees of an employer to accept or select such labor organization as their collective bargaining representative, unless such labor organization is currently certified as the representative of such employees:

(A) where the employer has lawfully recognized in accordance with this Act any other labor organization and a question concerning representation may not appropriately be raised under section 9(c) of this Act,

(B) where within the preceding twelve months a valid election under section 9(c) of this Act has been conducted, or

(C) where such picketing has been conducted without a petition under section 9(c) being filed within a reasonable period of time not to exceed thirty days from the commencement of such picketing: *Provided*, That when such a petition has been filed the Board shall forthwith, without regard to the provisions of section 9(c)(1) or the absence of a showing of a substantial interest on the part of the labor organization, direct an election in such unit as the Board finds to be appropriate and shall certify the results thereof: *Provided further*, That nothing in this subparagraph (C) shall be construed to prohibit any picketing or other publicity for the purpose of truthfully advising the public (including consumers) that an employer does not employ members of, or have a contract with, a labor organization, unless an effect of such picketing is to induce any individual employed by any other person in the course of his employment, not to pick up, deliver or transport any goods or not to perform any services.

Nothing in this paragraph (7) shall be construed to permit any act which would otherwise be an unfair labor practice under this section 8(b).

(c) The expressing of any views, argument, or opinion, or the dissemination thereof, whether in written, printed, graphic, or visual form, shall not constitute or be evidence of an unfair labor practice under any of the provisions of this Act, if such expression contains no threat of reprisal or force or promise of benefit.

(d) For the purposes of this section, to bargain collectively is the performance of the mutual obligation of the employer and the representative of the employees to meet at reasonable times and confer in good faith with respect to wages, hours, and other terms and conditions of employment, or the negotiation of an agreement or any question arising thereunder, and the execution of a written contract incorporating any agreement reached if requested by either party, but such obligation does not compel either party to agree to a proposal or require the making of a concession: *Provided*, That where there is in effect a collective-bargaining contract covering employees in an industry affecting commerce, the duty to bargain collectively shall also mean that no party to such contract shall terminate or modify such contract, unless the party desiring such termination or modification—

(1) serves a written notice upon the party to the contract of the proposed termination or modification sixty days prior to the expiration date thereof, or in the event such contract contains no expiration date, sixty days prior to the time it is proposed to make such termination or modification;

(2) offers to meet and confer with the other party for the purpose of negotiating a new contract or a contract containing the proposed modifications;

(3) notifies the Federal Mediation and Conciliation Service within thirty days after such notice of the existence of a dispute, and simultaneously therewith notifies any State or Territorial agency established to mediate and conciliate disputes within the State or Territory where the dispute occurred, provided no agreement has been reached by that time; and

(4) continues in full force and effect, without resorting to strike or lockout, all the terms and conditions of the existing contract for a period of sixty days after such notice is given or until the expiration date of such contract, whichever occurs later.

The duties imposed upon employers, employees, and labor organizations by paragraphs (2), (3), and (4) shall become inapplicable upon an intervening certification of the Board, under which the labor organization or individual, which is a party to the contract, has been superseded as or ceased to be the representative of the employees subject to the provisions of section 9(a), and the duties so imposed shall not be construed as requiring either party to discuss or agree to any modification of the terms and conditions contained in a contract for a fixed period, if such modification is to become effective before such terms and conditions can be reopened under the provisions of the contract. Any employee who engages in a strike within any notice period specified in this subsection, or who engages in any strike with the appropriate period specified in subsection (g) of this section, shall lose his status as an employee of the employer engaged in the particular labor dispute, for the purposes of sections 8, 9, and 10 of this Act, as amended, but such loss of status for such employee shall terminate if and when he is reemployed by such employer. Whenever the collective bargaining involves employees of a health care institution, the provisions of this section 8(d) shall be modified as follows:

(A) The notice of section 8(d)(1) shall be ninety days; the notice of section 8(d)(3) shall be sixty days; and the contract period of section 8(d)(4) shall be ninety days.

(B) Where the bargaining is for an initial agreement following certification or recognition, at least thirty days' notice of the existence of a dispute shall be given by the labor organization to the agencies set forth in section 8(d)(3).

(C) After notice is given to the Federal Mediation and Conciliation Service under either clause (A) or (B) of this sentence, the Service shall promptly communicate with the parties and use its best efforts, by mediation and conciliation, to bring them to agreement. The parties shall participate fully and promptly in such meetings as may be undertaken by the Service for the purpose of aiding in a settlement of the dispute.

(e) It shall be an unfair labor practice for any labor organization and any employer to enter into any contract or agreement, express or implied, whereby such employer ceases or refrains or agrees to cease or refrain from handling, using, selling, transporting or otherwise dealing in any of the products of any other employer, or to cease doing business with any other person, and any contract or agreement entered into heretofore or hereafter containing such an agreement shall be to such extent unenforceable and void: *Provided*, That nothing in this subsection (e) shall apply to an agreement between a labor organization and an employer in the construction industry relating to the contracting or subcontracting of work to be done at the site of the construction, alteration, painting, or repair of a building, structure, or other work: *Provided further*, That for the purposes of this subsection (e) and section 8(b)(4)(B) the terms "any employer," "any person engaged in commerce or in industry affecting commerce," and "any person" when used in relation to the terms "any other producer, processor, or manufacturer," "any other employer," or "any other person" shall not include persons in the relation of a jobber, manufacturer, contractor, or subcontractor working on the goods or premises of the jobber or manufacturer or performing parts of an integrated process of production in the apparel and clothing industry: *Provided further*, That nothing in this Act shall prohibit the enforcement of any agreement which is within the foregoing exception.

(f) It shall not be an unfair labor practice under subsections (a) and (b) of this section for an employer engaged primarily in the building and construction industry to make an agreement covering employees engaged (or who, upon their employment, will be engaged) in the building and construction industry with a labor organization of which building and construction employees are members (not established, maintained, or assisted by any action defined in section 8(a) of this Act as an unfair labor practice) because (1) the majority status of such labor organization has not been established under the provisions of section 9 of this Act prior to the making of such agreement, or (2) such agreement requires as a condition of employment, membership in such labor organization after the seventh day following the beginning of such employment or the effective date of the agreement, whichever is later, or (3) such agreement requires the employer to notify such labor organization of opportunities for employment with such employer, or gives such labor organization an opportunity to refer qualified applicants for such employment, or (4) such agreement specifies minimum training or experience qualifications for employment or provides for priority in opportunities for employment based upon length of service with such employer, in the industry or in the particular geographical area: *Provided*, That nothing in this subsection shall set aside the final proviso to section 8(a)(3) of this Act: *Provided further*, That any agreement which would be invalid, but for clause (1) of this subsection, shall not be a bar to a petition filed pursuant to section 9(c) or 9(e).

(g) A labor organization before engaging in any strike, picketing, or other concerted refusal to work at any health care institution shall, not less than ten days prior to such action, notify the institution in writing and the Federal Mediation and Conciliation Service of that intention, except that in the case of bargaining for an initial agreement following certification or recognition the notice required by this subsection shall not be given the expiration of the period specified in clause (B) of the last sentence of section 8(d) of this Act. The notice shall state the date and time that such action will commence. The notice, once given, may be extended by the written agreement of both parties.

Title VII of Civil Rights Act of 1964

DISCRIMINATION BECAUSE OF RACE, COLOR, RELIGION, SEX, OR NATIONAL ORIGIN

Section 703. (a) It shall be an unlawful employment practice for an employer—

(1) to fail or refuse to hire or to discharge any individual, or otherwise to discriminate against any individual with respect to his compensation, terms, conditions, or privileges of employment, because of such an individual's race, color, religion, sex, or national origin; or

(2) limit, segregate, or classify his employees or applicants for employment in any way which would deprive or tend to deprive any individual of employment opportunities or otherwise adversely affect his status as an employee, because of such individual's race, color, religion, sex, or national origin.

(b) It shall be an unlawful employment practice for an employment agency to fail or refuse to refer for employment, or otherwise to discriminate against, an individual because of his race, color, religion, sex, or national origin, or to classify or refer for employment any individual on the basis of his race, color, religion, sex, or national origin.

(c) It shall be an unlawful employment practice for a labor organization—

(1) to exclude or to expel from its membership, or otherwise to discriminate against, any individual because of his race, color, religion, sex, or national origin;

(2) to limit, segregate, or classify its membership or applicants for membership or to classify or fail or refuse to refer for employment any individual, in any way which would deprive or tend to deprive any individual of employment opportunities, or would limit such employment opportunities or otherwise adversely affect his status as an employee or as an applicant for employment, because of such an individual's race, color, religion, sex, or national origin; or

(3) to cause or attempt to cause an employer to discriminate against an individual in violation of this section.

(d) It shall be an unlawful employment practice for any employer, labor organization, or joint labor-management committee controlling apprenticeship or other training or retraining, including on-the-job training programs to discriminate against any individual because of his race, color, religion, sex, or national origin in admission to, or employment in, any program established to provide apprenticeship or other training.

(e) Notwithstanding any other provision of this title, (1) it shall not be an unlawful employment practice for an employer to hire and employ employees, for an employment agency to classify, or refer for employment any individual, or for any employer, labor organization, or joint labor-management committee controlling apprenticeship or other training or retraining programs to admit or employ any individual in any such program, on the basis of his religion, sex, or national origin in those certain instances where religion, sex, or national origin is a bona fide occupational qualification reasonably necessary to the normal operation of that particular business or enterprise, and (2) it shall not be an unlawful employment practice for a school, college, university, or other educational institution or institution of learning to hire and employ employees of a particular religion if such school, college, university, or other educational institution or institution of learning is, in whole or in substantial part, owned, supported, controlled, or managed by a particular religion or by a particular religious corporation, association, or society, or if the curriculum of such school, college, university, or other educational institution or institution of learning is directed toward the propagation of a particular religion.

(f) As used in this title, the phrase "unlawful employment practice" shall not be deemed to include any action or measure taken by an employer, labor organization, joint labor-management committee, or employment agency with respect to an individual who is a member of the Communist Party of the United States or of any other organization required to register as a Communist-action or Communist-front organization by final order of the Subversive Activities Control Act of 1950.

(g) Notwithstanding any other provision of this title, it shall not be an unlawful employment practice for an employer to fail or refuse to hire and employ any individual for any position, for an employer to discharge an individual from any position, or for any employment agency to fail or refuse to refer any individual for employment in any position, or for a labor organization to fail or refuse any individual for employment in any position, if—

(1) the occupancy of such position, or access to the premises in or upon which any part of the duties of such position is performed or is to be performed, is subject to any requirement imposed in the interest of the national security of the United States under any security program in effect pursuant to or administered under any statute of the United States or any Executive order of the President; and

(2) such individual has not fulfilled or has ceased to fulfill that requirement.

(h) Notwithstanding any other provision of this title, it shall not be an unlawful employment practice for an employer to apply different standards of compensation, or different terms, conditions, or privileges of employment pursuant to a bona fide seniority or merit system, or a system which measures earnings by quantity or quality of production or to employees who work in different locations, provided that such differences are not the result of an intention to discriminate because of race, color, religion, sex, or national origin; nor shall it be an unlawful employment practice for an employer to give and to act upon the results of any professionally developed ability test provided that such test, its administration or action upon the results is not designed, intended, or used to discriminate because of race, color, religion, sex,

or national origin. It shall not be an unlawful employment practice under this title for any employer to differentiate upon the basis of sex in determining the amount of wages or compensation paid or to be paid to employees of such employer if such differentiation is authorized by the provision of Section 6(d) of the Fair Labor Standards Act of 1938 as amended (29 U.S.C. 206(d)).

(i) Nothing contained in this title shall apply to any business or enterprise on or near an Indian reservation with respect to any publicly announced employment practice of such business or enterprise under which a preferential treatment is given to any individual because he is an Indian living on or near a reservation.

(j) Nothing contained in this title shall be interpreted to require any employer, employment agency, labor organization, or joint labor-management committee subject to this title to grant preferential treatment to any individual or to any group because of the race, color, religion, sex, or national origin of such individual or group on account of an imbalance which may exist with respect to the total number or percentage of persons of any race, color, religion, sex, or national origin employed by any employer, referred or classified for employment by any employment agency or labor organization, admitted to membership or classified by any labor organization, or admitted to, or employed in, any apprenticeship or other training program, in comparison with the total number or percentage of persons of such race, color, religion, sex, or national origin in any community, State, section, or other area, or in the available work force in any community, State, section, or other area.

The Sherman Antitrust Act

Section 1. *Trusts, etc., in restraint of trade illegal; penalty.* Every contract, combination in the form of trust or otherwise, or conspiracy, in restraint of trade or commerce among the several States, or with foreign nations, is declared to be illegal. Every person who shall make any contract or engage in any combination or conspiracy declared by sections 1 to 7 of this title to be illegal shall be deemed guilty of a felony, and, on conviction thereof,

shall be punished by fine not exceeding one million dollars if a corporation, or, if any other person, one hundred thousand dollars, or by imprisonment not exceeding three years, or by both said punishments, in the discretion of the court.

Section 2. *Monopolizing trade a felony; penalty.* Every person who shall monopolize, or attempt to monopolize, or combine or conspire with any other person or persons, to monopolize any part of the trade or commerce among the several States, or with foreign nations, shall be deemed guilty of a felony, and, on conviction thereof, shall be punished by fine not exceeding one million dollars if a corporation, or, if any other person, one hundred thousand dollars, or by imprisonment not exceeding three years, or by both said punishments, in the discretion of the court.

The Robinson-Patman Act*

Section 2. *Discrimination in price, services, or facilities.*

(a) Price; selection of customers.

It shall be unlawful for any person engaged in commerce, in the course of such commerce, either directly or indirectly, to discriminate in price between different purchases of commodities of like grade and quality, where either or any of the purchasers involved in such discrimination are in commerce, where such commodities are sold for use, consumption, or resale within the United States or any Territory thereof or the District of Columbia or any insular possession or other place under the jurisdiction of the United States, and where the effect of such discrimination may be substantially to lessen competition or tend to create a monopoly in any line of commerce, or to injure, destroy, or prevent competition with any person who either grants or knowingly receives the benefit of such discrimination, or with customers of either of them: *Provided,* That nothing herein contained shall prevent differentials which make only due allowance for differences in the cost of manufacture, sale, or delivery resulting from the differing methods or quantities in which such commodities are to such purchasers sold or delivered: *Provided, however,* That the Federal Trade Commission may, after due investigation and hearing to all interested parties, fix and establish quantity limits, and revise the same as it finds necessary as to particular commodities or classes of commodities, where it finds that available purchasers in greater quantities are so few as to render differentials on account thereof unjustly discriminatory or promotive of monopoly in any line of commerce; and the foregoing shall then not be construed to permit differentials based on differences in quantities greater than those so fixed and established: *And provided further,* That nothing herein contained shall prevent persons engaged in selling goods, wares, or merchandise in commerce from selecting their own customers in bona fide transactions and not in restraint of trade: *And provided further,* That nothing herein contained shall prevent price changes from time to time where in response to changing conditions affecting the market for or the market-ability of the goods concerned, such as but not limited to actual or imminent deterioration of perishable goods, obsolescence of seasonal goods, distress sales under court process, or sales in good faith in discontinuance of business in the goods concerned.

(b) Burden of rebutting prima-facie case of discrimination.

Upon proof being made, at any hearing on a complaint under this section, that there has been discrimination in price or services or facilities furnished, the burden of rebutting the prima-facie case thus made by showing justification shall be upon the person charged with a violation of this section, and unless justification shall be affirmatively shown, the Commission is authorized to issue an order terminating the discrimination: *Provided, however,* That nothing herein contained shall prevent a seller rebutting the prima-facie case thus made by showing that his lower price or the furnishing of services or facilities to any purchaser or purchasers was made in good faith to meet an equally low price of a competitor, or the services or facilities furnished by a competitor.

(c) Payment or acceptance of commission, brokerage or other compensation.

It shall be unlawful for any person engaged in commerce, in the course of such commerce, to pay or grant, or to receive or accept, anything of value as a commission, brokerage, or other compensation, or any allowance of discount in lieu thereof, except for services rendered in connection with the sale or purchase of goods, wares, or merchandise,

---

*Passed in 1936 to amend Section 2 of the Clayton Act.

either to the other party to such transaction or to an agent, representative, or other intermediary therein where such intermediary is acting in fact for or in behalf, or is subject to the direct or indirect control, of any party to such transaction other than the person by whom such compensation is so granted or paid.

(d) Payment for services of facilities for processing or sale.

It shall be unlawful for any person engaged in commerce to pay or contract for the payment of anything of value to or for the benefit of a customer of such person in the course of such commerce as compensation or in consideration for any services or facilities furnished by or through such customer in connection with the processing, handling, sale, or offering for sale of any products or commodities manufactured, sold, or offered for sale by such person, unless such payment of consideration is available on proportionally equal terms to all other customers competing in the distribution of such products or commodities.

(e) Furnishing services or facilities for processing, handling, etc.

It shall be unlawful for any person to discriminate in favor of one purchaser against another purchaser or purchasers of a commodity bought for resale, with or without processing, by contracting to furnish or furnishing, or by contributing to the furnishing of, any services or facilities connected with the processing, handling, sale, or offering for sale of such commodity so purchased upon terms not accorded to all purchasers on proportionally equal terms.

(f) Knowingly inducing or receiving discriminatory price.

It shall be unlawful for any person engaged in commerce, in the course of such commerce, knowingly to induce or receive a discrimination in price which is prohibited by this section.

The Clayton Antitrust Act

Section 3. *Sale, etc., on agreement not to use goods of competitor.* It shall be unlawful for any person engaged in commerce, in the course of such commerce, to lease or make a sale or contract for sale of goods, wares, merchandise, machinery, supplies, or other commodities, whether patented or unpatented, for use, consumption, or resale within the United States or any Territory thereof or the District of Columbia or any insular possession or other place under the jurisdiction of the United States, or fix a price charged thereof, or discount from, or rebate upon, such price, on the condition, agreement, or understanding that the lessee or purchaser thereof shall not use or deal in the goods, wares, merchandise, machinery, supplies, or other commodities of a competitor or competitors of the lessor or seller, where the effect of such lease, sale, or contract for sale or such condition, agreement or understanding may be to substantially lessen competition or tend to create a monopoly in any line of commerce.

Section 7. *Acquisition by one corporation of stock of another.* No corporation engaged in commerce shall acquire, directly or indirectly, the whole or any part of the stock or other share capital and no corporation subject to the jurisdiction of the Federal Trade Commission shall acquire the whole or any part of the assets of another corporation engaged also in commerce, where in any line of commerce in any section of the country, the effect of such acquisition may be substantially to lessen competition, or to tend to create a monopoly.

No corporation shall acquire, directly or indirectly, the whole or any part of the stock or other share capital and no corporation subject to the jurisdiction of the Federal Trade Commission shall acquire the whole or any part of the assets of one or more corporations engaged in commerce, where in any line of commerce in any section of the country, the effect of such acquisition, of such stocks or assets, or of the use of such stock by the voting or granting of proxies or otherwise, may be substantially to lessen competition, or to tend to create a monopoly.

This section shall not apply to corporations purchasing such stock solely for investment and not using the same by voting or otherwise to bring about, or in attempting to bring about, the substantial lessening of competition. Nor shall anything contained in this section prevent a corporation engaged in commerce from causing the formation of subsidiary corporations for the actual carrying on of their immediate lawful business, or the natural and legitimate branches or extensions thereof, or from owning and holding all or part of the stock of such subsidiary corporations, when the effect of such formation is not to substantially lessen competition.

Section 8. *Interlocking directorates and officers....*

No person at the same time shall be a director in any two or more corporations, any one of which has capital, surplus, and undivided profits aggregating more than $1,000,000, engaged in whole or in part in commerce, other than banks, banking associations, trust companies, and common carriers subject to the Act to regulate commerce approved February fourth, eighteen hundred and eighty-seven, if such corporations are or shall have been theretofore, by virtue of their business and location or operation, competitors, so that the elimination of competition by agreement between them would constitute a violation of any of the provisions of any of the antitrust laws. The eligibility of a director under the foregoing provision shall be determined by the aggregate amount of the capital, surplus, and undivided profits, exclusive of dividends declared but not paid to stockholders, at the end of the fiscal year of said corporation next preceding the election of the directors, and when a director has been elected in accordance with the provisions of this Act it shall be lawful for him to continue as such for one year thereafter.

The Federal Trade Commission Act

Section 5. *Unfair methods of competition unlawful; prevention by Commission—declaration.* Declaration of unlawfulness; power to prohibit unfair practices.

(a) (1) Unfair methods of competition in or affecting commerce, and unfair or deceptive acts or practices in or affecting commerce, are declared unlawful....

Penalty for violation of order, injunctions and other appropriate equitable relief.

(b) Any person, partnership, or corporation who violates an order of the Commission to cease and desist after it has become final, and while such order is in effect, shall forfeit and pay to the United States a civil penalty of not more than $5,000 for each violation, which shall accrue to the United States and may be recovered in a civil action brought by the Attorney General of the United States. Each separate violation of such an order shall be a separate offense, except that in the case of a violation through continuing failure or neglect to obey a final order of the Commission each day of continuance of such failure or neglect shall be deemed a separate offense.

APPENDIX E
UNITED NATIONS CONVENTION ON CONTRACTS
FOR THE INTERNATIONAL SALE OF GOODS (EXCERPTS)

The States Parties to this Convention,

Bearing in mind the broad objectives in the resolutions adopted by the sixth special session of the General Assembly of the United Nations on the establishment of a New International Economic Order,

Considering that the development of international trade on the basis of equality and mutual benefit is an important element in promoting friendly relations among States,

Being of the opinion that the adoption of uniform rules which govern contracts for the international sale of goods and take into account the different social, economic and legal systems would contribute to the removal of legal barriers in international trade and promote the development of international trade,

Have agreed as follows:

PART I. SPHERE OF APPLICATION AND GENERAL PROVISIONS

Chapter I. Sphere of Application

ARTICLE 1

(1) This Convention applies to contracts of sale of goods between parties whose places of business are in different States:

   (a) when the States are Contracting States; or

   (b) when the rules of private international law lead to the application of the law of a Contracting State.

(2) The fact that the parties have their places of business in different States is to be disregarded whenever this fact does not appear either from the

contract or from any dealings between, or from information disclosed by, the parties at any time before or at the conclusion of the contract.

(3) Neither the nationality of the parties nor the civil or commercial character of the parties or of the contract is to be taken into consideration in determining the application of this Convention.

ARTICLE 2

This Convention does not apply to sales:

(a) of goods bought for personal, family or household use, unless the seller, at any time before or at the conclusion of the contract, neither knew nor ought to have known that the goods were bought for any such use;

(b) by auction;

(c) on execution or otherwise by authority of law;

(d) of stocks, shares, investment securities, negotiable instruments or money;

(e) of ships, vessels, hovercraft or aircraft;

(f) of electricity

ARTICLE 3

(1) Contracts for the supply of goods to be manufactured or produced are to be considered sales unless the party who orders the goods undertakes to supply a substantial part of the materials necessary for such manufacture or production.

(2) This Convention does not apply to contracts in which the preponderant part of the obligations of the party who furnishes the goods consists in the supply of labour or other services.

ARTICLE 4

This Convention governs only the formation of the contract of sale and the rights and obligations of the seller and the buyer arising from such a contract. In particular, except as otherwise expressly provided in this Convention, it is not concerned with:

(a) the validity of the contract or of any of its provisions or of any usage;

(b) the effect which the contract may have on the property in the goods sold.

ARTICLE 5

This Convention does not apply to the liability of the seller for death or personal injury caused by the goods to any person.

ARTICLE 6

The parties may exclude the application of this Convention or, subject to article 12, derogate from or vary the effect of any of its provisions.

Chapter II. General Provisions

ARTICLE 7

(1) In the interpretation of this Convention, regard is to be had to its international character and to the need to promote uniformity in its application and the observance of good faith in international trade.

(2) Questions concerning matters governed by this Convention which are not expressly settled in it are to be settled in conformity with the general principles on which it is based or, in the absence of such principles, in conformity with the law applicable by virtue of the rules of private international law.

ARTICLE 8

(1) For the purposes of this Convention statements made by and other conduct of a party are to be interpreted according to his intent where the other party knew or could not have been unaware what that intent was.

(2) If the preceding paragraph is not applicable, statements made by and other conduct of a party are to be interpreted according to the understanding that a reasonable person of the same kind as the other party would have had in the same circumstances.

(3) In determining the intent of a party or the understanding a reasonable person would have had, due consideration is to be given to all relevant circumstances of the case including the negotiations, any practices which the parties have established between themselves, usages and any subsequent conduct of the parties.

ARTICLE 9

(1) The parties are bound by any usage to which they have agreed and by any practices which they have established between themselves.

(2) The parties are considered, unless otherwise agreed, to have impliedly made applicable to their contract or its formation a usage of which the parties knew or ought to have known and

which in international trade is widely known to, and regularly observed by, parties to contracts of the type involved in the particular trade concerned.

ARTICLE 10

For the purposes of this Convention:

(a) if a party has more than one place of business, the place of business is that which has the closest relationship to the contract and its performance, having regard to the circumstances known to or contemplated by the parties at any time before or at the conclusion of the contract;

(b) if a party does not have a place of business, reference is to be made to his habitual residence.

ARTICLE 11

A contract of sale need not be concluded in or evidenced by writing and is not subject to any other requirements as to form. It may be proved by any means, including witnesses.

ARTICLE 12

Any provision of article 11, article 29 or Part II of this Convention that allows a contract of sale or its modification or termination by agreement of any offer, acceptance or other indication of intention to be made in any form other than in writing does not apply where any party has his place of business in a Contracting State which has made a declaration under article 96 of this Convention. The parties may not derogate from or vary the effect of this article.

ARTICLE 13

For the purposes of this Convention "writing" includes telegram and telex.

PART II. FORMATION OF THE CONTRACT

ARTICLE 14

(1) A proposal for concluding a contract addressed to one or more specific persons constitutes an offer if it is sufficiently definite and indicates the intention of the offeror to be bound in case of acceptance. A proposal is sufficiently definite if it indicates the goods and expressly or implicitly fixes or makes provision for determining the quantity and the price.

(2) A proposal other than one addressed to one or more specific persons is to be considered merely as an invitation to make offers, unless the contrary is clearly indicated by the person making the proposal.

ARTICLE 15

(1) An offer becomes effective when it reaches the offeree.

(2) An offer, even if it is irrevocable, may be withdrawn if the withdrawal reaches the offeree before or at the same time as the offer.

ARTICLE 16

(1) Until a contract is concluded an offer may be revoked if the revocation reaches the offeree before he has dispatched an acceptance.

(2) However, an offer cannot be revoked:

(a) if it indicates, whether by stating a fixed time for acceptance or otherwise, that it is irrevocable; or

(b) if it was reasonable for the offeree to rely on the offer as being irrevocable and the offeree has acted in reliance on the offer.

ARTICLE 17

An offer, even if it is irrevocable, is terminated when a rejection reaches the offeror.

ARTICLE 18

(1) A statement made by or other conduct of the offeree indicating assent to an offer is an acceptance. Silence or inactivity does not in itself amount to acceptance.

(2) An acceptance of an offer becomes effective at the moment the indication of assent reaches the offeror. An acceptance is not effective if the indication of assent does not reach the offeror within the time he has fixed or, if no time is fixed, within a reasonable time, due account being taken of the circumstances of the transaction, including the rapidity of the means of communication employed by the offeror. An oral offer must be accepted immediately unless circumstances indicate otherwise.

(3) However, if, by virtue of the offer or as a result of practices which the parties have established between themselves or of usage, the offeree

may indicate assent by performing an act, such as one relating to the dispatch of the goods or payment of the price, without notice to the offeror, the acceptance is effective at the moment the act is performed, provided that the act is performed within the period of time laid down in the preceding paragraph.

ARTICLE 19

(1) A reply to an offer which purports to be an acceptance but contains additions, limitations or other modifications is a rejection of the offer and constitutes a counter-offer.

(2) However, a reply to an offer which purports to be an acceptance but contains additional or different terms which do not materially alter the terms of the offer constitutes an acceptance, unless the offeror, without undue delay, objects orally to the discrepancy or dispatches a notice to that effect. If he does not so object, the terms of the contract are the terms of the offer with the modifications contained in the acceptance.

(3) Additional or different terms relating, among other things, to the price, payment, quality and quantity of the goods, place and time of delivery, extent of one party's liability to the other or the settlement of disputes are considered to alter the terms of the offer materially.

ARTICLE 20

(1) A period of time for acceptance fixed by the offeror in a telegram or a letter begins to run from the moment the telegram is handed in for dispatch or from the date shown on the letter or, if no such date is shown, from the date shown on the envelope. A period of time for acceptance fixed by the offeror by telephone, telex or other means of instantaneous communication, begins to run from the moment that the offer reaches the offeree.

(2) Official holidays or non-business days occurring during the period for acceptance are included in calculating the period. However, if a notice of acceptance cannot be delivered at the address of the offeror on the last day of the period because that day falls on an official holiday or a non-business day at the place of business of the offeror, the period is extended until the first business day which follows.

ARTICLE 21

(1) A late acceptance is nevertheless effective as an acceptance if without delay the offeror orally so informs the offeree or dispatches a notice to that effect.

(2) If a letter or other writing containing a late acceptance shows that it has been sent in such circumstances that if its transmission had been normal it would have reached the offeror in due time, the late acceptance is effective as an acceptance unless, without delay, the offeror orally informs the offeree that he considers his offer as having lapsed or dispatches a notice to that effect.

ARTICLE 22

An acceptance may be withdrawn if the withdrawal reaches the offeror before or at the same time as the acceptance would have become effective.

ARTICLE 23

A contract is concluded at the moment when an acceptance of an offer becomes effective in accordance with the provisions of this Convention.

ARTICLE 24

For the purposes of this Part of the Convention, an offer, declaration of acceptance or any other indication of intention "reaches" the addressee when it is made orally to him or delivered by any other means to him personally, to his place of business or mailing address or, if he does not have a place of business or mailing address, to his habitual residence.

PART III. SALE OF GOODS

Chapter I. General Provisions

ARTICLE 25

A breach of contract committed by one of the parties is fundamental if it results in such detriment to the other party as substantially to deprive him of what he is entitled to expect under the contract, unless the party in breach did not foresee and a reasonable person of the same kind in the same circumstances would not have foreseen such a result.

ARTICLE 26

A declaration of avoidance of the contract is effective only if made by notice to the other party.

ARTICLE 27

Unless otherwise expressly provided in this Part of the Convention, if any notice, request or other communication is given or made by a party in accordance with this Part and by means appropriate in the circumstances, a delay or error in the transmission of the communication or its failure to arrive does not deprive that party of the right to rely on the communication.

ARTICLE 28

If, in accordance with the provisions of this Convention, one party is entitled to require performance of any obligation by the other party, a court is not bound to enter a judgment for specific performance unless the court would do so under its own law in respect of similar contracts of sale not governed by this Convention.

ARTICLE 29

(1) A contract may be modified or terminated by the mere agreement of the parties.

(2) A contract in writing which contains a provision requiring any modification or termination by agreement to be in writing may not be otherwise modified or terminated by agreement. However, a party may be precluded by his conduct from asserting such a provision to the extent that the other party has relied on that conduct.

Chapter II. Obligations of the Seller

* * * * *

ARTICLE 35

(1) The seller must deliver goods which are of the quantity, quality and description required by the contract and which are contained or packaged in the manner required by the contract.

(2) Except where the parties have agreed otherwise, the goods do not conform with the contract unless they:

(a) are fit for the purposes for which goods of the same description would ordinarily be used;

(b) are fit for any particular purpose expressly or impliedly made known to the seller at the time of the conclusion of the contract, except where the circumstances show that the buyer did not rely, or that it was unreasonable for him to rely, on the seller's skill and judgment;

(c) possess the qualities of goods which the seller has held out to the buyer as a sample or model;

(d) are contained or packaged in the manner usual for such goods or, where there is no such manner, in a manner adequate to preserve and protect the goods.

(3) The seller is not liable under subparagraphs (a) to (d) of the preceding paragraph for any lack of conformity of the goods if at the time of the conclusion of the contract the buyer knew or could not have been unaware of such lack of conformity.

ARTICLE 36

(1) The seller is liable in accordance with the contract and this Convention for any lack of conformity which exists at the time when the risk passes to the buyer, even though the lack of conformity becomes apparent only after that time.

(2) The seller is also liable for any lack of conformity which occurs after the time indicated in the preceding paragraph and which is due to a breach of any of his obligations, including a breach of any guarantee that for a period of time the goods will remain fit for their ordinary purpose or for some particular purpose or will retain specified qualities or characteristics.

ARTICLE 37

If the seller has delivered goods before the date for delivery, he may, up to that date, deliver any missing part or make up any deficiency in the quantity of the goods delivered, or deliver goods in replacement of any non-conforming goods delivered or remedy any lack of conformity in the goods delivered, provided that the exercise of this right does not cause the buyer unreasonable inconvenience or unreasonable expense. However, the buyer retains any right to claim damages as provided for in this Convention.

* * * * *

Chapter III. Obligations of the Buyer

* * * * *

Chapter IV. Passing of Risk

ARTICLE 66

Loss of or damage to the goods after the risk has passed to the buyer does not discharge him from his obligation to pay the price, unless the loss or damage is due to an act or omission of the seller.

ARTICLE 67

(1) If the contract of sale involves carriage of the goods and the seller is not bound to hand them over at a particular place, the risk passes to the buyer when the goods are handed over to the first carrier for transmission to the buyer in accordance with the contract of sale. If the seller is bound to hand the goods over to a carrier at a particular place, the risk does not pass to the buyer until the goods are handed over to the carrier at that place. The fact that the seller is authorized to retain documents controlling the disposition of the goods does not affect the passage of risk.

(2) Nevertheless, the risk does not pass to the buyer until the goods are clearly identified to the contract, whether by markings on the goods, by shipping documents, by notice given to the buyer or otherwise.

ARTICLE 68

The risk in respect of goods sold in transit passes to the buyer from the time of the conclusion of the contract. However, if the circumstances so indicate, the risk is assumed by the buyer from the time the goods were handed over to the carrier who issued the documents embodying the contract of carriage. Nevertheless, if at the time of the conclusion of the contract of sale the seller knew or ought to have known that the goods had been lost or damaged and did not disclose this to the buyer, the loss or damage is at risk of the seller.

ARTICLE 69

(1) In cases not within articles 67 and 68, the risk passes to the buyer when he takes over the goods or, if he does not do so in due time, from the time when the goods are placed at his disposal and he commits a breach of contract by failing to take delivery.

(2) However, if the buyer is bound to take over the goods at a place other than a place of business of the seller, the risk passes when delivery is due and the buyer is aware of the fact that the goods are placed at his disposal at that place.

(3) If the contract relates to goods not then identified, the goods are considered not to be placed at the disposal of the buyer until they are clearly identified to the contract.

ARTICLE 70

If the seller has committed a fundamental breach of contract, articles 67, 68 and 69 do not impair the remedies available to the buyer on account of the breach.

* * * * *

P ART IV. FINAL PROVISIONS

* * * * *

ARTICLE 96

A Contracting State whose legislation requires contracts of sale to be concluded in or evidenced by writing may at any time make a declaration in accordance with article 12 that any provision of article 11, article 29, or Part II of this Convention, that allows a contract of sale or its modification or termination by agreement or any offer, acceptance, or other indication of intention to be made in any form other than writing, does not apply where any party has his place of business in that State.

* * * * *

DONE at Vienna, this day of eleventh day of April, one thousand nine hundred and eighty, in a single original, of which the Arabic, Chinese, English, French, Russian and Spanish texts are equally authentic.

IN WITNESS WHEREOF the undersigned plenipotentiaries, being duly authorized by their respective Governments, have signed this Convention.

GLOSSARY

A

abstract a complete history of all documents which have been publicly recorded and which relate to a piece of property

account receivable money owed to a company by a customer

act of state doctrine the doctrine that governmental actions within a country cannot be challenged in the courts of another country

additur the court's order for more damages than the jury awarded

administrative law judge (ALJ) the trial examiner or hearing examiner for an agency

admiralty law the law of the sea

affidavit a sworn statement

agency shop a union–security device whereby all employees must pay dues to the union which represents them, whether or not the employee chooses to belong to that union

agent a person who has been authorized to conduct one or more business transactions for someone else

airbill the form of a bill of lading used when goods are transported by air

answer the defendant's version of the facts and denial of liability

apparent authority a situation in which the principal's words or actions have made it appear to a third party that agency authority exists

arbitration clause a clause in an agreement which permits the parties to select a person or a panel of persons who are experienced in the type of problem at issue, and who are trusted by both sides, to settle their dispute

assault a condition that occurs when one person's actions put another in fear of bodily harm

assign the legal term for transfer

assumption of risk a common law defense against a personal injury claim, which states that when an employee knows a job is dangerous but continues to perform the work, he or she could not collect damages

at will describing a relationship which either party may end at any time

attractive nuisance liability of a property owner who permits conditions on the property that lure young children onto the property and cause their injury

bail a sum of money left with the court to assure that a criminal defendant will appear for trial

bailee a person or warehouse who is in lawful possession of goods owned by another

bailment a situation in which one person has lawful possession of goods which are owned by another person; the temporary transfer of personal property

bailor transferor of goods into the lawful possession of another person in a bailment

battery unauthorized touching of another's body

bearer a person in possession of a negotiable instrument made payable to bearer, or of one which has been indorsed

bilateral contract a contract in which each party makes a promise to the other

bill of lading a document that serves as a contract for services, receipt for goods, and a means of transferring rights in goods without physically handling the goods themselves

BIOC the abbreviation for "buyer in the ordinary course of business"

blocking statute a statute that prevents the enforcement of a U.S. court order in another country

bond a long-term debt obligation

boycott refusal to buy a company's product or service

broker a third party, usually hired by the seller, whose job is to find buyers for property

burden of proof the responsibility for presenting evidence and for persuading the trier of fact

business judgment rule the courts' policy of imposing no liability for losses which resulted from the mistaken judgments of management

C

caveat emptor "Let the buyer beware."

caveat vendor "Let the seller beware."

CD an acknowledgement of receipt of money with an engagement to repay it; abbreviation for certificate of deposit

certificate of deposit an acknowledgement of receipt of money with an engagement to repay it; abbreviated as CD

certified check a check on which a bank has guaranteed payment

certiorari a petition which sets forth reasons for requesting the review of a case by the Supreme Court

challenge for cause a request from a party to a judge that a juror be excused for a specific reason

Chancery Court another name for Equity Court

charging order a court order for a partnership to pay one partner's share of the firm's profits to the court

check a draft drawn against a bank at which the drawer has an account, directing the drawee bank to pay money to a named payee

choice-of-law clause a contract provision which specifies what law will be used to decide any disputes

closed shop a company is prevented from hiring any nonunion members

closing the final meeting between the parties involved in a real estate transaction, at which money and documents are exchanged

cloture closure of debate

common carrier a company which holds itself out to the public as being willing to transport goods for anyone

comparable worth the doctrine that people who perform different jobs which have similar value to the employer must receive equal pay

comparative negligence the rule that the party who was mostly at fault must pay at least part of the other party's damages

complaint a document that states the plaintiff's version of the facts of a case and the legal basis for recovery from the defendant

conglomerate the combining of firms with unrelated businesses

consent decree the agreement of an accused company not to commit violations in the future

consequential secondary, as in the case of damages

consideration the thing of value that is given in exchange for a promise

contract an agreement between two or more parties which the law recognizes as binding

contribution the right of a surety to have cosureties pay their fair shares

contributory negligence a common law defense against a personal injury claim, which states that if an employee's own personal negligence had contributed to the employee's injury, he or she could not collect damages; any negligence by an injured party which contributed to causing the injury

convention a multinational agreement

conversion wrongful interference with an owner's right to personal property

corporate opportunity doctrine the doctrine that a business opportunity belongs to the corporation—not to the individual manager—if it is presented in the manager's official capacity, lies within the scope of the company's business, or is developed with the company's assets

corporation a separate and district legal entity, separate from the human beings who represent it and operate it

counterclaim the defendant's statement of a case against the plaintiff

counteroffer a proposal in different terms

countertrade a transaction in which a foreign firm is repaid for its investment with goods produced by the investment, or with local currency, which it uses to obtain local goods for export

countervailing duty an import duty imposed on goods whose manufacture is subsidized by the government of their country of origin

cover to purchase goods elsewhere and sue the seller for damages as a remedy against the seller's breach of contract

crime a wrong against society as a whole

D

dba the abbreviation for "doing business as"

debenture an unsecured bond; also called a debenture bond

debenture bond an unsecured bond; also called a debenture

debt financing borrowing funds from creditors, usually by selling corporate bonds

declaratory judgment a judgment which defines the rights of the parties without ordering anyone to do anything

deed a document transferring title to land

deed of trust a document which gives the buyer full use of land, but deeds the title to a trust company or bank which holds legal ownership until the buyer has paid the full purchase price

deposition a statement taken from a witness under oath

detrimental reliance a situation in which one party relies on a promise and makes a substantial change in legal position because of the promise

disability a physical or mental impairment, a past history of such impairments, or one's perception as a person who has such impairments

discharge petition writing in which members of one house order a bill out of committee for debate by the house

disclaimer a statement denying the existence of warranties

disparate impact a civil rights violation in which seemingly neutral job qualifications disqualify disproportionate numbers of a protected class of employees

disparate treatment a civil rights violation in which a specific person is treated differently because of race, color, religion, sex, or national origin

dissolution a required reorganization of a partnership after any change in its membership

diversity of citizenship case a case between citizens of different states

doctrine of precedent the assumption that the prior decision(s) made in a similar case should generally be followed

document of title a document which shows evidence of ownership of the goods it represents

domicile the place where a person's permanent home is located

draft a written order to someone else, usually a bank, to pay money to a third party

dumping selling goods at an unfairly low price to win market share or to injure or drive out

competitors in another country

duress pressure or force

emancipated free from parental control and support

employee a person who receives compensation for doing a job for another

Equity Court a supplementary court which gives special remedies

equity financing including additional investors as owners of a company

ethics the branch of philosophy which attempts to define standards for correct human behavior

exhaustion of administrative remedies the requirement to pursue all internal review procedures available within an agency before asking for court review

express authority authority which has been specifically stated in words

express warranty any affirmation of fact or promise which relates to the goods and which becomes part of the basis of a bargain

extra-hazardous job a job which by its very nature exposes members of the public to some risk

false imprisonment illegal interference with another's freedom of movement

federalism division of governmental authority between a national government and state or regional units

fellow servant another employee who injured the plaintiff employee

felony a serious crime, such as arson

fiduciary someone who is placed in a position of trust to manage money or property of another person

firm offer a written offer for goods, signed by a merchant, which states it will remain open for a specified time up to three months

force majeur the doctrine that excuses performance of a contract where an irresistible force, unforeseen by the parties, has substantially changed the situation

foreign corporation a corporation doing local business in a state other than its state of incorporation

forum the court in which a case has been filed

forum non conveniens a legal doctrine which permits courts to dismiss a lawsuit on the grounds of its being brought in an "inconvenient" location

forum-selection clause a contract provision which specifies where any disputes will be heard

fraud in the execution a situation where one party to a contract is deceived as to the very nature of the transaction so that the party does not realize a contract is being made

fraud in the inducement intentional misrepresentation of some facet of the contract that induces a party to enter the contract

full-line forcing the use of a tying contract

garnishee to force a third party in possession of defendant's property to turn that property over to the court

general average the doctrine that if a particular cargo is sacrificed to save the ship that is transporting it, the other cargo owners must contribute proportionately to pay for the loss

general partner the co-owner in a limited partnership who has full, unlimited liability

goods tangible, movable items

guarantor a cosigner who agrees that a creditor can collect from her or him only after attempting to collect from the principal debtor

guarantor of collectability a cosigner who only becomes liable if the creditor gets a judgment against the principal debtor and then is unable to collect it

H

habeas corpus a special procedure that tests the constitutionality of a person's imprisonment

HDC the abbreviation for "holder in due course"

hearing *en banc* a hearing before all the appeals judges in a circuit

holder in due course a person who buys a negotiable instrument in good faith and without notice of claims or defenses; also called an HDC

horizontal merger the combining of competing firms

hostile work environment a workplace situation in which some employees feel threatened or offended as a result of harassment

"hot cargo" agreement an agreement under which a company agrees not to handle non-union goods

I

implied authority authority given to an agent, but not stated in so many words

implied warranty of fitness the promise that goods are fit for a particular purpose

implied warranty of merchantability the promise that goods are of fair, average quality, reasonably fit for their normal use, properly packaged and labelled, that they conform to any promises made on the package or label, and that they will pass without objection in the trade under the contract description

impracticable economically unrealistic for requiring performance of a contract because of an unforeseen event

in pari delicto in equal wrong

indenture an agreement for using certain collateral to secure payment of a bond issue

independent contractor a separate person or business which is hired to do work for someone else

indictment a formal statement of criminal charges from a grand jury

indorsement a signature

information a prosecutor's formal statement of criminal charges

initiative a proposal to amend a state constitution which originates with the voters

injunction a court order

insider director, officer, or holder of ten percent or more of a company's stock

insurable interest a sufficient interest in specified goods to sustain insurance coverage in its favor

intellectual property a business's trade secrets, patents, copyrights, and trademarks

intentional infliction of emotional distress an action committed with the intent of disturbing another person's mental well-being

intentional interference with economic relations inducing a customer to breach an existing contract with a business's competitor

interest group a coalition of persons with similar interests or objectives; pressure group

interpretive rules official guidelines to an agency's enforcement policy

interrogatory a list of specific questions

interspousal immunity the doctrine which prohibits one spouse from suing the other

invasion of privacy disclosure of personal information or intrusion into personal space

investment contract an investment of money in a common enterprise with an expectation that profits will be derived primarily from the efforts of others

invitee a person who comes onto land for the benefit of the landowner

item veto power to refuse to sign into law specific parts of a bill while approving other parts

J

judgment the court's order disposing of a case

judgment N.O.V. judgment notwithstanding the verdict; a motion requesting the trial judge to enter a judgment for one side despite the jury's verdict for the other side

jurisdiction the power of a court to hear a case

justice of the peace a local judge with limited civil and criminal authority

L

land contract an arrangement under which the buyer has possession and use of land, but does not actually get a deed until the balance due on the purchase price is paid in full

legislative rules agency rules which set substantive legal requirements

letter of credit a promise by a bank that it "will honor drafts or other demands for payment upon compliance with the condition specified in the credit"

libel false information about someone published in written form

licensee a person who is on the premises with the owner's express or implied permission, but

not for the owner's benefit

lien the right to withhold goods until services rendered in connection with the goods have been paid for; a claim

limited partner the co-owner in a limited partnership who has limited liability

limited partnership a business organization in which one or more of the co-owners have limited liability, and one or more of the co-owners have unlimited liability

liquidation a proceeding in which a trustee is appointed to collect the debtor's assets, sell them, and pay off the creditors

LLC a business formed as a partnership with limited liability

lockout suspension of operations by an employer

"long-arm" statute a law that provides for limited personal jurisdiction over persons who have had certain minimum contacts with persons or things within the state

M

"mail-box" rule the presumption that an acceptance takes place when the communication is properly sent

malpractice the failure to measure up to professional standards

market share liability the doctrine that holds all producers of a generic product that has caused injury liable for their market share percentages

material fact a fact which might influence the decision of an average, reasonably prudent investor

mercantilism a government economic policy which emphasized a favorable balance of trade in order to accumulate gold and silver

merchant a dealer in goods, someone who is held out as having special knowledge of the goods, or someone represented by an agent who has special knowledge of the goods

merchantability a general guarantee of normal quality in a product

minor a legal infant

"mirror-image" rule a rule that states that in order for an acceptance to exist, the response must be a mirror-image of the offer

misdemeanor a less serious crime, such as disturbing the peace

Missouri Plan a system for appointing judges which combines features of the appointive system and the non-partisan election

moral consideration a situation in which one party owes the other a moral, but not legally enforceable, obligation

morals principles of proper human behavior

mortgage a contract giving the lender a claim against property as security for a loan

negligence failure to use reasonable care in performing activities

negotiable freely and fully transferable

nolo contendere a plea of no contest; the accused does not admit to guilt, but agrees to punishment

nominal consideration a statement of a token value in exchange for a real promise

non-compete agreement an agreement between an employer and an employee which restricts an employee who leaves the company from competing with the employer within a designated area and for a specified length of time

non-delegable duty a liability which cannot be avoided by hiring an independent contractor to do a job

nonnegotiable to be redelivered only to the bailor

note a promise by the maker of the note to pay money

nuisance a tort in which some part of a property owner's use of land interferes with other property owners' rights to use and enjoy their real estate

O

offer to purchase a form, signed by a buyer, which contains an offer to buy a parcel of land

option a preliminary contract, in which value is given to the offeror in exchange for keeping the offer open

order a direction to one party to pay another; an instrument in which one party is directed to pay a specific party or anyone else to whom that specific party transfers the instrument

P

parol oral or written proofs "outside a document"

partnership an association of two or more owners to carry on as co-owners of a business for profit

passing off copying the look of a competitor's product and passing one's own product off as theirs

past consideration things given or done previously

patent the exclusive right to manufacture an item

patronage government jobs, contracts, and projects

peremptory challenge a lawyer's right to dismiss a prospective juror without giving a specific reason

perjury lying under oath

personal jurisdiction the power of a court over an individual person

petition for certiorari a petition which sets forth reasons for requesting the review of a case by the Supreme Court

pledge a credit arrangement in which the items being used as collateral for the loan are left in the possession of the creditor

pocket veto presidential inaction on a bill at the end of a congressional session

power of attorney delegation of authority to an agent through signed writing

pre-existing duty rule the rule that promising to do something you would have to do anyway is not consideration for a promise made today

pre-trial conference a meeting between the judge, both parties, and their lawyers in an effort to settle a case before it goes to trial

pressure group a coalition of persons with similar interests or objectives; interest group

principal a person who hires another to act as an agent

privity of contract connection or relationship between contracting parties

procedural law law that specifies the steps by which a lawsuit is heard

procedural rules rules adopted by an agency to govern its own internal operations

promissory estoppel a situation in which one party's reliance on a promise prevents the promisor from denying the existence of a contract

promissory note a written promise to pay money at a future date

proof of claim a creditor's written, signed statement indicating the nature and amount of a bankrupt debtor's debt

prospectus the disclosure document given to investors

proximate cause the necessity for the plaintiff to show proof that the defendant's conduct caused the plaintiff's injury

proxy a written authorization to vote the owner's shares of stock

Q

quid pro quo a phrase loosely translated as "I will do that for you, if you will do this for me."

quitclaim deed a deed in which the seller makes no guarantees as to the title to the land, but merely transfers whatever claim he or she may have to the land

quota a quantity limit

R

ratify to approve

reasonable accommodation a workplace change made by an employer to enable a handicapped person to perform a job

referendum a proposal, originating in the state legislature, to amend a state constitution

registration statement the full disclosure document filed with the SEC

reimbursement the right of a surety to be repaid by the principal debtor

remand to send back

remittitur the court's order for lower damages than the jury awarded

reorganization a proceeding in which a business or individual debtor is given the opportunity to modify existing obligations and to develop a repayment plan

reply the plaintiff's response to the defendant's answer or counterclaim

res ipsa loquitur circumstantial evidence

right of exoneration the surety's right to force the principal debtor to pay the debt, so the surety

will not have to do so

ripeness for review agreement that a genuine case or controversy which demands court review has arisen

risk of loss an ownership interest in goods which determines which party is financially responsible if the goods are lost or damaged

rule of reason a policy under which a court examines the actual marketplace effect to make its ruling

S

sale a transaction in which ownership of goods is transferred in exchange for a consideration

secondary boycott a union requirement that a company not do business with another company with which the union has a labor dispute

security generally, any scheme in which the participants intend to make money from their passive investment of money rather than their own personal efforts

security interest the right of a creditor to repossess and resell collateral and to apply the proceeds to pay off the owner's loan

senatorial courtesy the practice of clearing judicial nominees with a state's senators

service mark any word (or words), symbol, or device which a company has adopted to identify its service

service of process notification to the defendant that a court case has begun

share of stock a percentage of basic ownership interest in a corporation

shipment contract a contract in which title passes to the buyer when the seller delivers the goods to the carrier for shipment

shop right an employer's right to non-exclusive use of a patent held by a non-research and development employee who developed an idea using the employer's facilities or personnel

short sale a contract to sell stock in one's own company which the seller does not currently own

short-swing profits rule the rule that any profits obtained from purchase and sale, or sale and purchase, of one's own company's securities within a six-month period must be turned over to the company

slander false information about someone conveyed in oral form

sole proprietorship a single owner business

sovereign immunity the doctrine that a government cannot be sued without its consent

special property interest a buyer's right to inspect goods, to recover damages caused by a third party's injury to the goods, and to recover the goods from the seller in special situations

specific performance a court order which requires a seller to perform a contract as agreed

standing the right to challenge an agency action

state of the art defense a manufacturer's defense that a product defect was not known or able to be known at the time the product was made

statute of frauds a law which requires a signed writing for enforcement of certain contracts

statute of limitations the limited time period after an occurrence in which a lawsuit must be filed

strict liability liability without proof of negligence or fault

strict scrutiny a test that requires a state to show a compelling reason for a regulation

Subchapter S corporation a corporation whose stockholders choose to be taxed as if they were partners, thus avoiding the assessment of corporate income tax

subject-matter jurisdiction the power of a court to hear particular types of cases

subrogation the right of a cosigner who has paid part of the principal's debt to acquire all the rights which the creditor had against the principal debtor

substantive law law that declares rights and duties

summary judgment a judgment in the defendant's favor without a trial

summons a court order to appear before the court

sunset legislation a law under which a program or agency would terminate automatically after a certain number of years unless reenacted by the legislature

surety a cosigner who cosigns as a full co-debter, agreeing that a creditor can take action directly against the surety without trying to collect from the principal debtor first

T

tariff a tax on imported goods

tender offer

terminate end a partnership's existence

title basic ownership interest

title insurance insurance in which the company agrees to defend the buyer's title to a piece of property, reimburse the buyer for the purchase price of the land if another party proves to have a better title, and cover other types of claims which would interfere with the buyer's ownership and enjoyment of the land

tort a civil wrong against a specific victim

trade dress a product's package size, shape, and color

trade secret any piece of non-public information, such as a customer list, formula, or business plan, which has commercial value

trademark any word (or words), symbol, or device which a company has adopted to identify its product

treaty an agreement between nations

trespass wrongful interference with an individual's person or property

trespasser a person who is on the premises without any right at all

tying contract a contract in which a customer is forced to buy a product he or she does not want in order to be allowed to buy the one he or she does want

unconscionability gross unfairness

undue influence a situation in which a dominant person, or a person in a position of trust and confidence, gives advice that robs another of free will

unenforceable contract a contract for which the law gives no court remedy

unilateral contract a contract in which one party makes a promise offering some benefit if another party performs a specified act

unilateral mistake an error made by only one of the parties to a contract

union shop an arrangement in which all employees must become union members after a probationary period

usury laws laws regulating interest rates

valid contract a contract which is fully enforceable against both parties

venue the location of a trial

verdict the decision of the jury

vertical merger the combining of firms in the same industry, but at different levels of the production/distribution process

vicarious liability liability for the acts of another person

vis major act-of-God; see *force majeur*

void agreement a contract totally without legal effect

voidable contract a contract in which one party has the option to disaffirm the bargain, or back out

voir dire the process of questioning potential jurors

warehouse receipt the acknowledgement of the transfer of goods to a warehouse and of the terms of the storage contract

warranty a specific guarantee

warranty deed a deed by which the seller guarantees that the title is clear and that the buyer will be able to use and enjoy the land

white collar crime a wrong, usually occurring in a business situation, which involves fraud or cheating

winding up the process of finishing up a firm's business, paying off its creditors, and dividing any remaining assets

Z

zoning governmental restriction of land use

CASE INDEX

SUBJECT INDEX